# COLLECTING BRITISH FIRST DAY COVERS

## 30th Edition 2011

*The complete guide to the variety of
first day covers and postmarks
available for each Royal Mail stamp issue.*

*Compiled, designed & edited by*
ADRIAN BRADBURY

GW00493659

## Published by A G BRADBURY
### 3 Link Road    Stoneygate    Leicester    LE2 3RA
Telephone: 0116 2705367    email brad@bfdc.co.uk    www.bfdc.co.uk

1st Edition - Dec 1981

| | |
|---|---|
| 2nd (revised) Edition - Oct 1982 | 3rd (revised) Edition - Oct 1983 |
| 4th (revised) Edition - Oct 1984 | 5th (revised) Edition - Oct 1985 |
| 6th (revised) Edition - Oct 1986 | 7th (revised) Edition - Oct 1987 |
| 8th (revised) Edition - Oct 1988 | 9th (revised) Edition - Oct 1989 |
| 10th (revised) Edition - Oct 1990 | 11th (revised) Edition - Oct 1991 |
| 12th (revised) Edition - Oct 1992 | 13th (revised) Edition - Oct 1993 |
| 14th (revised) Edition - Oct 1994 | 15th (revised) Edition - Oct 1995 |
| 16th (revised) Edition - Oct 1996 | 17th (revised) Edition - Oct 1997 |
| 18th (revised) Edition - Oct 1998 | 19th (revised) Edition - Oct 1999 |
| 20th (revised) Edition - Oct 2000 | 21st (revised) Edition - Dec 2000 |
| 22nd (revised) Edition - Oct 2001 | 23rd (revised) Edition - Oct 2002 |
| 24th (revised) Edition - Oct 2004 | 25th (revised) Edition - Oct 2005 |
| 26th (revised) Edition - Nov 2006 | 27th (revised) Edition - Nov 2007 |
| 28th (revised) Edition - Nov 2008 | 29th (revised) Edition - Nov 2009 |

30th (revised) Edition - Nov 2010

## ISBN 978-0-9540710-9-7

Origination by A G Bradbury

Printed by A. T. Shelley (Printers) Ltd., Leicester.

The original work of 1981 was compiled by Norman C. Porter.  His contribution is gratefully acknowledged.

*The purpose of this catalogue is to give the reader a guide to the variety of covers and postmarks
available for each stamp issue.  **It is NOT my price list.**  Prices are a guide - see the Introduction.
Whilst every care has been taken to ensure complete accuracy in the compilation of this catalogue, I
cannot accept responsibility for any errors or omissions.*

There are thousands of special handstamps listed in this catalogue: far too many to illustrate.
However for each commemorative stamp issue there are now files illustrating most of the
handstamps which were available for each issue  - these can be downloaded FREE from
www.bfdc.co.uk/postmarks

# FOREWORD

Welcome to this 30th edition of an annual favourite for collectors of British first day covers. I find it difficult to believe that I have compiled, designed and published this catalogue annually for thirty years. As collectors we have all seen many changes since the first edition in 1980 - not just in the catalogue format but the way in which we collect. These changes have been driven by the increasing number of new Royal Mail stamps issued each year, and their different types and formats.

For new readers, very briefly the catalogue lists all first day covers for all Royal Mail stamps. The commemoratives are listed in date order with the definitives in a separate section at the end of the catalogue. The illustrations are intended to give a broad overview of what is available. There are literally thousands more illustrated at www.bfdc.co.uk

In order to get the most from this catalogue it is important that you should read the Introduction which explains the concept of first day covers and provides valuable information about the different types of postmarks and covers, together with information about many of the cover producers.

From the Introduction you will appreciate that the hobby affords a choice like no other. The collector has such a wide range of postmarks and cover designs to choose from resulting in hundreds of different combinations for each Royal Mail stamp issue. It is a hobby where the collector is in the driving seat, being able to build a collection from many different perspectives, e.g. by postmark type or postmark location; by theme; by cover producer or cover series etc - or perhaps best of all to collect what takes their fancy. It is a hobby to be enjoyed. Do NOT buy for investment - if and when you decide to sell your collection, and if you do make a profit, that should be a bonus, not your aim. Having said that, always buy from a trusted source and only purchase covers in good condition. If you are new to the hobby, I hope that this catalogue will give you lots of ideas on how to create your own unique collection.

There is so much to learn about Britain by collecting first day covers, e.g. our history, transport, sports, royalty, literature, painters, culture, science, in essence, the whole British way of life. By collecting British stamps and first day covers, you are acquiring a part of our nation's heritage - Britain introduced postage stamps to the world, something to be proud of!

Adrian Bradbury.

# CONTENTS

# Introduction

This introduction should answer most of your questions concerning the hobby of *Collecting British First Day Covers*. After reading this section it will soon become apparent that this fascinating hobby can be both absorbing and rewarding. However before going any further it is important to understand precisely what constitutes a first day cover (FDC).

(1) The Envelope        (2) The Set of Stamps        (3) The Postmark

Three elements are brought together to create each first day cover: an envelope (or cover); the postage stamps and a postmark. In the above example, Royal Mail issued a new set of postage stamps on 10th March 2009 featuring pioneers of the Industrial Revolution. Several special envelopes and postmarks were designed for the issue - including the one shown above featuring George Stephenson's *Locomotion*. This catalogue, together with more specialised online material, describes the different first day covers and postmarks which have been designed for each Royal Mail stamp issue. Initially first day covers were only available on plain envelopes, with specially designed covers appearing regularly in the 1950s as the hobby grew in popularity.

It is important not to confuse first day covers with commemorative/souvenir covers, which are usually issued to coincide with the date of a special anniversary or event. First day covers are only issued on the first day of availability of a new set of postage stamps. This is the most common area of confusion for collectors. For example the set of stamps to mark the wedding of Charles and Camilla were issued on 8th April 2005. However many covers were also produced and postmarked on 9th April - the day of the wedding. Only those postmarked on 8th are first day covers, with those postmarked on the 9th being souvenir covers. This catalogue only provides information for first day covers!

The catalogue lists all first day covers for both commemorative and definitive stamps. The commemoratives are listed in date order with the definitives in a separate section at the end of the catalogue. The illustrations are intended to give a broad overview of what is available. There are many more thousands depicted on my website www.bfdc.co.uk

The prices quoted in the catalogue should be treated as a guide, and are for good clean covers with the full set of stamps. Earlier covers (up to the mid 1960s) are acceptable with neat hand written addresses; typed addresses from 1960s-1970s; and then unaddressed, small labels or printed addresses are the standard. Invariably older covers will be of inferior quality when compared to their more recent counterparts and allowance should be made for this. Very scarce covers may well retail at full or above catalogue value. **Please remember this catalogue is NOT my price list!**

# The Postmarks

The postmarks are listed for each commemorative stamp issue in the following order:

    1. Special Handstamps
    2. Ordinary FDI Postmarks
    3. CDS Postmarks
    4. Slogan Postmarks.

Not every stamp issue will have postmarks for each category. It is important to remember that for every postmark entry in the catalogue there will be several different covers available.

## 1. SPECIAL HANDSTAMPS

These are specially designed postmarks which are by far the most popular with collectors. Until the 1990s special handstamps were applied with hand held machines and the quality of impressions varied considerably. However, today's covers are serviced with more sophisticated pad canceller machines which give consistently good impressions, and allow for more intricate postmark designs.

Any member of the public is permitted to sponsor a special handstamp - at a current cost of £195 (plus VAT) - provided that they adhere to certain Royal Mail guidelines. The special handstamp remains the property of Royal Mail and is applied to philatelic items by trained Royal Mail staff.

All special handstamps are advertised in advance in the *British Postmark Bulletin* - a fortnightly newsletter issued by Royal Mail. By subscribing to the Bulletin collectors can find out before the stamp issue date which postmarks will be available. They can then send in to the appropriate Special Handstamp Centres requesting that particular special handstamps be applied to their own first day covers. This is known as the *re-posting facility*. In other words the sponsor does not get exclusive use of their postmark - it is freely available to anyone who wishes to send in their covers for cancelling with that postmark - even though they could be sending in many more than the sponsor!

Royal Mail operates five Special Handstamp Centres which, with a team of dedicated staff, provide an excellent service for dealers and collectors. All special handstamps are now applied at these Centres, each of which covers a specific area of the country, viz:

    Royal Mail London *(London & SE England)*
    Royal Mail Cardiff *(Wales & SW England)*
    Royal Mail Birmingham *(Midlands & East to the Wash)*
    Royal Mail Newcastle *(Northern England)*
    Royal Mail Glasgow *(Scotland & Northern Ireland)*

Since the decimal stamp issues of 1971 Royal Mail has provided one or more special handstamps for each of their commemorative stamp issues - see examples alongside. These special handstamps all bear the words *First Day of Issue*. It is not permitted for a private sponsor to use this wording on postmarks. There are normally two Royal Mail postmarks available, one from Tallents House (formerly the Philatelic Bureau), and another from a location relevant to the stamp issue, e.g. Windsor or London SW1 for royalty issues.

*A selection of recent Royal Mail covers and postmarks.*

For an additional fee, sponsors may have their handstamps applied in different coloured inks. In such cases it is usual for the sponsor's own covers to be cancelled in colour, with other covers submitted under the *re-posting facility* cancelled in black.

Under exceptional circumstances special postmarks in coloured ink are provided free of charge by Royal Mail. This occurs when it is appropriate to do so, e.g. for the 1992 Green issue, collectors had the choice of green or black ink. The designs of some stamps, especially in recent years, are particularly dark which makes it difficult to read the postmark. In these cases Royal Mail will give collectors the choice of silver ink, or the standard black ink.

In the early years handstamps were predominately circular or rectangular in shape, now all shapes are permitted. Similarly a special handstamp could only be sponsored to celebrate a significant anniversary or event. This rule has gradually been eroded over time so that postmarks can now be sponsored without such constraints. However, it should be noted that it is the handstamp sponsor's legal responsibility to ensure that their design does not infringe any copyright or intellectual property rights. Sponsors are required to sign a contract with Royal Mail accepting that they have the necessary permission to reproduce emblems, crests, logos etc, and they are often required to produce proof of such permission. When sponsoring postmarks for organisations it is always prudent to to make the organisation aware that their postmark is not exclusive and that other companies, stamp dealers etc are able to have use of the postmark, via the *re-posting facility* and without charge.

Another change which has occurred in recent times is the acceptance of covers for dual-postmarking. Collectors can submit covers, which have been previously postmarked, to a Special Handstamp Centre for cancelling with another postmark. Whilst there are a number of rules concerning this procedure, it can create some interesting covers.

All special handstamps in use on the first day of issue of a set of commemorative stamps are included in the catalogue whether relevant to an issue or not.

**Permanent Special Handstamps**

There are now numerous special handstamps available to the collector which are in use on each first day of issue of new postage stamps. These have not been listed under each stamp issue but are sometimes listed where relevant to the particular issue, e.g. the Buckingham Palace and Windsor Castle postmarks maybe found listed for royal issues. All of these handstamps, i.e. those still in use, are available under the *re-posting facility* from the Special Handstamp Centres.

These 'permanent' handstamps can briefly be categorised as follows:

Philatelic Counter & Royal Mail handstamps
Other permanent handstamps sponsored by Royal Mail
Permanent handstamps privately sponsored
Operational style handstamps

A few examples of each are shown overleaf:

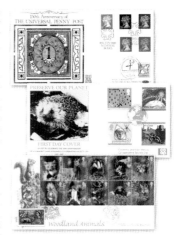

*Handstamps applied in coloured inks:*
*red = 1990 Penny Black*
*green = 1992 Green Issue*
*silver = 2004 Woodland Animals*

*Handstamps with unusual shapes.*

Restoration of Brunel's
BOX TUNNEL

*This cover was originally issued in 1986 to mark the restoration of Brunel's Box Tunnel. In 2006 Royal Mail issued a set of six stamps to mark the bicentenary of the birth of Brunel, one of which featured Box Tunnel. Some of these new Box Tunnel stamps were affixed to the 1986 covers and cancelled with a second Box Tunnel handstamp.*

3

### (a) Philatelic Counter & Royal Mail handstamps

When stamp collecting was at its zenith, there were no less than 67 Philatelic Counters scattered around the country situated inside main Post Offices - each with its own changeable date handstamp. These came in and out of use on various dates between 1981 until 1997. Each postmark bore the legend *Philatelic Counter* and depicted a local landmark or emblem.

These were replaced in 1997 with a series of 43 permanent philatelic handstamps, similar in style but with the legend *Royal Mail*. These are still in use today.

*Philatelic Counter handstamps*

### (b) Other permanent handstamps sponsored by Royal Mail

The first long-running changeable date handstamp was introduced at the National Postal Museum (NPM) in 1969. Since then a number of Royal Mail changeable date postmarks have come and gone. Over the years, several have changed in design - in particular Windsor, also the National Postal Museum as shown below.

*Royal Mail handstamps*

### (c) Permanent Handstamps privately sponsored

Private sponsorship of long-running special handstamps really took off in the late 1990s when cover producers realised that for very little extra expense, they could sponsor a postmark which could be in use for 365 days - instead of just one day! Each handstamp has a changeable date 'slug' at the foot of the design as can be seen in the example alongside. This Battle of the Somme cover has been franked with a Royal Mail FDI handstamp on the day of issue (right) on 9th

November. It has then been franked again with a Whitehall changeable date postmark on Remembrance Day (left). Note how the date is 'detached' from the design - an easy way to identify such postmarks.

### (d) Operational style handstamps

Royal Mail also provide a few circular date stamp postmarks for those collectors who prefer a more authentic style - most of these incorporate the initials *SHC* (Special Handstamp Centre) in the design.

### USEFUL PUBLICATIONS

*All About Postmarks* - from: Royal Mail Stamps and Collectibles
148 Old Street
London   EC1V 9HQ

*British Postmark Bulletin* - free sample copy from: Tallents House
21 South Gyle Crescent
Edinburgh   EH12 9PB

A pdf file listing all (and illustrating most) of these long-running postmaks is availale as a free download from: www.bfdc.co.uk/postmarks

## 2. ORDINARY FIRST DAY OF ISSUE POSTMARKS

These postmarks were introduced with the 1964 Shakespeare issue when the then GPO realised that there was a need for proper philatelic postmarking. Each postmark bears the wording *First Day of Issue*.

They are circular in design, incorporating the town name and date of stamp issue and were used in many towns and cities throughout the UK. The size of the postmark varied considerably with the original Stratford postmark (Shakespeare issue) being quite small. Subsequent issues were much larger, only to be replaced by a smaller size a few years later. In use for all commemorative issues and many definitive stamp issues, FDI postmarks were applied by Royal Mail staff using hand held machines. They were also available to collectors under the *re-posting facility*. Some covers have additional cachets applied by dealers to explain the significance of the postmarks.

These postmarks are listed from their introduction up to the 1970 Christmas issue. The start of the decimal period saw much wider use of special handstamps. However there were numerous examples of where no special handstamps were available at places with an obvious connection with the stamp issues. In such cases, where a FDI postmark was available, these have been listed. FDI postmarks were withdrawn by Royal Mail after the 1998 Christmas issue.

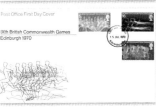

*Ordinary First Day of Issue postmarks*

## 3. COUNTER DATE STAMP POSTMARKS

Sometimes known as circular date stamps, these are standard everyday cancellations available at all Post Office counters. In most cases the only way to obtain these operational postmarks is to use Royal Mail's Special Delivery Services (formerly Registered Mail), although some Post Offices will cancel ordinary mail.

In the early years, pre-1960s, first day covers were generally only available with CDS or slogan postmarks and most had no relevance to the stamp issue.

During the 1960s and up to the present day, the collecting of relevant CDS postmarks has become a specialist interest. The criterion used for the inclusion of these postmarks is that they should have a bearing on the stamp issue. Items which are 'one-off' or have a dubious connection with the issue are not listed. CDS postmarks included (as far as I am aware) were available in reasonable quantities - i.e. twenty or more covers. Better quality covers will have additional cachets applied where the connection between the postmark and the stamp issue is not apparent.

The CDS postmarks are included even if there is a special handstamp or ordinary FDI postmark available for the same area because often the CDS postmarks are more valid. For example on the 2002 Airliners issue all Heathrow special handstamps were applied by the London Special Handstamp Centre, the only covers to be actually postmarked at Heathrow are the CDS postmarks of Terminal 2 & 4.

The best covers have a postmark completely on the envelope and better still a registered label which repeats the name, see the covers alongside - Rose and Stoke Charity.

*Counter Date Stamp Postmarks*

5

*Counter Date Stamp Postmarks*

The proliferation of CDS postmarks (from the 1979 Christmas issue) necessitated their classification into main and ancillary listings. Those postmarks which have a more direct connection to an issue are given a full listing. Other CDS postmarks are listed in italics below the main listing. From 1999 only the more relevant CDS postmarks are listed.

It should be noted that it is not always possible to get perfect postmark impressions. Post Office counter staff who agree to frank covers in this way do so for little or no reward. Quite often the metal counter date stamps are old or worn, or the ink pad may be under or over inked causing faint or smudged postmarks. The general rule is that at least one of the postmarks should provide a legible place name and date.

Broadly speaking, the criteria used to for determining whether a postmark is included in the main listing are as follows:

**(a) Name association**
The name of a Post Office has a strong link with the stamp issue, e.g. 1975 Charity stamp issue postmarked at Stoke Charity near Winchester.

**(b) Place association**
A Post Office is located in, or near to, a place which is commemorated on the stamp issue, e.g. 2002 Bridges of London issue postmarked at London Bridge Post Office. Where the connection is not obvious, better covers will have an explanatory cachet.

**(c) House of Commons & House of Lords**
These CDS postmarks are not usually available to members of the public, and are only listed where relevant, e.g.:
(i)   Where an issue commemorates the passing of legislation, e.g. the 1980 Birds issue celebrates the centenary of the Wild Bird Protection Act.
(ii)  Parliamentary issues, e.g. 1973 and 1975
(iii) Where a featured individual has a strong connection with parliament, e.g. 1965 and 1974 Churchill issues.
(iv)  Royalty issues.

**(d) Royal households**
Postal facilities at Buckingham Palace, Windsor Castle, Balmoral Castle, and Sandringham House are only available to members of the Royal Family or staff of the Royal Household. Whilst these postmarks on first day covers are extremely scarce, especially Balmoral and Sandringham, these are only listed where the stamp issue involves a royal theme, e.g. Royal Weddings.

**(e) Travelling Post Offices**
e.g. 1975, 1980, 1985 and 1994 train issues.

**(f) Paquebots (items posted at sea)**
European issues, e.g. 1973 EEC, 1979 European Elections usually with Calais postmarks.

## USEFUL PUBLICATIONS

As the collecting of CDS postmarks has now become a very specialised area, I have decided from mid 2009 not to list future issues. Current listings and values can be obtained from:
Mike Porter
48 Coalport Close
Harlow
CM17 9QA

## 4. SLOGAN POSTMARKS

These were machine cancellations applied to the vast majority of British mail. A slogan postmark consists of two parts, viz: a circle showing the time, date and sorting office; and more often than not, an advertising 'slogan'. These postmarks were advertised in advance in Royal Mail's *Postmark Bulletin* and were available under the *re-posting facility*. Three types of slogan have been available to the collector, viz:

### (a) First Day of Issue Slogans
First introduced in 1963, these were used on first day covers posted in special posting boxes at selected Post Offices. The slogan was in the style of the back of an envelope with the wording *First Day of Issue* - see the National Nature Week cover alongside. These were mostly replaced by the ordinary FDI handstamps (see page 5) when special posting boxes were provided for FDC collectors at most head post offices.

### (b) 'Wavy-line' machine postmarks
These have only been listed if the location at which they were used was connected to the stamp issue - see House of Commons postmark alongside.

### (c) Advertising slogans
The criterion used to determine whether a slogan should be included depends on its relevance to the stamp issue. Unlike CDS postmarks, the location of the Post Office at which a slogan was used was not as important as the wording or illustration of the slogan, which should have a good connection with the stamp issue. The proliferation of slogan postmarks (from 1979 Christmas issue) necessitated their classification into main and ancillary listings. Those postmarks which, in the opinion of the publisher, have a close or direct connection to an issue are given a full listing. Other slogan postmarks are listed in italics below the main listing.

### Late use of slogans
Slogan postmark campaigns were booked to run for a specified period and were advertised as such in the *Postmark Bulletin*. Sometimes slogans ran over their allotted time because there was no alternative available. This could result in a slogan being in use at the time of the first day of issue of a new set of stamps where the subject of the stamps and slogan were closely linked. This situation produced some very collectable covers.

### Proper siting of stamps
Earlier covers are usually only available with a slogan which obliterates the stamps which often makes the slogan difficult to read. However with effect from 1974 most covers were available with the stamps positioned in such a way as to make the slogan clearly legible. To achieve this the stamps had to be sited so that the slogan or its date slug only cancelled one stamp, the remaining stamps being franked with a CDS or FDI postmark. Once again, it should be stressed that it was not always possible to get good clean impressions. To obtain these postmarks the covers were fed through automatic franking machines which handled thousands of items per day. Royal Mail ceased to provide a *re-posting facility* for slogans after the 1996 Christmas issue, and now no longer accepts advertising slogans from firms or organisations.

*A selection of Slogan Postmarks*

# The Covers

## 1. ORDINARY or COMMERCIAL COVERS

These are produced primarily for the general FDC collector and are usually sold as 'blanks' (i.e. with no stamps affixed). They are available from most good stamp shops before the day of issue of the postage stamps. Collectors purchase the 'blanks', affix the stamps and arrange to have their covers postmarked under the *re-posting facility*. Royal Mail produce their own FDC which is available through Post Offices prior to the issue date. Three makes are currently available: Royal Mail, Cotswold and Stuart.

## 2. OFFICIAL or SPONSORED COVERS

**In the context of this catalogue**, 'official' covers are defined as covers produced by private organisations or cover producers, who at the same time sponsor a special handstamp to accompany their cover. Some official/sponsored covers are produced in small quantities and in some cases may not be available to collectors. Such covers are therefore rarer than the 'ordinary' covers with the same handstamp.

Sometimes an organisation will not affix the full set of stamps to their covers because not all of the stamps may be relevant. It may be possible in such cases to obtain the blank envelopes from the sponsor and affix your own stamps, thus creating a full set cover. However, where covers are only known to exist with an incomplete set, the official cover description in italics is suffixed with **(s)**.

Since the mid 1980s the rules governing the sponsorship of special handstamps has been relaxed with the result that there are now far more sponsored - mostly by first day cover producers. Anyone can sponsor handstamps depicting places such as Westminster Abbey or Windsor Castle. The covers used to accompany these handstamps are only 'official' in the context of this catalogue, i.e. in most cases no special sanction has been received from the places depicted. Therefore with effect from 1997 I have referred to such covers as 'sponsored' - a more meaningful description. Some would argue, and quite rightly so, that the only true OFFICIAL covers are those produced by Royal Mail.

The following list will give the reader an idea of just how many different makes and styles of cover have been available over the years - the list is not exhaustive - apologies to any producer not represented on the next few pages.

*Abbey:* Produced from 1969 until 1982 these covers were sold complete with the stamps and postmark and issued as numbered limited editions.

*Art Craft:* Based in America - the earliest cover I have seen was produced for the 1948 Olympic Games and the latest is this splendid set of 1974 Churchill FDCs.

*Arlington:* Normally official covers produced for companies or organisations. In some instances very few were serviced with the full set of stamps and as such command high prices.

At www.bfdc.co.uk you will find thousands more pictures of British first day covers.

8

*Benham Covers:* Benhams of Folkestone have dominated the British cover market since the late 1970s. There have been numerous different series. With the exception of the Woodcut series (1968-1978), and their Small Silk series, most covers have their own sponsored postmarks. The Small Silks which started in 1980 and are still running, are single stamp covers - i.e. individual covers for each postage stamp.

Benhams were the first cover producer to promote the concept of 'official' covers. The idea of being able to purchase fully serviced first day covers for each stamp issue quickly caught on with collectors as a trouble free way of collecting. Initially, most of the covers were linked to organisations connected with the stamp issue. The Benham Official Cover Series (BOCS) commenced with the 1978 Energy issue and ran through to Christmas 1984. The 'silk' cachet covers became the standard from the 1982 issues. The Benham Large Silk (BLS) ran in tandem with the BOCS series until the end of 1984. The start of 1985 saw the commencement of the Benham Luxury Cover Series (BLCS), and the Benham Gold 500 series - both of which have continued through to the present day. www.benhamcovers.com

Woodcut Series

BOCS Series

BLS Series

BLCS Series

Small Silk Series

Coin Series

*Bletchley Park PO:*
The series started in 1994. (D-Day issue). Most have sponsored Bletchley Park postmarks.

*Bradbury Covers:* My LFDC series commenced in 1980 and continued through to the last issue of 2000 when it was replaced by the Sovereign Series in 2001. My Victorian Prints series ran from1985 to 2000. The Britannia Series, Anniversaries & Events Series, and Windsor Series also started in 2001. In addition I have produced many others, both first day covers and souvenir covers. In 2008 I consolidated all the series into one *BFDC* series. View all of my covers at: www.bfdc.co.uk/producers/bradbury

LFDC Series

Sovereign Series

Britannia Series

Anniversaries & Events Series

*Brazier:* Mike Brazier's pubs series started with these two issues in 1999 and continued until 2007. Most are limited to 100 or less with their own sponsored postmarks.

*Buckingham Covers:* Tony and Cath Buckingham founded Benhams (see page 9), sold the business, and then went on to create Internetstamps and Buckingham Covers in 2001. Each cover has specially sponsored postmarks. www.buckinghamcovers.com

*Cambridge Stamp Centre:* Covers are mostly related to the cinema or military, with sponsored handstamps. Many are produced as single stamp covers with very few having the full set.

*Cameo:*
The Cameo Stamp Centre produced a few covers in 1970 and 1971.

*Colorano Silks:* These were first produced for the 1974 Horse Chestnut issue and continued until the Christmas 1987 issue.

*Connoisseur:* Published between 1963-1970 and bearing an Old English 'C' logo - sometimes on the reverse, these were marketed by R F Grover of Fareham, Hants.

**Cotswold Covers:** Cotswold die-stamped covers first appeared with the 1970 Christmas issue and are still in production. A large square 'C' border is common to all their designs. In the main, these are sold as blank envelopes.

**CoverCraft:** Produced by Rafael deSwarte, mostly for companies or organisations, his covers span a twenty year period from 1983 - 2003.

**Dawn Covers:** Produced by Stuart Renshaw who specializes in Football and Transport covers and is sometimes able to combine the two as in these examples of trains named after football clubs!
www.footballcover.co.uk

**Fine Art Covers:**
This series only ran for a short period from 1984 - 1986. The covers reproduced specially commissioned paintings and were limited to 850 numbered copies. Most were signed by the artist and were franked with their own sponsored postmark. In many cases they were supplied in special presentation folders with a special wax seal applied to the front of the envelope.

**Forces Covers:** Most forces covers are produced in numbered series - and in the main have special postmarks applied by the Philatelic Section at the Forces Post Office (Philatelic), Mill Hill. Many have been flown in military aircraft or carried on board naval ships and are pilot signed or signed by distinguished military personnel. The majority are backstamped and have the flight/carried details printed on the cover. In addition to the first day covers series, examples illustrated below, there have also been numerous series of souvenir covers. The driving force behind many of these series is Bill Randle.

Use the Advanced Search at www.bfdc.co.uk and sort by Cover Producer, Series, Stamp Issue etc

*Fourpenny Post:* Produced by Susannah and John Strettle, this attractive series ran from 1996 to 2003 and were sold as blanks. A number of official covers were produced, in particular for the millennium issues of 1999-2000.

*GBFDC:* This series commenced in 1995 and should not be confused with the occasional *Association of GB FDC Collectors* series which started with the 2000 People & Place issue.

*Havering Covers:* Founded by Terry Hurlstone in 1979.

*Hawkwood Covers:* Produced by Trevor Dyke of Chingford, these were issued for most of the 1980-86 issues.

*Historic Relics:* Produced from 1969 to 1992.

*Mercury Die-stamped:* Published from 1972 to 1993 by Harry Allen of Rickmansworth, these die-stamped covers bear a distinctive 'Mercury' logo.

*Philart:* Produced from 1964 Geographical issue through to 1990. The Philart 'Luxury' die-stamped covers were available from the 1969 Ships issues until the early 1980s - these were printed on vellum type paper.

12

**Phil Stamp Covers:** Love them or hate them, this series is most certainly different from the rest and will add a new dimension to your collection! Find out more at: www.philstampcovers.co.uk

**Pilgrim Covers:** Produced in Canterbury by Ken Jaggers, mainly for the RNLI and the British Library with many sponsored postmarks. Production ceased in 1995.

**Presentation Philatelic Services (PPS):** The series was started by Roy Bywater of Earl Shilton (Leics) with their first blank cover for the 1981 Butterflies issue. Christmas 1981 saw their first 'silk' cover which continued through to Christmas 1983. The series was then taken over by Antony Grodecki of London Road Stamps in 1984, who continued production as the Sotheby's 'silk' series which ran until the 1995 Christmas issue. The Cigarette Cards 'silks' were produced for all issues from 1988 to 1994.

PPS Covers     HERALDRY     Sotheby 'Silks'     THE AGE OF STEAM     Cigarette Card Series

**PTS/BPA:** The Philatelic Traders Society and the British Philatelic Association jointly produced a number of covers from the 1948 Olympics issue through to the 1966 World Cup.

**Railway Societies:** Below are a few examples of covers produced by railway societies and private railway companies. Many also incorporate Railway Letter Stamps which are then franked with various cachets. As you will see Christmas is a popular time to issue such covers.

At www.bfdc.co.uk you will find around 25,000 British FDCs available. This visual resource allows you to search by cover producer, cover series, stamp type, postmark - and much more.

*Royal Mail/Post Office:* The first PO cover appeared for the 1964 Shakespeare issue and for all issues to date with the exception of 1965 Salvation Army, Joseph Lister, Arts, UN, ITU and 1966 England Winners. All of the covers illustrated on pages 2 and 5 are Royal Mail/Post Office covers. For more details of their latest issues go to: www.royalmail.com

*Save the Children:*
These were produced for the earlier decimal issues commencing with the 1973 Royal Wedding.

*Sheridan Covers:*
Sponsored covers issued from 1999 to date, with some having additional meter marks appropriate to the stamp issue.

*Peter Scot:* These larger covers were produced from the 1978 Energy through to 1988 to accommodate a full set of gutter pairs on the one cover and were also useful for double dating.

*Steven Scott:*
Produced from the Stamp Centre on the Strand since 1996, these official covers are still in production. For more details go to:
www.stamp-centre.co.uk

*Stamp Publicity:*
Produced in Worthing by Mel Brown from the late 1960s until 2003 - most of the more recent covers relate to cricket.

*Stewart Petty:*
Stewart produced a series of official covers from 1981, but like many at the time, fell by the wayside after only a few years in production. His covers were in the main die-stamped.

**Stuart:**
First produced for the 1965 Churchill issue, this series is still available as blank envelopes and now published by Cotswold covers. The envelopes are die-stamped and feature a 'thistle' logo.

*Thames:* First issue in 1968 and continuing through to the 1974 Christmas issue, the covers had a similar appearance to die-stamping. The earlier issues were printed with a 'Thames estuary' logo on the envelope flap.

**Trident:**
Produced for some 1969/70 issues and bearing a 'Trident' logo.

**Wessex:**
Printed with a 'wyvern' logo, these were first produced for the 1967 EFTA issue and then regularly until 1975. A few have been produced since, most notably the 1977 Jubilee.

**The Westminster Collection:**
This company is a major player in the collectibles field and produces first day covers for each stamp issue, including an autographed and hand painted series.

# Summary

From this introduction you will appreciate that the hobby affords a choice like no other. The collector has such a wide range of postmarks and cover designs to choose from resulting in hundreds of different combinations for each Royal Mail stamp issue. It is a hobby where the collector is in the driving seat, being able to build a collection from many different perspectives, e.g. by postmark type or postmark location; by theme; by cover producer or cover series etc - or perhaps best of all to collect what takes your fancy. It is a hobby to be enjoyed. Do NOT buy for investment - if and when you decide to sell your collection, and if you do make a profit, that should be a bonus, not your aim. Having said that, always buy from a trusted source and only purchase covers in good condition. If you are new to the hobby, I hope that this introduction will give you lots of ideas on how to create your own collection.

# HOW TO USE THIS CATALOGUE

③ Description of stamp designs and values. Reference to these will often explain the significance of many of the postmarks

④ Selection of cover illustrations. NB The numbers refer to the postmark **NOT** the cover.

① Official date of issue of stamps

Remember the same postmark can appear on several cover designs.

② Title of stamp issue

⑤

**21st June 1988 – AUSTRALIAN BICENTENARY**
18p Historical - Early Settler and Clipper ship;   **ordinary**    **official**
18p Constitutional - The Queen & Parliament;    **covers**    **covers**
34p Sports - W.G.Grace and Tennis    £    £
34p The Arts – Lennon, Shakespeare, Sydney Opera Hse;

⑨ **SPECIAL HANDSTAMPS**
| | | | |
|---|---|---|---|
| (1) | First Day of Issue – Philatelic Bureau | 3 | – Royal Mail |
| (2) | First Day of Issue – Portsmouth | 3 | – Royal Mail |
| (3) | Bicentenary of Australia, SW1 | 12 | 20 LFDC 69 |
| (4) | Australian Bicentenary, Portsmouth | 12 | 40 BenSG5 |
| (5) | James Cook Museum, Marton-in-Cleveland | 12 | 15 S. Muscroft |
| (6) | Links with Australia, Amy Johnson, Hull | 12 | 50 Bradbury |
| (7) | GB Cricketing Links, Old Trafford | 12 | 75 S.P. |
| (8) | GB Cricketing Links, Edgbaston | 12 | 75 S.P. |
| (9) | GB Cricketing Links, Trent Bridge | 12 | 75 S.P. |
| (10) | GB Cricketing Links, The Oval, SE11 | 12 | 75 S.P. |
| (11) | GB Cricketing Links, Headingley | 12 | 75 S.P. |
| (12) | GB Cricketing Links, Lords | 12 | 15 S.P. |
| (13) | Wedgwood Australian Bicentenary Barlaston | 12 | 50 Arlington |
| (14) | Botany Bay, Enfield | 12 | 30 Ben500(33) |
| (15) | Bombardment of Bardia, BF 2178 PS | 12 | 25 FAAMuseum |
| (16) | Australian Bicentennial, EC | 12 | 35 CoverCraft |
| (17) | Lawn Tennis Museum, SW19 | 12 | 25 H.R. |
| (18) | R.A.F. Cottesmore, TTT3, BF 2177 PS | 12 | 15 RFDC 64 |

⑨ **C.D.S. POSTMARKS**
| | | |
|---|---|---|
| (19) | Bathampton – Capt.Phillip/first Gov. of NSW. | 15 |
| (20) | Botany Bay or Penny Lane | 15 |
| (21) | Downend (Grace) or Whitby (Cook) ........each | 20 |
| (22) | Hambledon – birthplace of English Cricket | 20 |
| (23) | House of Commons or Lords | 30 |
| (24) | Portsmouth or Ryde - First Fleet | 15 |
| (25) | Stratford-upon-Avon or Windsor | 15 |

*Also: Buckingham Palace, Croydon, Headingley, Kennington Park, Marton, Melbourne, Queen Elizabeth Ave., St. Bravels, Sydney Rd, Wimbledon. From £12.*

⑨ **SLOGAN POSTMARKS**
| | | |
|---|---|---|
| (26) | 1588-1788-1988 Tobormory 200, Oban | 250 |

*In addition: Royal Mail/Glasgow G.F.; Ullapool Bicentenary. Prices from £15.*

(5) Two column price structure:
    *1924-1961    illustrated or plain covers*
    *1962-1967    non-phosphor or phosphor stamps*
    *1967- to date   ordinary or official/sponsored cover*

(6) Brief description of official cover & series number

(7) Abbreviated wording of postmarks.

(8) Price guide.

(9) Type of postmark.

The above is just an example of the thousands of illustrations of postmarks which I have available.
Users of this catalogue can download **FREE** files for each commemorative issue from: www.bfdc.co.uk/postmarks

## Abbreviations

| | | | |
|---|---|---|---|
| *BFPS/Forces* | - British Forces Postal Services | *LFDC* | - Leicester First Day Covers |
| *BL* | - British Library with BL pmks | *n.k.* | - not known |
| *BLCS* | - Benham luxury cover | *n.o.c./n.s.c.* | - no official cover/no sponsored cover |
| *BLS* | - Benham large 'silk' | *NYMoorsRly* | - North York Moors Railway |
| *BenL* | - Benham limited edition | *NVRly* | - Nene Valley Railway |
| *BenSG* | - Benham Special Gold | *P.P.S.* | - Presentation Philatelic Services |
| *Ben500* | - Benham 500 series | *RAF FDC* | - Forces First Day Covers |
| *BOCS* | - Benham official cover series | *RAF (P&P)* | - RAF Planes & Places |
| *Cam S.C.* | - Cambridge Stamp Centre | *RH/RHDR* | - Rly History/Romney, Hythe & Dym. Rly |
| *D.F.* | - David Fletcher of Coventry | *RN Cvrs Gp* | - Royal Naval Covers Group |
| *D.G.T.* | - D. G. Taylor of Harrow | *RFDC* | - Forces first day covers |
| *(f)* | - denotes forerunner to the series | *(s)* | - covers only known with single stamp |
| *F.A.A.* | - Fleet Air Arm Museum | *S.P.* | - Stamp Publicity |
| *FDP Co* | - First Day Publishing Co. | *VP* | - Victorian Prints |
| *GBFDC* | - Assoc. GB FDC | *W & W* | - Warwick & Warwick |
| *H.R.* | - Historic Relics | | |

## 23rd April 1924 – WEMBLEY EXHIBITION
*1d, 1¹/₂ d Wembley Lion*

| | illustrated £ | plain £ |
|---|---|---|
| **SPECIAL HANDSTAMPS** | | |
| (1) Empire Exhibition, Wembley Park, 1924 .................. | – | 300 |
| (2) Palace of Engineering or Palace of Industry .....*each* | – | 1000 |
| **SLOGAN POSTMARKS** | | |
| (3) Wembley Park.............(*Harmer display cover £350*) | – | 300 |
| (4) British Empire.......................................................... | – | 450 |
| (5) British Industries Fair .....................*1¹/₂ d value only* | – | 50 |
| **POSTAL STATIONERY** | | |
| (6) 1d Postcard – Wembley special h/s or slogan.......... | – | 150 |
| (7) 1¹/₂d Postcard (foreign) – Wembley h/s or slogan... | – | 275 |
| (8) 1¹/₂d Printed env. or lettercard – Wembley pmk...... | – | 200 |

## 9th May 1925 – WEMBLEY EXHIBITION
*1d, 1¹/₂ d Wembley Lion*

| | | |
|---|---|---|
| **SPECIAL HANDSTAMPS** | | |
| (1) British Empire Exhib., Wembley or Wembley Park... | – | 1,250 |
| (2) Empire Exhibition Wembley, Palace of Industry...... | – | 1,750 |
| **SLOGAN POSTMARKS** | | |
| (3) Wembley Park (Lion) 1925 ......................................... | – | 1,500 |
| **POSTAL STATIONERY** | | |
| (4) 1d Postcard – Wembley special h/s or slogan.......... | – | 350 |
| (5) 1¹/₂d Postcard (foreign) – Wembley h/s or slogan... | – | 400 |
| (6) 1¹/₂d Printed env. or lettercard – Wembley pmk...... | – | 350 |

## 10th May 1929 – POSTAL UNION CONGRESS
*¹/₂d, 1d, 1¹/₂d, 2¹/₂d King George V; £1 St. George and the Dragon*

| | | |
|---|---|---|
| **C.D.S. POSTMARKS** | | |
| (1) Postal Union Congress, London – £1 value ............. | – | 8,500 |
| (2) Postal Union Congress, London – 4 low values........ | – | 750 |
| (3) -do- on P.U.C. stationery or env. (crest on flap)....... | – | 900 |
| (4) -do- on P.U.C. stationery – all 5 values.................... | – | 5,500 |
| (5) Registered P.U.C., London (oval) – 4 low values..... | – | 1,000 |
| (6) Any other postmark – £1 value ................................. | – | 4,000 |
| (7) Any other postmark – 4 low values .......................... | – | 350 |
| (8) Any other postmark – all five values ........................ | – | 4,000 |
| **SLOGAN POSTMARKS** | | |
| (9) Any postmark – 4 low values ..................................... | – | 250 |

## 7th May 1935 – KING GEORGE V SILVER JUBILEE
*¹/₂d, 1d, 1¹/₂d, 2¹/₂d King George V*

| | | |
|---|---|---|
| **C.D.S. POSTMARKS** (1) Windsor, Berks...................... | 800 | 300 |
| (2) London. SW1...................................................... | 525 | 150 |
| (2a) -do- on Westminster Stamp Co. cover...................... | 550 | – |
| **SLOGAN POSTMARKS** | | |
| (3) London SW1 or Windsor – wavy line pmks...*each* | 50(s) | 20 |
| **ANY OTHER POSTMARK (CDS or Slogan)** .........*from* | 400 | 75 |

## 13th May 1937 – KING GEORGE VI CORONATION
*1¹/₂d King George VI and Queen Elizabeth*

| | | |
|---|---|---|
| **C.D.S. POSTMARKS** (1) Windsor, Berks...................... | 150 | 25 |
| (2) Hampton Court Camp or Kensington Gdns Camp...... | 200 | 100 |
| (3) Pirbright Camp – used for troops for Coronation...... | 180 | 75 |
| (4) Regents Park Camp – for troops for Coronation...... | – | 100 |
| (5) Any other SW postmark........................................... | 35 | 8 |
| (6) London & New York (Anglo/American Air Mail) .. | – | 45 |
| **SLOGAN POSTMARKS** | | |
| (7) Windsor – wavy line ................................................. | 150 | 30 |
| (8) London SW1 – wavy line........................................... | 35 | 7 |
| **ANY OTHER POSTMARK (CDS or Slogan)** .........*from* | 30 | 2 |

## 6th May 1940 – POSTAGE STAMP CENTENARY
*¹/₂d, 1d, 1¹/₂d, 2¹/₂d, 3d Victoria & George VI*

| | | |
|---|---|---|
| **SPECIAL HANDSTAMPS** | | |
| (1) 27th Philatelic Congress, Bournemouth .................. | 125 | 20 |
| (2) Adhesive Stamp Centenary Exhib., Bournemouth .. | 50 | 7 |
| (3) Stamp Centenary (Red Cross) Exhib., London........ | 55 | 7 |
| (3a) -do- on Perkins Bacon cover ....................................... | 95 | – |
| (4) Pavilion, Bournemouth.............................................. | 35 (s) | 150 |
| **C.D.S. POSTMARKS** | | |
| (5) Dundee – James Chalmers, first adhesive stamps..... | 170 | – |
| (6) Kidderminster - birthplace of Rowland Hill .............. | – | 20 |
| **SLOGAN POSTMARKS** | | |
| (7) Post Early in the Day................................................. | 175 | 50 |
| **ANY OTHER POSTMARK (CDS or Slogan)** .........*from* | 25 | 4 |

*1924 postmarks*

*1925 postmarks*

## 11th June 1946 – VICTORY

*2¹/₂ d, 3d Peace and Reconstruction*

| | illustrated £ | plain £ |
|---|---|---|
| **C.D.S. POSTMARKS** | | |
| (1) Any central London postmark | 60 | 5 |
| (2) House of Commons, London SW1 | 125 | 30 |
| (3) Jersey or Guernsey – German occupation ......*each* | 70 | 10 |
| (3a) Canadian Overseas or British Fleet Mail ..........*each* | n.k. | 100 |
| **SLOGAN POSTMARKS** | | |
| (4) Don't Waste Bread–Others Need It | 75 | 15 |
| **ANY OTHER POSTMARK (CDS or Slogan)** .........*from* | 40 | 3 |

## 26th April 1948 – SILVER WEDDING

*2¹/₂ d, £1 Photographic portraits of the King and Queen.*

| | illustrated | plain |
|---|---|---|
| **C.D.S. POSTMARKS** | | |
| (1) Georgetown, Jersey | 500 | 275 |
| (2) Any central London postmark | 400 | 110 |
| (3) Any other postmark | 350 | 90 |
| **SLOGAN POSTMARKS** | | |
| (4) London SW1 or Windsor - wavy line pmks | 40(s) | 15(s) |
| (5) Any other postmark | 275 | 60 |

## 10th May 1948 – CHANNEL ISLANDS LIBERATION

*1d, 2¹/₂ d Gathering Vraic (seaweed)*

| | illustrated | plain |
|---|---|---|
| **C.D.S. POSTMARKS** | | |
| (1) Guernsey or Jersey .....................................*each* | 35 | 4 |
| (2) Sark or Alderney ........................................*each* | 75 | 10 |
| (3) British Industries Fair, Birmingham (registered) ...... | 70 | 25 |
| **SLOGAN POSTMARKS** | | |
| (4) Guernsey or Jersey–wavy line pmks ...................*each* | 25 | 4 |
| (5) A Distinguished Career–Nursing | 80 | 20 |
| (6) British Industries Fair, Birmingham | 125 | 35 |
| **ANY OTHER POSTMARK (CDS or Slogan)** .........*from* | 30 | 10 |

## 29th July 1948 – OLYMPIC GAMES, WEMBLEY

*2¹/₂ d, 3d, 6d, 1s Olympic Symbols*

| | illustrated | plain |
|---|---|---|
| **C.D.S. POSTMARKS** | | |
| (1) Wembley, Middx. (double ring metal cancel) | 120 | 20 |
| (1a) ditto–used at Games (nos.11 to 16 in pmk.) | 100 | 30 |
| **SLOGAN POSTMARKS** | | |
| (2) Olympic Games, Wembley (often with cds pmk) | 50 | 15 |
| **ANY OTHER POSTMARK (CDS or Slogan)** .........*from* | 40 | 10 |

## 10th October 1949 – UNIVERSAL POSTAL UNION

*2¹/₂ d Two Hemispheres; 3d UPU Monument, Berne;*
*6d Goddess Concordia; 1s Posthorn and Globe*

| | illustrated | plain |
|---|---|---|
| **C.D.S. POSTMARKS** | | |
| (1) London Chief Office–postal headquarters | 100 | 30 |
| **ANY OTHER POSTMARK (CDS or Slogan)** .........*from* | 70 | 12 |

## 3rd May 1951 – FESTIVAL OF BRITAIN

*2¹/₂ d Commerce and Prosperity; 4d Festival Symbol*

| | illustrated | plain |
|---|---|---|
| **C.D.S. POSTMARKS** | | |
| (1) British Industries Fair, B'ham or Earl's Court | n.k. | 40 |
| (2) Registered B.I.F. Birmingham (oval) | n.k. | 40 |
| (3) Battersea SW11 – Festival Gardens | 70 | 15 |
| (4) Buckingham Palace, SW1 or Windsor | 250 | 50 |
| (5) London SE1 – Festival site was on the South Bank | 75 | 15 |
| **SLOGAN POSTMARKS** | | |
| (6) Battersea, SW11–wavy line | 50 | 15 |
| (7) Festival of Britain May 3-Sept 30 (used at Cardiff) ... | 300 | 175 |
| **ANY OTHER POSTMARK (CDS or Slogan)** .........*from* | 35 | 8 |

*A Festival handstamp and slogan were in use on the opening day of the festival, 4th May. These are commemorative covers **NOT** first day covers.*

## 3rd June 1953 – CORONATION

*2¹/₂ d, 4d, 1s 3d, 1s 6d Portraits of Queen Elizabeth/Regalia*

| | illustrated | plain |
|---|---|---|
| **C.D.S. POSTMARKS** | | |
| (1) Arundel–Earl Marshal/Coronation arrangements.... | 200 | – |
| (2) Buckingham Palace, Windsor Castle or Sandringham.. | 1850 | 250 |
| (3) House of Commons or House of Lords | 250 | 50 |
| (4) Windsor, Berks. | 250 | 50 |
| (5) Queen's Head, Queensbury (or similar) .........*each* | 12(s) | |
| (6) London SW | 75 | 25 |
| (7) Any other postmark | 50 | 10 |
| **SLOGAN POSTMARKS** | | |
| (8) Long Live the Queen, Windsor | 550 | 40 |
| (9) Long Live the Queen, London SW1 | 85 | 20 |
| (10) Long Live the Queen, any other location | 65 | 15 |
| **ANY OTHER POSTMARK (CDS or Slogan)** .........*from* | 30 | 7 |

## 1st August 1957 – SCOUT JUBILEE JAMBOREE
*2¹/₂ d, 4d, 1s 3d Scouting Symbols*

|  |  | illustrated | plain |
|---|---|---|---|
| **C.D.S. POSTMARKS** |  | £ | £ |
| (1) | Sutton Coldfield | 150 | 20 |
| **SLOGAN POSTMARKS** |  |  |  |
| (2) | World Scout Jubilee Jamboree, Sutton Coldfield | 25 | 5 |
| (3) | -do- different design (see illustration) | 35(s) | 10(s) |
| (4) | Wavy line cancellation–Sutton Coldfield | 125 | 5 |
| | **ANY OTHER POSTMARK (CDS or Slogan)** ........*from* | 15 | 3 |

## 12th Sept 1957 – PARLIAMENTARY CONFERENCE
*4d Overprinted definitive*

| **SPECIAL HANDSTAMPS** |  |  |  |
|---|---|---|---|
| (1) | 46th Parliamentary Conference, London SW1 ........ | 100 | 20 |
| *Forged London W1 handstamps exist for this issue.* |  |  |  |
| **C.D.S. POSTMARKS** |  |  |  |
| (2) | House of Commons or Lords, London SW1 ........... | 300 | – |
| (3) | Northern Parliament, Belfast | 225 | 80 |
| (4) | Any London SW postmark | 75 | 20 |
| **SLOGAN POSTMARKS** |  |  |  |
| (5) | London SW1 - wavy line postmark | 125 | n.k. |
| | **ANY OTHER POSTMARK (CDS or Slogan)** ........*from* | 65 | 7 |

## 18th July 1958 – COMMONWEALTH GAMES
*3d, 6d, 1s 3d Welsh Dragon & Games Emblem*

| **C.D.S. POSTMARKS** |  |  |  |
|---|---|---|---|
| (1) | Empire Games Village, Barry (double ring pmk) ..... | 250 | 125 |
| (2) | Empire Games Village, Barry (single ring) | 325 | 90 |
| (3) | Empire Games Village, Barry ('hooded' pmk) | 300 | 75 |
| (3a) | -do- on R.A.F.A. Philatelic Society cover | 600 | – |
| (4) | Games Mobile Post Office | 1200 | 350 |
| (5) | Empire Games Village, Barry Parcel Post | n.k. | 25(s) |
| **SLOGAN POSTMARKS** |  |  |  |
| (7) | British Empire & Comm. Games | 85 | 25 |
| (8) | British Empire & Comm. Games 18th-26th July | n.k. | 75 |
| | **ANY OTHER POSTMARK (CDS or Slogan)** ........*from* | 30 | 5 |

## 7th July 1960 – THE GENERAL LETTER OFFICE
*3d, 1s 3d Post boy and Post horn of 1660*

| **C.D.S. POSTMARKS** |  |  |  |
|---|---|---|---|
| (1) | Lombard Street, EC3 – General Letter Office | 70 | 20 |
| (2) | London Chief Office, EC – postal headquarters | 90 | 20 |
| **SLOGAN POSTMARKS** |  |  |  |
| (3) | International Postal Conference, Eastbourne | 150 | 50 |
| | **ANY OTHER POSTMARK (CDS or Slogan)** ........*from* | 40 | 5 |

## 19th Sept. 1960 – 'EUROPA'
*6d, 1s 6d Conference Emblem*

| **C.D.S. POSTMARKS** |  |  |  |
|---|---|---|---|
| (1) | Lombard Street, EC3 – General Letter Office | 100 | 20 |
| (2) | London Chief Office, EC – postal headquarters | 100 | 20 |
| (3) | Norwich – first use of post codes in 1960 | 110 | 20 |
| (4) | London F.S. (Foreign Section) | 110 | 25 |
| **SLOGAN POSTMARKS** |  |  |  |
| (5) | Express Good Wishes by Greeting's Telegram | 200 | 20 |
| (6) | London EC - wavy line | 40 | n.k. |
| | **ANY OTHER POSTMARK (CDS or Slogan)** ........*from* | 35 | 5 |

## 28th August 1961 – SAVINGS BANK CENTENARY
*2¹/₂ d, 3d, 1s 6d Thrift Plant and Growth of Savings*

| **C.D.S. POSTMARKS** |  |  |  |
|---|---|---|---|
| (1) | Blythe Rd., W14 – HQ of the P.O.S.B. | 300 | 75 |
| (2) | London Chief Office, EC – postal headquarters | 175 | 25 |
| (3) | Any London postmark | 100 | 20 |
| **SLOGAN POSTMARKS** |  |  |  |
| (4) | Express Good Wishes by Greeting's Telegrams | 175 | 20 |
| (5) | West Kensington, W14 - wavy line postmark | 300 | 75 |
| | **ANY OTHER POSTMARK (CDS or Slogan)** ........*from* | 65 | 6 |

## 18th September 1961 – CEPT
*2d, 4d, 10d Doves and CEPT Emblem*

| **C.D.S. POSTMARKS** |  |  |  |
|---|---|---|---|
| (1) | London Chief Office, EC – postal headquarters | 30 | n.k. |
| (2) | Torquay – Conference venue | 40 | n.k. |
| **SLOGAN POSTMARKS** |  |  |  |
| (3) | CEPT European Conference, Torquay | 15 | 5 |
| (4) | Post Office Savings Bank 1861-1961 | 200 | 25 |
| (5) | Express Good Wishes by Greeting's Telegram | n.k. | 25 |
| | **ANY OTHER POSTMARK (CDS or Slogan)** ........*from* | 10 | 2 |

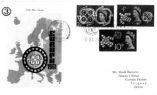

## 25th September 1961 – PARLIAMENT
*6d Hammer Beam Roof, Westminster Hall;*
*1s 3d Palace of Westminster*

|  | illustrated covers | plain covers |
|---|---|---|
| **C.D.S. POSTMARK** | £ | £ |
| (1) House of Commons, SW1 | 375 | 45 |
| (2) House of Lords, SW1 | 400 | 60 |
| (3) Parliament St or Westminster Bridge Rd, SW1 | 200 | 30 |
| (4) London SW1 | 100 | 20 |
| **SLOGAN POSTMARKS** |  |  |
| (5) Commonwealth Parliamentary Conference | 75 | 10 |
| **ANY OTHER POSTMARK (CDS or Slogan)**......*from* | 45 | 5 |

1962 - 67 stamps were printed with & without phosphor bands. All prices are now for illustrated covers. Plain covers are worth much less.

|  | non-phos. covers | phos. covers |
|---|---|---|

## 14th Nov. 1962 – NATIONAL PRODUCTIVITY YEAR
*2¹/2d, 3d, 1s 3d Productivity Emblems*

|  | £ | £ |
|---|---|---|
| **SLOGAN POSTMARKS** |  |  |
| (1) National Productivity Year, Nov 1962-63 | 60 | 130 |
| (2) Export & Prosper, NW1 | 375 | n.k. |
| (3) Southampton T – wavy line cancel | 125 | 110 |
| **ANY OTHER POSTMARK (CDS or Slogan)**......*from* | 50 | 90 |

## 21st March 1963 – FREEDOM FROM HUNGER
*2¹/2d, 1s 3d Campaign Emblems*

|  |  |  |
|---|---|---|
| **SPECIAL HANDSTAMPS** |  |  |
| (1) Tenth Anniversary Stampex 1963, SW1 | 85 | 85 |
| **SLOGAN POSTMARKS** |  |  |
| (2) Freedom From Hunger Week 17-24 March 1963 | 35 | 40 |
| (3) Southampton T – wavy line cancel | n.k. | 35 |
| **ANY OTHER POSTMARK (CDS or Slogan)**......*from* | 30 | 35 |

## 7th May 1963 – PARIS POSTAL CONFERENCE
*6d 'Paris Conference'*

|  |  |  |
|---|---|---|
| **SPECIAL HANDSTAMPS** |  |  |
| (1) Post Office Tercentenary, Dover Packet Service | 30 | 450 |
| (1a) - ditto - Dover Philatelic Society official cover | 45 | n.k. |
| **SLOGAN POSTMARKS** |  |  |
| (2) First Day of Issue–any office | 20 | 25 |
| (3) Norwich Addresses Need Post Codes | 250 | n.k. |
| (4) Southampton T–wavy line cancel | n.k. | 30 |
| **ANY OTHER POSTMARK (CDS or Slogan)**......*from* | 15 | 25 |

## 16th May 1963 – NATIONAL NATURE WEEK
*3d Posy of Flowers; 4¹/2d Woodland Life*

|  |  |  |
|---|---|---|
| **SPECIAL HANDSTAMPS** |  |  |
| (1) Brownsea Island Opening Week, Poole, Dorset | 140 | 140 |
| (2) Esperanto Kongresso, Stoke | 300 | n.k. |
| (2a) -ditto- Esperanto Kongresso official cover | 350 | n.k. |
| **C.D.S. POSTMARKS** |  |  |
| (3) Botanic Gardens, Belfast, Forest Row etc | – | 150 |
| (4) Selborne – 'Natural History of Selborne' | 120 | 120 |
| **SLOGAN POSTMARKS** |  |  |
| (5) First Day of Issue–any office | 20 | 25 |
| (6) Southampton T–wavy line cancel | n.k. | 25 |
| **ANY OTHER POSTMARK (CDS or Slogan)**......*from* | 20 | 25 |

## 31st May 1963 – LIFEBOAT CONFERENCE
*2¹/2d Rescue at Sea; 4d Lifeboat; 1s 6d Lifeboatmen*

|  |  |  |
|---|---|---|
| **C.D.S. POSTMARKS** |  |  |
| (1) Edinburgh | 125 | n.k. |
| (2) Lifeboat or RN Stations, e.g. Cromer etc | 125 | 125 |
| **SLOGAN POSTMARKS** |  |  |
| (3) International Lifeboat Conference, Edinburgh | 60 | 85 |
| (4) Southampton T–wavy line cancel | n.k. | 45 |
| (5) First Day of Issue–Edinburgh | 50 | 55 |
| **ANY OTHER POSTMARK (CDS or Slogan)**......*from* | 30 | 40 |

## 15th August 1963 – RED CROSS CENTENARY
*3d, 1s 3d, 1s 6d Red Cross*

|  |  |  |
|---|---|---|
| **SPECIAL HANDSTAMPS** |  |  |
| (1) World Union of Catholic Teachers | 500 | n.k. |
| **C.D.S. POSTMARKS** |  |  |
| (2) West Wellow, Romsey – Florence Nightingale | 125 | 150 |
| (3) Any hospital Post Office | 175 | 175 |
| **SLOGAN POSTMARKS** |  |  |
| (4) Red Cross Centenary – A Century of Service | 70 | 100 |
| (5) Southampton T–wavy line cancel | n.k. | 65 |
| **ANY OTHER POSTMARK (CDS or Slogan)**......*from* | 40 | 55 |

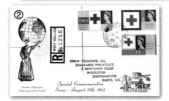

## 3rd December 1963 - COMMONWEALTH CABLE

*1/6d Commonwealth Cable (COMPAC)*

| | non-phos. covers £ | phos. covers £ |
|---|---|---|
| **SLOGAN POSTMARKS** | | |
| (1) First Day of Issue – Philatelic Bureau GPO, EC1 ... | 50 | 55 |
| (2) Southampton T – wavy line cancel ............................ | 50 | 50 |
| (3) First Day of Issue – any other office ........................ | 30 | 35 |
| (4) London WC FDI on Standard Telephones cover..... | 125 | n.k. |
| **ANY OTHER PMK (FDI, CDS or Slogan)**.............*from* | 20 | 30 |

The 'Ordinary F.D.I. postmarks' were introduced with effect from the 1964 Shakespeare issue. In general, these were collected in preference to the F.D.I slogan (envelope design).

## 23rd April 1964 - SHAKESPEARE FESTIVAL

*3d, 6d, 1s 3d, 1s 6d + 2s 6d (non-phos. only) scenes from plays*

| | | |
|---|---|---|
| **SPECIAL HANDSTAMPS** | | |
| (1) Shakespeare 400th Anniversary, Stratford................ | 35 | 35 |
| **ORDINARY F.D.I. POSTMARKS** | | |
| (2) Stratford-upon-Avon, Wks............................................ | 15 | 20 |
| **CDS POSTMARKS** | | |
| (2a) Field Post Office 1050 (Sited in Stratford)................ | 65 | 75 |
| (2b) London SE1 (Site of the Globe)................................... | nk | 75 |
| **SLOGAN POSTMARKS** | | |
| (3) Shakespeare Anniversary Year, Stratford.................. | 975 | 975 |
| (4) First Day of Issue, Stratford......................................... | 15(s) | 15(s) |
| **ANY OTHER PMK (FDI, CDS or Slogan)**.............*from* | 10 | 15 |

## 1st July 1964 - GEOGRAPHICAL CONGRESS

*2¹/₂d Flats; 4d Shipbuilding; 8d Forestry; 1s 6d Nuclear Power.*

| | | |
|---|---|---|
| **SPECIAL HANDSTAMPS** | | |
| (1) Lawn Tennis Championships AELTC, Wimbledon . | 250 | n.k. |
| **ORDINARY F.D.I. POSTMARKS** | | |
| (2) Philatelic Bureau ........................................................... | 25 | 35 |
| (3) London................................................................................ | 25 | 35 |
| **C.D.S. POSTMARKS** | | |
| (4) South Kensington – Royal Geographical Society.. | 150 | 150 |
| (5) Forest Row, Colliers Wood, Newtown or similar..... | 100 | 100 |
| **SLOGAN POSTMARKS** | | |
| (6) F.D.I. – Greenwich or SE10 (with triangle)......*each* | 300 | 300 |
| (7) Ralph Allen of Bath, Postal Pioneer.......................... | 400 | n.k. |
| (8) The Country Code–Leave no litter.............................. | 350 | n.k. |
| (9) Great Southampton Show............................................. | n.k. | 75 |
| **ANY OTHER PMK (FDI, CDS or Slogan)**.............*from* | 20 | 30 |

## 5th August 1964 - BOTANICAL CONGRESS

*3d Spring Gentian; 6d Dog Rose; 9d Honeysuckle; 1s 3d Water Lily*

| | | |
|---|---|---|
| **SPECIAL HANDSTAMPS** | | |
| (1) 10th International Botanical Congress, Edinburgh.. | 300 | 350 |
| **ORDINARY F.D.I. POSTMARKS** | | |
| (2) Philatelic Bureau or Edinburgh................................... | 30 | 50 |
| (3) Kingston-upon-Thames (local F.D.I. for Kew) ......... | 30 | 50 |
| **C.D.S. POSTMARKS** | | |
| (4) Forest Row, Wood Green or similar ........................... | 150 | 150 |
| (5) Kew Gardens or Primrose Valley, Filey ...........*each* | 200 | 200 |
| (6) Richmond & Twickenham (local CDS for Kew)...... | 175 | n.k. |
| **SLOGAN POSTMARKS** | | |
| (7) FDI–Richmond & Twickenham (Kew) ..................... | 200 | 200 |
| **ANY OTHER PMK (FDI, CDS or Slogan)**.............*from* | 25 | 35 |

## 4th September 1964 –FORTH ROAD BRIDGE

*3d, 6d Forth Road Bridge*

| | | |
|---|---|---|
| **SPECIAL HANDSTAMPS** | | |
| (1) Forth Road Bridge, North Queensferry ..................... | 45 | 125 |
| (2) Forth Road Bridge, South Queensferry..................... | 35 | 90 |
| (3) Apostolatus Maris – Int. Congress, Liverpool.......... | n.k. | 325 |
| **ORDINARY F.D.I. POSTMARKS** | | |
| (4) Philatelic Bureau........................................................... | 20 | 30 |
| (5) Edinburgh (local F.D.I. for Forth Rd Bridge)........... | 20 | 30 |
| **C.D.S. POSTMARKS** | | |
| (6) Balmoral Castle – The Queen proceeded to Balmoral after opening the Forth Road Bridge........ | 225 | 225 |
| (7) South Queensferry, West Lothian................................ | 90 | 90 |
| (8) North Queensferry, Fife................................................. | 125 | 125 |
| **SLOGAN POSTMARKS** | | |
| (9) F.D.I. – Edinburgh ......................................................... | 60 | 60 |
| (10) Midlothian for Industrial Sites................................... | 75 | 80 |
| (11) Edinburgh – wavy line cancellation ......................... | 40 | n.k. |
| **ANY OTHER PMK (FDI, CDS or Slogan)**.............*from* | 15 | 20 |

SHELLEY STAMPS,
COLLEGE HILL CHAMBERS,
COLLEGE HILL, LONDON, E.C.4

## 8th July 1965 - SIR WINSTON CHURCHILL
*4d, 1s 3d Silhouettes of Churchill*

| | non-phos. covers £ | phos. covers £ |
|---|---|---|
| **ORDINARY F.D.I. POSTMARKS** | | |
| (1) Bladon, Oxford – Churchill buried at Bladon ......... | 25 | 30 |
| (2) London SW1 ................................................................... | 10 | 15 |
| (3) Philatelic Bureau ....................................................... | 9 | 15 |
| **C.D.S. POSTMARKS** | | |
| (4) Churchill, Bristol or Oxford.................................*each* | 95 | 100 |
| (5) Any Field or RAF Post Office ................................... | 75 | n.k. |
| (6) House of Commons, SW1 .......................................... | 95 | 95 |
| (7) House of Lords, SW1................................................. | 145 | 145 |
| (8) Marlborough – the Churchill ancestral home.......... | 200 | n.k. |
| (9) Woodford Green – MP for Woodford...................... | 200 | n.k. |
| **SLOGAN POSTMARKS** | | |
| (10) First Day of Issue–Westminster, London SW1........ | 95 | 95 |
| (11) London SW1–wavy line cancellation ...................... | 50 | n.k. |
| **ANY OTHER PMK (FDI, CDS or Slogan)**............*from* | 8 | 9 |

## 19th July 1965 - 700th ANNIV. of PARLIAMENT
*6d De Montfort's Seal; 2s 6d (non-phos. only) Parliament*

| **ORDINARY F.D.I. POSTMARKS** | | |
|---|---|---|
| (1) Dover or Lincoln – first to be represented | | |
| at the Parliament by commoners......................*each* | 40 | 40 |
| (2) Evesham – Simon De Montfort killed here.............. | 35 | 35 |
| (3) London SW...................................................................... | 20 | 20 |
| (4) Leicester – De Montfort was Earl of Leicester....... | 35 | 35 |
| (5) Oxford – Parliament sometimes met at Oxford....... | 35 | 35 |
| (6) Philatelic Bureau ....................................................... | 15 | 15 |
| (7) Any other office ........................................................ | 12 | 12 |
| **C.D.S. POSTMARKS** | | |
| (8) Buckingham Palace, SW1 .......................................... | 200 | 150 |
| (9) Dover or Lincoln (see note above) ...................*each* | 60 | 60 |
| (10) Evesham – Simon De Montfort killed.................... | 125 | 100 |
| (11) House of Commons, SW1......................................... | 100 | 100 |
| (12) House of Lords, SW1............................................... | 125 | 125 |
| (13) North Warnborough – De Montfort's home........... | 275 | 275 |
| (14) London SW1 or Parliament Street, SW1 ................ | 75 | 75 |
| **SLOGAN POSTMARKS** | | |
| (15) London SW1 – wavy line cancel .............................. | 30 | n.k. |
| **ANY OTHER PMK (FDI, CDS or Slogan)**............*from* | 10 | 10 |

## 9th August 1965 – SALVATION ARMY
*3d, 1s 6d*

| **SPECIAL HANDSTAMPS** | | |
|---|---|---|
| (1) Portsmouth & District Philatelic Society ................. | 125 | 125 |
| (1a) -ditto- on Philatelic Society official cover .............. | 100 | 100 |
| **ORDINARY F.D.I. POSTMARKS** | | |
| (2) London EC – HQ of Salvation Army........................ | 35 | 40 |
| (3) Nottingham – Birthplace of William Booth ............. | 75 | 75 |
| **ANY OTHER PMK (FDI, CDS or Slogan)**............*from* | 25 | 35 |

## 1st September 1965 – JOSEPH LISTER (Antiseptic Surgery)
*4d Carbolic Spray; 1s Lister*

| **SPECIAL HANDSTAMPS** | | |
|---|---|---|
| (1) Eyam Plague Commemoration ................................... | 200 | n.k. |
| (1a) -ditto- (Eyam Plague official cover)........................... | 550 | n.k. |
| **ORDINARY F.D.I. POSTMARKS** | | |
| (2) Edinburgh – Professor of Clinical Surgery.............. | 50 | 50 |
| (2a) - ditto - (Royal Infirmary special cover).................. | 70 | 70 |
| (3) Glasgow – Lister was Professor of Surgery here...... | 60 | 50 |
| (4) GPO Philatelic Bureau, London EC1 ....................... | 30 | 30 |
| **C.D.S. POSTMARKS** | | |
| (5) Royal Infirmary Edinburgh (Royal Infirmary cvr).... | 225 | 225 |
| (6) Glasgow – Lister was Professor of Surgery here ..... | 125 | 150 |
| **SLOGAN POSTMARKS** | | |
| (7) First Day of Issue – Edinburgh................................... | 125 | 125 |
| **ANY OTHER PMK (FDI, CDS or Slogan)**............*from* | 25 | 25 |

## 1st Sept. 1965 – COMMONWEALTH ARTS FESTIVAL
*6d Trinidad Carnival Dancers; 1s 6d Canadian Folk Dancers*

| **SPECIAL HANDSTAMPS** | | |
|---|---|---|
| (1) Eyam Plague Commemoration ................................... | 150 | n.k. |
| (1a) -ditto- (Eyam Plague official cover)........................... | 700 | n.k. |
| **ORDINARY F.D.I. POSTMARKS** | | |
| (2) Cardiff, Glasgow, Liverpool or London..................... | 30 | 30 |
| **C.D.S. POSTMARKS** | | |
| (3) Balmoral Castle – Duke of Edinburgh travelled | | |
| from Balmoral Castle to open the Festival................. | 150 | 150 |
| (4) Buckingham Palace ...................................................... | 125 | n.k. |
| (5) Stratford-upon-Avon (on Arts Centre cover) ........... | 125 | n.k. |

| Commonwealth Arts (contd.) | non-phos. covers £ | phos. covers £ |
|---|---|---|
| **SLOGAN POSTMARKS** | | |
| (6)  Commonwealth Arts Festival, Glasgow ...................... | 700 | 800 |
| (7)  Commonwealth Arts Festival, Liverpool ................... | 700 | 800 |
| (8)  Commonwealth Arts Festival – any other office  ..... | 500 | 600 |
| (9)  4th Bach Festival Bath, October 1965, Bath ........... | 550 | n.k. |
| **ANY OTHER PMK (FDI, CDS or Slogan)**..............from | 20 | 25 |

### 13th Sept. 1965 – THE BATTLE OF BRITAIN
*6 x 4d; 9d, 1s 3d Battle scenes*

| | | |
|---|---|---|
| **ORDINARY F.D.I. POSTMARKS** | | |
| (1)  Philatelic Bureau............................................................. | 20 | 25 |
| **C.D.S. POSTMARKS** | | |
| (2)  Biggin Hill (packet pmk), Westerham or Cranwell.. | 100 | 100 |
| (3)  Biggin Hill (single or double ring metal pmk)........... | 150 | 150 |
| (4)  Churchill, Bristol.......................................................... | 75 | n.k. |
| (5)  Dover, Kent.................................................................... | 60 | 75 |
| (6)  Any RAF, RN or Field Post Office (FPO) pmk........ | 150 | 150 |
| **ANY OTHER PMK (FDI, CDS or Slogan)**..............from | 20 | 20 |

### 8th October 1965 – POST OFFICE TOWER
*3d Georgian Bldgs & Tower; 1s 3d Nash Terrace & Tower*

| | | |
|---|---|---|
| **SPECIAL HANDSTAMPS** | | |
| (1)  Leicester Philatelic Society Diamond Jubilee ......... | 75 | 85 |
| (1a) ditto – on Leicester Philatelic Soc. official cover ..... | 85 | 95 |
| **ORDINARY F.D.I. POSTMARKS** | | |
| (2)  London WC – Site of P.O. Tower.............................. | 20 | 20 |
| (3)  Philatelic Bureau......................................................... | 15 | 15 |
| **C.D.S. POSTMARKS** | | |
| (4)  Gt. Portland St. – nearest P.O. to the Tower............ | 125 | 125 |
| (5)  London W1 – site of P.O. Tower ................................ | 30 | 30 |
| **SLOGAN POSTMARKS** | | |
| (6)  Have you taken out your licence for Radio-TV?...... | 75 | 50 |
| (7)  London W1 (wavy line) – site of P.O. Tower............ | 20 | 20 |
| **ANY OTHER PMK (FDI, CDS or Slogan)**..............from | 15 | 15 |

### 25th Oct. 1965 – U.N. & INT. CO-OPERATION YEAR
*3d U.N. Emblem; 1s 6d I.C.Y. Emblem*

| | | |
|---|---|---|
| **SPECIAL HANDSTAMPS** | | |
| (1)  Leicester Philatelic Society Diamond Jubilee .......... | 70 | 80 |
| (1a) ditto – on Leicester Philatelic Soc. official cover .... | 80 | 90 |
| **ORDINARY F.D.I. POSTMARKS** | | |
| (2)  London SW – U.N. London HQ................................. | 25 | 35 |
| **C.D.S. POSTMARKS** | | |
| (3)  House of Commons, London SW1............................. | 50 | 65 |
| (4)  Royal Courts of Justice, Bow WC2 ............................ | 200 | n.k. |
| **SLOGAN POSTMARKS** | | |
| (5)  International Co-operation Year, Reading................. | 550 | 550 |
| **ANY OTHER PMK (FDI, CDS or Slogan)**..............from | 20 | 25 |

### 15th Nov. 1965 – INT. TELECOMMUNICATIONS
*9d Telecommunications; 1s 6d Radio Waves*

| | | |
|---|---|---|
| **C.D.S. POSTMARKS** | | |
| (1)  Helston – Goonhilly Downs Ground Station .......... | 325 | 325 |
| **SLOGAN POSTMARKS** | | |
| (2)  Have you taken out your licence for Radio-TV?...... | 275 | n.k. |
| **ANY OTHER PMK (FDI, CDS or Slogan)**..............from | 20 | 25 |

### 25th January 1966 – ROBERT BURNS
*4d, 1s 3d Portraits of Burns*

| | | |
|---|---|---|
| **SPECIAL HANDSTAMPS** | | |
| (1)  The friend of man to vice alone a foe – Dumfries.... | 20 | 20 |
| (2)  That man to man the warld o'er..... – Alloway........ | 15 | 15 |
| (3)  That man to man the warld o'er..... – Ayr ................. | 15 | 15 |
| (4)  That man to man the warld o'er..... – Edinburgh  ... | 20 | 20 |
| (5)  That man to man the warld o'er..... – Glasgow....... | 20 | 20 |
| (6)  That man to man the warld o'er..... – Greenock....... | 35 | 40 |
| (7)  That man to man the warld o'er..... – Kilmarnock .. | 20 | 20 |
| (8)  That man to man the warld o'er..... – Mauchline ..... | 35 | 40 |

*These special handstamps were sponsored by the Post Office. Various organisations produced covers using these handstamps but they are not 'official' as described in the General Notes. However, they do command a premium.*

| | | |
|---|---|---|
| **ORDINARY F.D.I. POSTMARKS** | | |
| (9)  Any Scottish postmark ................................................. | 8 | 10 |
| **C.D.S. POSTMARKS** | | |
| (10) Burns Statue, Ayr......................................................... | 275 | 275 |
| (11) Ayr - Carlisle TPO ....................................................... | 225 | n.k. |
| **ANY OTHER PMK (FDI, CDS or Slogan)**..............from | 7 | 8 |

## 28th February 1966 – WESTMINSTER ABBEY
*3d Abbey; 2s 6d (non-phos. only) Henry VII Chapel*

| | non-phos covers £ | phos. covers £ |
|---|---|---|
| **ORDINARY F.D.I. POSTMARKS** | | |
| (1) London SW | 25 | 25 |
| (2) Philatelic Bureau | 15 | 15 |
| **C.D.S. POSTMARKS** | | |
| (3) Buckingham Palace | 150 | 150 |
| (4) House of Commons or Parliament St. SW1 | 125 | 100 |
| (5) House of Lords | 155 | 135 |
| **SLOGAN POSTMARKS** | | |
| (6) Westminster Abbey 900th Anniversary Year | 150 | 120 |
| (7) First Day of Issue – Westminster, London SW1 | 160 | 100 |
| (8) London SW1 - wavy line postmark | 50 | 15 |
| ANY OTHER PMK (FDI, CDS or Slogan)............*from* | 15 | 15 |

## 2nd May 1966 – BRITISH LANDSCAPES
*4d Sussex; 1s 3d Harlech; ls 6d The Cairngorms*

| | | |
|---|---|---|
| **ORDINARY F.D.I. POSTMARKS** | | |
| (1) Lewes, Sussex – appropriate for 4d value | 75 | 75 |
| (2) Harlech, Merioneth – appropriate for 1s 3d | 150 | 90 |
| (3) Coleraine – appropriate for 6d value | 150 | 90 |
| (4) Grantown-on-Spey – appropriate for 1s 6d | 150 | 125 |
| (5) GPO Philatelic Bureau, London EC1 | 15 | 15 |
| **C.D.S. POSTMARKS** | | |
| (6) Antrim – appropriate for 6d value | 135 | 135 |
| (7) Coleraine – appropriate for 6d value | 135 | 135 |
| (8) Grantown-on-Spey – appropriate for 6d value | 135 | 135 |
| (9) Harlech – appropriate for 1s 3d value | 135 | 135 |
| (10) Forest Row, Heath Common or similar | 75 | 75 |
| ANY OTHER PMK (FDI, CDS or Slogan)............*from* | 10 | 10 |
| **SET** 4 single stamp covers with appropriate pmks | | |
| – usually (1), (2), (3) and (4) | 30 | 40 |

## 1st June 1966 – WORLD CUP FOOTBALL
*4d, 6d, 1s 3d Football scenes*

| | | |
|---|---|---|
| **ORDINARY F.D.I. POSTMARKS** | | |
| (1) Wembley, Middx | 35 | 45 |
| (2) Philatelic Bureau | 20 | 25 |
| (3) B'ham, Liverpool, Manchester, Middlesbrough, Sheffield, Sunderland – World Cup Games ......*each* | 35 | 45 |
| **SLOGAN POSTMARKS** | | |
| (4) First Day of Issue – Harrow & Wembley | 100 | 80 |
| (5) World Cup City, Sheffield, City of Steel | 650 | n.k. |
| (6) The Dairy Festival, Time for Sport | 400 | n.k. |
| (7) World Cup Sunderland .................*plain cover* | 250 | n.k. |
| ANY OTHER PMK (FDI, CDS or Slogan)............*from* | 15 | 25 |

## 8th August 1966 – BRITISH BIRDS
*4 x 4d Black-headed Gull; Blue Tit; Robin; Blackbird*

| | | |
|---|---|---|
| **SPECIAL HANDSTAMPS** | | |
| (1) Poloniae Millennium - Jamboree Lilford Park | 300 | – |
| **ORDINARY F.D.I. POSTMARKS** | | |
| (2) Philatelic Bureau | 30 | 30 |
| **C.D.S. POSTMARKS** | | |
| (3) Birdbrook (or similar) | 325 | – |
| ANY OTHER PMK (FDI, CDS or Slogan)............*from* | 20 | 20 |

## 18th August 1966 – 'ENGLAND WINNERS'
*4d World Cup stamp overprinted 'England Winners' (non-phosphor only)*

| | | |
|---|---|---|
| **SPECIAL HANDSTAMPS** | | |
| (1) World Methodist Conference, SW1 | 275 | – |
| (2) Opening of the Tay Road Bridge, Dundee | 50 | – |
| (2a) - do - on official cover | 175 | – |
| (3) Ballater Highland Games (official cover) | 125 | – |
| **ORDINARY F.D.I. POSTMARKS** | | |
| (4) Harrow & Wembley | 20 | – |
| (5) B'ham, Liverpool, Manchester, Middlesbrough Sheffield, Sunderland - World Cup Games ......*each* | 25 | – |
| **C.D.S. POSTMARKS** | | |
| (6) Harrow & Wembley, Middx | 35 | – |
| **SLOGAN POSTMARKS** | | |
| (7) Harrow & Wembley - wavy line cancel | 30 | – |
| ANY OTHER PMK (FDI, CDS or Slogan)............*from* | 10 | – |

*Some double-dated covers exist with the set of World Cup stamps postmarked 1st June and the England Winners stamp postmarked 18th August*

| | | |
|---|---|---|
| (1) Harrow & Wembley FDI double dated | 275 | |
| (2) B'ham, Liverpool, Manchester, Middlesbrough Sheffield or Sunderland – double dated | 125 | |
| ANY OTHER PMK (FDI, CDS or Slogan)............*from* | 70 | |

## 19th September 1966 – BRITISH TECHNOLOGY

*4d Jodrell Bank; 6d Motor Cars; 1s 3d Hovercraft;*
*1s 6d Nuclear Power*

| | | non-phos. covers £ | phos. covers £ |
|---|---|---|---|
| **ORDINARY F.D.I. POSTMARKS** | | | |
| (1) | Philatelic Bureau | 15 | 15 |
| (2) | B'ham, Coventry, Oxford, Liverpool - car industry.. | 30 | 35 |
| (3) | Carlisle, Cumberland - Windscale Reactor | 30 | 35 |
| (4) | Manchester - Jodrell Bank | 30 | 35 |
| (5) | Newport, Isle of Wight - Hovercraft | 30 | 35 |
| (6) | Portsmouth - Hovercraft | 30 | 35 |
| (7) | Luton, Beds - car industry | 30 | 35 |
| **C.D.S. POSTMARKS** | | | |
| (8) | Macclesfield, Cheshire (with Jodrell Bank cachet) .. | 150 | 175 |
| (9) | Cowes, I.O.W. (British Hovercraft Corp. cover) | 175 | 150 |
| (10) | Calderbridge, Seascale - Windscale reactor | 10(s) | – |
| (11) | Lower Withington - Jodrell Bank | 10(s) | – |
| **SLOGAN POSTMARKS** | | | |
| (12) | Build Your New Factory at Grimsby | 60 | – |
| (13) | Remploy (steering columns for the mini) | 125 | – |
| (14) | Stop Accidents (with road sign) | 175 | – |
| **ANY OTHER PMK (FDI, CDS or Slogan)**..............*from* | | 10 | 10 |
| **SET** 4 single stamp covers with appropriate pmks | | | |
| – usually (2), (3), (4) and (5) | | 30 | 45 |

## 14th October 1966 – BATTLE OF HASTINGS

*6 x 4d, 6d, 1s 3d Battle Scenes*

| **SPECIAL HANDSTAMPS** | | | |
|---|---|---|---|
| (1) | Battle of Hastings 900th Anniv. Battlefield | 12 | 15 |
| **ORDINARY F.D.I. POSTMARKS** | | | |
| (2) | Battle, Sussex | 12 | 15 |
| (3) | Hastings | 10 | 12 |
| (4) | Philatelic Bureau | 10 | 12 |
| (5) | Guernsey or Jersey.................................*each* | 10 | 10 |
| **C.D.S. POSTMARKS** | | | |
| (6) | Battle | 50 | 50 |
| (7) | Harold Hill or Normandy .....................*each* | 275 | 250 |
| (7a) | Hastings | 550 | 475 |
| **SLOGAN POSTMARKS** | | | |
| (8) | Les Iles Normandes, Guernsey (on 2 covers) | 400 | 400 |
| (9) | Les Iles Normandes, Jersey (on 2 covers) | 400 | 400 |
| (10) | Hastings Popular with Visitors since 1066 | 30(s) | 30(s) |
| **ANY OTHER PMK (FDI, CDS or Slogan)**..............*from* | | 10 | 10 |

## 1st December 1966 – CHRISTMAS

*3d, 1s 6d Children's Paintings*

| **SPECIAL HANDSTAMPS** | | | |
|---|---|---|---|
| (1) | British Stamp Exhibition, BF 1000 PS | 40 | 40 |
| (1a) | – ditto – on BFPS official cover | 25 | 25 |
| **ORDINARY F.D.I. POSTMARKS** | | | |
| (2) | Bethlehem, Llandeilo, Carms | 10 | 10 |
| (3) | Philatelic Bureau | 10 | 10 |
| **C.D.S. POSTMARKS** | | | |
| (4) | Bethlehem or Nazareth.........................*each* | 300 | 275 |
| (5) | Isle of Whithorn – first seat of Christianity | 150 | n.k. |
| (6) | St. Nicholas, Guildford | 150 | n.k. |
| **SLOGAN POSTMARKS** | | | |
| (7) | Britain Leads the World in Helping Spastics | 75 | 60 |
| (8) | Reedham School Caring for Children | 90 | n.k. |
| (9) | John Groom's Cares for the Disabled | 80 | 50 |
| (10) | Post Early for Christmas | 250 | n.k. |
| **ANY OTHER PMK (FDI, CDS or Slogan)**..............*from* | | 5 | 5 |

## 20th Feb. 1967 – EUROPEAN FREE TRADE AREA

*9d Sea Freight; 1s 6d Air Freight*

| **SPECIAL HANDSTAMPS** | | | |
|---|---|---|---|
| (1) | Radiation Biology Conference,Portmadoc | 30 | 30 |
| **ORDINARY F.D.I. POSTMARKS** | | | |
| (2) | Philatelic Bureau or London SW | 8 | 8 |
| (3) | Hounslow - Heathrow Airport | 15 | 15 |
| (4) | Hull, Grimsby or Newcastle – EFTA Ports | 25 | 25 |
| **C.D.S. POSTMARKS** | | | |
| (5) | Boston or similar  – EFTA Ports | 20 | 25 |
| (6) | House of Commons or House of Lords, SW1 | 60 | 55 |
| **SLOGAN POSTMARKS** | | | |
| (7) | Ship Early Through the Port of London | 175 | 175 |
| (8) | Southend, Sunderland or Liverpool slogans | 50 | 50 |
| (9) | Tees Side Means Business .................*plain covers* | 15 | 15 |
| (10) | Are you under insured? | 50 | 50 |
| **ANY OTHER PMK (FDI, CDS or Slogan)**..............*from* | | 8 | 8 |

## 24th April 1967 – WILD FLOWERS
*4 x 4d, 9d & 1s 9d Wild Flowers*

| | non-phos. | phos. |
|---|---|---|
| **SPECIAL HANDSTAMPS** | £ | £ |
| (1) RSH Health Congress, Eastbourne | 250 | 250 |
| (1a) -ditto- on official cover | 400 | n.k. |
| **ORDINARY F.D.I. POSTMARKS** | | |
| (2) Philatelic Bureau | 10 | 10 |
| (3) Kingston-upon-Thames (local F.D.I. for Kew) | 15 | 15 |
| **C.D.S. POSTMARKS** | | |
| (4) Bluebell Hill, Flore, Hawthorn or Primrose St | 175 | 175 |
| (5) Kew Gardens or Flowery Field | 150 | 150 |
| (6) Hedgend, Forest Row, Welwyn Gdn City etc | 75 | 75 |
| **ANY OTHER PMK (FDI, CDS or Slogan)** ......*from* | 12 | 15 |

# OFFICIAL OR ORDINARY?

The most frequently asked question: *'What is the difference between official covers and ordinary covers?'*

SEE PAGE 8 FOR MORE DETAILS

*The two covers on the left are official and the two on the right are ordinary.*

*However both pairs have identical postmarks.*

### OFFICIAL or SPONSORED COVERS
In the context of this catalogue, 'official' or 'sponsored' covers are defined as covers produced by private organisations or cover producers, who at the same time sponsor a special handstamp to accompany their cover. In the above two examples *Markton Stamps* of Norfolk produced a cover for the Norfolk Naturalists' Trust and sponsored a special postmark, and the Police cover was produced for the Metropolitan Police Force by *Cotswold Covers*.

### ORDINARY or COMMERCIAL COVERS
These are produced primarily for the general FDC collector and are usually sold as 'blanks' (i.e with no stamps affixed). They are available from most good stamp shops before the day of issue of the postage stamps. The Wildlife cover was produced by *Philart Covers*, and the Police cover by *Stuart Covers* - both were available as blanks. Collectors purchase the covers, affix the stamps, and then send their covers to the Royal Mail Special Handstamp Centres requesting that their covers be postmarked with any of the privately sponsored handstamps. See the General Notes for more details.

*FROM THE NEXT ISSUE PRICES ARE GIVEN FOR BOTH TYPES OF COVER (where available)*

## 10th July 1967 – PAINTINGS
*4d 'Master Lambton' (Lawrence); 9d Stubbs; 1s 6d 'Children Coming Out of School' (Lowry)*

| | ordinary covers | official covers | |
|---|---|---|---|
| **SPECIAL HANDSTAMPS** | £ | £ | |
| (1) Art on Stamps Exhibition,WC2 | 35 | 125 | *P.R. O'Connell* |
| **ORDINARY F.D.I. POSTMARKS** | | | |
| (2) Philatelic Bureau | 10 | | |
| (3) Bishop Auckland -'Master Lambton' | 50 | | |

## 24th July 1967 – SIR FRANCIS CHICHESTER
*1s 9d Gipsy Moth IV*

| | | | |
|---|---|---|---|
| **SPECIAL HANDSTAMPS** | | | |
| (1) Philatelic Bureau | 10 | – | *Post Offfice* |
| (2) Greenwich, SE10 | 10 | – | *Post Office* |
| (3) Plymouth | 10 | – | *Post Office* |
| (4) International Camp, E. Mersea | 250 | – | *n.o.c.* |
| **ORDINARY F.D.I. POSTMARKS** | | | |
| (5) Barnstaple – Birthplace of Chichester | 20 | | |
| (6) Chichester, Sussex or Gosport, Hants ......*each* | 15 | | |
| **C.D.S. POSTMARKS** | | | |
| (7) Barnstaple or Selsey, Chichester | 25 | | |
| (8) Chichester Road, Portsmouth. | 400 | | |
| (9) House of Commons (Outward Bound cover) | 25 | | |
| (10) Shirwell – ancestral home of Chichester | 150 | | |
| **SLOGAN POSTMARKS** | | | |
| (11) Ship through the Port of London | 125 | | |

## 19th September 1967 – BRITISH DISCOVERY
*4d Radar; 1s Penicillin;*
*1s 6d Jet Engine; 1s 9d Television*

|  |  | ordinary covers £ | official covers £ |
|---|---|---|---|
| **SPECIAL HANDSTAMPS** | | | |
| (1) | Penicillin/Sir Alexander Fleming, W2 | 25 | – *n.o.c.* |
| (2) | HMS Discovery, WC | 20 | – *n.o.c.* |
| (3) | BF 1000 PS (used at RAF Bruggen) | 80 | 110 *Forces* |
| **ORDINARY F.D.I. POSTMARKS** | | | |
| (4) | Philatelic Bureau | 5 | |
| (5) | Coventry – birthplace of Whittle | 15 | |
| (6) | Hounslow (jet) or Hastings (first TV images) | 15 | |
| (7) | London SW (British Drug Houses cover) | 25 | |
| (8) | Paddington W2 – discovery of penicillin | 15 | |
| (9) | Plymouth (with Westward TV logo) | 20 | |
| (10) | Any other office | 5 | |
| **C.D.S. POSTMARKS** | | | |
| (11) | Benenden Chest Hospital, Cranbrook | 375 | |
| (12) | Brechin – birthplace of Watson-Watt | 25(s) | |
| (13) | Darvel – birthplace of Fleming | 25(s) | |
| (14) | Helensburgh – birthplace Baird | 150 | |
| **SLOGAN POSTMARKS** | | | |
| (15) | First Day of Issue – Paddington W2 | 100 | |
| **SET** | 4 single stamp covers with appropriate pmks | | |
| | – usually (5), (12), (13) and (14) | 45 | |

## 18th October 1967 – CHRISTMAS
*4d 'Madonna and Child'*

|  |  | £ |
|---|---|---|
| **ORDINARY F.D.I. POSTMARKS** | | |
| (1) | Bethlehem, Llandeilo, Carms | 5 |
| (2) | Philatelic Bureau | 3 |
| **C.D.S. POSTMARKS** | | |
| (3) | Bethlehem, Nasareth or Jericho | 150 |
| (4) | St. Nicholas | 75 |
| **SLOGAN POSTMARKS** | | |
| (5) | First Day of Issue – Bethlehem | 10 |
| (6) | Oxfam - 25th Year | 25 |
| (7) | Visit Roman Bath | 100 |

## 27th November 1967 – CHRISTMAS
*3d, 1s 6d 'Adoration of the Shepherds'*

|  |  | | |
|---|---|---|---|
| **SPECIAL HANDSTAMPS** | | | |
| (1) | Dulwich Millennium | 125 | 225 |
| **ORDINARY F.D.I. POSTMARKS** | | | |
| (2) | Philatelic Bureau | 2 | |
| (3) | Bethlehem, Llandeilo, Carms | 5 | |
| **C.D.S. POSTMARKS** | | | |
| (4) | Bethlehem or Nasareth | 200 | |
| (5) | St. Nicholas, Starcross or similar | 225 | |
| **SLOGAN POSTMARKS** | | | |
| (6) | First Day of Issue – Bethlehem | 75 | |
| (7) | Christmas Illuminations, Cheltenham | 325 | |
| (8) | First Ever Christmas Present, Londonderry | 375 | |
| (9) | Oxfam - 25th Year | 50 | |
| (10) | Visit Roman Bath (plain cover) | 25 | |

*Some **double-dated** covers exist with the 4d stamp postmarked 18th October
and the 3d & 1s 6d stamps postmarked 27th November*

| (1) | Bethlehem First Day of Issue | 30 |
|---|---|---|
| (2) | Any other postmark | 20 |

## 29th April 1968 – BRITISH BRIDGES
*4d Tarr Steps, Dulverton; 9d Aberfeldy Bridge;*
*1s 6d Menai Bridge; 1s 9d M4 Viaduct, Chiswick*

|  |  | | |
|---|---|---|---|
| **SPECIAL HANDSTAMPS** | | | |
| (1) | First Day of Issue - Philatelic Bureau | 10 | – *Post Office* |
| (2) | First Day of Issue - Bridge | 10 | – *Post Office* |
| (3) | RSH Health Congress, Eastbourne | 200 | 300 *R.S.H.* |
| **ORDINARY F.D.I. POSTMARKS** | | | |
| (4) | Perth (Aberfeldy) or Exeter (Dulverton) | 25 | |
| (5) | Bath (Pulteney Bridge cover) | 30 | |
| (6) | Lincoln or Windsor (on special covers) | 25 | |
| **C.D.S. POSTMARKS** | | | |
| (7) | Aberfeldy – featured on 9d value | 150 | |
| (8) | Chiswick – featured on 1s 9d value | 175 | |
| (9) | Dulverton – featured on 4d value | 250 | |
| (10) | Menai – featured on 1s 6d value | 125 | |
| **SLOGAN POSTMARKS** | | | |
| (11) | First Day of Issue – Bridge, Canterbury | 80 | |
| (12) | First Day of Issue – Menai Bridge | 80 | |
| (13) | First Day of Issue – Aberfeldy | 80 | |
| (14) | Chiswick – wavy line cancellation | 150 | |
| (15) | Harlow - Motorists Week (known on 2 cvrs) | 350 | |
| **SET** | 4 single stamp covers with appropriate pmks | | |
| | – usually (8), (9), (12) and (13) | 40 | |

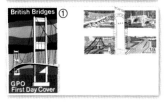

## 29th May 1968 – BRITISH ANNIVERSARIES

*4d TUC; 9d Votes for Women;*
*1s RAF; 1s 9d James Cook*

| | | ordinary covers £ | official covers £ |
|---|---|---|---|
| **SPECIAL HANDSTAMPS** | | | |
| (1) | First Day of Issue, Manchester TUC 100 ........ | 80 | – *Post Office* |
| (2) | First Day of Issue, Women's Suffrage .............. | 80 | – *Post Office* |
| (3) | First Day of Issue, Hendon, NW4 ................... | 80 | – *Post Office* |
| (4) | First Day of Issue, Whitby .............................. | 80 | – *Post Office* |
| (5) | 50th Anniversary RAF Leuchars, Fife............... | 250 | 20 *Forces(s)* |
| (6) | 50th Anniv. RAF Medmenham......................... | 190 | – *n.o.c.* |
| (7) | RAF 50th Anniv. Fylingdales ............................ | 190 | 20 *Forces(s)* |
| (8) | RAF 50th Anniv. RAF College Cranwell........... | 250 | 20 *Forces(s)* |
| (9) | RAF Escaping Society, BF 1067 PS.................. | 190 | 20 *Forces(s)* |
| (10) | BF 1000 PS (used at RAF Laarbrucke) ............. | 190 | – *n.o.c.* |
| (11) | P.O. Engineering Union 100000, Ealing........... | 250 | 30 *P.O.E.U.(s)* |
| (12) | RNIB Centenary , London SW1 ...................... | 350 | – *n.o.c.* |
| **ORDINARY F.D.I. POSTMARKS** | | | |
| (13) | Philatelic Bureau ............................................ | 10 | |
| (14) | Any other office.............................................. | 8 | |
| **C.D.S. POSTMARKS** | | | |
| (15) | Hendon ........................................................... | 30 | |
| (16) | House of Commons or Lords, SW1 ................. | 45 | |
| (17) | Forces P.O. or any Field Post Office ............... | 50 | |
| (18) | Digby Aerodrome or Trinity (Montrose Airbase)... | 75 | |
| (19) | Marton-in-Cleveland – b/place Captain Cook. | 10(s) | |
| (20) | Any R.A.F. Post Office e.g. Hawkinge ............. | 100 | |
| (21) | Tolpuddle, Dorset – Tolpuddle Martyrs ........... | 250 | |
| **SLOGAN POSTMARKS** | | | |
| (22) | Bicentenary Captain Cook ......*(on four covers)* | 75 | |
| **SET** 4 single stamp covers with appropriate pmks | | | |
| – usually (1), (2), (3) and (4)........................................ | | 15 | |

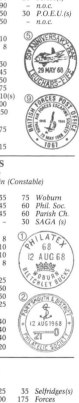

## 12th August 1968 – BRITISH PAINTINGS

*4d Elizabeth I (artist unknown); 1s Pinkie (Lawrence);*
*1s 6d Ruins of St. Mary le Port (Piper); 1s 9d Hay Wain (Constable)*

| | | | |
|---|---|---|---|
| **SPECIAL HANDSTAMPS** | | | |
| (1) | Philatex 68 Woburn, Bletchley ....................... | 35 | 75 *Woburn* |
| (2) | Portsmouth & District Philatelic Society ......... | 45 | 60 *Phil. Soc.* |
| (3) | Parish Church Restoration Kettering ................ | 45 | 60 *Parish Ch.* |
| (4) | SAGA (Scouts & Guides), Beeley..................... | – | 30 *SAGA (s)* |
| **ORDINARY F.D.I. POSTMARKS** | | | |
| (5) | Philatelic Bureau ............................................ | 8 | |
| (6) | Bristol – Birthplace of Lawrence ..................... | 10 | |
| (7) | Ipswich – F.D.I. for 'Constable Country'.......... | 10 | |
| (8) | Any other office.............................................. | 8 | |
| **C.D.S. POSTMARKS** | | | |
| (9) | Blackheath SE3 – Queen Elizabeth ................. | 225 | |
| (10) | East Bergholt – Constable's birthplace ............. | 450 | |
| (11) | Greenwich, SE10 – Birthplace of Elizabeth I.. | 250 | |
| (12) | Richmond – 'Pinkie'........................................ | 225 | |
| **SLOGAN POSTMARKS** | | | |
| (13) | F.D.I. – Hatfield – Hatfield Hse ....................... | 40 | |
| (14) | F.D.I. – London SE1 – B/place of Elizabeth ... | 40 | |
| (15) | F.D.I. – London W1 – Art galleries ................. | 40 | |
| **SET** 4 single stamp covers with appropriate pmks.. | | 20 | |

## 25th November 1968 – CHRISTMAS

*4d, 9d, 1s 6d Childrens Toys*

| | | | |
|---|---|---|---|
| **SPECIAL HANDSTAMPS** | | | |
| (1) | Selfridges Toy Fair, London W1 ...................... | 25 | 35 *Selfridges(s)* |
| (2) | HMS Hermes, BF 1074 PS .............................. | 100 | 175 *Forces* |
| **ORDINARY F.D.I. POSTMARKS** | | | |
| (3) | Philatelic Bureau ............................................ | 4 | |
| (4) | Bethlehem, Llandeilo, Carms........................... | 8 | |
| (5) | Any other office.............................................. | 3 | |
| **SLOGAN POSTMARKS** | | | |
| (6) | First Day of Issue – Bethlehem ........................ | 40 | |
| (7) | Christmas Illuminations, Cheltenham................ | 10(s) | |

## 15th January 1969 – BRITISH SHIPS

*5d 'Queen Elizabeth 2'; 9d 'Cutty Sark'; 9d Elizabethan Galleon;*
*9d East Indiaman; 1s 'SS Great Britain'; 1s RMS 'Mauretania'*

| | | | |
|---|---|---|---|
| **SPECIAL HANDSTAMPS** | | | |
| (1) | Lloyd's New Coffee House EC3........................ | 90 | – *n.o.c.* |
| (2) | Cutty Sark , Greenwich SE10............................ | 35 | – *n.o.c.* |
| **ORDINARY F.D.I. POSTMARKS** | | | |
| (3) | Philatelic Bureau ............................................ | 15 | |
| (4) | Belfast, Glasgow or Newcastle – Shipbuilding | 25 | |
| (5) | Bristol, Liverpool, Plymouth or Portsmouth .... | 25 | |
| (6) | London EC or SE1.......................................... | 20 | |
| (7) | Southampton (QE2) or Dover (Channel port) ... | 20 | |
| (8) | Any other office.............................................. | 12 | |

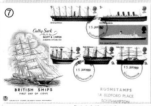

| Ships (contd.) | ordinary covers | official covers |
|---|---|---|
| C.D.S. POSTMARKS | £ | £ |
| (9) Clydebank or Maritime Mail ......................*each* | 250 | |
| (10) The Quarterdeck or British Fleet Mail ............. | 150 | |
| (11) Southampton, Plymouth or Seaview.........*each* | 50 | |
| **SLOGAN POSTMARKS** | | |
| (12) F.D.I. Greenwich or Great Britain W2.............. | 20 | |

## 3rd March 1969 - CONCORDE
*4d in flight, 9d plan & elevation, 1s 6d nose & tail*

| ORDINARY F.D.I. POSTMARKS | | |
|---|---|---|
| (1) Filton Bristol............................................................ | 15 | |
| (1a) -do- with 'Conseil de L'Europe' postmark ....... | 30 | |
| (2) Hounslow, Middx - Heathrow............................ | 25 | |
| (3) Philatelic Bureau or any other office ................ | 4 | |
| **C.D.S. POSTMARKS** | | |
| (4) Bristol.................................................................... | 40 | |
| (5) Farnborough ....................................................... | 75 | |

## 2nd April 1969 – NOTABLE ANNIVERSARIES
*5d Alcock & Brown, 9d Europa; 1s International Labour Organisation;*
*1s 6d NATO; 1s 9d 1st England/Australia flight*

| SPECIAL HANDSTAMPS | | | |
|---|---|---|---|
| (1) Alcock & Brown, Manchester ...................... | 35 | 20 | *Man.Airp.(s)* |
| (2) NATO HQ BF 1080 PS .................................. | 250 | 325 | *N.A.T.O.* |
| (3) NATO SHAPE BF 1081 PS ........................... | 250 | 325 | *N.A.T.O* |
| (4) Hoverlloyd, Pegwell Bay .............................. | 425 | 25 | *Hoverlloyd(s)* |
| (5) BF 1000 PS (used at Mill Hill) .................... | 250 | 150 | *Forces* |
| (6) Grammar School Centenary, Doncaster. | 175 | 200 | *DonGramSch* |
| **ORDINARY F.D.I. POSTMARKS** | | | |
| (7) Hounslow or Manchester ............................. | 25 | | |
| (8) London SW – Int. Labour Org....................... | 15 | | |
| (9) Philatelic Bureau ......................................... | 6 | | |
| (10) Any other office............................................ | 3 | | |
| **C.D.S. POSTMARKS** | | | |
| (11) Farnborough, Hants ..................................... | 125 | | |
| (12) Field Post Office postmarks ........................ | 25 | | |
| **SLOGAN POSTMARKS** | | | |
| (13) Manchester Airport/Alcock & Brown.............. | 40(s) | | |
| (14) Fly the Prestwick Way ................................. | 50 | | |
| **SET** 5 single stamp covers with appropriate pmks .. | 15 | | |

## 28th May 1969 – BRITISH CATHEDRALS
*4 x 5d – Durham, York, Canterbury, Edinburgh; 9d St. Paul's; 1s 6d Liverpool*

| SPECIAL HANDSTAMPS | | | |
|---|---|---|---|
| (1) Metropolitan Cathedral, Liverpool.................... | 30 | 35 | *Stampex(s)* |
| (2) Philatex St. Pauls, London EC.......................... | 25 | – | *n.o.c.* |
| (3) York Minster ................................................... | 40 | 50 | *York Mins.* |
| (4) Lewis's Stamp Exhibition, Manchester 1 ...... | 300 | – | *n.o.c.* |
| (5) Croeso 69 Tywyn Merioneth .......................... | 40 | 50 | *Tywyn* |
| (6) German British Culture Week BF 1078 PS...... | 40 | 40 | *Forces* |
| (7) Ulster Recruiting BF 1085 PS ........................ | 40 | 40 | *Forces* |
| **ORDINARY F.D.I. POSTMARKS** | | | |
| (8) GPO Philatelic Bureau, Edinburgh 1 ............... | 6 | | |
| (9) London EC – St. Paul's or York ...................... | 15 | | |
| (10) Canterbury, Durham, Edinburgh or Liverpool | 15 | | |
| (11) Any other office............................................... | 5 | | |
| **C.D.S. POSTMARKS** | | | |
| (12) Alcester (Alcester Church Restoration cvr) ...... | 175 | | |
| (13) Durham or Winchester ...............................*each* | 50 | | |
| **SET** single stamp covers with appropriate pmks....... | 15 | | |

## 1st July 1969 – PRINCE OF WALES
*3 x 5d Caernarvon Castle; 9d Celtic Cross; 1s Prince Charles*

| SPECIAL HANDSTAMPS | | | |
|---|---|---|---|
| (1) Croes Geltaidd, Margam Abbey ......................... | 120 | – | *n.o.c.* |
| (2) Croeso 69, Investiture Day, Cardiff ................ | 120 | – | *n.o.c.* |
| (3) Talyllyn Railway, Tywyn, Merioneth ................. | 45 | 50 | *Tywyn* |
| (4) Nettleham, Lincoln ......................................... | 120 | 80 | *Nettleham* |
| (5) BF 1000 PS (troop camp for Investiture)......... | 175 | 175 | *Forces* |
| (6) Lawn Tennis Championships............................ | 475 | – | *n.o.c.* |
| **ORDINARY F.D.I. POSTMARKS** | | | |
| (7) GPO Philatelic Bureau, Edinburgh 1 ............... | 5 | | |
| (8) London SW, Windsor or Cardiff....................... | 5 | | |
| (9) Truro (Duchy of Cornwall) or Chester (Earl) .. | 25 | | |
| (10) Day of Investiture, Caernarvon ....................... | 5 | | |
| **C.D.S. POSTMARKS** | | | |
| (11) Buckingham Palace or Windsor Castle ............ | 275 | | |
| (12) Catterick (Royal Lancers PoWales's cover)...... | 150 | | |
| (13) House of Commons or Lords......................*each* | 65 | | |
| **SLOGAN POSTMARKS** | | | |
| (14) Dydd yr Arwisgo, Investiture Day..................... | 275 | | |
| (15) Wales Tomorrow Exhibition, Cardiff................ | 20(s) | | |

### 13th August 1969 - GANDHI

*1s 6d Mahatma Gandhi*

| | | ordinary covers | official covers |
|---|---|---|---|
| **SPECIAL HANDSTAMPS** | | £ | £ |
| (1) | Gandhi Centenary Year HCRC, E8.................. | 5 | 30 *Hackney CRC* |
| (2) | Trade Fair & Exhibition Llanelli, Carms ......... | 250 | – *n.o.c.* |
| (3) | International Youth Camp, Colchester.............. | 250 | – *n.o.c.* |
| **ORDINARY F.D.I. POSTMARKS** | | | |
| (4) | Philatelic Bureau or any other office ................ | 2 | |

### 1st October 1969 - POST OFFICE TECHNOLOGY

*5d Giro; 9d & 1s Telecommunications; 1s 6d Automatic Sorting*

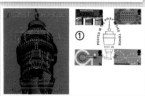

| | | | |
|---|---|---|---|
| **SPECIAL HANDSTAMPS** | | | |
| (1) | Posted in the Post Office Tower, W1 ................ | 7 | – *n.o.c.* |
| (2) | P.O. Technology University College, WC1 ....... | 7 | – *n.o.c.* |
| (3) | Philatelic Stand Ideal Homes, Birmingham..... | 250 | – *n.o.c.* |
| (4) | Southampton Boat Show, Mayflower Park ..... | 175 | 35 *Boat Show(s)* |
| (5) | National Postal Museum, EC1...................... | 110 | – *Post Office* |
| **ORDINARY F.D.I. POSTMARKS** | | | |
| (6) | Philatelic Bureau or any other office ................ | 3 | |
| (7) | Norwich – first use of postal coding ............... | 10 | |
| (8) | London EC (British Week in Tokyo cover)...... | 20 | |
| **C.D.S. POSTMARKS** | | | |
| (9) | Bootle – Giro HQ - featured on 5d value......... | 20(s) | |
| **SLOGAN POSTMARKS** | | | |
| (10) | Muncipal Bank Golden Jubilee Birmingham ... | 150 | |
| (11) | Remember to use the Postcode ........................ | 300 | |
| **SET** 4 single stamp covers with appropriate postmarks | | | |
| – usually (1), (2), (7) and (9) ........................ | | 25 | |

### 26th November 1969 - CHRISTMAS

*4d, 5d, 1s 6d The Nativity*

| | | | |
|---|---|---|---|
| **SPECIAL HANDSTAMPS** | | | *Temple of* |
| (1) | Jerusalem, Skellingthorpe, Lincs ....................... | 40 | 40 *Jerusalem* |
| **ORDINARY F.D.I. POSTMARKS** | | | |
| (2) | GPO Philatelic Bureau, Edinburgh l................ | 3 | |
| (3) | Bethlehem, Llandeilo, Carms............................ | 3 | |
| (4) | Any other office ............................................... | 2 | |
| **C.D.S. POSTMARKS** | | | |
| (5) | Bethlehem, Llandeilo, Carms ........................... | 200 | |
| (6) | Nasareth, Gwynedd ....................................... | 150 | |
| **SLOGAN POSTMARKS** | | | |
| (7) | First Day of Issue – Bethlehem ......................... | 60 | |
| (8) | Christmas Illuminations in Cheltenham .......... | 40(s) | |
| (9) | Christmas Dick Whittington, Lewisham .......... | 225 | |
| (10) | National Childrens Home .................................. | 50 | |
| (11) | Elgin (depicts cathedral)................*plain cover* | 20 | |

### 11th February 1970 - BRITISH RURAL ARCHITECTURE

*5d Fife harling; 9d Cotswold limestone; 1s Welsh stucco; 1s 6d Ulster thatch*

| | | | |
|---|---|---|---|
| **ORDINARY F.D.I. POSTMARKS** | | | |
| (1) | Philatelic Bureau..................................... | 4 | |
| (2) | Aberaeron – 1s Welsh stucco............................ | 12 | |
| (3) | Belfast (1s 6d) or Dunfermline (5d).........*each* | 12 | |
| (4) | Edinburgh (5d) or Gloucester (9d) ..........*each* | 12 | |
| (5) | Any other office ............................................... | 2 | |
| **C.D.S. POSTMARKS** | | | |
| (6) | Auchtermuchty, Fife – 5d Fife harling .............. | 125 | |
| (7) | Bibury or Chipping Campden – 9p.................. | 125 | |
| (8) | Criccieth (Criccieth Philatelic Soc cover) ........ | 40 | |
| (9) | Cirencester or Stroud – 9d Cotswold limestone ... | 75 | |
| (10) | Culross, Fife – 5d Fife harling............................ | 80 | |
| (11) | Holywood, Co. Down – 1s 6d Ulster thatch .... | 125 | |
| **SLOGAN POSTMARKS** | | | |
| (12) | Keep Britain Green – Conservation Year ........ | 175 | |
| (13) | 1970 Furniture Show........................*plain cover* | 20 | |
| **SET** 4 single stamp covers with appropriate pmks ... | | 12 | |

### 1st April 1970 - GENERAL ANNIVERSARIES

*5d Declaration of Arbroath; 9d Florence Nightingale;1s Co-operative Alliance; 1s 6d Mayflower; 1s 9d Royal Astronomical Society*

| | | | |
|---|---|---|---|
| **SPECIAL HANDSTAMPS** | | | |
| (1) | Anniversary Stamps, Canterbury...................... | 20 | – *n.o.c.* |
| (2) | Florence Nightingale Hospital NW1................. | 60 | – *n.o.c.* |
| (3) | Florence Nightingale Exhibition, SE1.............. | 45 | 50 *F.N. Cttee* |
| (4) | The Crimean War, BF 1206 PS.......................... | 350 | 15 *Forces(s)* |
| (5) | Florence Nightingale, BF 1121 PS..................... | 175 | 15 *Forces(s)* |
| (6) | Florence Nightingale, BF 1205 PS..................... | 300 | 15 *Forces(s)* |
| (7) | London Co-op Golden Year, E15...................... | 275 | 20 *Co-op(s)* |
| (8) | Int. Co-operative Alliance ICA, W1.................. | 250 | – *n.o.c.* |
| (9) | Mayflower '70, Scrooby, Doncaster.................. | 275 | 30 *Scrooby(s)* |
| (10) | Sir William Herschel, Slough............................ | 80 | – *n.o.c.* |
| (11) | Air-sea Warfare Dev. Unit, RAF Ballykelly ...... | 225 | 350 *RAF Ballykelly* |
| (12) | Air Mountains Base, Gibraltar, BF 1112 PS..... | 225 | 20 *Forces(s)* |

*General Anniversaries (contd.)*

| | ordinary covers | official covers |
|---|---|---|
| **ORDINARAY F.D.I. POSTMARKS** | £ | £ |
| (13) Philatelic Bureau or any other office ............... | 3 | |
| (14) Arbroath – 5d Declaration of Arbroath........... | 45 | |
| (15) Billericay or Boston – 'Mayflower' associations...... | 15 | |
| (16) London W1 – World HQ of ICA..................... | 12 | |
| (17) Plymouth – 1s 6d Pilgrim Fathers.................... | 12 | |
| (17a)-do- on special Plymouth cover ..................... | 25 | |
| (18) Rochdale – first Co-op.................................... | 25 | |
| (19) Slough – Sir William Herschel..................... | 20 | |
| (20) Southampton – Pilgrim Fathers........................ | 15 | |
| (20a)-do- on Southampton City Council cover......... | 25 | |
| **C.D.S. POSTMARKS** | | |
| (21) Immingham or Scrooby – Pilgrim Fathers........... | 20(s) | |
| (22) Southampton – Pilgrim Fathers.................... | 35 | |
| (23) Forces P.O. (Florence Nightingale/Crimea) ...... | 35 | |
| **SLOGAN POSTMARKS** | | |
| (24) Plymouth Mayflower 70................................. | 35(s) | |
| (25) Boston Lincs. Mayflower 70 ........................... | 35(s) | |
| (26) Rochdale – wavy line postmark ........................ | 35(s) | |
| (27) London W1 wavy line - HQ of ICA.................. | 25 | |
| **SET** 5 single stamp covers with appropriate pmks... | 15 | |

## 3rd June 1970 – LITERARY ANNIVERSARIES

*4 x 5d Dickens characters; 1s 6d Wordsworth*

**SPECIAL HANDSTAMPS**

| | | | |
|---|---|---|---|
| (1) E78 Chigwell, Essex ....................................... | 60 | 95 | *Chigwell* |
| (2) Dickens Fellowship, Broadstairs ...................... | 50 | 90 | *Broadstairs\** |
| (3) Old Curiosity Shop, WC2 .......................... | 20 | 30 | *Cameo* |
| (4) Dickens Centenary, Pickwick, Corsham .......... | 70 | 150 | *Corsham* |
| (5) David Copperfield, Winterbourne.................. | 60 | 90 | *Winterbourne\** |
| (6) Living Exhibition '70, Sheffield ...................... | n.k. | 150 | *Sheffield Living* |

*\* These two official covers are only known with the 4 Dickens stamps*

**ORDINARY F.D.I. POSTMARKS**

| | |
|---|---|
| (7) British Philatelic Bureau, Edinburgh 1 ............. | 5 |
| (8) Broadstairs – 'Bleak House' ........................... | 15 |
| (9) Cambridge – Wordsworth educated here........... | 15 |
| (10) Cockermouth – b/place of Wordsworth........... | 25 |
| (10a)-do- on special Wordsworth House cover......... | 75 |
| (11) Portsmouth – b/place of Dickens ................... | 15 |
| (12) Rochester – Dickens died here in 1870........... | 15 |
| (13) Any other office....................................... | 5 |

**C.D.S. POSTMARKS**

| | |
|---|---|
| (14) Ambleside – Wordsworth/Rydal Mount .......... | 200 |
| (15) Grasmere – Wordsworth/Dove Cottage........... | 150 |
| (16) Portsmouth – Dickens born here in 1812........ | 80 |

**SLOGAN POSTMARKS**

| | |
|---|---|
| (17) First Day of Issue – Broadstairs ...................... | 90 |
| (18) Int. Stamp Exhibition (4 x 5d only)................. | 25 |
| **PAIR** of covers with appropriate pmks.............*from* | 10 |

Set of 5

## 15th July 1970 – COMMONWEALTH GAMES

*5d Runners; 1s 6d Swimmers; 1s 9d Cyclists*

**SPECIAL HANDSTAMPS**

| | | | |
|---|---|---|---|
| (1) Centenary RCT, BF 1123 PS ...................... | 225 | 15 | *Forces(s)* |
| (2) Enterprise Exhibition, Nottingham ................. | 165 | 25 | *NottFest.(s)* |
| (3) Thos. Becket 1170-1970, Canterbury............. | 165 | 25 | *C.Cath.(s)* |
| (4) Cardigan Secondary School ........................... | 165 | 175 | *Card. Sch.* |
| (5) Assembly of Euro Municipalities, SE1............. | 225 | – | *n.o.c.* |
| (6) Great Yorkshire Show, Harrogate ................... | 165 | 250 | *G.Y. Show* |
| (7) Victoria Cross, BF 1210 PS .......................... | 250 | 15 | *Forces(s)* |
| (8) Rorke's Drift, BF 1211 PS ......................... | 250 | 15 | *Forces(s)* |

**ORDINARY F.D.I. POSTMARKS**

| | |
|---|---|
| (9) Philatelic Bureau ......................................... | 3 |
| (10) Edinburgh................................................ | 10 |
| (11) Any other office........................................ | 2 |

**C.D.S. POSTMARKS**

| | |
|---|---|
| (12) Edinburgh Mobile Post Office ........................ | 125 |

**SLOGAN POSTMARKS**

| | |
|---|---|
| (13) The National Postal Museum........................... | 100 |
| (14) FDI – Edinburgh, Great Britain ..................... | 55 |
| (15) Edinburgh – wavy line................................ | 25 |

First Day Cover

## 18th September 1970 – 'PHILYMPIA'

*5d (Penny Black); 9d (1s Green); 1s 6d (4d Carmine)*

**SPECIAL HANDSTAMPS**

| | | | |
|---|---|---|---|
| (1) Philatelic Bureau........................................ | 2 | – | *Post Office* |
| (2) Philympia Day, London ............................... | 6 | – | *Post Office* |
| (3) First Flight, Philympia, Calne........................... | 200 | 35 | *B.N.I.(s)* |
| (4) First Flight, Philympia, Bembridge................. | 200 | 35 | *B.N.I.(s)* |
| (5) 23 Base Workshop REME, BF 1136 PS.......... | 50 | 50 | *Forces* |
| (6) National Postal Museum................................. | 75 | – | *n.o.c.* |

| Philympia (contd.) | ordinary covers | official covers |
| --- | --- | --- |
| **ORDINARAY F.D.I. POSTMARKS** | £ | £ |
| (7)   London W1 (local F.D.I. for Philympia) .......... | 6 | |
| (8)   Any other office................................................ | 1 | |
| **C.D.S. POSTMARKS** | | |
| (9)   House of Commons, SW1 (Postage Act)........... | 40 | |
| (10)  Olympia W14................................................... | 275 | |
| **SLOGAN POSTMARKS** | | |
| (11)  Int Stamp Exhibition, Philympia 70 ................. | 500 | |
| (12)  Any Postcode slogans ..................................... | 35 | |

## 25th November 1970 – CHRISTMAS
*4d, 5d, 1s 6d The Nativity*

| **SPECIAL HANDSTAMPS** | | | |
| --- | --- | --- | --- |
| (1)   Philatelic Bureau............................................ | 3 | – | *Post Office* |
| (2)   First Day of Issue – Bethlehem ...................... | 6 | – | *Post Office* |
| (3)   Lilleshall Parish Church AD670-1970 .............. | 175 | 200 | *Lill. P.Ch.* |
| **ORDINARY F.D.I. POSTMARKS** | | | |
| (4)   Any office ...................................................... | 2 | | |
| **SLOGAN POSTMARKS** | | | |
| (5)   First Day of Issue – Bethlehem ...................... | 100 | | |
| (6)   Fairfield Christmas Circus ............................. | 150 | | |
| (7)   Christmas Illuminations, Cheltenham.............. | 40(s) | | |

# COMMEMORATIVES: Decimal 1971-1998

Ordinary F.D.I. pmks are now only listed if relevant to a stamp issue.

## 16th June 1971 – ULSTER '71 PAINTINGS
*3p, 7½p, 9p Landscapes*

| **SPECIAL HANDSTAMPS** | | | |
| --- | --- | --- | --- |
| (1)   First Day of Issue – Philatelic Bureau............... | 3 | – | *Post Office* |
| (2)   First Day of Issue – Belfast................................. | 8 | – | *Post Office* |
| (3)   First Day of Issue – Londonderry ...................... | 40 | – | *Post Office* |
| (4)   First Day of Issue – Coleraine ........................... | 175 | – | *Post Office* |
| (5)   First Day of Issue – Newry ................................ | 175 | – | *Post Office* |
| (6)   First Day of Issue – Ballymena ......................... | 175 | – | *Post Office* |
| (7)   First Day of Issue – Armagh ............................. | 175 | – | *Post Office* |
| (8)   First Day of Issue – Portadown ......................... | 175 | – | *Post Office* |
| (9)   First Day of Issue – Cookstown ........................ | 175 | – | *Post Office* |
| (10)  First Day of Issue – Omagh .............................. | 175 | – | *Post Office* |
| (11)  First Day of Issue – Enniskillen......................... | 175 | – | *Post Office* |
| (12)  Ulster 71 Exhibition Botanic Gardens, Belfast | 75 | – | *n.o.c.* |
| (13)  Ulster Paintings Day, Norwich ......................... | 50 | 75 | *Phil Cong* |
| **C.D.S. POSTMARKS** | | | |
| (14)  Dungiven, Hilltown & Newcastle | | | |
|     *situated close to the scenes on stamps*............. | 100 | (set of three) | |
| (15)  Newcastle, Portadown or Northern Parliament .... | 125 | | |

## 28th July 1971 – LITERARY ANNIVERSARIES
*3p Keats; 5p Gray; 7½p Scott*

| **SPECIAL HANDSTAMPS** | | | |
| --- | --- | --- | --- |
| (1)   First Day of Issue – Philatelic Bureau ............. | 4 | – | *Post Office* |
| (2)   First Day of Issue – London EC ....................... | 8 | – | *Post Office* |
| (3)   John Keats, Shanklin 1819, Isle of Wight ....... | 110 | 250 | *Shank Library* |
| (4)   Thomas Gray Bicentenary, Stoke Poges......... | 35 | 125 | *Stoke Court* |
| (4a)  -do- with Carried by Mailcoach cachet ............ | 50 | 125 | *Stoke Court* |
| (5)   National Collectors Fair, Horticultural Hall .... | 225 | – | *n.o.c.* |
| (6)   Ulster 71 Exhib, Botanic Gardens, Belfast....... | 150 | – | *n.o.c.* |
| **ORDINARY F.D.I. POSTMARKS** | | | |
| (7)   Edinburgh – birthplace of Sir Walter Scott ...... | 15 | | |
| **C.D.S. POSTMARKS** | | | |
| (8)   Melrose (7½p) – Scott/Abbotsford, Melrose...... | 5(s) | | |
| **SET** 3 single stamp covers with appropriate pmks ... | 15 | | |

## 25th August 1971 – GENERAL ANNIVERSARIES
*3p British Legion; 7½p City of York; 9p Rugby Football Union*

| **SPECIAL HANDSTAMPS** | | | |
| --- | --- | --- | --- |
| (1)   First Day of Issue – Philatelic Bureau ............. | 3 | – | *Post Office* |
| (2)   First Day of Issue – Twickenham ..................... | 15 | – | *Post Office* |
| (3)   First Day of Issue – Maidstone ........................ | 15 | – | *Post Office* |
| (4)   First Day of Issue – York ................................. | 15 | – | *Post Office* |
| (5)   Rugby Football Union, Twickenham................. | 200 | 375 | *R.F.U.* |
| (6)   Rugby Football Union, Rugby .......................... | 225 | 300 | *Rugby School* |
| (7)   Royal British Legion, BF 1182 PS ................... | 230 | 250 | *Brit. Legion* |
| (8)   Royal Aero Club, BF 1170 PS .......................... | 300 | 25 | *RAF (s)* |
| (9)   Ulster 71 Exhibition, Botanic Gdens, Belfast.... | 160 | – | *n.o.c.* |
| (10)  Sir Walter Scott Bicentenary, Abbotsford ........ | 160 | – | *n.o.c.* |

**ORDINARY F.D.I. POSTMARKS**
(11) Rugby ................................................. 35
**C.D.S. POSTMARKS**
(12) Any Field Post Office ............................................. 20
(13) Richmond & Twickenham .................................... 75
**SET** 3 single stamp covers with appropriate pmks
 – usually (2), (3) and (4) ..................................... 12

## 22nd September 1971 – UNIVERSITIES

| *3p Aberystwyth; 5p Southampton* | **ordinary** | **official** |
| *7¹⁄₂p Leicester; 9p Essex* | **covers** | **covers** |
| **SPECIAL HANDSTAMPS** | **£** | **£** |
| (1) First Day of Issue – Philatelic Bureau............... | 3 | – *Post Office* |
| (2) First Day of Issue – Aberystwyth ....................... | 13 | – *Post Office* |
| (3) First Day of Issue – Colchester........................... | 13 | – *Post Office* |
| (4) First Day of Issue – Leicester............................. | 13 | – *Post Office* |
| (5) First Day of Issue – Southampton .................... | 13 | – *Post Office* |
| (6) Postal Management College, Rugby ................... | 200 | 300 *P. Man. Coll.* |
| (7) Sir Walter Scott Bicentenary, Abbotsford........ | 150 | – *n.o.c.* |
| **SET** 4 single stamp covers with appropriate pmks | | |
| – usually (2), (3), (4) and (5) ............................ | 10 | |

## 13th October 1971 – CHRISTMAS

*2¹⁄₂p, 3p, 7¹⁄₂p Stained Glass at Canterbury Cathedral*
**SPECIAL HANDSTAMPS**
| (1) First Day of Issue – Philatelic Bureau ............. | 4 | – *Post Office* |
| (2) First Day of Issue – Bethlehem ........................ | 10 | – *Post Office* |
| (3) First Day of Issue – Canterbury........................ | 10 | – *Post Office* |
| (4) Commonwealth Postal Conference, SW1 ........ | 275 | – *n.o.c.* |
| (5) 1900th Anniv. Emperor Serverus, York ........... | 225 | 250 *Emp. Serv.* |

## 16th February 1972 – POLAR EXPLORERS

*3p Ross; 5p Frobisher; 7¹⁄₂p Hudson; 9p Scott*
**SPECIAL HANDSTAMPS**
| (1) First Day of Issue – Philatelic Bureau............... | 10 | – *Post Office* |
| (2) First Day of Issue – London WC ...................... | 15 | – *Post Office* |
**ORDINARY F.D.I. POSTMARKS**
| (3) Plymouth................................................................ | 20 | |
**C.D.S. POSTMARKS**
| (4) Reykjavik BFPS (Backstamped) FPO 376 ........ | 800 | |
| (5) FPO 129 - used in Norway................................ | 400 | |
| (6) Gravesend, Kent (7¹⁄₂p)...................................... | 25(s) | |
| (7) Greenwich B.O. S.E.10 ...................................... | 25(s) | |
| **SET** of 4 single stamp covers with appropriate pmks | | |
| – usually (2), (3), (5) and (6)............................. | 35 | |

## 26th April 1972 – GENERAL ANNIVERSARIES

*3p Tutankhamun; 7¹⁄₂p HM Coastguard; 9p Ralph Vaughan Williams*
**SPECIAL HANDSTAMPS**
| (1) First Day of Issue – Philatelic Bureau............... | 3 | – *Post Office* |
| (2) First Day of Issue – London EC........................ | 8 | – *Post Office* |
| (3) Treasures of Tutankhamun Exhib. WC.............. | 35 | 75 *Tut. Exhib.* |
| (4) Vaughan Williams., Down Ampney ................. | 35 | 50 *D. Ampney(s)* |
| (5) H .M. Coastguard., Hartland Point ................. | 35 | 40 *Philart* |
| (6) Hovercraft Trials BF 1270 PS............................ | 125 | 400 *Hovercraft* |
**SLOGAN POSTMARKS**
| (7) Treasures of Tutankhamun British Museum...... | 250 | |
| **SET** 3 single stamp covers with appropriate pmks | | |
| – usually (3), (4) and (5)..................................... | 15 | |

## 21st June 1972 – VILLAGE CHURCHES

*3p Greensted; 4p Earls Barton; 5p Letheringsett;*
*7¹⁄₂p Helpringham; 9p Huish Episcopi.*
**SPECIAL HANDSTAMPS**
| (1) First Day of Issue – Philatelic Bureau............... | 6 | – *Post Office* |
| (2) First Day of Issue – Canterbury........................ | 8 | – *Post Office* |
| (3) World's Oldest Wooden Church, Greensted.... | 35 | 95 *St. Andrew's* |
| (4) Village Churches, AD 970 Earls Barton ........... | 25 | 50 *Earls Barton* |
| (5) First Day of Issue Exhib. Huish Episcopi........ | 35 | 95 *St. Mary's* |
| (6) Village Churches, Helpringham, Sleaford ........ | 35 | 90 *Helpringham* |
| (7) Village Churches, Letheringsett, Holt ............. | 35 | – *n.o.c.* |
| (8) Parish Church of St. Mary, Langley ................. | 150 | 250 *Philart* |
| (9) St. Augustine's Church, Kilburn, NW6 ............ | 150 | 250 *St.Augustine's* |
| (10) Festival of Berkswell, Coventry ...................... | 170 | 250 *Berkswell* |
| (11) Treasures of Tutankhamun Exhibition, WC ..... | 100 | – *n.o.c.* |
| (12) Royal Eng. Military Aeronautics, BF 1312 PS...... | 175 | 175 *Royal Eng. 3* |
**C.D.S. POSTMARKS**
| (13) Earls Barton, Northampton.............................. | 125 | |
| (14) Church Street, Harwich .................................... | 225 | |
| (15) New Romney, Kent (St. Nicholas Cover) ........ | 75 | |
| **SET** 5 single stamp covers with appropriate pmks | | |
| – usually (3), (4), (5), (6) and (7)...................... | 25 | |

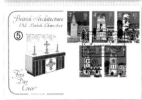

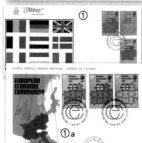

### 13th September 1972 – B.B.C.
*3p, 5p, 7½p BBC; 9p Marconi/Kemp*

|  |  | ordinary covers £ | official covers £ |  |
|---|---|---|---|---|
| **SPECIAL HANDSTAMPS** | | | | |
| (1) | First Day of Issue – Philatelic Bureau | 5 | – | *Post Office* |
| (2) | First Day of Issue – London W1 | 12 | – | *Post Office* |
| (3) | Marconi-Kemp Experiments, Chelmsford | 35 | 100 | *Mar. Phil Soc* |
| (4) | Royal Engineers, Army Wireless, BF 1326 PS | 70 | 80 | *Royal Eng. 4* |
| (5) | Marconi's First Wireless, Flatholm Island | 35 | 170 | *Barry College* |
| (6) | BBC Radio Leicester, 5th Anniversary Year | 60 | 100 | *Radio Leics* |
| (7) | 21st Anniv TV Network Opened Gloucester | 75 | 375 | *British Relay* |
| (8) | Humberside's Own Home Service, Hull | 75 | 175 | *Radio Hull* |
| (9) | BBC 50th Anniversary, Pebble Mill | 475 | * | *Pebble Mill* |
| (10) | John Knox – Philatelic Bureau | 150 | – | *n.o.c.* |
| (11) | Manchester City FC Kick-Off in UEFA Cup | 175 | 575 | *Dawn* |
| (12) | Treasures of Tutankhamun Exhibition, WC | 160 | – | *n.o.c.* |

*\*Two types of Pebble Mill official covers exist:*
  *– covers with BBC logo only @ £170; and fully illustrated covers @ £425.*

| **ORDINARY F.D.I. POSTMARKS** | | | |
|---|---|---|---|
| (13) | Brighton (BBC Radio Brighton cover) | 30 | |
| (14) | Chelmsford (Marconi Philatelic Soc cover) | 20 | |
| **SLOGAN POSTMARKS** | | | |
| (15) | Medium Wave BBC Radio Brighton | 425 | |
| PAIR covers (3p,5p,7½p on one; 9p on the other) | | 12 | |

### 18th October 1972 – CHRISTMAS
*2½p, 3p, 7½p Angels*

| **SPECIAL HANDSTAMPS** | | | | |
|---|---|---|---|---|
| (1) | First Day of Issue – Philatelic Bureau | 5 | – | *Post Office* |
| (2) | First Day of Issue – Bethlehem | 8 | – | *Post Office* |
| (3) | Treasures of Tutankhamun Exhibition, WC | 100 | – | *n.o.c.* |
| (4) | Rowntree's Philatelic Exhib. Scarborough | 200 | – | *n.o.c.* |
| (5) | John Knox , Philatelic Bureau | 125 | – | *n.o.c.* |
| (6) | Borough Jubilee 1922-1972, Watford | 250 | 150 | *WatfordBC (card)* |

### 20th November 1972 – SILVER WEDDING
*3p, 20p H.M. The Queen and Prince Philip*

| **SPECIAL HANDSTAMPS** | | | | |
|---|---|---|---|---|
| (1) | First Day of Issue – Philatelic Bureau | 4 | – | *Post Office* |
| (2) | First Day of Issue – Windsor | 8 | – | *Post Office* |
| (3) | Silver Wedding, Westminster Abbey, SW1 | 25 | 25 | *Philart ACC 6* |
| (4) | Silver Wedding, BF 1307 PS | 25 | 40 | *RAF M/Batten* |
| (5) | 16th/5th Queens Royal Lancers, BF 1922 PS | 60 | 80 | *R. Lancers* |
| (6) | Royal Regiment of Artillery, BF 1340 PS | 50 | 160 | *R.R.A.* |
| (7) | Royal Engineers Military Tanks, BF 1338 PS | 50 | 175 | *Royal Eng. 7* |
| (8) | Charlton Athletic, FA Cup Winners | 110 | 300 | *Phil. Prom.\** |
| (9) | Fiftieth Anniv. of the BBC, W1 | 200 | – | *n.o.c.* |
| (10) | Treasures of Tutankhamun Exhibition, WC | 125 | – | *n.o.c.* |
| (11) | John Knox, Philatelic Bureau | 125 | – | *n.o.c.* |

*\*Beware forged official covers exist*

| **C.D.S. POSTMARKS** | | | |
|---|---|---|---|
| (12) | Buckingham Palace, S.W.1 | 150 | |
| (13) | House of Commons, S.W.1 | 40 | |
| (14) | House of Lords,S.W.1 | 50 | |
| (15) | Windsor Castle, Windsor, Berks | 200 | |

### 3rd January 1973 – EUROPEAN COMMUNITIES
*3p, 2 x 5p Maps of Europe (jig-saw design)*

| **SPECIAL HANDSTAMPS** | | | | |
|---|---|---|---|---|
| (1) | First Day of Issue – Philatelic Bureau | 4 | – | *Post Office* |
| (1a) | Conseil de l'Europe Strasbourg | 20 | | |
| (2) | New Parcel Office, Southampton | 55 | 140 | *I.D.C.* |
| (3) | Royal Eng. Brennan Torpedo, BF 1343 PS | 40 | 60 | *Royal Eng. 8* |
| **ORDINARY F.D.I. POSTMARKS** | | | | |
| (4) | Dover or Folkestone | 10 | | |
| (4a) | -do- with PAQUEBOT markings | 20 | | |
| (5) | Harrow & Wembley ('Fanfare for Europe' cvr) | 65 | | |
| **C.D.S. POSTMARKS** | | | | |
| (6) | Calais with PAQUEBOT markings | 40 | | |
| (7) | Harwich (Gateway to Europe cover) | 75 | | |
| (8) | House of Commons, S.W.1 | 50 | | |
| (9) | House of Lords, S.W.1 | 60 | | |
| (10) | Harrow & Wembley (Britain v. EEC cachet) | 40 | | |

### 28th February 1973 – BRITISH TREES – THE OAK
*9p Oak Tree*

| **SPECIAL HANDSTAMPS** | | | | |
|---|---|---|---|---|
| (1) | First Day of Issue – Philatelic Bureau | 5 | – | *Post Office* |
| (2) | Stampex 73, Royal Horticultural Hall | 10 | 30 | *Stampex* |
| (3) | Hatfield Broad Oak, Plant a Tree | 20 | – | *n.o.c.* |
| (4) | Tree Planting, Westonbirt Arboretum, | 20 | 25 | *Cotswold (g)* |
| **C.D.S. POSTMARKS** | | | | |
| (5) | Oakham, Four Oaks, Sevenoaks etc ......*each* | 110 | | |

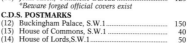

## 18th April 1973 – BRITISH EXPLORERS

*2 x 3p Livingstone & Stanley; 5p Drake;*
*7½p Raleigh; 9p Sturt*

| | | ordinary covers | official covers |
|---|---|---|---|
| **SPECIAL HANDSTAMPS** | | £ | £ |
| (1) | First Day of Issue – Philatelic Bureau........... | 10 | – *Post Office* |
| (2) | Drake's Island Adventure Centre, Plymouth....... | 35 | 175 *Cotswold* |
| (3) | Sir Walter Raleigh, Budleigh Salterton.............. | 35 | – *n.o.c.* |
| **ORDINARY F.D.I. POSTMARKS** | | | |
| (4) | Plymouth, Devon.................................................. | 25 | |
| (5) | Blantyre – birthplace of Livingstone................. | 40 | |
| (6) | Denbigh – birthplace of Stanley........................ | 40 | |
| (7) | Gloucestershire – Sturt buried here .................. | 50 | |
| **C.D.S. POSTMARKS** | | | |
| (8) | Mildenhall (Scientific Explorers Soc cover) ..... | 250 | |
| (9) | Livingston, W Lothian ........................................ | 90 | |
| **SET** 5 single stamp covers with appropriate pmks........ | | 8 | |

British Explorers

## 16th May 1973 – COUNTY CRICKET CENTENARY

*3p, 7½p, 9p W.G. Grace - sketches by Harry Furniss*

| **SPECIAL HANDSTAMPS** | | | |
|---|---|---|---|
| (1) | First Day of Issue – Philatelic Bureau............... | 4 | – *Post Office* |
| (2) | First Day of Issue – Lord's London NW.......... | 6 | – *Post Office* |
| (3) | English County Cricket Exhibition, Lord's ...... | 15 | 20 *TCCB** |
| (4) | County Cricket Centenary, Chelmsford........... | 30 | 45 *TCCB** |
| (5) | Surrey C.C.C., The Oval, SE11 ........................ | 30 | 45 *TCCB** |
| (6) | Sussex C.C.C., Hove ......................................... | 30 | 45 *TCCB** |
| (7) | Birthplace of County Cricket, Hambledon ...... | 60 | 400 *Porton Serv* |
| (8) | Downend Cricket Club, W.G. Grace ............... | 25 | 35 *Cotswold (g)* |
| (9) | Yorkshire v. Hamps, Headingley, Leeds........... | 30 | 45 *TCCB** |
| (10) | IBRA Exhibition Munich, BF 1400 PS ............ | 60 | 350 *BFPS** |
| **ORDINARY F.D.I. POSTMARKS** | | | |
| (11) | Derby – Derbyshire C.C.C.* ............................... | 15 | |
| (12) | Cardiff – Glamorgan C.C.C.* ............................ | 15 | |
| (13) | Bristol or Gloucestershire - Glos. C.C.C.* ....... | 15 | |
| (14) | Southampton – Hampshire C.C.C.* ................... | 15 | |
| (15) | Canterbury – Kent C.C.C.* ................................ | 15 | |
| (16) | Manchester – Lancashire C.C.C.* ..................... | 15 | |
| (17) | Leicester – Leicestershire C.C.C.* .................... | 15 | |
| (18) | Northampton – Northamptonshire C.C.C.* ....... | 15 | |
| (19) | Nottingham – Nottinghamshire C.C.C.* ........... | 15 | |
| (20) | Taunton – Somerset C.C.C.* .............................. | 15 | |
| (21) | Birmingham – Warwickshire C.C.C.* ............... | 15 | |
| (22) | Worcester – Worcestershire C.C.C.* ................. | 15 | |

*\*Note: Stamp Publicity of Worthing produced a set of 18 covers for the TCCB (Test & County Cricket Board). The set of 18 is valued at around £250.*

| **C.D.S. POSTMARKS** | | | |
|---|---|---|---|
| (23) | Hambledon - Birthplace of County Cricket......... | 70 | |

County Cricket

## 4th July 1973 – BRITISH PAINTINGS

*3p, 7½p Sir Joshua Reynolds; 5p, 9p Sir Henry Raeburn*

| **SPECIAL HANDSTAMPS** | | | |
|---|---|---|---|
| (1) | First Day of Issue – Philatelic Bureau ............. | 5 | – *Post Office* |
| (2) | Sir Joshua Reynolds, Royal Academy, W1....... | 15 | 75 *R. Academy* |
| (3) | Douglas, Isle of Man ......................................... | 40 | 50 *Post Office* |
| (4) | Whitehaven, Cumberland ................................... | 60 | 3 *Post Office(s)* |
| (5) | 1973 AELTC, Wimbledon .................................. | 225 | – *n.o.c.* |
| (6) | Monarchy 1000, Bath ......................................... | 250 | – *n.o.c.* |
| (7) | Death of General Sikorski Exhibition, SW7 ...... | 250 | – *n.o.c.* |
| (8) | Llangollen International Musical Eisteddfod ... | 250 | 35 *Eisteddfod(s)* |
| (9) | APEX 1973, Manchester................................... | 200 | 200 *APEX* |
| (10) | Royal Stoneleigh (metal circular stamp)... | 300 | – *n.o.c.* |
| **ORDINARY F.D.I. POSTMARKS** | | | |
| (11) | Edinburgh - birthplace of Raeburn .................... | 15 | |
| (12) | Plymouth - birthplace of Reynolds ................... | 15 | |
| **C.D.S. POSTMARKS** | | | |
| (13) | Raeburn Place, Edinburgh.......*(incomplete set)* | 75 | |

British Paintings

## 15th August 1973 – INIGO JONES

*3p St. Paul's, Covent Garden; 3p Court Masque Costumes;*
*5p Prince's Lodging, Newmarket; 5p Court Masque Stage Scene*

| **SPECIAL HANDSTAMPS** | | | |
|---|---|---|---|
| (1) | First Day of Issue – Philatelic Bureau................ | 5 | – *Post Office* |
| (2) | Inigo Jones Exhib. Wilton House, Salisbury..... | 15 | 25 *Cotswold (g)* |
| (3) | 400th Anniv. of Inigo Jones, Newmarket.......... | 15 | 150 *Rotary* |
| (4) | Livestock Market Centenary, Northampton..... | 350 | – *n.o.c.* |
| (5) | Monarchy 1000, Bath ........................................ | 325 | – *n.o.c.* |
| (6) | Third Int. Orthodontic Congress, SE ................ | 350 | 150 *I.O.C.* |
| **ORDINARY F.D.I. POSTMARKS** | | | |
| (7) | London W.C. ...................................................... | 5 | |
| **SLOGAN POSTMARKS** | | | |
| (8) | Inigo Jones Banqueting House (on 2 covers)... | 450 | |

## 12th Sept 1973 – PARLIAMENT

*8p, 10p Palace of Westminster*

| SPECIAL HANDSTAMPS | ordinary covers £ | official covers £ | |
|---|---|---|---|
| (1) First Day of Issue – Philatelic Bureau .............. | 4 | – | *Post Office* |
| (2) Houses of Parliament, London SW1................. | 6 | – | *n.o.c.* |
| (3) Monarchy 1000, Bath ........................................ | 250 | – | *n.o.c.* |
| (4) British Pharmaceutical Conference WC.......... | 300 | – | *n.o.c.* |
| (5) Surrey's Sixth Form College, Farnham............. | 300 | 135 | *Farn. Coll.* |
| **C.D.S. POSTMARKS** | | | |
| (6) Balmoral Castle................................................... | 150 | | |
| (7) Buckingham Palace or Windsor Castle ............. | 100 | | |
| (8) House of Commons or Lords.....................*each* | 75 | | |

## 14th November 1973 – ROYAL WEDDING

*3½p, 20p Princess Anne and Captain Mark Phillips*

| SPECIAL HANDSTAMPS | | | |
|---|---|---|---|
| (1) First Day of Issue – Philatelic Bureau................ | 3 | – | *Post Office* |
| (2) First Day of Issue – Windsor ............................. | 6 | – | *Post Office* |
| (3) First Day of Issue – Westminster Abbey ........... | 6 | – | *Post Office* |
| (4) Royal Wedding, Great Somerford....................... | 15 | – | *n.o.c.* |
| (5) Queens Dragoon Guards BF 1434 PS ............... | 25 | 10 | *Dragoons(s)* |
| (6) Royal Engineers, Gibraltar, BF 1387 PS ........... | 25 | 40 | *Royal Eng. 17* |
| (7) The Chinese Exhibition, London W1................. | 40 | 150 | *Ch. Exhib.* |
| **C.D.S. POSTMARKS** | | | |
| (8) Buckingham Palace or Windsor Castle ............. | 175 | | |
| (9) Great Somerford or Badminton ........................ | 30 | | |
| (10) House of Commons or House of Lords ....*each* | 35 | | |
| (11) Sandhurst, Camberley ...................................... | 30 | | |

## 28th November 1973 – CHRISTMAS

*5 x 3p; 3½p 'Good King Wenceslas'*

| SPECIAL HANDSTAMPS | | | |
|---|---|---|---|
| (1) First Day of Issue – Philatelic Bureau................ | 4 | – | *Post Office* |
| (2) First Day of Issue – Bethlehem ........................ | 8 | – | *Post Office* |
| (3) 141st Anniv. Lewis Carroll, Daresbury.............. | 250 | 90 | *ChesHist(set of 6)* |
| (4) The Chinese Exhibition, London W1................. | 75 | 75 | *Ch. Exhib.* |

## 27th February 1974 – THE HORSE CHESTNUT

*10p Horse Chestnut*

| SPECIAL HANDSTAMPS | | | |
|---|---|---|---|
| (1) First Day of Issue – Philatelic Bureau................ | 5 | – | *Post Office* |
| (2) Stampex, Royal Horticultural Hall SW1 .......... | 8 | 15 | *Stampex* |

## 24th April 1974 – FIRST FIRE SERVICE LEGISLATION

*3½p, 5½p, 8p, 10p Early Fire Engines*

| SPECIAL HANDSTAMPS | | | |
|---|---|---|---|
| (1) First Day of Issue – Philatelic Bureau .............. | 5 | – | *\*Post Office* |
| (2) Binns Philatelic & Fire Exhib. Sunderland....... | 40 | – | *n.o.c.* |
| (3) Avon County Fire Brigade, Bristol.................... | 30 | 35 | *Cotswold (g)* |
| (4) Cambridgeshire Fire & Rescue Service ............ | 40 | 200 | *Cambs C.C.* |
| (5) Lansing Bagnall 25 Years at Basingstoke......... | 200 | 700 | *Lan. Bag.* |
| (6) MCC v Hampshire, NW8 ................................... | 200 | 200 | *S.P.* |
| *\*Overprinted: 'Merryweather' £10 or 'Science Museum' £45.* | | | |
| **ORDINARY F.D.I. POSTMARKS** | | | |
| (7) London S.E.1 – H.Q. London Fire Brigade...... | 30 | | |
| (8) Bognor Regis (West Sx Fire cvr) or similar ...... | 40 | | |
| **C.D.S. POSTMARKS** | | | |
| (9) Burnt House Lane, Exeter .................................. | 675 | | |
| (10) Hose, Melton Mowbray.................................... | 350 | | |
| (11) House of Commons or House of Lords ........... | 45 | | |
| (12) Tooley St., SE l – Insurance Co. brigade.......... | 300 | | |
| **SLOGAN POSTMARKS** | | | |
| (13) The Fire Brigade Needs Men of Courage.......... | 625 | | |

## 12th June 1974 – UNIVERSAL POSTAL UNION

*3½p P&O Packet Steamer; 5½p First Official Airmail;*
*8p Air mail Blue Van and Postbox; 10p Imperial Airways Flyingboat*

| SPECIAL HANDSTAMPS | | | |
|---|---|---|---|
| (1) First Day of Issue – Philatelic Bureau................ | 5 | – | *Post Office* |
| (1a) -do- with 'INTERNABA' cachet ........................ | 10 | – | *Post Office* |
| (2) Imp. Airways Flying Boat, Southampton .......... | 15 | 250 | *Imp. Air.* |
| (3) Visit of Golden Hind ll, London E.C................. | 300 | – | *n.o.c.* |
| (4) Churchill Centenary Somerset House, WC ...... | 300 | – | *n.o.c.* |
| (5) NPM (reprinted 1890 Jubilee cover) ................. | 75 | – | *n.o.c.* |
| **ORDINARY F.D.I. POSTMARKS** | | | |
| (6) Windsor – First Official Airmail......................... | 20 | | |
| (7) Southampton – Flyingboat. .................................. | 20 | | |
| **C.D.S. POSTMARKS** | | | |
| (8) Harwich (Amsterdam Paquebot cover) ............. | 200 | | |
| (9) Southampton – Flyingboat ................................. | 25 | | |
| (10) Windsor Castle – First Official Airmail ............ | 200 | | |
| **SLOGAN POSTMARKS** | | | |
| (11) Any Post Code slogans.................................*from* | 150 | | |

## 10th July 1974 – GREAT BRITONS

*4½p Robert the Bruce; 5½p Owain Gyndwr;*
*8p Henry V; 10p Edward of Woodstock*

| | | ordinary covers £ | official covers £ | |
|---|---|---|---|---|
| **SPECIAL HANDSTAMPS** | | | | |
| (1) | First Day of Issue – Philatelic Bureau | 6 | – | Post Office |
| (2) | Robert the Bruce, Bannockburn | 40 | 175 | Scot N.T. |
| (3) | Robert the Bruce, Dunfermline Abbey | 40 | 175 | Dun. Abbey |
| (4) | Glyndwr's Parliament House, Machynlleth | 40 | 150 | Ow. Glyn. |
| (5) | Royal Tournament, BF 1974 PS | 70 | 70 | Royal T. |
| (6) | Visit of Golden Hind II, London EC | 275 | – | n.o.c. |
| (7) | Churchill, Centenary Somerset House, WC | 275 | – | n.o.c. |
| (8) | Open Golf, Lytham St. Annes | 275 | 40 | LythamGC(s) |
| (9) | Trustee Savings Bank, Sunderland | 275 | 25 | T.S.B. (s) |
| **ORDINARY F.D.I. POSTMARKS** | | | | |
| (10) | Canterbury, Windsor, Dunfermline or Gwent | 15 | | |
| (11) | Sunderland FDI on TSB official cover | 150 | | |
| **C.D.S. POSTMARKS** | | | | |
| (12) | Calais with PAQUEBOT markings | 175 | | |
| (13) | Cardross – Robert the Bruce died (4½p) | 125 | | |
| (14) | Glyndyfrdwy – Owain Glyndwr (5½p) | 30(s) | | |
| (15) | House of Commons, S.W.1 | 35 | | |
| (16) | House of Lords, S.W.1 | 45 | | |
| (17) | Woodstock – Edward of Woodstock (10p) | 20(s) | | |

## 9th October 1974 – WINSTON CHURCHILL

*4½p, 5½p, 8p, 10p Portraits of Churchill*

| | | | | |
|---|---|---|---|---|
| **SPECIAL HANDSTAMPS** | | | | |
| (1) | First Day of Issue – Philatelic Bureau | 6 | – | Post Office |
| (2) | FDI – Blenheim, Woodstock | 10 | – | Post Office |
| (3) | FDI – House of Commons, SW1 | 10 | – | Post Office |
| (4) | Woodford Green, Action This Day | 30 | 60 | See Note* |
| (5) | Churchill's First Constituency, Oldham | 30 | 30 | Old.Conserv. |
| (6) | RAF Honington, BF 1874 PS | 30 | 20 | RAF(s) |
| (7) | Churchill Centenary Somerset House, WC | 50 | 125 | Som. Hse. |
| (8) | Universal Postal Union 1874, Clitheroe | 250 | – | n.o.c. |
| (9) | Oldest Post Office In Britain Sanquhar | 80 | 200 | Sanq. PO |
| (10) | Rotary Club of Paddington, Golden Jubilee | 150 | 250 | Padd. R.C. |
| (11) | Gold Jubilee of Local Radio, Nottingham | 175 | 250 | BBC |
| *Two official Wanstead & Woodford covers exist:Conservative Assoc'n & Synagogue* | | | | |
| **ORDINARY F.D.I. POSTMARKS** | | | | |
| (12) | Tunbridge Wells (with 'Chartwell' cachet) | 30 | | |
| (13) | Medway (HMS Churchill Submarine cover) | 75 | | |
| **C.D.S. POSTMARKS** | | | | |
| (14) | Bladon, Oxford – Churchill is buried here | 175 | | |
| (15) | Churchill, Bristol | 175 | | |
| (16) | Churchill, Oxford | 175 | | |
| (17) | House of Commons, S.W.1 | 90 | | |
| (18) | House of Lords, S.W.1 | 125 | | |
| (19) | Marlborough – Churchill's ancestral home | 250 | | |
| (20) | Normandy, Guildford | 100 | | |
| (21) | Rye – Lord Warden of the Cinque Ports | 50 | | |
| (22) | Sandhurst – Churchill went to Sandhurst | 75 | | |
| (23) | Winston, Darlington | 250 | | |

## 27th November 1974 – CHRISTMAS

*3½p York Minster; 4½p St. Helens, Norwich;*
*8p Ottery St. Mary; 10p Worcester Cathedral*

| | | | | |
|---|---|---|---|---|
| **SPECIAL HANDSTAMPS** | | | | |
| (1) | First Day of Issue – Philatelic Bureau | 4 | – | Post Office |
| (2) | First Day of Issue – Bethlehem | 7 | – | Post Office |
| (3) | St. Helen's Church, Great Hospital, Norwich | 25 | 45 | Gt. Hosp. |
| (4) | The Collegiate Church, Ottery St. Mary | 25 | 45 | St. Mary |
| (5) | Salvation Army Christmas Supermarkets | 80 | 350 | Sal. Army |
| (6) | Oldest Post Office in Britain Sanquhar | 60 | 200 | Sanq. PO |
| (7) | Churchill County Sec. School, Woking | 120 | 120 | W.C. Sch. |
| **ORDINARY F.D.I. POSTMARKS** | | | | |
| (8) | Norwich, Worcester or York | each 25 | | |

## 22nd January 1975 – CHARITY

*4½p + 1½p donation to charities*

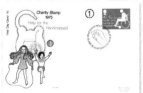

| | | | | |
|---|---|---|---|---|
| **SPECIAL HANDSTAMPS** | | | | |
| (1) | First Day of Issue – Philatelic Bureau | 3 | – | Post Office |
| (2) | Oldest Post Office in Britain Sanquhar | 25 | 150 | Sanq. PO |
| **ORDINARY F.D.I. POSTMARKS** | | | | |
| (3) | Kettering (Winged Fellowship Trust cover) | 12 | | |
| (4) | Oxford - Oxfam HQ | 15 | | |
| **C.D.S. POSTMARKS** | | | | |
| (5) | Stoke Charity, Winchester, Hants | 300 | | |
| **SLOGAN POSTMARKS** | | | | |
| (6) | Menphys Love the Handicapped | 90 | | |
| (7) | Tenovus Cares, Cardiff | 300 | | |
| (8) | Barnardo's Cares About Children | 300 | | |
| (9) | Seat Belts, Chelmsford | 100 | | |

| *Social Reformers (contd.)* | | ordinary covers | official covers |
|---|---|---|---|
| **C.D.S. POSTMARKS** | | £ | £ |
| (8) | House of Commons, S.W. 1 | 30 | |
| (9) | House of Lords, S.W. 1 | 40 | |
| (10) | Magdalen St., Norwich – Fry's b/place | 80 | |
| (11) | Newton, Powys – b/place of Robert Owen | 60 | |
| (12) | Parkhurst, I.O.W. – top security prison | 80 | |
| (13) | New Lanark – Robert Owen | 125 | |
| (14) | Lanark – Robert Owen | 70 | |
| (15) | Pelton, Durham – Hepburn's birthplace | 185 | |
| (16) | Shaftesbury, Dorset | 150 | |
| (17) | Wimborne St. Giles – Earl of Shaftesbury | 125 | |

## 2nd June 1976 – U.S.A. BICENTENARY
*11p Benjamin Franklin*
**SPECIAL HANDSTAMPS**

| (1) | First Day of Issue – Philatelic Bureau | 2 | – | *Post Office* |
|---|---|---|---|---|
| (1a) | Ditto with 'Interphil 76 ' cachet | 15 | – | *Post Office* |
| (2) | American Independence, BF 1776 PS | 12 | 20 | *BFPS* |
| (3) | USA Independence, Washington | 15 | 20 | *Wash. Old Hall* |
| (4) | 1776 Exhibition, Nati Maritime Museum | 15 | 25 | *Pilgrim* |
| (5) | American Museum, Bath | 15 | 20 | *Clav. Manor* |
| (6) | 58th Philatelic Congress Plymouth | 20 | 60 | *Phil. Cong.* |
| (7) | World of Islam Festival, London SW7 | 75 | 200 | *Pilgrim* |
| **ORDINARY F.D.I. POSTMARKS** | | | | |
| (8) | Boston, Lincs | 25 | | |
| (9) | Plymouth, Devon – Pilgrim Fathers | 25 | | |
| **C.D.S. POSTMARKS** | | | | |
| (10) | Bunker's Hill, Lincoln | 150 | | |
| (11) | Dallas, Forres, Morayshire | 150 | | |
| (12) | Denver, Downham Market | 150 | | |
| (13) | House of Commons, S.W.1 | 30 | | |
| (14) | House of Lords, S.W.1 | 40 | | |
| (15) | New York, Lincoln | 175 | | |
| (16) | Northborough – links with U.S.A. | 50 | | |
| (17) | Sulgrave – ancestors of George Washington | 60 | | |
| (18) | Washington, Pulborough, West Sussex | 100 | | |

## 30th June 1976 – ROSES
*8½p Elizabeth of Glamis; 10p Grandpa Dickson;*
*11p Rosa Mundi; 13p Sweet Briar*
**SPECIAL HANDSTAMPS**

| (1) | First Day of Issue – Philatelic Bureau | 4 | – | *Post Office* |
|---|---|---|---|---|
| (2) | Year of the Rose, Northampton | 15 | 60 | *N'ton Ph Soc* |
| (3) | Year of the Rose, Bath | 15 | 40 | *City of Bath* |
| (4) | Royal National Rose Society, Oxford | 15 | – | *n.o.c.* |
| (5) | Royal National Rose Society, St. Albans | 15 | – | *n.o.c.* |
| (6) | Royal Norfolk Show, Norwich | 35 | 200 | *Daniels* |
| (7) | The Mothers' Union Centenary, SW1 | 45 | 100 | *Mothers Un.* |
| (8) | The Championships AELTC Wimbledon | 225 | – | *n.o.c.* |
| (9) | USA Independence, Washington | 225 | – | *n.o.c.* |
| (10) | Warton Bicentennial Commem., Carnforth | 225 | – | *n.o.c.* |
| (11) | 1776 Exhibition, Nat Maritime Museum | 225 | – | *n.o.c.* |
| (12) | First Flight Britain/Australia, BF 1535 PS | 225 | – | *n.o.c.* |
| **ORDINARY F.D.I. POSTMARKS** | | | | |
| (13) | Tunbridge Wells ('Sissinghurst' cachet) | 25 | | |
| **C.D.S. POSTMARKS** | | | | |
| (14) | Glamis, Forfar – 'Elizabeth of Glamis' (8½p) | 100 | | |
| (15) | Kew Gardens, Richmond | 175 | | |
| (16) | Rose, Truro or Rose Cottage, Hull ........*each* | 150 | | |
| (17) | Rosebush, or Rosebank ........................*each* | 75 | | |

## 4th August 1976 – BRITISH CULTURAL TRADITIONS
*8½p & 13p Eisteddfod; 10p Morris Dancing; 11p Highland Gathering*
**SPECIAL HANDSTAMPS**

| (1) | First Day of Issue – Philatelic Bureau | 3 | – | *Post Office* |
|---|---|---|---|---|
| (2) | First Day of Issue – Cardigan | 4 | – | *Post Office* |
| (3) | Eisteddfod Genedlaethol Frenhinol Cymru | 10 | 125 | *Philart* |
| (4) | Bristol Morris Men, 25th Anniversary | 10 | 150 | *Bristol MM* |
| (5) | 1776 Exhibition, Nat Maritime Museum | 150 | – | *n.o.c.* |
| (6) | USA Independence, Washington | 150 | – | *n.o.c.* |
| (7) | Story of a Cathedral Exhibition, Canterbury | 100 | – | *n.o.c.* |
| (8) | Colchester Tattoo, 20th June | 150 | – | *n.o.c.* |
| (9) | Europa 6 Cantat, Leicester | 150 | 250 | *Cantat 6* |
| **ORDINARY F.D.I. POSTMARKS** | | | | |
| (10) | Exeter ('Sidmouth Folk Festival' cachet) | 30 | | |
| **C.D.S, POSTMARKS** | | | | |
| (11) | Abbots Bromley – horn dancing | 50 | | |
| (12) | Abingdon, Bampton, Britannia (Bacup), Chipping Campden or Headington Quarry – famous morris teams | 50 | | |
| (13) | Padstow – famous for its 'Hobby Horse' | 50 | | |
| (14) | Sidmouth ('Sidmouth Folk Festival' cachet) | 50 | | |

| Cultural Traditions (contd.) | ordinary covers | official covers |
|---|---|---|
| | £ | £ |

(15) Thaxted – Morris Ring meet here annually ..... 50
(16) Caerwys, Carmarthen or Corwen
 – famous eisteddfods ..................................... 50
(17) Llangollen – International Musical Eisteddfod 60
(18) Braemar – Royal Highland Gathering .............. 60
(19) Dunoon – Cowal Highland Gathering ............. 50

BRISTOL MORRIS MEN
④ 25ᵀᴴ ANNIVERSARY
4ᵀᴴ AUGUST 1976 · BRISTOL

**SLOGAN POSTMARKS**
(20) Teeside International Eisteddfod........................ 25 (s)

## 29th September 1976 – WILLIAM CAXTON
*8¹⁄₂p 'Canterbury Tales'; 10p Caxton's type-faces;*
*11p Game of Chess; 13p Printing Press*
**SPECIAL HANDSTAMPS**
(1) First Day of Issue – Philatelic Bureau.............. 3 – *Post Office*
(2) First Day of Issue – London SW1 .................... 4 – *Post Office*
(3) 500 Years of British Printing, Westminster...... 20 25 *Br Pr Ind Fed*
(4) Caxton Exhibition, British Library, WC .......... 20 50 *BL 1*
(5) William Caxton, Plymouth ............................... 20 150 *Ply. Coll.*
(6) Paper & Printing Study Group, SE1 ................ 20 100 *Philart*
(7) NATSOPA, Caxton House, SE1........................ 20 100 *NATSOPA*
(8) De Montfort Press, Leicester............................. 20 100 *DeM. Press*
(9) British Philatelic Exhibition, London W1........ 20 25 *B.P.E.*
(10) School Centenary, Stoke Poges, Bucks............ 30 75 *S.P. Sch.*
(11) 1776 Exhibition, Nat Maritime Museum.......... 75 – *n.o.c.*
(12) Royal Charter , Stow-on-the-Wold.................. 40 125 *S-o-t-W Sch.*
(13) Manchester United v. Ajax, UEFA Cup............ 90 25 *Dawn (s)*
**ORDINARY F.D.I. POSTMARKS**
(14) Bristol – Associated Graphics cover ................ 50
(15) Canterbury – 'Canterbury Tales'....................... 20
(16) Colwyn Bay – The Rydal Press special cover.. 50
(17) Derby – Bemrose Printing Derby spec cover ... 50
**C.D.S. POSTMARKS**
(18) Abingdon – first printing for Abbot of Abingdon .... 110
(19) Caxton, Cambridge.......................................... 100
(20) Fleet St., E.C.4 – home of British printing....... 110
(21) House of Commons – buried in Chapel........... 50
(22) Radcliffe - East Lancs Paper Mill cover .......... 75
(23) Tenterden – presumed birthplace .................... 85

## 24th November 1976 – CHRISTMAS
*6¹⁄₂p, 8¹⁄₂p, 11p, 13p Embroideries*
**SPECIAL HANDSTAMPS**
(1) First Day of Issue – Philatelic Bureau.............. 3 – *Post Office*
(2) First Day of Issue – Bethlehem ....................... 4 – *Post Office*
(3) Pompeii AD79, Royal Academy of Arts ........... 20 60 *PompExh*
(4) Tonic to the Nation, Victoria & Albert ............. 20 60 *H R*
(5) 1st British Corps, Bielefeld, BF 1923 PS ......... 30 60 *Forces*
(6) 1st British Corps, Aldershot, BF 1901 PS ........ 30 60 *Forces*
(7) Caxton Exhibition, British Library, WC ............ 50 – *n.o.c.*
**C.D.S. POSTMARKS**
(8) Angel Hill, Sutton .............................................. 50
(9) Pincushion, Boston – embroideries ................... 50

## 12th January 1977 – RACKET SPORTS
*8¹⁄₂p Lawn Tennis; 10p Table Tennis; 11p Squash; 13p Badminton*
**SPECIAL HANDSTAMPS**
(1) First Day of Issue – Philatelic Bureau .............. 3 – *Post Office*
(2) The Badminton Association, Badminton ......... 10 95 *Badm. Assoc.*
(3) Squash Rackets Association, Harrow ............... 10 95 *Philart*
(4) Pompeii AD 79, Royal Academy of Arts ......... 30 95 *PompExh*
(5) Caxton, Exhibition British Library, WC ........... 50 – *n.o.c.*
**ORDINARY F.D.I. POSTMARKS**
(6) Battersea – Head PO for Wimbledon ............... 20
(7) Birmingham – World Table Tennis at NEC ..... 20
(8) Hastings – English Table Tennis Assoc'n......... 20
(9) Warwick & Leamington – 1st Tennis Club ..... 20
**C.D.S. POSTMARKS**
(10) Wimbledon SW19 ............................................... 250

## 2nd March 1977 – CHEMISTRY
*8¹⁄₂p Steroids (Barton);10p Vitamin C (Haworth);*
*11p Starch (Martin & Synge); 13p Salt (Bragg)*
**SPECIAL HANDSTAMPS**
(1) First Day of Issue – Philatelic Bureau.............. 3 – *Post Office*
(2) Royal Institute of Chemistry 1877-1977........... 8 35 *RI of Chem.*
(3) Starch Derivatives for Industry, Battersea ....... 8 35 *Garton Ltd*
(4) Royal Silver Jubilee, Stampex, SW1 ................ 8 60 *Stampex*
(5) Pompeii AD 79, Royal Academy of Arts .......... 30 60 *Pomp Exh.*
(6) Tonic to the Nation, Victoria & Albert ............. 35 200 *H.R.*

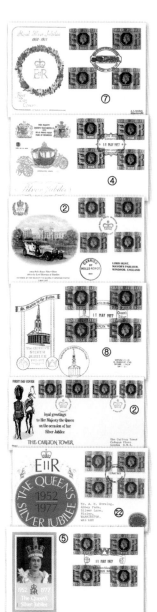

**Chemistry (contd.)**

| | | ordinary covers £ | official covers £ |
|---|---|---|---|
| **ORDINARAY F.D.I. POSTMARKS** | | | |
| (7) | Liverpool – birthplace of R.L.M. Synge............. | 20 | |
| **C.D.S. POSTMARKS** | | | |
| (8) | Barton – Barton on 8½p val................................. | 60 | |
| (9) | Gravesend – birthplace of D H. R. Barton ....... | 60 | |
| (10) | Haworth – Haworth on 10p value ....................... | 60 | |
| (11) | Martin – Martin on 11p value ............................ | 60 | |
| (12) | Pill, Bristol........................................................... | 60 | |
| (13) | Wigton – birthplace of W. H. Bragg................. | 60 | |

## 11th May 1977 – SILVER JUBILEE

*8½p, 10p, 11p, 13p Portrait of H.M. The Queen*

| | | ordinary | official | |
|---|---|---|---|---|
| **SPECIAL HANDSTAMPS** | | | | |
| (1) | First Day of Issue – Philatelic Bureau ............. | 3 | – | *Post Office* |
| (2) | First Day of Issue – Windsor ............................. | 3 | – | *Post Office* |
| (3) | Jubilee Exhibition, Bath, England ...................... | 15 | 30 | *City of Bath* |
| (4) | A Royal Jubilee Exhibition, British Library ...... | 15 | 50 | *BL 2* |
| (5) | Croydon Celebrates Queen's Silver Jubilee....... | 15 | 150 | *Croydon* |
| (6) | Stamp Collecting Promotion Council, SE1........ | 15 | – | *n.o.c.* |
| (7) | Queen Elizabeth II, RHDR, Hythe..................... | 15 | 40 | *RHDR 1* |
| (8) | St. Martin-in-the-Fields, Silver Jubilee.............. | 15 | 150 | *Historic Relics* |
| (9) | Hayling Island Philatelic Soc............................. | 25 | 175 | *HI Phil Soc* |
| (10) | Duke of Edinburgh's Award, SW1...................... | 10 | 10 | *DoEAScheme* |
| (11) | Stamp of Royalty Exhibition, Glasgow ............. | 15 | 30 | *Pal. of Art* |
| (12) | Weymouth & Portland, Philatelic Exhibition .. | 15 | 75 | *W & P Exhib* |
| (13) | Tenth Conference, Dixieme Congress, W1 ....... | 25 | 200 | *ICTWO* |
| (14) | Exercise Makefast XXV BF 1952 PS .................. | 15 | 30 | *Royal Eng.* |
| (15) | Bristol Bordeaux, 30th Anniversary .................. | 25 | 150 | *BB Assoc* |
| (16) | Milton Keynes Arts Association ......................... | 25 | 250 | *MK Festival* |
| **ORDINARY F.D.I. HANDSTAMPS** | | | | |
| (17) | Aberdeen ('Balmoral Castle' cachet).................. | 20 | | |
| (18) | Croydon (Woldingham special cover) ................ | 50 | | |
| (19) | King's Lynn ('Sandringham' cachet) .................. | 35 | | |
| (20) | Leicester (Littleton special cover)...................... | 50 | | |
| (20a) | North Devon (North Devon special cover)...... | 50 | | |
| (21) | Portsmouth – Review of the Fleet..................... | 20 | | |
| (22) | Warrington (Warrington Festival cover) .......... | 50 | | |
| **C.D.S. POSTMARKS** | | | | |
| (23) | Buckingham Palace or Windsor Castle ............ | 200 | | |
| (24) | House of Commons or Lords ............................. | 35 | | |
| (25) | Jubilee Cres, Jubilee Oak or Jubilee Fields....... | 25 | | |
| (26) | Queen Elizabeth Avenue, Walsall ..................... | 50 | | |
| (27) | Queen's Parade, or Queen's Head...................... | 40 | | |
| (28) | Silver Link, Tamworth........................................ | 30 | | |
| **SLOGAN POSTMARKS** | | | | |
| (29) | Silver Jubilee Appeal, Belfast ............................ | 110 | | |
| (30) | Silver Jubilee Philatelic Exhib., Cardiff ............ | 125 | | |
| (31) | Silver Jubilee Philatelic Exhib., Edinburgh ...... | 125 | | |
| (32) | Silver Jubilee Philatelic Exhib., NPM, EC........ | 125 | | |
| (33) | Review of Fleet (Jubilee logo) Portsmouth ...... | 150 | | |
| (34) | St. Neots Jubilee Riverside Festival ................. | 200 | | |
| (35) | Portsmouth & Southsea (Jubilee logo)............... | 10(s) | | |

## 8th June 1977 – COMMONWEALTH MEETING

*13p 'Gathering of Nations'*

| | | ordinary | official | |
|---|---|---|---|---|
| **SPECIAL HANDSTAMPS** | | | | |
| (1) | First Day of Issue – Philatelic Bureau................ | 2 | – | *Post Office* |
| (2) | First Day of Issue – London SW........................ | 2 | – | *Post Office* |
| (3) | Girl Guides Association, Open Days .................. | 20 | 50 | *Girl Guides* |
| (4) | St. Martin-in-the-Field, Silver Jubilee................ | 20 | 50 | *St. M-i-t-F* |
| (5) | A Royal Jubilee Exhibition, British Library ...... | 20 | – | *n.o.c.* |
| (6) | Croydon Celebrates Queens Silver Jubilee ...... | 20 | 40 | *Croydon* |
| (7) | British Genius Exhibition, Battersea ................. | 20 | – | *n.o.c.* |
| (8) | 6000 King George V, Hereford ........................... | 20 | – | *n.o.c.* |
| (9) | City of Leicester, Silver Jubilee, EIIR............... | 20 | – | *n.o.c.* |
| (10) | Jubilee Exhibition, North Devon ...................... | 20 | – | *n.o.c.* |
| (11) | Royal Image Exhibition, Bristol ........................ | 20 | – | *n.o.c.* |
| (12) | The Prince of Wales Division, BF 8677 PS ...... | 20 | 50 | *BFPS* |
| (13) | The Queens Silver Jubilee, Windsor.................. | 20 | 50 | *WindsorBC* |
| (14) | Silver Jubilee Train, Newcastle.......................... | 20 | – | *n.o.c.* |
| (15) | Queen's Silver Jubilee, Merseyside Police......... | 20 | – | *n.o.c.* |
| (16) | Silver Jubilee Festival, Canon Hill Park ........... | 20 | – | *n.o.c.* |
| – | *n.o.c.* | | | |
| **C.D.S. POSTMARKS** | | | | |
| (17) | House of Commons, S.W.1 ................................ | 50 | | |
| (18) | House of Lords, S.W.1 ....................................... | 60 | | |
| (19) | Queen Elizabeth Ave, Walsall ........................... | 20 | | |
| (20) | Buckingham Palace or Windsor Castle ............. | 75 | | |
| **SLOGAN POSTMARKS** | | | | |
| (21) | Queen's Silver Jubilee Appeal............................ | 20 | | |
| (22) | House of Commons (wavy line cancel)............. | 15 | | |

## 15th June 1977 – SILVER JUBILEE
*9p Portrait of H.M. The Queen*

| | | ordinary covers £ | official covers £ | |
|---|---|---|---|---|
| **SPECIAL HANDSTAMPS** | | | | |
| (1) | First Day of Issue – Philatelic Bureau............... | 2 | – | *Post Office* |
| (2) | First Day of Issue – Windsor......................... | 2 | – | *Post Office* |
| (3) | Borough of Blackburn, Silver Jubilee................ | 10 | 135 | *BlackburnBC* |
| (4) | Jubilee Exhibition, North Devon...................... | 10 | 50 | *N. Devon* |
| (5) | Silver Jubilee Exhibition, Trafalgar Square ...... | 10 | – | *n.o.c.* |
| (6) | Royal Jubilee Exhibition, British Library.......... | 10 | 40 | *BL 2* |
| (7) | City of Leicester, Silver Jubilee, EIIR .............. | 10 | 10 | *City of Leics* |
| (8) | Nuneaton Council, 1952 EIIR 1977................ | 10 | 50 | *NuneatonBC* |
| (9) | Croydon Celebrates/Queen's Silver Jubilee ..... | 10 | 50 | *Croydon* |
| (10) | Royal Image Exhibition, Bristol...................... | 25 | 60 | *Royal Image* |
| (11) | British Genius Exhibition Battersea SW11...... | 15 | – | *n.o.c.* |
| **ORDINARY F.D.I. POSTMARKS** | | | | |
| (12) | Crewe (Sandbach special cover) ................... | 30 | | |
| (13) | Portsmouth – Review of Fleet....................... | 5 | | |
| **C.D.S. POSTMARKS** | | | | |
| (14) | Buckingham Palace or Windsor Castle ........... | 75 | | |
| (15) | House of Commons, S.W.1 ............................ | 10 | | |
| (16) | House of Lords, S.W.1 ................................. | 10 | | |
| (17) | Jubilee Oak; Jubilee Cresc.; Jubilee Fields...... | 20 | | |
| (18) | Silver Link; Queens Head; Queens Parade ...... | 20 | | |
| (19) | Queen Elizabeth Avenue, Walsall.................. | 15 | | |
| **SLOGAN POSTMARKS** | | | | |
| (20) | The Queen's Silver Jubilee Appeal.................. | 15 | | |
| (21) | Review of the Fleet (Jubilee logo).................. | 20 | | |
| (22) | Silver Jubilee Philatelic Exhib., Cardiff ........... | 20 | | |
| (23) | Silver Jubilee Philatelic Exhib., Edinburgh ...... | 20 | | |
| (24) | Silver Jubilee International Air Tattoo .............. | 50 | | |
| (25) | Portsmouth & Southsea (Jubilee logo) ............ | 30 | | |

*Some **double-dated** covers exist with the set of Silver Jubilee stamps postmarked 11th May and the additional 9p value postmarked 15th June.*

| | | | |
|---|---|---|---|
| (1) | special h/s (11 May) + FDI pmk (15 June)....... | 30 | 30 |
| (2) | special h/s (11 May) + special h/s (15 June) ... | 40 | 30 |
| (3) | appropriate CDS (both dates on one cover) ... | 50 | |

## 5th October 1977 – BRITISH WILDLIFE
*5 x 9p: Hedgehog, Hare, Red Squirrel, Otter, Badger*

| | | | | |
|---|---|---|---|---|
| **SPECIAL HANDSTAMPS** | | | | |
| (1) | First Day of Issue – Philatelic Bureau............... | 4 | – | *Post Office* |
| (2) | Badger Beer, Blandford, 200th Anniversary..... | 15 | 35 | *Hall&Wdhse (s)* |
| (3) | SCT (Shropshire Conservation Trust)................ | 15 | 250 | *SCT* |
| (4) | Norfolk Wildlife in Trust, Norwich ................... | 15 | 15 | *Markton (NNT)* |
| (5) | Port Lympne, Wildlife Sanctuary, Hythe ......... | 10 | 15 | *RHDR 3* |
| (6) | 11-13 Broad Court, Covent Garden, WC2 ...... | 10 | 20 | *Garden Studio* |
| (7) | Darley's, 150 Years of Print, Burton ............... | 45 | 650 | *Darley's* |
| (8) | Sir Francis Drake, British Library, WC ........... | 50 | – | *n.o.c.* |
| (9) | British Genius Exhibition, London SW11 ......... | 50 | – | *n.o.c.* |
| (10) | Army & Navy, Victoria, SW1 ......................... | 45 | 200 | *A&N(set of 5)* |
| (11) | Manchester United, FA Cup Winners............... | 50 | 45 | *Dawn(set of 5)* |
| **C.D.S. POSTMARKS** | | | | |
| (12) | Badgers Mount, Sevenoaks ........................... | 75 | | |
| (13) | Forest Row, East Sussex................................ | 30 | | |
| (14) | Foxton, Leics ............................................. | 75 | | |
| (15) | Haresfield, Harefield or Harewood...........*each* | 75 | | |
| (16) | Hedge End, Southampton .............................. | 15 | | |
| (17) | Nettleham – Royal Soc Nature Conservation.. | 35 | | |
| (18) | Otterburn, Otterbourne, Ottery St Mary...*each* | 40 | | |
| (19) | Otter Ferry, Tighnabruaich............................ | 50 | | |
| (20) | Squirrels Heath, Romford .............................. | 75 | | |

## 23rd November 1977 – CHRISTMAS
*5 x 7p; 9p 'The Twelve Days of Christmas'*

| | | | | |
|---|---|---|---|---|
| **SPECIAL HANDSTAMPS** | | | | |
| (1) | First Day of Issue – Philatelic Bureau............... | 4 | – | *Post Office* |
| (2) | First Day of Issue – Bethlehem ...................... | 5 | – | *Post Office* |
| (3) | Christmas Greetings, Blackpool ...................... | 20 | 40 | *Blackpool(s)* |
| (4) | Sir Francis Drake, British Library, WC ............ | 20 | 50 | *Br. Lib.* |
| (5) | First Mail Flight, Lerwick, Shetland ................. | 30 | 35 | *B.Airways(s)* |
| (6) | First Mail Flight, Dyce, Aberdeen .................... | 30 | 35 | *B.Airways(s)* |
| **ORDINARY F.D.I. POSTMARKS** | | | | |
| (7) | Cambridge–Trinity College/original manuscript... | 15 | | |
| **C.D.S. POSTMARKS** | | | | |
| (8) | House of Lords – 'Ten Lords a-leaping'............ | 35 | | |
| (9) | Lordship Lane, Dulwich ................................. | 45 | | |
| (10) | Partridge Green or Pear Tree............................ | 45 | | |
| **SLOGAN POSTMARK** | | | | |
| (11) | Collect through Philatelic Bureau..................... | 50 | | |

43

## 25th January 1978 – ENERGY

*9p Oil; 10½p Coal; 11p Gas; 13p Electricity*

| SPECIAL HANDSTAMPS | ordinary covers £ | official covers £ | |
|---|---|---|---|
| (1) First Day of Issue – Philatelic Bureau | 5 | – | *Post Office* |
| (2) KW Claymore 'A' Project Team, Peterhead | 50 | 200 | *Claymore* |
| (3) Institute of Fuel, Golden Jubilee Year, W1 | 10 | 15 | *Cotswold (g)* |
| (4) Coal is Precious, Ellistown | 15 | 20 | *Green(s)* |
| (5) Oil is Precious, Melton Mowbray | 15 | 20 | *Green(s)* |
| (6) British Speedway, Gulf Oil League, W4 | 15 | – | *n.o.c.* |
| (7) SEGAS, a part of British Gas Croydon | 15 | – | *n.o.c.* |
| (8) Forties Field, BP, Aberdeen | 10 | 35 | *BOCS 1* |
| (9) West Sole Field, BP, Hull | 10 | 30 | *BOCS 1* |
| (10) 21 Years Nuclear Electricity, Dungeness | 10 | 15 | *RHDR 4* |
| (11) Haroldswick permanent special handstamp | 50 | – | *n.o.c.* |
| **ORDINARY F.D.I. POSTMARKS** | | | |
| (12) Aberdeen (Taylor Woodrow cover) | 35 | | |
| (13) Battersea – Power Station | 35 | | |
| **C.D.S. POSTMARKS** | | | |
| (14) Bacton – North Sea gas pipeline | 75 | | |
| (15) Coalville, Coal Aston, Coalpit Heath or Selby | 75 | | |
| (16) Cruden Bay – Forties Field oil pipeline | 75 | | |
| (17) Seascale – first nuclear power station | 100 | | |
| **SLOGAN POSTMARK** | | | |
| (18) Collect through Philatelic Bureau | 30 | | |

## 1st March 1978 – HISTORIC BUILDINGS

*9p Tower of London; 10½p Holyroodhouse;*
*11p Caernarvon Castle; 13p Hampton Court*

| SPECIAL HANDSTAMPS | | | |
|---|---|---|---|
| (1) First Day of Issue – Philatelic Bureau | 3 | – | *Post Office* |
| (2) First Day of Issue – London EC | 3 | – | *Post Office* |
| (3) Tower of London, BF 9000 PS | 10 | 25 | *Tower of Lon* |
| (4) British Architecture, British Library, WC | 10 | 20 | *BL 5* |
| (5) Royal Heritage, Hampton Court Palace | 10 | 25 | *BOCS 2* |
| (6) Hampton Court, Oldest Tennis Court | 10 | 70 | *S.P.* |
| (7) Wells Cathedral, 800th Anniversary | 12 | 15 | *Cotswold (g)* |
| (8) 1953-1978 Stampex, Silver Jubilee, SW1 | 15 | 40 | *Stampex* |
| (9) Portland 900th, Dorset | 20 | 50 | *Portland* |
| (10) Northwest Genius, Manchester | 90 | – | *n.o.c.* |
| **ORDINARY F.D.I. POSTMARKS** | | | |
| (11) Caernarfon or Kingston-upon-Thames | 25 | | |
| (12) King's Lynn ('Sandringham' cachet) | 35 | | |
| **C.D.S. POSTMARKS** | | | |
| (13) Holyrood, Edinburgh 8 | 60 | | |
| (14) Corfe Castle (on Saint Edward 1000 cover) | 25 (s) | | |

## 1st March 1978 – HISTORIC BUILDINGS

*Miniature Sheet - same postmarks as stamp issue*

| SPECIAL HANDSTAMPS | | | |
|---|---|---|---|
| (1) First Day of Issue – Philatelic Bureau | 5 | – | *Post Office* |
| (2) First Day of Issue – London EC | 5 | – | *Post Office* |
| (3) Tower of London, BF 9000 PS | 15 | 20 | *Tower of Lon* |
| (4) British Architecture, British Library, WC | 15 | 25 | *BL 5* |
| (5) Royal Heritage, Hampton Court Palace | 15 | 100 | *BOCS 2d* |
| (6) Hampton Court, Oldest Tennis Court | 15 | – | *n.o.c.* |
| (7) Wells Cathedral, 800th Anniversary | 20 | 75 | *Cotswold (g)* |
| (8) 1953-1978 Stampex, Silver Jubilee, SW1 | 15 | 75 | *Stampex* |
| (9) Portland 900th, Dorset | 25 | 60 | *Portland* |
| (10) Northwest Genius, Manchester | 125 | – | *n.o.c.* |
| **ORDINARY F.D.I. POSTMARKS** | | | |
| (11) Caernarfon or Kingston-upon-Thames | 25 | | |
| **C.D.S. POSTMARKS** | | | |
| (12) Earl's Court SW5 - venue of London 1980 | 40 | | |
| (13) Holyrood, Edinburgh 8 | 60 | | |

## 31st May 1978 – 25th ANNIVERSARY of CORONATION

*9p, 10½p, 11p, 13p Coronation Regalia*

| SPECIAL HANDSTAMPS | | | |
|---|---|---|---|
| (1) First Day of Issue – Philatelic Bureau | 3 | – | *Post Office* |
| (2) First Day of Issue – London SW | 3 | – | *Post Office* |
| (3) 1953 Coronation 1978, British Library, WC | 8 | 25 | *BL 7* |
| (4) Cameo Stamp Centre, WC2 | 8 | 12 | *Cameo* |
| (5) RAF Wattisham, BF 1953 PS | 8 | 60 | *RAF Watt.* |
| (6) Queen Elizabeth II, RHDRailway | 8 | 10 | *RHDR 6* |
| (7) Caernarfon (depicting castle) | 25 | – | *n.o.c.* |
| (8) Official Opening, Prince of Wales, Newcastle | 25 | 50 | *Freeman Hosp.* |
| (9) British Philatelic Fed. Congress, Worthing | 25 | 75 | *B.P.F.* |
| (10) Union of PO Workers, Blackpool | 25 | 75 | *U.P.O.W.* |
| (11) RAF Hospital Wegberg, BF 1612 PS | 25 | 50 | *Forces* |
| (12) Lewis's Celebrate 21 Years in Bristol | 25 | 125 | *Lewis's* |
| (13) Mint, Sutton, Surrey | 25 | 100 | *Mint* |
| (14) The Gatwick Park, Horley | 25 | 150 | *G. Park Hotel* |

| | ordinary covers | official covers |
|---|---|---|
| | £ | £ |

(15) Assoc. Dairies, Royal Opening, Newcastle ..... 25 — 300 *Assoc.Dairies*
(16) Visit of Prince of Wales, Newton Aycliffe...... 25 — 175 *Newton Aycl.*
(17) Temple of Jerusalem, Leicester ............................ 25 — 275 *Grand Priory*

**ORDINARAY F.D.I. POSTMARKS**
(18) Windsor, Berks ................................................. 10
(19) Crewe (Sandbach special cover) ........................ 25
(20) King's Lynn ('Sandringham' cachet) ................. 35

**C.D.S. POSTMARKS**
(21) Benson RAF Station (Queen's Flight)................ 50
(22) Buckingham Palace or Windsor Castle ............ 150
(23) Coronation Road, Parade or Square ................... 25
(24) House of Commons or Lords ............................. 30
(25) Queen Elizabeth Avenue or Crown View ......... 25
(26) Scone – Stone of Scone/Coronation Chair ...... 175

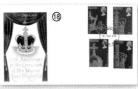

## 5th July 1978 – SHIRE HORSE SOCIETY
*9p Shire Horse; 10½p Shetland Pony; 11p Welsh Pony; 13p Thoroughbred*
**SPECIAL HANDSTAMPS**
(1) First Day of Issue – Philatelic Bureau ............. 3 — – *Post Office*
(2) First Day of Issue – Peterborough ................... 4 — – *Post Office*
(3) Havering Park Riding School ............................ 15 — 40 *Havering (f)*
(4) Tribute to the Horse, Market Weighton Sch.... 15 — 30 *MW School*
(5) Horses of Britain, British Library, WC ............ 10 — 40 *BL 8*
(6) Courage Shire Horse Centre, Maidenhead ...... 10 — 65 *BOCS 4*
(7) The Royal Show, 1878-1978, Kenilworth ........ 15 — 40 *S.P.*
(8) The Sport of Kings, Brighton ............................ 15 — 50 *B.Racecourse*
(9) Shetland Pony Stud Book Society .................... 15 — 50 *Pilgrim*
(10) Home of the Derby, Epsom .............................. 10 — – *Post Office*
(11) World Dressage Championships Goodwood .... 20 — 75 *W Dressage*
(12) 700th Anniv. of the Cinque Ports, Hythe ........ 10 — 15 *RHDR 7*
(13) RNLl Clacton 1878-1978, Clacton ................. 25 — 30 *Pilgrim*
(14) Ars Gratia Artis, London W1 ........................... 30 — 250 *MGM*
(15) Royal Scots Dragoon Guards, BF 1678 PS...... 20 — 5 *S.P.(s)*
(16) Royal Irish Rangers, BF 1621 PS ..................... 20 — 70 *Roy.Ir.Rang.*
(17) Lawn Tennis Championships, Wimbledon ...... 20 — – *n.o.c.*
(18) Salvation Army, Wembley ............................... 20 — 375 *Salvation Army*
(19) Sutton-on-Trent Comprehensive School.......... 20 — 70 *Sutton Sch*
(20) Big Four Rly Museum, Bournemouth ............. 20 — – *n.o.c.*
(21) Llangollen International Musical Eisteddfod.... 20 — 250 *Eisteddfod*
(22) Caernarfon (depicting castle).............................. 15 — – *n.o.c.*

**ORDINARY F.D.I. POSTMARKS**
(23) Aberystwyth ('Welsh Pony Express' cover)...... 35
(24) Aylesbury (Amersham Horse Show cover)...... 25
(25) Bournemouth ('Railway Horses' cover)............ 25
(26) King's Lynn ('Sandringham' cachet) ................. 25

**C.D.S. POSTMARKS**
(27) Aintree or Ascot................................................. 90
(28) Blackhorse, Old Roan or Horsebridge.............. 20
(29) Darley – 'Darley Arabian' ................................. 60
(30) Godolphin Cross – 'Goldolphin Arabian'......... 60
(31) Epsom Downs – home of the Derby.................. 100
(32) Gt. Yarmouth (Anna Sewell cover) ................... 45
(33) Horsefair – Kidderminster or Rugeley......*each* 35
(34) Lerwick – Shetland pony................................... 80
(35) Riding Hill, Paddock or Shireoaks ..........*each* 40
(36) Stud Farm, Studlands or Newmarket.......*each* 45

## 2nd August 1978 – CYCLING CENTENARY
*9p Penny Farthing; 10½p Touring Bicycles;*
*11p Modern Bikes; 13p Road Racers*
**SPECIAL HANDSTAMPS**
(1) First Day of Issue – Philatelic Bureau ............. 3 — – *Post Office*
(2) First Day of Issue – Harrogate ........................ 3 — – *Post Office*
(3) BCF Centenary Meeting, Leicester ................... 10 — 35 *City Council*
(4) Tl Raleigh, Bicycle Manufacturer, Nott'gham .. 10 — 30 *BOCS 5*
(5) Tl Raleigh, Tour de France, Nottingham.......... 10 — 25 *BOCS 5*
(6) 1953 Coronation 1978, British Library, WC .... 12 — 40 *B. Library*
(7) Colchester Searchlite Tattoo, BF 1606 PS ....... 30 — 150 *C.S. Tattoo*
(8) Self-righting Lifeboat, Science Museum ........... 40 — – *n.o.c.*
(9) Caernarfon (depicting castle) ............................ 30 — – *n.o.c.*
(10) 700th Anniv. of the Cinque Ports, Hythe ......... 20 — 40 *RHDR 7*

**ORDINARY F.D.I. POSTMARKS**
(11) Dumfries – invention of the bicycle .................. 45
(12) Guildford (Surrey Police 'Bike Safe' cover)...... 30
(13) London SE1 (Holdsworthy Cycles promo cvr)........ 30

**C.D.S. POSTMARKS**
(14) Charlbury – Tandem Club ................................. 90
(15) Godalming – Cyclists' Touring Club ................. 90
(16) Meriden – Cyclists' War Memorial................... 90
(17) Raleigh, Torpoint, Cornwall ............................. 250

**SLOGAN POSTMARKS**
(18) Driver – Mind that Bike........................................ 125

45

## 22nd Nov 1978 – CHRISTMAS

*7p, 9p, 11p, 13p Carols*

| | | ordinary covers £ | official covers £ | |
|---|---|---|---|---|
| **SPECIAL HANDSTAMPS** | | | | |
| (1) | First Day of Issue – Philatelic Bureau .............. | 2 | – | *Post Office* |
| (2) | First Day of Issue – Bethlehem ......................... | 3 | – | *Post Office* |
| (3) | Carols for Christmas, British Library, WC ...... | 10 | 30 | *BL 9* |
| (4) | Kings College Cambridge.................................... | 10 | 20 | *BOCS 6* |
| (5) | Parish of Dalgety, Dunfermline ......................... | 10 | 20 | *Dal Parish* |
| (6) | Music for All, Romford....................................... | 10 | 15 | *Havering (f)* |
| (7) | History of Philately Exhibition, Warwick ........ | 10 | 30 | *W & W* |
| (8) | Meet Your Post Office, Dunfermline................ | 25 | – | *n.o.c.* |
| (9) | Meet Your Post Office, Portsmouth .................. | 125 | – | *n.o.c.* |
| (10) | 50 Years of Rotary in Clacton ........................... | 20 | 60 | *Rotary* |
| (11) | Gold of Eldorado, Royal Academy, W1 ........... | 20 | 75 | *Pilgrim* |
| (12) | Croeso Cymru I'r Crysau Duon, Cardiff........... | 20 | 450 | *All Blacks* |
| **ORDINARY F.D.I. POSTMARKS** | | | | |
| (13) | Oxford – Boars Head Carol Queens College...... | 30 | | |
| **C.D.S. POSTMARKS** | | | | |
| (14) | Boars Head, Wigan or Nasareth ....................... | 125 | | |
| (15) | Fairy Cross, Fir Tree or Hollybush.............*each* | 40 | | |

## 7th February 1979 – DOGS

*9p Old English Sheepdog; 10½p Welsh Springer Spaniel; 11p West Highland Terrier; 13p Irish Setter*

| | | | | |
|---|---|---|---|---|
| **SPECIAL HANDSTAMPS** | | | | |
| (1) | First Day of Issue – Philatelic Bureau .............. | 2 | – | *Post Office* |
| (2) | First Day of Issue – London SW ....................... | 3 | – | *Post Office* |
| (3) | Spillers Congratulate Kennel Club, EC4 .......... | 8 | 12 | *BOCS 7* |
| (4) | New Zealand Exhibition, Warwick .................... | 10 | 40 | *W & W* |
| (5) | Gold of Eldorado, Royal Academy, W1 ............ | 10 | 65 | *Pilgrim* |
| (6) | England v. N. Ireland, Wembley....................... | 15 | 40 | *Dawn(set of 4)* |
| **ORDINARY F.D.I. POSTMARKS** | | | | |
| (7) | Battersea – Battersea Dogs Home .................... | 25 | | |
| (8) | Brighton (Brighton & Hove Stadium cover).... | 50 | | |
| (9) | London W1 (Dulux paints cover) ...................... | 75 | | |
| (10) | Paddington (CIBA-GEIGY cover) ...................... | 45 | | |
| (11) | Redhill (P.D.S.A. cover) ..................................... | 45 | | |
| **C.D.S. POSTMARKS** | | | | |
| (12) | Barking or Dogsthorpe ...................................... | 40 | | |
| (13) | Battersea Park Road – Dogs Home................... | 95 | | |
| (14) | Black Dog or Hounds Hill ................................. | 100 | | |
| (15) | Dog & Gun, Dog Kennel Lane or Isle of Dogs ... | 120 | | |

## 21st March 1979 – BRITISH FLOWERS

*9p Primrose; 10½p Daffodil; 11p Bluebell; 13p Snowdrop*

| | | | | |
|---|---|---|---|---|
| **SPECIAL HANDSTAMPS** | | | | |
| (1) | First Day of Issue – Philatelic Bureau .............. | 2 | – | *Post Office* |
| (2) | Royal Botanic Gardens, Kew, Richmond......... | 8 | 30 | *Botanic Gdns* |
| (3) | Bath Floral City Exhibition .............................. | 8 | 10 | *Cotswold (g)* |
| (4) | Flower Arrangers Soc., St. Marys..................... | 6 | 9 | *BOCS 8* |
| (5) | Flower Arrangers Soc., Penzance...................... | 6 | 9 | *BOCS 8* |
| (6) | Founders Day, Bluebell Railway, Uckfield....... | 10 | 20 | *RHDR 8* |
| (7) | Rural Blisworth Exhibition, Northampton ...... | 10 | 35 | *Blisworth* |
| (8) | W.I. Canterbury (Women's Institute) ................ | 15 | 60 | *W.I.* |
| (9) | Egypt Postage Stamp Exhibition, Warwick ..... | 15 | 35 | *W & W* |
| **C.D.S. POSTMARKS** | | | | |
| (10) | Blue Bell Hill, Huddersfield ............................. | 50 | | |
| (11) | Botanic Gardens, Belfast or Flowery Field ...... | 50 | | |
| (12) | Isles of Scilly or Snow Hill .............................. | 40 | | |
| (13) | Kew Gardens, Richmond ................................... | 100 | | |
| (14) | Primrose, Jarrow ............................................... | 60 | | |
| (15) | Spring Gardens, Lytham St. Annes ................... | 40 | | |
| **SLOGAN POSTMARKS** | | | | |
| (16) | Bath – Europe's Floral City ............................... | 85 | | |
| (17) | 21st Spalding Flower Parade ............................. | 85 | | |

## 9th May 1979 – EUROPEAN ELECTIONS

*9p, 10½p, 11p, 13p Flags of Member Nations*

| | | | | |
|---|---|---|---|---|
| **SPECIAL HANDSTAMPS** | | | | |
| (1) | First Day of Issue – Philatelic Bureau................ | 3 | – | *Post Office* |
| (2) | First Day of Issue – London SW....................... | 3 | – | *Post Office* |
| (3) | Strasbourg – Leicester's Twin City ................... | 6 | 15 | *City Council* |
| (4) | British European Elections, SW1....................... | 7 | 15 | *BOCS 10* |
| (5) | Entente Cordiale, Stowmarket......................... | 225 | 150 | *Stow. Tw. Com.* |
| (6) | Cameo Stamp Centre, WC2 .............................. | 6 | 10 | *Cameo* |
| (7) | Inst. of Gas Engineers, SW............................... | 10 | 40 | *Gas Eng.* |
| (8) | Worth Valley Rly Letter Service, Keighley....... | 10 | 40 | *W V Rly* |
| (9) | Lions Holiday, 79 District, Hayling Island ...... | 10 | 100 | *Lions* |
| (10) | Barbados Postage Stamps Exhib. Warwick ...... | 10 | 25 | *W & W* |
| (11) | Nat. Assoc. Flower Arrangers, Blackpool ........ | 10 | 10 | *BOCS 8* |
| (12) | Derby 200 Exhibition, Royal Academy, W1..... | 10 | 10 | *BOCS 9* |
| (13) | British Chess Federation, Norwich................... | 10 | 35 | *Chess Fed* |
| **ORDINARY F.D.I. POSTMARKS** | | | | |
| (14) | Folkestone – Gateway to Europe....................... | 10 | | |

| European Elections (contd.) | ordinary covers £ | official covers £ |
|---|---|---|
| (15) Colchester (Clacton on Sea twinning cover).... | 20 | |

**C.D.S. POST.MARKS**

| | | |
|---|---|---|
| (16) Blackrod, Bolton.......................................... | 35 | |
| (17) Dover or Harwich – Gateways to Europe ........ | 15 | |
| (18) House of Commons or Lords ........................... | 25 | |
| (19) Newhaven with PAQUEBOT markings ........... | 15 | |
| (20) Dieppe with PAQUEBOT markings................. | 12 | |
| (21) Parliament St. or Northern Parliament............ | 25 | |
| (22) Weymouth – Gateway to Europe...................... | 15 | |

**SLOGAN POSTMARKS**

| | | |
|---|---|---|
| (23) Are you on the Voters List?, Lincoln ............... | 600 | |
| (24) Bath – Europe's Floral City................................ | 135 | |

## 6th June 1979 – HORSE RACING

*9p The Derby; 10½p Aintree; 11p Newmarket; 13p Windsor*

**SPECIAL HANDSTAMPS**

| | | | |
|---|---|---|---|
| (1) First Day of Issue – Philatelic Bureau.............. | 3 | – | Post Office |
| (2) First Day of Issue – Epsom, Surrey .................. | 3 | – | Post Office |
| (3) Jockey Club, Newmarket ................................... | 6 | 30 | S.P. |
| (4) Derby 200 Exhibition, Royal Academy, W1..... | 6 | 9 | BOCS 9 |
| (5) Derby 200, Epsom, Surrey................................. | 6 | 10 | BOCS 11 |
| (6) England's Oldest Horse Race, Kiplingcotes...... | 8 | 20 | MW School |
| (7) Derbyshire Festival, Matlock............................ | 10 | 150 | Derbys Fest. |
| (8) Newbury Show, Berks ....................................... | 8 | 20 | New. Ag. Soc |
| (9) Chigwell School, 1629-1979............................. | 10 | 50 | Chigwell Sch |
| (10) Nauru Postal History Exhibition, Warwick ..... | 20 | 30 | W & W |
| (11) Norwich Union First Class Insurance.............. | 20 | 70 | Norwich.Un. |
| (12) 35th Anniv. of D-Day, Southampton ............... | 20 | – | n.o.c. |
| (13) 35th Anniv. Operation Neptune, BF 3544 PS . | 20 | – | n.o.c. |
| (14) First Collection, Edinburgh Eurocrest Hotel.... | 20 | 90 | Euro Hotel |
| (15) First Collection, Glasgow Eurocrest Hotel ....... | 20 | 90 | Euro Hotel |

**ORDINARY F.D.I. POSTMARKS**

| | | |
|---|---|---|
| (16) Derby, Doncaster or Liverpool.......................... | 15 | |
| (17) King's Lynn (Sandringham' cachet)................. | 25 | |
| (18) Windsor - Dorsett Ferry, Windsor (13p) .......... | 15 | |

**C.D.S. POSTMARKS**

| | | |
|---|---|---|
| (19) Aintree, Ascot or Epsom Downs....................... | 85 | |
| (20) Derby or Horse Fair......................................... | 25 | |
| (21) Langholm (Rotary/Red Rum cover).................. | 75 | |
| (22) Newmarket, Stud Farm or Studlands................ | 50 | |
| (23) Tattenham Corner – Epsom racecourse ........... | 250 | |

**SLOGAN POSTMARKS**

| | | |
|---|---|---|
| (24) Come Racing at Great Yarmouth ..................... | 75 | |
| (25) Derby Fiesta July 3rd-7th, Derby ..................... | 85 | |
| (26) Derbyshire Festival.......................................... | 150 | |

## 11th July 1979 – YEAR OF THE CHILD

*9p Peter Rabbit – Beatrix Potter; 10½p Wind in the Willows – Kenneth Grahame; 11p Winnie the Pooh – A. A . Milne; 13p Alice – Lewis Caroll*

**SPECIAL HANDSTAMPS**

| | | | |
|---|---|---|---|
| (1) First Day of Issue - Philatelic Bureau ............... | 2 | – | Post Office |
| (2) Yardley Primary School, Chingford................... | 8 | 35 | Walth. Forest |
| (3) NSPCC, Bethlehem ........................................... | 8 | 15 | BOCS Sp 1 |
| (4) Kent & East Sussex Rly, Tenterden................... | 8 | 10 | RH 9 |
| (5) Winnie the Pooh, Hartfield ............................ | 8 | 25 | BOCS 12 |
| (6) Beatrix Potter, Near Sawrey, Ambleside........ | 8 | – | Post Office |
| (7) Great Ormonde St., WC1.................................. | 15 | – | n.o.c. |
| (8) Palitoy Diamond Jubilee, Leicester ................. | 25 | 350 | Palitoy |
| (9) New Parks Boys School Leicester..................... | 10 | 50 | NPB School |
| (10) Lewis Carroll Society, Daresbury..................... | 10 | 40 | L.C. Soc |
| (11) Alice in Wonderland, Llandudno ..................... | 10 | 50 | Llan Town C |
| (12) Cub Country, Birkenhead ................................. | 10 | 30 | Dawn |
| (13) Year of the Child, Wokingham ......................... | 10 | 30 | Dawn |
| (14) IYC, Westminster Cathedral, SW1 .................. | 10 | 30 | Cotswold |
| (15) Wisbech Grammar School................................. | 10 | 95 | Wisbech GS |
| (16) Mother & Baby Life Care, Leamington............ | 35 | 30 | LIFE |
| (17) Royal Tournament, BF 1979 PS ....................... | 10 | 30 | BFPS |
| (18) 1979 Anniversaries, British Library................. | 10 | 50 | BL 10 |
| (19) Home International Bowls Pontypool .............. | 15 | 50 | Pilgrim |
| (20) Rhodesia Philatelic Exhib. Warwick ............... | 20 | 25 | W & W |

**ORDINARY F.D.I. POSTMARKS**

| | | |
|---|---|---|
| (21) Birmingham (IYC Scout Conference cover)..... | 35 | |
| (22) Edinburgh – b/place Kenneth Grahame ........... | 15 | |
| (23) Exeter (Exeter Childrens Orchestra cover)....... | 25 | |
| (24) Hartfield – home of A. A. Milne ...................... | 15 | |
| (25) London WC (F Warne cover)............................ | 55 | |
| (26) London WC (Org. of Good Templars cover) ... | 35 | |
| (27) Oxford – Lewis Carroll.................................... | 15 | |
| (28) Stourbridge – designer of PO cover ................. | 15 | |

| | ordinary covers £ | official covers £ |
|---|---|---|
| **C.D.S. POSTMARKS** | | |
| (29) Child Okeford or Child's Hill | 50 | |
| (30) Far Sawrey – home of Beatrix Potter | 70 | |
| (31) Hartfield – home of A. A. Milne | 30 | |
| (32) Playing Place, Truro | 70 | |
| **SLOGAN POSTMARKS** | | |
| (33) Barnardo's Care about Children | 60 | |
| (34) Give a Child a Home Leeds | 100 | |

## 22nd August 1979 – SIR ROWLAND HILL

*10p Sir Rowland Hill; 11½p General Post c 1839;*
*13p London Post c 1839; 15p Uniform Postage 1840*

| **SPECIAL HANDSTAMPS** | | |
|---|---|---|
| (1) First Day of Issue – Philatelic Bureau | 2 | – *Post Office* |
| (2) First Day of Issue – London EC | 2 | – *Post Office* |
| (3) London EC Chief Office | 6 | – *n.o.c.* |
| (4) National Postal Museum (Maltese Cross) | 6 | – *n.o.c.* |
| (5) Bruce Castle Museum, Tottenham N17 | 10 | 45 *Haringey* |
| (6) Sir Rowland Hill, Kidderminster Art Gallery | 6 | – *n.o.c.* |
| (7) Bath Postal Museum, Centenary Exhib. | 6 | 25 *BP Museum* |
| (8) Mail Coach Run, Kidderminster | 6 | 10 *BOCS 13* |
| (9) Mail Coach Run, Birmingham | 6 | 10 *BOCS 13* |
| (10) Commemorative Delivery, Rayleigh | 10 | 200 *WigginsTeape* |
| (11) Rowland Hill 1795-1879, Coventry | 6 | – *n.o.c.* |
| (12) Rowland Hill 1795-1879, Stratford | 6 | – *n.o.c.* |
| (13) Rowland Hill 1795-1879, Warwick | 6 | – *n.o.c.* |
| (14) First Day of Issue, Kidderminster | 6 | – *n.o.c.* |
| (15) 1979 Anniversaries, British Library, WC | 10 | 40 *BL 11* |
| (16) Military Tattoo, Edinburgh | 10 | 75 *M Tattoo* |
| (17) York Races, Tote Ebor Handicap, York | 10 | 25 *S.P.(s)* |
| (18) Pier Centenary, Bournemouth | 10 | 90 *Philatex* |
| (19) Skirrid Energy Drive, SW1 | 10 | 70 *Skirrid* |
| (20) Codesort - Manchester or Liverpool | 15 | – *n.o.c.* |
| (21) Haddo House, Aberdeen | 10 | 20 *Scot N.T.* |
| **ORDINARY F.D.I. POSTMARKS** | | |
| (22) Kidderminster– b/place of Rowland Hil | 8 | |
| (23) Sanquhar – Britain's oldest Post Office | 8 | |
| **C.D.S. POSTMARKS** | | |
| (24) Belsize Park or Hampstead | 30 | |
| (25) Bruce Grove – Bruce Castle | 25 | |
| (26) House of Commons or Lords | 20 | |
| (27) Kidderminster – b/place of Rowland Hill | 20 | |
| (28) PAQUEBOTS – introduced by Rowland Hill | 20 | |
| (29) Rowlands Castle, Hants | 25 | |
| **SLOGAN POSTMARKS** | | |
| (30) International Stamp Exhib., Earls Court, EC | 80 | |
| (31) Datapost D – a new postal service, Enfield | 90 | |
| (32) Remember to use the Postcode or similar | 30 | |

## 26th Sept. 1979 – POLICE

*10p Local 'bobby'; 11½p Traffic Control; 13p Mounted police; 15p Police Launch*

| **SPECIAL HANDSTAMPS** | | |
|---|---|---|
| (1) First Day of Issue – Philatelic Bureau | 2 | – *Post Office* |
| (2) First Day of Issue – London SW | 2 | – *Post Office* |
| (3) New Scotland Yard, Metropolitan Police | 4 | 10 *Cotswold* |
| (4) Port of London Police, E16 | 10 | 250 *Port London* |
| (5) Devon & Cornwall Constabulary, Exeter | 10 | 40 *D & C Const.* |
| (6) West Yorks Metropolitan Police, Wakefield | 10 | 10 *BOCS 14* |
| (7) Sir Robert Peel, Tamworth | 10 | – *n.o.c.* |
| (8) RAF Police, Bruggen, BF 1665 PS | 10 | 30 *RAF Police* |
| (9) 1979 Anniversaries, British Library, WC | 10 | 40 *BL 12* |
| (10) Shooting First Enemy Aircraft, BF 1662 PS | 10 | – *n.o.c.* |
| (11) Zeppelin Mail Exhibition, NPC Warwick | 10 | 25 *W & W* |
| (12) Sir John Gielgud at Blackpool | 10 | 25 *Blk Theatre* |
| **ORDINARY F.D.I. POSTMARKS** | | |
| (13) Bedford (Bedfordshire Police cover) | 25 | |
| (14) Bolton & Bury (Manchester Police cover) | 60 | |
| (15) Bury St Edmunds (Suffolk Police cover) | 60 | |
| (16) Lincoln (Lincolnshire Police cover) | 60 | |
| (17) Norwich (Norfolk Constabulary cover) | 45 | |
| (18) Oxford (Police Training Centre cover) | 60 | |
| (19) Warrington (Cheshire Constabulary cover) | 60 | |
| **C.D.S. POSTMARKS** | | |
| (20) Bow Street, Dyfed – Bow Street Runners | 85 | |
| (21) Bury, Lancs – birthplace of Sir Robert Peel | 40 | |
| (22) Constable Burton, Leyburn North Yorks | 60 | |
| (23) Constable Road, Sheffield | 50 | |
| (24) Crook, Co. Durham | 35 | |
| (25) Hendon – Police Training School | 30 | |
| (26) House of Commons, S.W.1 | 25 | |
| (27) House of Lords, S.W.1 | 35 | |

**Police (contd.)**

| | ordinary covers £ | official covers £ |
|---|---|---|
| (28) Law, Carluke........................................................ | 50 | |
| (29) Tamworth – Home of Robert Peel...................... | 20 | |
| (30) Wapping, E.1 – River Police HQ....................... | 50 | |
| (31) Eynsham (Police Training Centre cover) ......... | 40 | |
| (32) Field Post Office 999 (NY Police cover) .......... | 150 | |
| **SLOGAN POSTMARKS** | | |
| (33) Durham 800 Years a City ................................. | 150 | |

## 24th October 1979 – SIR ROWLAND HILL
*Miniature sheet*

**SPECIAL HANDSTAMPS**

| | | |
|---|---|---|
| (1) First Day of Issue – Philatelic Bureau............... | 2 | – *Post Office* |
| (2) First Day of Issue – London EC......................... | 2 | – *Post Office* |
| (3) London EC Chief Office.................................... | 8 | – *n.o.c.* |
| (4) National Postal Museum................................... | 8 | – *n.o.c.* |
| (5) Bruce Castle Museum, Tottenham..................... | 20 | 50 *Haringey* |
| (6) London & Brighton Rly Co............................... | 8 | 10 *BOCS 16* |
| (7) Cartoonists Club Gatwick Airport..................... | 8 | 10 *BOCS Sp 2* |
| (8) 1979 Anniversaries, British Library.................. | 10 | 30 *BL 11a* |
| (9) PUC 1929 Exhibition NPC Warwick................. | 10 | – *n.o.c.* |
| (10) Codesort - Manchester or Liverpool ............... | 15 | – *n.o.c.* |
| **ORDINARY F.D.I. POSTMARKS** | | |
| (11) Kidderminster – b/place of Rowland Hill........ | 10 | |
| (12) Sanquhar – Britain's oldest Post Office............ | 10 | |
| **C.D.S. POSTMARKS** | | |
| (13) Hampstead NW3 - where he died ..................... | 15 | |
| (14) House of Commons or Lords ............................ | 15 | |
| (15) Kidderminster – b/place of Rowland Hill .......... | 10 | |
| (16) Rowlands Castle, Hants................................... | 25 | |
| **SLOGAN POSTMARKS** | | |
| (17) Int. Stamp Exhib., Earls Court............................ | 75 | |

*Some **double-dated** covers exist with the set of Rowland Hill stamps postmarked 22nd August and the miniature sheet postmarked 24th October. Prices from £40.*

## 21st November 1979 – CHRISTMAS
*8p, 10p, 11½p, 13p, 15p The Nativity*

**SPECIAL HANDSTAMPS**

| | | |
|---|---|---|
| (1) First Day of Issue – Philatelic Bureau............... | 2 | – *Post Office* |
| (2) First Day of Issue – Bethlehem ......................... | 2 | – *Post Office* |
| (3) Christmas, British Library, WC ........................ | 8 | 25 *BL 13* |
| (4) 25th Anniv After the Ball, Blackpool................ | 8 | 25 *Blk Theatre* |
| (5) Cheriton & Morehall Christmas Lights.............. | 8 | 10 *CM Traders* |
| (6) Father Christmas Special, K. & E. S. Rly ......... | 8 | 10 *RH 10* |
| (7) Centenary of the War Cry, EC4 ........................ | 8 | 50 *H.R.* |
| (8) Rotary Club of Swansea .................................... | 8 | 35 *Rotary* |
| (9) Stamp & Coin Exhib. Coventry......................... | 8 | 35 *D.F.* |
| (10) Naming Ceremony Margate Lifeboat................. | 8 | 20 *Pilgrim* |
| (11) Air Mails, 1920-1950 NPC ,Warwick............... | 10 | 25 *W & W* |
| (12) BIPEX, London SW......................................... | 10 | – *n.o.c.* |
| (13) England v. Bulgaria, Wembley.......................... | 10 | 50 *Dawn* |
| **C.D.S. POSTMARKS** | | |
| (14) Nasareth, Caernarfon......................................... | 50 | |

*Also: Angel Hill, Holy Island, Kings Road, Star, Starcross, Shepherds Bush. Prices from £10*

**SLOGAN POSTMARKS**

| | | |
|---|---|---|
| (15) Milton Keynes, Xmas Shopping ......................... | 100 | |

*Also: Barnardos Cares About Children; Postcode It. Prices from £40.*

## 16th January 1980 – BRITISH BIRDS
*10p Kingfisher; 11½p Dipper; 13p Moorhen; 15p Yellow Wagtail*

**SPECIAL HANDSTAMPS**

| | | |
|---|---|---|
| (1) First Day of Issue – Philatelic Bureau............... | 2 | – *Post Office* |
| (2) First Day of Issue – Sandy, Beds....................... | 2 | – *Post Office* |
| (3) Essex Field Club, Centenary, Chelmsford ........ | 8 | 10 *Havering 5* |
| (4) Leicestershire & Rutland Ornithological Soc .. | 8 | 20 *LFDC (f)* |
| (5) West Midlands Bird Club, 51st Anniversary .... | 8 | 10 *P.P.S.* |
| (6) Wildfowl Trust, Arundel.................................... | 8 | 10 *BOCS 17* |
| (7) Wildfowl Trust, Washington ............................. | 8 | 15 *BOCS 17* |
| (8) Wildfowl Trust, Peakirk .................................... | 8 | 10 *BOCS 17* |
| (9) Wildfowl Trust, Martin Mere ........................... | 8 | 10 *BOCS 17* |
| (10) Wildfowl Trust, Slimbridge .............................. | 8 | 10 *BOCS 17* |
| (11) Pioneers in Bird Protection, RSPB Sandy........ | 8 | 25 *R.S.P.B.* |
| (12) Hull Natural History Society ............................ | 8 | 20 *MW School* |
| (13) NNT Wild Birds Protection Act, Norwich........ | 8 | 15 *Markton* |
| (14) 10th Anniv., Cotswold Wild Park ............... | 8 | 20 *Cotswold (g)* |
| (15) Wintertime, British Library, WC ...................... | 15 | 80 *BL 14* |
| (16) The Salvation Army, 100, Harwich .................. | 15 | 95 *H.R.* |
| (17) The Royal Image Exhibition, NPC, Warwick.... | 15 | 40 *W & W* |
| (18) Queens School Rheindahlen, BF 1671 PS........ | 15 | 150 *Queens Sch* |

**Birds (contd.)**

|  | ordinary covers £ | official covers £ |
|---|---|---|

**C.D.S. POSTMARKS**

| | ordinary | official |
|---|---|---|
| (19) Fair Isle – famous bird observatory ................. | 40 | |
| (20) House of Commons or Lords ............................ | 30 | |
| (21) Sandy, Beds. – R.S.P.B. Headquarters .............. | 40 | |

*Also: Birds Edge, Cley, Eagle, Heron Cross, Hickling, Holme, Partridge Green, Ranworth, Swallownest, Wing, Wren's Nest. Prices range from £20 each.*

**SLOGAN POSTMARKS**

| | | |
|---|---|---|
| (22) Dovecot Arts Centre (depicting doves)............. | 500 | |

*Also: Collect British Stamps £30.*

## 12th March 1980 – LIVERPOOL & MANCHESTER RAILWAY

*5 x 12p 'The Rocket' and various railway carriages*

**SPECIAL HANDSTAMPS**

| | | | |
|---|---|---|---|
| (1) First Day of Issue – Philatelic Bureau.............. | 2 | – | *Post Office* |
| (2) First Day of Issue – Manchester....................... | 2 | – | *Post Office* |
| (3) First Day of Issue – Liverpool ........................ | 2 | – | *Post Office* |
| (4) Great Railway Exposition, Manchester ............ | 10 | – | *n.o.c.* |
| (5) Main Line Steam Trust, Loughborough ........... | 10 | 15 | *LFDC (f)* |
| (6) Newton-le-Willows, Earlstown......................... | 10 | 75 | *Newton 150* |
| (7) 80th Anniversary Rother Rly, Tenterden.......... | 10 | 12 | *RH 11* |
| (8) The Railway Age, Coventry............................. | 10 | 40 | *D.F.* |
| (9) To London 1980 by Rail, BF 1682 PS ............... | 10 | 25 | *Forces(set of 5)* |
| (10) Havering's own Railway.................................. | 10 | 15 | *Havering 6* |
| (11) Bressingham Steam Museum, Diss.................. | 10 | 10 | *Markton* |
| (12) T.P.O. Exhibition, Crewe ............................... | 10 | 50 | *Dawn* |
| (13) Manchester (Kelloggs) ................................... | 10 | 35 | *Kelloggs* |
| (14) Austro-Hungarian Postal History, Warwick.... | 15 | 75 | *W & W* |
| (15) Volvo Diplomat Sales Consult the Experts...... | 15 | 225 | *Volvo* |
| (16) LSP Ammeraal, Ware Herts............................ | 15 | 225 | *LSP* |
| (17) Wintertime, British Library, WC ..................... | 15 | 75 | *BL 16* |
| (18) Daily Mail, Ideal Home Exhib., SW5.............. | 15 | 150 | *Pilgrim* |
| (19) Codesort Comes to Manchester, or Liverpool. | 20 | – | *Post Office* |

**ORDINARY F.D.I. POSTMARKS**

| | | |
|---|---|---|
| (20) Aberystwyth (Talyllyn Railway cover)............ | 45 | |
| (21) Bournemouth (Big Four Railway Museum) .... | 35 | |
| (22) Bradford (Worth Valley Railway cover).......... | 45 | |
| (23) Caernarfon (Llanberis or Festiniog Rly cvrs) ... | 45 | |
| (24) Any other FDI on private railway covers........ | 45 | |

**C.D.S. POSTMARKS (inc. T.P.O. CANCELS)**

| | | |
|---|---|---|
| (25) Crowthorne Stn – station Post Office ............. | 20 | |
| (26) Rainhill, Prescot – 'Rainhill Trials' ................. | 35 | |
| (27) The Rocket, Liverpool or Wylam.................... | 75 | |
| (28) Sheringham (North Norfolk Railway cover).... | 45 | |
| (29) Any other CDS on private railway covers ....... | 45 | |
| (30) Any TPO (travelling post office) postmarks ..... | 20 | |

**SLOGAN POSTMARKS**

| | | |
|---|---|---|
| (31) 150 Years of Mail by Rail ............................... | 50 | |

## 9th April 1980 – LONDON 1980 STAMP EXHIBITION

*50p Montage of London Buildings*

**SPECIAL HANDSTAMPS**

| | | | |
|---|---|---|---|
| (1) First Day of Issue – Philatelic Bureau.............. | 2 | – | *Post Office* |
| (2) First Day of Issue – London S.W..................... | 2 | – | *Post Office* |
| (3) Cameo Stamp Centre ..................................... | 8 | 10 | *Cameo* |
| (4) London Tourist Board Victoria ...................... | 8 | 10 | *BOCS 19* |
| (5) West Country-Liverpool, Inaugural Flight ......... | 8 | 20 | *RoyalMail* |
| (6) Trafalgar Square or London Chief Office ........ | 8 | – | *n.o.c.* |
| (7) National Postal Museum................................. | 8 | – | *n.o.c.* |
| (8) G.B. Major Errors Exhibition, Warwick........... | 6 | 25 | *W & W* |
| (9) Springtime, British Library, WC...................... | 6 | 25 | *BL 17* |
| (10) C.S./R.I.C. Annual Congress, Durham............ | 6 | 45 | *CS/RIC* |

**C.D.S. POSTMARKS**

| | | |
|---|---|---|
| (11) Earls Court B.O. ............................................ | 75 | |
| (12) House of Commons or Lords ......................... | 15 | |

**SLOGAN POSTMARKS**

| | | |
|---|---|---|
| (13) Collect British Stamps ................................... | 40 | |
| (14) Int. Stamp Exh. Earls Court – Leeds................ | 60 | |

## 7th May 1980 – LONDON 1980

*50p Miniature Sheet*

**SPECIAL HANDSTAMPS**

| | | | |
|---|---|---|---|
| (1) First Day of Issue – Bureau (Eros) ................. | 2 | – | *Post Office* |
| (2) First Day of Issue – Bureau (London 1980)..... | 2 | – | *Post Office* |
| (3) First Day of Issue – Kingston.......................... | 2 | – | *Post Office* |
| (4) First Day of Issue – London SW ...................... | 2 | – | *Post Office* |
| (5) Stamps Magazine/London 1980 ...................... | 8 | – | *n.o.c.* |
| (6) Supersonically/London 1980 BF 7580 PS .......... | 8 | 20 | *BOCS 20* |
| (7) London Union of Youth Clubs......................... | 8 | – | *n.o.c.* |
| (8) Leicester Philatelic Society............................. | 8 | 50 | *LFDC Sp 1* |
| (9) London Stamp Fair, London SW1 ................... | 8 | 20 | *Showpiece* |
| (10) Post Office Day, London 1980, SW ................ | 8 | 20 | *POCommCvr* |
| (11) Royal Opera House, Covent Garden ............... | 8 | – | *n.o.c.* |
| (12) Warwick Penny Post Exhibition,..................... | 15 | – | *n.o.c.* |
| (13) Festival Fringe, Brighton................................. | 15 | – | *n.o.c.* |

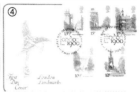

**London 1980 (contd.)**

| | ordinary covers | official covers |
|---|---|---|
| | £ | £ |
| (14) Salvation Army, 1880-1980, Belfast ................. | 15 | 75 *Sal Army* |
| (15) Freedom of Plymouth, BF 1694 PS .................. | 15 | – *n.o.c.* |
| (16) Parish Church, Hampton-in-Arden .................. | 20 | – *n.o.c.* |
| (17) Springtime, British Library, London ................ | 10 | 35 *BL 17a* |
| **C.D.S. POSTMARKS** | | |
| (18) Earl's Court, S.W.5 ........................................... | 50 | |
| (19) House of Commons or Lords ....................*each* | 25 | |
| (20) Little London, Basingstoke ................................ | 20 | |
| **SLOGAN POSTMARKS** | | |
| (21) Collect British Stamps ...................................... | 30 | |

*Some **double-dated** covers exist with both the 50p stamp postmarked
9th April and the miniature sheet postmarked 7th May. Prices from £30.*

## 7th May 1980 – LONDON LANDMARKS

*10½p Buckingham Palace; 12p Albert Memorial;
13½p Royal Opera House; 15p Hampton Court; 17½p Kensington Palace*

**SPECIAL HANDSTAMPS**

| | | |
|---|---|---|
| (1) First Day of Issue – Bureau (Eros) .................. | 2 | – *Post Office* |
| (2) First Day of Issue – Bureau (London 1980)..... | 2 | – *Post Office* |
| (3) First Day of Issue – Kingston-upon-Thames .... | 2 | – *Post Office* |
| (4) First Day of Issue – London SW...................... | 2 | – *Post Office* |
| (5) Stamps Magazine/London 1980, Brentwood... | 8 | – *n.o.c.* |
| (6) Supersonically to London 1980 BF 7580 PS ... | 8 | 5 *RAF Mus.(s)* |
| (7) London Union of Youth Clubs.......................... | 8 | 15 *S.P. (Card)* |
| (8) Leicester Philatelic Society ............................... | 8 | 10 *LFDC 1* |
| (9) London Stamp Fair, London SW1 ................... | 8 | 25 *Showpiece* |
| (10) Post Office Day London 1980, London SW ... | 8 | 20 *POCommCvr* |
| (11) Royal Opera House, Covent Garden, WC ...... | 8 | 30 *Cotswold* |
| (12) Warwick Penny Post, Postal History Exhib...... | 8 | 40 *W & W* |
| (13) Festival Fringe, Brighton ................................. | 10 | 30 *BrightonFF(s)* |
| (14) Salvation Army, 1880-1980, Belfast ................. | 12 | 75 *S. Army* |
| (15) Freedom of Plymouth, BF 1694 PS ................. | 10 | 25 *R. Marine(s)* |
| (16) Parish Church, Hampton-in-Arden .................. | 10 | 90 *H-i-A Church* |
| (17) Springtime, British Library, London WC ......... | 10 | 40 *BL 18* |
| **C.D.S. POSTMARKS** | | |
| (18) Buckingham Palace, S.W.1................................ | 90 | |
| (19) Buckingham Gate, S.W.1.................................. | 60 | |
| (20) Earl's Court – posted at the Exhibition ........... | 50 | |
| (21) House of Commons or Lords ....................*each* | 35 | |
| (22) Little London, Piccadilly or Kensington........... | 30 | |

## 9th July 1980 – FAMOUS PEOPLE

*12p Charlotte Brontë – Jane Eyre; 13½p George Eliot – Mill on the Floss;
15p Emily Brontë – Wuthering Heights; 17½p Mrs. Gaskell – North & South*

**SPECIAL HANDSTAMPS**

| | | |
|---|---|---|
| (1) First Day of Issue – Philatelic Bureau.............. | 2 | – *Post Office* |
| (2) First Day of Issue – Haworth, Keighley............ | 2 | – *Post Office* |
| (3) International Society, Mrs Gaskell ..................... | 8 | 25 *Int. Society* |
| (4) Elizabeth Gaskell Chelsea, SW3 ....................... | 8 | 30 *Hawkwood* |
| (5) Leicester Writers' Club ..................................... | 8 | 10 *LFDC 2* |
| (6) The Elms, Country Home of George Eliot....... | 8 | 25 *The Elms* |
| (7) George Eliot Centenary, Nuneaton ................... | 8 | 50 *D.F.* |
| (8) Dent/Charlotte & Emily Brontë, Haworth........ | 8 | 15 *BOCS 22* |
| (9) Women Christian Temperance Union .............. | 15 | – *n.o.c.* |
| (10) Rush & Tompkins, Swindon ............................ | 10 | 275 *R & T* |
| (11) Summertime, British Library, WC .................... | 10 | 25 *BL 19* |
| (12) William Shakespeare, Stratford ........................ | 10 | – *n.o.c.* |
| (13) Channel Isles Occupation Exhib. Warwick ...... | 10 | 20 *W & W* |
| (14) Llangollen International Musical Eisteddfod ... | 10 | 275 *Eisteddfod* |
| (15) Royal Tournament Centenary, BF 1980 PS...... | 10 | 30 *BFPS* |
| **ORDINARY F.D.I. POSTMARKS** | | |
| (16) Altrincham (with Knutsford P.O. cachet) ........ | 20 | |
| **C.D.S. POSTMARKS** | | |
| (17) Chilvers Coton – birthplace of George Eliot.... | 25 | |
| (18) Cranford – Mrs Gaskell's novel *Cranford* ........ | 25 | |
| (19) Haworth – home of Brontë sisters.................... | 25 | |
| (20) Inkpen, Newbury, Berks ................................... | 20 | |
| (21) Knutsford – Mrs Gaskell's *Cranford* ................ | 25 | |
| (22) Thornton – birthplace of Brontë sisters............ | 25 | |
| **SLOGAN POSTMARKS** | | |
| (23) Knutsford, Mrs Gaskell's 'Cranford'................ | 50 | |
| (24) Central Library & Museum, Sunderland............ | 225 | |

## 4th August 1980 – QUEEN MOTHER'S 80th BIRTHDAY

*12p Portrait of the Queen Mother*

**SPECIAL HANDSTAMPS**

| | | |
|---|---|---|
| (1) First Day of Issue – Philatelic Bureau ............. | 2 | – *Post Office* |
| (2) First Day of Issue – Glamis, Forfar.................. | 2 | – *Post Office* |
| (3) Queen Mother's 80th Birthday, BF 8080 PS.... | 8 | 40 *BFPS* |
| (4) Clarence House...................................................... | 8 | 12 *Havering 11* |
| (5) St. Paul's Walden Flower Festival, Hitchin ...... | 8 | 25 *Hawkwood* |

## Queen Mother (contd.)

| | | ordinary covers £ | official covers £ | |
|---|---|---|---|---|
| (6) | St. Mary's Church, Ware | 8 | 50 | St. Mary's |
| (7) | Grand Theatre Blackpool | 8 | 30 | Blk Theatre |
| (8) | Queen Mother's 80th Birthday, Windsor | 8 | 25 | Sumner |
| (9) | Queen Mother's 80th Birthday, York | 8 | 25 | Sumner |
| (10) | FDCs of Royalty Exhibition, Leicester | 8 | 10 | LFDC 3 |
| (11) | Hitchin Salutes the Queen Mother | 8 | – | n.o.c. |
| (12) | Happy Birthday, British Library, WC | 8 | 20 | BL 20 |
| (13) | Lord Warden of Cinque Ports, Walmer | 8 | 12 | BOCS 25 |
| (14) | St. Paul's Walden | 8 | 25 | Sumner |
| (15) | 100 Years of GMT, Greenwich, SE10 | 8 | 50 | GMT |
| (16) | Poppy Appeal cares all year, Richmond | 8 | 10 | Poppy Appeal |
| (17) | Forces Help Soc/Lord Roberts Workshops | 8 | 15 | Cotswold |
| (18) | Hull Kingston Rovers, Hull | 8 | 15 | MW School |
| (19) | RNLI Station Calshott | 8 | 15 | Pilgrim |
| (20) | Great Railway Exposition, Manchester | 8 | – | n.o.c. |
| (21) | Paramins 50 Years, Southampton | 10 | 325 | Paramins |
| (22) | Rother Railway, Tenterden | 10 | 10 | RH 11 |
| (23) | 1980 Promenade Concerts, SW7 | 10 | – | n.o.c. |
| (24) | Recro '80, Kenilworth | 10 | 40 | D.F. |
| (25) | Anglo-Boer War Exhibition, Warwick | 10 | 40 | W & W |
| (26) | British Chess Congress, Brighton | 10 | 50 | Chess Fed |

### ORDINARY F.D.I. POSTMARKS
| | | | |
|---|---|---|---|
| (27) | King's Lynn ('Sandringham' cachet) | 20 | |
| (28) | Windsor, Berks | 8 | |

### C.D.S. POSTMARKS
| | | | |
|---|---|---|---|
| (29) | Bowes – Bowes-Lyon (family name) | 15 | |
| (30) | Buckingham Palace, S.W.1 | 120 | |
| (31) | Glamis – Queen Mother's ancestral home | 30 | |
| (32) | House of Commons or Lords | 25 | |
| (33) | Mey (Castle of Mey) or Buckingham Gate | 35 | |
| (34) | Queen Elizabeth Avenue, Walsall | 20 | |
| (35) | Windsor Castle, Windsor, Berks | 150 | |

### SLOGAN POSTMARKS
| | | | |
|---|---|---|---|
| (36) | Isle of Man, Queen Mother Crowns | 15 | |

*Also: Elizabethan Banquets; Collect British Stamps; Post Code It. Prices from £15.*

## 10th September 1980 – BRITISH CONDUCTORS

*12p Sir Henry Wood; 13½p Sir Thomas Beecham;*
*15p Sir Malcolm Sargent; 17½p Sir John Barbirolli*

### SPECIAL HANDSTAMPS

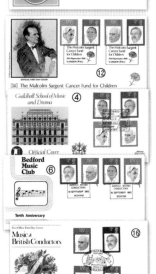

| | | | | |
|---|---|---|---|---|
| (1) | First Day of Issue – Philatelic Bureau | 2 | – | Post Office |
| (2) | First Day of Issue – London SW | 2 | – | Post Office |
| (3) | Royal Opera House, WC2 | 8 | 20 | Cotswold |
| (4) | Guildhall School of Music & Drama, EC2 | 8 | 10 | Benham |
| (5) | Leicester Symphony Orchestra | 8 | 10 | LFDC 4 |
| (6) | Famous British Conductors, Bedford | 8 | 50 | Bed Music Club |
| (7) | Conductors of the Halle, Manchester | 8 | 15 | P.P.S. |
| (8) | 1980 Promenade Concerts, SW7 | 8 | 10 | BOCS 24 |
| (9) | BBC Symphony Orchestra, SW7 | 8 | 10 | BOCS 24 |
| (10) | Royal Philharmonic Orchestra, SE1 | 8 | 20 | S.P. |
| (11) | Anaesthesia 1980, Royal Festival Hall, SE1 | 8 | 15 | Hawkwood |
| (12) | Sir Malcolm Sargent Cancer Fund, SW3 | 8 | 10 | Havering 12 |
| (13) | Birthplace Sir Thomas Beecham, St. Helens | 8 | 55 | Th Beecham |
| (14) | CBSO (City of Birmingham Symp. Orch.) | 8 | 5 | C.B.S.O. |
| (15) | TI Commemorates CBSO Birmingham | 8 | 15 | C.B.S.O. |
| (16) | Sir Thomas Beecham Rossall Sch. Fleetwood | 8 | 3 | Benham(s) |
| (17) | Fairfield, Croydon | 8 | 35 | Fairfield |
| (18) | Summertime, British Library, WC | 10 | 45 | BL 21 |
| (19) | Sponne School 550th Anniv., Towcester | 10 | 40 | Sponne Sch |
| (20) | Flower Arrangements Nottingham | 10 | 55 | NFFA |
| (21) | Moorlands Festival, Leek | 10 | 120 | Festival |
| (22) | From Tom-Tom to Telex , NPC Warwick | 10 | 80 | W & W |
| (23) | Sir Geoffrey De Havilland, Hatfield | 10 | 85 | MosquitoMus |
| (24) | England v. Norway, World Cup, Wembley | 10 | 30 | Dawn |
| (25) | Great Railway Exposition, Manchester | 15 | – | n.o.c. |

### C.D.S. POSTMARKS
| | | | |
|---|---|---|---|
| (26) | Hitchin, Herts – Sir Henry Wood died here | 15 | |
| (27) | Marylebone, W1 – Royal Academy of Music | 15 | |
| (28) | New York – N.Y. Philharmonic (Barbirolli) | 15 | |
| (29) | Southampton Row – birthplace of Barbirolli | 15 | |
| (30) | Stamford – birthplace of Sargent | 15 | |
| (31) | St. Helens – birthplace of Beecham | 15 | |

**SLOGAN POSTMARK** *B.P.E. Wembley. Prices range from £50.*

## 10th October 1980 – SPORTING ANNIVERSARIES

*12p Athletics; 13½p Rugby; 15p Boxing; 17½p Cricket*

### SPECIAL HANDSTAMPS

| | | | | |
|---|---|---|---|---|
| (1) | First Day of Issue – Philatelic Bureau | 2 | – | Post Office |
| (2) | First Day of Issue – Cardiff | 2 | – | Post Office |
| (3) | W.R.U. Centenary, Cardiff Arms Park | 8 | 20 | W.R.U. |
| (4) | The Saints 1880-1980, Northampton | 8 | 50 | Saints RFC |
| (5) | King Henry VIII, Rugby Centenary, Coventry | 8 | 30 | D.F. |
| (6) | Leicester Football Club | 8 | 10 | LFDC 5 |

### Sport (contd.)

| | ordinary covers £ | official covers £ | |
|---|---|---|---|
| (7) | Norfolk County F. A. Centenary, Norwich...... | 8 | 10 | *Markton* |
| (8) | Middlesex CCC, NW8 ......................................... | 8 | 10 | *Havering 13* |
| (9) | PO XI v Cricket Writers/Vic Lewis Xl Lord's...... | 8 | 10 | *VicLewis(s)* |
| (10) | Centenary Tour, 1880-1980, Lord's, NW8....... | 8 | 300 | *S.P.* |
| (11) | Century of Tests, England v Australia, Oval.... | 8 | 10 | *Hawkwood* |
| (12) | London Union of Y.C./London Sportsmen...... | 8 | – | *n.o.c.* |
| (13) | Amateur Athletic Assoc., Crystal Palace........ | 8 | 10 | *BOCS 23* |
| (14) | Amateur Boxing Assoc., Wembley, M'sex........ | 8 | 20 | *BOCS Sp 3* |
| (15) | St. John Ambulance l880-1980, Manchester .... | 10 | 35 | *Cotswold* |
| (16) | Autumntime, British Library, WC................... | 10 | 45 | *BL 22* |
| (17) | New Zealand Exhibition, Warwick.................. | 10 | 35 | *W & W* |
| (18) | Post Office Philatelic Centre, Plymouth ........... | 10 | – | *n.o.c.* |
| (19) | Nearest & Dearest, Blackpool ........................... | 10 | 45 | *Blk Theatre* |

**ORDINARY F.D.I. POSTMARKS**

| (20) | Oxford, Rugby or Twickenham ........................... | 10 | | |
|---|---|---|---|---|

**C.D.S. POSTMARKS**

| (21) | Hambledon, Kennington, Llanelli or Neath..... | 30 | | |
|---|---|---|---|---|

*In addition: Boycott, Bowling, Box, Brecon, Lampeter, Jump, Llandovery, Pontypool, Rugby, The Oval, Welford Road, Wells. Prices from £15.*

**SLOGAN POSTMARKS** *Leicester Speedway. £150.*

## 19th November 1980 – CHRISTMAS
*10p, 12p, 13½p, 15p, 17½p Christmas decorations*

**SPECIAL HANDSTAMPS**

| (1) | First Day of Issue – Philatelic Bureau.............. | 2 | – | *Post Office* |
|---|---|---|---|---|
| (2) | First Day of Issue – Bethlehem ......................... | 3 | – | *Post Office* |
| (3) | 950 Years of Worship,Waltham Abbey.............. | 8 | 15 | *Hawkwood* |
| (4) | 1980 Christmas, British Library, WC................ | 8 | 25 | *BL 23* |
| (5) | Regent Street Association, W1 ........................... | 8 | 10 | *Havering 14* |
| (6) | Christmas Carols, Ivybridge ............................. | 8 | – | *n.o.c.* |
| (7) | Merry Christmas, Hollybush ............................. | 8 | – | *n.o.c.* |
| (8) | Norway's Christmas Gift, Trafalgar Square ..... | 8 | 10 | *BOCS 26* |
| (9) | Commonwealth Christmas Stamps, Warwick.. | 8 | 25 | *W & W* |
| (10) | Fire Service Charity Appeal, Leicester.............. | 8 | 10 | *LFDC 6* |
| (11) | Salvation Army, Mount Cross, Bramley ........... | 10 | 75 | *H.R.* |
| (12) | England v Switzerland World Cup, Wembley | 10 | 60 | *Dawn* |

**C.D.S. POSTMARKS**

| (13) | Bethlehem or Nasareth ....................................... | 35 | | |
|---|---|---|---|---|
| (14) | Glastonbury – conversions to Christianity...... | 35 | | |

*Also: Fairy Cross, Holly Bush, Holly Hall, Holy Island, Ivybridge, Ivychurch, Magdalen, Star. Prices from £15 each.*

**SLOGAN POSTMARKS** *Shopping By Post. £40.*

## 6th February 1981 – FOLKLORE
*14p St. Valentine's Day; 18p Morris Dancers; 22p Lammastide; 25p Medieval Mummers*

**SPECIAL HANDSTAMPS**

| (1) | First Day of Issue – Philatelic Bureau.............. | 2 | – | *Post Office* |
|---|---|---|---|---|
| (2) | First Day of Issue – London WC ....................... | 2 | – | *Post Office* |
| (3) | My Valentine, Lover, Salisbury ......................... | 8 | 10 | *Cotswold (g)* |
| (4) | Valentines at the British Library, WC............... | 8 | 75 | *BL 25* |
| (5) | Valentines Card Exhibition, Leicester.............. | 8 | 20 | *LFDC 7* |
| (6) | English Folk Song & Dance Society, SW1....... | 8 | 8 | *BOCS (2) 1* |
| (7) | Headington Morris Dancers, Oxford................ | 8 | 15 | *Hawkwood* |
| (8) | Thaxted Morris Men .......................................... | 8 | 15 | *Havering 15* |
| (9) | Dunmow Flitch, Little Dunmow........................ | 8 | 15 | *Havering Sp 1* |
| (10) | Robin Hood Society, Nottingham .................... | 8 | 30 | *Bradbury* |
| (11) | Radley College, St. Helens, Abingdon ............. | 8 | 50 | *Radley Coll* |
| (12) | Royal Mail Stampede, Hornsea Pottery............ | 10 | – | *n.o.c.* |
| (13) | Aviation History at Hendon, BF 1725 PS......... | 10 | 15 | *RFDC 1* |
| (14) | Orient F.C. Centenary, E10................................ | 10 | 40 | *Hawkwood* |
| (15) | Victoria Cross Exhib., Postal Museum.............. | 15 | – | *n.o.c.* |
| (16) | George VI, Sandringham ................................... | 15 | – | *n.o.c.* |

**C.D.S. POSTMARKS**

| (17) | Gretna Green or Lover ........................................ | 40 | | |
|---|---|---|---|---|
| (18) | Headington Quarry or Thaxted ......................... | 25 | | |

*Also: Bampton, Chipping Campden, Davey Place, Honiton, Padstow, Robin Hood, St. George's, Tintagel, Widecombe-in-the-Moor. Prices from £15 each.*

## 25th March 1981 – YEAR OF DISABLED PEOPLE
*14p Guide Dog; 18p Sign Language; 22p Wheelchair; 25p Foot Artist*

**SPECIAL HANDSTAMPS**

| (1) | First Day of Issue – Philatelic Bureau.............. | 2 | – | *Post Office* |
|---|---|---|---|---|
| (2) | First Day of Issue – Windsor ............................ | 2 | – | *Post Office* |
| (3) | Oaklands PH School, Salford ............................ | 8 | 90 | *Oaklands* |
| (4) | Guide Dogs Jubilee, Wallasey ........................... | 8 | 10 | *BOCS (2) 2* |
| (5) | Menphys Celebrate IYDP, Leicester ................. | 8 | 20 | *LFDC 8* |
| (6) | MS, Exeter & District Branch ............................ | 8 | 25 | *Exeter MS* |
| (7) | IYDP Toynbee Hall, D.I.G., E1........................... | 8 | 10 | *Havering 16* |
| (8) | Leicestershire Committee/IYDP ....................... | 8 | 20 | *P.P.S.* |
| (9) | Le Court: First Cheshire Home, Petersfield...... | 8 | 40 | *Cotswold* |

1981 International Year of the Disabled

The International Year of Disabled People 1981

British Butterflies Exhibition
OFFICIAL FIRST DAY COVER

CASTLE MUSEUM
OFFICIAL FIRST DAY COVER

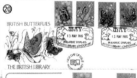

BRITISH BUTTERFLIES

THE BRITISH LIBRARY

Butterflies

Butterflies

LINGHOLM GARDENS

ST KILDA DETACHMENT
RA RANGE HEBRIDES

| Year of the Disabled (contd.) | ordinary covers £ | official covers £ | |
|---|---|---|---|
| (10) Cambridge & District Hard of Hearing............ | 8 | 35 | Cam. HHA |
| (11) Arthritis Care, London SW1 ............................. | 8 | 175 | Arlington |
| (12) RAF Headley Court, BF 1726 PS..................... | 8 | 15 | RFDC 2 |
| (13) Stoke Mandeville, Spinal Unit........................ | 8 | 15 | Hawkwood |
| (14) Coventry Sports Association, Charity Walk .... | 8 | 25 | D.F. |
| (15) Disabled Drivers Motor Club, W3 .................. | 8 | 35 | D.D.M.C. |
| (16) The Royal British Legion, SW1 ...................... | 8 | 175 | Brit. Leg. |
| (17) Stars for the Disabled, Peterborough ............. | 8 | 35 | Stars |
| (18) Carters (J & A), IYDP, Westbury ................... | 8 | 25 | P.P.S. |
| (19) Donington Park, 1931-1981, Derby................. | 10 | 175 | Don. Park |
| (20) Daily Mail Ideal Home, Earls Court, SW5 ..... | 10 | 40 | Pilgrim |
| (21) Swansea Philatelic Counter............................. | 10 | 175 | Cotswold |
| (22) March Philatelic Displays British Library........ | 10 | 40 | BL 24 |
| (23) Victoria Cross Exhib., Postal Museum............ | 12 | – | n.o.c. |

**ORDINARY F.D.I. POSTMARKS**

| | | |
|---|---|---|
| (24) Dudley (Redhill Disabled cvr)...........or similar | 25 | |
| (25) Maidstone (Leeds Castle Disabled cover) ........ | 25 | |
| (26) Fylde & Blackpool (Blind Society cover) ........ | 25 | |

**C.D.S. POSTMARKS**

| | | |
|---|---|---|
| (27) Any Hospital postmark ................................. | 25 | |
| (28) Leeds, Maidstone (Leeds Castle/Disabled cvr) .... | 40 | |
| (29) Stoke Mandeville – Spinal Injury Unit.............. | 25 | |

*Also: Bethesda, Guide,Leeds, St. Dunstans, Stoke Charity, Tredegar, Wallasey. Prices from £15 each.*

**SLOGAN POSTMARKS**

| | | |
|---|---|---|
| (30) 'Can Disabled People Go Where You Go?' ..... | 35 | |
| (31) St. Loyes College Exeter................................... | 50 | |
| (32) The British Deaf Association, Carlisle .............. | 35 | |

## 13th May 1981 – BUTTERFLIES
*14p Small Tortoiseshell; 18p Large Blue; 22p Peacock; 25p Chequered Skipper*
**SPECIAL HANDSTAMPS**

| | | | |
|---|---|---|---|
| (1) First Day of Issue – Philatelic Bureau............. | 3 | – | Post Office |
| (2) First Day of Issue – London SW.................... | 3 | – | Post Office |
| (3) Large Blue,Quorn ........................................ | 10 | 15 | BOCS (2) 3 |
| (4) Chequered Skipper, Bourton ...................... | 10 | 15 | BOCS (2) 3 |
| (5) Peacock, Sherborne ...................................... | 10 | 15 | BOCS (2) 3 |
| (6) Wildfowl Trust, Slimbridge........................... | 10 | 15 | BOCS (2) 3 |
| (7) World Wide Butterflies, Sherborne .............. | 10 | 15 | Havering Sp 2 |
| (8) Nottingham Trust, Eakring Meadows............ | 10 | 15 | Bradbury |
| (9) Margaret Fountaine Exhib., Norwich .............. | 10 | 15 | Markton |
| (10) Leics. Museums British Butterflies Exhib........ | 10 | 15 | LFDC 9 |
| (11) British Naturalist Assoc., Woodwalton............ | 10 | 15 | Hawkwood |
| (12) National Butterfly Museum, Bramber............. | 10 | 50 | S.P. |
| (13) Mtce Unit Conservamus, BF 1738 PS............. | 10 | 15 | RFDC 3 |
| (14) 25 Years Freedom, RAF Locking.................... | 15 | 100 | RAF(set of 4) |
| (15) Sub-Postmasters Conf., Scarborough ............. | 25 | – | n.o.c. |
| (16) Victorian Postbox Postcards, Liverpool .......... | 25 | – | n.o.c. |
| (17) Victorian Postbox Postcards, Keswick............. | 25 | – | n.o.c. |
| (18) Victorian Postbox Postcards, Buxton.............. | 25 | – | n.o.c. |
| (19) Rochdale's Unique Pillar Box ........................ | 25 | 175 | Toad Lane Mus |
| (20) May Philatelic Displays, British Library .......... | 15 | 75 | BL 26 |
| (21) Inauguration Wood Green Shopping.............. | 15 | 25 | Havering 17 |
| (22) 25th Christian Aid Week, Preston .................. | 15 | 35 | Chr. Aid |

**ORDINARY F.D.I. POSTMARKS**

| | | |
|---|---|---|
| (23) Basildon (Marks Hill Nature Reserve cover) ... | 40 | |
| (24) Hemel Hempstead (Herts Nature cover) ......... | 40 | |

**C.D.S. POSTMARKS**

| | | |
|---|---|---|
| (25) Peacock Cross, Hamilton ................................ | 35 | |
| (26) Quorn – HQ British Butterflies Society ........... | 25 | |

*Also: Castle Acre, Dousland, Kings Norton, Nettlebed, Nettleham, Spring Gardens. Prices from £15*

**SLOGAN POSTMARKS**

| | | |
|---|---|---|
| (27) National Butterfly Museum Bramber ................. | 50 | |

*Also: Whipsnade Zoo. Prices from £40.*

## 24th June 1981 – NATIONAL TRUSTS
*14p Glenfinnan; 18p Derwentwater; 20p Stackpole Head;*
*22p Giant's Causeway; 25p St. Kilda*
**SPECIAL HANDSTAMPS**

| | | | |
|---|---|---|---|
| (1) First Day of Issue – Philatelic Bureau............. | 3 | – | Post Office |
| (2) First Day of Issue – Keswick......................... | 3 | – | Post Office |
| (3) First Day of Issue – Glenfinnan ..................... | 3 | – | Post Office |
| (4) National Trust, Derwentwater....................... | 10 | 12 | BOCS Sp 4 |
| (5) National Trust for Scotland, Glenfinnan.......... | 10 | 12 | BOCS Sp 4 |
| (6) National Trust for Scotland, St. Kilda............. | 10 | 12 | BOCS Sp 5 |
| (7) National Trust, Stackpole Head..................... | 10 | 8 | Benham(s) |
| (8) National Trust, Giants Causeway .................. | 10 | 8 | Benham(s) |
| (9) N.T. Leicester, Sir Robert Shirley's Church...... | 10 | 20 | LFDC 10 |
| (10) Oakham Castle, 800 Years, Rutland.................. | 10 | 35 | Oakham Castle |
| (11) Lingholm Gardens, Open Day, Keswick............ | 10 | 20 | Hawkwood |
| (12) Geology of Causeway Coast, Nottingham........ | 10 | 35 | Bradbury |
| (13) Robin Hood Society, Nottingham Castle ......... | 10 | 30 | Bradbury |
| (14) St. Kilda, 25 Years BF 1750 PS....................... | 10 | 25 | BFPS |
| (15) The N.T. Scotland, Charlecote, Warwick.......... | 10 | 30 | Charlecote |

54

| National Trusts (contd.) | ordinary covers | | official covers |
|---|---|---|---|
| (16) London International Stamp Centre, WC2 ..... | 10 | 15 | *Stamp Centre* |
| (17) Lyke Wake Walk, BF 1739 PS ........................... | 10 | 15 | *RFDC 4* |
| (18) Friends of the Earth, Olympia W14 ................ | 10 | 15 | *Havering 18* |
| (19) Jaguar Drivers Club, 1956-1981, Luton........... | 15 | 25 | *Jaguar DC* |
| (20) Crane Schools Golden Jubilee, Nottingham..... | 15 | 150 | *Crane Sch.* |
| (21) Holkham Hall, Norfolk...................................... | 15 | 15 | *Markton* |
| (22) Lawn Tennis Museum, SW19 ........................... | 15 | 35 | *Lawn Tennis* |
| (23) Christianity in Otley, Leeds.............................. | 15 | 35 | *Parish Church* |
| (24) June Philatelic Displays, British Library.......... | 15 | 45 | *BL 27* |
| (25) Scottish Council for Spastics ........................... | 15 | 275 | *Spastics* |
| (26) ANTAR Service in BAOR, BF 1724 PS............. | 15 | 30 | *Army (s)* |
| (27) Humber Bridge Hull, Open to Traffic............... | 25 | 300 | *Scarboro'* |

**C.D.S. POSTMARKS**

| | |
|---|---|
| (28) Alfriston – first building acquired by N.T........ | 20 |
| (29) Barmouth – first site acquired by N.T............. | 20 |
| (30) Buckland Monachorum – Buckland Abbey ..... | 25 |
| (31) Culross – first building/N.T. for Scotland ........ | 20 |
| (32) Glenfinnan, Stackpole, or Causeway Head ...... | 25 |
| (33) Tintagel – PO is National Trust property......... | 25 |
| (34) Haslemere – Sir Robert Hunter (founder) ........ | 30 |
| (35) Lower Shiplake – Canon Rawnsley (founder).... | 30 |
| (36) Wisbech – b/place of Octavia Hill (founder) .. | 30 |
| (37) Land's End & John O' Groats.....................*pair* | 95 |

**SLOGAN POSTMARKS** *Bluebell Rly; Gawsworth Hall; Sandwich; The Pantiles; Hagley Hall. Prices from £75.*

## 22nd July 1981 – ROYAL WEDDING
*14p, 25p Prince of Wales and Lady Diana Spencer*
**SPECIAL HANDSTAMPS**

| | | | |
|---|---|---|---|
| (1) First Day of Issue – Philatelic Bureau................ | 2 | – | *Post Office* |
| (2) First Day of Issue – London EC........................ | 2 | – | *Post Office* |
| (3) First Day of Issue – Caernarfon ........................ | 2 | – | *Post Office* |
| (4) Royal Wedding Celebrations, Leicester ............ | 8 | 15 | *LFDC 11* |
| (5) Royal Wedding, Chingford Old Church ............ | 8 | 15 | *Hawkwood* |
| (6) Royal Wedding, St. Paul's Cathedral................ | 8 | 15 | *Havering 19* |
| (7) Royal Wedding, Stamp Exhibition, Exeter....... | 8 | 10 | *Ex StampCentre* |
| (8) Royal Wedding, Cameo Stamp Centre ............. | 8 | 20 | *Cameo* |
| (9) First Prince of Wales, Lincoln Cathedral ........ | 10 | 60 | *Lin. Cath* |
| (10) Greetings from Watton-at-Stone, Hertford ..... | 10 | 60 | *Watton Church* |
| (11) Prince of Wales & Lady Diana, Caernarfon ... | 8 | 20 | *BOCS (2) 6* |
| (12) Royal Wedding Greetings, Canterbury ............ | 10 | – | *n.o.c.* |
| (13) Canoe 81/Royal Wedding, Nottingham ........... | 10 | 20 | *Bradbury* |
| (14) RAF St. Clement Danes, BF 1932 PS .............. | 10 | 25 | *RFDC 5* |
| (15) Royal Wedding, Althorp, Northampton ........... | 10 | 40 | *Althorp* |
| (16) Loyal Greetings, Lullingstone Silk Farm ........ | 10 | 80 | *Benham L1* |
| (17) St. Pauls, EC4 (changeable date) ...................... | 10 | 40 | *H.R.* |
| (18) East of England Show, Peterborough ............... | 10 | 35 | *S.P.* |
| (19) Congratulations, Todd Scales, Cambridge ...... | 10 | 50 | *Todd Scales* |
| (20) Royal Tournament, BF 1805 PS........................ | 10 | 25 | *BFPS* |
| (21) Mayors Charity, City of Exeter ....................... | 10 | 20 | *ExMayor* |
| (22) Centenary Postcard, Cornhill P.O., Ipswich..... | 10 | 25 | *Corn'l p.card* |
| (23) Keswick/National Trust ................................... | 10 | – | *n.o.c.* |
| (24) South Lakeland/National Trust ........................ | 15 | – | *n.o.c.* |
| (25) July Philatelic Displays, British Library, WC..... | 10 | 30 | *BL 28* |
| (26) East Midlands CBI, Head P.O., Leicester ........ | 10 | – | *n.o.c.* |
| (27) Lifeboat Week 1981, Lyme Regis...................... | 10 | 25 | *Pilgrim* |
| (28) Gredington Jamboree, Whitchurch................... | 20 | 200 | *Jamboree* |
| (29) Port Sunlight, Liverpool ................................. | 10 | 50 | *Lever Bros* |
| (30) Windsor, Berks................................................ | 10 | – | *n.o.c.* |

**ORDINARY F.D.I. POSTMARKS**

| | |
|---|---|
| (31) Chester – Prince Charles is Earl of Chester .... | 15 |
| (32) Gloucestershire (Highgrove House cover) ......... | 25 |
| (33) King's Lynn (Sandringham special cover) ........ | 30 |
| (34) Windsor ......................................................... | 15 |

**C.D.S. POSTMARKS**

| | |
|---|---|
| (35) Buckingham Palace or Windsor Castle ............. | 175 |
| (36) Great Brington ............................................... | 100 |
| (37) House of Commons or Lords ............................ | 25 |
| (38) Prince Charles Ave or Prince of Wales Ave .... | 25 |
| (39) Princetown .................................................... | 35 |
| (40) Romsey, Tetbury or Buckingham Gate.............. | 35 |

*Also: Caernarfon, Charlestown, Dartmouth, Diss, Duffus, Highgrove, Sevenoaks, Spencers Wood, St. Paul's, Trinity St. From £20.*

**SLOGAN POSTMARKS**

| | |
|---|---|
| (41) Prince Charles/Lady Diana, IoM Crowns........ | 30 |
| (42) Exhibition of Royal Pagentry, Hagley Hall ...... | 75 |
| (43) Royal Westminster Exhibition ........................... | 100 |

*In addition: The Pantiles. £25.*

**NOTE:** *Double dated covers* exist with 22 July handstamp and 29 July (Wedding Day) handstamp. Each handstamp cancelling both stamps. *Prices from £20*
In addition, *triple dated covers* were serviced with 22 July, 28 July (Wedding Fireworks) and 29 July (Wedding Day) handstamps. Each handstamp cancelling both stamps. *Prices from £30*

National Trust - Leicester Centre

LINCOLN CATHEDRAL

## 12th August 1981 – DUKE OF EDINBURGH'S AWARD

*14p Expeditions; 18p Skills;*        **ordinary covers**   **official covers**
*22p Service; 25p Recreation*                 £        £

**SPECIAL HANDSTAMPS**

| | | ordinary | official | |
|---|---|---|---|---|
| (1) | First Day of Issue – Philatelic Bureau ............. | 2 | – | *Post Office* |
| (2) | First Day of Issue – London W2 ...................... | 2 | – | *Post Office* |
| (3) | Duke of Edinburgh's Award, Belfast................. | 8 | 25 | *Cotswold* |
| (4) | Duke of Edinburgh's Award, Cardiff................. | 8 | 25 | *Cotswold* |
| (5) | Duke of Edinburgh's Award, Edinburgh .......... | 8 | 25 | *Cotswold* |
| (6) | Duke of Edinburgh's Award, EC4 ................... | 8 | 25 | *Cotswold* |
| (7) | Duke of Edinburgh's Award, SW1................... | 8 | 25 | *Cotswold* |
| (8) | Duke of Edinburgh's Award, Devon ................ | 8 | 15 | *Devon DoEAS* |
| (9) | Duke of Edinburgh's Award, Winchmore Hill | 8 | 10 | *Havering 20* |
| (10) | RAF Canadian Rockies, BF 1740 PS............... | 8 | 15 | *RFDC 6* |
| (11) | Duke of Edinburgh's Award, Hull ................... | 8 | 25 | *HullDoEAS* |
| (12) | Leics Girl Guides Association ......................... | 8 | 10 | *LFDC 12* |
| (13) | August Philatelic Displays, British Library ...... | 10 | 40 | *BL 29* |
| (14) | Royal Mail House, Wakefield .......................... | 10 | 40 | *Wakefield* |
| (15) | Cardiff Searchlight Tattoo, BF 1747 PS........... | 10 | 45 | *BFPS* |
| (16) | Stoke Mandeville Games, Aylesbury................. | 8 | 15 | *Hawkwood* |
| (17) | Military Tattoo,Edinburgh .............................. | 10 | 40 | *M Tattoo* |
| (18) | Keswick/National Trust .................................. | 10 | – | *n.o.c.* |
| (19) | South Lakeland/National Trust ....................... | 10 | – | *n.o.c.* |
| (20) | Royal Wedding, St. Pauls Cathedral, EC4........ | 10 | 75 | *H.R.* |

**C.D.S. POSTMARKS**

| | | | | |
|---|---|---|---|---|
| (21) | Buckingham Palace or Windsor Castle ............ | 100 | | |
| (22) | Balmoral Castle ............................................ | 150 | | |
| (23) | Pathfinder Village, Exeter .............................. | 20 | | |

*Also: Calshot, Duffus, Dukestown, Edinburgh, Gateshead, Holyrood, Hse of Lords, Okehampton, Phillipstown. From £15*

**SLOGAN POSTMARKS**

| | | | | |
|---|---|---|---|---|
| (24) | Duke of Edinburgh's Award Crowns................ | 25 | | |

*Also: Cardiff Tattoo; Highland Games; Royal Westminster Exhib. Prices from £25*

## 23rd September 1981 – FISHING

*14p Cockle dredging; 18p Hauling in a Trawl Net;*
*22p Lobster Potting; 25p Hoisting a Seine Net*

**SPECIAL HANDSTAMPS**

| | | | | |
|---|---|---|---|---|
| (1) | First Day of Issue – Philatelic Bureau ............. | 2 | – | *Post Office* |
| (2) | First Day of Issue – Hull ................................ | 2 | – | *Post Office* |
| (3) | Catch '81, Falmouth ...................................... | 8 | 30 | *Catch '81* |
| (4) | Manchester Weather Centre ............................ | 8 | 15 | *Dawn* |
| (5) | Mission Deep Sea Fishermen, Aberdeen ........ | 8 | 10 | *BOCS (2) 5* |
| (6) | Heart of Scotland's Fishing Industry, Buckie . | 8 | 25 | *Fish.Mut.Ass.* |
| (7) | Fishing Fleets of Brixham ............................... | 8 | 225 | *Pandora Press* |
| (8) | Leics. Amalgamated Society of Anglers .......... | 8 | 25 | *LFDC 13* |
| (9) | Centuries of Trading, Billingsgate, EC3 ......... | 8 | 25 | *Hawkwood* |
| (10) | Ocean Tapestry, BF 1741 PS, St. Mawgan ..... | 8 | 25 | *RFDC 7* |
| (11) | Fishmonger's Company, EC4........................... | 8 | 15 | *S. Petty 1* |
| (12) | Sept. Philatelic Displays, British Library ......... | 10 | 35 | *BL 30* |
| (13) | Transporter Bridge, Newport............................ | 10 | 100 | *Newport BC* |
| (14) | Langley Grammar School, Slough.................... | 10 | 100 | *Langley Sch* |

**ORDINARY F.D.I. POSTMARKS**

| | | | | |
|---|---|---|---|---|
| (15) | Grimsby or any other fishing port FDI .....*each* | 15 | | |

**C.D.S. POSTMARKS**

| | | | | |
|---|---|---|---|---|
| (16) | Lighthouse. Fleetwood .................................... | 50 | | |
| (17) | Six Bells or The Wharf ..............................*each* | 35 | | |

*Also: Crab Lane, Dousland, Eyemouth, Fisherie Turriff, Fisherow, Fisher's Pond, Fishpool, Fishguard, Fleetwood, The Harbour, Hull, Milford Haven, Stafford, St. Peter's St., The Salmon Leap, Whale Hill, Whiting Bay. Prices from £15 each.*

**SLOGAN POSTMARKS**

| | | | | |
|---|---|---|---|---|
| (18) | Hastings/Resort for all seasons (depicts boat) . | 60 | | |

*In addition: Visit Sandwich. Price from £35*

## 18th November 1981 – CHRISTMAS

*11½p, 14p,18p, 22p, 25p Childrens Paintings*

**SPECIAL HANDSTAMPS**

| | | | | |
|---|---|---|---|---|
| (1) | First Day of Issue – Philatelic Bureau............... | 2 | – | *Post Office* |
| (2) | First Day of Issue – Bethlehem ....................... | 2 | – | *Post Office* |
| (3) | Children First Canterbury................................ | 8 | 10 | *BOCS (2) 8* |
| (4) | Children's Christmas Book Show Blackwells .. | 8 | 30 | *Hawkwood* |
| (5) | Friends of Leicester Cathedral.......................... | 8 | 25 | *LFDC 14* |
| (6) | Church of St. Mary-at-Hill, EC3...................... | 8 | 20 | *S. Petty 2* |
| (7) | Stamp Magazine Link House, Croydon .......... | 8 | 5 | *Benham(s)* |
| (8) | Happy Xmas from Big C Appeal Norwich ...... | 8 | 25 | *Big C Appeal* |
| (9) | Princess of Wales Regent St., W1 ................... | 8 | 10 | *Havering 22* |
| (10) | Pillar Box Postcards – Preston......................... | 20 | – | *n.o.c.* |
| (11) | Pillar Box Postcards – Oldham........................ | 20 | – | *n.o.c.* |
| (12) | Pillar Box Postcards – Manchester.................. | 20 | – | *n.o.c.* |
| (13) | Pillar Box Postcards – Blackpool..................... | 20 | – | *n.o.c.* |
| (14) | Nov. Philatelic. Displays British Library ......... | 10 | 45 | *BL 31* |
| (15) | England v. Hungary, Wembley.......................... | 10 | 55 | *Dawn* |

**C.D.S. POSTMARKS**

| | | | | |
|---|---|---|---|---|
| (16) | Bethlehem or Nasareth ...............................*each* | 25 | | |

*Christmas (contd.)*     ordinary covers    official covers
                                     £      £

(17) Rhoose, Ramridge, Clutton, Horsham or Fulwood
      – homes of stamp designers ................. 20

*Also: Angel Hill, Holy Island, Kings Road, Star, Starcross, St. Nicholas, Trinity. Prices from £10*

## 10th February 1982 – CHARLES DARWIN
*15½p Giant Tortoises; 19½p Iguanas; 26p Finch; 29p Skulls*

**SPECIAL HANDSTAMPS**

| | | | | |
|---|---|---|---|---|
| (1) | First Day of Issue – Philatelic Bureau ............... | 2 | – | *Royal Mail* |
| (2) | First Day of Issue – Shrewsbury ........................ | 2 | – | *Royal Mail* |
| (3) | Darwin Centenary, RSPB, Sandy ..................... | 8 | 25 | *R.S.P.B.* |
| (4) | Maer Hall Tribute to Charles Darwin ................ | 8 | 150 | *Maer Hall* |
| (5) | Charles Darwin 1809-1882, Slimbridge ............ | 8 | 10 | *BOCS(2)9* |
| (6) | Charles Darwin 1809-1882, Cambridge ........... | 8 | 10 | *BOCS(2)9* |
| (7) | Charles Darwin 1809-1882, Shrewsbury ........... | 8 | 10 | *BOCS(2)9* |
| (8) | Down House, Charles Darwin Memorial ......... | 8 | 15 | *S. Petty 3* |
| (9) | Charles Darwin, Westminster Abbey, SW1 ...... | 8 | 15 | *Hawkwood* |
| (10) | Voyage of HMS Beagle, Plymouth ................... | 8 | 10 | *BLS 1* |
| (11) | Man of Vision, London, SW7 ........................... | 8 | 10 | *Havering 23* |
| (12) | HMS Beagle, BF 1762 PS ................................ | 8 | 15 | *RFDC 9* |
| (13) | 1809-1882 Charles Darwin Centenary, NW1 .. | 8 | 35 | *London Zoo* |
| (14) | Leicester University Jubilee Year ..................... | 10 | 15 | *LFDC 15* |
| (15) | February Philatelic Displays, British Library.... | 10 | 40 | *BL 32* |
| (16) | Valentines at Harrods, SW1 ............................. | 10 | 75 | *Pilgrim* |

**C.D.S. POSTMARKS**

| | | | |
|---|---|---|---|
| (17) | Downe – Darwin's home or The Lizard ............ | 15 | |
| (18) | Frankwell – near to Darwin's birthplace .......... | 30 | |

*Also: Atcham, Falmouth, Frog Island, Oxford, Piltdown, Sandown, Shrewsbury, Slimbridge, Stonehouse, Whipsnade. From £12*

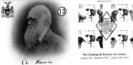

Charles Darwin
1809–1882

## 24th March 1982 – YOUTH ORGANISATIONS
*15½p Boys' Brigade; 19½p Girls' Brigade; 26p Scouts; 29p Girl Guides*

**SPECIAL HANDSTAMPS**

| | | | | |
|---|---|---|---|---|
| (1) | First Day of Issue – Philatelic Bureau ............... | 2 | – | *Royal Mail* |
| (2) | First Day of Issue – Glasgow ............................. | 2 | – | *Royal Mail* |
| (3) | First Day of Issue – London SW ........................ | 2 | – | *Royal Mail* |
| (4) | St. Mary's 8th Hendon, NW4 ............................ | 8 | 20 | *Havering 24* |
| (5) | Year of the Scout Celebrations, Peterborough . | 8 | 40 | *Peteb. Scouts* |
| (6) | Lord Baden Powell, Westminster Abbey ........... | 8 | 15 | *Hawkwood* |
| (7) | Loughborough, Year of Scout ........................... | 8 | 25 | *Loughb. Scouts* |
| (8) | Scout Movement W. Europe, BF 1742 PS ....... | 8 | 50 | *Forces* |
| (9) | 75th Anniversary of Scouting, Glasgow ........... | 8 | 40 | *Glasgow Scouts* |
| (10) | Scouting for Boys, Baden-Powell House ........... | 8 | 35 | *Scouts Council* |
| (11) | 75th Anniversary of Scouting, Caterham ......... | 8 | 35 | *Cat'm Scouts* |
| (12) | The Girls Brigade, SW6 ................................... | 8 | 12 | *BOCS (2) 10b* |
| (13) | Girl Guides Association, SW1 .......................... | 8 | 20 | *Cotswold* |
| (14) | First for Boys, SW6 ......................................... | 8 | 15 | *BOCS (2) 10a* |
| (15) | Young Enterprise, Folkestone ........................... | 8 | 45 | *S. Kent Coll.* |
| (16) | National Association of Youth Clubs ................. | 8 | 30 | *Bradbury* |
| (17) | National Youth Bureau, Leicester ..................... | 8 | 20 | *LFDC 16* |
| (18) | 1982 (Huyton) Sqd ATC, BF 5282 PS ............ | 8 | 15 | *RFDC 10* |
| (19) | St. Donats Castle, Llantwit Major ................... | 8 | 20 | *S. Petty 4* |
| (20) | Yorkshire County Bowling Assoc., York .......... | 10 | 20 | *Yorks CBA* |
| (21) | Motorway Sub P.O., Rank M6 Forton .............. | 15 | 140 | *Rank M6* |
| (22) | First Postbus in Yorkshire, Masham ................. | 15 | – | *n.o.c.* |
| (23) | Four Marks Golden Jubilee, Alton ................... | 10 | 65 | *FourMarksPO* |
| (24) | March Philatelic Displays, British Library ........ | 10 | 35 | *BL 33* |
| (25) | Norwich Union, Mail Coach to Rayleigh .......... | 10 | 75 | *Norwich Un.* |
| (26) | Daily Mail, Ideal Home, Earls Court, SW5 ...... | 10 | 70 | *Pilgrim* |

**ORDINARY F.D.I. POSTMARKS**

| | | | |
|---|---|---|---|
| (27) | Sunderland (Sunderland Scouts cover) ............ | 25 | |
| (28a) | Sheffield (Sheffield Boys Brigade cover) .......... | 35 | |
| (28) | Enfield - Boys Brigade on 15½p stamp ............ | 25 | |

**C.D.S. POSTMARKS**

| | | | |
|---|---|---|---|
| (29) | Bentley, Euston, Paddington or House of Lords .. | 20 | |
| (30) | Fleur-de-lis – the scout's emblem .................... | 95 | |
| (31) | Guide, Pathfinder Village or The Camp ........... | 25 | |
| (32) | West Hampstead – girl guide on 29p value ...... | 25 | |

*Also: Chingford, Pinkneys Road, Poole, Sandbanks, Scouthead, Scout Hill, Thurso. From £10.*

**SLOGAN POSTMARKS**

| | | | |
|---|---|---|---|
| (33) | Scouts help others – any office ........................... | 20 | |

## 28th April 1982 – BRITISH THEATRE
*15½p Ballet; 19½p Harlequin; 26p Drama; 29p Opera*

**SPECIAL HANDSTAMPS**

| | | | | |
|---|---|---|---|---|
| (1) | First Day of Issue – Philatelic Bureau ............... | 2 | – | *Royal Mail* |
| (2) | First Day of Issue – Stratford-upon-Avon ........ | 2 | – | *Royal Mail* |
| (3) | John Gay, Westminster Abbey ......................... | 8 | 15 | *Hawkwood* |
| (4) | Royal Shakespeare Theatre, Stratford .............. | 8 | 15 | *BOCS (2) 11* |
| (5) | Royal Opera House, Covent Garden ................ | 8 | 7 | *BLS 3* |
| (6) | Arts Theatre, Cambridge ................................ | 10 | 45 | *Arts Theatre* |
| (7) | Theatre Royal Restoration, Bath ..................... | 10 | 30 | *Cotswold* |
| (8) | Queens Theatre, Hornchurch ......................... | 10 | 15 | *Havering 25* |
| (9) | Tavistock Repertory Co., London N1 .............. | 10 | 30 | *Tav. Rep.* |
| (10) | Leicester Drama Society ................................... | 10 | 50 | *LFDC 17* |

LEICESTER DRAMA SOCIETY

official first day cover

**Theatre (contd.)**

| | | ordinary covers £ | official covers £ | |
|---|---|---|---|---|
| (11) | Theatre Royal, Norwich | 10 | 45 | *Th. Royal* |
| (12) | Mercury Theatre, Colchester | 10 | 45 | *Mercury Th.* |
| (13) | Shakespeare, Southwark Cathedral, SE1 | 10 | 15 | *S. Petty 5* |
| (14) | New Theatre, Hull | 10 | 45 | *New Theatre* |
| (15) | Worthing Operatic Society | 10 | 35 | *S.P.* |
| (16) | Barbican Centre, EC2 | 10 | 50 | *Barbican* |
| (17) | S.C.D.A., Pitlochry | 10 | 60 | *S.C.D.A.* |
| (18) | Theatr Clwyd, Ebrill, Yr Wyddgrug, Mold | 25 | – | *n.o.c.* |
| (19) | William Shakespeare, Stratford | 15 | – | *n.o.c.* |
| (20) | Royal Air Force Central Band, BF 1773 PS | 10 | 20 | *RFDC 11* |
| (21) | Rating & Valuation Association, SW1 | 10 | 60 | *Bradbury* |
| (22) | Queen Victoria's Visit of Epping Forest | 15 | 35 | *Hawkwood* |

**ORDINARY F.D.I. POSTMARKS**

| | | | |
|---|---|---|---|
| (23) | Basingstoke (Horseshoe Theatre Co. cover) | 40 | |
| (24) | Bury St Edmunds (Threatre Royal cover) | 40 | |
| (25) | Northampton (Royal Theatre cover) | 40 | |
| (26) | Leeds (Grand Theatre cover) | 60 | |
| (27) | Swindon (Wyvern Theatre card) | 40 | |

**C.D.S. POSTMARKS**

| | | | |
|---|---|---|---|
| (28) | Barnstaple – birthplace of John Gay | 15 | |
| (29) | Ben Jonson Road or Shakespeare St | 25 | |
| (30) | Great Yarmouth – first theatre | 10 | |
| (31) | Stratford-upon-Avon | 15 | |
| (32) | The Harlequin – harlequin (19½p ) | 25 | |

*Also: Aldeburgh, Amesbury, Barbican, Bishopgate, Blackfriars, Broadway, Globe Road, Hereford, Macduff, Shoreditch, Stafford, The Circle. Prices from £10.*

**SLOGAN POSTMARKS**

| | | | |
|---|---|---|---|
| (33) | Eden Court – The Theatre of the Highlands | 30 | |
| (34) | Dickens Festival – Rochester | 90 | |

*Also: Dunfermline Festival; Congleton Carnival. Aldershot Army Display.  Prices from £30.*

## 16th June 1982 – MARITIME HERITAGE

*15½p Henry VIII; 19½p Blake; 24p Nelson; 26p Fisher; 29p Cunningham*

**SPECIAL HANDSTAMPS**

| | | | | |
|---|---|---|---|---|
| (1) | First Day of Issue – Philatelic Bureau | 3 | – | *Royal Mail* |
| (1a) | -do- with PhilexFrance'82 Paris cachet | 10 | – | *Royal Mail* |
| (2) | First Day of Issue – Portsmouth | 3 | – | *Royal Mail* |
| (3) | Birthplace of Nelson, Burnham Thorpe | 10 | 30 | *Hawkwood* |
| (4) | National Maritime Museum, Greenwich | 10 | 12 | *BLS 4* |
| (5) | Lloyds Register of Shipping, EC3 | 10 | 45 | *S. Petty 6* |
| (6) | Maritime Heritage, Lloyds, EC3 | 10 | 45 | *Cotswold* |
| (7) | Britannia's Maritime Heritage, Dartmouth | 10 | 90 | *B.R.N.C.* |
| (8) | Maritime Heritage Stamp Exhibition, Exeter | 10 | 25 | *Exeter Cvrs* |
| (9) | Maritime England Year, Poole | 10 | 60 | *Poole Mar Tr* |
| (10) | Nottinghamshire Lifeboat Appeal | 10 | 20 | *Pilgrim* |
| (11) | Axe Valley Maritime 82, Seaton | 10 | 75 | *Fire Ser NBF* |
| (12) | WeymouthChamber of Commerce | 10 | 60 | *Ch. of Comm.* |
| (13) | Capt Matthew Flinders, Port Lincoln | 10 | 90 | *LincolnCath2* |
| (14) | Cook's Endeavour Salutes Nelson's Victory | 10 | 20 | *B. Travers* |
| (15) | Maritime Heritage Cruise, Penarth | 10 | 20 | *Post Office* |
| (16) | Missions to Seamen, Stratford | 10 | 50 | *Eng. T. Board* |
| (17) | Historic Ships, St. Katherines Dock, E1 | 10 | 20 | *Havering 26* |
| (18) | Missions to Seamen, Portsmouth | 10 | 50 | *S.P.* |
| (19) | Cinque Ports Exhibition, Dover | 10 | 75 | *Cinque Ports* |
| (20) | Mountbatten Memorial Trust, Broadlands | 10 | 12 | *S. Petty 7* |
| (21) | Leicester Sea Cadets | 10 | 30 | *LFDC 18* |
| (22) | RAF Marine Branch, BF 1779 PS | 10 | 30 | *RFDC 12* |
| (23) | Peru Hovercraft Expedition, BF 1956 PS | 10 | 45 | *Forces* |
| (24) | Worshipful Co. of Shipwrights, EC | 10 | 10 | *BOCS (2) 12* |
| (25) | Centenary Forces Postal Service, BF 8282 PS | 10 | 25 | *Forces* |
| (26) | Trafalgar Sq. Philatelic Counter | 12 | – | *n.o.c.* |
| (27) | Philatelic Counter Opening, Coventry | 12 | – | *n.o.c.* |
| (28) | Royal Shakespeare, Barbican, EC2 | 12 | 250 | *Barbican* |

**ORDINARY F.D.I. POSTMARKS**

| | | | |
|---|---|---|---|
| (29) | Exeter (Exeter Maritime special cover) | 40 | |
| (30) | Any other FDI on special maritime covers | 40 | |

**C.D.S. POSTMARKS**

| | | | |
|---|---|---|---|
| (31) | Bridgwater – birthplace of Blake | 10 | |
| (32) | Buckingham Palace, S.W.1 | 75 | |
| (33) | Burnham Thorpe – birthplace of Nelson | 20 | |
| (34) | Castle Rd. Southsea – Mary Rose | 20 | |
| (35) | Devonport or Naval Barracks, Chatham | 25 | |
| (36) | Falkland or Victory Street, Devonport | 30 | |
| (37) | Flotta, Orkney – Scapa Flow (Home Fleet) | 20 | |
| (38) | Fleet Mail Office Portsmouth or Devonport | 35 | |
| (39) | Greenwich, London S.E.10 | 15 | |
| (40) | House of Lords, SW1 | 25 | |
| (41) | Marazion – b/place of Sandy Woodward | 25 | |
| (42) | Nelson, Portsmouth or Trafalgar | 20 | |
| (43) | The Quarterdeck or Westward Ho! | 15 | |

*Also: Blakes Corner, Blake Street, Bridgwater, Britannia, The Chart, Clyde Submarine Base, Cunningham Crescent, Dartmouth, Deptford High Street, The Docks (Bridgwater), Fisher's Pond, Fleet, Henry St., Marton-in-Cleveland, Nelson (Lancs), Portsmouth, Portsmouth Dock Yard, St. Andrew's Cross (Plymouth), Tavistock. From £10.*

*Maritime (contd.)*

| | ordinary covers £ | official covers £ |
|---|---|---|
| **SLOGAN POSTMARKS** | | |
| (44) See the Tall Ships in Southampton | 45 | |
| (45) Maritime Bristol | 70 | |
| (46) Tower Bridge Open to the Public | 75 | |

## 23rd July 1982 – BRITISH TEXTILES

*15½p 'Strawberry Thief' (Morris); 19½p 'Scarlet Tulips' (Steiner);*
*26p 'Cherry Orchard' (Nash); 29p 'Chevrons' (Foster)*

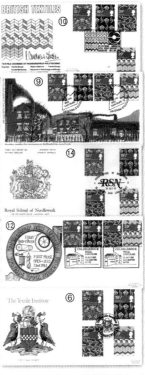

**SPECIAL HANDSTAMPS**

| | | | |
|---|---|---|---|
| (1) First Day of Issue – Philatelic Bureau | 3 | – | *Royal Mail* |
| (2) First Day of Issue – Rochdale | 3 | – | *Royal Mail* |
| (3) William Morris, Water House, E17 | 10 | 15 | *Hawkwood* |
| (4) Sir Richard Arkwright, Preston | 10 | 12 | *BOCS (2) 13* |
| (5) Hockley Mill, Nottingham | 10 | 15 | *Cotswold (g)* |
| (6) Textile Institute, Manchester | 10 | 15 | *Pilgrim* |
| (7) School of Textiles, Leicester | 10 | 50 | *Bradbury* |
| (8) Textile Exhibition, Bradford | 10 | 15 | *Peter Scot* |
| (9) Leek, Centre of Textile Industry | 10 | 90 | *Staffs C.C.* |
| (10) Textile Design, Huddersfield Polytechnic | 10 | 70 | *Hudd.Poly* |
| (11) Textiles on Stamps, Liberty, W1 | 10 | 12 | *BLS 5* |
| (12) Coldharbour Mill, Uffculme | 10 | 90 | *Coldhbr. Mill* |
| (13) Leicester & District Knitting Industry | 10 | 50 | *LFDC 19* |
| (14) Royal School of Needlework, SW7 | 10 | 15 | *S. Petty 8* |
| (15) No.2 Squadron RAF Regiment, BF 1781 PS | 10 | 20 | *RFDC 13* |
| (16) Arkwright Anniv., Cromford Mills, Matlock | 10 | 30 | *Ark. Soc.* |
| (17) British Philatelic Federation, Southampton | 10 | 20 | *B.P.F.* |
| (18) European Floral City, Exeter | 10 | 30 | *Exeter C.C.* |
| (19) Papal Visits in Philately, SW1 | 10 | 45 | *Bradbury* |
| (20) Royal Tournament, BF 1840 PS | 10 | 35 | *Forces* |
| (21) International Scout Camp, Blair Atholl | 10 | 35 | *Scot Scouts* |
| (22) Life Boat Week, Lyme Regis | 10 | 25 | *Pilgrim* |
| (23) Open Days, RNLI HQ, Poole | 10 | 25 | *Pilgrim* |
| (24) Caldey Island, Pope John Paul, Wales | 10 | 35 | *Caldey Isl.* |

**C.D.S. POSTMARKS**

| | | |
|---|---|---|
| (25) Cherry Orchard or Silk Street | 15 | |
| (26) Forest Rd., E17 – b/place of Wm. Morris | 10 | |
| (27) Hall-ith-Wood – later named Spinning Mule | 25 | |
| (28) Hammersmith W6 – home of Wm. Morris | 10 | |
| (29) Preston – birthplace of Richard Arkwright | 10 | |
| (30) Stanhill – James Hargreaves 'Spinning Jenny' | 15 | |
| (31) Walthamstow, E17 – b/place of Wm. Morris | 9 | |

*Also: All Saints (Derby), Arkwright Town, Axminster, Bobbers Mill, Coat, Coggeshall, Cotton Tree, Draperstown, Fair Isle, Harris, Lechlade, Merton, Milltown, New Invention, Shaftesbury,Tweed Rd, Weaver Lodge, Wilton, Wool, Worstead. Prices from £10 each.*

**SLOGAN POSTMARKS** *Collect British Stamps, Hull. £15.*

## 8th September 1982 – INFORMATION TECHNOLOGY

*15½p History of Communications; 26p Technology Today*

**SPECIAL HANDSTAMPS**

| | | | |
|---|---|---|---|
| (1) First Day of Issue – Philatelic Bureau | 2 | – | *Royal Mail* |
| (2) First Day of Issue – London WC | 2 | – | *Royal Mail* |
| (3) Intelpost Head Post Office, E1 | 8 | 15 | *Hawkwood* |
| (4) Computertown, Croydon | 10 | 50 | *Croy. Lib.* |
| (5) World Trade Centre | 10 | 10 | *Havering 28* |
| (6) Information Technology Year, Bedford | 10 | 55 | *Texas Instr.* |
| (7) RAF Supply Centre, BF 1787 PS | 10 | 15 | *RFDC 14* |
| (8) Best of Prestel, Martlesham | 10 | 12 | *Prestel* |
| (9) Artificial Earth Satellites, Jodrell Bank | 10 | 12 | *BLS 6* |
| (10) Information Technology UMIST, Manchester | 10 | 12 | *BOCS (2) 14* |
| (11) University of Leicester | 10 | 25 | *LFDC 20* |
| (12) Ashville College, Computer Age, Harrogate | 10 | – | *n.o.c.* |
| (13) Exercise British Prince, 82 BF 1882 PS | 10 | 15 | *Forces* |
| (14) Anaesthesiology, Royal Festival Hall, SE1 | 10 | 25 | *Assoc Anaesth* |
| (15) 1982 Museum of the Year, Stoke | 10 | 25 | *Stoke Museum* |
| (16) Military Tattoo, Edinburgh | 10 | 45 | *Mil. Tattoo* |
| (17) Trishaw Marathon, Kent Fire Brigade | 10 | 45 | *Kent Fire B.* |
| (18) King's Cup Air Race, BF 1788 PS | 10 | 55 | *MosqMus.* |

**ORDINARY F.D.I. POSTMARKS**

| | | |
|---|---|---|
| (19) London EC (Orbital Test Satellite/FT cover) | 35 | |
| (20) Norwich (Hotel Norwich IT82 Exhib. cover) | 35 | |
| (21) Milton Keynes (Milton Keynes IT cover) | 35 | |
| (22) Brighton (Brighton Congress cover) | 35 | |

**C.D.S. POSTMARKS**

| | | |
|---|---|---|
| (23) Helston, Mawgan, Mullion-Goonhilly Downs | 10 | |
| (24) Martlesham – British Telecom Research | 20 | |
| (25) New Invention, Willenhall | 10 | |

*In addition: Bean, Bletchley, Bracknell, Caversham, Cheltenham, Edinburgh, Felixstowe, Helensburg, Lovelace Rd Mount Pleasant, National Insurance Blgs (Newcastle), Newton St (Manchester), Oldland Common, Oxford, The Rocket, Rosetta, South Kensington, Stock Exchange, Taunton,Telephone House, Totnes, Walworth Road. Prices from £10.*

**SLOGAN POSTMARKS**

| | | |
|---|---|---|
| (26) Post Code It, Norwich | 25 | |

*Also: Radio Gwent; Beat Crime Dial 999; Collect British Stamps; any Postcode slogans. From £15.*

## 13th October 1982 – BRITISH MOTOR CARS

*15½p Metro & Austin Seven;*    **ordinary covers**    **official covers**
*19½p Ford Escort & Model T;*            £            £
*26p Jaguar XJ6 & SS1; 29p Rolls-Royce Silver Spirit & Silver Ghost*

**SPECIAL HANDSTAMPS**

| | | | | |
|---|---|---|---|---|
| (1) | First Day of Issue – Philatelic Bureau | 3 | – | *Royal Mail* |
| (2) | First Day of Issue – Birmingham | 3 | – | *Royal Mail* |
| (3) | First Day of Issue – Crewe | 3 | – | *Royal Mail* |
| (4) | National Motor Museum, Beaulieu | 10 | 20 | *Beaulieu* |
| (5) | Metro, World Trade Centre, E1 | 10 | 15 | *Havering 29* |
| (6) | Year of the Car, Woodford Green | 10 | 130 | *Havering* |
| (7) | Millionth New Ford Escort, Halewood | 10 | 25 | *Ford* |
| (8) | Nuffield College, Oxford | 10 | 25 | *Univ. Covers* |
| (9) | Royal Flying Corps, BF 1789 PS | 10 | 25 | *RFDC 15* |
| (10) | Worshipful Company of Coachmakers | 10 | 25 | *S. Petty 10* |
| (11) | Ford Sierra, Launch Day, Chippenham | 10 | 200 | *Cotswold* |
| (12) | Cycle & Car Museum, Stanford Hall | 10 | 25 | *LFDC 21* |
| (13) | Austin 7, Brooklands, Weybridge | 10 | 10 | *BLS 7* |
| (14) | Transport Centenary, Chesterfield | 10 | 20 | *Dawn* |
| (15) | Heritage Collection, Syon Park, Brentford. | 10 | 20 | *Hawkwood* |
| (16) | Dagenham, Home of Ford | 10 | 25 | *Dag. Motors* |
| (17) | Sixty Years of Jaguar Cars, Coventry | 10 | 15 | *BOCS (2) 15* |
| (18) | 35 Years of Silverstone Circuit | 10 | 35 | *Silverstone* |
| (19) | Rolls-Royce Enthusiasts', Paulerspury | 10 | 40 | *Bradbury* |
| (20) | Wiltshire Radio, Wootton Bassett | 10 | 75 | *Wilts Radio* |
| (21) | Tile Hill Wood School, Coventry | 10 | 75 | *Tile Hill* |

**ORDINARY F.D.I. POSTMARKS**

| | | | |
|---|---|---|---|
| (22) | Manchester – where Rolls met Royce | 15 | |

**C.D.S. POSTMARKS**

| | | | |
|---|---|---|---|
| (23) | Amersham – b/place of Sir Herbert Austin | 20 | |
| (24) | Alwalton – birthplace of Henry Royce | 25 | |
| (25) | Austin, Plymouth | 20 | |
| (26) | Brighton & Knightsbridge – car rally........pair | 20 | |
| (27) | Dagenham – Dagenham Motors (Ford) | 20 | |
| (28) | Dover Paquebot – car ferry | 20 | |
| (29) | Foleshill – original Jaguar SS production | 20 | |
| (30) | Ford, Liverpool or Shrewsbury | 25 | |
| (31) | Halewood or Longbridge | 25 | |
| (32) | Leyland – birthplace of Leyland Motors | 25 | |
| (33) | Mount Street, W1 – b/place of Charles Rolls | 20 | |
| (34) | N.E.C. Birmingham – Motor Show | 75 | |
| (35) | R.A.C. London SW1 | 525 | |
| (36) | Rank Forton Services – first motorway PO | 60 | |
| (37) | Trafford Park – U.K. assembly for Model T | 40 | |

*Also: Allesley, Battery, Beaulieu, Bentley, Crewe, Dunlop, Fender, Hulme, Lanchester, Lewisham, Milton, Rockfield, Saltley, Silverstone, Sparkbrook (Birmingham), St. James' St., Tooting, Vauxhall, Walthamstow. From £15.*

**SLOGAN POSTMARKS**

| | | | |
|---|---|---|---|
| (41) | Hella of Banbury, Motor Show | 55 | |

## 17th November 1982 – CHRISTMAS

*12½p, 15½p, 19½p, 26p, 29p Christmas Carols*

**SPECIAL HANDSTAMPS**

| | | | | |
|---|---|---|---|---|
| (1) | First Day of Issue – Philatelic Bureau | 3 | – | *Royal Mail* |
| (2) | First Day of Issue – Bethlehem | 3 | – | *Royal Mail* |
| (3) | We Three Kings, Star, Glenrothes | 8 | 10 | *BLS 8* |
| (4) | I Saw Three Ships, Hythe | 8 | 10 | *BOCS (2) 16* |
| (5) | Good King Wenceslas, Salisbury | 8 | 10 | *Benham* |
| (6) | Seasons Greetings, Norwich Cathedral | 8 | 25 | *Nor. Cath.* |
| (7) | Seasons Greetings, Cutty Sark, SE10 | 8 | 10 | *Havering 30* |
| (8) | Salvation Army, Leicester | 8 | 25 | *LFDC 22* |
| (9) | Christmas Carol, Dickens House, WC1 | 8 | 25 | *Hawkwood* |
| (10) | St. John Ambulance, Leicester | 8 | 35 | *St. John Am.* |
| (11) | Sir Christopher Wren, East Knoyle | 8 | 20 | *S. Petty 11* |
| (12) | 1st Highams Park Girl Guides, E4 | 8 | 30 | *Girls Brig.* |
| (13) | North Atlantic Assembly, SW | 10 | – | *n.o.c.* |
| (14) | HMS Brilliant, Freedom of Tunbridge Wells | 10 | 80 | *H.R.* |

**C.D.S. POSTMARKS**

| | | | |
|---|---|---|---|
| (15) | Bethlehem or Nasareth | 25 | |

*In addition: Chipping Campden, East Grinstead, Fleet Street, Holly Bank, Hollybush, Holy Island, Holytown, Ivy Bush, Ivychurch, Kingsway, Kingsworthy, London SE1, Noel Road, Orient Road, St. Erth, St. Nicholas, St. Stephen, Shepherds Hill, Shepherdswell, Star, Starcross, Theobalds Road BO, Three Kingham. From £10.*

## 26th January 1983 – BRITISH RIVER FISH

*15½p Salmon; 19½p Pike; 26p Trout; 29p Perch*

**SPECIAL HANDSTAMPS**

| | | | | |
|---|---|---|---|---|
| (1) | First Day of Issue – Philatelic Bureau | 2 | – | *Royal Mail* |
| (2) | First Day of Issue – Peterborough | 2 | – | *Royal Mail* |
| (3) | Fishing the Teign, Newton Abbot | 12 | – | *Royal Mail* |
| (4) | Display of River Fish, Salisbury | 12 | – | *Royal Mail* |
| (5) | 400 years of Fishing Tackle, Redditch | 12 | – | *Royal Mail* |
| (6) | British Waterways Board | 12 | 15 | *D. Taylor* |
| (7) | Cinque Ports Angling Society, Hythe | 12 | 15 | *BOCS (2) 17* |
| (8) | Pike Anglers Club, Norwich | 12 | 40 | *Pike Anglers* |
| (9) | London Anglers Association, E17 | 12 | 25 | *Havering 1* |

*River Fish (contd.)*          ordinary covers   official covers
                                    £               £

(10) Izaak Walton, River Itchen, Winchester .......... 12 | 20 *S. Petty 12*
(11) RAF Stafford Angling Club, BF 1798 PS ......... 12 | 30 *RFDC 17*
(12) Tisbury Fish Farm, Romford .............................. 12 | 30 *Havering*
(13) National Anglers Council, EC4 .......................... 12 | 25 *NAC*
(14) House of Hardy Exhibition, Pall Mall, SW1 .... 12 | 25 *Hawkwood*
(15) Return of the Salmon, Thames Water, EC....... 12 | 20 *Thames Water*
(16) 100 years of Salmon Fishing, Salmon Leap..... 12 | 10 *BLS (83) 1*
(17) Douglas Bader Angling Club, Leicester ........... 12 | 50 *Bradbury*
(18) Birmingham Anglers Association ...................... 12 | 50 *Bradbury*
(19) Izaak Walton Tercentenary, Stafford .............. 12 | 60 *Staff. Museum*
(20) Izaak Walton, 1593-1683, Stafford .................. 12 | 15 *LFDC 23*
(21) I.E.W. National Postal Museum ........................ 12 | – *n.o.c.*

**C.D.S. POSTMARKS**
(22) Fleet Street – 'The Compleat Angler' ................ 20
(23) Itchen – Izaak Walton................................. 20
(24) The Salmon Leap or Troutbeck.......................... 20
(25) Stafford – Izaak Walton's birthplace ............. 20
(26) Walton, Stafford...................................... 25
(27) Winchester, Hants – Walton's burial place ...... 25

*In addition: Alnwick, Angle, Bream, Coldstream, Fishbourne, Fishguard, Fishers Pond, Fishlake, Fishponds, Freshwater, Hook, Lochawe, Newton Solney, Norton Bridge, Oulton Broads, Pike Hill Pike Road, River, Potters Heigham, Romsey, Salmon Lane, Walton-on-Thames. From £15.*

## 9th March 1983 – COMMONWEALTH
*15½p Topical Island; 19½p Arid Desert; 26p Temperate Climate; 29p Mountains*

**SPECIAL HANDSTAMPS**
(1) First Day of Issue – Philatelic Bureau.............. 2 | – *Royal Mail*
(2) First Day of Issue – London SW ...................... 2 | – *Royal Mail*
(3) Commonwealth Institute, W8 .......................... 8 | 15 *LFDC 24*
(4) Capt. Cook's Voyages of Discovery, Whitby ... 8 | 15 *B. Travers*
(5) William Wilberforce, Hull ............................ 8 | 75 *Wilb. Council*
(6) World Trade Centre, E1 ............................... 8 | 15 *Havering 2*
(7) Royal Commonwealth Society, WC2 ................ 8 | 15 *D. Taylor*
(8) Romsey, Mahatma Gandhi, 1869-1948 ........... 8 | 15 *S. Petty 13*
(9) No 24 Squadron, BF 1799 PS.......................... 8 | 25 *RFDC 18*
(10) British Airways, London Airport W. Sussex..... 8 | 12 *BOCS (2) 18*
(11) Geographical Magazine, London .................... 8 | 20 *Hawkwood*
(12) Association of Cricket Umpires, Leicester ....... 10 | 75 *Assoc. C.U.*
(13) Dunsmore Boy's School, Rugby ...................... 10 | 75 *Dunsmore Sch.*
(14) Daily Mail Ideal Home Exhibition, SW .......... 10 | 45 *Pilgrim*
(15) Sixty years of Jaguar Cars, Coventry .............. 8 | 10 *Benham*

**C.D.S. POSTMARKS**
(16) Buckingham Palace, S.W.1 .............................. 80
(17) Gleneagles Hotel – 'Gleneagles Agreement'..... 60
(18) House of Commons or Lords ........................... 30
(19) Parliament Street BO. SW1............................ 20
(20) Marldon – b/place of Sir Humphrey Gilbert ... 15

*Also: The Beach, Blantyre, Dartmouth, Falklands, Forest Town, Hull, India St., Kensington High St High St, Marton-in-Cleveland, Melbourne, Mountain Ash, Queen Elizabeth Ave., Queen Victoria Rd, Romsey, Summit, Toronto,Windsor, Whitby. Prices from £10.*

## 25th May 1983 – ENGINEERING
*16p Humber Bridge; 20½p Thames Barrier; 28p Energy Support Vessel – Iolair*

**SPECIAL HANDSTAMPS**
(1) First Day of Issue – Philatelic Bureau ............. 2 | – *Royal Mail*
(1a) -do- with 'British Post Office Tembal' cachet .. 5 | – *Royal Mail*
(2) First Day of Issue – Hull.............................. 2 | – *Royal Mail*
(3) Institution of Civil Engineers, SW1 ................ 10 | 35 *LFDC 25*
(4) Eng. Achievement, Thames Flood Barrier ....... 10 | 20 *G & P*
(5) CTH, Thames Flood Barrier, SE7.................... 10 | 20 *Havering 3*
(6) GLC Thames Barrier, Woolwich Reach............ 10 | 45 *Des. Enc.*
(7) Engineering Achievements, AUEW, SE15........ 10 | 30 *AUEW*
(8) British Shipbuilders Iolair, SW7.................... 10 | 10 *BOCS (2) 19*
(9) BP Contribution Iolair, Aberdeen .................. 10 | 10 *BOCS (2) 19*
(10) Technology to greater depths, UDI, Aberdeen. 10 | 25 *UDI*
(11) Humber Bridge, Longest Single Span............ 10 | 15 *Hawkwood*
(12) Humber Bridge, Opened 17 July 1981, Barton 10 | 10 *BLS (83) 3*
(13) Institute of Mechanical Engineers, SW1 ......... 10 | 15 *Pilgrim*
(14) Printing Shares the fruits of Human Genius .... 10 | 20 *Havering*
(15) RAF Cosford, BF 1806 PS ............................ 10 | 25 *RFDC 19*
(16) The Harrier, Kingston upon Thames................ 10 | 25 *S. Petty 14*
(17) 30 Years engineering, Dan Air London Airport 10 | 15 *Benham*
(18) Post Office Philatelic Counter, Grimsby........... 12 | 110 *Royal Mail*
(19) Telecom Technology Showcase, EC4.............. 12 | – *n.o.c.*
(20) Chester-le-Street Co. Durham........................ 12 | 35 *C. leS. Council*
(21) The Wilberforce Council, Hull ...................... 12 | 45 *Wilb. Council*
(22) Children's Hospital, Chippenham.................... 12 | 45 *Rotary*

**C.D.S. POSTMARKS**
(23) Coalbrookdale – b/place of Ind. Revolution ... 15
(24) Eagle – 'Iolair' is gaelic for eagle .................. 10
(25) Hessle & Barton – Humber Bridge............*pair* 30
(26) Ironbridge – the world's first iron bridge ....... 20
(27) New Bridge Road, Hull ............................... 20

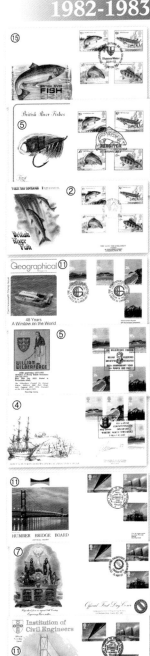

**Engineering** *(contd.)*

| | | ordinary covers £ | official covers £ |
|---|---|---|---|
| (28) | Port Glasgow – 'Iolair' was built here | 35 | |
| (29) | Silvertown & Woolwich – Barrier...............*pair* | 20 | |
| (30) | Silvertown & Charlton – Barrier...............*pair* | 20 | |

*Also: Bacton, Bridge, Clydebank, Cleveland, Cruden Bay, Dundee, Hatfield, Langholm, Portsmouth, Rigside, Rotherham, Saltash, Stock Exchange, Telford. From £12.*

**SLOGAN POSTMARKS**

| (31) | GLC Thames Barrier.................... | 25 | |
|---|---|---|---|
| (32) | Collect British Stamps Humberside.................... | 50 | |

*In addition: Middlesbrough Philatelic Counter; Royal Mail Helping Business on Merseyside; World Communications Year. Prices from £20.*

## 6th July 1983 – BRITISH ARMY

*16p The Royal Scots; 20½ Royal Welch Fusiliers; 26p Royal Green Jackets; 28p Irish Guards; 31p Parachute Regiment*

**SPECIAL HANDSTAMPS**

| (1) | First Day of Issue – Philatelic Bureau .............. | 3 | – | *Royal Mail* |
|---|---|---|---|---|
| (2) | First Day of Issue – Aldershot .................... | 3 | – | *Royal Mail* |
| (2a) | -do- with Carried by Red Devils cachet............ | 12 | – | *Royal Mail* |
| (3) | Regimental Stamp Display, Glasgow............ | 12 | – | *Royal Mail* |
| (4) | The British Army Series, BF 1983 PS ................. | 12 | 15 | *Army* |
| (5) | The Royal Scots, BF 0350 PS .................... | 12 | 35 | *Army* |
| (6) | The Royal Welch Fusiliers, BF 0294 PS ........... | 12 | 35 | *Army* |
| (7) | The Royal Greenjackets, BF 1800 PS ........... | 12 | 35 | *Army* |
| (8) | The Irish Guards, BF 1900 PS.................... | 12 | 35 | *Army* |
| (9) | The Parachute Regiment, BF 2000 PS ........... | 12 | 35 | *Army* |
| (10) | 75th Anniversary/TA in Wales, BF 1908 PS ... | 12 | 50 | *Forces* |
| (11) | Rheindahlen Allied Marches, BF 1810 PS....... | 12 | 60 | *Forces* |
| (12) | Royal Military Academy, Sandhurst............ | 12 | 20 | *G & P* |
| (13) | Queen's Own Hussars, Warwick ............ | 12 | 35 | *LFDC 26* |
| (14) | Duke of York's Royal Military Sch. Dover...... | 12 | 15 | *BenL2* |
| (15) | Blenheim Palace, Woodstock .................... | 12 | 20 | *Havering 4* |
| (16) | Soldier Print Soc., Worthing .................... | 12 | 45 | *S.P.* |
| (17) | National Army Museum 1971-1983, SW3......... | 12 | 15 | *BOCS (2) 20* |
| (18) | Ensign Model Soldier Exhib., Boston ........... | 12 | 35 | *Hawkwood* |
| (19) | Duke of Edinburgh's Reg. Museum, Salisbury . | 12 | 30 | *S. Petty 15* |
| (20) | Ancient Order of Foresters, Rugeley ............ | 15 | 60 | *A.O.F.* |
| (21) | Richard III 500th Anniv., Middleham ............ | 15 | 50 | *R III Soc* |
| (22) | Llangollen International Eisteddfod ............ | 15 | 150 | *Eist'd* |
| (23) | Telecom Technology Showcase, EC4............ | 15 | 75 | *Brit Tele* |
| (24) | Royal Show, Kenilworth .................... | 15 | | |
| | – *n.o.c.* | | | |

**C.D.S. POSTMARKS**

| (25) | Aldershot – Parachute Regiment HQ .............. | 15 | | |
|---|---|---|---|---|
| (26) | Battle, or Battlefield.................... *each* | 12 | | |
| (27) | Broadway, SW1 – Irish Guards Reg HQ ......... | 15 | | |
| (28) | Buckingham Palace, SW1.................... | 75 | | |
| (29) | Catterick Garrison, N Yorks .................... | 15 | | |
| (30) | Duke of York's School, Dover – Military Sch. | 20 | | |
| (31) | Edinburgh – Royal Scots Regimental HQ........ | 15 | | |
| (32) | Hightown – Royal Welch Fusiliers Reg HQ..... | 15 | | |
| (33) | Marlborough, Wilts .................... | 15 | | |
| (34) | Sandhurst – Royal Military Academy ............ | 15 | | |
| (35) | Wilton, Salisbury – HQ UK Land Forces ....... | 15 | | |
| (36) | Winchester – Royal Greenjackets Reg HQ...... | 15 | | |
| (37) | Army POs (Worthy Down, etc) .................... | 15 | | |
| (38) | Any Field or Forces Post Office cancellations | 20 | | |

*Also: Athelstaneford, Bannockburn, Barracks, Brunswick Road (Pirbright Camp), Bunkers Hill, Chelsea Royal Hospital, Falkland, Guard House, Gunhill, Huntingdon, Major's Green, Montgomery, Naseby, St. Andrews, Sentry Corner, Terriers, Tidworth, Waterloo, Wellington, Woodstock, Woolwich, York, Yorktown. Prices from £12.*

**SLOGAN POSTMARKS**

| (39) | Join Territorial Army 75th Anniversary............ | 525 | | |
|---|---|---|---|---|
| (40) | National Army Museum - London SW ......... | 25 | | |

## 24th August 1983 – BRITISH GARDENS

*16p Sissinghurst; 20½ Biddulph Grange; 28p Blenheim; 31p Pitmedden*

**SPECIAL HANDSTAMPS**

| (1) | First Day of Issue – Philatelic Bureau............... | 3 | – | *Royal Mail* |
|---|---|---|---|---|
| (2) | First Day of Issue – Oxford .................... | 3 | – | *Royal Mail* |
| (3) | Capability Brown at Bowood, Calne................. | 12 | – | *Royal Mail* |
| (4) | Queen's Gardens, Croydon .................... | 12 | 75 | *Croydon BC* |
| (5) | Capability Brown, Kew Gardens.................... | 12 | 20 | *LFDC 27* |
| (6) | National Trust, Sissinghurst Castle.................... | 12 | 15 | *BOCS (2) 21* |
| (7) | League of Friends, The Grange, Biddulph ....... | 12 | 35 | *League of F* |
| (8) | Blenheim Palace, Woodstock .................... | 12 | 15 | *Havering 5* |
| (9) | National Trust for Scotland, Pitmedden ........... | 12 | 15 | *BLS (83) 5* |
| (10) | Capability Brown, Esher, Claremont.................. | 12 | 60 | *Arlington* |
| (11) | Roses in August, Syon Park, Brentford............ | 12 | 15 | *Hawkwood* |
| (12) | Lancelot Capability Brown, Fenstanton ........... | 12 | 35 | *Fenst Par Ch* |
| (13) | National Trust for Scotland, Crathes Castle..... | 12 | 12 | *BenL4* |
| (14) | National Trust, Lyme Park, Disley .................... | 12 | 15 | *BenL3* |
| (15) | Capability Brown, Kirkharle, Newcastle ........... | 12 | 35 | *Landscape Ins.* |
| (16) | Capability Brown, GRBS, Hampton Court....... | 12 | 25 | *S. Petty 16* |
| (17) | Celebration of English Gardens, SW1............ | 12 | 25 | *DGT* |
| (18) | RAF Gardens, Runnymede, BF 1814 PS........... | 12 | 25 | *RFDC 21* |

*Gardens (contd.)*

| | | ordinary covers £ | official covers £ | |
|---|---|---|---|---|
| (19) | International camp, BB 83, Perth ..................... | 12 | 100 | *Boys Brig.* |
| (20) | Military Tattoo Edinburgh.................................. | 12 | 25 | *Mil. Tattoo* |
| (21) | Hornchurch Cricket Club.................................... | 20 | 75 | *H.C.C.* |

**C.D.S. POSTMARKS**

| | | | |
|---|---|---|---|
| (22) | Biddulph – featured on 20½p value................... | 20 | |
| (23) | Botanic Gardens, Belfast................................. | 25 | |
| (24) | Fenstanton – Capability Brown buried here..... | 20 | |
| (25) | Kew Gardens, Richmond................................... | 35 | |
| (26) | Kirkwhelpington – b/place Capability Brown . | 20 | |
| (27) | Mayfair, W1 – Capability Brown died here...... | 20 | |
| (28) | Sissinghurst – featured on 16p value............... | 20 | |
| (29) | Udny, Ellon – Pitmedden (31p)......................... | 20 | |
| (30) | Woodstock – Blenheim Palace (28p)................ | 20 | |

*In addition, covers are known with the following CDS pmks: Garden Suburb, Garden Village, Glamis, Harewood, Headstone Gardens, Petworth, Rake, Royal Hospital Chelsea, Sledmere, The Allotments, Trentham, Welwyn Garden City. Prices from £15.*

**SLOGAN POSTMARKS**

| | | | |
|---|---|---|---|
| (31) | Back Beautiful Britain ......................................... | 40 | |
| (32) | Chamber of Commerce – Devizes in Bloom .... | 40 | |
| (33) | Your Garden Isle is Beautiful – Isle of Wight.. | 50 | |
| (34) | Leicester City Show at Abbey Park ................... | 80 | |

*In addition: Beautiful Bath. £30.*

## 5th October 1983 – BRITISH FAIRS

*16p Merry-go-round; 20½p Menageries and rides; 28p Side shows; 31p Early trade and produce fairs*

**SPECIAL HANDSTAMPS**

| | | | | |
|---|---|---|---|---|
| (1) | First Day of Issue – Philatelic Bureau............... | 3 | – | *Royal Mail* |
| (2) | First Day of Issue – Nottingham ....................... | 3 | – | *Royal Mail* |
| (3) | St. Bartholomew the Great, EC........................ | 12 | 20 | *Havering 6* |
| (4) | Butchers Charitable Institution, EC1 ............... | 12 | 15 | *Hawkwood* |
| (5) | Showmen's Guild, Staines ................................. | 12 | 50 | *S. Guild* |
| (6) | Goose Fair, Tavistock ....................................... | 12 | 25 | *S. Petty 17* |
| (7) | Chipperfield's Circus, EC.................................. | 12 | 15 | *BLS (83) 6* |
| (8) | NABMA (Markets Authority) Birmingham ...... | 12 | 20 | *Des. Enc.* |
| (9) | Fairfield, Croydon............................................. | 12 | 35 | *Fairfield* |
| (10) | Turner's Northampton........................................ | 12 | 12 | *BOCS (2) 21* |
| (11) | Goose Fair 1983, Nottingham........................... | 12 | 25 | *LFDC 28* |
| (12) | World's First Air Fair, BF 1815 PS.................. | 12 | 15 | *RFDC 22* |
| (13) | Rowell Lions, Rothwell, Kettering ................... | 12 | 50 | *RothwellLions* |
| (14) | British Philatelic Federation, Bath .................. | 12 | 20 | *BPF* |
| (15) | Samuel Pepys, Cambridge ................................. | 12 | 20 | *Univ. Covers* |
| (16) | The Boys Brigade Centenary, Cardiff ............... | 12 | 60 | *BB Wales* |
| (17) | MMB (Milk Marketing Board) Newcastle........ | 12 | 25 | *MMB* |
| (17a) | -do- spelling error: Newcastlf.......................... | – | 125 | *MMB (s)* |
| (18) | Exhibition Garden City, Letchworth................ | 12 | – | *n.o.c.* |

**C.D.S. POSTMARKS**

| | | | |
|---|---|---|---|
| (19) | Borough High Street, S.E.1 – Southwark Fair. | 15 | |
| (20) | Cambridge or Chesterton – Sturbridge Fair...... | 15 | |
| (21) | Horse Fair...................................................... | 15 | |
| (22) | London Chief Office – Bartholomew Fair ........ | 15 | |
| (23) | St. Giles, Oxford – largest surviving wake ....... | 20 | |
| (24) | Scarborough..................................................... | 15 | |
| (25) | Tavistock – Goose Fair..................................... | 25 | |
| (26) | Widecombe-in-the-Moor................................... | 15 | |
| (27) | Winchester – Bishops Fair-oldest Charter Fair .... | 15 | |

*Also: Abingdon, Alford, Appleby-in-Westmorland, Barrus Bridge, Big Top, Brigg, Elephant & Castle, Exeter, Frome, Greenwich, Honiton, Hyson Green, King's Lynn, Marlborough, Market Sidmouth, Mayfair, North End, St. Ives, Stow-on-the-Wold, Stratford-upon-Avon, Ulverston, Warwick, Wookey Hole, Woodkirk, Yarm. Prices from £12 each.*

**SLOGAN POSTMARKS** *Wonderland of Wales; Magnum World of Entertainment. From £85.*

## 16th November 1983 – CHRISTMAS

*12½p, 16p, 20½p, 28p, 31p Peace and Goodwill*

**SPECIAL HANDSTAMPS**

| | | | | |
|---|---|---|---|---|
| (1) | First Day of Issue – Philatelic Bureau ............. | 3 | – | *Royal Mail* |
| (2) | First Day of Issue – Bethlehem ....................... | 3 | – | *Royal Mail* |
| (3) | Peace and Goodwill, Nasareth .......................... | 10 | 25 | *LFDC 29* |
| (4) | Minster Gatehouse, Sheppey............................. | 10 | 25 | *Hawkwood* |
| (5) | Leicestershire Society for the Blind.................. | 10 | 5 | *L. Blind Soc* |
| (6) | Winchester Cathedral....................................... | 10 | 15 | *S. Petty 18* |
| (7) | Peace on Earth, Peacehaven ............................ | 10 | 10 | *BLS (83) 7* |
| (8) | St. Mary le Strand, WC2................................... | 10 | 15 | *Havering 7* |
| (9) | Telecom Technology Showcase, EC4................ | 10 | 60 | *Brit Tele* |
| (10) | Lyminge Parish Church, Festival Year ............. | 10 | 10 | *BOCS (2) 23* |
| (11) | T.C. (Tandy Corporation), Walsall ................... | 15 | 220 | *T.C.* |

**C.D.S. POSTMARKS**

| | | | |
|---|---|---|---|
| (12) | Bethlehem, Nasareth or Peacehaven ................ | 35 | |

*Also: Birdsall, Blackbird Leys, Canterbury, Chapel, Chester-le-Street, Christchurch, Dovecot, Dove Holes, Dove House Lane, Holy Island, Kingsworthy, Minster, Quakers Rd., St. Augustine's, St. Nicholas, Star. Prices from £12.*

**SLOGAN POSTMARKS**

| | | | |
|---|---|---|---|
| (13) | Hastings, Resort for All Seasons (Xmas scene).... | 90 | |

*In addition: Royal Mail Special Services, Hull. £30.*

63

## 17th January 1984 – HERALDRY

*16p College of Arms; 20½p Richard III;*
*28p The Earl Marshal; 31p City of London*

| | | ordinary covers £ | official covers £ | |
|---|---|---|---|---|
| **SPECIAL HANDSTAMPS** | | | | |
| (1) | First Day of Issue – Philatelic Bureau | 3 | – | Royal Mail |
| (2) | First Day of Issue – London EC | 4 | – | Royal Mail |
| (3) | Heraldry Guildhall, City of London, EC | 12 | – | Royal Mail |
| (4) | College of Arms, London EC4 | 12 | 35 | Cotswold |
| (5) | The Heraldry Society, WC | 12 | 15 | BOCS (2) 24 |
| (6) | Richard III Society, Leicester | 12 | 35 | LFDC 30 |
| (7) | Richard III, Fotheringhay Castle | 12 | 45 | LFDC 30 |
| (8) | Richard III Celebration, Scarborough | 12 | 40 | Pilgrim |
| (9) | The City of London, The Square Mile, EC | 12 | 25 | G&P |
| (10) | Deputy Norroy, King of Arms, York | 12 | 25 | Hawkwood |
| (11) | Friary Meux Kings Arms, Godalming | 12 | 25 | Hawkwood |
| (12) | Coat of Arms Granted in 1890, Belfast | 12 | 30 | BLS (84) 1 |
| (13) | Coat of Arms Granted in 1906, Cardiff | 10 | 30 | BLS (84) 1 |
| (14) | Coat of Arms Granted in 1975, Edinburgh | 12 | 30 | BLS (84) 1 |
| (15) | Spencer of Althorp | 12 | 40 | Althorp |
| (16) | Heirlooms, 1 Hayhill, Berkeley Sq., W1 | 12 | 15 | Havering |
| (17) | Arthurian Legend, Camelot, Tintagel | 12 | 25 | S. Petty 19 |
| (18) | 1st RAF Badge, BF 1826 PS | 12 | 15 | RFDC 24 |
| (19) | NSPCC Centenary, EC4 | 12 | 75 | NSPCC |
| (20) | High Wycombe, Stamp Printing | 12 | 15 | Harrisons |
| (21) | Lincoln Philatelic Counter Opened | 25 | – | n.o.c. |
| (22) | Marks & Spencer, 100 Years, W1 | 12 | 15 | DGT |
| (23) | Berkswell Parish Church | 12 | 35 | Parish Ch. |
| (24) | Good News People, Martin, Aylesbury | 12 | 90 | Martins |
| (25) | Story of the Poppy, Maidstone | 12 | 25 | Brit. Legion |
| (26) | London SW1 (Buckingham Palace) | 12 | – | n.o.c. |
| **ORDINARY F.D.I. POSTMARKS** | | | | |
| (27) | Stratford (Shakespeare Coat of Arms cover) | 35 | | |
| **C.D.S. POSTMARKS** | | | | |
| (28) | Arundel – home of the Earl Marshal | 20 | | |
| (29) | Cannon St., EC4 – near to College of Arms | 20 | | |
| (30) | Fore St., EC2 – near to the Guildhall | 20 | | |
| (31) | Market Bosworth – Richard III | 35 | | |
| (32) | Middleham – Richard III's castle | 35 | | |

*Also: Barony, Chester, College Town, Coneysthorpe, Fleur-de-Lis, Godalming, Gloucester, Harewood, King Arthur's Way, Leadenhall St., Lombard St., Ludgate Circus, Ludlow, Queen Elizabeth Ave., Richmond, St. Georges Cross, Sloane Square, Stock Exchange, York. From £15.*

## 6th March 1984 – BRITISH CATTLE

*16p Highland Cow; 20½p Chillingham Wild Bull; 26p Hereford Bull;*
*28p Welsh Black Bull; 31p Irish Moiled Cow*

| | | | | |
|---|---|---|---|---|
| **SPECIAL HANDSTAMPS** | | | | |
| (1) | First Day of Issue – Philatelic Bureau | 4 | – | Royal Mail |
| (2) | First Day of Issue – Oban EC | 4 | – | Royal Mail |
| (3) | Highland Cattle Society, Edinburgh | 10 | 12 | BOCS (2) 25 |
| (4) | Chateau Impney, Highland Cattle, Droitwich.. | 15 | – | Royal Mail |
| (5) | Last Stronghold of the Chillingham Bull | 10 | 10 | BLS (84) 2 |
| (6) | Home of the Chillingham Wild Cattle | 10 | 25 | CWC Assoc |
| (7) | Hereford Herd Book Society | 10 | 25 | DGT |
| (8) | Welsh Black Cattle Society, Caernarfon | 10 | 25 | DGT |
| (9) | Irish Moiled Cattle Society, Ballynahinch | 10 | 25 | DGT |
| (10) | British Friesian Cattle Soc Rickmansworth | 10 | 25 | DGT |
| (11) | Livestock Show, Tring | 15 | – | Royal Mail |
| (12) | Farming the Backbone of Britain, SW1 | 10 | 25 | DGT |
| (13) | Rare Breeds Survival Trust, Stoneleigh | 10 | 12 | LFDC 31 |
| (14) | Butcher's Charitable Institution, EC1 | 10 | 10 | Hawkwood |
| (15) | Earl's Court – Royal Smithfield Show, SW5 .. | 10 | 10 | Havering |
| (16) | Royal Veterinary College, NW1 | 10 | 10 | S. Petty 20 |
| (17) | Farmers Weekly Golden Jubilee, Sutton | 10 | 80 | Des. Enc. |
| (18) | Dairy Crest Honours British Cattle, Crewe | 10 | 70 | MMB |
| (19) | RAF Hereford, BF 1828 PS | 10 | 15 | RFDC 25 |
| (20) | The Martyrs, Tolpuddle | 10 | 20 | TUC |
| (21) | Stampex, London, SW1 | 10 | 50 | Stampex |
| (22) | Daily Mail, Ideal Home Exhibition, SW | 15 | 45 | Pilgrim |
| (23) | 767 Another 1st from Britannia | 20 | 225 | Brit. Airw. |

*A special handstamp 'Maiden Flight Skyship 600, Cardington' was used on 6th March, but no covers are known to exist with the British Cattle Stamps affixed.*

| | | | |
|---|---|---|---|
| **C.D.S. POSTMARKS** | | | |
| (24) | Ballynahinch or Saintfield–Irish Moiled Cow | 20 | |
| (25) | Black Bull St., Leeds | 20 | |
| (26) | Bull Farm, Red Cow or Cattle Market | 25 | |
| (27) | Caernarfon – Welsh Black Cattle | 20 | |
| (28) | Chillingham – Chillingham Wild Cattle | 20 | |
| (29) | Hereford | 20 | |
| (30) | Kyle, Kyleakin or Oban – Highland Cattle | 25 | |

*Also: Bovey Tracey, Bull Bay, Bull Brook, Cowfold, Cowplain, Dolgellau, Heriot, Lavenham, Lincoln, Moy, Oxen Park, Royal College St., Stoneleigh, Terling, Thames Ditton, The Markets, Thirsk. From £12.*

**SLOGAN POSTMARKS** *Collect British Stamps; Any Royal Mail slogans. From £10.*

## 10th April 1984 – URBAN RENEWAL

*16p Liverpool Garden Festival;*  **ordinary**  **official**
*20½ Milburngate Centre, Durham;*  **covers**  **covers**
*28p City Docks, Bristol; 31p Commercial St, Perth*  **£**  **£**

**SPECIAL HANDSTAMPS**

| | | | |
|---|---|---|---|
| (1) | First Day of Issue – Philatelic Bureau............... | 3 | – *Royal Mail* |
| (2) | First Day of Issue – Liverpool ........................... | 3 | – *Royal Mail* |
| (3) | International Garden Festival, Liverpool......... | 10 | 12 *BOCS (2) 26* |
| (4) | Abbey National Building Society ...................... | 10 | 15 *G&P* |
| (5) | Urban Renewal, City of Durham....................... | 10 | 25 *C of Durham* |
| (6) | Laing Development, Durham.............................. | 10 | 70 *Laing* |
| (7) | Urban Renewal, BDP, W1 .................................. | 10 | 25 *BDP* |
| (8) | Bush House, Arnolfini Gallery, Bristol............. | 10 | 25 *C of Bristol* |
| (9) | Commercial Street Redevelopment, Perth ....... | 10 | 25 *G&P* |
| (10) | Landscape Institute, Liverpool........................ | 10 | 25 *Lans. Inst.* |
| (11) | RIBA, Festival of Architecture, York ............... | 10 | 45 *Cotswold* |
| (12) | RIBA, Festival of Architecture, W1 ................. | 10 | 45 *Cotswold* |
| (13) | St. John the Evangelist, (RIBA), E15 ............... | 10 | 15 *Hawkwood* |
| (14) | Festival of Architecture, Guildhall, EC2.......... | 10 | – *Royal Mail* |
| (15) | Year of Building, CIOB, Ascot .......................... | 10 | 25 *DGT* |
| (16) | DIADEM, Dundee Inst. of Architects............... | 10 | 25 *D.I.A.* |
| (17) | Letchworth the First Garden City..................... | 10 | 15 *LFDC 32* |
| (18) | London Docklands, Isle of Dogs, E14............... | 10 | 25 *Havering* |
| (19) | Covent Garden Market, WC............................. | 10 | 25 *S. Petty 21* |
| (20) | Cheshire Gibson, Surveyors, Birmingham ....... | 15 | – *n.o.c.* |
| (21) | Wigan Pier Project.............................................. | 15 | 50 *Wigan Coun.* |
| (22) | Bristol Scout, BF 1835 PS .................................. | 12 | 15 *RFDC 26* |

**C.D.S. POSTMARKS**

| | | |
|---|---|---|
| (23) | Aigburth, or Cockburn St. – near to the IGF... | 12 |
| (24) | Ascot – Chartered Inst. of Building................... | 12 |
| (25) | Brigend, Perth – Commercial St........................ | 12 |
| (26) | Letchworth – First Garden City......................... | 12 |
| (27) | New Buildings, Londonderry.............................. | 45 |
| (28) | North Rd., Durham – Milburngate Centre....... | 12 |
| (29) | Prince St., Bristol – near to Arnolfini Gallery.. | 12 |

*Also: Fore St., Isle of Dogs, Red House, Southampton Street, Telford, Tingley, Welwyn Garden City. Prices from £10.*

**SLOGAN POSTMARKS**

| | | |
|---|---|---|
| (30) | International Garden Festival Liverpool 84 ..... | 15 |

*In addition: Royal Mail, Hull; Beautiful Bath; Sunderland. Prices from £20.*

## 15th May 1984 – EUROPA

*2 x 16p; 2 x 20½p CEPT 25th anniversary logo and the abduction of Europa*

**SPECIAL HANDSTAMPS**

| | | | |
|---|---|---|---|
| (1) | First Day of Issue – Philatelic Bureau............... | 3 | – *Royal Mail* |
| (2) | First Day of Issue – London SW........................ | 3 | – *Royal Mail* |
| (3) | European Elections, London, SW...................... | 10 | 15 *Havering* |
| (4) | Second British European Elections, SW1......... | 10 | 7 *BLS (84) 4* |
| (5) | Sealink, Bridge with Europe, Folkestone ......... | 10 | 12 *BOCS (2) 27* |
| (6) | 1606-1984 Dover Harbour Board...................... | 10 | 15 *LFDC 33* |
| (7) | Hawkwood Covers, Europa E1 ......................... | 10 | 15 *Hawkwood* |
| (8) | D-Day + 40 Portsmouth...................................... | 10 | 15 *S. Petty 22* |
| (9) | 35th Anniv. Formation of NATO, BF 1949 PS | 12 | 20 *RFDC 27* |
| (10) | Mosquito Aircraft Museum, Hatfield ................ | 10 | 75 *M.A. Mus.* |

**C.D.S. POSTMARKS**

| | | |
|---|---|---|
| (11) | Bridge or Postbridge ...................................*each* | 15 |
| (12) | Dover, Folkestone, Harwich, Weymouth......... | 15 |
| (13) | House of Commons or Lords ............................ | 15 |
| (14) | Mark Cross, Crowborough ............................... | 75 |
| (15) | Newhaven plus PAQUEBOT.............................. | 15 |
| (16) | Boulogne, Calais or Dieppe + PAQUEBOT..... | 25 |
| (17) | Parliament Street ................................................ | 15 |

*Also: Felixstowe, Holland Fen, Montgomery, Normandy, Northern Parliament, Poling Corner, Portsmouth, Portsmouth Dockyard, York. Prices from £10.*

**SLOGAN POSTMARKS** *Milk on your Doorstep; Historic Sandwich; Any Royal Mail slogans; Collect British Stamps. Prices from £20.*

## 5th June 1984 – LONDON ECONOMIC SUMMIT

*31p Lancaster House*

**SPECIAL HANDSTAMPS**

| | | | |
|---|---|---|---|
| (1) | First Day of Issue – Philatelic Bureau............... | 2 | – *Royal Mail* |
| (2) | First Day of Issue – London SW........................ | 2 | – *Royal Mail* |
| (3) | Economic Summit, SW1 (50p shaped globe)... | 8 | 8 *LFDC 34* |
| (4) | London Economic Summit, SW1 ...................... | 8 | 10 *Havering* |
| (5) | London Welcomes the Economic Summit ....... | 8 | 7 *BOCS (2) 29* |
| (6) | Sterling Travellers Cheques, Croydon............... | 8 | – *Post Office* |
| (7) | TSB, Chingford.................................................... | 8 | 15 *Hawkwood* |
| (8) | Brit. Philatelic Cover Producers Assoc., SW1... | 8 | 20 *BPCPA* |
| (9) | London Underwriters Centenary, EC3.............. | 8 | 35 *Cotswold* |
| (10) | 75th Rotary Convention, Birmingham.............. | 8 | 25 *Int. Rotary* |
| (11) | The Queen Embarks Britannia, Portsmouth .... | 10 | 50 *Rembrandt* |

**C.D.S. POSTMARKS**

| | | |
|---|---|---|
| (12) | Dollar .................................................................. | 40 |
| (13) | Lombard St. B.O.................................................. | 30 |

65

**Economic Summit (contd.)**

| | ordinary covers £ | official covers £ |
|---|---|---|
| (14) Pounds or Summit ......each | 15 | |
| (15) St. James's St. – near to Lancaster House........ | 8 | |
| (16) Stock Exchange............ | 25 | |

*Also: Bretton, The Forum, Lancaster, Moneyhill, Parliament Street BO. Prices from £6.*

**SLOGAN POSTMARKS** *Sunderland Loans & Grants; Shopping by Post; Any Royal Mail slogans;Inverness Conference Capital; Sandwell Industrial. From £30.*

## 26th June 1984 – GREENWICH MERIDIAN

*16p Astronomy; 20½p Navigation; 28p The Observatory; 31p Time*

**SPECIAL HANDSTAMPS**

| | | |
|---|---|---|
| (1) First Day of Issue – Philatelic Bureau............... | 3 | – *Royal Mail* |
| (2) First Day of Issue – Greenwich........................ | 3 | – *Royal Mail* |
| (3) World's Prime Meridian, Greenwich, SE10...... | 10 | 12 *BOCS (2) 28* |
| (4) Greenwich Mean Time, EC4............................. | 20 | – *n.o.c.* |
| (5) Geographical Magazine.................................. | 10 | 15 *Hawkwood* |
| (6) Royal Naval College...................................... | 10 | 25 *RNC* |
| (7) Meridian Road 0° 00' 00" Longitude, Boston.... | 15 | – *Royal Mail* |
| (8) Greenwich Meridian, East Lindsey, Louth...... | 12 | 35 *L. Rotary* |
| (9) Royal Naval Staff College, BF 1838 PS............ | 12 | 35 *RFDC 28* |
| (10) Longitude Zero, Somersham, Huntingdon....... | 12 | 35 *PO overprint cvr* |
| (11) Meridian County School, Comberton.............. | 12 | 45 *MCP Sch.* |
| (12) Meridian Day, 0° MG GM, Swavesey.............. | 12 | 35 *MG Owners* |
| (13) Peacehaven, Newhaven................................. | 12 | 150 *P'haven P.O.* |
| (14) British Horological Institute, Newark............ | 10 | 15 *LFDC 35* |
| (15) John Longitude Harrison, Barrow .................. | 10 | 85 *Lincoln Cath.* |
| (16) British Astronomical Association, W1 ........... | 10 | 15 *DGT* |
| (17) National Physical Laboratory, Teddington...... | 10 | 200 *NPL* |
| (18) Captn. Cook Study Unit, Whitby .................... | 10 | 35 *B. Travers* |
| (19) Lloyds List, Greenwich, SE10 ....................... | 10 | 35 *Lloyds* |
| (20) National Federation of Women's Institutes...... | 10 | 250 *Arlington* |
| (21) Steve Davis Embassy World Champion............ | 10 | 35 *Havering* |
| (22) Ladies Centenary Year  Lawn Tennis Museum... | 15 | 35 *AELTC* |

**C.D.S. POSTMARKS**

| | | |
|---|---|---|
| (23) Alnwick – birthplace of Sir George Airy.......... | 15 | |
| (24) Chingford – longitudinal obelisk.................... | 15 | |
| (25) Clock Face, St. Helens.................................. | 40 | |
| (26) Hartland – Magnetic Observatory .................. | 25 | |
| (27) Herstmonceux – new observatory .................. | 20 | |
| (28) Greenwich or The Chart................................ | 20 | |
| (29) Meridian Centre, Peacehaven......................... | 140 | |
| (30) Playford, Ipswich – home of Sir George Airy .. | 15 | |

*In addition: Cleethorpes, Comberton, East Grinstead, Globe Rd, Great Ayton, Great Portland St., Louth, Macclesfield, Station Rd (Oxted), Swavesey, Washington, World's End. Prices from £12.*

**SLOGAN POSTMARKS** *Magyar Philatelic Society.  £65.*

## 31st July 1984 – THE ROYAL MAIL

*5 x 16p: The Bath Mail Coach; Attack on Exeter Mail Coach;*
*Norwich Mail Coach in a thunderstorm; Holyhead & Liverpool Mail Coaches;*
*Edinburgh Mail Coach Snowbound*

**SPECIAL HANDSTAMPS**

| | | |
|---|---|---|
| (1) First Day of Issue – Philatelic Bureau............... | 3 | – *Royal Mail* |
| (1a) -do- with Bristol-London coach run cachet ..... | 5 | – *Royal Mail* |
| (2) First Day of Issue – Bristol............................. | 3 | – *Royal Mail* |
| (2a) -do- with Bristol-London coach run cachet ..... | 10 | – *Royal Mail* |
| (3) Bath Mail Coach Commemorative Run ............ | 10 | 12 *BOCS (2) 30* |
| (4) Golden Age of Coaching, Bath........................ | 10 | 15 *LFDC 36* |
| (5) Interlink Express Parcels Co, Bristol................ | 10 | 15 *Hawkwood* |
| (6) Royal Mail Transport, Leicester...................... | 10 | 50 *Mus. of Tech.* |
| (7) Manchester – Altrincham Mail Coach Run....... | 10 | 12 *BLS (84) 7* |
| (8) Liverpool Mail Coach.................................... | 10 | 12 *BLS (84) 7* |
| (9) British Air Mail Service, BF 1845 PS............... | 10 | 15 *RFDC 30* |
| (10) The Islington Society, N1 ............................. | 10 | 15 *Havering* |
| (11) Worshipful Company of Coachmakers, WC2.. | 10 | 30 *Cotswold* |
| (12) Royal Mail Commemoration, Holyhead Mail.. | 10 | – *Royal Mail* |
| (13) North Eastern Parcel Centre, Washington....... | 15 | 20 *Royal Mail* |
| (14) St. James's Church Piccadilly, W1 .................. | 15 | 60 *St. J. Church* |
| (15) Island of Portland Heritage Trust................... | 15 | 60 *PHT* |
| (16) International Essex Jamboree, Chelmsford....... | 15 | 60 *Scouts* |
| (17) National Postal Museum - permanent h/s........ | 15 | – *n.o.c.* |

**C.D.S. POSTMARKS**

| | | |
|---|---|---|
| (18) Bath, Bristol, Edinburgh, Exeter, Holyhead, Liverpool or Norwich.................................. | 20 | |
| (19) Fleet Street, EC4 – 'Bolt-in-Tun' Inn ............. | 15 | |
| (20) Holyhead or Dun Laoghaire PAQUEBOTS..... | 20 | |
| (21) Islington, N1 – 'The Angel Inn'...................... | 15 | |
| (22) London Chief Office, EC1............................. | 15 | |
| (23) Marlborough – provided Bath Mail horses...... | 15 | |
| (24) Moffat – snowbound Edinburgh Mail............ | 15 | |
| (25) Newmarket – Norwich Mail in thunderstorm . | 15 | |
| (26) Thatcham – provided Bath Mail horses .......... | 15 | |
| (27) Winterslow or Lopcombe Corner – scene of the attack on the Exeter Mail .... | 15 | |

*In addition: Black Horse, Coach Road, Devonport. Prices from £10.*

*The Royal Mail (contd.)*

| | ordinary covers £ | official covers £ |
|---|---|---|
| **SLOGAN POSTMARKS** | | |
| (28) Collect British Stamps | 30 | |
| (29) Be Properly Addressed, Post Code It | 40 | |
| (30) Magyar Philatelic Society | 75 | |
| (31) Take a Break in Beautiful Bath | 50 | |

## 25th September 1984 – THE BRITISH COUNCIL
*17p Medicine; 22p Arts; 31p Construction; 34p Language*

**SPECIAL HANDSTAMPS**

| | | | |
|---|---|---|---|
| (1) First Day of Issue – Philatelic Bureau | 3 | – | *Royal Mail* |
| (2) First Day of Issue – London SW | 3 | – | *Royal Mail* |
| (3) The British Council, SW | 8 | 15 | *G&P* |
| (4) Oxford Dictionary Exhibition | 8 | 15 | *Hawkwood* |
| (5) Ausipex 84, Melbourne | 8 | 10 | *BOCS (2) 31* |
| (6) RBPD, Sutton | 8 | 15 | *Des. Enc.* |
| (7) Samuel Johnson, Lichfield | 8 | 15 | *LFDC 37* |
| (8) Battle of Britain, BF 1850 PS | 8 | 15 | *RFDC 31* |
| (9) St. James's Church, Piccadilly, W1 | 8 | – | *Royal Mail* |
| (10) Mail Coach Service, National Postal Musuem. | 10 | – | *n.o.c.* |
| (11) Beagles Congratulate Daley Thompson, E13 ... | 10 | 20 | *Havering* |

**C.D.S. POSTMARKS**

| | | |
|---|---|---|
| (12) Southampton St. – 1st Meeting | 15 | |
| (13) St. James's St. – inaugurated at Palace | 15 | |
| (14) Trafalgar Sq. BO – near to British Council | 15 | |
| (15) Wadhurst – 'The Midsummer Marriage' | 15 | |
| (16) Walton St., Oxford – Oxford Eng Dictionary .. | 15 | |
| (17) Westminster Bdg. Rd. – Tippett, Morley Coll .. | 15 | |

*Also: Aberystwyth, Burgh, Dundee, King Edward VII Hospital,Lichfield, Limpsfield, Lower Broadheath, Melbourne, Oxford. From £10.*

**SLOGAN POSTMARKS** *Doctor Johnson, Lichfield; Collect British Stamps. £25.*

## 20th November 1984 – CHRISTMAS
*13p, 17p, 22p, 31p, 34p the Nativity*

**SPECIAL HANDSTAMPS**

| | | | |
|---|---|---|---|
| (1) First Day of Issue – Philatelic Bureau | 3 | – | *Royal Mail* |
| (2) First Day of Issue – Bethlehem | 3 | – | *Royal Mail* |
| (3) Christian Heritage Year – Durham | 10 | 25 | *BOCS (2) 32* |
| (4) Christian Heritage Year – Ely | 10 | 25 | *BOCS (2) 32* |
| (5) Christian Heritage Year – Norwich | 10 | 12 | *BLS (84) 6* |
| (6) Christian Heritage Year – Liverpool | 10 | 12 | *BLS (84) 6* |
| (7) Christmas, Isle of Iona | 10 | 15 | *Pilgrim* |
| (8) Glastonbury Abbey | 10 | 35 | *Fine Arts 1* |
| (9) Christmas Greetings, World Trade Centre | 10 | 12 | *Havering* |
| (10) Christmas, Weybridge | 10 | 25 | *S. Petty 25* |
| (11) Christmas, Theatre Royal, Stratford, E15 | 10 | 15 | *Hawkwood* |
| (12) Telecom Technology Showcase, EC4 | 15 | – | *n.o.c.* |
| (13) John Wycliffe, Lutterworth | 10 | 15 | *LFDC 38* |
| (14) The Lindisfarne Gospels, Holy Island | 10 | 15 | *S. Muscroft* |
| (15) Samuel Johnson, Lichfield | 10 | 35 | *Bradbury* |
| (16) Mail Coach Service, Nat Postal Museum | 12 | – | *n.o.c.* |
| (17) North Eastern Parcel Centre, Washington | 12 | – | *n.o.c.* |

**ORDINARY F.D.I. POSTMARKS**

| | |
|---|---|
| (18) Hemel Hempstead (St. Mary's cvr) | 20 |

**C.D.S. POSTMARKS**

| | |
|---|---|
| (19) Bethlehem or Nasareth | 25 |

*In addition: Canterbury, Glastonbury, Holy Island, Holytown, Horbury Bridge, Jarrow, Lutterworth, Shepherd's Bush, Shepherd's Hill, Three Kingdom. £10 each.*

**SLOGAN POSTMARKS**

| | |
|---|---|
| (20) Hastings – Resort for All Seasons (snowman) . | 40 |
| (21) Halfpenny Green – Christmas 1984 | 50 |

*In addition: Late Night Shopping, Exeter. Prices from £25.*

**CHRISTMAS DISCOUNT BOOKLET:** Covers bearing a pair or block of 4 x 13p Christmas stamps from booklet with relevant postmark ......................... 10

## 22nd January 1985 – FAMOUS TRAINS
*17p Flying Scotsman; 22p Golden Arrow; 29p Cheltenham Flyer; 31p Royal Scot; 34p Cornish Riviera*

**SPECIAL HANDSTAMPS**

| | | | |
|---|---|---|---|
| (1) First Day of Issue – Philatelic Bureau | 5 | – | *Royal Mail* |
| (1a) -do- carried on Orient Express cachet | 7 | – | *Royal Mail* |
| (2) First Day of Issue – Bristol | 5 | – | *Royal Mail* |
| (3) Steamtown Railway Museum, Carnforth | 15 | 25 | *LFDC 39* |
| (4) Flying Scotsman, Doncaster | 15 | 25 | *LFDC 39* |
| (5) Flying Scotsman, King's Cross, N1 | 15 | 70 | *BenL6* |
| (6) Flying Scotsman, Scotrail, Edinburgh | 25 | – | *n.o.c.* |
| (7) Golden Arrow, Dover | 15 | 70 | *BenL8* |
| (8) Golden Arrow, VSOE, Victoria, SW1 | 15 | 25 | *G&P* |
| (9) VSOE Stops at Denham Station | 25 | – | *Royal Mail* |
| (10) GWR 150, Paddington Stn., London, W2 | 15 | 75 | *CoverCraft* |
| (11) Great Western Hotel, Paddington, W2 | 15 | 75 | *Fine Arts 2* |
| (12) Cheltenham Flyer, Cheltenham | 15 | 125 | *Ben500(1)* |
| (13) Great Western Town, Swindon | 15 | 30 | *Hawkwood* |

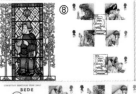

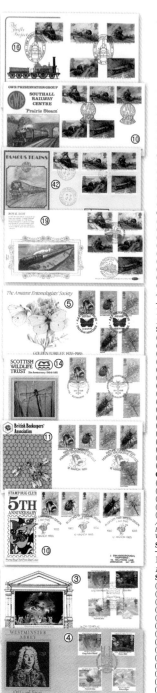

*Famous Trains (contd.)*

| | ordinary covers £ | official covers £ | |
|---|---|---|---|
| (14) GWR Didcot, Oxon | 15 | 25 | *814 TPO Gp* |
| (15) GWR Preservation Gp, Southall Rly Centre .... | 15 | 25 | *DGT* |
| (16) Firefly Project, Swindon | 15 | 25 | *Cotswold* |
| (17) King George V, Hereford | 25 | – | *Royal Mail* |
| (18) ScotRail Royal Scot, Glasgow | 25 | – | *n.o.c.* |
| (19) Royal Scot, Euston, NW1 | 15 | 70 | *BenL7* |
| (20) Cornish Riviera, Paddington | 15 | 60 | *BLCS 1* |
| (21) Cornish Riviera, Penzance | 15 | 60 | *BLCS 1* |
| (22) National Railway Museum, York | 20 | – | *Royal Mail* |
| (23) York Station, Rail Riders | 15 | 20 | *DGT* |
| (24) North Staffs Rly. Co. Ltd., Leek | 15 | 85 | *NSRly* |
| (25) Railway Loco's, British Legion, Maidstone | 15 | 40 | *Brit. Leg.* |
| (26) Hendon Spitfire, BF 1857 PS | 15 | 40 | *RFDC 33* |
| (27) Rowland Hill Loco, Crewe | 30 | – | *Royal Mail* |
| (28) National Assoc'n Boys' Clubs, Blenheim | 30 | 70 | *NABC* |

**ORDINARY F.D.I. POSTMARKS**

| | | |
|---|---|---|
| (29) Aberysthwyth (Talyllyn Railway cover) | 30 | |
| (30) Ashford (Romney Hythe Railway cover) | 30 | |
| (31) Bradford (Worth Valley Railway cover) | 30 | |
| (32) Carlisle (Ravenglass & Eskdale Rly cover) | 30 | |
| (33) Darlington (Darlington Preserv. Soc cover) | 30 | |
| (34) Any other railway society covers with FDIs | 30 | |

**C.D.S. POSTMARKS (inc. T.P.O. CANCELS)**

| | | |
|---|---|---|
| (35) Carnforth or Doncaster | 25 | |
| (36) Cheltenham, Penzance or Swindon........ each | 25 | |
| (37) Didcot – GWR centre | 25 | |
| (38) Euston, King's Cross or Paddington. .......each | 25 | |
| (39) Railway Place, Coleraine | 25 | |
| (40) Saltash – Brunel's famous GWR bridge | 25 | |
| (41) Any 'station' pmk e.g. Crowthorne | 25 | |
| (42) Any connected T.P.O. | 25 | |
| (43) Any other T.P.O. cancellations | 20 | |

*Also: Bristol, Corby, Edinburgh, Glasgow, Haverthwaite, Portsmouth, Silver Link, The Rocket. £15.*

## 12th March 1985 – BRITISH INSECTS

*17p Bumble Bee; 22p Ladybird; 29p Bush-Cricket; 31p Stag Beetle; 34p Dragonfly*

**SPECIAL HANDSTAMPS**

| | | | |
|---|---|---|---|
| (1) First Day of Issue – Philatelic Bureau | 4 | – | *Royal Mail* |
| (2) First Day of Issue – London SW | 4 | – | *Royal Mail* |
| (3) Royal Entomological Soc., Meadow Bank | 7 | 50 | *Ben500(2)* |
| (4) Royal Entomological Soc., SW7 | 7 | 20 | *BLCS 2* |
| (5) A.E.S. Golden Jubilee, Feltham | 12 | 30 | *LFDC 40* |
| (6) Selborne Society Centenary, Alton | 12 | 25 | *Cotswold* |
| (7) Writhlington School, Radstock | 15 | 100 | *Writh. Sch.* |
| (8) British Museum, Natural History, SW7 | 10 | 20 | *BLCS 2* |
| (9) Stamp Bug Club, High Wycombe | 15 | 50 | *SB Club* |
| (10) Bugford, I AM FIVE | 20 | 80 | *SB Club* |
| (11) Nature Conservation, Hummer Sherborne | 15 | – | *Post Office* |
| (12) Enfield Butterfly Centre | 12 | 25 | *Hawkwood* |
| (13) Robert Hooke, Freshwater | 12 | 40 | *Fine Arts 3* |
| (14) Scottish Wildlife Trust, Edinburgh | 12 | 25 | *Pilgrim* |
| (15) Mosquito Aircraft, BF 1862 PS | 12 | 15 | *RFDC 34* |
| (16) Pestalozzi Children's Village | 35 | – | *n.o.c.* |
| (17) National Assoc'n Boys' Clubs, Abercrave | 15 | 50 | *NABC* |

**C.D.S. POSTMARKS**

| | | |
|---|---|---|
| (18) Buckfastleigh – Abbey monks bee-keepers | 25 | |
| (19) Nettleham – Soc for Nature Conservation | 25 | |
| (20) St. Bees | 25 | |
| (21) St. James's St., or South Kensington. | 25 | |
| (22) Selborne – 'Natural History of Selborne' | 25 | |

*Also: Alexandra Park, Alexandra, Beeston, Bugbrooke, Bugthorpe, Church St., Enfield, Dunkeld, Duns, Feltham, Fleet St., Kingsstag, Lady, Meadow Bank, Northam, Sedgfield, Sheerness, Wickham, Writhlington. Prices from £15.*

**SLOGAN POSTMARKS** *Collect British Stamps. £15.*

## 14th May 1985 - COMPOSERS

*17p Handel; 22p Holst; 31p Delius; 34p Elgar*

**SPECIAL HANDSTAMPS**

| | | | |
|---|---|---|---|
| (1) First Day of Issue – Philatelic Bureau | 3 | – | *Royal Mail* |
| (2) First Day of Issue – Worcester | 3 | – | *Royal Mail* |
| (3) Handel's Birthday, Royal Opera House | 6 | 20 | *BLCS 3* |
| (4) Handel, Westminster Abbey, SW1 | 12 | 20 | *LFDC 41* |
| (5) St. Paul's Cathedral, 850 Years of Music | 12 | 40 | *St. Paul's* |
| (6) Holst Birthplace Museum, Cheltenham | 12 | 35 | *H.B. Museum* |
| (7) Holst, European Music Year, Cheltenham. | 12 | 50 | *Ben500(3)* |
| (8) Stagenhoe Park, Mikado, Hitchin | 12 | 15 | *Hawkwood* |
| (9) Delius Festival, Bradford | 12 | 25 | *P. Scott* |
| (10) Sir Edward Elgar, Birmingham | 12 | – | *n.o.c.* |
| (11) Sir Michael Tippett, Bournemouth | 12 | 25 | *Pilgrim* |
| (12) British Composers, Royal Festival Hall, SE1 | 12 | 15 | *G.L.C.* |
| (13) European Music Year, High Wycombe | 12 | – | *n.o.c.* |
| (14) Scottish National Orchestra, Aberdeen | 12 | 30 | *BenL9* |
| (15) Scottish National Orchestra, Dundee | 12 | 30 | *BenL10* |

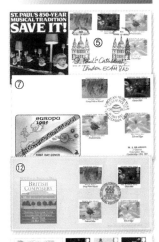

| Composers (contd.) | ordinary covers £ | official covers £ | |
|---|---|---|---|
| (16) Royal Military School of Music, BF 2128 PS... | 12 | 20 | RFDC 35 |
| (17) Music Year, National Postal Museum, EC1 .... | 12 | – | n.o.c. |
| (18) Leicester Philharmonic Society ........................ | 12 | 25 | L.P.O. |
| (19) 1st Ruislip Guides............................................... | 12 | 40 | Ruislip GG |
| (20) St. David's Hall, Cardiff ..................................... | 12 | 30 | Pilgrim |
| (21) Haddo House, Aberdeen.................................... | 12 | 30 | Pilgrim |
| (22) Lennon & McCartney, Composers of Today.... | 12 | 60 | Fine Arts 4 |
| (23) Philatelic Counter – Worcester ......................... | 12 | – | n.o.c. |
| (24) Centenary of SSAFA, SW1................................ | 15 | 25 | Benham |
| (25) Royal Visit, The Princess of Wales, E13 .......... | 15 | 25 | Havering |
| (26) Ultramar Fifty Years, EC.................................... | 15 | 250 | CoverCraft |
| (27) National Assoc'n Boys' Clubs, Edinburgh....... | 15 | 50 | NABC |
| (28) 700th Mayoral Anniversary, High Wycombe ... | 15 | 40 | High Wyc DC |

**ORDINARY F.D.I. POSTMARKS**

| (29) Birmingham (CBSO/M&B SimonRattle cvr)... | 20 |
|---|---|

**C.D.S. POSTMARKS**

| (30) Chichester – Holst buried in Cathedral.......... | 15 |
|---|---|
| (31) Hammersmith – Holst wrote 'Planets' here...... | 15 |
| (32) Limpsfield – Delius is interred here ................ | 15 |
| (33) Lower Broadheath – Elgar's birthplace............ | 15 |
| (34) Lowesmoor – Elgar died here .......................... | 15 |
| (35) Pittville or Thaxted – Holst............................... | 15 |
| (36) South Molton St., W1 – Handel lived here ...... | 15 |
| (37) University, Bradford – near Delius's b/place ... | 15 |
| (38) Malvern – Elgar buried nearby........................ | 15 |

*In addition: Brigg, Chelsea, Hereford, Whitwell. Prices from £5.*

**SLOGAN POSTMARKS**

| (39) CBSO Proms, Birmingham ......(on two covers) | 50 |
|---|---|
| (40) Delius Festival, Bradford .........(on two covers) | 50 |

*In addition: Hereford Cathedral; North Wiltshire Entertains. Prices from £50.*

## 18th June 1985 – SAFETY AT SEA

*17p Lifeboat; 22p Lighthouse; 31p Satellite; 34p Buoy*

**SPECIAL HANDSTAMPS**

| (1) First Day of Issue – Philatelic Bureau............... | 3 | – | Royal Mail |
|---|---|---|---|
| (2) First Day of Issue – Eastbourne, E. Sussex....... | 3 | – | Royal Mail |
| (3) The Plimsoll Line, Bristol ................................. | 12 | – | Royal Mail |
| (4) Spurn Head Lifeboat, Hull ............................... | 12 | – | Royal Mail |
| (5) Lifeboat Dedication, Cromer ........................... | 12 | 25 | RNLI |
| (6) Lifeboat Display, Poole, Dorset........................ | 12 | 25 | RNLI |
| (7) Berwick-upon-Tweed Lifeboat ......................... | 12 | 55 | B.u.T. Lifeboat |
| (8) Appledore, RNLI Lifeboat Station .................... | 12 | 50 | Appledore LS |
| (9) Earliest Lifeboat Design, Lowestoft.................. | 12 | 50 | Ben500(4) |
| (10) Grace Darling Museum, Bamburgh.................. | 12 | 15 | LFDC 42 |
| (11) Lukin's Patent for Lifeboat Design, Hythe ...... | 12 | 25 | BLCS 4 |
| (12) Lighthouse Club, Whitley Bay ......................... | 12 | 40 | Light. Club |
| (13) Nore Lightship, E1 ........................................... | 12 | 45 | Fine Arts 5 |
| (14) Global Maritime, Safety at Sea, WC2 .............. | 12 | 50 | Global |
| (15) Maritime Museum, SE10 ................................. | 12 | 12 | BLCS 4 |
| (16) Schermuly, Greenwich, SE10 .......................... | 12 | 50 | Schermuly |
| (17) Sealion Shipping, City of London.................... | 12 | 125 | Sealion |
| (18) The Geographical Magazine, SW7 ................... | 12 | 12 | Hawkwood |
| (19) No. 22 Squadron, RAF BF 1890 PS ................. | 12 | 20 | RFDC 36 |
| (20) British Film Year, Bristol ................................. | 12 | 75 | CoverCraft |
| (21) The Ashes Tour, NW8 ...................................... | 12 | 15 | S.P. |
| (22) London Welsh Rugby, Richmond ..................... | 12 | 25 | LondonWelsh |
| (23) Lawn Tennis Museum, Wimbledon, SW19 ...... | 12 | 12 | AELTA |
| (24) Nat. Assoc. of Boys' Clubs, Worcester ........... | 12 | 40 | NABC |
| (25) GWR 150 Exhibition Train, Shrewsbury ........ | 12 | 25 | BLCS 4 |
| (26) Scottish National Orchestra, Glasgow.............. | 12 | – | n.o.c. |

**ORDINARY F.D.I. POSTMARKS**

| (27) Grimsby & Cleethorpes (Humber RNLI cvr) .. | 35 |
|---|---|

**C.D.S. POSTMARKS**

| (28) Anstruther or Cromer ...................................... | 15 |
|---|---|
| (29) Austhorpe – b/place of Smeaton (Eddystone). | 15 |
| (30) Bamburgh – first lifeboat station .................... | 15 |
| (31) Cawsand, Toward Point, Whitley Bay .............. | 15 |
| (32) Daventry – first successful radar experiments.. | 15 |
| (33) Dover – lighthouse built by the Romans.......... | 15 |
| (34) E. Dean or Grand Hotel Blgs – Beachy Head .... | 15 |
| (35) Hawes – birthplace of RNLI founder ............... | 25 |
| (36) Hythe – Lionel Lukin is buried here................ | 15 |
| (37) Lighthouse, Fleetwood .................................... | 25 |
| (38) Little Dunmow – birthplace of Lionel Lukin... | 15 |
| (39) Poole – Headquarters of RNLI......................... | 15 |
| (40) Redcar – The 'Zetland' oldest lifeboat............. | 15 |
| (41) Richmond – H. Greathead – 'Zetland'.............. | 15 |
| (42) Seething Lane, EC3 – near to Trinity House ... | 20 |
| (43) Culdrose or Yeovilton RN Air Stns ................. | 15 |
| (44) Any RAF or RN (Air-Sea Rescue) Station ....... | 15 |

*Also: Beacon, Marton-in-Cleveland, Sheerness, Six Bells, The Rocket, Thorpe Esplanade, Yeovil. £10*

**SLOGAN POSTMARKS**

| (45) Relax at Sunny Weymouth ................................ | 75 |
|---|---|

## 30th July 1985 – THE ROYAL MAIL

*17p Datapost; 22p Postbus;*
*31p Parcel Post; 34p Letter Post*

| | | ordinary covers £ | | official covers £ |
|---|---|---|---|---|
| **SPECIAL HANDSTAMPS** | | | | |
| (1) | First Day of Issue – Philatelic Bureau................ | 3 | – | *Royal Mail* |
| (2) | First Day of Issue – Bagshot ............................... | 3 | – | *Royal Mail* |
| (2a) | -do- carried on helicopter by Prince Charles ... | 5 | – | *Royal Mail* |
| (3) | P.O. Archives, 23 Glass Hill St., SE1................ | 12 | 75 | *Fine Arts 6* |
| (4) | National Postal Museum, 350 Years Service.... | 12 | – | *Royal Mail* |
| (5) | Thomas Witherings Postmaster, 1635................. | 12 | 40 | *St. Andrew's* |
| (6) | Royal Mail London Post, 1635-1985, EC1 ....... | 12 | – | *Post Office* |
| (7) | UCWA Public Service Union, SW4................. | 12 | 15 | *BLCS 5* |
| (8) | Royal Mail 350 Years of Service, EC ................ | 12 | – | *Royal Mail* |
| (9) | Royal Mail SEPR Postcards, Bagshot................. | 12 | – | *Royal Mail* |
| (10) | Royal Mail SEPR Postcards, Windsor............... | 12 | – | *Royal Mail* |
| (11) | Royal Mail 350 Exhibition, Bristol .................... | 12 | – | *Royal Mail* |
| (12) | Post Paid, Healey & Wise, EC4........................... | 12 | 40 | *H & W* |
| (13) | Intelpost, Head Post Office, E1.......................... | 12 | 15 | *Hawkwood* |
| (14) | Postal Museum, Bath ........................................... | 12 | 50 | *Ben500(5)* |
| (15) | National Postal Museum (Maltese Cross)......... | 15 | – | *Royal Mail* |
| (16) | North Eastern Parcels Centre .............................. | 15 | – | *Royal Mail* |
| (17) | 10 Downing Street, SW1 ..................................... | 12 | 35 | *LFDC 43* |
| (18) | British Legion, SW1............................................. | 12 | 35 | *Brit. Leg.* |
| (19) | The Cardiff Tattoo, BF 1879 PS ......................... | 12 | 45 | *Forces* |
| (20) | Norton 100, 1885-1985, Leicester ...................... | 12 | 150 | *N. Clipper* |
| (21) | GWR 150 Steam Special, Gloucester.................. | 12 | – | *n.o.c.* |
| (22) | M.C.C. Cricket Festival, Uxbridge..................... | 12 | 50 | *MCC* |
| (23) | The Ashes Tour, NW8........................................... | 12 | 25 | *S.P.* |
| (24) | Nat. Assoc. of Boys' Clubs, Trentham Gdns..... | 12 | 50 | *NABC* |
| (25) | Ptarmigan Equipment, BF 3254 PS .................... | 12 | 20 | *RFDC 37* |
| **ORDINARY F.D.I. POSTMARKS** | | | | |
| (26) | Bromley (Bromley Post Office cover) ................ | 45 | | |
| (27) | Leeds (Yorkshire Parcel Centre cover)............. | 45 | | |
| **C.D.S. POSTMARKS** | | | | |
| (28) | Aberfeldy – postbus............................................ | 20 | | |
| (29) | Bagshot – Charles I Proclamation ..................... | 20 | | |
| (30) | Buckingham Palace, SW1.................................... | 40 | | |
| (31) | Hornchurch – T. Witherings, 1st postmaster .. | 25 | | |
| (32) | Letter, Enniskillen .............................................. | 30 | | |
| (33) | Llangurig or Llandloes – first ever postbus ..... | 30 | | |
| (34) | Cannon Street or Lombard Street ...................... | 20 | | |
| (35) | Mount Pleasant – sorting office......................... | 20 | | |
| (36) | Sanquhar – Britain's oldest Post Office............ | 20 | | |
| (37) | Stock Exchange – Royal Exchange (17p) ......... | 20 | | |

*Also: Brighton, Dunfermline, Edinburgh, FPO postmarks, Henfield,*
*House of Commons, Kidderminster, Kingstanding, Postbridge. From £20.*

| | | | | |
|---|---|---|---|---|
| **SLOGAN POSTMARKS** | | | | |
| (38) | Royal Mail 350 Years Service to the Public ..... | 20 | | |
| (39) | Make any Post Office in Cleveland, etc.......... | 50 | | |
| **OTHER POSTMARKS** | | | | |
| (40) | Parcel Post cancel – Chingford, London E4 .... | 75 | | |
| **ROYAL MAIL DISOUNT BOOKLET** | | | | |
| Covers bearing a pair or block of 4 x 17p 'Datapost' | | | | |
| stamps from booklet with relevant pmk.............. | | 8 | | |
| Covers with complete pane and relevant postmark.. | | 15 | | |

## 3rd September 1985 – ARTHURIAN LEGEND

*17p Arthur & Merlin; 22p Lady of the Lake;*
*31p Guinevere & Lancelot; 34p Sir Galahad;*

| | | | | |
|---|---|---|---|---|
| **SPECIAL HANDSTAMPS** | | | | |
| (1) | First Day of Issue – Philatelic Bureau................ | 3 | – | *Royal Mail* |
| (2) | First Day of Issue – Tintagel ............................. | 3 | – | *Royal Mail* |
| (3) | The Sword & The Stone, St. Paul's, EC4 ......... | 12 | 40 | *Fine Arts 7* |
| (4) | Old Post Office ,Tintagel................................... | 12 | 20 | *BenL12* |
| (5) | The Legendary Camelot, Winchester.................. | 12 | 15 | *BLCS 6* |
| (6) | Morte D'Arthur, Mere, Warminster................... | 12 | 50 | *Ben500(6)* |
| (7) | The Great Hall, Winchester................................. | 12 | 30 | *Hants CC* |
| (8) | Exhibition of Celtic Legend, Glastonbury........ | 12 | 35 | *Arth. Exh.* |
| (9) | St. Margaret's Church, SW1................................ | 12 | 20 | *Hawkwood* |
| (10) | King Arthur's Avalon, Glastonbury ................... | 12 | 15 | *LFDC 44* |
| (11) | Royal Fleet Auxiliary, BF 1880 PS.................... | 12 | 15 | *RFDC 38* |
| (12) | Leith Hall, Huntly ............................................... | 12 | 20 | *Pilgrim* |
| (13) | Stockton on Tees, Town Hall .............................. | 12 | 25 | *Town Counc.* |
| (14) | Nat. Assoc. of Boys' Clubs, Guildhall, EC3 ..... | 12 | 50 | *NABC* |
| (15) | BI Centenary Cricket, Schaw Park ..................... | 12 | 25 | *Scot. Cricket* |
| (16) | 23 BASE WKSP REME, BF 2340 PS ............... | 12 | 20 | *Forces* |
| **ORDINARY F.D.I. POSTMARKS** | | | | |
| (17) | Cardiff or Newport.............................................. | 6 | | |
| **C.D.S. POSTMARKS** | | | | |
| (18) | Amesbury – Guinevere became a nun here...... | 15 | | |
| (19) | Bamburgh – Lancelot's Castle ........................... | 15 | | |
| (20) | Bodmin – Dozmary Pool/Excalibur ................... | 15 | | |
| (21) | Camelford – Arthur mortally wounded ............ | 15 | | |

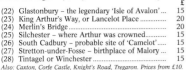

# 1985-1986

| Arthurian Legends (contd.) | ordinary covers £ | | official covers £ |
|---|---|---|---|
| (22) Glastonbury – the legendary 'Isle of Avalon' ... | 15 | | |
| (23) King Arthur's Way, or Lancelot Place .............. | 20 | | |
| (24) Merlin's Bridge........................................................ | 20 | | |
| (25) Silchester – where Arthur was crowned........... | 15 | | |
| (26) South Cadbury – probable site of 'Camelot'..... | 15 | | |
| (27) Stretton-under-Fosse – birthplace of Malory ... | 15 | | |
| (28) Tintagel or Winchester ....................................... | 15 | | |

*Also: Caxton, Corfe Castle, Knight's Road, Tregaron. Prices from £10.*
**SLOGAN POSTMARKS** *Carlisle – worth a closer look. £60.*

## 8th October 1985 – BRITISH FILM YEAR
*17p Peter Sellers; 22p David Niven; 29p Charles Chaplin;*
*31p Vivien Leigh; 34p Alfred Hitchcock*
**SPECIAL HANDSTAMPS**

| | | | |
|---|---|---|---|
| (1) First Day of Issue – Philatelic Bureau................ | 4 | – | *Royal Mail* |
| (2) First Day of Issue – London WC ....................... | 4 | – | *Royal Mail* |
| (3) British Film Year, MCMLXXXV, W1 ................ | 12 | 15 | *LFDC 45* |
| (4) British Film Year, Bradford............................... | 12 | 50 | *BLCS 7* |
| (5) British Film Year, Richmond .............................. | 12 | 100 | *Ben500(7)* |
| (6) British Film Year, Leicester Sq (rectangular) ... | 12 | 20 | *Arlington* |
| (7) British Film Year, Goldcrest London W1 ......... | 12 | 15 | *G&P* |
| (8) British Film Year, David Niven .......................... | 12 | 35 | *Cotswold* |
| (9) British Film Year, Leicester Sq (Pink Panther)... | 12 | 60 | *BLCS 7* |
| (10) Equity, Harley Street, W1 .................................. | 12 | 45 | *Fine Arts 8* |
| (11) 50 Years, National Film Archives, W1 ............. | 12 | 40 | *N.F.A.* |
| (12) Dambusters, BF 2101 PS ................................... | 12 | 50 | *RFDC 39* |
| (13) Alfred Hitchcock, Leytonstone, E11 ................. | 12 | 20 | *Hawkwood* |
| (14) Charrington Bass, LVNH Denham .................... | 12 | 35 | *Havering* |
| (15) Nat. Post. Museum, Film Festival, EC1 ........... | 12 | – | *n.o.c.* |
| (16) Brian Reeve New Stamp Shop, WC2................. | 12 | 15 | *DGT* |
| (17) Perth Theatre ....................................................... | 12 | 160 | *Perth* |
| (18) Opening Arndale Centre, Luton........................ | 12 | 50 | *EPR(postcard)* |
| (19) Nat. Assoc. of Boys' Clubs, Belfast ................... | 12 | 50 | *NABC* |

**C.D.S. POSTMARKS**

| | | |
|---|---|---|
| (20) Any film studio, e.g. Pinewood, Ealing ........... | 15 | |
| (21) Castle Road, Southsea – b/place/Peter Sellers | 15 | |
| (22) Down Special T.P.O. – P.O. film 'Night Mail'...... | 25 | |
| (23) East St., Walworth – b/place/Charles Chaplin .. | 15 | |
| (24) Hollywood, Birmingham................................... | 15 | |
| (25) Kirriemuir – home of David Niven .................. | 15 | |
| (26) Lacock – Fox Talbot (photographic negative) . | 15 | |
| (27) Leytonstone – b/place of Alfred Hitchcock ..... | 15 | |
| (28) Maida Vale – Friese Green (inventor of cine) . | 15 | |
| (29) Victoria St., SW1 – b/place of David Niven .... | 15 | |

*Also: Chancery Lane, Goonhaven, Queens Rd., Shamley Green, Sloane Square, Star. From £10.*
**SLOGAN POSTMARKS** *Eden Court Theatre. £65.*

## 19th November 1985 – CHRISTMAS
*12p 17p, 22p, 31p, 34p Pantomime;*
**SPECIAL HANDSTAMPS**

| | | | |
|---|---|---|---|
| (1) First Day of Issue – Philatelic Bureau................ | 3 | – | *Royal Mail* |
| (2) First Day of Issue – Bethlehem .......................... | 3 | – | *Royal Mail* |
| (3) Telecom Technology Showcase, EC4................. | 12 | – | *n.o.c.* |
| (4) Aladdin, Nottingham Theatre ............................ | 12 | 15 | *LFDC 46* |
| (5) English Pantomime, Drury Lane, WC2 .............. | 12 | 35 | *Ben500(8)* |
| (6) Peace on Earth, Sewardstone Church, E4 ........ | 12 | 15 | *Hawkwood* |
| (7) Mother Goose, Biddenden .................................. | 12 | 15 | *BLCS 8* |
| (8) Cinderella at the Palladium, W1 ........................ | 12 | 45 | *Fine Arts 9* |
| (9) North Eastern Parcel Centre .............................. | 12 | – | *n.o.c.* |
| (10) Nat. Assoc. of Boys' Clubs, Althorp ................. | 12 | 50 | *NABC* |

**C.D.S. POSTMARKS**

| | | |
|---|---|---|
| (11) Bethlehem, Nasareth or The Harlequin ........... | 30 | |

*Also: Holy Island, Lilliput, Old Whittington, Robin Hood, Star, The Circle, Whittington. From £10.*
**SLOGAN POSTMARKS** *Eastgate or Exeter Shopping; Eden Court; Explorer Bus Tickets. £20.*
**CHRISTMAS BOOKLET:** Covers with pair or block
of 4 x 12p stamps from bklet with special h/s........5

## 14th January 1986 – INDUSTRY YEAR
*17p Energy; 22p Health; 31p Leisure; 34p Food*
**SPECIAL HANDSTAMPS**

| | | | |
|---|---|---|---|
| (1) First Day of Issue – Philatelic Bureau................ | 3 | – | *Royal Mail* |
| (2) First Day of Issue – Birmingham ...................... | 3 | – | *Royal Mail* |
| (3) Birthplace of Industry, Ironbridge ..................... | 8 | 25 | *LFDC 47* |
| (4) Rank Taylor Hobson, Leicester ......................... | 8 | 100 | *RTH* |
| (5) Osram, A Leading Light, Wembley .................. | 15 | 225 | *G&P* |
| (6) British Steel, Industry Year, SE1...................... | 10 | 85 | *CoverCraft* |
| (7) Purveyors of Flour, Hovis, Windsor ................ | 15 | 325 | *CoverCraft* |
| (8) The Workers Playground, Blackpool ................ | 10 | 15 | *BLCS 9* |
| (9) Farming Feeds the Nation, Wheatacre .............. | 10 | 25 | *Ben500(9)* |
| (10) British Steel Smelters Assoc'n, WC1 ............... | 10 | 75 | *BSSA* |
| (11) Ulcer Therapy, Welwyn..................................... | 15 | 225 | *Smith Kline* |
| (12) All Industrious People are Happy, Blackwells ..... | 10 | 20 | *Hawkwood* |

71

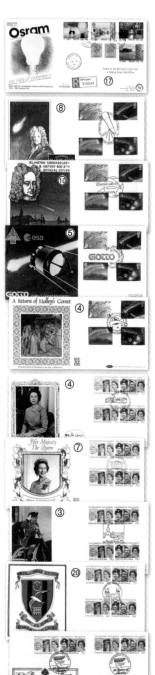

**Industry Year (contd.)**

| | ordinary covers £ | official covers £ | |
|---|---|---|---|
| (13) Industry Year, BP, EC | 10 | 45 | BP |
| (14) World Leading Energy Technology, Aberdeen | 10 | 45 | Conoco(s) |
| (15) British Aerospace Companies BF 2105 PS | 10 | 25 | RFDC 41 |
| (16) The Salvation Army, Hoxton, N1 | 10 | 90 | H.R. |

**C.D.S. POSTMARKS**

| | | |
|---|---|---|
| (17) Any Trading/Industrial Estate | 20 | |
| (18) Clydebank – shipbuilding | 10 | |
| (19) Cruden Bay – North Sea oil pipeline | 10 | |
| (20) Furnace, Furnace End or Ironbridge | 10 | |
| (21) Greenock – birthplace of James Watt | 15 | |
| (22) Sunderland – Joseph Swan (light bulb) | 15 | |
| (23) Steel or Steel City House | 20 | |

*Also: Bacton, Bakewell, NEC, New Invention, Pill. Prices from £7.*

**SLOGAN POSTMARKS** *Clydebank; Sedgemoor has the Edge; Nissan. From £35.*

## 18th February 1986 – HALLEY'S COMET

*17p Halley; 22p Giotto; 31p Twice in a Lifetime; 34p Comet*

**SPECIAL HANDSTAMPS**

| | | | |
|---|---|---|---|
| (1) First Day of Issue – Philatelic Bureau | 4 | – | Royal Mail |
| (2) First Day of Issue – London SE10 | 4 | – | Royal Mail |
| (3) Old Royal Observatory, SE10 | 10 | 20 | BLCS 10 |
| (4) A Return of Halley's Comet, Star | 10 | 30 | Ben500(10) |
| (5) Giotto, Halley's Comet Interceptor, Bristol | 10 | 30 | CoverCraft |
| (6) Halley's Comet Society, SE10 | 12 | 25 | HC Soc. |
| (7) Islington Home of Halley, N1 | 12 | 20 | Hawkwood |
| (8) London Planetarium, NW1 | 12 | 20 | LFDC 48 |
| (9) Interplanetary Society, SW | 12 | 20 | DGT |
| (10) Edmund Halley born 1656, Haggerston | 12 | 35 | Fine Arts 11 |
| (11) Royal Greenwich Observatory, Herstmonceux | 12 | 25 | K&D |
| (12) Skynet 4A Satellite, BF 2109 PS | 12 | 25 | RFDC 42 |
| (13) Royal Mail Fiveways, Tunbridge Wells | 15 | – | Royal Mail |
| (14) Royal Mail SEPR Postcards, Brighton | 12 | – | Royal Mail |
| (15) Ripon 1100 AD 886-1986 | 12 | 60 | Ripon Counc. |

**C.D.S. POSTMARKS**

| | |
|---|---|
| (16) Battle – Bayeux Tapestry/Halley's Comet | 25 |
| (17) Filton – Giotto Project Team | 20 |
| (18) Greenwich or Herstmonceux – observatories | 25 |
| (19) Hartland – Magnetic Observatory | 25 |
| (20) Helston – Goonhilly Downs | 20 |
| (21) Islington – home of Edmund Halley | 20 |
| (22) Lower Withington or Macclesfield | 20 |
| (23) Seven Sisters or Star | 20 |
| (24) Shoreditch – birthplace of Edmund Halley | 20 |

*In addition: Kingsland Road. Prices from £10.*

**SLOGAN POSTMARKS** *Shop at Post Office; Zone Tickets; Industry Year. From £18.*

## 21st April 1986 – H.M. THE QUEEN'S 60th BIRTHDAY

*2 x 17p; 2 x 34p Portraits of the Queen*

**SPECIAL HANDSTAMPS**

| | | | |
|---|---|---|---|
| (1) First Day of Issue – Philatelic Bureau | 4 | – | Royal Mail |
| (2) First Day of Issue – Windsor | 4 | – | Royal Mail |
| (3) Birthday Greetings, London SW1 (square) | 10 | 20 | LFDC 49 |
| (4) Queen's Birthday, Sandringham, Norfolk | 10 | 15 | BLCS 11 |
| (5) Queen's Birthday, London SW1 (circular) | 10 | 15 | BLCS 11 |
| (6) Lombard North Central, 17 Bruton St., W1 | 10 | 20 | G&P |
| (7) Queen's Birthday, Windsor | 10 | 35 | Ben500(11) |
| (8) Radio Times, W1 | 10 | 25 | Arlington |
| (9) Queen's 60th Birthday, SW1 (rectangular) | 10 | 25 | Arlington |
| (10) Southend Pier Train | 10 | 15 | Hawkwood |
| (11) Queen's Flight, BF 2106 PS | 10 | 25 | RFDC 43 |
| (12) Queen's 60th Birthday Bruton St., W1 | 10 | 25 | K&D |
| (13) Queen's Birthday, Balmoral | 10 | 20 | BenSG1 |
| (14) Loyal Greetings, City of London | 10 | – | n.o.c. |
| (15) Many Happy Returns Nat. Postal Museum | 10 | 15 | NPM card |
| (16) Lord High Admiral, BF 2113 PS | 10 | 75 | Royal Navy |
| (17) Royal British Legion, SW1 | 10 | 35 | Brit. Leg. 26 |
| (18) London SW1 or Windsor permanent h/s | 15 | – | n.o.c. |
| (19) British Forces 1000 | 15 | – | n.o.c. |
| (20) Tower Hill or Broadlands – permanent h/s | 15 | – | n.o.c. |
| (21) Royal Academy of Dancing, SW11 | 10 | 50 | CoverCraft |
| (22) N. Ireland £1 Coin, Royal Mint | 10 | – | n.o.c. |
| (23) Women's Institutes, Denham College | 10 | 35 | Fed. WI |
| (24) Durham County Schools Society | 10 | 40 | DCSS |
| (25) Licensed Victuallers Soc., Horsham | 12 | 175 | RumMerc |
| (26) G&J Swingler Ltd., Birmingham | 10 | 40 | G&J Sw. |
| (27) BNAI Brith District 15, London WC1 | 10 | 40 | B.B. |
| (28) Austin Rover, Birmingham | 10 | 40 | A. Rover |
| (29) Open Days Broadlands | 10 | 20 | Broadlands |

**C.D.S. POSTMARKS**

| | |
|---|---|
| (30) Aldershot – HM Queen enroled in A.T.S | 20 |
| (31) Badminton – Horse Trials | 20 |
| (32) Buckingham Palace or Windsor Castle | 100 |

*Queen's 60th Birthday (contd.)*     ordinary covers     official covers
£       £

| | | ordinary | official |
|---|---|---|---|
| (33) | Camberley | 20 | |
| (34) | House of Commons or Lords | 30 | |
| (35) | Mount Street, W1 – near Queen's birthplace... | 15 | |
| (36) | Romsey (honeymoon) or Crathie (Balmoral)... | 25 | |
| (37) | Queen Elizabeth Ave | 20 | |
| (38) | Queen's Parade or Queensway | 20 | |
| (39) | Windsor Great Park or Windsor | 25 | |
| (40) | RAF Benson – The Queen's Flight | 20 | |

## 20th May 1986 – NATURE CONSERVATION
*17p Barn Owl; 22p Pine Marten; 31p Wild Cat; 34p Natterjack Toad*

**SPECIAL HANDSTAMPS**

| | | | | |
|---|---|---|---|---|
| (1) | First Day of Issue – Philatelic Bureau | 4 | – | *Royal Mail* |
| (2) | First Day of Issue – Lincoln | 4 | – | *Royal Mail* |
| (3) | Ramblers' Association, SW8 | 12 | 20 | *LFDC 50* |
| (4) | Barn Owl, Endangered Species, Owlsmoor | 12 | 40 | *Ben500(12)* |
| (5) | RSPB, Endangered Species, Sandy | 12 | 15 | *BLCS 12* |
| (6) | Life & Landscape, Norfolk Broads | 12 | 45 | *Bus. Inf. Ltd.* |
| (7) | The Wildfowl Trust, Slimbridge | 12 | 15 | *BLCS 12* |
| (8) | Friends of the Earth, EC1 | 12 | 15 | *F.o.t.E.* |
| (9) | Royal Society for Nature Conservation, EC4 | 12 | 20 | *Arlington* |
| (10) | Species at Risk, Hants & IOW | 12 | 45 | *H&IOW NT* |
| (11) | Herpetological Society, Studland | 12 | 15 | *Hawkwood* |
| (12) | Cornish Wildlife, CTNC, Truro | 12 | 25 | *CTNC* |
| (13) | Royal Society for Nature Conservation, W1 | 12 | 25 | *Arlington* |
| (14) | Lady's Slipper Orchid, Grassington | 12 | 25 | *Fine Arts 13* |
| (15) | Friends of Arundel Castle CC | 12 | 25 | *FACCC* |
| (16) | Big Ack, BF 2111 PS | 12 | 15 | *RFDC 44* |
| (17) | British Naval Anniversary, Plymouth | 12 | – | *n.o.c.* |
| (18) | Caring & Sharing, Colchester Co-op | 12 | 40 | *Col. Co-op* |
| (19) | Hawk 200, First Flight, Godalming | 12 | 110 | *V.A.F.A.* |

**C.D.S. POSTMARKS**

| | | |
|---|---|---|
| (20) | Aviemore, Kinloch, or Tummel Bridge – Wildcat | 15 |
| (21) | Beddgelert or Kilnlochewe – Pine Marten | 15 |
| (22) | Lincoln or Nettleham – RSNC | 15 |
| (23) | Park Road, Regents Park – London Zoo | 15 |
| (24) | Selbourne – Gilbert White/famous naturalist | 15 |

*Also: Cheltenham; Ecclestone St., SW1; Eagle; Eaglescliffe; Fair Isle;Frog Island; Isle of Rhum; Otterburn; Otterferry; Owlsmoor; Paddock Wood; Studland and Willsbridge. From £10.*

**SLOGAN POSTMARKS**

| | | |
|---|---|---|
| (25) | Lincs. & Humberside Nature | 70 |
| (26) | Natureland Marine Zoo Skegness | 70 |

*In addition: Stoke Garden Festival (2 versions). Prices from £40.*

## 17th June 1986 - MEDIEVAL LIFE
*17p Serf; 22p Freeman; 31p Knight; 34p Baron*

**SPECIAL HANDSTAMPS**

| | | | | |
|---|---|---|---|---|
| (1) | First Day of Issue – Philatelic Bureau | 4 | – | *Royal Mail* |
| (2) | First Day of Issue – Gloucester | 4 | – | *Royal Mail* |
| (3) | Domesday Book MLXXXVI, Winchester | 12 | 15 | *LFDC 51* |
| (4) | Freemen of England, Oswestry | 12 | 45 | *Bradbury* |
| (5) | Cub Scouts Medieval Pageant, Worthing | 12 | 45 | *Worthing Cubs* |
| (6) | Crofters Act, Inverness | 12 | 75 | *CroftersComm* |
| (7) | Crofters Act, Edinburgh | 12 | 75 | *CroftersComm* |
| (8) | Medieval Life Stamps/Tayburn, Edinburgh | 15 | – | *n.o.c.* |
| (9) | Medieval Life Stamps/Tayburn, W14 | 15 | – | *n.o.c.* |
| (10) | Domesday, 900th Anniversary, WC2 | 12 | 15 | *Cotswold* |
| (11) | Charter Celebrations, Port of Penryn | 12 | 50 | *Penryn* |
| (12) | Domesday Survey 900 Years, Battle | 12 | 25 | *Ben500(13)* |
| (13) | Hereward Country, Isle of Ely | 12 | 40 | *E.CambsDC* |
| (14) | Hereward Country, Peterborough | 12 | 40 | *E.CambsDC* |
| (15) | The Great Hall, Domesday 900, Winchester | 12 | 25 | *Cotswold* |
| (16) | 900th Anniversary, Domesday Survey, Exeter | 12 | 12 | *BLCS 13* |
| (17) | Chapter Hse, Abbey of St. Peter, Gloucester | 12 | 50 | *Fine Arts 14* |
| (18) | Blackwells Childrens Bookshop, Oxford | 12 | 25 | *Hawkwood* |
| (19) | Battle, East Sussex (permanent handstamp) | 12 | – | *n.o.c.* |
| (20) | Hastings (permanent handstamp) | 12 | – | *n.o.c.* |
| (21) | Ripon 1100, AD 886-1986 | 12 | 35 | *Ripon* |
| (22) | Harrow Heritage Trust | 12 | 25 | *HHT* |
| (23) | Tattershall Castle, BF 2116 PS | 12 | 20 | *RFDC 45* |
| (24) | Legal & General, London EC4 | 12 | 275 | *CoverCraft* |
| (25) | Stamplink '86, Portsmouth | 12 | 35 | *Brit. Ferries* |
| (26) | Blair Castle, Pitlochry | 12 | 35 | *Pilgrim* |
| (27) | Friends of Arundel Castle | 12 | 45 | *S.P.* |

**ORDINARY F.D.I. POSTMARKS**

*For this issue only, many Post Offices used special F.D.I. postmarks. These were non-pictorial and incorporated both the modern and medieval spelling of the town name. Such covers (unaddressed) are valued at £15 each.*

**C.D.S. POSTMARKS**

| | | |
|---|---|---|
| (28) | Battle – William's battle with Harold | 25 |
| (29) | Bosham – Manor reserved by William | 20 |
| (30) | Braunton or Laxton – ancient farming | 40 |
| (31) | Chancery Lane, WC2 – Domesday Book | 25 |
| (32) | Cherbourg PAQUEBOT – Duke of Normandy | 25 |

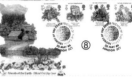

| | | ordinary covers £ | official covers £ |
|---|---|---|---|

(33) Kingsholm – Domesday survey instigated.......... 50
(34) Winchester – Domesday Book compiled........... 15

*In addition: Castle Acre, Castle Rising, Castleton, Chertsey, Egham, Ettington, Guernsey or Jersey Paquebots, Hastings, Knight's Road, Oswestry, Saxon Ave., The Barony, Westham. From £10.*

**SLOGAN POSTMARKS**
(35) Hereward Country – Fen Heritage ..................... 80
*In addition: Crofter's Act. Prices from £45.*

## 15th July 1986 – SPORTS
*17p Athletics; 22p Rowing; 29p Weight Lifting; 31p Shooting; 34p Hockey*

**SPECIAL HANDSTAMPS**
(1) First Day of Issue – Philatelic Bureau................ 4 – *Royal Mail*
(2) First Day of Issue – Edinburgh........................... 4 – *Royal Mail*
(3) Amateur Rowing Association, W6..................... 10 15 *LFDC 53*
(4) British Rowing, Henley-on-Thames................... 10 25 *Ben500(14)*
(5) Cosford Arena, BF 2119 PS ............................... 15 15 *RFDC 46*
(6) 6th World Hockey Cup, NW10........................... 10 25 *Cotswold*
(7) Scottish Brewers, Edinburgh............................. 10 15 *DGT*
(8) The Royal British Legion, SW1.......................... 10 35 *Brit.Leg.28*
(9) Amateur Athletic Association, SW1 .................. 10 15 *DGT*
(10) Commonwealth Games, MAC, Edinburgh ....... 10 15 *DGT*
(11) Waltham Forest, London Youth Games, E17... 10 15 *Hawkwood*
(12) The Royal Tournament, BF 2118 PS................. 12 – *n.o.c.*
(13) England v. N. Zealand, NW8 ............................ 10 25 *S.P.*
(14) England v. India, NW8 ...................................... 10 25 *S.P.*
(15) Medieval Life Stamps/Tayburn, Edinburgh...... 10 – *n.o.c.*
(16) Medieval Life Stamps/Tayburn, W14 .............. 10 – *n.o.c.*
(17) Domesday 900th Anniversary, WC2 ................ 10 – *n.o.c.*
(18) Blair Castle, Pitlochry ....................................... 10 25 *Pilgrim*

**C.D.S. POSTMARKS**
(19) Edinburgh, Jock's Lodge, Leith Walk, Murrayfield, Musselborough, Newbridge, North Motherwell or Norton Park – venues of Games events*each* 15
(20) Bisley or Henley............................................... 15
(21) Gleneagles Hotel – 'Gleneagles Agreement'..... 20
(22) Mobile P.O. 2 Edinburgh – Games Village........ 125
(23) Willesden – World Hockey Championships ..... 15

*Also: Badminton, Bowling Green, Clarkston, Fulham Rd, Gun Hill, Shooting Common. From £10.*

## 22nd July 1986 - ROYAL WEDDING
*12p & 17p Prince Andrew & Sarah Ferguson*

**SPECIAL HANDSTAMPS**
(1) First Day of Issue – Philatelic Bureau................ 2 – *Royal Mail*
(2) First Day of Issue – London SW1...................... 2 – *Royal Mail*
(3) Dummer (depicts horseshoe and church)......... 7 15 *G&P*
(4) Westminster Abbey (circular - front of Abbey). 7 15 *LFDC 52*
(5) Royal Wedding Greetings, Windsor ................. 7 40 *Ben500(15)*
(6) Loyal Greetings from York................................ 7 25 *BenSG2*
(7) The Royal Wedding, EC4................................... 7 15 *Arlington*
(8) Westminster Abbey (circular - twin towers)...... 7 15 *Arlington*
(9) Loyal Greetings from Lullingstone Silk Farm.... 7 15 *Benham L14*
(10) Debretts Recording Royal History, SW6........... 20 15 *Fine Arts 16*
(11) Westminster Abbey (vertical - front of Abbey). 7 10 *Havering*
(12) The Royal Wedding, London EC ...................... 7 – *Royal Mail*
(13) Dummer (depicts bell)...................................... 7 20 *K&D*
(14) The Lewis Carroll Society................................. 7 20 *Hawkwood*
(15) Royal Wedding, XIII Commonwealth Games... 7 15 *DGT*
(16) Westminster Abbey (rectangular - four bells).... 7 15 *DGT*
(17) Woman's Weekly, SE1...................................... 7 75 *CoverCraft*
(18) Open Days Broadlands, Romsey........................ 7 25 *Broadlands*
(19) London SW1 (Palace) – permanent h/s............. 7 – *n.o.c.*
(20) Windsor (Castle) Philatelic Counter h/s .......... 7 – *n.o.c.*
(21) Blair Castle, Pitlochry ...................................... 10 20 *Pilgrim*
(22) Wednesbury Sport Union ................................ 10 20 *Wed.SportsUnion*
(23) Lifeboat Week, Lyme Regis............................... 10 20 *Pilgrim*
(24) Brooklands, Daily Mail Air Race...................... 10 75 *V.A.F.A.*
(25) Head Post Office, Hemel Hempstead ................ 10 125 *H.H.P.O.*
(26) Royal Tournament, BF 2118 PS ........................ 10 – *n.o.c.*
(27) Amateur Athletic Association, SW1.................. 10 20 *DGT*

**C.D.S. POSTMARKS**
(28) Ascot – Andrew and Sarah, schools.................. 10
(29) Buckingham Palace, SW1.................................. 100
(30) Dummer – home of Sarah Ferguson................. 15
(31) Great Portland St/Portman Sq – Sarah's b/place.. 10
(32) House of Commons or Lords ........................... 20
(33) Kelso – where Andrew proposed to Sarah........ 15
(34) Windsor or Windsor Great Park .............*each* 15
(35) Windsor Castle, Berks ..................................... 130

*Also: Culdrose RNAS, Dartmouth, Duffus, Duke of York's School, Ferguson's Lane, Princetown, Romsey, St. Aldates, St. Andrews, Yeovilton RNAS. From £6.*

**SLOGAN POSTMARKS**
*St. Anne's Church, Naval Base Portsmouth; Collect British Stamps; Victorian Rose Gdn. From £15.*

## 19th August 1986 – PARLIAMENTARY CONFERENCE
*34p Stylised Cross and Ballot Paper*

| | ordinary covers | official covers | |
|---|---|---|---|
| **SPECIAL HANDSTAMPS** | £ | £ | |
| (1) First Day of Issue – Philatelic Bureau................. | 2 | – | *Royal Mail* |
| (2) First Day of Issue – London SW1 ...................... | 2 | – | *Royal Mail* |
| (3) Common'lth Parl. Conf., Houses of Parliament..... | 8 | 10 | *LFDC 54* |
| (4) Common'lth Parl. Assoc., 32nd Conf., SW1...... | 8 | 15 | *BLCS 16* |
| (5) St. Margaret's Parish Church, SW1 .................... | 8 | 20 | *Hawkwood* |
| (6) London SW1 (Palace) permanent h/s ............... | 8 | – | *n.o.c.* |
| (7) Dumfries Octocentenary 1186-1986 ................. | 8 | 45 | *Dumfries* |
| (8) World Chess Championship, W1 ...................... | 10 | 55 | *H.Murray* |
| **ORDINARY F.D.I. POSTMARKS** | | | |
| (9) London N1 (Finchley Conservative cover)....... | 10 | | |
| **C.D.S. POSTMARKS** | | | |
| (10) Buckingham Palace, SW1.................................... | 75 | | |
| (11) Gleneagles Hotel – 'Gleneagles Agreement'...... | 15 | | |
| (12) House of Commons, SW1 ................................... | 45 | | |
| (13) House of Lords, SW1 ........................................ | 55 | | |
| (14) Huntingdon – birthplace of Oliver Cromwell... | 12 | | |
| (15) Kensington High St. W8 – Comm. Institute...... | 10 | | |
| (16) Queen Elizabeth Ave., Walsall ......................... | 10 | | |
| (17) Westminster Bridge Rd., SE1 – venue/Conf. .... | 15 | | |

**SLOGAN POSTMARKS** *Inverness Conference Capital; British Presidency. From £15.*

## 16th September 1986 – THE ROYAL AIR FORCE
*17p Dowding/Hurricane; 22p Tedder/Typhoon; 29p Trenchard/DH 9A;*
*31p Harris/Lancaster; 34p Portal/Mosquito*

| **SPECIAL HANDSTAMPS** | | | |
|---|---|---|---|
| (1) First Day of Issue – Philatelic Bureau................. | 5 | – | *Royal Mail* |
| (2) First Day of Issue – Farnborough ...................... | 5 | – | *Royal Mail* |
| (3) 46th Anniversary Battle of Britain, Uxbridge..... | 7 | 10 | *LFDC 55* |
| (4) Hawkinge Aerodrome, Spitfire........................... | 15 | 100 | *Ben500(17)* |
| (5) RAF Scampton, Lincoln ..................................... | 15 | 30 | *BLCS 17* |
| (6) Spitfire, 1936-1986, Eastleigh ............................ | 15 | 20 | *Bradbury* |
| (7) RAFA, Andover, Hants ....................................... | 15 | 15 | *Cotswold* |
| (8) Kenley Aerodrome.............................................. | 15 | 30 | *Fine Arts 18* |
| (9) Re-organisation of RAF, BF 2114 PS ................. | 15 | 20 | *RFDC 49* |
| (10) The Battle of Britain, BF 2123 PS ..................... | 15 | 15 | *Forces* |
| (11) Newark on Trent, RAF........................................ | 15 | 35 | *Newark* |
| (12) Duxford Aviation Society .................................. | 15 | 15 | *Havering* |
| (13) British Philatelic Federation, Norwich .............. | 15 | – | *n.o.c.* |
| (14) Marx Memorial Library, EC1.............................. | 15 | 10 | *Hawkwood* |
| (15) British Forces 1000 ............................................ | 15 | – | *n.o.c.* |
| **C.D.S. POSTMARKS** | | | |
| (16) RAF Biggin Hill *(Biggin Hill village see (22))* . | 100 | | |
| (17) Any other RAF station postmark................*each* | 25 | | |
| (18) Any Field or Forces Post Office..................*each* | 20 | | |
| (19) House of Lords, SW1 ........................................ | 25 | | |
| (20) Moffat, Killearn, Taunton, Cheltenham or Hungerford – birthplaces of Commanders on stamps ......*each* | 25 | | |
| (21) Gravesend, Hawkinge, Digby Aerodrome, Manston, Kenley or Oakington – connected with aircraft featured on stamps........................................*each* | 25 | | |
| (22) Biggin Hill, Cosford Camp, Cranwell, Duxford, Honington Camp or Leuchars – RAF connections .....*each* | 25 | | |

*Also: Churchill, Eastleigh, Gatenby, The Hyde, Hendon, Lancaster, Middle Wallop, Northolt,*
*Pathfinder Village, Stanmore. Prices from £12.*

## 18th November 1986 – CHRISTMAS
*13p The Glastonbury Thorn; 18p The Tanad Valley Plygain;*
*22p The Hebrides Tribute; 31p The Dewsbury Church Knell;*
*34p The Hereford Boy Bishop*

| **SPECIAL HANDSTAMPS** | | | |
|---|---|---|---|
| (1) First Day of Issue – Philatelic Bureau................. | 3 | – | *Royal Mail* |
| (2) First Day of Issue – Bethlehem, Llandeilo........ | 3 | – | *Royal Mail* |
| (3) The Hebrides Tribute, Stornaway ...................... | 10 | 25 | *Ben500(18)* |
| (4) The Devil's Knell, Dewsbury.............................. | 10 | 45 | *DewsburyPC* |
| (5) Christmas Greetings, Folkestone........................ | 10 | 15 | *BenL15* |
| (6) St. Margaret's, Westminster, SW1...................... | 10 | 12 | *Hawkwood* |
| (7) The Glastonbury Thorn....................................... | 10 | 12 | *LFDC 56* |
| (8) English Folk, Dance & Song Soc., Sheffield ..... | 10 | 10 | *BLCS 18* |
| (9) Telecom Technology Showcase, EC1................. | 15 | – | *n.o.c.* |
| (10) Seasons Greetings/Railway Societies, WC1 ...... | 15 | – | *n.o.c.* |
| (11) Christmas, Hereford .......................................... | 10 | 10 | *BLCS 18* |
| (12) NE Parcels Centre, Washington ........................ | 12 | – | *Royal Mail* |
| (13) Lloyd's of London, EC3..................................... | 12 | 40 | *CoverCraft* |
| (14) Battle of the Somme, BF 2124 PS ...................... | 12 | 90 | *RAF (JSF3)* |
| (15) Leicester Circuits .............................................. | 12 | 60 | *L. Circuits* |
| **C.D.S. POSTMARKS** | | | |
| (16) Bethlehem or Nasareth.............................*each* | 15 | | |
| (17) Dewsbury, Glastonbury or Hereford .........*each* | 15 | | |
| (18) Llanrhaeadr-ym-Mochnant (Welsh Plygain) ..... | 15 | | |
| (19) Lochboisdale or Lochmaddy (Hebrides)......*each* | 15 | | |

*In addition: Holy Island, St. Nicholas. Prices from £10.*

**SLOGAN POSTMARKS** *10th Anniversary Codesort. Prices from £20*

## 2nd December 1986 – CHRISTMAS

*12p The Glastonbury Thorn*

| | | ordinary covers £ | | official covers £ |
|---|---|---|---|---|
| **SPECIAL HANDSTAMPS** | | | | |
| (1) | First Day of Issue – Philatelic Bureau................ | 1 | – | *Royal Mail* |
| (2) | The Glastonbury Thorn (changeable date) ....... | 7 | 10 | *LFDC 56* |
| (3) | The Glastonbury Thorn, Glastonbury SC ......... | 7 | 10 | *Cotswold* |
| (4) | Christmas, Glastonbury, Somerset.................... | 7 | 15 | *Ben500(19)* |
| (5) | Telecom Technology Showcase, EC1................. | 10 | – | *n.o.c.* |
| (6) | Biggin Hill, BF 2130 PS ..................................... | 10 | 10 | *RFDC 51* |
| (7) | Submarine 2400, Upholder, Barrow................. | 15 | 200 | *Vickers* |
| **C.D.S. POSTMARKS** | | | | |
| (8) | Bethlehem or Nasareth ..................................... | 25 | | |
| (9) | Glastonbury or Holy Island .............................. | 10 | | |
| **SLOGAN POSTMARKS** | | | | |
| (10) | Happy Christmas The Post Office..................... | 10 | | |

*Note: On the same day of issue, 2nd December, a special Christmas stamp pack was issued containing 36 x 13p Glastonbury Thorn Christmas stamps. These were identical to the 18th November 13p issue. Many of the covers produced for this issue bore both 12p and 13p values – the prices quoted above reflect this. Some covers exist with a complete pane of 18 x 13p stamps. Price from £15.*

*Some **double-dated** covers exist with the set of Christmas stamps postmarked 18th November, and 12p value postmarked 2nd December. Prices from £30.*

## 20th January 1987 – FLOWERS

*18p Gaillardia; 22p Echinops; 31p Echeveria; 34p Colchium*

| | | | | |
|---|---|---|---|---|
| **SPECIAL HANDSTAMPS** | | | | |
| (1) | First Day of Issue – Philatelic Bureau................ | 4 | – | *Royal Mail* |
| (2) | First Day of Issue – Richmond, Surrey.............. | 4 | – | *Royal Mail* |
| (3) | Flowers, Flore, Northampton............................. | 10 | 30 | *Ben500(20)* |
| (4) | Nat. Assoc. Flower Arrangement Soc., SW1 ..... | 10 | 15 | *LFDC 57* |
| (5) | Chelsea Flower Shows, SW3 .............................. | 10 | 25 | *BOCS (3) 1* |
| (6) | Westminster Shows, SW1 ................................... | 10 | 25 | *BOCS (3) 1* |
| (7) | The Lindley Library, SW1 .................................. | 10 | 25 | *BOCS (3) 1* |
| (8) | Wisley Gardens, Royal Hort. Society, .............. | 10 | 25 | *BOCS (3) 1* |
| (9) | Royal Botanical Gardens, Kew.......................... | 10 | 10 | *BLCS 20* |
| (10) | Stephen Thomas Flora & Fauna, Ovingdean .... | 10 | 10 | *G & P* |
| (11) | KEB Horticultural Society, EC1A ...................... | 10 | 35 | *KEB H.S.* |
| (12) | GQT BBC Manchester ........................................ | 10 | 60 | *CoverCraft* |
| (13) | Royal College of Art, SW1................................ | 10 | 60 | *CoverCraft* |
| (14) | Reformation 77 Squadron, BF 2150 PS ............ | 10 | 15 | *RFDC 52* |
| (15) | Bradbury Blinds, Northampton ......................... | 10 | 175 | *BradBlinds* |
| **C.D.S. POSTMARKS** | | | | |
| (16) | Botanic Gdns, Belfast, Kew Gardens or Kew ... | 30 | | |
| (17) | Flowery Field or Spring Gardens....................... | 15 | | |
| (18) | Royal Hospital, Chelsea – Flower Show ........... | 15 | | |
| (19) | Sissinghurst or Ripley – Wisley Gardens .......... | 15 | | |

*Also: Botany Bay, Ipswich, Mickleton, Ovingdean, Saffron Walden, St. Bees, Thistle Hill, Tresco. £10.*

## 24th March 1987 – SIR ISAAC NEWTON

*18p Principia; 22p Motion of Bodies; 31p Opticks; 34p The System of the World*

| | | | | |
|---|---|---|---|---|
| **SPECIAL HANDSTAMPS** | | | | |
| (1) | First Day of Issue – Philatelic Bureau................ | 3 | – | *Royal Mail* |
| (2) | First Day of Issue – Woolsthorpe, Lincs .......... | 3 | – | *Royal Mail* |
| (3) | Isaac Newton, Woolsthorpe, Grantham............ | 10 | 15 | *LFDC 58* |
| (4) | Trinity College, Cambridge................................ | 10 | 35 | *Ben500(21)* |
| (5) | The Old Royal Observatory, SE10...................... | 10 | 17 | *BLCS 21* |
| (6) | Weston Favell Upper School, Northampton ..... | 10 | 15 | *WF School* |
| (7) | Isaac Newton, Grantham.................................... | 10 | 40 | *Maths Assoc* |
| (8) | The George, Newton's Tercentenary, Grantham... | 10 | 50 | *George Hotel* |
| (9) | Apple's 10th Anniversary, Hemel Hempstead ... | 10 | 80 | *Arlington* |
| (10) | Sir Isaac Newton, Science Museum, SW7........ | 10 | 20 | *Cotswold* |
| (11) | Sir Isaac Newton, Royal Society, EC4............... | 10 | – | *n.o.c.* |
| (12) | London College of Music, W1........................... | 10 | 60 | *CoverCraft* |
| (13) | Parachute Descent, BF 2151 PS......................... | 10 | 15 | *RFDC 53* |
| (14) | Taunton Philatelic Sales (depicts apple) ........... | 15 | – | *n.o.c.* |
| **C.D.S. POSTMARKS** | | | | |
| (15) | Colsterworth, Lincs. – Woolsthorpe Manor..... | 15 | | |
| (16) | Grantham – Newton attended King's School ... | 12 | | |
| (17) | Greenwich – Royal Observatory ....................... | 15 | | |
| (18) | House of Commons–MP for Cambridge Univ .. | 12 | | |
| (19) | Kensington – where Newton died ..................... | 12 | | |
| (20) | Newton – Cambridge, Swansea or Wisbech ..... | 12 | | |
| (21) | Regent St., SW1 – Newton's home.................... | 12 | | |
| (22) | Trinity St., Cambridge – Trinity College.......... | 12 | | |

*In addition: Globe Road and Seething Lane EC3. Prices from £10.*

## 12th May 1987 – BRITISH ARCHITECTS IN EUROPE

*18p Ipswich (Foster); 22p Paris (Rogers & Piano);*
*31p Stuttgart (Stirling & Wilford); 34p Luxembourg (Lasdun)*

| | | | | |
|---|---|---|---|---|
| **SPECIAL HANDSTAMPS** | | | | |
| (1) | First Day of Issue – Philatelic Bureau................ | 3 | – | *Royal Mail* |
| (2) | First Day of Issue – Ipswich.............................. | 3 | – | *Royal Mail* |

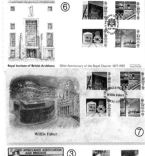

## Architects in Europe (contd.)

| | ordinary covers £ | official covers £ | |
|---|---|---|---|
| (3) British Architects in Europe, W1 | 10 | 10 | LFDC 59 |
| (4) The Clore Gallery, SW1 | 10 | 20 | Ben500(22) |
| (5) R.I.B.A., Macclesfield | 10 | 10 | BLCS 22 |
| (6) R.I.B.A., Royal Charter, W1 | 10 | 15 | CoverCraft |
| (7) Willis Faber, Heritage & Progress, Ipswich | 10 | 25 | CoverCraft |
| (8) Clinical Biochemists, Eastbourne | 12 | 25 | A.C.B. |
| (9) Royal Engineers, BF 1987 PS | 12 | 12 | RFDC 54 |
| (10) Gallantry Awards RNLI, SE1 | 12 | 40 | Pilgrim |
| (11) London - Venice, Orient Express, Folkestone | 12 | 60 | BenSG3 |

**C.D.S. POSTMARKS**

| | |
|---|---|
| (12) Ascot – Chartered Institute of Building | 10 |
| (13) Euston Centre BO – James Stirling | 10 |
| (14) Gt. Portland St. – R.I.B.A. | 10 |
| (15) Hammersmith W6 – Richard Rogers | 10 |
| (16) Ipswich – Willis Faber Building | 10 |
| (17) New Buildings, Londonderry | 25 |
| (18) Vauxhall Bridge Rd. – Denys, Lasdun | 10 |

*Also: Buxton Road, Macclesfield; Kirkwall; Paris Ave.; Stirling;Town Centre. From £8.*

**SLOGAN POSTMARKS**

*St. Magnus Cathedral; The Copthorne; Arndale Centre; Collect British Stamps; Nissan. From £35.*

### 16th June 1987 – ST. JOHN AMBULANCE

*18p Early Duties; 22p Wartime; 31p Pop Concert; 34p Transplant Organ Flight*

**SPECIAL HANDSTAMPS**

| | | | |
|---|---|---|---|
| (1) First Day of Issue – Philatelic Bureau | 3 | – | Royal Mail |
| (2) First Day of Issue – London EC1 | 3 | – | Royal Mail |
| (3) St. John's Gate, SJA Exhibition, EC1 | 12 | 15 | LFDC 60 |
| (4) 2nd Oldest Div. SJA Brigade, Heywood | 12 | 15 | Cotswold |
| (5) St. John Ambulance, Hyde Park, SW1 | 12 | 30 | Ben50023 |
| (6) St. John Ambulance, Stansted | 12 | 15 | BLCS 23 |
| (7) St. John Ambulance Brigade, SW1 | 12 | 15 | Arlington |
| (8) St. Margaret's Hospital, Epping | 12 | 15 | Arlington |
| (9) London - Venice, Orient Express, Folkestone | 15 | 125 | BenSG3 |
| (10) Maiden Voyage, Waverley, Glasgow | 15 | 50 | Benham |

**ORDINARY F.D.I. POSTMARKS**

| | |
|---|---|
| (11) Southport (Southport SJA Centre cover) | 20 |

**C.D.S. POSTMARKS**

| | |
|---|---|
| (12) Ashford – John Furley, Founder/Birthplace | 15 |
| (13) Bow or Coventry – The Blitz (22p) | 15 |
| (14) Epping or Stansted – The Airwing (34p) | 15 |
| (15) Farringdon Rd. or London EC – St. John's Gate | 15 |
| (16) Harrow – First road accident attended by SJA | 15 |
| (17) Margate (1st Corp) or Woolwich (1st Centre) | 15 |
| (18) Mount St., W1 – Hyde Park (31p) | 15 |
| (19) Papworth – Transplant surgery (34p) | 15 |
| (20) RAF Benson – First flight of Air Wing (34p) | 20 |
| (21) St. John's or St. John's Chapel | 15 |

*Also: GWR TPO 'Up', House of Commons, House of Lords, Muswell Hill, Oldham, Orthopaedic Hospital, Royal Hospital School, and Windsor Great Park. From £10.*

**SLOGAN POSTMARKS** *British Deaf Assoc.; Postcode your Property. From £5.*

### 21st July 1987 – SCOTTISH HERALDRY

*18p Lord Lyon King of Arms; 22p HRH The Duke of Rothesay;
31p Royal Scottish Academy; 34p Royal Society of Edinburgh*

**SPECIAL HANDSTAMPS**

| | | | |
|---|---|---|---|
| (1) First Day of Issue – Philatelic Bureau | 4 | – | Royal Mail |
| (2) First Day of Issue – Rothesay, Isle of Bute | 4 | – | Royal Mail |
| (3) Order of the Thistle, Edinburgh | 12 | 25 | Ben500(24) |
| (4) Drum Castle, Banchory | 12 | 15 | BLCS 24 |
| (5) Crathes Castle, Banchory | 12 | 12 | BLCS 24 |
| (6) Dunkeld, Perthshire | 12 | 15 | BLCS 24 |
| (7) Bannockburn, Stirling | 12 | 12 | BLCS 24 |
| (8) Mary Queen of Scots, Fotheringhay | 12 | 15 | LFDC 61 |
| (9) Royal Scottish Academy, Edinburgh | 12 | 40 | CoverCraft |
| (10) Lord Cameron of Balhousie, BF 2144 PS | 12 | 12 | RFDC 56 |
| (11) Glasgow Herald | 15 | 25 | Pilgrim |
| (12) Duke & Duchess of York | 15 | 35 | Y. Minster |
| (13) Queen's School Rheindahlen, BF 21787 PS | 15 | 45 | Queens Sch |
| (14) The Royal Tournament, BF 2142 PS | 15 | 25 | Forces |

**C.D.S. POSTMARKS**

| | |
|---|---|
| (15) Banff – home of Lord Lyon King of Arms | 15 |
| (16) Bannockburn – famous battle | 15 |
| (17) Buckingham Palace, London SW1 | 50 |
| (18) Edinburgh | 15 |
| (19) Frederick St., Edinburgh – Royal Soc. of Ed. | 15 |
| (20) Holyrood – Royal residence in Edinburgh | 16 |
| (21) House of Lords, SW1 | 15 |
| (22) Largs or Luncarty – adoption of Thistle | 15 |
| (23) Rothesay – arms of Duke of Rothesay (22p) | 15 |
| (24) Scone – Scone Palace | 35 |
| (25) St. Andrews – Patron Saint of Scotland | 20 |
| (26) St. Mary St., Edinburgh – Royal Scot. Academy | 15 |

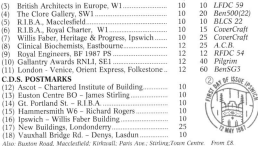

1987

*Also: Caledonian TPO, Dingwall, Elgin, Gordon, Kintore, Linlithgow, Prince Charles Ave, Selkirk, Thistle Hill, Ullapool. Prices from £10.*

**SLOGAN POSTMARKS**
*Etterick & Lauderdale: Aberdeen Youth Fest; Inverness Conf Capital;St. Magnus Cathedral. £25.*

---

## 8th September 1987 – VICTORIAN BRITAIN

*18p Great Exhibition: 'Monarch of the Glen'; Grace Darling*
*22p 'Great Eastern'; Prince Albert; Mrs. Beeton*
*31p Albert Memorial; Benjamin Disraeli; Ballot Box*
*34p Relief of Mafeking; Marconi Wireless; Diamond Jubilee*

**SPECIAL HANDSTAMPS**

| | | | |
|---|---|---|---|
| (1) | First Day of Issue – Philatelic Bureau | 4 | – Royal Mail |
| (2) | First Day of Issue – Newport, Isle of Wight | 4 | – Royal Mail |
| (3) | N.T. for Scotland, Edinburgh | 12 | 20 BLCS 25 |
| (4) | Victorian Britain VA, SW7 | 12 | 15 BLCS 25 |
| (5) | Queen Victoria, 1837-1901, SW1 | 12 | 15 LFDC 62 |
| (6) | Victorian Britain, Balmoral | 12 | 30 Ben500(25) |
| (7) | Victorian Britain, Windsor | 12 | 50 BenSG4 |
| (8) | Southampton Victorian Post Office | 15 | – Royal Mail |
| (9) | Historic Worcester Postmarks Picture Card | 15 | – Royal Mail |
| (10) | Mrs. Beeton's, W1 | 20 | 75 Arlington |
| (11) | Calderdale's Victorian Inheritance, Halifax | 20 | – Post Office |
| (12) | Marconi Philatelic Society, Gt Baddow | 12 | 20 G & P |
| (13) | Victorian Britain, Edensor, Bakewell | 12 | 40 CoverCraft |
| (14) | Henry Archer, Festiniog Rly., Porthmadog | 20 | 50 BenL16 |
| (15) | National Postal Museum, 1966 -1987, EC1 | 12 | – n.o.c. |
| (16) | Ballooning in British Army, BF 2156 PS | 12 | 15 RFDC 57 |
| (17) | Ballymena Rugby Football Club | 12 | 40 Bally RFC |
| (18) | London SW (permanent handstamp) | 12 | – n.o.c. |
| (19) | Royal Navy Equip. Exhib., BF 2187 PS | 12 | 25 Forces |

**C.D.S. POSTMARKS**

| | | |
|---|---|---|
| (20) | Balmoral Castle | 325 |
| (21) | Bamburgh – Grace Darling | 15 |
| (22) | Beaconsfield – Disraeli/Lord Beaconsfield | 15 |
| (23) | Buckingham Palace, SW1 | 150 |
| (24) | East Cowes – near to Osborne House | 15 |
| (25) | Fleet St., – 'Mafeking' on newspaper hoarding. | 15 |
| (26) | Hatch End, Pinner – Mrs. Beeton | 15 |
| (27) | House of Commons or Lords | 15 |
| (28) | Hughenden Valley – home of Disraeli | 25 |
| (29) | Kensington – V & A, Albert Memorial etc | 15 |
| (30) | Maida Vale – Landseer 'Monarch of the Glen' | 15 |
| (31) | Old Windsor or Windsor Great Park | 15 |
| (32) | Prince Consort Rd., Queen Victoria Rd etc | 15 |
| (33) | St. Margaret's Bay, Dover – wireless | 30 |
| (34) | Theobald's Road – birthplace of Disraeli | 15 |
| (35) | West Ferry Rd., Millwall – 'The Great Eastern' | 15 |
| (36) | Westow St., Norwood – resited Crystal Palace. | 15 |

*In addition: Britannia, Paddington, Nelson, Woburn. Prices from £10.*

**SLOGAN POSTMARKS** *Church of Latter Day Saints; The Times. From £20.*

## 13th OCTOBER 1987 – STUDIO POTTERY

*18p Bernard Leach; 26p Elizabeth Fritsch; 31p Lucie Rie; 34p Hans Coper*

**SPECIAL HANDSTAMPS**

| | | | |
|---|---|---|---|
| (1) | First Day of Issue – Philatelic Bureau | 3 | – Royal Mail |
| (2) | First Day of Issue – St. Ives, Cornwall | 3 | – Royal Mail |
| (3) | Craftsmen Potters Assoc'n, W1 | 10 | 10 LFDC 63 |
| (4) | Studio Pottery, Potters Corner, Ashford | 10 | 15 Ben500(26) |
| (5) | Studio Pottery, VA, SW7 | 10 | 10 BLCS 26 |
| (6) | Designed by Tony Evans, Shrewsbury | 10 | 30 Tony Evans |
| (7) | Stoke-on-Trent, Philatelic Counter | 10 | – n.o.c. |
| (8) | Battle of Britain, BF 2154 PS | 9 | 15 RFDC 58 |
| (8a) | Stoke Philatelic Counter | 15 | 40 Goss Coll. Club |

**C.D.S. POSTMARKS**

| | | |
|---|---|---|
| (9) | Carbis Bay, St. Ives – home of Bernard Leach . | 25 |
| (10) | Chelsea, London SW3 – annual Craft Fair | 10 |
| (11) | Frome, Somerset – Hans Coper's studio | 10 |
| (12) | Marble Arch, W1 – Lucie Rie's studio | 10 |
| (13) | Poplar, E14 – Elizabeth Fritsch's studio | 10 |
| (14) | South Kensington – V&A Museum | 10 |
| (15) | St. Ives – home of studio pottery | 12 |
| (16) | Stennack, St. Ives – Leach's pottery | 25 |
| (17) | Welwyn Garden – Elizabeth Fritsch | 10 |
| (18) | Whitchurch – birthplace of Elizabeth Fritsch | 10 |

*Also: Barlaston, Bathwick St., Dartington, Digswell, Euston Centre, Leach Ln, Potters Bar, Pottery Rd. From £8.*

**SLOGAN POSTMARKS** *Redhill Philatelic Soc.; Royal Mail Code Show. From £15.*

## 17th November 1987 – CHRISTMAS

*13p, 18p, 26p, 31p, 34p A child's view of Christmas*

**SPECIAL HANDSTAMPS**

| | | | |
|---|---|---|---|
| (1) | First Day of Issue – Philatelic Bureau | 4 | – Royal Mail |
| (2) | First Day of Issue – Bethlehem, Llandeilo | 4 | – Royal Mail |

*1987 Christmas (contd.)*     **ordinary covers**     **official covers**

| | | £ | | £ |
|---|---|---|---|---|
| (3) | Christmas, Toys Hill, Westerham | 10 | 25 | *Ben500(27)* |
| (4) | 175th Anniv. Birth of Charles Dickens | 10 | 15 | *LFDC 64* |
| (5) | Hamley's Toy Shop, W1 | 10 | 35 | *CoverCraft* |
| (6) | Christmas Common, Oxford | 10 | 17 | *BLCS 27* |
| (7) | Holy Cross Church, Pattishall | 10 | 30 | *HC Church* |
| (8) | Christmas, Christleton, Chester | 10 | 10 | *Benham* |
| (9) | Christmas 1987, Star Underprint, Star | 10 | 17 | *B'ham500(28)* |
| (10) | Telecom Technology Showcase, EC4 | 15 | – | *n.o.c.* |
| (11) | RFA Argus, BP 2157 PS | 10 | 20 | *FAAMuseum* |

**C.D.S. POSTMARKS**

| | | |
|---|---|---|
| (12) | Bethlehem or Nasareth | 20 |
| (13) | Regent St – near to Hamley's Toy Shop | 15 |

*Also: Child Okeford, Childs Hill, Fir Tree, Holy Island, Noel Road,
Playing Place, St. Nicholas, Snowshill, Star, Sidmouth. From £10.*

**SLOGAN POSTMARKS**

| | | |
|---|---|---|
| (14) | Gold Angels for Xmas – Pobjoy Mint | 75 |
| (15) | Church of Jesus Christ of Latter Day Saints | 40 |
| (16) | Christmas Shopping is Fun, Nottingham | 140 |
| (17) | Gold Angels available from Jewellers | 10(s) |

**CHRISTMAS DISCOUNT 13P MINIATURE SHEET**

| | |
|---|---|
| Covers with gutter pair from sheet and special h/s | 4 |
| Covers with whole miniature sheet and special h/s | 20 |

## 19th January 1988 – THE LINNEAN SOCIETY
*18p Bull-rout (fish); 26p Yellow Waterlily; 31p Bewick's Swan; 34p Morel (fungus)*
**SPECIAL HANDSTAMPS**

| | | | | |
|---|---|---|---|---|
| (1) | First Day of Issue – Philatelic Bureau | 3 | – | *Royal Mail* |
| (2) | First Day of Issue – Burlington House, W1 | 3 | – | *Royal Mail* |
| (3) | 1788-1988 The Linnean Society | 12 | 20 | *LFDC 65* |
| (4) | British Natural History, Waterside | 12 | 25 | *Ben500(29)* |
| (5) | The Wildfowl Trust, Welney | 12 | 20 | *BLCS 29* |
| (6) | The Wildfowl Trust, Swan Lake | 12 | 15 | *BLCS 29* |
| (7) | Sir Thomas Sopwith, BF 2158 PS | 12 | 15 | *RFDC 60* |
| (8) | The Emperor's Warriors Exhibition, SW1 | 12 | 30 | *Pilgrim* |

**C.D.S. POSTMARKS**

| | | |
|---|---|---|
| (9) | Broadwick St., W1 – first meeting of Society | 12 |
| (10) | Norwich – B/place of founder Sir J. E. Smith | 12 |
| (11) | Fleur-de-lis – flower of the lily | 15 |
| (12) | Gotenburg, Sweden PAQUEBOT | 50 |
| (13) | POs near to Burlington House, W1 | 12 |
| (14) | Holloway – Edward Lear (illustration 31p) | 12 |
| (15) | Kew Gardens or Slimbridge | 35 |
| (16) | Lambeth – James Sowerby (illustration 34p) | 12 |
| (17) | Ovingham & Mickley Sq., North'land – Bewick | 12 |
| (18) | Polperro – Dr. Jonathan Couch (manuscript 18p) | 20 |

*Also: Abbotsbury, Badger's Mount, Bosherton, House of Commons, Lillies Leaf, Nettleham,
Selbourne, Swanpool, Waterside, Welney. From £12.*

## 1st March 1988 – THE WELSH BIBLE 1588-1988
*18p William Morgan; 26p William Salesbury;
31p Richard Davies; 34p Richard Parry*
**SPECIAL HANDSTAMPS**

| | | | | |
|---|---|---|---|---|
| (1) | First Day of Issue – Philatelic Bureau | 4 | – | *Royal Mail* |
| (2) | First Day of Issue – Ty Mawr Wybrnant | 4 | – | *Royal Mail* |
| (3) | Bible Society, St. David's Day, St. Asaph | 10 | 15 | *LFDC 66* |
| (4) | Welsh Bible, Caernarfon Castle | 10 | 30 | *Ben500(30)* |
| (5) | Y Beibl Yn Gymraeg, Llanrhaeadr | 10 | 15 | *BLCS 30* |
| (6) | Translators of Welsh Bible, St. Asaph | 10 | 13 | *BLCS 30* |
| (7) | Soldiers' Scripture Assoc., BF 2159 PS | 10 | 15 | *RFDC 61* |
| (8) | 1588-1988 Ty Mawr Wybrnant, Gwynedd | 10 | 20 | *CoverCraft* |
| (9) | Spring Stampex, SW1 | 10 | – | *Post Office* |

**C.D.S. POSTMARKS**

| | | |
|---|---|---|
| (10) | Abergwili, Bala, Conway, Cwm, Dyserth, Llandaff, Llanrhaeadr Ym, Llansanffraid, Llansannan, Penmachno, Welshpool all associated with Bible translators | 15 |
| (11) | Bethlehem, St Davids or St. Asaph | 25 |
| (12) | House of Commons or Lords | 25 |

*In addition: Ruthin, Trinity St. Prices from £5.*

**SLOGAN POSTMARKS**

| | | |
|---|---|---|
| (13) | Jesus is Alive! | 75 |

*In addition: Oldham Education Week. £95.*

## 22nd March 1988 – SPORT
*18p Gymnastics; 26p Skiing; 31p Lawn Tennis; 34p Association Football*
**SPECIAL HANDSTAMPS**

| | | | | |
|---|---|---|---|---|
| (1) | First Day of Issue – Philatelic Bureau | 4 | – | *Royal Mail* |
| (2) | First Day of Issue – Wembley | 4 | – | *Royal Mail* |
| (3) | 100 Years Ago Accrington | 10 | 60 | *Dawn* |
| (4) | 100 Years of League Football, Aston Villa | 10 | 60 | *Dawn* |

79

## Sport (contd.)

| | | ordinary covers £ | official covers £ |
|---|---|---|---|
| (5) | 100 Years of League Football, Wolves | 10 | 50 *Dawn* |
| (6) | 100 Years of League Football, Everton | 10 | 50 *Dawn* |
| (7) | Record Holders, Liverpool FC | 10 | 60 *Dawn* |
| (8) | Manchester United | 10 | 60 *Dawn* |
| (9) | Record Holders, Tottenham Hotspur | 10 | 20 *BLCS 31* |
| (10) | Record Holders, Arsenal FC | 10 | 20 *BLCS 31* |
| (11) | Preston North End Football Club, Preston | 10 | 12 *LFDC 67* |
| (12) | Lawn Tennis at Edgbaston | 10 | 35 *Ben500(31)* |
| (13) | The Lawn Tennis Association, W14 | 10 | 20 *Cotswold* |
| (14) | Amateur Gymnastics Assoc., Slough | 10 | 20 *Cotswold* |
| (15) | 'A Question of Sport', Manchester | 10 | 15 *CoverCraft* |
| (16) | Physical Training Corps, BF 2161 PS | 10 | 15 *RFDC 62* |

**C.D.S. POSTMARKS**

| | | |
|---|---|---|
| (17) | Accrington, Blackburn, Bolton, Burnley, Derby, Preston, Stoke – founder members of League .. | 15 |
| (18) | Aviemore – ski centre | 15 |
| (19) | Deepdale Rd., Preston – Preston North End ... | 15 |
| (20) | Eccleston St., SW1 – HQ of Ski Association .... | 15 |
| (21) | Edgbaston – first lawn tennis court | 15 |
| (22) | Fleet St. – first meeting of Football League | 15 |
| (23) | Any Wimbledon pmk | 20 |
| (24) | Leamington Spa – world's first tennis club | 15 |
| (25) | Lilleshall – National Gymnastics Centre | 15 |
| (26) | Liverpool – most successful League Club | 10 |
| (27) | Lytham – HQ of the Football League | 15 |
| (28) | Meadow Lane – Notts County FC | 20 |
| (29) | Slough – HQ/Amateur Gymnastics Assoc'n .... | 12 |
| (30) | Villa Road – near to Aston Villa FC | 50 |
| (31) | Wembley B.O. | 12 |
| (32) | Wembley Park | 20 |

*In addition: Highbury, North End Road W14. Prices from £10.*

## 10th May 1988 – TRANSPORT & COMMUNICATIONS

*18p 'Mallard'; 26p 'Queen Elizabeth'; 31p Glasgow Tram; 34p Handley Page*

**SPECIAL HANDSTAMPS**

| | | | |
|---|---|---|---|
| (1) | First Day of Issue – Philatelic Bureau | 3 | – *Royal Mail* |
| (2) | First Day of Issue – Glasgow | 3 | – *Royal Mail* |
| (3) | Nat Postal Museum Railways and the Post | 7 | – *n.o.c.* |
| (4) | Mallard, National Rly. Museum, York | 12 | 25 *BLCS 32* |
| (5) | Mallard, Rail Riders, York | 12 | 75 *CoverCraft* |
| (6) | T.P.O. 150 Anniversary, Peterborough | 12 | 50 *Nene V. Rly* |
| (7) | The Jessop Collection, Diss | 12 | 20 *P.P.S.* |
| (8) | Sheffield & Rotherham Railway | 12 | 85 *Br. Rail* |
| (9) | Video Cinecosse Film, Ellen | 12 | 125 *Cinecosse* |
| (10) | R.M.S. Queen Elizabeth, SW1 | 12 | 20 *Arlington* |
| (11) | R.M.S. Queen Elizabeth, Southampton | 12 | 15 *LFDC 68* |
| (12) | First Atlantic Convoy, BF 2165 PS | 12 | 25 *FAA Museum* |
| (13) | The Museum of Transport, Glasgow | 12 | 20 *BLCS 32* |
| (14) | Imperial Airways, Rochester | 12 | 35 *Ben500(32)* |
| (15) | Croydon Airport Terminal, BF 2162 PS | 12 | 20 *RFDC 63* |
| (16) | National Postal Museum (AirMail routes) | 12 | – *n.o.c.* |
| (17) | TGWU, SW1 | 12 | 40 *CoverCraft* |
| (18) | Laser, 1973-1988, Hythe | 12 | 25 *G&P* |
| (19) | Illustrated by Andrew Davidson, Bromley | 12 | – *n.o.c.* |
| (20) | Designed by Carroll Dempsey & Thirkell | 12 | 35 *CD&T(card)* |
| (21) | Lloyd's of London, EC3 | 12 | 30 *CoverCraft* |
| (22) | 19th Century Post Box Discovery, Spilsby | 12 | 30 *SpilsbyCofT* |
| (23) | Transams By Technology, WC1 | 12 | 125 *Transams* |
| (24) | Heathrow or NE Parcel Centre changeable date .. | 12 | – *n.o.c.* |

**C.D.S. POSTMARKS (inc. T.P.O. CANCELS)**

| | | |
|---|---|---|
| (25) | Berkhamsted – first use of T.P.O. apparatus ... | 15 |
| (26) | Central Stn., Edinburgh; or Nunthorpe Stn | 15 |
| (27) | Croydon or Purley – Croydon Airport | 30 |
| (28) | Clydebank – 'Queen Elizabeth' built here | 15 |
| (29) | Cricklewood – Handley Page HP42 built here | 15 |
| (30) | Doncaster – where 'Mallard' was built | 15 |
| (31) | Essendine – 'Mallard'/speed record | 15 |
| (32) | Garden Festival – Glasgow's trams | 25 |
| (33) | Hong Kong BFPO 1 – 'Queen Elizabeth' | 100 |
| (34) | Mosspark, Glasgow – tram destination (31p).. | 10 |
| (35) | Southampton – home port/'Queen Elizabeth' .. | 15 |
| (36) | Springburn, Glasgow – first tram route | 15 |
| (37) | Tiverton – where HP42 ended its days | 15 |
| (38) | York – home of 'Mallard' | 15 |
| (39) | Any TPO postmark ...................................*from* | 15 |

*Also:Crich, Forton Services, Heathrow Airport, Hope St., New York, Queen Elizabeth Ave. From £10.*

**SLOGAN POSTMARKS**

| | | |
|---|---|---|
| (40) | Only Fools Play on Railway Lines | 25 |
| (41) | Paisley 500 (Paisley's last tram No. 146) | 20 |
| (42) | Royal Mail/Garden Festival | 25 |
| (43) | Grampians – Going Places – Aberdeen | 30 |
| (44) | West Midlands 100 Great Days Out | 35 |

*In addition: Postcode your Property; Tobormory. Prices from £15.*

## 21st June 1988 – AUSTRALIAN BICENTENARY

*18p Historical - Early Settler and Clipper ship;* **ordinary** **official**
*18p Constitutional - The Queen & Parliament;* **covers** **covers**
*34p Sports - W.G.Grace and Tennis* **£** **£**
*34p The Arts – Lennon, Shakespeare, Sydney Opera Hse;*

**SPECIAL HANDSTAMPS**

| | | | |
|---|---|---|---|
| (1) | First Day of Issue – Philatelic Bureau............... | 3 | – *Royal Mail* |
| (2) | First Day of Issue – Portsmouth............................ | 3 | – *Royal Mail* |
| (3) | Bicentenary of Australia, SW1............................ | 12 | 20 *LFDC 69* |
| (4) | Australian Bicentenary, Portsmouth.................. | 12 | 40 *BenSG5* |
| (5) | James Cook Museum, Marton-in-Cleveland.......... | 12 | 15 *S. Muscroft* |
| (6) | Links with Australia, Amy Johnson, Hull ......... | 12 | 50 *Bradbury* |
| (7) | GB Cricketing Links, Old Trafford.................... | 12 | 75 *S.P.* |
| (8) | GB Cricketing Links, Edgbaston........................ | 12 | 75 *S.P.* |
| (9) | GB Cricketing Links, Trent Bridge.................... | 12 | 75 *S.P.* |
| (10) | GB Cricketing Links, The Oval, SE11 ............. | 12 | 75 *S.P.* |
| (11) | GB Cricketing Links, Headingley .................... | 12 | 75 *S.P.* |
| (12) | GB Cricketing Links, Lords.............................. | 12 | 15 *S.P.* |
| (13) | Wedgwood Australian Bicentenary Barlaston .. | 12 | 50 *Arlington* |
| (14) | Botany Bay, Enfield........................................ | 12 | 30 *Ben500(33)* |
| (15) | Bombardment of Bardia, BF 2178 PS.............. | 12 | 25 *FAAMuseum* |
| (16) | Australian Bicentennial, EC............................. | 12 | 35 *CoverCraft* |
| (17) | Lawn Tennis Museum, SW19............................ | 12 | 25 *H.R.* |
| (18) | R.A.F. Cottesmore, TTT3, BF 2177 PS ............. | 12 | 15 *RFDC 64* |

**C.D.S. POSTMARKS**

| | | |
|---|---|---|
| (19) | Bathampton – Capt.Phillip/first Gov. of NSW . | 15 |
| (20) | Botany Bay or Penny Lane............................... | 15 |
| (21) | Downend (Grace) or Whitby (Cook) ........*each* | 20 |
| (22) | Hambledon – birthplace of English Cricket ..... | 20 |
| (23) | House of Commons or Lords............................. | 30 |
| (24) | Portsmouth or Ryde -  First Fleet ..................... | 15 |
| (25) | Stratford-upon-Avon or Windsor...................... | 15 |

*Also: Buckingham Palace, Croydon, Headingley, Kennington Park, Marton-in-Cleveland, Melbourne, Queen Elizabeth Ave., St. Bravels, Sydney, Road, Wimbledon. Prices from £12.*

**SLOGAN POSTMARKS**

| | | |
|---|---|---|
| (26) | 1588-1788-1988 Tobormory 200, Oban ............. | 275 |

*In addition: Royal Mail/Glasgow G.F.; Ullapool Bicentenary. Prices from £15.*

**DOUBLE POSTMARKED COVERS**
This issue was the first 'joint issue' involving Royal Mail.  Arrangements were made for British collectors to send their British first day covers to Australia where the Australia stamps were affixed and cancelled on 21st June 1988. Prices below are for covers with the FULL SET of both British & Australian stamps.

| | | |
|---|---|---|
| (1) | Any British handstamp + Australian h/s .......... | 35 |
| (2) | Any British C.D.S. + Australian handstamp....... | 40 |

## 19th July 1988 – THE ARMADA 1588

*5 x 18p stamps show the progress of the Armada, viz:*
*The Lizard; Plymouth; Isle of Wight; Calais; and North Sea.*

**SPECIAL HANDSTAMPS**

| | | | |
|---|---|---|---|
| (1) | First Day of Issue – Philatelic Bureau............... | 3 | – *Royal Mail* |
| (2) | First Day of Issue – Plymouth ............................ | 3 | – *Royal Mail* |
| (3) | Royal Naval College, SE10................................ | 12 | 40 *CoverCraft* |
| (4) | Spanish Armada Tilbury (Elizabeth on horse).. | 12 | 40 *BenSG6* |
| (5) | Spanish Armada, Effingham.............................. | 12 | 30 *Ben500(34)* |
| (6) | Sighting of Armada, BF 2179 PS ...................... | 12 | 15 *RFDC 65* |
| (7) | Armada 400 Plymouth (circular)...................... | 12 | 15 *PlyPhilSoc* |
| (8) | Armada 400 Years, Plymouth (rectangular)...... | 12 | – *n.o.c.* |
| (9) | Armada Anniversary, Tavistock........................ | 12 | 25 *TavBkShop* |
| (10) | First Armada 400 Beacon, The Lizard............... | 12 | 30 *BenL19* |
| (11) | Armada 400, Battle of Gravelines, Dover ......... | 12 | 10 *BLCS 34* |
| (12) | Spanish Armada, Tilbury (Tudor Rose)............. | 12 | 20 *LFDC 70* |
| (13) | John Hurleston, Mariner, Chester..................... | 12 | 10 *Havering* |
| (14) | Royal Tournament, BF 2181 PS ........................ | 12 | 25 *Forces* |
| (15) | Scout Camp, Blair Atholl, Pitlochry................. | 12 | 20 *Scouts* |
| (16) | Merriott Mouldings Ltd.................................... | 12 | 125 *Cotswold* |
| (17) | Plymouth Philatelic Counter (Drake) ............... | 25 | – *n.o.c.* |
| (18) | Portsmouth Philatelic Counter (Mary Rose) ..... | 15 | – *n.o.c.* |

**C.D.S. POSTMARKS**

| | | |
|---|---|---|
| (19) | Altofts - birthplace of Sir Martin Frobisher...... | 25 |
| (20) | Buckland Monachorum – home of Drake......... | 25 |
| (21) | Calais or Dover + PAQUEBOT markings.*each* | 35 |
| (22) | Drake, Plymouth.............................................. | 300 |
| (23) | Effingham – b/place of Lord Howard .............. | 20 |
| (24) | Greenwich – b/place of Queen Elizabeth I....... | 20 |
| (25) | Maritime Mail I.S. London............................... | 100 |
| (26) | Paquebot, London or Santander ...................... | 50 |
| (27) | Portland, Southwell, or Bonchurch – battles ... | 20 |
| (28) | Plymouth or West Hoe, Plymouth ................... | 20 |
| (29) | Sandwich – prepared to meet invasion ........... | 20 |
| (30) | St. Mary's, Isle of Scilly – first sighting........... | 20 |
| (31) | Tavistock – birthplace of Sir Francis Drake...... | 20 |
| (32) | The Lizard & Berwick – first & last beacons ... | 15 |
| (33) | Tilbury – where Elizabeth rallied her troops..... | 15 |
| (34) | Tobormory, Hope and Fair Isle – wreck sites .... | 25 |

*Also: Beacon, Drakes Broughton, House of Commons, House of Lords. From £12.*

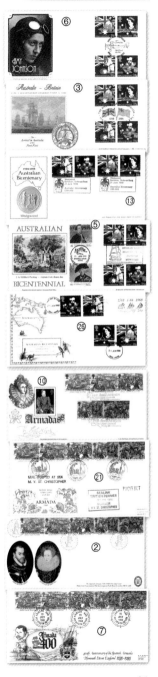

| Armada (contd.) | ordinary covers £ | official covers £ |
|---|---|---|

**SLOGAN POSTMARKS**

| | | |
|---|---|---|
| (35) 400th Anniv. of Spanish Armada | 50 | |
| (36) Tobomory 200, 1588-1788-1988 | 375 | |

*In addition: Isle of Skye; Royal Mail Letters Supports G.G.F. Prices from £25.*

## 6th September 1988 – EDWARD LEAR
*19p 'The Owl and the Pussycat'; 27p Pen Sketch; 32p Alphabet 'C'; 35p Rhyme*

**SPECIAL HANDSTAMPS**

| | | | |
|---|---|---|---|
| (1) | First Day of Issue – Philatelic Bureau | 4 | – *Royal Mail* |
| (2) | First Day of Issue – London N7 | 4 | – *Royal Mail* |
| (3) | Edward Lear, Foss Rampant, Learmouth | 12 | 30 *Ben500(35)* |
| (4) | Edward Lear Centenary, Knowsley | 12 | 15 *LFDC 71* |
| (5) | Hull Schools Reorganization | 12 | 20 *HullSchools* |
| (6) | Birthplace of Edward Lear, Holloway, N7 | 12 | 15 *BLCS 35* |
| (7) | Designed by the Partners, Edward Lear, EC1 | 12 | – *n.o.c.* |
| (8) | Knowsley, from Menagerie to Safari Park | 12 | 25 *CoverCraft* |
| (9) | Coeliac Symposium, St. Batholomew's, EC1 | 12 | 175 *St. Barts* |
| (10) | Farnborough International, BF 2173 PS | 10 | 15 *RFDC 66* |

**C.D.S. POSTMARKS**

| | | |
|---|---|---|
| (11) | Camden, or Theobald's Rd. – homes of Lear | 15 |
| (12) | Chester, Gretna, Portree, Ryde – Lear's rhymes | 15 |
| (13) | Holloway – birthplace of Lear | 15 |
| (14) | Knowsley – Lear wrote his nonsense verse | 15 |
| (15) | Regents Park Rd–Lear drew birds & animals at the Zoological Gardens | 15 |

*Also: Catsfield, Catshill, Derry Hill, East Cowes, Foss Mount, Freshwater, Luimneach, Owlsmoor, Petworth, Victoria St, Winchelsea. From £10.*

**SLOGAN POSTMARKS** *Isle of Skye; Brighton Guide; Guide Dog Week; Tobomory. From £15.*

## 27th September 1988 – EDWARD LEAR
*Miniature Sheet*

**SPECIAL HANDSTAMPS**

| | | | |
|---|---|---|---|
| (1) | First Day of Issue – Philatelic Bureau | 5 | – *Royal Mail* |
| (2) | First Day of Issue – London, N22 | 5 | – *Royal Mail* |
| (3) | Edward Lear, Foss Rampant, Learmouth | 12 | 20 *BLCS 36* |
| (4) | Edward Lear Centenary, Knowsley | 12 | 15 *LFDC 72* |
| (5) | Edward Lear Centenary, Stampex, SW | 12 | 12 *BLCS 36* |
| (6) | Birthplace of Edward Lear, Holloway, N7 | 12 | 35 *Ben500(36)* |
| (7) | Stampway to the World, Liverpool | 15 | – *n.o.c.* |
| (8) | Autumn Stampex/BPE, SW1 | 12 | 20 *Stampex* |
| (9) | Royal Mail Exhibition Card, Stampex/BPE | 12 | – *Royal Mail* |
| (10) | Cancer & Leukaemia, BF 2182 PS | 12 | 15 *RFDC 67* |
| (11) | 150 Wolverton, Milton Keynes | 12 | – *n.o.c.* |
| (12) | HMS Leamington, BF 2189 PS | 12 | 25 *FAAMuseum* |
| (13) | RMS Queen Elizabeth, Clydebank | 12 | 50 *Clydebank* |
| (14) | Royal Academy of Arts, Henry Moore, W1 | 12 | 25 *Pilgrim* |

**C.D.S. POSTMARKS**

| | | |
|---|---|---|
| (15) | Alexandra Park Rd – 'Stamp World 1990' | 20 |
| (16) | Chester, Gretna, Portree, Ryde–Lear's rhymes | 20 |
| (17) | Holloway, N7 – birthplace of Lear | 20 |
| (18) | Knowsley – Lear/nonsense verse | 20 |
| (19) | Park Rd., Regent's Park – Lear drew birds and animals at the Zoological Gdns | 20 |
| (20) | Portman Square – home of Lear | 20 |

*In addition: Catsfield, Catshill, Derry Hill, East Cowes, Foss Mount, Freshwater, Luimneach, Owlsmoor, Petworth, Victoria St., Winchelsea. Prices from £10.*

**SLOGAN POSTMARKS**

| | | |
|---|---|---|
| (21) | Autumn Stampex/BPE | 20 |
| (22) | Great Ormonde St. Candle | 15 |
| (23) | Philatelic Bulletin 25th Anniversary | 25 |

*In addition: Isle of Skye; Brighton Guide; Guide Dog Week. Prices from £12.*

*Some **double-dated** covers exist with the set of stamps postmarked 6th September and the miniature sheet postmarked 27th September. Prices from £35.*

## 15th Nov 1988 - CHRISTMAS
*14p, 19p, 27p, 32p, 35p Christmas Cards*

**SPECIAL HANDSTAMPS**

| | | | |
|---|---|---|---|
| (1) | First Day of Issue – Philatelic Bureau | 4 | – *Royal Mail* |
| (2) | First Day of Issue – Bethlehem, Llandeilo | 4 | – *Royal Mail* |
| (3) | St. Alban The Martyr, Northampton | 12 | 35 *Ch. of St. A.* |
| (4) | Guinea Pig Club, BF 2184 PS | 12 | 10 *RFDC 68* |
| (5) | York Minster Commemoration | 12 | 25 *CoverCraft* |
| (6) | Christmas Card Mailcoach Run, Box | 12 | 12 *BLCS 37* |
| (7) | Christmas Card Mailcoach Run, Luton | 12 | 12 *BLCS 37* |
| (8) | Christmas Card Mailcoach Run, Bath | 12 | 15 *BLCS 37* |
| (9) | Victorian Christmas Cards Postling, Hythe | 12 | 25 *Ben500(37)* |
| (10) | Saint Dunstan Millennium, Canterbury | 12 | 15 *LFDC 73* |
| (11) | Cartmel Priory, Grange, Cumbria | 12 | 50 *Bradbury* |
| (12) | Telecom Technology Showcase, EC4 | 12 | – *n.o.c.* |
| (13) | Scanner, HRH Princess Margaret, Romford | 12 | 20 *OldchHosp* |
| (14) | Royle, Royle, Royle, N1 | 20 | 200 *Arlington* |
| (15) | Stampway to the World, Liverpool | 12 | – *n.o.c.* |

| *Christmas (contd.)* | ordinary covers £ | official covers £ | |
|---|---|---|---|
| (16) Royal Academy of Arts, Henry Moore, W1 ...... | 12 | 9 | *Pilgrim* |
| (17) The Green Howards, BF 2183 PS ...................... | 12 | 75 | *Forces* |
| (18) Railways and the Post, Postal Museum ............. | 12 | – | *Royal Mail* |
| (19) Holmfirth Postcard Museum............................... | 25 | | |
| – *n.o.c.* | | | |

**C.D.S. POSTMARKS**

| | | |
|---|---|---|
| (20) Kensington Church St. – first Xmas card........... | 15 | |
| (21) Nasareth, Gwynedd................................................ | 25 | |

*Also: Angel Hill, Bath, Holy Island, Lancelot Place SW7, Noel Road W3,*
*St. Nicholas, Shepherds Bush W12, Shepherds Hill, Star. Prices from £10.*

**SLOGAN POSTMARKS**

| | |
|---|---|
| (22) Washington Apples/Bigger Christmas Crunch . | 20 |

*In addition: Stampway; BBC Children in Need. Prices from £15.*

## 17th January 1989 – SEA BIRDS

*19p Puffin; 27p Avocet; 32p Oyster Catcher; 35p Gannet*

**SPECIAL HANDSTAMPS**

| | | | |
|---|---|---|---|
| (1) First Day of Issue – Philatelic Bureau.............. | 4 | – | *Royal Mail* |
| (2) First Day of Issue – Sandy, Bedfordshire.......... | 4 | – | *Royal Mail* |
| (3) Famous Gannet Colony, Bass Rock .................... | 12 | 12 | *BenSG8* |
| (4) Leics. & Rutland Ornithological Society........... | 12 | 30 | *LFDC 74* |
| (5) Lundy Island, Bideford...................................... | 12 | 60 | *Lundy P.B.* |
| (6) British Sea Birds, Dungeness ........................... | 12 | 30 | *Ben500(38)* |
| (7) St. Kilda – Puffin Colony ................................. | 12 | 17 | *BLCS 38* |
| (8) RSPB, Action for Birds, Sandy. .......................... | 12 | 25 | *CoverCraft* |
| (9) No. 201 Squadron, BF 2193 PS ......................... | 12 | 12 | *RFDC 69* |
| (10) HMS Quorn, BF 2194 PS................................... | 12 | 20 | *FAA Museum* |

**C.D.S. POSTMARKS**

| | |
|---|---|
| (11) Balivanich, Bempton, Papa Westray or Rathlin Is. – Puffin colonies ...................................*each* | 15 |
| (12) Didsbury Village – RSPB founded here............ | 25 |
| (13) Fair Isle or Ness – Gannet colonies...........*each* | 25 |
| (14) Orford – near to Minsmere (Avocet)............... | 15 |
| (15) Sandy or Slimbridge.......................................... | 15 |
| (16) Snettisham or Westleton – Oystercatcher........ | 15 |
| (17) Tring – British Trust for Ornithology................ | 35 |

*Also: Bideford, Birdsedge, Heron Cross, Kinlochleven, Redhill, Swallow's Nest, Wren's Nest. From £10.*

**SLOGAN POSTMARK** *Visit the Isle of Skye. £35.*

## 31st January 1989 – GREETINGS STAMPS

*5 x 19p: rose, cupid, sailing boat, bowl of fruit and teddy bear.*

**SPECIAL HANDSTAMPS**

| | | | |
|---|---|---|---|
| (1) First Day of Issue – Philatelic Bureau.............. | 8 | – | *Royal Mail* |
| (2) First Day of Issue – Lover, Salisbury ................. | 8 | – | *Royal Mail* |
| (3) Teddy Bear Museum, Ironbridge........................ | 15 | 20 | *BLCS 39* |
| (4) St. Valentine's, Lover......................................... | 15 | 30 | *Ben500(39)* |
| (5) Flowery Field, Hyde............................................ | 15 | 15 | *BLCS 39* |
| (6) Commission 'Postes' CEPT, Edinburgh ............. | 15 | – | *n.o.c.* |
| (7) No. 6 Squadron, BF 2192 PS............................. | 15 | 20 | *RDFC 70* |
| (8) Up-Helly-A, Lerwick.......................................... | 15 | 35 | *UpHellyA* |
| (10) Holmfirth Postcard Museum............................. | 25 | – | *n.o.c.* |

**C.D.S. POSTMARKS**

| | |
|---|---|
| (11) Bearpark, Cowes, Flowery Field, Greet, Greetland, Gretna Green, Kew Gardens, Lover, Orchard, Pudsey, Rose, Rosehearty, Seaside, or Strawberry Hill........... | 25 |

**SLOGAN POSTMARKS** *Burns, Dumfries; Visit the Isle of Skye. Prices from £20.*

## 7th March 1989 – FOOD & FARMING YEAR

*19p Fruit & vegetables; 27p Meat & Fish;32p Dairy produce; 35p Cereals*

**SPECIAL HANDSTAMPS**

| | | | |
|---|---|---|---|
| (1) First Day of Issue – Philatelic Bureau.............. | 4 | – | *Royal Mail* |
| (2) First Day of Issue – Kenilworth ......................... | 4 | – | *Royal Mail* |
| (3) BVA Animal Welfare Foundation, W1 ............... | 10 | 10 | *LFDC 75* |
| (4) British Food & Farming, Isle of Grain.............. | 10 | 25 | *Ben500(40)* |
| (5) Min. of Agriculture, Fisheries and Food, SW1.. | 10 | 25 | *CoverCraft* |
| (6) Women's Land Army, BF 2195 PS...................... | 10 | 20 | *RFDC 71* |
| (7) Royal Agricultural Soc., Stoneleigh ................... | 10 | 10 | *BLCS 40* |
| (8) Purveyors of Flour, Hovis, Windsor.................... | 10 | 250 | *Arlington* |
| (9) Taunton tourist h/s (features apple)................... | 25 | – | *n.o.c.* |

**ORDINARY F.D.I. POSTMARKS**

| | |
|---|---|
| (10) Chichester (Weald & Downland Museum cvr).... | 45 |

**C.D.S. POSTMARKS**

| | |
|---|---|
| (11) Any Farm Post Offices........................................ | 20 |
| (12) Cheddar, Stilton or Wensley.........................*each* | 15 |
| (13) Corn Exchange or Market Place....................*each* | 15 |
| (14) Farmers, Dyfed or Tile Farm, Orpington......... | 15 |
| (15) Ham or Melton Mowbray – pork pies .......*each* | 15 |
| (16) Isle of Grain, Rochester .................................... | 15 |
| (17) Leek or Bramley.............................................*each* | 15 |
| (18) Ivymeade, High Wycombe – shopping centre P.O. | 20 |
| (19) Savacentre – Supermarket Post Office .............. | 40 |
| (20) Stoneleigh – Royal Show ................................... | 15 |

*Also: The Allotments, Bakers Ln, Bakewell, Butterton, Evesham, The Orchard, Wheatley. From £10.*

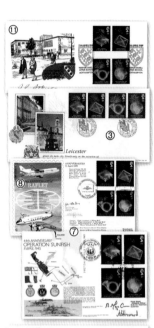

*Food & Farming (contd.)*

| | ordinary covers £ | official covers £ |
|---|---|---|

**SLOGAN POSTMARKS**

(21) Collect British Stamps–Bradford (sheep's head).... 25

*In addition: York Collect British Stamps; Wild about Worcestershire; Hooked on Herefordshire; County Councils; Industry Matters. Prices from £12.*

## 11th April 1989 – ANNIVERSARIES

*19p Public Education (150th Anniversary); 19p European Parliament; 35p Postal Telegraph & Telephones Congress; 35p Inter-Parliamentary Union*

**SPECIAL HANDSTAMPS**

| | | ord | off | |
|---|---|---|---|---|
| (1) | First Day of Issue – Philatelic Bureau.................. | 4 | – | *Royal Mail* |
| (2) | First Day of Issue – SW London ...................... | 4 | – | *Royal Mail* |
| (3) | Strasbourg – Leicester's Twin City ................... | 10 | 15 | *LFDC 76* |
| (4) | 26th World Congress PTTI, W1 ...................... | 10 | 25 | *Ben500(41)* |
| (5) | Inter Parliamentary Union, SW1 ..................... | 10 | 20 | *BLCS 41* |
| (6) | Direct Elections, Downing St. ........................ | 10 | 20 | *BLCS 41* |
| (7) | Operation Sunfish, S.E.A.C., BF 2202 PS ......... | 10 | 40 | *FAAMuseum* |
| (8) | RAFLET, BF 2197 PS ................................. | 10 | 15 | *RFDC 72* |
| (9) | Centenary Derbys County Council, Matlock...... | 10 | 35 | *DerbysCC* |
| (10) | Stampway to the World, Manchester................ | 10 | 15 | *S.P.Board* |
| (11) | Weston Favell School, Northampton................. | 10 | 20 | *WFUS* |
| (12) | Evesham Corps, Centenary Blood & Fire ......... | 10 | 20 | *H.R.* |

**C.D.S. POSTMARKS**

| | | | |
|---|---|---|---|
| (13) | Brighton – PTTI Conference.......................... | 12 | |
| (14) | Brighton Centre, Brighton – PTTI Conference . | 80 | |
| (15) | Broadway, SW1 – site of IPU Congress .......... | 12 | |
| (16) | Dover or Calais + PAQUEBOT cachet.....*each* | 15 | |
| (17) | Hope Street, Edin. – b/place A. Graham Bell .. | 15 | |
| (18) | House of Commons and Lords ...................... | 25 | |
| (19) | Mark Cross or Northern Parliament................ | 20 | |
| (20) | Duke of York's Sch. or Royal Hospital Sch..... | 15 | |
| (21) | Telephone House, Birmingham...................... | 20 | |
| (22) | Temple Hill, Dartford – Unwin Pyrotechnics .. | 12 | |
| (23) | Heathrow – main UK airport serving Europe.... | 30 | |
| (24) | University pmks: Bath, Bradford, Essex, Lancaster, | | |
| | Liverpool, Norwich & Swansea.....*each* | 20 | |

*Also: Clapham Common, College Rd, Eton, Fareham, Grange Hill, Harwich, Regent St, Rochdale, Scholar Green, Sussex Coast, World's End. From £10.*

**SLOGAN POSTMARKS**

| | | |
|---|---|---|
| (25) | University of Durham, Dept. of Geography ..... | 20 |
| (26) | Mailing and Communications Show, London .. | 20 |
| (27) | Liverpool Mechanised Office – use postcodes.. | 20 |
| (28) | Remember to use the Postcode – Ipswich ...... | 15 |
| (29) | Edinburgh Festival of Science & Technology .. | 20 |
| (30) | NATO Fortieth Anniversary........................... | 95 |

*Also: Lead Free; Derbyshire C.C.; Inverness Confe. Capital; BBC Wilts Sound; Stampway. From £14.*

## 16th May 1989 – GAMES AND TOYS

*19p train and plane; 27p building blocks; 32p board games; 35p boat, robot and doll's house*

**SPECIAL HANDSTAMPS**

| | | ord | off | |
|---|---|---|---|---|
| (1) | First Day of Issue – Philatelic Bureau................ | 4 | – | *Royal Mail* |
| (2) | First Day of Issue – Leeds ........................... | 4 | – | *Royal Mail* |
| (3) | Putting Children First, NSPCC, EC.................. | 10 | 10 | *CoverCraft* |
| (4) | Lewis Carrol, 1832-1898, Oxford ................... | 10 | 75 | *Zanders* |
| (5) | The Teddybears' Picnic, Ironbridge................. | 10 | 20 | *BLCS 42* |
| (6) | Pollock's Toy Museum, W1............................ | 10 | 15 | *LFDC 77* |
| (7) | Toys Hill, Westerham ................................. | 10 | 20 | *Ben500(42)* |
| (8) | Stampway to the World, Manchester................ | 10 | 15 | *S.P.Board* |
| (9) | Postal Museum, Uniform Exhibition, EC.......... | 10 | – | *n.o.c.* |
| (10) | Rotary Diamond Charter, Newcastle ............... | 10 | 20 | *Rotary* |
| (11) | Guisborough Priory.................................... | 10 | 10 | *S. Muscroft* |
| (12) | Royal Naval Air Service, BF 2200 PS............... | 10 | 15 | *RFDC 73* |
| (13) | RNLI Gallantry Awards, SE1......................... | 10 | 15 | *Pilgrim* |
| (14) | History of the Royal Navy, Plymouth ............... | 12 | – | *n.o.c.* |

**C.D.S. POSTMARKS**

| | | |
|---|---|---|
| (15) | Fforestfach, Swansea – 'Corgi' toys ............... | 10 |
| (16) | Hornby, Waddington or Playing Place ............ | 12 |
| (17) | Mt Pleasant Liverpool–b/place Frank Hornby..... | 10 |
| (18) | Old Swan, Liverpool – 'Hornby' factory .......... | 12 |
| (19) | Regent St., W1 – Hamley's Toy Shop ............. | 12 |
| (20) | Any TPO postmark .................................... | 10 |
| (21) | Woodlesford or Rothwell – Waddington Games. | 10 |

*In addition: Bathampton, Bethnal Green, Bowling, Bunny, Butlin's Holiday Camp, Child's Hill, Ironbridge, Kirton, Market, Mulberry Parade, Paddington. Prices from £8*

**SLOGAN POSTMARKS**

| | | |
|---|---|---|
| (22) | 'Chess board' – Bradford ........................... | 75 |
| (23) | Save the Children Week ............................. | 40 |

*Also: Medway & Swale Child Safety; 40 Years Council of Europe; Lead Free; Spotless; 0Robin Hood; Train slogans; The Archers. From £12.*

## 4th July 1989 – INDUSTRIAL ARCHAEOLOGY
*19p Ironbridge; 27p St. Agnes;*
*32p New Lanark; 35p Pontcysyllte Aqueduct*

| | | ordinary covers £ | official covers £ |
|---|---|---|---|
| **SPECIAL HANDSTAMPS** | | | |
| (1) | First Day of Issue – Philatelic Bureau | 4 | – *Royal Mail* |
| (2) | First Day of Issue – Telford | 4 | – *Royal Mail* |
| (3) | Isambard Kingdom Brunel, Bristol | 10 | 50 *Zanders* |
| (4) | Water Powered Mills at New Lanark | 10 | 20 *Ben500(43)* |
| (5) | Pontcysyllte Aqueduct, Llangollen | 10 | 20 *BenL21* |
| (6) | New Lanark Conservation | 10 | 15 *LFDC 78* |
| (7) | Our Industrial Heritage, St. Agnes | 10 | 17 *BLCS 43* |
| (8) | Birthplace of British Industry, Ironbridge | 10 | 15 *BLCS 43* |
| (9) | Aberdulais Falls, W. Glam. | 10 | 15 *CoverCraft* |
| (10) | Penfold Box Waterways Museum, Gloucester | 10 | – *n.o.c.* |
| (11) | Philatelic Counter, Bolton ('Spinning Mule') | 20 | – *n.o.c.* |
| (12) | Philatelic Counter, Bradford (industial mills) | 20 | – *n.o.c.* |
| (13) | Philatelic Counter, Stoke (kiln) | 20 | – *n.o.c.* |
| (14) | Yorkshire Museum, York | 10 | – *n.o.c.* |
| (15) | Killiecrankie, National Trust Scotland | 10 | 75 *NT for Scotland* |
| (16) | Trenchard-Keyes Agreement, BF 2208 PS | 10 | 25 *FAAMuseum* |
| (17) | Lawn Tennis Museum | 10 | 20 *H.R.* |
| (18) | The Royal Show, Stoneleigh | 10 | – *n.o.c.* |
| (19) | No. 72 Squadron, BF 2201 PS | 10 | 10 *RFDC 74* |
| **C.D.S. POSTMARKS** | | | |
| (20) | Froncysyllte or Trevor – Pontcysyllte aqueduct | 15 | |
| (21) | Ironbridge (19p) | 15 | |
| (22) | Langholm – birthplace of Thomas Telford | 15 | |
| (23) | New Lanark (32p) | 15 | |
| (24) | St. Agnes (27p) | 15 | |

*Also: Arkwright Town, Bolton, Camborne, Chirk, Highway, Illogen, Liverton Mines, Newtown, Preston, Saltaire, Shrewsbury, Stewarton. From £10.*

**SLOGAN POSTMARKS£**
| (25) | Aveling Barford – The Earthmovers | 20 |
| (26) | Collect British Stamps – Bradford (mills) | 25 |

*Also: Marine Engineers; Teesside Talent; Richmond Fest.; Post Code; Post Early; York, the Distinct Advantage. From £10.*

## 25th July 1989 – INDUSTRIAL ARCHAEOLOGY
*Miniature Sheet*

| | | | | |
|---|---|---|---|---|
| **SPECIAL HANDSTAMPS** | | | | |
| (1) | First Day of Issue – Philatelic Bureau | 4 | – *Royal Mail* |
| (2) | First Day of Issue – New Lanark | 4 | – *Royal Mail* |
| (3) | Water Powered Mills at New Lanark | 10 | 20 *BenL22* |
| (4) | Pontcysyllte Aqueduct, Llangollen | 10 | 35 *Ben500(44)* |
| (5) | Assoc'n for Ind. Archaeology, Ironbridge | 10 | 10 *LFDC 79* |
| (6) | Our Industrial Heritage, Redruth | 10 | 20 *BLCS 44* |
| (7) | Birthplace of British Industry, Ironbridge | 10 | 25 *BLCS 44* |
| (8) | National Postal Museum, SWL90, EC | 10 | – *n.o.c.* |
| (9) | Killiecrankie, National Trust Scotland | 10 | 25 *Scot.N.T.* |
| (10) | International Scout Camp, Gosford | 10 | 35 *Scouts* |
| (11) | Aircraft Archaeology, BF 1968 PS | 10 | 12 *RFDC 75* |
| (12) | Royal Tournament, BF 2196 PS | 10 | 12 *Forces* |
| (13) | Philatelic Counter, Bolton ('Spinning Mule') | 15 | – *n.o.c.* |
| (14) | Philatelic Counter, Bristol (Suspension Bridge) | 15 | – *n.o.c.* |
| (15) | Philatelic Counter, Bradford (industrial mills) | 15 | – *n.o.c.* |
| (16) | Philatelic Counter, Stoke (kiln) | 15 | – *n.o.c.* |
| **C.D.S. POSTMARKS** | | | |
| (17) | Froncysyllte or Trevor – Pontcysyllte aqueduct | 15 | |
| (18) | Ironbridge, New Lanark or St. Agnes | 15 | |
| (19) | Langholm – birthplace of Thomas Telford | 15 | |

*In addition: Alexandra Park Road, Arkwright Town, Camborne, Chirk, Illogen, Liverton Mines, Muswell Hill Newtown, Preston, Saltaire, Stewarton. Prices from £10.*

**SLOGAN POSTMARKS**
| (20) | Aveling Barford – The Earthmovers | 25 |
| (21) | Collect British Stamps – Bradford (mills) | 20 |

*Also: Marine Engineers; Teesside Talent Ability; Please Post Early;Post Code. From £10.*

*Some **double-dated** covers exist with both the sets of stamps postmarked 4th July and the miniature sheet postmarked 25th July. Prices range from £25.*

Now you can digitally record your collection of British first day covers by using STAMP ORGANISER. Find out how by downloading a free trial version from

**www.bfdc.co.uk/so**

This program includes around 26,000 images of British stamps, FDCs, presentation packs, PHQ cards and stamp books.

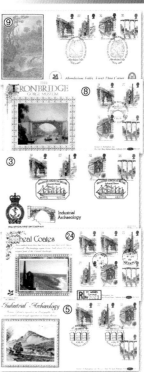

## 5th Sept. 1989 – MICROSCOPES

*19p Snowflake; 27p Fly; 32p Blood; 35p Microchip*

| | ordinary cvrs £ | official covers £ |
|---|---|---|
| **SPECIAL HANDSTAMPS** | | |
| (1) First Day of Issue – Philatelic Bureau | 4 | – *Royal Mail* |
| (2) First Day of Issue – Oxford | 4 | – *Royal Mail* |
| (3) Royal Microscopical Soc Oxford | 10 | 30 *Bradbury* |
| (4) Royal Microscopical Soc 1839-1989 Oxford | 10 | 30 *Bradbury* |
| (5) Cambridge Instruments | 10 | 40 *Bradbury* |
| (6) Year of the Microscope, SW7 | 10 | 30 *LFDC 80* |
| (7) Year of Microscope Exh. Science Museum | 10 | 15 *BLCS 45* |
| (8) Year of the Microscope, Cambridge | 10 | 15 *Ben500(45)* |
| (9) Marconi Electronic Devices, Lincoln | 10 | 10 *Cotswold* |
| (10) Dr. Robert Hooke, Freshwater | 10 | 85 *Zanders* |
| (11) IMLS Conference, Warwick University | 10 | 20 *H.R.* |
| (12) UK North Sea Oil, Aberdeen | 10 | 75 *Arlington* |
| (13) Jeol (UK), NW9 | 10 | 75 *Arlington* |
| (14) Dormeuil, The World's Best Cloths, SW1 | 10 | 40 *Dormeuil* |
| (15) Battle of Britain, BF 2209 PS | 10 | 12 *RFDC 76* |
| (16) Inter-Parliamentary Union Conf., SW1 | 9 | 9 *BLCS 41* |
| **C.D.S. POSTMARKS** | | |
| (17) Church or Freshwater – Robert Hooke | 20 | |
| (18) Regent St., W1 – first meeting of Society | 12 | |
| (19) St. Clements, Oxford – Society HQ | 12 | |
| (20) South Kensington, SW7 – Science Museum | 12 | |
| (21) Whitechapel – first meeting of Society | 12 | |

*Also: Alnwick, Holloway, Houndsditch, Lancaster, London Chief Office,
Rotherhithe Lower Rd, Royal Hospital School, Snowhill, Stoke Newington,
Wollaston. Prices from £10.*

**SLOGAN POSTMARKS**

| | | |
|---|---|---|
| (22) Army – 50 Years of Blood Transfusion | 20 | |
| (23) CARE '89 | 18 | |
| (24) Europe Against Cancer Year 1989 | 20 | |

*Also: Europe's Univ.; Royal Mail, Winchester; Collect British Stamps, Milton Keynes. £10.*

## 17th October 1989 – THE LORD MAYOR'S SHOW

*5 x 20p Scenes from the procession*

| **SPECIAL HANDSTAMPS** | | |
|---|---|---|
| (1) First Day of Issue – Philatelic Bureau | 4 | – *Royal Mail* |
| (1a) -do- carried in the Lord Mayor's Show | 6 | – *Royal Mail* |
| (2) First Day of Issue – London EC4 | 4 | – *Royal Mail* |
| (3) Richard Whittington's Birthplace, Pauntley | 10 | 110 *Bradbury* |
| (4) Dick Whittington, Thrice Lord Mayor, EC | 10 | 10 *LFDC 81* |
| (5) Lord Mayor's Show, EC (trumpet) | 10 | 15 *BenSG9* |
| (6) The Lord Mayor, City of London, EC (crest) | 10 | 15 *BLCS 46* |
| (7) Exhibition at the Museum of London, EC | 10 | 20 *Ben500(46)* |
| (8) Royal Mail Open Day, WC1 | 10 | – *n.o.c.* |
| (9) Royal Mail Exhibition Card 3, Stampex/BPE | 10 | – *n.o.c.* |
| (10) Autumn Stampex/BPE, 1989, SW1 | 10 | 25 *Stampex* |
| (11) National Postal Museum, SWL90, EC | 10 | – *n.o.c.* |
| (12) Berlin Airlift, BF 2210 PS | 10 | 12 *RFDC 77* |
| (13) Sevastopol, BF 1782 PS | 10 | 15 *FAA Museum* |
| (14) Town Hall Centenary, Middlesbrough | 10 | 15 *S.Muscroft* |
| (15) Art of Photography, W1 | 10 | 12 *Pilgrim* |
| (16) City of London (crest) permanent handstamp | 25 | – *Royal Mail* |
| **C.D.S. POSTMARKS** | | |
| (17) Bovingdon–Hugh Bidwell (1989 Lord Mayor) | 15 | |
| (18) Fore St.; Lombard St.; Stock Exchange; Cannon St.; London Chief Office; Fleet St. | | |
| – nearest POs to scenes on the stamps | 20 | |
| (19) Ludgate Circus or Moorgate – on the route | 20 | |
| (20) Newent or Redmarley – Dick Whittington | 20 | |
| (21) Whittington, Lichfield | 20 | |

*Also: House of Lords, Richmond, Wickham, Wimbledon Park. From £18.*

**SLOGAN POSTMARKS**

*Stampex; Cancer; Stampway; Gloucester Cathedral; Robin Hood; Aveling Barford; From £15.*

## 14th November 1989 – CHRISTMAS

*15p, 15p+1p, 20p+1p, 34p+1p, 37p+1p Ely Cathedral*

| **SPECIAL HANDSTAMPS** | | |
|---|---|---|
| (1) First Day of Issue – Philatelic Bureau | 4 | – *Royal Mail* |
| (2) First Day of Issue – Bethlehem, Llandeilo | 4 | – *Royal Mail* |
| (3) First Day of Issue – Ely | 4 | – *Royal Mail* |
| (4) 'Thomas' Invites you to Nene Valley | 10 | 40 *N.V.Rly* |
| (5) Christmas 1989, Gloucester | 10 | 20 *Bradbury* |
| (6) Telecom Technology Showcase, EC4 | 10 | – *n.o.c.* |
| (7) Christmas 1989, Ely, Cambs. | 10 | 15 *LFDC 82* |
| (8) Norman Nave, Ely Cathedral, (Mitre) | 10 | 35 *Ben500(47)* |
| (9) Norman Nave, Ely Cathedral, (3 Keys) | 10 | 20 *BLCS 47* |
| (10) Mailcoach Run, Cambridge – Ely Cathedral | 10 | 25 *BLCS 47* |
| (11) Christmas Greetings, HM Ships, BF 2214 PS | 10 | 20 *FAA Museum* |
| (12) Whitby Abbey | 10 | 15 *S.Muscroft* |
| (13) RAF Gliding Assoc'n., BF 2212 PS | 10 | 10 *RFDC 78* |
| (14) Art of Photography 1839-1989, W1 | 10 | 15 *Pilgrim* |

| *Christmas (contd.)* | ordinary covers | official covers |
|---|---|---|

**C.D.S. POSTMARKS** £ £

| | | |
|---|---|---|
| (15) Barnack - Cathedral stone | 15 | |
| (16) Ely, Cambs | 15 | |
| (17) Exning - Etheldreda, Cathedral Founder | 15 | |
| (18) Primrose Hill, Tonbridge - Charities Aid HQ | 12 | |
| (19) Stoke Charity | 20 | |
| (20) Walsingham - Alan de Walsingham, architect | 18 | |

*Also: Angel Hill, Canterbury, Holy Island, Nasareth, Northwold. From £10.*

**SLOGAN POSTMARKS**

| | | |
|---|---|---|
| (21) Gloucester Cathedral | 20 | |
| (22) Choose Charity Stamps or Children in Need | 20 | |
| (23) Luton Carol Aid '89 | 40 | |

*Also: Unicef Cards; Beautiful Bath; Bath Royal Charter; Liverpool MLO; Collect British Stamps; Stampway. £10.*

④

## 10th January 1990 - PENNY BLACK ANNIVERSARY
*15p, 20p, 29p, 34p, 37p Queen Victoria & Queen Elizabeth II*

**SPECIAL HANDSTAMPS**

| | | | |
|---|---|---|---|
| (1) First Day of Issue - Philatelic Bureau | 4 | – | *Royal Mail* |
| (2) First Day of Issue - Windsor | 4 | – | *Royal Mail* |
| (3) First Roadside Pillar Box, Carlisle | 12 | 75 | *Carlisle P.O.* |
| (4) Postal Museum, 1840-1990, EC | 12 | – | *n.o.c.* |
| (5) Postal Museum, SWL90, Rowland Hill | 12 | 25 | *NPM postcard* |
| (6) Victorian Letterbox, Dean Heritage Museum | 12 | 75 | *CoverCraft* |
| (7) Uniform Penny Post, B.P.F., EC1 | 12 | 25 | *CoverCraft* |
| (8) Uniform Penny Postage, Kidderminster | 12 | 25 | *CoverCraft* |
| (9) Sir Rowland Hill, Kidderminster | 12 | 15 | *LFDC 83* |
| (10) Perkins, Bacon & Co., Penny Black, Fleet St | 12 | 75 | *Bradbury* |
| (11) 1840-1990 Uniform Penny Postage, SW1 | 12 | 50 | *Bradbury* |
| (12) Etchingham Festival | 12 | 45 | *Et'ham P.C.* |
| (13) 150th Anniversaries, SG Plymouth | 12 | 25 | *BLCS 48* |
| (14) Windsor, Berks. (Maltese Cross) | 12 | 30 | *Ben500(48)* |
| (15) Stampway to the World, Newcastle | 12 | 50 | *S.P.Board* |

**C.D.S. POSTMARKS**

| | | |
|---|---|---|
| (16) Botchergate, Carlisle - first roadside postbox | 30 | |
| (17) Buckingham Palace, SW1 | 75 | |
| (18) Fleet Street - Perkins, Bacon (Penny Black) | 25 | |
| (19) House of Commons or Lords - Postage Act | 35 | |
| (20) Kidderminster - b/place of Sir Rowland Hill | 15 | |
| (21) Sanquhar - oldest Post Office | 25 | |
| (22) Windsor, Berks | 25 | |
| (23) Windsor Castle, Berks | 95 | |

*Also: Arbroath, Bath, Birmingham, Holyrood, London Chief Office, Lordship Lane N17, Queen Elizabeth Ave, Queensbury, Queen's Parade, Queen Victoria Rd, Scone, Seething Lane EC3, Stoke-on-Trent, Victoria Rd. From £15.*

**SLOGAN POSTMARKS**

| | | |
|---|---|---|
| (24) Collect British Stamps: Philatelic Counters | 25 | |
| (25) Collect British Stamps - World's Greatest Hobby | 20 | |
| (26) Be Properly Addressed, Postcode It | 20 | |
| (27) Pass on your Postcode | 20 | |
| (28) Get the Most From Your Post - Code It! | 20 | |
| (29) Remember to use the Postcode | 20 | |
| (30) Post Early in the Day | 20 | |
| (31) Liverpool is a Mechanised Letter Office | 20 | |
| (32) Senders Name & Address /back of envelopes | 20 | |
| (33) Write Now! - Say it Better in a Letter | 75 | |
| (34) Stampway to the World - Newcastle | 95 | |

*Also available: Great Expectations; Beautiful Bath. Prices from £10.*

## 23rd January 1990 - R.S.P.C.A.
*20p Kitten; 29p Rabbit; 34p Duckling; 37p Puppy*

**SPECIAL HANDSTAMPS**

| | | | |
|---|---|---|---|
| (1) First Day of Issue - Philatelic Bureau | 4 | – | *Royal Mail* |
| (2) First Day of Issue - Horsham | 4 | – | *Royal Mail* |
| (3) Bunny, Nottingham | 12 | 75 | *Bradbury* |
| (4) Battersea, London SW8 | 12 | 25 | *LFDC 84* |
| (5) RSPCA, 150 Years, Horsham | 12 | 25 | *CoverCraft* |
| (6) RSPCA, Pett, Hastings | 12 | 60 | *Ben500(49)* |
| (7) Cats Protection League, Middlesbrough | 12 | 40 | *S. Muscroft* |
| (8) Cat World Magazine, Shoreham | 12 | 50 | *BLCS 49* |
| (9) Provincial Grand Masters, Hadleigh | 10 | 35 | *Masons* |
| (10) Ekowe, Naval Brigade, BF 2215 PS | 10 | 35 | *FAAMuseum* |
| (11) No. 24 Squadron, BF 2216 PS | 10 | 20 | *RFDC 79* |

**C.D.S. POSTMARKS**

| | | |
|---|---|---|
| (12) Battersea, or Battersea Park Road | 25 | |
| (13) Bunny, Nottingham | 25 | |
| (14) Dog & Gun, Dog Kennel Lane or Isle of Dogs | 25 | |
| (15) Horsham - RSPCA headquarters | 15 | |
| (16) Sidmouth - birthplace of founder of RSPCA | 15 | |
| (17) Trafalgar Sq - near to RSPCA's first meeting | 12 | |

*Also: Ballynahinch, Black Dog, Catsfield, Catshill, Catsfield, Ducklington, Duckworth Ln, Middlesbrough, Regent St. From £15.*

③

④

④

⑦

⑬

⑤

87

**RSPCA (contd.)**      ordinary covers    official covers

**SLOGAN POSTMARKS**      £      £

(18) Collect British Stamps, Bradford (ram's head) .   25

(19) Aveling Barford, the Earthmovers (horse) ........   80

*Also: Collect British Stamps; Liverpool MLO; Write Now etc. Prices from £7.*

## 6th February 1990 – GREETINGS STAMPS

*10 x 20p Famous 'Smiles':*
*Teddy Bear; Dennis the Menace, Mr. Punch, Cheshire Cat, Man in the Moon,*
*Laughing Policeman; Clown, Mona Lisa, Queen of Hearts, Stan Laurel.*

**SPECIAL HANDSTAMPS**

(1) First Day of Issue – Philatelic Bureau...............   8    –   *Royal Mail*

(2) First Day of Issue – Giggleswick ....................   15    –   *Royal Mail*

(3) Greetings, Clowne, Chesterfield ......................   15   35   *BenD135*

(4) Greetings, Puncheston, Haverfordwest.............   15   20   *Benham*

(5) Greetings, The Teddy Bear Shop, Ironbridge.....   15   50   *Ben500(50)pair*

(6) Greetings, Hartford, Cheshire...........................   15   40   *BLCS 50 pair*

(7) No.604 Squadron, BF 2217 PS..........................   15   20   *RFDC 80*

**C.D.S. POSTMARKS**

(8) Bearpark, Catsfield, or Pudsey .................*each*   25

(9) Bow St., Constable Rd., Constable Burton, or Law ..   25

(10) Fleet Street – where 'Beano' is published .........   25

(11) Giggleswick................................................   25

(12) Greet, Birmingham......................................   25

(13) Oxford – Lewis Carrol/'Alice in Wonderland' .   25

(14) Ulverston – birthplace of Stan Laurel...............   25

*Also: Colemore Circus, Greets Green, Big Top, Merry Hill, Laurel Ln,*
*Puncheston, London E.C. £20.*

**SLOGAN POSTMARKS**

(15) Take a Bite Out of Crime, Newcastle ...............   30

(16) Collect British Stamps, Lincoln ('Lincoln Imp') ...   30

*Also: Darlington Open Day; Stampex; Collect British Stamps. Prices from £15.*

## 6th March 1990 – EUROPA

*20p Alexandra Palace; 29p British Philatelic Bureau;*
*20p Glasgow School of Art; 37p Templeton Carpet Factory, Glasgow*

**SPECIAL HANDSTAMPS**

(1) First Day of Issue – Philatelic Bureau...............   4    –   *Royal Mail*

(2) First Day of Issue – Glasgow ......................   4    –   *Royal Mail*

(3) Cultural Capital, Glasgow...............................   10   25   *Arlington*

(4) Europa, Stamp World, N22......   10   15   *BLCS 51*

(5) Modern Movement Blg. in Europe, Glasgow...   10   35   *Ben500(51)*

(6) British Philatelic Bureau, Edinburgh..............   10   10   *Bureau (s)*

(7) 1st Int. Stamp Exhibition, BPF, N22..............   10   15   *BPF*

(8) Alexandra Palace, Victorian Heritage, N22......   10   20   *CoverCraft*

(9) Europa 1990, Edinburgh...............................   10   10   *LFDC 85*

(10) Alexandra Palace, Europa 1990, N22.............   10   15   *Bradbury*

(11) Oldest Post Office, Sanquhar.....................   10   50   *Bradbury*

(12) Forth Bridge Centennial, S. Queensferry .........   10   45   *Bradbury*

(13) No.8 Squadron, BF 2219 PS..........................   10   20   *RFDC 81*

**C.D.S. POSTMARKS**

(14) Alexandra Park Rd – venue of Stamp World....   10

(15) Bridgeton – Templeton Carpet Factory.............   10

(16) Cowcadden, City Branch, or Hope St.

    – near to Glasgow School of Art......*each*   10

(17) Warriston – near to Philatelic Bureau ...............   10

*Also: Cove, Craigpark, Duke St., Edinburgh, Glasgow, Glasgow Airport Helensburgh, London EC1,*
*Paisley, Sanquhar, Templeton, The Scotlands. From £8.*

**SLOGAN POSTMARKS**

(18) There's a lot of Glasgowing on..........................   20

(19) Collect British Stamps – World's Greatest Hobby ..   20

(20) Lincoln or Bradford Philatelic Counters ...*each*   20

*Also: Burgh of Lanark; Scottish Blood Trans; Liverpool MLO. Prices from £10.*

## 10th April 1990 – QUEEN'S AWARDS TO INDUSTRY

*2 x 20p, 2 x 37p Export & Technology Award emblems*

**SPECIAL HANDSTAMPS**

(1) First Day of Issue – Philatelic Bureau...............   4    –   *Royal Mail*

(2) First Day of Issue – SW London ....................   4    –   *Royal Mail*

(3) Queen's Awards to Industry, SW1......................   10   30   *Ben500(52)*

(4) Queen's Award, SAGA, Folkestone.................   10   15   *SAGA*

(5) Laboratory of the Gov. Chemist.......................   10   25   *CoverCraft*

(6) William Grant & Sons, Glenfiddich..................   10   95   *Arlington*

(7) CBI, Silver Jubilee, Investing in Success............   10   20   *LFDC 86*

(8) Paper for the Penny Black, Northampton ........   10   75   *D.Rutt*

(9) No. 10 Squadron, BF 2220 PS..........................   10   15   *RFDC 82*

(10) Konigsberg, BF 2224 PS..........................   10

20   *FAAMuseum*

**C.D.S. POSTMARKS**

(11) Buckingham Palace, SW1..................................   75

(12) Dover, Gatwick or Heathrow – exports ...*each*   10

(13) Golders Green – Abram Games (stamp designer) ..   10

(14) New Invention or Queen Elizabeth Avenue .....   15

(15) Tufton Street, SW1 – Queen's Award Office ...   15

(16) Turnpike Estate, Newbury – Quantel Ltd.,

     (Computer Graphic artwork for stamps)....   15

**Queen's Awards (contd.)** ordinary covers £  official covers £

(17) Windsor Castle, Windsor, Berks ......................... 50

*Also: Aycliffe Trading Estate, Broadway SW1, Derby, Globe Road E1, House of Commons, Jubilee Crescent, Lombard St., London EC, NEC Birmingham, Newbury, Silver Link, South Lambeth SW8. Prices from £12.*

**SLOGAN POSTMARKS**

(19) Invest in Sunderland – Enterprise Zone ........... 20

*In addition: British Steel; Aveling Barford; Hastings Exhibition; Stamp World; Sure Plumber; Collect British Stamps; Penny Black Coin. Prices from £10.*

## 3rd May 1990 – PENNY BLACK ANNIVERSARY
*Miniature Sheet: 20p + Facsimile of Penny Black*

**SPECIAL HANDSTAMPS**

| | | | |
|---|---|---|---|
| (1) | First Day of Issue – Philatelic Bureau................ | 4 | – *Royal Mail* |
| (2) | First Day of Issue – City of London................... | 4 | – *Royal Mail* |
| (3) | First Day of Issue – Alexandra Palace, N22...... | 15 | – *Royal Mail* |
| (4) | First Roadside Pillar Box, Carlisle ...................... | 10 | 60 *Carlisle P.O.* |
| (5) | Postal Museum, 1840-1990, EC ......................... | 10 | – *n.o.c.* |
| (6) | Royal Mail Exhib. Card No. 4, Edinburgh........ | 10 | – *n.o.c.* |
| (7) | Int. Stamp Exhibition, Stamp World, N22 ........ | 10 | – *n.o.c.* |
| (8) | Postal Museum, SWL90, EC .............................. | 10 | – *n.o.c.* |
| (9) | Penny Black, Rowland Hill, Kidderminster....... | 10 | 30 *CoverCraft* |
| (10) | Penny Black, William Wyon, Birmingham ....... | 10 | 30 *CoverCraft* |
| (11) | 1d Black, Bruce Castle Museum, N17 .............. | 10 | 30 *CoverCraft* |
| (12) | Jacob Perkins, Printer of the Penny Black........ | 10 | 30 *CoverCraft* |
| (13) | British Philatelic Federation, N22 ..................... | 10 | 30 *CoverCraft* |
| (14) | Sir Rowland Hill, Kidderminster....................... | 10 | 15 *LFDC 87* |
| (15) | Perkins Bacon & Co., Fleet St. ......................... | 10 | 25 *Bradbury* |
| (16) | 'Rule Britannia', SW1 ....................................... | 10 | 20 *Bradbury* |
| (17) | Penny Black, Alexandra Palace, N22................. | 10 | 20 *BenSG10* |
| (18) | The Penny Black, Bath...................................... | 10 | 45 *Ben500(53)* |
| (19) | Stanley Gibbons, Stamp World, N22................. | 10 | 50 *BLCS53* |
| (20) | Perkins, Bacon, Southwark Bdge....................... | 10 | 20 *BLCS53* |
| (21) | Etchingham Stamp Festival ................................ | 10 | 35 *Etc'ham P.C.* |
| (22) | The First Adhesive Stamp on Cover, Bath........ | 10 | 25 *S. Muscroft* |

**C.D.S. POSTMARKS**

| | | |
|---|---|---|
| (23) | Alexandra Park Road – 'Stamp World' ............. | 10 |
| (24) | Britannia, Bacup or Porth..........................*each* | 10 |
| (25) | Buckingham Palace, SW1 .................................. | 40 |
| (26) | Fleet Street – Perkins, Bacon (Penny Black) .... | 10 |
| (27) | House of Commons, SW1 – Postage Act........... | 25 |
| (28) | House of Lords, SW1 – Postage Act................. | 35 |
| (29) | Kidderminster – b/place of Sir Rowland Hill ... | 10 |
| (30) | Sanquhar – oldest Post Office .......................... | 10 |
| (31) | Wood Green – Mobile PO, 'Stamp World'......... | 12 |
| (32) | Windsor, Windsor Gt Park or Old Windsor ..... | 65 |
| (33) | Windsor Castle ................................................. | 125 |

*In addition: Cobham, Etchingham, Horsefair, London Chief Office, Lordship Lne N17, Queen Elizabeth Ave., South Kensington, Queen Victoria Rd, Victoria Rd. Prices from £15.*

**SLOGAN POSTMARKS**

| | | |
|---|---|---|
| (34) | Visit Stamp World, Alexandra Palace................ | 15 |
| (35) | Write Now! or Post Early in the Day................ | 30 |
| (36) | Any Postcode slogan ........................................ | 30 |
| (37) | Senders name & address on back of envelopes ... | 30 |
| (38) | New Sunday Collections, Royal Mail, B'ham ... | 15 |
| (39) | Liverpool is a Mechanised Letter Office .......... | 20 |
| (40) | Postman of the Year ......................................... | 35 |
| (41) | Queen Victoria School ...................................... | 20 |

*Also: Aveling Barford; Cunard; 6 May Code Change; Help Police, Postcode Valuables. From £7.*

## 5th June 1990 – KEW GARDENS
*20p Cycad + Joseph Banks Blg; 29p Stone Pine + Conservatory; 34p Willow Tree + Palm House; 37p Cedar + Pagoda*

**SPECIAL HANDSTAMPS**

| | | | |
|---|---|---|---|
| (1) | First Day of Issue – Philatelic Bureau................ | 4 | – *Royal Mail* |
| (2) | First Day of Issue – Kew, Richmond................. | 4 | – *Royal Mail* |
| (3) | Arboricultural Assoc., Sevenoaks...................... | 10 | 12 *BLCS54* |
| (4) | 150th Anniv. Royal Botanic Gardens, Kew....... | 10 | 25 *Ben500(54)* |
| (5) | Royal Botanic Gdns, Given to the Nation, 1840.. | 10 | 15 *LFDC 88* |
| (6) | Royal Botanic Gdns, Kew 1840-1990................. | 10 | 15 *LFDC 88* |
| (7) | Botanical Society, SW7 ..................................... | 10 | 20 *CoverCraft* |
| (8) | The Conservation Trust, Reading....................... | 10 | 20 *CoverCraft* |
| (9) | Nat. Garden Festival (changeable date) ............. | 12 | – *Royal Mail* |
| (10) | Nat. Garden Festival Tyne and Wear ............... | 12 | – *Royal Mail* |
| (11) | Church in the Wood, St. Leonards on Sea ........ | 10 | 50 *Bradbury* |
| (12) | Forth Bridge Centennial ................................... | 10 | 35 *Bradbury* |
| (13) | Torquay Philatelic Counter (Palm Tree)............ | 20 | – *n.o.c.* |
| (14) | 10th Anniversary, TTTE, BF 2247 PS ................ | 7 | 15 *RFDC 84* |

**C.D.S POSTMARKS**

| | | |
|---|---|---|
| (15) | Kew Gardens, Richmond, Surrey....................... | 30 |
| (16) | Ash, Beech, Cherry Tree, Elm, Hatfield Broad Oak, Fir Tree, Orange Tree, Pear Tree, Yew Tree.. | 20 |

*Also: Botanic Gdns, Broad Oak, Cedar Road, Chestnut Terrace, Forest Rd, The Firs, Glasshouses, Green Willows, Hawkhurst, Pinewoods, Sevenoaks, The Forest, The Green, The Willows, Wood End, Woodlands. Prices from £15.*

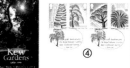

**Kew Gardens (contd.)**

|  | ordinary covers £ | official covers £ |
|---|---|---|

**SLOGAN POSTMARKS**

| | | |
|---|---|---|
| (17) Royal Botanic Gardens, Kew | 40 | |
| (18) Richmond, Twin Towns, Twickenham | 20 | |
| (19) Dronfield & District Feast of Flowers | 15 | |

*Also: Steam Rally & Country Show; Royal Mail Derby/ESTF; Royal Mail Uxbridge New Sorting Office; Chester Business Park; Post Code; Collect British Stamps. Prices from £5.*

## 10th July 1990 – THOMAS HARDY

*20p Portrait of Hardy with Clyffe Clump, Dorset*

**SPECIAL HANDSTAMPS**

| | | | |
|---|---|---|---|
| (1) First Day of Issue – Philatelic Bureau | 2 | – | *Royal Mail* |
| (2) First Day of Issue – Dorchester | 2 | – | *Royal Mail* |
| (3) Thomas Hardy Society, Higher Bockhampton | 8 | 10 | *LFDC 89* |
| (4) Marnhull, Tess of the D'Urbervilles | 8 | 12 | *Bradbury* |
| (5) Dorchester, Mayor of Casterbridge | 8 | 12 | *Bradbury* |
| (6) Thomas Hardy, Stinsford | 8 | 12 | *Bradbury* |
| (7) 150th Anniv. Thomas Hardy, Bockhampton | 8 | 20 | *Ben500(55)* |
| (8) Thomas Hardy, Wessex Poet & Novelist | 8 | 10 | *BLCS 55* |
| (9) Puddletown, Hardy's Weatherbury | 8 | 15 | *A. Pearce* |
| (10) Thomas Hardy, Dorchester | 8 | 15 | *Havering* |
| (11) Thomas Hardy, Higher Bockhampton | 8 | 20 | *CoverCraft* |
| (12) Nelson with Capt. Hardy, BF 2248 PS | 8 | 15 | *FAA Museum* |
| (13) Gibbons Stamp Monthly, Ringwood | 8 | 10 | *BenL24* |
| (14) Royal Navy Series, Plymouth | 8 | 10 | *Marriott* |
| (15) RAF Station Northolt, BF 2250 PS | 8 | 10 | *RFDC 85* |
| (16) Wimbledon, Lawn Tennis Museum | 8 | 20 | *H.R.* |

**C.D.S. POSTMARKS**

| | |
|---|---|
| (17) Bere Regis (*Kingsbere*); Dorchester (*Casterbridge*); Maiden Newton (*Chalk Newton*); Puddletown (*Weatherbury*); Salisbury (*Melchester*); Shaftesbury (*Shaston*); Sherborne (*Sherton Abbas*); Sturminston Newton (*Stourcastle*); Weymouth (*Budmouth*); Winfrith (*Haggard Egden*) .......................................*each* | 10 |
| (18) Harrow Rd or Westbourne Pk Rd – London home. | 10 |
| (19) Fordington – wrote many of his works here | 10 |

*Also: Amesbury, Hardy Lane, Owermoigne, Piddlinghton, Wimborne. From £15.*

**SLOGAN POSTMARKS**

*Royal Mail Derby; Postcode, Dorchester; Say it Better in a Letter; Post Early; Various Post Code slogans; Uxbridge Sorting Office. Prices from £8.*

## 2nd August 1990 – THE QUEEN MOTHER'S 90th BIRTHDAY

*20p Queen Elizabeth The Queen Mother; 29p Queen Elizabeth; 34p Elizabeth Duchess of York; 37p Lady Elizabeth Bowes-Lyon*

**SPECIAL HANDSTAMPS**

| | | | |
|---|---|---|---|
| (1) First Day of Issue – Philatelic Bureau | 4 | – | *Royal Mail* |
| (2) First Day of Issue – City of Westminster | 4 | – | *Royal Mail* |
| (3) St. Paul's, Walden, Herts – (square) | 10 | 15 | *LFDC 90* |
| (4) Clarence House, SW1 – (square) | 10 | 15 | *LFDC 90* |
| (5) Glamis, Tayside – (square) | 10 | 15 | *LFDC 90* |
| (6) Clarence House – (oval) | 10 | 15 | *BLCS 56* |
| (7) Glamis Castle – (oval) | 10 | 25 | *Ben500(56)* |
| (8) Windsor Castle – (oval) | 10 | 20 | *BLCS 56* |
| (9) St. Paul's, Hitchin – (oval) | 10 | 15 | *BenSG11* |
| (10) The Queen Mother, Woman & Home, SE1 | 10 | 20 | *BLCS 56* |
| (11) Heartiest Congratulations, BF 1990 PS | 10 | 15 | *RFDC 86* |
| (12) Royal Mail, Birmingham | 10 | 25 | *RM B'ham* |
| (13) Queen Mother, Bowes Museum | 10 | 15 | *S. Muscroft* |
| (14) 90th Birthday HM The Queen Mother, W1 | 10 | 30 | *CoverCraft* |
| (15) Glamis Castle – (circle) | 10 | 45 | *CoverCraft* |
| (16) Clarence House – (circle) | 10 | 45 | *CoverCraft* |
| (17) Royal Wolverhampton School | 10 | 35 | *LFDC 90* |
| (18) RNLI, Thurso Lifeboat | 10 | 35 | *Pilgrim* |
| (19) Royal Doulton, The Potteries | 10 | 20 | *P.Withers* |

**C.D.S. POSTMARKS**

| | |
|---|---|
| (20) Barnard Castle or Bowes | 8 |
| (21) Buckingham Palace or Windsor Castle | 100 |
| (22) Glamis – Queen Mother's ancestral home | 25 |
| (23) House of Commons or Lords | 25 |
| (24) Mey – Castle of Mey | 25 |
| (25) Queen Elizabeth Ave. or Queen's Rd. | 10 |
| (26) Whitwell, Hitchin – Bowes-Lyon family | 10 |
| (27) Windsor, Old Windsor or Windsor Gt Park | 10 |

*Also: Albemarle St, Crathie, Holyrood, Rose, Scone, Walmer, York. From £15.*

**SLOGAN POSTMARKS**

*Queen Victoria School; Royal Engineers Museum; Cunard; Forres Europe in Bloom; Alder Hey; Royal Mail – Car Secure; Royal Botanic Gardens. Prices from £7.*

There are thousands of special handstamps listed in this catalogue: too many to illustrate. However for each commemorative stamp issue there is a file illustrating most of the handstamps available FREE from www.bfdc.co.uk/postmarks

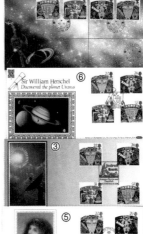

## 11th Sept. 1990 – GALLANTRY

*5 x 20p: Distinguished Service Cross & Medal*
*Distinguished Flying Cross & Medal*
*Military Cross & Military Medal; Victoria Cross; George Cross*

|  |  | ordinary cvrs | official covers |  |
|---|---|---|---|---|
|  |  | £ | £ |  |

### SPECIAL HANDSTAMPS

| | | | | |
|---|---|---|---|---|
| (1) | First Day of Issue – Philatelic Bureau................. | 4 | – | *Royal Mail* |
| (2) | First Day of Issue – City of Westminster........... | 4 | – | *Royal Mail* |
| (3) | St. George, Bristol ..................................... | 12 | 30 | *Bradbury* |
| (4) | The Spirit of Britain, SW1 ................................. | 12 | 15 | *LFDC 91* |
| (5) | Battle of Britain, Hawkinge............................... | 12 | 25 | *BLCS 57* |
| (6) | Battle of Britain, Biggin Hill, Westerham ........ | 12 | 35 | *BLCS 57* |
| (7) | Victoria Cross for Valour, SW ........................... | 12 | 60 | *Ben500(57)* |
| (8) | George Cross for Gallantry, SW ....................... | 12 | 30 | *BenSG12* |
| (9) | Military Medal for Bravery, Chichester ............. | 12 | 25 | *BenL26* |
| (10) | Distinguished Service Medal, Liverpool............ | 12 | 25 | *BenL25* |
| (11) | Battle of Britain, BF 2232 PS ........................... | 12 | 25 | *Forces (s)* |
| (12) | Royal Navy Series, Plymouth............................. | 12 | 2 | *Marriott(s)* |
| (13) | Victoria Cross, National Postal Museum .......... | 20 | – | *n.o.c.* |
| (14) | World War II, Far East, BF 2251 PS ................. | 12 | 20 | *FAA Museum* |
| (15) | Defence of Rorke's Drift.................................... | 12 | 35 | *S. Muscroft* |
| (16) | Battle of Britain, RAF Bentley Priory................ | 12 | 45 | *CoverCraft* |
| (17) | Battle of Britain, BBMF, RAF Coningsby.......... | 12 | 35 | *CoverCraft* |
| (18) | Battle of Britain, RAF Coltishall........................ | 12 | 10 | *Markton* |
| (19) | George Cross, Island Siege, Bell Fund, Malta... | 12 | 125 | *Cam.S.C.* |
| (20) | Baden-Powell House............................................ | 12 | 10 | *Havering* |
| (21) | Sunderland AFC ................................................... | 12 | 15 | *Dawn* |
| (22) | Torquay, Birthplace of Agatha Christie ............. | 12 | 85 | *CoverCraft* |

### C.D.S. POSTMARKS

| | | |
|---|---|---|
| (23) | High Cross, Ware – b/place of first VC & Bar . | 20 |
| (24) | Biggin Hill, or RAF Biggin Hill............................ | 30 |
| (25) | Any Field Post Office or RAF Station................ | 20 |
| (26) | Portsmouth - Royal Navy ................................... | 15 |
| (27) | Sandhurst – Royal Military Academy ................. | 25 |
| (28) | Royal Hospital Chelsea – Chelsea Pensioners.. | 25 |
| (29) | St. George, Bristol or St. Georges, Telford .... | 25 |
| (30) | St. George's Cross, Glasgow .............................. | 20 |
| (31) | Hawkinge or Duxford........................................... | 20 |
| (32) | Maritime Mail....................................................... | 40 |

*Also: Albemarle St. W1, Battle, Battlefield, Battlefield Rd., Battlehill,*
*Buckingham Palace, Churchill, Cove Bay, Duke of York Sch., Dunkirk,*
*Falklands, Gun End, House of Commons, House of Lords,*
*Immingham Dock, King George Rd, Manor Park, Memorial Rd,*
*Mount Ephriam, Normandy, Queen's Cross, Richmond, Sebastopol,*
*Three Crosses, Victoria Rd, Walton-on-Thames, Wargrave,*
*Waterloo, Windsor Castle, Wortley. From £15.*

### SLOGAN POSTMARKS

| | | |
|---|---|---|
| (33) | Royal Engineers Museum ................................... | 20 |
| (34) | RAF Finningley Air Show ..................................... | 20 |

*In addition: Nth Yorks Police; Queen Victoria Sch; Croydon. Prices from £8.*

## 16th October 1990 – ASTRONOMY

*22p Armagh Observatory; Jodrell Bank and La Palma telescopes;*
*26p Moon and tides; Herschel's telescope;*
*31p Greenwich Old Observatory and early Astronomical equipment;*
*37p Stonehenge: gyroscope and navigation by the stars*

### SPECIAL HANDSTAMPS

| | | | | |
|---|---|---|---|---|
| (1) | First Day of Issue – Philatelic Bureau................. | 4 | – | *Royal Mail* |
| (2) | First Day of Issue – Armagh .............................. | 4 | – | *Royal Mail* |
| (3) | Jodrell Bank Science Centre ............................... | 10 | 15 | *LFDC 92* |
| (4) | Old Royal Observatory, Greenwich ................... | 10 | 15 | *BLCS 58* |
| (5) | Heavens Declare the Glory of God, Armagh.... | 10 | 10 | *BLCS 58* |
| (6) | Sir William Herschel, Slough............................... | 10 | 30 | *Ben500(58)* |
| (7) | Woolsthorpe, Birthplace of Isaac Newton........ | 10 | 50 | *CoverCraft* |
| (8) | Astronomical Alignments, Stonehenge .............. | 10 | 60 | *Bradbury* |
| (9) | Old Royal Observatory, Greenwich (globe) ...... | 10 | 15 | *Arlington* |
| (10) | British Astronomical Assoc., Burlington Hse.... | 10 | 65 | *Cam.S.C.* |
| (11) | British Astronomical Assoc., Royal Observatory . | 10 | 95 | *Cam.S.C.* |
| (12) | Autumn Stampex/BPE, London SW1 ................. | 10 | – | *Royal Mail* |
| (13) | Royal Mail Exhibition Card No. 4....................... | 10 | – | *Royal Mail* |
| (14) | No. 249 Squadron BF 2253 PS ......................... | 10 | 15 | *RFDC 88* |

### C.D.S. POSTMARKS

| | | |
|---|---|---|
| (15) | Armagh – Armagh Observatory .......................... | 20 |
| (16) | Macclesfield etc – Jodrell Bank.......................... | 20 |
| (17) | Greenwich, Herstmonceux, Castle St. Cambridge | |
| | – Royal Observatory.................. | 15 |
| (18) | Larkhill or Amesbury – Stonehenge................... | 20 |
| (19) | Albemarle St. – Burlington House...................... | 15 |
| (20) | Meridian Centre, Peacehaven............................. | 20 |

*Also: Archer Road, Barnard Castle, Blackford Avenue Edinburgh, Ceres, Colsterworth,*
*Comberton, The Crescent, Crown View, Denby, Five Points, Flamstead End, Globe Rd., Helston,*
*Moore, Newton, North Pole, Oldland Common, The Rocket, Seven Sisters, Southern Cross,*
*Starcross. From £12.*

### SLOGAN POSTMARKS

*PO Mercurycard; Stampex; New World Dom. Appliances; Car Secure; Smugglers; Isle of Skye;*
*Royal Soc of Chemistry; Sunderland Illuminations. Prices from £12.*

## 13th November 1990 – CHRISTMAS

*17p Children building snowman;*
*22p Bringing home the Christmas tree;*
*26p Carol singers; 31p Tobogganing; 37p Skating*

|  |  | ordinary cvrs £ | official covers £ |
|---|---|---|---|
| **SPECIAL HANDSTAMPS** | | | |
| (1) | First Day of Issue – Philatelic Bureau | 4 | – Royal Mail |
| (2) | First Day of Issue – Bethlehem, Llandeilo | 4 | – Royal Mail |
| (3) | Church Bell Ringers, St. Paul's, EC4 | 10 | 35 Bradbury |
| (4) | Church Bell Ringers, Duffield | 10 | 35 Bradbury |
| (5) | Birmingham Cathedral | 10 | 20 Bradbury |
| (6) | 25 Years Christmas Stamps, Bethlehem | 10 | 35 LFDC 93 |
| (7) | 150 Years of Stamps, Nasareth | 10 | 35 CoverCraft |
| (8) | 150 Years of Stamps, London EC1 | 10 | 35 CoverCraft |
| (9) | Nat. Postal Museum, Post Early for Christmas | 10 | 20 Friends of NPM |
| (10) | Benham, First Day Covers, Folkestone | 10 | 15 BLCS 59 |
| (11) | Christmas Mailcoach Run, Windsor | 10 | 10 BLCS 59 |
| (12) | Christmas Tradition, Snowdown, Dover | 10 | 20 Ben500(59) |
| (13) | Stanley Gibbons Catalogue, Ringwood | 10 | 25 BenL27 |
| (14) | Christmas 1990, Cambridge | 10 | 95 Cam.S.C. |
| (15) | Stampway to the World, Glasgow | 10 | 25 S.P. Board |
| (16) | Bishop Vesey, Sutton Coldfield | 10 | 25 BVGS |
| (17) | Blood & Fire in Darkest England, EC1 | 10 | 15 S.Army |
| (18) | Royal Navy Series, Plymouth | 15 | – n.o.c. |
| **C.D.S. POSTMARKS** | | | |
| (19) | Church, Hollybush, Fir Tree or Playing Place... | 15 | |
| (20) | Nasareth | 25 | |

*In addition: Aviemore, Churchfield, Church Hill, Church Village,*
*Holy Island, Jericho, Jerusalem St., Merry Hill, Noel Road,*
*St. Nicholas, Trafalgar Square, Winter Hey. Prices from £10.*

| **SLOGAN POSTMARKS** | | | |
|---|---|---|---|
| (21) | Birmingham Cathedral | 20 | |
| (22) | Happy Christmas – Please Post Early | 40 | |
| (23) | Nadolig Llawen – Happy Christmas | 40 | |

*Also: Stampway; Candlelighters; Control your Dog; Coventry/Friendship; Alder Hey. Prices from £8.*

**CHRISTMAS BOOKLET**
Covers bearing pair or block of 4 x 17p from booklet with spec h/s
(straight edges at top and bottom) .......... 5
Full pane of ten stamps on cover .......... 20

## 8th January 1991 – DOGS (George Stubbs)

*22p King Charles Spaniel; 26p A Pointer; 31p Two Hounds in a Landscape;*
*33p A Rough Dog; 37p Fino and Tiny*

| **SPECIAL HANDSTAMPS** | | | |
|---|---|---|---|
| (1) | First Day of Issue – Philatelic Bureau | 4 | – Royal Mail |
| (2) | First Day of Issue – Birmingham | 4 | – Royal Mail |
| (3) | PDSA, Telford | 10 | 15 LFDC 94 |
| (4) | Tate Gallery, London, SW1 | 10 | 25 Bradbury |
| (5) | Birmingham Dogs Home | 10 | 30 Bradbury |
| (6) | Best of British Dogs, Birmingham | 10 | 30 Bradbury |
| (7) | RVC, 200 Years, NW1 | 10 | 25 Bradbury |
| (8) | Crufts Dog Show, Birmingham (badge) | 10 | 10 BLCS 60 |
| (9) | Centenary Crufts Dog Show, Birmingham | 10 | 40 Ben500(60) |
| (10) | Pawprints, Stoke-on-Trent | 10 | 20 P. Withers |
| (11) | Birthplace of George Stubbs, Liverpool | 10 | 25 CoverCraft |
| (12) | National Canine Defence League, NW1 | 10 | 30 CoverCraft |
| (13) | Dog World, Crufts, NEC, Birmingham | 10 | 20 R. Skinner |
| (14) | Police Guard Dog School, BF 2257 PS | 10 | 20 RFDC 90 |
| (15) | Stampway to the World, Glasgow | 10 | 20 S.P. Board |
| **C.D.S. POSTMARKS** | | | |
| (16) | Barking, Black Dog or Dogsthorpe........each | 20 | |
| (17) | Battersea or NEC | 20 | |
| (18) | Dog & Gun, Dog Kennel Ln or Isle of Dogs... | 25 | |
| (19) | Odiham – RVC founded by Odiham Agr Soc... | 15 | |
| (20) | Portman Square – Stubb's studio | 15 | |
| (21) | Royal College St – Royal Veterinary College .... | 15 | |
| (22) | Stubb's Cross | 15 | |

*Also: Airedale, Corn Exchange, Houndsditch, Newmarket, Pant. From £12.*

| **SLOGAN POSTMARKS** | | | |
|---|---|---|---|
| (23) | Pawprints Appeal | 20 | |
| (24) | Take a Bite out of Crime | 20 | |

*In addition: Stampway to the World. Prices from £8.*

## 5th February 1991 – GREETINGS STAMPS

*10 designs of '1st Class' stamps featuring good luck symbols*

| **SPECIAL HANDSTAMPS** | | | |
|---|---|---|---|
| (1) | First Day of Issue – Philatelic Bureau | 5 | – Royal Mail |
| (2) | First Day of Issue – Greetwell, Lincs. | 5 | – Royal Mail |
| (3) | Good Luck, Rainow, Macclesfield | 10 | 30 BLCS 61 |
| (4) | Good Luck, Good Easter, Chelmsford | 10 | 25 Ben500(61) |
| (5) | Good Luck, Wishford, Salisbury | 10 | 10 BenD158 |
| (6) | Good Luck, Glenrothes, Fife | 10 | 40 BLCS 61 |
| (7) | Good Luck, Magpie, Yelverton | 10 | 40 BLCS 61 |
| (8) | Good Luck, Luckington, Chippenham | 10 | 15 Bradbury |
| (9) | Rescue Services, BF 2258 PS | 10 | 15 RFDC 91 |

*Greetings (contd.)*
**C.D.S. POSTMARKS**

<table>
<tr><td></td><td>ordinary covers £</td><td>official covers £</td></tr>
</table>

(10) Acorn St., Bell Green, Boot, Branch End, Bridge, Catsfield, Clover Rd., Cross Keys, Drakes Broughton, Ducklington, Frog Island, Frogpool, Goldenacre, Greet, Greetland, Gretna Green, Jacob's Well, Keyworth, Klondyke, Luckington, Merlin's Bridge, Primrose Hill, Silverwell, Sky Crescent, Starcross, Swallow's Nest, Well, Wing, Wren's Nest..................................*each*  15

**POSTMARK SLOGANS**
*Pawprints; Samaritans; Alder Hey; Magic of British Music; Royal Mail/Post Code. From £15.*

## 5th March 1991 – SCIENTIFIC ACHIEVEMENTS
*22p Michael Faraday – electricity; 22p Charles Babbage – computers;*
*31p Robert Watson-Watt – radar; 37p Frank Whittle – jet engine*

**SPECIAL HANDSTAMPS**

| | | | | |
|---|---|---|---|---|
| (1) | First Day of Issue – Philatelic Bureau | 4 | – | *Royal Mail* |
| (2) | First Day of Issue – South Kensington, SW7 | 4 | – | *Royal Mail* |
| (3) | Charles Babbage, Science Museum, SW7 | 10 | 20 | *Bradbury* |
| (4) | Royal Society of Chemistry, W1 | 10 | 20 | *Bradbury* |
| (5) | Society British Aerospace Companies, SW1 | 10 | 20 | *Bradbury* |
| (6) | The Royal Institution, W1 | 10 | 20 | *Bradbury* |
| (7) | Sir Frank Whittle, Lutterworth | 10 | 15 | *LFDC 95* |
| (8) | Marconi Radar Systems, Chelmsford | 10 | 20 | *Bradbury* |
| (9) | Michael Faraday, Electrical Discovery, SW | 10 | 17 | *Ben500(62)* |
| (10) | A.E.U. General Office, SE15 | 10 | 20 | *R. Skinner* |
| (11) | Loughborough University | 10 | 20 | *S. Muscroft* |
| (12) | Michael Faraday/Charles Babbage, IEE | 10 | 45 | *Cam.S.C.* |
| (13) | Industrial Soc., Peter Runge House | 10 | 20 | *P. Withers* |
| (14) | First Aircraft Turbo Jet Engine, BF 2260 PS | 10 | 20 | *Forces* |
| (15) | First Flight of Jet, Cranwell, BF 2259 PS | 10 | 20 | *RFDC 92* |
| (16) | Computer Innovation, Wembley | 10 | 135 | *Arlington* |
| (17) | Electricity, Hove | 10 | 160 | *Arlington* |
| (18) | Royal Signals & Radar, Malvern | 10 | 160 | *Arlington* |
| (19) | RMA Woolwich, Sandhurst | 10 | 160 | *Arlington* |

**C.D.S. POSTMARKS**

| | | |
|---|---|---|
| (20) | Albermarle Street, W1 – Royal Institution | 15 |
| (21) | Cranwell – first official flight of the jet engine.. | 15 |
| (22) | Daventry – radar experiments | 15 |
| (23) | Exhibition Road, SW7 – Science Museum | 15 |
| (24) | Hucclecote – Gloster Meteor was built here | 20 |
| (25) | Lutterworth – jet engine was built here | 20 |
| (26) | New Invention | 20 |
| (27) | Weedon – first successful radar demonstrated . | 20 |

*Also: Alderton, Banbury, Brechin, Brockworth, Broomfield Rd, Caversham, Earlsden, Elephant & Castle, Faraday St, Loughborough, Seascale, Southcliff, Totnes, Trinity St., Walworth Road. From £12.*

**SLOGAN POSTMARKS**

| | | |
|---|---|---|
| (28) | Philips – a hundred years ahead | 15 |
| (29) | Loughborough University | 15 |

*In addition: Sunderland Enterprise Zone £8.*

## 26th March 1991 – GREETINGS STAMPS
*Same 'smiles' designs as 6th Feb. 1990 – values changed from 20p to '1st Class'*

**SPECIAL HANDSTAMPS**

| | | | | |
|---|---|---|---|---|
| (1) | First Day of Issue – Philatelic Bureau | 5 | – | *Royal Mail* |
| (2) | First Day of Issue – Laughterton, Lincs. | 5 | – | *Royal Mail* |
| (3) | Puncheston, Haverfordwest, Dyfed | 10 | 20 | *BenD159* |
| (4) | Greetings, The Teddy Bear Shop, Ironbridge | 10 | 25 | *BLCS 63* |
| (5) | Greetings, Clowne, Chesterfield | 10 | 30 | *BLCS 63* |
| (6) | Greetings, Hartford, Cheshire | 10 | 20 | *Ben500(63)* |
| (7) | Birthplace of Stan Laurel, Ulverston | 10 | 15 | *Bradbury* |
| (8) | Battle of Cape Matapan, BF 2262 PS | 10 | – | *n.o.c.* |

**C.D.S. POSTMARKS**

| | | |
|---|---|---|
| (9) | Bearpark, or Catsfield | 12 |
| (10) | Constable Road, or Fleet Street | 12 |
| (11) | Giggleswick, Greet or Laughterton | 12 |
| (12) | Puncheston, Clowne or Queen's Head | 12 |
| (13) | Ulverston – birthplace of Stan Laurel | 12 |

**SLOGAN POSTMARKS**

| | | |
|---|---|---|
| (14) | Take a Bite out of Crime | 15 |

*In addition: The Samaritans; Alder Hey. Prices from £7.*

## 23rd April 1991 – EUROPE IN SPACE
*2 x 22p Man looking into space; 2 x 37p Space looking at man*

**SPECIAL HANDSTAMPS**

| | | | | |
|---|---|---|---|---|
| (1) | First Day of Issue – Philatelic Bureau | 4 | – | *Royal Mail* |
| (2) | First Day of Issue – Cambridge | 4 | – | *Royal Mail* |
| (3) | Soft Moon Landing, Jodrell Bank | 10 | 20 | *BLCS 64* |
| (4) | Vostok 1, Yuri Gargarin, The Rocket | 10 | 20 | *BLCS 64* |
| (5) | First Man in Space, Harwell | 10 | 25 | *Ben500(64)* |
| (6) | Kettering Boys School | 10 | 20 | *P. Withers* |
| (7) | Space: The Final Frontier, W1 | 10 | 25 | *Bradbury* |
| (8) | Hubble Space Telescope, Cambridge | 10 | 50 | *Bradbury* |

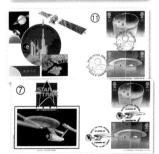

Rugby Union World Cup

**Europe in Space (contd.)** — ordinary covers £ — official covers £

| | ord. | off. | |
|---|---|---|---|
| (9) Royal Aeronautical Society, W1 | 10 | 10 | *Bradbury* |
| (10) British Interplanetary Society, SW8 1SZ | 10 | 15 | *Bradbury* |
| (11) BNSC – Britain's Space Agency, SW1 | 10 | 10 | *LFDC 96* |
| (12) Jodrell Bank Science Centre, Macclesfield | 10 | 45 | *CoverCraft* |
| (13) VC10 in Military Service, BF 2272 PS | 10 | 20 | *RFDC 93* |
| (14) Centre for Crop Circle Studies, Guildford | 10 | 20 | *S. Muscroft* |
| (15) Prince & Princess of Wales, Brazil | 10 | 125 | *Forces* |
| (16) Salvation Army Match Factory, E3 | 10 | 30 | *S.Army* |

**C.D.S. POSTMARKS**

| | |
|---|---|
| (17) Comberton – Mullard Radio Astron. Observatory | 10 |
| (18) Greenwich or Cambridge – Royal Observatory | 10 |
| (19) Helston – Goonhilly Downs Earth Station | 10 |
| (20) The Rocket | 15 |
| (21) Siddington, Goostrey, Macclesfield – Jodrell Bank | 10 |
| (22) South Lambeth Rd – Interplanetary Soc | 10 |
| (23) Surbiton–Helen Sharman/Britain's first astronaut | 15 |

*Also: Chilton, Eye, Farnborough, Neville's Cross, Oldland Common, S. Wonston, Upton Lea. From £10.*

**SLOGAN POSTMARKS**

| | |
|---|---|
| (24) Squint Awareness Week | 25 |

*Also: Loughborough Univ; BBC Radio; Samaritans; Sunday Collections; Please Control your Dog; Beat the Burglar; Postcode it. £8.*

## 11th June 1991 – SPORTS

*22p Fencing; 26p Hurdling; 31p Diving; 39p Rugby*

**SPECIAL HANDSTAMPS**

| | ord. | off. | |
|---|---|---|---|
| (1) Philatelic Bureau | 4 | – | *Royal Mail* |
| (2) First Day of Issue – Sheffield | 4 | – | *Royal Mail* |
| (3) Rugby Football, 'Grand Slam', Twickenham | 10 | 15 | *Sajal Phil* |
| (4) If it's on, it's in Radio Times, W1 | 10 | 20 | *Radio Times* |
| (5) Home of Welsh Rugby, Cardiff Arms Park | 10 | 12 | *BLCS 65* |
| (6) Home of Scottish Rugby, Murrayfield | 10 | 15 | *BLCS 65* |
| (7) Home of English Rugby, Twickenham | 10 | 12 | *BLCS 65* |
| (8) 1991 Year of Sport, Sheffield | 10 | 30 | *Ben500(65)* |
| (9) Rugby School | 10 | 10 | *LFDC 97* |
| (10) William Webb Ellis: Game of Rugby | 10 | 40 | *VP 59* |
| (11) Inter. Olympic Committee, Birmingham | 10 | 15 | *Bradbury* |
| (12) Sport for All, Wembley | 10 | 20 | *Bradbury* |
| (13) World Student Games, Sheffield | 10 | 25 | *WSGames* |
| (14) Avon Pride, 1977-1991, Bristol | 10 | 375 | *Avon Pride* |
| (15) Lawn Tennis Museum | 10 | 25 | *AELT* |

**C.D.S. POSTMARKS**

(16) The Hayes (Cardiff); Kingsholm (Gloucester); Kneller Rd. (Twickenham); Murrayfield (Edinburgh); Ravenhill Park (Belfast); Sandygate (Llanelli); Welford Rd. (Leicester); Otley; Pontypool; Pontypridd – Rugby World Cup

| | |
|---|---|
| ...............................................each | 20 |
| (17) Rugby – Rugby School | 15 |
| (18) Sheffied – World Student Games | 15 |

*Also: The University Bath, Fence, Jump, First Lane, Loughborough, University Bradford. From £8.*

**SLOGAN POSTMARKS**

| | |
|---|---|
| (19) Birmingham Welcomes IOC Committee | 15 |
| (20) Cardiff Just Capital | 20 |
| (21) Federation Cup, Nottingham Tennis Centre | 25 |

*Also: Loughborough University; Convention Centre B'ham; Cub Scouting;London Docklands. £10.*

## 16th July 1991 – ROSES

*22p Silver Jubilee; 26p Mme. Alfred Carriere; 31p Rosa Moyesii; 33p Harvest Fayre; 37p Rosa Mutabilis*

**SPECIAL HANDSTAMPS**

| | ord. | off. | |
|---|---|---|---|
| (1) Philatelic Bureau | 4 | – | *Royal Mail* |
| (2) First Day of Issue – Belfast | 4 | – | *Royal Mail* |
| (3) Royal National Rose Society, St. Albans | 10 | 15 | *LFDC 98* |
| (4) Royal Botanic Gardens, Kew | 10 | 15 | *Bradbury* |
| (5) World Rose Convention, Belfast | 10 | 40 | *VP 60* |
| (6) O, My Luve's Like a Red, Red Rose | 10 | 20 | *Bradbury* |
| (7) Roses on Stamps, Rose, Truro | 10 | 20 | *Bradbury* |
| (8) The Gardener, Chelsea, SW3 | 10 | 20 | *BLCS 66* |
| (9) Rosebush, Clynderwen, Dyfed | 10 | 25 | *Ben500(66)* |
| (10) Rose Garden, Drum Castle, Banchory | 10 | 22 | *BLCS 66* |
| (11) Henry VIII, Hampton Court | 10 | 15 | *BenSG13* |
| (12) Hampton Court Palace, Int. Flower Show | 10 | 60 | *CoverCraft* |
| (13) National Gallery, WC2 | 10 | 85 | *CoverCraft* |
| (14) Royal Tournament, Earls Court, BF 2292 PS | 10 | 10 | *Forces* |
| (15) London Economic Summit, SW1 | 10 | 50 | *Arlington* |

**C.D.S. POSTMARKS**

| | |
|---|---|
| (16) Botanic Gardens, Belfast or Kew Gardens | 25 |
| (17) Newtonards – 'Harvest Fayre' bred here | 15 |
| (18) Rose, Truro | 25 |
| (19) Roseacre, Rosebank, Rosebush, Rosedale Abbey, Rosehearty, Rose Green, Rose Hill, Roseland, Rosemarket, Roses Lane Ends ....................each | 25 |
| (20) Royal Hospital – Chelsea Flower Show | 25 |

*In addition: Chipping Campden, Glamis, Leaves Green. Prices from £12.*

Roses *(contd.)*

|  | ordinary covers £ | official covers £ |
|---|---|---|

**SLOGAN POSTMARKS**
(21) Beechwood Place – Shopping in full bloom ..... 20
*Also: Belfast 1991; Control your dog; Mansfield Show; Postcodes. Prices from £7.*

## 20th August 1991 – DINOSAURS
*22p Iguanodon; 26p Stegosaurus; 31pTyrannosaurus;
33p Protoceratops; 37p Triceratops*

**SPECIAL HANDSTAMPS** (1) Philatelic Bureau ..... 4  – *Royal Mail*
(2) First Day of Issue – Plymouth ............................. 4  – *Royal Mail*
(3) Dinosaur Museum, Dorchester........................... 15  15 *BLCS 67*
(4) The Last Dinosaur? The Loch Ness Monster ... 15  25 *BLCS 67*
(5) Iguanodon Mantelli , Maidstone....................... 15  15 *BenL28*
(6) 150th Anniv. of the Word Dinosaur, Oxford .... 15  18 *B'ham (500)67*
(7) First Discovery of Iguanodon, Cuckfield............ 15  45 *VP 61*
(8) Natural History Museum, Dinosaurs, SW7 ....... 15  20 *LFDC 99*
(9) First use of Word Dinosaur, Plymouth............... 15  35 *Bradbury*
(10) Farewell Shackletonsaurus, BF 2299 PS ........... 15  20 *RFDC 96*
(11) Plymouth Museums & Art Gallery .................... 15  65 *Arlington*
(12) Franklin & Andrew, London, EC4 ..................... 15  150 *Arlington*

**C.D.S. POSTMARKS**
(13) Plymouth – first use of Word 'Dinosaur'........... 20
(14) Cuckfield, Lyme Regis, Maidstone, Stonesfield
      or Tilgate – dinosaur remains ................*each*  20
(15) Dorchester – Dinosaur Museum ........................ 20
(16) Exhibition Rd. – Natural History Museum........ 20
(17) The Lizard .......................................................... 20
*Camels Head, Lancaster, Lewes, Oxford, Ness, Stonewell, Sydenham.
From £15.*

**SLOGAN POSTMARKS** *Pawprints; Control Your Dog; Guide Dogs; Bite/Crime.£10.*

## 17th September 1991 – MAPS
*24p, 28p, 33p, 39p – Hamstreet as depicted on Ordnance Survey maps.*

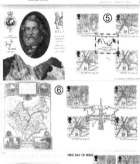

**SPECIAL HANDSTAMPS** (1) Philatelic Bureau ..... 4  – *Royal Mail*
(2) First Day of Issue – Southampton ..................... 4  – *Royal Mail*
(3) Visit the Nene Valley Railway .......................... 12  55 *N.V. Rly.*
(4) Maps and the Post Office, NPM, EC ................ 12  110 *NPMuseum*
(5) Sir George Everest, Surveyor, Greenwich.......... 12  45 *Bradbury*
(6) Birthplace of Tourism, Leicester ...................... 12  35 *Bradbury*
(7) RICS, London, SW1 .......................................... 12  12 *Bradbury*
(8) Ordnance Survey, Hamstreet ............................ 12  12 *LFDC 100*
(9) Ordnance Survey Act, Westminster, SW1 ........ 12  35 *VP 62*
(10) Ordnance Survey, Hamstreet (oast house) ........ 12  15 *Ben500(68)*
(11) Hamstreet D490................................................ 12  15 *BLCS 68*
(12) Darling Buds of May, Hamstreet ...................... 12  12 *BLCS 68*
(13) Ordnance Survey OS, Southampton................... 12  75 *CoverCraft*
(14) Royal Observer Corps BF 2301 PS.................... 12  12 *RFDC 97*
(15) Tower of London, EC3....................................... 12  10 *Sunday Mag.*
(16) Salvation Army, Hadleigh.................................. 12
15  *S. Army*

**C.D.S. POSTMARKS**
(17) Ham Street, Ashford ......................................... 25
(18) House of Commons – Ordnance Survey Act .... 20
(19) House of Lords – Ordnance Survey Act ........... 30
(20) John O'Groats/Land's End ..........................*pair*  50
(21) Maybush – Ordnance Survey HQ ..................... 15
(22) Newlyn – OS Tidal Observatory ....................... 15
(23) Pathfinder Village or Ordnance Road............... 15
(24) Seething Lane – original HQ of OS .................. 15
*In addition: The Chart, Chartham, Cross Roads, Hereford, Junction, Marshfield, Meridian Centre,
Richmond, Roman Way, The Triangle, Tingley, World's End. Prices from £10.*

**SLOGAN POSTMARKS**
(25) Royal Scottish Geographical Society ................ 25
*Also: New Postage Rates; Yellow Brick Road; Royal Mail/Community; Control Your Dog. From £7.*

## 12th November 1991 – CHRISTMAS
*18p, 24p, 28p, 33p, 39p Illuminated Manuscripts (Bodleian Library).*

Bodleian Library

**SPECIAL HANDSTAMPS** (1) Philatelic Bureau ..... 4  – *Royal Mail*
(2) First Day of Issue – Bethlehem, Llandeilo......... 4  – *Royal Mail*
(3) Dean & Chapter Library, Durham Cathedral ... 10  15 *LFDC 101*
(4) Holy Island, Berwick ........................................ 10  15 *Bradbury*
(5) Illuminated Manuscripts, Bodleian Library ...... 10  35 *Bradbury*
(6) Illuminated Manuscripts, Bethlehem ................ 10  35 *VP 63*
(7) Cadfael Omnibus, Christmas, Shrewsbury........ 10  15 *BLCS 69*
(8) Christmas Manuscripts, Fountain's Abbey......... 10  15 *Ben500(69)*
(9) Christmas, Jerusalem, Skellingthorpe.................. 10  20 *C. Cooke*
(10) Lindisfarne Gospels, Holy Island...................... 10  25 *S. Muscroft*
(11) Happy Christmas Royal Mail City of London... 10  – *n.o.c.*
(12) Nat. Postal Museum Post Early for Christmas.. 10  50 *Friends of NPM*
(13) Christmas 1991, Cambridge .............................. 10  60 *Cam. S.C.*
(14) Joy to the World, The Salvation Army, SW1 .... 10  15 *S. Army*
(15) Hercules, BF 2304 PS........................................ 10  20 *RFDC 98*
(16) Henry VIII, Greenwich, SE1 ............................ 10  15 *BLCS 69*
(17) New Hoylake Lifeboat, Liverpool ..................... 10  20 *Pilgrim*

*Christmas (contd.)*

| | ordinary covers | official covers |
|---|---|---|
| **C.D.S. POSTMARKS** | £ | £ |

(18) Exeter – birthplace of Sir Thomas Bodley ......... 15
(19) Holy Island or Oxford (Bodleian Library)......... 15

*Angel Hill, Bolton Abbey, Caldey Is., Jerusalem St., Kings Rd, Nasareth, St.Nicholas, Threekingham. £10.*

**SLOGAN POSTMARKS**
*Newcastle Brown; Clatterbridge Superscan; JVC Video Letter; Northsound Charity; Control Your Dog; Pulse Trust Appeal; Shopping in Full Bloom; Glasgow Court Hall; Alder Hey; Write Now etc. £7.*

**CHRISTMAS BOOKLET:** Covers bearing pair or block of 4 x 18p stamps from booklet with special handstamp (these have straight edges at top and bottom)...*each* 3
Full pane of ten stamps on cover..........................*each* 15

## 14th January 1992 – WINTERTIME
*18p Deer; 24p Hare; 28p Fox; 33p Redwing; 39p Welsh Sheep.*

| | | | |
|---|---|---|---|
| **SPECIAL HANDSTAMPS** (1) Philatelic Bureau ..... | 4 | – | *Royal Mail* |
| (2) First Day of Issue – Brecon................................ | 4 | – | *Royal Mail* |
| (3) Emmerdale, Arncliffe, Skipton ........................... | 12 | – | *n.o.c.* |
| (4) Wintertime, Richmond Park ................................ | 10 | 15 | *B. Reeve 1* |
| (5) Wintertime, Owlsmoor, Camberley .................... | 10 | 15 | *LFDC 102* |
| (6) Wintertime, Haresfield ...................................... | 10 | 45 | *Bradbury* |
| (7) Wintertime, New Forest ..................................... | 10 | 25 | *VP 64* |
| (8) The Monarch of the Glen, Glenbuck.................. | 10 | 25 | *Ben500(70)* |
| (9) Wildlife in Winter, Thrushwood, Keswick........ | 10 | 10 | *BLCS 70* |
| (10) Wild About Animals, EC .................................. | 10 | 15 | *Benham* |
| (11) World Wide Fund for Nature, Godalming........ | 10 | 20 | *BLCS 70* |
| (12) British Wintertime, Brecon ............................. | 10 | 20 | *BLCS 70* |
| (13) Foxearth, Suffolk (or Sufflok)......................... | 10 | 20 | *BenSG14* |
| (14) Sittingbourne's New Postbus ........................... | 10 | 20 | *RM postcard* |
| (15) Chester Cathedral ............................................ | 10 | – | *n.o.c.* |
| (16) RAF Fylingdales, BF 2281 PS .......................... | 10 | 20 | *RFDC 99* |
| **C.D.S. POSTMARKS** | | | |
| (17) Deerpark, New Deer or Old Deer.............*each* | 20 | | |
| (18) Harefield, Harehills or Harewood.............*each* | 20 | | |
| (19) Foxhole or Fox Lane .................................*each* | 20 | | |
| (20) Sheepridge, Sheepwash or Sheepy.............*each* | 20 | | |
| (21) Sheepscombe – farm Post Office ...................... | 25 | | |
| (22) Brecon – sheep stamp set in Brecon area......... | 20 | | |

*Also: Coldridge, Frosterley, Freezywater, Godalming, Lairg, Lyndhurst, Nettleham, Wing, Winterbourne, Winter Hey, Winter Rd. Winterton. Prices from £15.*

**SLOGAN POSTMARKS** *Control your dog; Ynys Mon Isle of Anglesey; Pawprints.£12.*

## 28th January 1992 – GREETINGS STAMPS
*10 designs of 1st Class stamps on the theme of Memories.*

| | | | |
|---|---|---|---|
| **SPECIAL HANDSTAMPS** (1) Philatelic Bureau ..... | 5 | – | *Royal Mail* |
| (2) First Day of Issue – Whimsey ........................... | 5 | – | *Royal Mail* |
| (3) The Good Old Days, London Colney.................. | 10 | 12 | *BenD182* |
| (4) The Good Old Days, Surbiton............................ | 10 | 25 | *Ben500(71)* |
| (5) The Good Old Days, Brighton............................ | 10 | 30 | *BLCS 71* |
| (6) The Good Old Days, Kings Cross ...................... | 10 | 30 | *BLCS 71* |
| (7) The Good Old Days, Oxford............................... | 10 | 30 | *BLCS 71* |
| (8) Harrogate, Yorks ............................................... | 10 | 30 | *BLCS 71* |
| (9) Portobello Road, W11 ....................................... | 10 | 15 | *Bradbury* |
| (10) Chester Cathedral ............................................ | 10 | – | *n.o.c.* |
| (11) Up Helly AA Lerwick ....................................... | 10 | 40 | *A. Moncrief* |
| (12) Eastbourne Judgement, Salvation Army............ | 10 | 25 | *S. Army* |
| **C.D.S. POSTMARKS** | | | |
| (13) Bala – featured on the map.............................. | 12 | | |
| (14) Greet, Lover, Letter, Rose, or Seaside ............ | 12 | | |
| (15) Portobello Road – famous antiques market...... | 12 | | |

*Cargreen, Keyford, Kings Road, Chelsea, Market Place, Maypole, Ordnance Rd, Penny Lne. From £10.*

| **SLOGAN POSTMARKS** | | |
|---|---|---|
| (16) Southend on Sea Borough Centenary................. | 20 | |

*In addition: Westmoreland; VW Audi; Please control your dog; Write Now etc. Prices from £12.*

## 6th February 1992 – HAPPY & GLORIOUS
*5 x 24p: Her Majesty as:- Head of State; Head of the Church of England; Head of the Royal Family; Head of Armed Forces; & Head of the Commonwealth.*

| | | | |
|---|---|---|---|
| **SPECIAL HANDSTAMPS** (1) Philatelic Bureau ..... | 3 | – | *Royal Mail* |
| (2) First Day of Issue – Buckingham Palace........... | 3 | – | *Royal Mail* |
| (3) Happy & Glorious, National Postal Museum ..... | 10 | – | *Royal Mail* |
| (4) Happy & Glorious, Brian Reeve, Windsor ........ | 10 | 12 | *B. Reeve 2* |
| (5) Happy & Glorious, London, SW1 ...................... | 10 | 15 | *VP 65* |
| (6) Happy & Glorious, Church Bell Ringers........... | 10 | 10 | *LFDC 103* |
| (7) Happy & Glorious, Commonwealth Institute... | 10 | 15 | *Bradbury* |
| (8) Happy & Glorious, Windsor .............................. | 10 | 35 | *Bradbury* |
| (9) Happy & Glorious, TV Times, SW1 .................. | 10 | 25 | *Benham* |
| (10) 40th Anniv. Accession, Sandringham.............. | 10 | 25 | *BLCS 72* |
| (11) 40th Anniv. Accession, Windsor Castle........... | 10 | 25 | *BLCS 72* |
| (12) 40th Anniv. Accession, Buckingham Palace .... | 10 | 15 | *BenSG15* |
| (13) 40th Anniv. Accession, Balmoral Castle ......... | 10 | 20 | *BenSG15* |
| (14) 40th Anniv. Accession, Westminster Abbey...... | 10 | 35 | *Ben500(72)* |
| (15) MAJESTY, London, W1.................................... | 10 | 45 | *CoverCraft* |

*Happy & Glorious (contd.)*      ordinary covers    official covers

| | | £ | £ | |
|---|---|---|---|---|
| (16) | Long Live the Queen, SW1 | 10 | 20 | *CoverCraft* |
| (17) | Sooty World Museum | 10 | 85 | *Arlington* |
| (18) | Queen's Flight, BF 1992 PS | 10 | 15 | *RFDC 100* |
| (19) | City of London, 40 Happy & Glorious Years | 10 | 5 | *MGN/SG/RMail* |
| (20) | London SW1 or Windsor (permanent h/s) | 10 | - | *Royal Mail* |

**C.D.S. POSTMARKS**

| | | |
|---|---|---|
| (21) | Buckingham Palace or Windsor Castle | 120 |
| (22) | Canterbury or York – Head of Church | 20 |
| (23) | Catterick Garrison – Head of Armed Forces | 25 |
| (24) | Duke of Yorks School | 15 |
| (25) | Any Field Post Office | 15 |
| (26) | House of Commons or Lords | 20 |
| (27) | Kensington High St. – Com'wealth Institute | 15 |
| (28) | Sandringham | 300 |
| (29) | Scone – the Coronation Chair stone | 20 |
| (30) | Terminal 2 or 4, Heathrow | |
| | – H.M. first set foot on British soil as Queen | 20 |
| (31) | West Newton – near to Sandringham House | 15 |
| (32) | Windsor or Windsor Great Park | 15 |

*Also: Coronation Parade, Crown Town, Queen Elizabeth Ave., Queens Parade, Queens Road, Queen Street, Royal Parade, Trafalgar Square. Prices from £12.*

**SLOGAN POSTMARKS**
*Control your dog; Alder Hey; Royal School for Deaf Children; Post Code Windsor. Prices from £7.*

## 10th March 1992 – TENNYSON

*24p 'Vivien'; 28p 'The Miller's Daughter'; 33p 'The Lady of Shalott'; 39p 'Mariana'.*

| | | | | |
|---|---|---|---|---|
| **SPECIAL HANDSTAMPS** | (1) | Philatelic Bureau | 3 | – | *Royal Mail* |
| (2) | First Day of Issue – Isle of Wight | 3 | – | *Royal Mail* |
| (3) | Tennyson Centenary, Grange de Lings | 10 | 20 | *Ben500(73)* |
| (4) | Charge of the Light Brigade, Winchester | 10 | 10 | *BLCS 73* |
| (5) | Tennyson, The Revenge, Bude | 10 | 12 | *BLCS 73* |
| (6) | Idylls of the King, Tintagel | 10 | 10 | *BenL29* |
| (7) | Tennyson, Brian Reeve, Isle of Wight | 10 | 15 | *B Reeve 3* |
| (8) | The Poetry Society, SW1 | 10 | 25 | *CoverCraft* |
| (9) | Lord Tennyson, Freshwater, Isle of Wight | 10 | 15 | *VP 66* |
| (10) | Lord Tennyson, Haslemere | 10 | 15 | *Bradbury* |
| (11) | Lord Tennyson, Hagworthingham | 10 | 25 | *Bradbury* |
| (12) | The Tennyson Society, Somersby | 10 | 12 | *LFDC 104* |
| (13) | The Salvation Army, Newport | 10 | 15 | *S. Army* |
| (14) | Number 60 Squadron, BF 2318 PS | 10 | 10 | *RAF FDC 1* |

**ORDINARY F.D.I. POSTMARKS**

| | | | |
|---|---|---|---|
| (15) | Lincoln (Somersby/Tennyson special cover) | 20 |

**C.D.S. POSTMARKS**

| | | |
|---|---|---|
| (16) | Freshwater – Tennyson's home (Farringford) | 15 |
| (17) | Haslemere – Tennyson's home (Aldworth) | 15 |
| (18) | House of Lords, London SW1 | 35 |
| (19) | Louth – where he attended Grammar School | 15 |
| (20) | Tetford – near to Somersby, his birthplace | 15 |
| (21) | Tintagel – inspired 'Idylls of the King' | 15 |
| (22) | Trinity St., Cambridge – Trinity College | 15 |

*Also: King Arthurs Way, Sebastopol, Tennyson Rd., Tennyson Ave., Trumpington, Winchester. From £15.*

**SLOGAN POSTMARKS** *Glasgow's Alive; Control your dog; Write Now!. Prices from £8.*

## 7th April 1992 – EUROPA

*24p Columbus; 24p Olympics; 24p Paralympics; 39p Operation Raleigh; 39p Expo.*

| | | | | |
|---|---|---|---|---|
| **SPECIAL HANDSTAMPS** | (1) | Philatelic Bureau | 3 | – | *Royal Mail* |
| (2) | First Day of Issue – Liverpool | 3 | – | *Royal Mail* |
| (3) | Landfall of the Americas, Columbus, Bristol | 5 | – | *n.o.c.* |
| (4) | Columbus 500, Brian Reeve, Liverpool | 10 | 15 | *B Reeve 4* |
| (5) | Columbus Quincentenary, Greenwich | 10 | 15 | *Bradbury* |
| (6) | America, Yours to Discover, New York | 10 | 15 | *LFDC 105* |
| (7) | America, Yours to Discover, California | 10 | 25 | *VP 67* |
| (8) | Columbus, Discovery of America, Portsmouth | 10 | 25 | *Ben500(74)* |
| (9) | Columbus, Discovery of America, Greenwich | 10 | 15 | *BLCS 74* |
| (10) | Captain Cook's Endeavour, Whitby | 10 | 20 | *S. Muscroft* |
| (11) | Peterborough, City of Europe | 10 | 50 | *N V Rly* |
| (12) | King George's Fund for Sailors, SW1 | 10 | 95 | *CoverCraft* |
| (13) | 1992 Olympic Games, Manchester | 10 | 15 | *BLCS 74* |
| (14) | No. 56 Squadron, BF 2319 PS | 10 | 15 | *RAF FDC 2* |
| (15) | Royal Belfast Hospital for Sick Children | 10 | 50 | *R.B.H.S.C.* |
| (16) | Walk Through Space, Jodrell Bank | 8 | 40 | *Bradbury* |

**C.D.S. POSTMARKS**

| | | |
|---|---|---|
| (17) | Chelsea – HQ of 'Operation Raleigh' | 15 |
| (18) | Croydon – HQ of British Paralympics | 15 |
| (19) | Maritime Mail, London I.S. | 15 |
| (20) | Raleigh | 10 |
| (21) | Stoke Mandeville or Orthopaedic Hospital | 10 |
| (22) | Wandsworth – British Olympic Assoc | 10 |

*Also: Boston, Hagley Road, Birmingham, Lilleshall, Liverpool, Much Wenlock, New York, The Chart, The Quarterdeck, Washington, Westward Ho!, Whitechapel. Prices from £8.*

**SLOGAN POSTMARKS**

| | | |
|---|---|---|
| (23) | Arcadian Festival, Birmingham | 25 |

*Also: Control your dog; Post Haste; Tenovus; Hearts of Oak; Rly History; PO Charter; Impact. £7.*

## 16th June 1992 – ENGLISH CIVIL WAR

*24p Pikeman; 28p Drummer*       **ordinary covers**     **official covers**
*35p Musketeer; 39p Standard Bearer*       £         £

| | | |
|---|---|---|
| **SPECIAL HANDSTAMPS** (1) Philatelic Bureau... | 3 | – *Royal Mail* |
| (2) First Day of Issue – Banbury, Oxfordshire ....... | 3 | – *Royal Mail* |
| (3) Civil War, The Sealed Knot, Edgehill ................ | 12 | 15 *Bradbury* |
| (4) Civil War, Edgehill Battle Museum, Banbury .. | 12 | 15 *Bradbury* |
| (5) Civil War, The Commandery, Worcester .......... | 12 | 15 *Bradbury* |
| (6) Civil War, Cromwell Museum, Huntingdon...... | 12 | 15 *LFDC 106* |
| (7) Civil War, Naseby......................................... | 12 | 25 *VP 68* |
| (8) Civil War, National Army Museum.................... | 12 | 12 *BLCS 75* |
| (9) Civil War, Robert Devereaux, Newbury............ | 12 | 12 *BenL30* |
| (10) Civil War, Oliver Cromwell, Huntingdon ......... | 12 | 12 *BLCS 75* |
| (11) Civil War, Prince Rupert, London EC............... | 12 | 25 *Ben500(75)* |
| (12) Civil War, Raising of the Standard, Nottingham . | 12 | 12 *BenSG17* |
| (13) Civil War, History Today, Kineton .................. | 12 | 12 *BLCS 75* |
| (14) Start & Finish Civil War, Bredon Covers.......... | 12 | 15 *Bredon Cvrs* |
| (15) Whitefriars, Coventry..................................... | 12 | 40 *Coventry CC* |
| (16) English Civil War Society, Hull........................ | 12 | 30 *CoverCraft* |
| (17) Navy Goes Over to Parliament, Portsmouth..... | 12 | 12 *BenL30* |
| (18) Edgehill, Brian Reeve .................................... | 12 | 15 *B Reeve 5* |
| (19) Lawn Tennis Museum .................................... | 12 | 20 *L.T.Museum* |
| (20) 75th Anniversary of 101 Squadron.................. | 12 | 15 *RAF FDC 3* |

**C.D.S. POSTMARKS**
(21) Castle Boulevard – Raising of the Standard..... 20
(22) House of Commons or Lords ......................... 30
(23) Huntingdon – Birthplace of Oliver Cromwell .. 20
(24) Kineton, Warks – near to Edgehill.................. 20
(25) Marston – Battle of Marston Moor ................. 20
(26) Naseby – Battle of Naseby.............................. 20
(27) Battle sites: Dunbar, Lostwithiel, Newbury, Powick, Ribbleton, Sidbury, Stow-on-the-Wold, Wash Common .................................................*each* 20
(28) Oliver's Battery, Winchester ........................... 20
(29) Southwell – where Charles I surrendered.......... 20

*Also:Battle, Battlehill, Buckingham Palace, Castle Donington, Charles St., Cropredy, Edgehill (Scarborough), Hull, Kingsland, Lichfield, Northern Parliament, Oxford, Preston, Ratley, Windsor Castle, Worcester. Prices from £15.*

**SLOGAN POSTMARKS**
(30) Storming of Preston – Battle and Pageant......... 20
(31) Hull Festival 1992 ......................................... 20
*Also: Guild Preston; Hearts of Oak; North Yorks Moors Rly. Prices from £8.*

## 21st July 1992 – GILBERT & SULLIVAN

*18p Yeoman of the Guard; 24p The Gondoliers;*
*28p The Mikado; 33p Pirates of Penzance; 39p Iolanthe*

| | | |
|---|---|---|
| **SPECIAL HANDSTAMPS** (1) Philatelic Bureau... | 3 | – *Royal Mail* |
| (2) First Day of Issue – D'Oyly Carte...................... | 3 | – *Royal Mail* |
| (3) D'Oyly Carte Opera Company, Birmingham .... | 12 | 20 *LFDC 107* |
| (4) Lambeth Walk, SE11...................................... | 12 | 20 *VP 69* |
| (5) Royal Academy of Music, NW1...................... | 12 | 20 *Bradbury* |
| (6) The Gilbert & Sullivan Society, WC2............... | 12 | 25 *Bradbury* |
| (7) Birthplace of Richard D'Oyly Carte, Soho ....... | 12 | 35 *Bradbury* |
| (8) Mikado, Savoy, WC2..................................... | 12 | 25 *Ben500(76)* |
| (9) Yeoman of the Guard, The Tower, EC1............ | 12 | 10 *BLCS 76* |
| (10) Pirates of Penzance, Penzance ........................ | 12 | 20 *BLCS 76* |
| (11) Iolanthe, The Sullivan Society, SW7................. | 12 | 20 *BenL32* |
| (12) Gondoliers, The Sullivan Society, Weybridge .. | 12 | 20 *BenL31* |
| (13) Sir Arthur Sullivan Sesquicentenary, Savoy ..... | 12 | 30 *CoverCraft* |
| (14) Ruddigore, etc., G & S Operas, Halifax ..... | 12 | 30 *Savoyards* |
| (15) Damart, Gilbert & Sullivan, Bingley .............. | 12 | 20 *Arlington* |
| (16) Gilbert & Sullivan Society, Paignton .............. | 12 | 35 *G&S Torbay* |
| (17) Symphony of Stamps, Nat Postal Museum....... | 12 | 12 *N.P.M.(s)* |
| (18) The Salvation Army, Penzance....................... | 12 | 15 *H.R.* |
| (19) Sir Arthur Sullivan, 1842-1992, SE11.............. | 12 | 15 *B Reeve 6* |
| (20) No.47 Squadron, BF 2321 PS......................... | 12 | 12 *RAF FDC 4* |
| (21) Royal Tournament, BF 2330 PS...................... | 12 | 60 *Forces* |
| (22) Hampton Court Palace................................... | 12 | 65 *CoverCraft* |
| (23) Shoreham-by-Sea Station .............................. | 12 | 20 *BenhamR7* |
| (24) Pad Cancelling Machine at SHC, Cardiff.......... | 35 | – *Royal Mail* |

**C.D.S. POSTMARKS**
(25) Birmingham – D'Oyly Carte Opera Co. ......... 15
(26) House of Commons – Iolanthe 39p value ........ 15
(27) House of Lords – Iolanthe 39p value .............. 20
(28) Kingsway (TV House) – Savoy Theatre............ 15
(29) Lambeth Walk – B/place Sir Arthur Sullivan... 15
(30) Paignton or Penzance - Pirates of Penzance...... 15
(31) Regent St – where G & S first met.................. 15
(32) Trafalgar Sq. – near to Birthplace of Gilbert..... 15

*Also: Broadwick Street, Castle Green, The Circle, Gilbertstone, Harrow & Wealdstone, Haymarket, London EC, Old Windsor, Pindore Street, Seething Lane, Temple, West End. Prices from £10.*

**SLOGAN POSTMARKS**
(33) Smugglers' Adventure, Hastings......................... 25
*Also: Mansfield Show; Maritime Mail; Belfast Harpers; PO Charter; BBC Radio Llandudno; Edinburgh Tattoo; Royal Mail Preston; Royal Mail Cardiff; Southend Borough Centenary. From £6.*

## 15th September 1992 – GREEN ISSUE

*24p Acid Rain; 28p Ozone Layer* · **ordinary covers** · **official covers**
*33p Greenhouse Effect; 39p Bird of Hope* · £ · £

| | | | |
|---|---|---|---|
| SPECIAL HANDSTAMPS (1) Philatelic Bureau... | 3 | – | *Royal Mail* |
| (2) First Day of Issue – Torridon............................ | 3 | – | *Royal Mail* |
| (3) Without conservation..., Red Squirrel............... | 10 | 15 | *BLCS 77* |
| (4) Without conservation..., Cardigan ..................... | 10 | 15 | *BLCS 77* |
| (5) Without conservation..., Bristol Zoo................. | 10 | 15 | *BLCS 77* |
| (6) Without conservation..., Marsh Fritilary........... | 10 | 15 | *BLCS 77* |
| (7) Without conservation..., London Zoo.............. | 10 | 15 | *BLCS 77* |
| (8) Without conservation..., The Osprey.............. | 10 | 18 | *BLCS 77* |
| (9) Without conservation..., Howletts.................... | 10 | 15 | *BLCS 77* |
| (10) Without conservation..., The Dormouse........... | 10 | 15 | *Ben500(77)* |
| (11) Brownsea Island ............................................... | 10 | 15 | *BLCS 77* |
| (12) Water Wildlife, Otterhampton........................... | 10 | 70 | *SEC & RM* |
| (13) Sutton Ecology Centre..................................... | 10 | 30 | *CoverCraft* |
| (14) The Barn Owl Trust, Ashburton....................... | 10 | 25 | *LFDC 108* |
| (15) Green Charter, City of Plymouth ..................... | 10 | 20 | *VP 70* |
| (16) Greenacres, Aylesford...................................... | 10 | 40 | *Bradbury* |
| (17) Preserve our Planet, Coventry Co-op................ | 10 | 20 | *Bradbury* |
| (18) Leicester on top of the World.......................... | 10 | 40 | *Bradbury* |
| (19) Carsington Water.............................................. | 10 | 15 | *B Reeve 7* |
| (20) Green Issue, Fair Isle....................................... | 10 | 15 | *Dawn* |
| (21) Manchester Metrolink....................................... | 10 | 12 | *RAF FDC 5* |
| (22) No.74 Squadron, BF 2322 PS........................... | 10 | 150 | *P.P.S.* |
| (23) Shell UK, Cowdenbeath................................... | 10 | 15 | *S. Army* |
| (24) Salvation Army, Greenford............................... | 10 | – | *Royal Mail* |
| (25) National Postal Museum, London...................... | 15 | | |

**C.D.S. POSTMARKS**

| | |
|---|---|
| (26) Balham, SW12 – Green Party HQ ...................... | 15 |
| (27) Glasshouses, Greenacres, Greenhill, Greenfields, Green Island, Greenlands, Green St., Forest Green, The Green............................*each* | 15 |
| (28) Islington, N1 – Green Peace Headquarters......... | 15 |
| (29) Kew Gardens – conservation and seed bank .... | 25 |
| (30) Leicester – first Environment City...................... | 20 |
| (31) Paradise............................................................... | 25 |

*Also: Boat of Garton, Globe Road, Greeness, Greenlaw, Greenside, Hope, Hopes Green, Nettleham, Park Road, Rainhill, Shepherd's Bush, Slimbridge, Sunnyside, World's End, Wren's Nest. From £10.*

**SLOGAN POSTMARKS**

| | |
|---|---|
| (32) Leicester – Environment City .............................. | 15 |
| (33) Skegness is SO Bracing....................................... | 15 |
| (34) Enrico Fermi Controlled Nuclear Fission........... | 100 |
| (35) Tropical Places – exotic holiday specialists ....... | 15 |
| (36) Schools Poster Campaign, Glasgow ................... | 25 |

*Also: Wall's virtually fat free; Stamp Collecting Greatest Hobby; Please Control your Dog. From £6.*

## 13th October 1992 – SINGLE EUROPEAN MARKET

*24p Artist's interpretation of British star on European flag*

| | | | |
|---|---|---|---|
| SPECIAL HANDSTAMPS (1) Philatelic Bureau... | 2 | – | *Royal Mail* |
| (2) First Day of Issue – Westminster......................... | 2 | – | *Royal Mail* |
| (3) First Day of Issue – Europe '92 London ........... | 8 | – | *Royal Mail* |
| (4) Autumn Stampex, London SW1 ......................... | 8 | – | *Royal Mail* |
| (5) British Presidency, Downing Street..................... | 8 | 15 | *Ben500(78)* |
| (6) The Single Market, Westminster, SW1............... | 8 | 10 | *BLCS 78* |
| (7) European Arts Festival, Edinburgh..................... | 8 | 15 | *BLCS 78* |
| (8) CBI Investing for the New Europe, WC1 ......... | 8 | 10 | *LFDC 109* |
| (9) Single European Market, Dover.......................... | 8 | 10 | *VP 71* |
| (10) Single European Market, Parliament Street...... | 8 | 10 | *B Reeve 8* |
| (11) European Commemorative 50 Pence................... | 8 | 10 | *Royal Mint* |
| (12) Liverpool FC – FA Cup Winners – In Europe.. | 8 | 12 | *Dawn* |
| (13) Manchester United in Europe, UEFA Cup ........ | 8 | 12 | *Dawn* |
| (14) Leeds Utd – League Champions into Europe ... | 8 | 12 | *Dawn* |
| (15) Saltaire, 1853 Gallery ....................................... | 8 | 30 | *1853 Gallery* |
| (16) No.111 Squadron, BF 2336 PS.......................... | 8 | 10 | *RAF FDC 6* |
| (17) HMC International............................................... | 8 | 35 | *HMC Int.* |

**C.D.S. POSTMARKS**

| | |
|---|---|
| (18) Birmingham – venue for European Summit...... | 10 |
| (19) House of Commons, SW1 ................................... | 20 |
| (20) House of Lords, SW1 ......................................... | 25 |
| (21) Industrial and Trading Estates – various ...*each* | 10 |
| (22) Lombard Street, or Stock Exchange..........*each* | 15 |
| (23) Maritime Mail...................................................... | 10 |
| (24) Market, Market Place or Newmarket........*each* | 10 |
| (25) Newbridge or Aycliffe, Dover ............................ | 10 |
| (26) Paquebot – various ..........................................*each* | 10 |

*In addition: Mastrick, Northern Parliament, Parliament Street, Pound, Runcorn (Shopping Centre), Saltaire, Starcross, Summit. Prices from £8.*

**SLOGAN POSTMARKS**

| | |
|---|---|
| (27) Birmingham (surrounded by circle of stars) ...... | 10 |
| (28) Europe for Workers Safety and Health ............... | 25 |
| (29) The Visaservice – Passports Renewed ................ | 10 |
| (30) Maritime Mail...................................................... | 10 |

*Also: WHSmiths; Royal Mail Children in Cities; Post Haste; Hearts of Oak; Times & Star. From £4.*

## 10th November 1992 – CHRISTMAS

*18p St. James's, Pangbourne*
*24p St. Mary's Bibury;*
*28p & 39p Our Lady & St. Peter's, Leatherhead; 33p All Saint's, Porthcawl*

| | | ordinary covers £ | official covers £ | |
|---|---|---|---|---|
| **SPECIAL HANDSTAMPS** | (1) Philatelic Bureau... | 3 | – | *Royal Mail* |
| (2) | First Day of Issue – Bethlehem, Llandeilo........ | 3 | – | *Royal Mail* |
| (3) | First Day of Issue – Pangbourne ...................... | 3 | – | *Royal Mail* |
| (4) | Stained Glass at Canterbury Cathedral ............. | 10 | 10 | *BLCS 79* |
| (5) | Stained Glass, Castle Howard, York................. | 10 | 12 | *BLCS 79* |
| (6) | All Saints, Middleton Cheney........................... | 10 | 15 | *BenL33* |
| (7) | St. Peter & St. Paul, Cattistock....................... | 10 | 15 | *BenL33* |
| (8) | St. Michaels Church, Forden ........................... | 10 | 15 | *BenL34* |
| (9) | All Hallows Church, Allerton ........................... | 10 | 10 | *BenL34* |
| (10) | St. Martin's Church, Brampton ........................ | 10 | 15 | *BenL33* |
| (11) | Christchurch, Cambridge .................................. | 10 | 15 | *Ben500(79)* |
| (12) | Bethlehem, Dyfed, Victorian Print No.72........ | 10 | 15 | *VP 72* |
| (13) | Church of the Lily Cross, Godshill.................... | 10 | 10 | *LFDC 110* |
| (14) | Our Lady & St. Peter's, Leatherhead ................ | 10 | 20 | *Bradbury* |
| (15) | St. Mary's Bibury, Glos ................................... | 10 | 50 | *CoverCraft* |
| (16) | Peace on Earth, All Saint's, Porthcawl ............. | 10 | 30 | *CoverCraft* |
| (17) | Stained Glass Museum, Ely, Cambs .................. | 10 | 30 | *CoverCraft* |
| (18) | Christmas, Canterbury Cathedral...................... | 10 | 15 | *B Reeve 9* |
| (19) | Cambridge, Christmas 1992 .............................. | 10 | 40 | *Cam. S.C.* |
| (20) | Christmas Blessings, Salvation Army ................ | 10 | 15 | *S. Army* |
| (21) | National Postal Museum, EC ............................ | 10 | 30 | *FriendsNPM* |
| (22) | Happy Christmas, Royal Mail, EC1.................. | 10 | – | *n.o.c.* |
| (23) | Seasons Greetings from Liverpool FC............... | 10 | 25 | *Dawn* |
| (24) | Seasons Greetings from Newcastle United........ | 10 | 25 | *Dawn* |
| (25) | CEAC 7, COSAC, London................................. | 10 | – | *n.o.c.* |
| (26) | No.84 Squadron, BF 2338 PS............................ | 10 | 15 | *RAF FDC 7* |

**C.D.S. POSTMARKS**

(27) Bibury, Leatherhead, Pangbourne or Porthcawl . 20
*Also: All Saints Church, Ely, Glasshouses, Holy Island, Jerusalem St., Nasareth, St. James, St. Marys, St. Nicholas, St. Peters, Threekingham. From £12.*

**SLOGAN POSTMARKS**

(28) Leeds Light Up – Illuminations............................ 20
(29) Happy Christmas, Please Post Early – Inverness.. 25
(30) A Happy Christmas, The Post Office – Wick........ 25
(31) Jesus is Alive! – Manchester ............................... 175
*Also: Shetland for 93; Please control your Dog; Write now etc.; From £5.*

**CHRISTMAS BOOKLET:** Covers bearing pair or block
of 4 x 18p stamps from booklet with relevant postmark
(these have margin at top and bottom) ..............*each* 3
Full pane of ten stamps on cover.....................*each* 10

## 19th January 1993 – SWANS

*Abbotsbury Swannery:- 18p Mute Swan Cob; 24p Cygnets;*
*28p Mute Swan Breeding Pair; 33p Mute Swans Eggs; 39p Winter Mute Swans*

| **SPECIAL HANDSTAMPS** | (1) Philatelic Bureau... | 4 | – | *Royal Mail* |
|---|---|---|---|---|
| (2) | First Day of Issue – Abbotsbury......................... | 4 | – | *Royal Mail* |
| (3) | First Day of Issue – London .............................. | 4 | – | *Royal Mail* |
| (4) | Wildfowl & Wetlands, Caerlaverock.................. | 12 | 15 | *BLCS 80* |
| (5) | Wildfowl & Wetlands, Castle Espie ................... | 12 | 15 | *BLCS 80* |
| (6) | Wildfowl & Wetlands, Martin Mere................... | 12 | 20 | *BLCS 80* |
| (7) | Wildfowl & Wetlands, Slimbridge ..................... | 12 | 12 | *BLCS 80* |
| (8) | Wildfowl & Wetlands, Llanelli........................... | 12 | 12 | *BLCS 80* |
| (9) | 600th Anniv. Abbotsbury Swannery................... | 12 | 25 | *BenSG18* |
| (10) | Bird Watching Magazine, Peterborough ........... | 12 | 20 | *Benham* |
| (11) | Stratford upon Avon ........................................ | 12 | 20 | *Ben500(80)* |
| (12) | Dyers' Hall, London, EC4 ................................. | 12 | 35 | *LFDC 111* |
| (13) | Vintners' Company, London, EC4..................... | 12 | 25 | *VP 73* |
| (14) | Swan Sanctuary, Egham ................................... | 12 | 25 | *Bradbury* |
| (15) | Independent Chapel, Swanland ......................... | 12 | 35 | *S'land Priory* |
| (16) | Old Swan Corps, Liverpool............................... | 12 | 25 | *S. Army* |
| (17) | Swan Lifeline, Eton.......................................... | 12 | 35 | *CoverCraft* |
| (18) | Swan Trust, Berwick......................................... | 12 | 25 | *CoverCraft* |
| (19) | No.115 Squadron, BF 2347 PS.......................... | 12 | 15 | *RAF FDC 8* |
| (20) | People in the Post, National Postal Museum .... | 12 | – | *n.o.c.* |
| (21) | William Shakespeare Stratford (swan) .............. | 12 | – | *n.o.c.* |

**C.D.S. POSTMARKS**

(22) Abbotsbury, Egham, Sandy or Slimbridge ......... 25
(23) Swanland, Swanpool or Old Swan ............*each* 25
(24) Thetford – British Trust for Ornithology............ 25
*Also: Comber, Fleet, Hanley Swan, Henley-on-Thames, House of Lords, Ilchester, Mickley, Old Berwick, Swanmore, Swansea. Prices from £15.*

**SLOGAN POSTMARKS**
*Postcode, Doncaster; Colourful Greetings Stamps; Gloucester Citizen; Control your Dog. From £10.*

There are thousands of special handstamps listed in this
catalogue: too many to illustrate. However for each
commemorative stamp issue there is a file illustrating most of the
handstamps available FREE from www.bfdc.co.uk/postmarks

## 2nd Feb 1993 - GREETINGS

*10 x 1st Class: Long John Silver, Peter Rabbit,*
*Tweedledee & Tweedledum, Just William, Toad and Mole,*
*Bash Street Kids, the Snowman, Big Friendly Giant, Rupert Bear, Aladdin*

| | ordinary covers £ | official covers £ | |
|---|---|---|---|
| **SPECIAL HANDSTAMPS** (1) Philatelic Bureau... | 3 | – | *Royal Mail* |
| (2) First Day of Issue – Greetland............................ | 5 | – | *Royal Mail* |
| (3) First Day of Issue – London .............................. | 5 | – | *Royal Mail* |
| (4) Badger............................................................... | 12 | 6 | *DailyExp(s)* |
| (5) Daresbury, Warrington...................................... | 12 | 25 | *Bradbury* |
| (6) Scottish Literary Museum.................................. | 12 | 25 | *BLCS 81* |
| (7) Beatrix Potter, Kensington, W8......................... | 12 | 25 | *BLCS 81* |
| (8) Big Friendly Giant, Great Missenden ................ | 12 | 25 | *BLCS 81* |
| (9) Aladdin, Manchester......................................... | 12 | 20 | *BenD191* |
| (10) Alice in Wonderland, Oxford ........................... | 12 | 3 | *Benham(s)* |
| (11) Rivers Corner, Sturminster Newton ................. | 12 | 15 | *Ben500(81)* |
| (12) Peter Rabbit Centenary, Near Sawrey............... | 12 | 125 | *CoverCraft (pair)* |
| (13) Waterstone's, London....................................... | 12 | 15 | *Waterstone's* |

**C.D.S. POSTMARKS**

| | | |
|---|---|---|
| (14) Far Sawrey – home of Beatrix Potter................. | 15 | |
| (15) Fleet Street – where the 'Beano' is published ... | 15 | |
| (16) Greet, Birmingham........................................... | 15 | |
| (17) Oxford – home of Lewis Carroll ....................... | 15 | |

*Also: Badger's Mount, Bearpark, Blackfriars Rd, Braemar, Bromley Common,*
*Bunny, Cross Hands, Earls Court, Exchange, Fulham Palace Road,*
*Great Missenden, Hassocks, Kensington High St, Molehill Green, Portobello Rd*
*Rupert Street, Stock Exchange, Tweedle, Waterston, William Street,*
*The Willows. Prices from £10.*

**SLOGAN POSTMARKS**

| | | |
|---|---|---|
| (18) Use Colourful Greetings Stamps ....................... | 20 | |

*In addition: Write Now, etc; Radio Nottingham.   Prices from £5.*

## 16th February 1993 - MARINE TIMEKEEPERS

*24p, 28p, 33p, 39p: Four layer's of Harrison's 'H4' Clock*

| | | | |
|---|---|---|---|
| **SPECIAL HANDSTAMPS** (1) Philatelic Bureau... | 3 | – | *Royal Mail* |
| (2) First Day of Issue – Greenwich......................... | 3 | – | *Royal Mail* |
| (3) First Day of Issue – John Harrison, London ..... | 3 | – | *Royal Mail* |
| (4) Queen Elizabeth 2, Southampton...................... | 12 | 3 | *Benham(s)* |
| (5) RMS Queen Mary, Southampton ....................... | 12 | 3 | *Benham(s)* |
| (6) The Cutty Sark, Greenwich................................ | 12 | 15 | *BLCS 82* |
| (7) SS Great Britain, Bristol................................... | 12 | 40 | *BenL35* |
| (8) Marine Chronometer, Portsmouth..................... | 12 | 3 | *Benham(s)* |
| (9) Marine Chronometer, Plymouth ....................... | 12 | 25 | *Ben500(82)* |
| (10) HMS Belfast, London SE1 ............................... | 12 | 3 | *Benham(s)* |
| (11) HMS Victory, Portsmouth................................ | 12 | 15 | *BLCS 82* |
| (12) Antiquarian Horological Soc., Ticehurst........... | 12 | 25 | *Bradbury* |
| (13) British Watch & Clockmaker's Gd, Burnham .. | 12 | 20 | *LFDC 112* |
| (14) British Horological Institute, Newark............... | 12 | 20 | *VP 74* |
| (15) John Harrison Tercentenary, Greenwich........... | 12 | 20 | *CoverCraft* |
| (16) British Sailors' Society, Southampton.............. | 12 | 20 | *SP* |
| (17) No.1 Squadron, BF 2346 PS............................. | 12 | 15 | *RAF FDC 9* |
| (18) Salvation Army, Medical Fellowship, EC4........ | 12 | 15 | *S. Army* |
| (19) First Day of Sale, Windsor .............................. | 12 | – | *n.o.c.* |

**C.D.S. POSTMARKS**

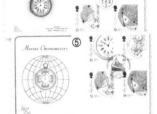

| | | |
|---|---|---|
| (20) Clockface or Clock House Parade...................... | 10 | |
| (21) Greenwich or Any Paquebot.............................. | 15 | |
| (22) Maritime Mail, London I.S............................... | 15 | |
| (23) Meridian Centre, Newhaven............................. | 40 | |
| (24) New Invention, Willenhall, West Midlands ...... | 10 | |
| (25) New Crofton – near to B/place of Harrison ...... | 10 | |

*Also: The Chart, Cog Lane, Hampstead, Marine Parade, Marton-in-*
*Cleveland, The Quarterdeck, Theobalds Rd, Watchet, Whitby. From £8.*

**SLOGAN POSTMARKS**

| | | |
|---|---|---|
| (26) Maritime Mail, London I.S............................... | 30 | |
| (27) SWATCH Swatch the World............................... | 250 | |

*Also: Bedford Council/Waste Watchers; Glos. Citizen; Safeway, Plymouth; Royal Mail/Business. £6.*

## 16th March 1993 - ORCHIDS

*18p, 24p, 28p, 33p, 39p Species of Orchids*

| | | | |
|---|---|---|---|
| **SPECIAL HANDSTAMPS** (1) Philatelic Bureau... | 3 | – | *Royal Mail* |
| (2) First Day of Issue – Glasgow ............................ | 3 | – | *Royal Mail* |
| (3) First Day of Issue – London ............................. | 3 | – | *Royal Mail* |
| (4) Royal Botanic Gardens, Kew............................ | 12 | 20 | *BLCS 83* |
| (5) Botanical Gardens, Birmingham....................... | 12 | 17 | *BLCS 83* |
| (6) Botanic Gardens, Glasgow................................ | 12 | 17 | *BLCS 83* |
| (7) Botanic Gardens, Belfast ................................. | 12 | 17 | *BLCS 83* |
| (8) Royal Botanic Garden, Edinburgh.................... | 12 | 17 | *BLCS 83* |
| (9) Oldest Botanic Gardens, Oxford ...................... | 12 | 17 | *BLCS 83* |
| (10) Royal Orchid Service, Thai Airways ................ | 12 | 25 | *BenSG20* |
| (11) World Orchid Conference, Glasgow.................. | 12 | 15 | *Ben500(83)* |
| (12) Worshipful Company of Gardeners, EC............ | 12 | 25 | *LFDC 113* |
| (13) Royal Botanic Gardens, Edinburgh.................. | 12 | 25 | *VP 75* |
| (14) Orchid Society of Great Britain ....................... | 12 | 55 | *CoverCraft* |
| (15) No.30 Squadron, BF 2348 PS........................... | 12 | 12 | *RAF FDC 10* |
| (16) Derwentside LDO, Consett .............................. | 12 | – | *n.o.c.* |
| (17) New Post Office, Southend-on-Sea................... | 12 | 75 | *Bradbury* |

**Orchids (contd.)**

| | ordinary covers £ | official covers £ |
|---|---|---|
| **C.D.S. POSTMARKS** | | |
| (18) Botanic Gardens, Belfast or Kew Gardens | 25 | |
| (19) Glasgow – World Orchid Conference | 20 | |
| (20) Royal Hospital – Chelsea Flower Show | 20 | |

*In addition: Bloomfield, Flore, Flowery Field, Glasgow Airport, Glasshouses, Montague Terrace, Edinburgh, Queen Elizabeth Ave., Paradise, Ripley, Spring Gardens. From £5.*

**SLOGAN POSTMARKS** *Daffodil Day; Royal Concert Hall; Postcodes; Royal Mail. From £5*

## 11th May 1993 – ART IN THE 20th CENTURY

*24p Henry Moore – Family Group; 28p Edward Bawden – Kew Gardens; 33p Stanley Spencer – St. Francis & the Birds; 39p Ben Nicholson – Odyssey 1*

| | | | |
|---|---|---|---|
| **SPECIAL HANDSTAMPS** (1) Philatelic Bureau... | 3 | – | *Royal Mail* |
| (2) First Day of Issue – London SW | 3 | – | *Royal Mail* |
| (3) First Day of Issue – London | 3 | – | *Royal Mail* |
| (4) Courtauld Institute, WC2 | 8 | 12 | *BLCS 84* |
| (5) Paul Nash, Dymchurch, | 8 | 17 | *Ben500(84)* |
| (6) Henry Moore, Leeds | 8 | 10 | *BenSG21* |
| (7) Ben Nicholson, St. Ives, | 8 | 3 | *Benham(s)* |
| (8) Stanley Spencer, Cookham, | 8 | 3 | *Benham(s)* |
| (9) Edward Bawden, Saffron Walden, | 8 | 3 | *Benham(s)* |
| (10) National Portrait Gallery, London WC2 | 8 | 15 | *Westminster* |
| (11) Royal College of Art, SW7 | 8 | 25 | *LFDC 114* |
| (12) Sir Joshua Reynolds, London W1 | 8 | 15 | *VP 76* |
| (13) Swiss National Tourist Office | 8 | 20 | *CoverCraft* |
| (14) British Council, Promoting Britain Abroad | 8 | 20 | *CoverCraft* |
| (15) Frank Wootton Artist, Lympne | 8 | 10 | *BLCS 84* |
| (16) No.216 Squadron, BF 2349 PS | 8 | 15 | *RAF FDC 11* |
| (17) Cyprus, Malaya and Suez, BF 2368 PS | 8 | – | *n.o.c.* |
| (18) The Salvation Army, Sunbury, | 6 | 20 | *S. Army* |
| **C.D.S. POSTMARKS** | | | |
| (19) Albemarle Street – near to Royal Academy | 8 | | |
| (20) Braintree – birthplace of Edward Bawden | 8 | | |
| (21) Carbis Bay – home of Ben Nicholson | 8 | | |
| (22) Castleford – birthplace of Henry Moore | 8 | | |
| (23) Cookham – birthplace of Stanley Spencer | 8 | | |
| (24) Denham Green – birthplace of Ben Nicholson | 8 | | |
| (25) Great Bardfield – home of Edward Bawden | 8 | | |
| (26) Kew Gardens or The Galleries | 20 | | |
| (27) Much Hadham – Henry Moore Foundation | 8 | | |

*Also: Moore, Pembroke St., Bedford; Plympton St. Maurice; Trafalgar Square; Tufton Street, SW1; Vauxhall Bridge Road, SW1. Prices from £6.*

**SLOGAN POSTMARKS**

| | | |
|---|---|---|
| (28) Barnes Cray School Arts Week | 25 | |
| (29) Royal Mail Supports the Arts, Glasgow | 25 | |
| (30) Milton Keynes, Festival Folk Art | 75 | |

*In addition: Royal Mail Can Help Your Business; Postcodes. Prices from £5.*

## 15th June 1993 – ROMAN BRITAIN

*24p Claudius (Gold Coin, British Museum) found at Bredgar, Kent; 28p Hadrian (Bronze Sculpture, British Museum) found in the River Thames; 33p Roma (Gemstone, Legionian Museum, Caerleon) found at Caerleon; 39p Christ (Mosaic, British Museum) from a villa at Hinton St. Mary*

| | | | |
|---|---|---|---|
| **SPECIAL HANDSTAMPS** (1) Philatelic Bureau... | 3 | – | *Royal Mail* |
| (2) First Day of Issue – Caerllion | 3 | – | *Royal Mail* |
| (3) First Day of Issue – London | 3 | – | *Royal Mail* |
| (4) Ermine Street Guard, York | 12 | 20 | *LFDC 115* |
| (5) Camulodunum, Roman Britain, Colchester | 12 | 25 | *VP 77* |
| (6) Roman Britain, Caerleon | 12 | 20 | *BenL37* |
| (7) Roman Britain, Chester | 12 | 20 | *BenL37* |
| (8) Roman Britain, Newcastle | 12 | 12 | *BenSG21* |
| (9) Roman Britain, Bath | 12 | 9 | *BenSG21* |
| (10) Roman Britain, Colchester | 12 | 20 | *BenL37* |
| (11) Roman Britain, Invasion A.D. 43, Canterbury | 12 | 20 | *BenL37* |
| (12) White Cliffs Experience, Dover | 12 | 10 | *BenL36* |
| (13) Largest Roman Palace in Britain, Fishbourne | 12 | 10 | *BLCS 85* |
| (14) Roman Villa, Chedworth | 12 | 10 | *BLCS 85* |
| (15) Roman Britain, Cirencester | 12 | 20 | *BenL37* |
| (16) Roman Britain, Walbrook, EC4 | 12 | 20 | *BenL37* |
| (17) Roman Britain, St. Albans | 12 | 15 | *Ben500(85)* |
| (18) Museum of Antiquities, Newcastle | 12 | 35 | *CoverCraft* |
| (19) Museum of London, London Wall | 12 | 30 | *CoverCraft* |
| (20) Lactodorum, Towcester, | 12 | 40 | *Sponne School* |
| (21) Royal Air Force Locking, Weston-super-Mare | 12 | 200 | *RAF Locking* |
| (22) New Relief Lifeboat, Fleetwood | 12 | 20 | *Pilgrim* |
| (23) Salvation Army, International Headquarters | 12 | 20 | *S. Army* |
| (24) No. 120 Squadron | 75 | – | *n.o.c.* |
| **C.D.S. POSTMARKS** | | | |
| (25) Bowness or Heddon – Hadrian's Wall | 15 | | |
| (26) Bredgar – Claudius gold coin (24p) | 15 | | |
| (27) Britannia – Roman name for Britain | 15 | | |
| (28) Caerlon – Roma gemstone (33p) | 15 | | |
| (29) London Bdge – Hadrian sculpture (28p) | 15 | | |
| (30) Roman Way Caerlon – Roma gemstone (33p) | 25 | | |
| (31) Sturminster – Mosaic of Christ (39p) | 15 | | |

*Roman Britain (contd.)*     ordinary covers    official covers
                                £            £

*Also: Bacchus Road, Bath, Camp, Colchester, Eastgate, Ermine Street, Fishbourne, Fort Augustus, Garrison, High Holborn, Jerusalem, Micklegate, Occupation Rd, Prettygate, Northgate, Roman Road, Russell Square, Sandwich, Southampton Row, Southgate, Temple, The Forum, Villa Road, Wall, Wallsend, Watling Street, Westgate, York. Prices from £8.*

**SLOGAN POSTMARKS**
(32) Christian Aid Week................................................. 35
*In addition: Stenna Sealink; Any Royal Mail slogans. Prices from £5.*

## 20th July 1993 – INLAND WATERWAYS
*24p Grand Junction Canal; 28p Stainforth & Keadby Canal; 33p Brecknock & Abergavenny Canal; 39p Crinan Canal*

| | | | |
|---|---|---|---|
| **SPECIAL HANDSTAMPS** (1) Philatelic Bureau... | 3 | – | *Royal Mail* |
| (2) First Day of Issue – Gloucester .................... | 3 | – | *Royal Mail* |
| (3) First Day of Issue – London ........................... | 3 | – | *Royal Mail* |
| (4) Inland Waterways Assoc'n, Mkt Harborough... | 15 | 35 | *LFDC 116* |
| (5) Grand Union Canal, Foxton ............................. | 15 | 35 | *VP 78* |
| (6) Canal Museum, Stoke Bruerne....................... | 15 | 20 | *Benham(s)* |
| (7) Conserving..., The Wharf, Braunston ............ | 15 | 3 | *Benham(s)* |
| (8) Conserving..., Lochgilphead, Argyll .............. | 15 | 20 | *BLCS 86* |
| (9) Conserving..., Sheffield, Yorks...................... | 15 | 20 | *BLCS 86* |
| (10) Conserving..., Newport, Gwent ..................... | 15 | 20 | *BLCS 86* |
| (11) Canals 200, Grand Junction Canal ................. | 15 | 20 | *BLCS 86* |
| (12) Canals 200, Crinan Canal.............................. | 15 | 20 | *BLCS 86* |
| (13) Canals 200, Stainforth & Keadby Canal......... | 15 | 20 | *BLCS 86* |
| (14) Canals 200, Brecknock & Abergavenny........... | 15 | 20 | *BLCS 86* |
| (15) Grand Junction Canal, London North .......... | 15 | 20 | *Ben500(86)* |
| (16) Canals Bicentenary, Regents Canal, London ... | 15 | – | *n.o.c.* |
| (17) Canals Bicentenary, Watford, Herts............... | 15 | – | *n.o.c.* |
| (18) New Lanark Visitor Centre, Lanark................. | 15 | – | *n.o.c.* |
| (19) The Mary-Anne Worsley Marina ..................... | 15 | 20 | *S. Army* |
| (20) No. 51 Squadron, BF 2383 PS........................ | 15 | 15 | *RAF FDC 13* |
| (21) Royal Tournament, BF 2385 PS...................... | 15 | 110 | *Forces* |
| **ORDINARY F.D.I. POSTMARKS** | | | |
| (22) Milton Keynes (*Leighton Lady* PO cachet) ...... | 40 | | |
| **C.D.S. POSTMARKS** | | | |
| (23) Abergavenny, Brecon or Pontymoile – | | | |
|      – Brecknock & Abergavenny Canal................ | 15 | | |
| (24) Ardrishaig or Bellanoch – Crinan Canal.......... | 15 | | |
| (25) Brentford or Braunston – Grand Junction...... | 15 | | |
| (26) Stainforth or Keadby...................................... | 15 | | |
| (27) Ellesmere Port – Inland Waterways Museum... | 15 | | |
| (28) House of Commons or Lords .......................... | 30 | | |

*Also: Anderton, Bingley, Birchvale, Bridgwater, Burnley, Froncysllte, Lochgilphead, Locks Bottom, Locks Lane, Marsden, Patricroft, Shelton Lock, Sugar Island, Towcester, Waterside. Prices from £8.*
**SLOGAN POSTMARKS**
*Postbus; 60 Yrs Passenger Service; Royal Mail slogans; Sunbury. Prices from £4.*

## 14th September 1993 – AUTUMN
*18p Horse Chestnut; 24p Blackberry; 28p Hazel Nut; 33p Mountain Ash; 39p Pear*

| | | | |
|---|---|---|---|
| **SPECIAL HANDSTAMPS** (1) Philatelic Bureau... | 3 | – | *Royal Mail* |
| (2) First Day of Issue – Taunton........................... | 3 | – | *Royal Mail* |
| (3) First Day of Issue – London ............................ | 3 | – | *Royal Mail* |
| (4) Autumn – Rowanburn...................................... | 10 | 15 | *Benham L38* |
| (5) Autumn – Pear Tree......................................... | 10 | 15 | *Benham L38* |
| (6) Autumn – Berry Hill........................................ | 10 | 15 | *Benham L38* |
| (7) Autumn – Nutfield ........................................... | 10 | 15 | *Ben500(87)* |
| (8) Autumn – Hazelwood ...................................... | 10 | 15 | *BLCS 87* |
| (9) Stourhead House & Garden ............................. | 10 | 15 | *BLCS 87* |
| (10) Worshipful Company of Fruiterers.................. | 10 | 15 | *LFDC 117* |
| (11) Worshipful Company of Gardeners, EC............ | 10 | 15 | *VP 79* |
| (12) Battle of Britain, BF 2384 PS.......................... | 10 | 15 | *RAF FDC 14* |
| (13) Peterborough, NVR, Wansford Stn ................. | 10 | 45 | *NVRly* |
| (14) National Postal Museum, 1793-1993 ................. | 10 | – | *n.o.c.* |
| **C.D.S. POSTMARKS** | | | |
| (15) Chestnut Grove or Chestnut Terrace ................ | 20 | | |
| (16) Hazel Grove, Mountain Ash or Pear Tree ........ | 20 | | |
| (17) Kew Gdns or Savacentre (supermarket PO) ..... | 25 | | |
| (18) The Allotments or The Orchards ...................... | 25 | | |

*Also: Berry Hill, Berrylands, Cherry Tree, Evesham, Faversham, Forest Row, Garden Fm, Hazelslade, Oundle, Peel Green, Pershore, Plantation, Rowanburn, Woodlands, Woodside, Worcester. From£15 .*
**SLOGAN POSTMARKS** *Autumn Concerts; £££s Paid for Stamp Collections; Philatelic Cong.; Safeway; Any Royal Mail slogans. Prices from £10.*

## 12th October 1993 – SHERLOCK HOLMES
*5 x 24p stamps: The Reigate Squire; The Hound of the Baskervilles; The Six Napoleons; The Greek Interpreter; The Final Problem*

| | | | |
|---|---|---|---|
| **SPECIAL HANDSTAMPS** (1) Philatelic Bureau... | 3 | – | *Royal Mail* |
| (2) First Day of Issue – 221B Baker St, NW1 ........ | 3 | – | *Royal Mail* |
| (3) First Day of Issue – London ............................ | 3 | – | *Royal Mail* |
| (4) First Day of Issue – Autumn Stampex, SW1 ..... | 15 | – | *Royal Mail* |
| (5) Conan Doyle Society (silhouette) ...................... | 15 | 30 | *VP 80* |
| (6) Windlesham Manor, Crowborough.................... | 15 | 30 | *Bradbury* |

103

**Sherlock Holmes (contd.)**

| | ordinary covers £ | | official covers £ |
|---|---|---|---|
| (7) Sherlock Holmes Museum (silhouette) | 15 | 35 | LFDC 118 |
| (8) St. Bartholomew's Hospital | 15 | 20 | H. Murray |
| (9) Sherlock Holmes Society, London | 15 | 35 | CoverCraft |
| (10) Adventures of Sherlock Holmes, 221B Baker St. | 15 | 35 | CoverCraft |
| (11) POID Bicentenary, EC | 15 | 75 | POID |
| (12) Baker Street Post Office, W1 | 15 | – | n.o.c. |
| (13) Radio Times, Sherlock Holmes, Baker St. | 15 | 30 | Benham |
| (14) Sherlock Holmes, Baker St. NW1 (silhouette) | 15 | 20 | Benham |
| (15) Hound of the Baskervilles, Black Dog | 15 | 50 | Ben500(88) |
| (16) Burial Place of Conan Doyle, Minstead | 15 | 10 | Benham(s) |
| (17) The Strand, WC2 | 15 | 10 | Benham(s) |
| (18) Jeremy Brett/Sherlock Holmes, Granada TV | 15 | 20 | BLCS 88 |
| (19) Sherlock Holmes, Granada TV, Manchester | 15 | 25 | BLCS 88 |
| (20) Arthur Conan Doyle Society, ACD | 15 | 35 | BenL39 |
| (21) Conan Doyle Establishment, Crowborough | 15 | 35 | BenL39 |
| (22) Autumn Stampex, SW1 (changeable date) | 15 | – | n.o.c. |
| (23) Sherlock Holmes Memorabilia Company | 15 | 75 | SHMCo |
| (24) Province of Suffolk, Ipswich | 15 | 35 | Arlington |
| (25) No. 100 Squadron, BF 2388 PS | 8 | 20 | RAF FDC 15 |

**C.D.S. POSTMARKS**

| | | |
|---|---|---|
| (26) Baker Street – home of Sherlock Holmes | 35 | |
| (27) Elm Row Edinburgh – B/place Conan-Doyle | 35 | |
| (28) Beckenham, Kennington, Newhaven, Princetown, Reigate, Walkhampton, Widecombe-in-the-Moor: – locations connected with novels on stamps | 35 | |
| (29) Crowborough, Hindhead, or South Norwood: – homes of Arthur Conan-Doyle | 35 | |
| (30) Swiss Valley Park (The Final Problem) | 45 | |

*Also: Crook; Constable Burton; Dog and Gun; Elm Grove, Southsea; Forest Row; Holmes Chapel; Minstead; Nicholson St., Edinburgh; Stonyhurst; North East TPO Down; The Strand. Prices from £20.*

**SLOGAN POSTMARKS**

| | |
|---|---|
| (31) Post Office Investigation Dept | 25 |
| (32) Autumn Stampex – features Sherlock Holmes | 25 |
| (33) Please Control your Dog – features a Hound | 45 |

*In addition: £££s Paid for Stamp Collections; Postbus Silver Jubilee; Exeter Automated Processing; Collect British Stamps; Any Royal Mail slogans. Prices from £5.*

## 9th November 1993 - CHRISTMAS

*A Christmas Carol: 19p Bob Cratchit & Tiny Tim; 25p Mr & Mrs Fezziwig; 30p Scrooge; 35p Prize Turkey; 41p Mr Scrooge's Nephew*

**SPECIAL HANDSTAMPS**

| | | | |
|---|---|---|---|
| (1) Philatelic Bureau | 3 | – | Royal Mail |
| (2) First Day of Issue – Bethlehem | 3 | – | Royal Mail |
| (3) First Day of Issue – City of London (top hat) | 3 | – | Royal Mail |
| (4) First Day of Issue – London (cracker) | 3 | – | Royal Mail |
| (5) The Dickens Fellowship, London WC1 | 10 | 15 | LFDC 119 |
| (6) Birthplace of Dickens, Portsmouth | 10 | 15 | VP 81 |
| (7) Scrooge & Bob Cratchit, Rochester | 10 | 25 | Bradbury |
| (8) Dickens House Museum | 10 | 25 | CoverCraft |
| (9) Visit of Charles Dickens to Newcastle | 12 | 35 | N'stle RoyalMail |
| (10) A Christmas Carol – Rochester, Kent | 10 | 15 | BenL41 |
| (11) A Christmas Carol – Portsmouth | 10 | 20 | Ben500(89) |
| (12) A Christmas Carol – Broadstairs | 10 | 15 | BenL41 |
| (13) A Christmas Carol – Pickwick | 10 | 15 | BenL41 |
| (14) A Christmas Carol – Chatham | 10 | 15 | BenL41 |
| (15) A Christmas Carol – Old Curiosity Shop | 10 | 10 | BLCS 89 |
| (16) A Christmas Carol – Radio Times | 10 | 15 | Benham |
| (17) A Christmas Carol – Rochester, Medway | 10 | 12 | BLCS 89 |
| (18) Scrooge's Mailcoach Run, Rochester | 10 | 12 | BLCS 89 |
| (19) Gads Hill, Higham-by-Rochester | 10 | 15 | BenL40 |
| (20) The Salvation Army | 10 | 15 | SouthportCorps |
| (21) Happy Christmas, Royal Mail, EC1 | 10 | – | n.o.c. |
| (22) A Happy Christmas, News of the World | 10 | 20 | CoverCraft |
| (23) National Postal Museum, Christmas Postcards | 10 | 20 | Friends of NPM |
| (24) No.10 Squadron, BF 2389 PS | 10 | 15 | RAF FDC 16 |

**C.D.S. POSTMARKS**

| | |
|---|---|
| (25) Broadstairs; Marylebone; Gad's Hill or Mid-Higham; Rochester; Sultan Road, Portsmouth; Theobalds Road, London – near to the homes of Dickens | 15 |
| (26) Camden Town – 'home' of Bob Cratchit | 15 |

*Holybush, Jerusalem St, London Chief Office, Nasareth, St. Nicholas. From £8.*

**SLOGAN POSTMARKS**

| | |
|---|---|
| (27) Christmas Shopping at Rainbow Superstore | 20 |

*BT; Safeway; Postbus; Collect British Stamps; Royal Mail slogans. From £5.*

**£2.50 & £3.80 CHRISTMAS BOOKS OF STAMPS**

| | | |
|---|---|---|
| With pair or block of four 19p & 25p stamps | ....pair | 7 |
| With complete panes of 19p & 25p stamps | ......pair | 15 |

There are thousands more pictures of British first day covers at www.bfdc.co.uk where you can sort by stamp issue, theme, cover producer, stamp type - and much more!

## 18th January 1994 – THE AGE OF STEAM
*19p Bridge of Orchy; 25p "Amadis" at King's Cross;*
*30p Turntable at Blyth North;*
*35p Irlam into Wigan Central;*
*41p "Devizes Castle" across Worcester & B'ham Canal*

|  |  | ordinary covers | official covers |
|---|---|---|---|
|  |  | £ | £ |

**SPECIAL HANDSTAMPS**

| | | ordinary | official | |
|---|---|---|---|---|
| (1) | Philatelic Bureau... | 3 | – | *Royal Mail* |
| (2) | First Day of Issue – York | 3 | – | *Royal Mail* |
| (3) | First Day of Issue – Bridge of Orchy | 3 | – | *Royal Mail* |
| (4) | First Day of Issue – London | 10 | – | *Royal Mail* |
| (5) | The Age of Steam, Waterloo, SE1 | 15 | 20 | *VP 82* |
| (6) | The Age of Steam, Derby | 15 | 20 | *LFDC 120* |
| (7) | Peterborough NVR, Wansford Station | 15 | 25 | *Nene V. Rly* |
| (8) | All Aboard Now, Collectors' Club | 15 | 40 | *C.Club (RMail)* |
| (9) | North Yorkshire Moors Railway | 15 | 25 | *CoverCraft* |
| (10) | Britain's Railway History, RMT, Euston | 15 | 25 | *CoverCraft* |
| (11) | Britain's Railway Heritage, Ian Allen | 15 | 40 | *CoverCraft* |
| (12) | Football Locomotives, Manchester United | 15 | 20 | *Dawn* |
| (13) | Football Locomotives, Newcastle United | 15 | 20 | *Dawn* |
| (14) | Great Central Railway, Loughborough | 15 | 50 | *Bradbury* |
| (15) | Adventures of Sherlock Holmes, Paddington | 15 | 40 | *Bradbury* |
| (16) | Midland Fox, Leicester | 15 | 75 | *Bradbury* |
| (17) | Redhill, the Town and its Railway | 15 | 50 | *Redhill 150* |
| (18) | Railway Mania, GWR Dainton Tunnel | 15 | 30 | *BenSG22* |
| (19) | South Eastern Railway, Folkestone | 15 | 35 | *Ben500(90)* |
| (20) | North British Rly., Edinburgh | 15 | 20 | *BLCS 90* |
| (21) | Midland Railway, Euston | 15 | 20 | *BLCS 90* |
| (22) | London, Brighton & South Coast Rly | 15 | 20 | *Ben500(90a)* |
| (23) | Didcot, Great Western Railway Co. | 15 | 25 | *BenL43* |
| (24) | Great Eastern Railway, Great Yarmouth | 15 | 20 | *BenL42* |
| (25) | L.N.E.R., Railway Mania, Peterborough | 15 | 20 | *BenL42* |
| (26) | LXX Sqn. Est. LXXVII, BF 2393 PS | 15 | 20 | *RAF FDC 17* |

**ORDINARY F.D.I. POSTMARKS**

| | | | |
|---|---|---|---|
| (27) | Aberystwyth (Talyllyn Railway cover) | 35 | |
| (28) | Caernarfon (Festiniog Railway cover) | 35 | |

**C.D.S. POSTMARKS**

| | | | |
|---|---|---|---|
| (29) | Any Station postmark (e.g. Crowthorne) | 20 | |
| (30) | Any TPO (Travelling Post Office) postmark | 20 | |
| (31) | Blyth (or Cambois); Bridge of Orchy; King's Cross; Wigan; Worcester (or Lowesmoor) – sites on stamps... | 20 | |

*Also: Branch End, Bright St. York, Carlisle, Carnforth, Darlington, Derby, Didcot, Euston, Gifford, Mallaig, Paddington, Quainton, Rainhill, The Rocket, Settle, Stephenson Square, Stockton, Swindon, Wylam. Prices from £15.*

**SLOGAN POSTMARKS**

| | | | |
|---|---|---|---|
| (32) | Sixty Years Passenger Service for the Capital... | 85 | |

*In addition: British Philatelic Bulletin; Postbus. Prices from £5.*

## 1st February 1994 – GREETINGS
*10 x 1st Class – 'Messages':- Dan Dare, The Three Bears, Rupert Bear, Alice, Noggin the Nog, Peter Rabbit, Red Riding Hood, Orlando, Biggles, Paddington Bear.*

**SPECIAL HANDSTAMPS**

| | | ordinary | official | |
|---|---|---|---|---|
| (1) | Philatelic Bureau... | 3 | – | *Royal Mail* |
| (2) | First Day of Issue – Penn, Wolverhampton | 4 | – | *Royal Mail* |
| (3) | First Day of Issue – London | 12 | – | *Royal Mail* |
| (4) | Greetings, Daresbury | 12 | 35 | *Bradbury* |
| (5) | Greetings from Paddington Bear, W2 | 12 | 20 | *BLCS 91* |
| (6) | Greetings from Rupert, SE1 | 12 | 20 | *BLCS 91* |
| (7) | Orlando, the Marmalade Cat, W1 | 12 | 15 | *BenD223* |
| (8) | Teddy Bear Times, Steyning | 12 | 15 | *BenD223* |
| (9) | The Tale of Peter Rabbit, Keswick | 12 | 15 | *BenD223* |
| (10) | Noggin the Nog, Canterbury | 12 | 20 | *Ben500(91)* |
| (11) | Little Red Riding Hood, Wolfsdale | 12 | 15 | *BenD223* |
| (12) | Bearsden | 12 | 10 | *ExpNews pc(s)* |
| (13) | Evening Sentinel, Stoke on Trent | 12 | 45 | *Dawn(set of 10)* |

**C.D.S. POSTMARKS**

| | | | |
|---|---|---|---|
| (14) | Fleet St – newspapers characters | 15 | |
| (15) | Greet, Letter, or Paddington | 15 | |
| (16) | Oxford – home of Lewis Carroll | 15 | |

*Also: Bear Park, Bearsden, Biggleswade, Blackfriars Bridge Rd, Bunny, Catsfield, Catshill, Dunkeld, Eagle, Epsom Downs, Fulham Palace Rd, Letterston, Mount Nod, Penn, Rupert St., Wolf's Castle. £10.*

**SLOGAN POSTMARKS**

| | | | |
|---|---|---|---|
| (17) | Write Now, Say it Better in a Letter | 20 | |

*In addition: Octagon Theatre; Any Royal Mail slogans. Prices from £5.*

## 1st March 1994 – THE PRINCE OF WALES
*19p Chirk Castle; 25p Ben Arkle; 30p Mourne Mountains;*
*35p Dersingham; 41p Dolwyddelan Castle*

**SPECIAL HANDSTAMPS**

| | | ordinary | official | |
|---|---|---|---|---|
| (1) | Philatelic Bureau... | 3 | – | *Royal Mail* |
| (2) | First Day of Issue – Caernarfon | 3 | – | *Royal Mail* |
| (3) | First Day of Issue – London | 10 | – | *Royal Mail* |
| (4) | Caernarfon, St. David's Day | 10 | 15 | *Royal Mint* |
| (5) | St. David's Day, Caernarfon Castle | 10 | 15 | *LFDC 121* |
| (6) | St. David's Day, Caernarfon | 10 | 15 | *VP 83* |
| (7) | St. David's, Haverfordwest (daffodils) | 10 | – | *Royal Mail* |
| (8) | Investiture, Caernarfon (circle) | 10 | 25 | *CoverCraft* |

105

**Prince of Wales (contd.)**

| | ordinary covers £ | official covers £ | |
|---|---|---|---|
| (9) Investiture, Caernarfon (oval) | 10 | 15 | BLCS 92 |
| (10) Investiture, Highgrove | 10 | 17 | BLCS 92 |
| (11) Investiture, Windsor | 10 | 17 | BLCS 92 |
| (12) Radio Times, Buckingham Palace, SW1 | 10 | 12 | Benham |
| (13) MAJESTY, Investiture, W1 | 10 | 20 | Benham |
| (14) HRH Prince of Wales, Cardiff | 10 | 17 | Ben500(92) |
| (15) Buckingham Palace, London, SW1A 1AA | 10 | 45 | Prince'sTrust |
| (16) Prince Charles Ave. Post Office, Derby | 10 | – | Royal Mail |
| (17) Spring Stampex, SW1 | 10 | – | Royal Mail |
| (18) Byddin Yr etc., Caernarfon | 10 | 20 | S. Army |
| (19) Football Locomotive Paintings, Sunderland | 8 | 15 | Dawn |
| (20) Richard I, Nottingham | 8 | 25 | BenSG23 |
| (21) New £2 Coin, Bank of England, EC2 | 8 | – | n.o.c. |
| (22) 24 Squadron, BF 2409 PS | 8 | 15 | RAF FDC 18 |

**C.D.S. POSTMARKS**

| | |
|---|---|
| (23) Achfary, Lairg – near to Ben Arkle (25p) | 25 |
| (24) Buckingham Palace or Windsor Castle | 85 |
| (25) Caernarfon or Windsor | 15 |
| (26) Chirk (19p) or Dersingham (35p) | 15 |
| (27) Dolwyddelan – (41p) | 25 |
| (28) House of Commons or Lords | 20 |
| (29) Nettleham – first Investiture | 15 |
| (30) Newcastle (or Donard St., Newcastle) – (30p) | 15 |
| (31) Prince Charles Ave., Derby | 15 |
| (32) St. David's – issued on St. David's Day | 15 |
| (33) St. David's Road, Caernarfon | 15 |

*Also: Mount Charles, Prince Consort Rd, Princeville, Rhiconich, Tetbury, The Hayes, Wales. From £10.*

**SLOGAN POSTMARKS** *Newry 850; Any Royal Mail slogans. Prices from £15.*

## 12th April 1994 – PICTORIAL POSTCARDS 1894–1994

*19p Blackpool Tower; 25p "Where's my little lad";*
*30p "Wish you were here!"; 35p Punch and Judy; 41p Tower Bridge.*

**SPECIAL HANDSTAMPS**

| | | | |
|---|---|---|---|
| (1) Philatelic Bureau | 3 | – | Royal Mail |
| (2) First Day of Issue – Blackpool | 3 | – | Royal Mail |
| (3) First Day of Issue – London | 12 | – | Royal Mail |
| (4) Wish you were here, Blackpool | 12 | 20 | LFDC 122 |
| (5) Wish you were here, Broadstairs | 12 | 20 | VP 84 |
| (6) Wish you were here, Scarborough | 12 | 20 | Bradbury |
| (7) Blackpool Tower Centenary Year | 12 | 15 | Bradbury |
| (8) Picture Postcard Centenary, SW1 | 12 | 15 | BLCS 93 |
| (9) Tower Bridge Centenary, SE1 | 12 | 15 | BLCS 93 |
| (10) Picture Postcards Centenary, Brighton | 12 | 15 | Ben500(93) |
| (11) Football Locomotive Postcards, Arsenal | 12 | 15 | Dawn |
| (12) FA Cup Winners, Arsenal in Europe | 12 | 25 | Dawn |

**C.D.S. POSTMARKS**

| | |
|---|---|
| (13) Any Seaside town, e.g. Scarborough | 15 |
| (14) Any Butlin's Holiday Camp Post Office | 50 |
| (15) Grand Hotel Buildings, Eastbourne | 15 |
| (16) North Shore, or South Shore Blackpool | 20 |
| (17) Sands, Sandy or The Strand | 15 |
| (18) Seaside, Seaview, The Beach or The Pier | 25 |
| (19) Whitecliff, Poole | 12 |

*Also: Bare, Blackheath, Broadbottom, Crab Lane, Freezywater, Giggleswick, Holmfirth, Littlehampton, Pratt's Bottom, Rock, Seething Ln, Tower Hill. Prices from £10.*

**SLOGAN POSTMARKS**

| | |
|---|---|
| (20) Le Shuttle, Folkestone to Calais | 10 |
| (21) Portsmouth 800 | 15 |

*In addition: Collect British Stamps; Isle of Skye; Postcodes. Prices from £6.*

## 3rd May 1994 – CHANNEL TUNNEL

*25p, 41p British Lion and Le Coq; 25p, 41p Joined hands over a speeding train.*

**SPECIAL HANDSTAMPS**

| | | | |
|---|---|---|---|
| (1) Philatelic Bureau | 3 | – | Royal Mail |
| (2) First Day of Issue – Folkestone (map) | 3 | – | Royal Mail |
| (3) First Day of Issue – Folkestone (Big Ben) | 3 | – | Royal Mail |
| (4) First Day of Issue – London | 3 | – | Royal Mail |
| (5) Institution of Civil Engineers, SW1 | 12 | 15 | LFDC 123 |
| (6) British Tunnelling Society, SW1 | 12 | 15 | VP 85 |
| (7) Channel Tunnel (lion and cock), Folkestone | 12 | 15 | Bradbury |
| (8) Brush Traction, Loughborough | 12 | 15 | Bradbury |
| (9) Le Shuttle, The Channel Tunnel, Folkestone | 12 | 35 | BLCS 94 pair |
| (10) Celebrating the Channel Tunnel, Folkestone | 12 | 35 | BLCS 94 pair |
| (11) Euro Tunnel Celebration '94, Folkestone | 12 | 75 | Ben500(94)pr |
| (12) Opening of the Channel Tunnel, Folkestone | 12 | 25 | BLCS 94 pair |
| (13) Radio Times, Folkestone | 12 | 30 | Benham |
| (14) First through the Tunnel, Laser, Folkestone | 12 | 50 | Benham |
| (15) Tarmac Construction Ltd, Wolverhampton | 12 | – | n.o.c. |
| (16) Design Consultants, London | 12 | 200 | CoverCraft |
| (17) No. 33 Squadron, BF 2421 PS | 12 | 15 | RAF FDC 20 |
| (18) Woodhead Tunnel, Sheffield Wednesday | 12 | 20 | Dawn |
| (19) Busways E.S.O.P., Newcastle | 12 | 20 | Dawn |
| (20) Peterborough NVR, Wansford Station | 12 | 25 | Nene V. Rly |

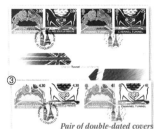

| Channel Tunnel (contd.) | ordinary covers | official covers |
|---|---|---|

**C.D.S. POSTMARKS** £ £
(21) Cheriton or Folkestone – tunnel terminal ........ 15
(22) Ashford – international terminal......................... 15
(23) King's Cross – proposed new terminal ............... 15
(24) Waterloo Road, SE1 – existing terminal ........... 15
(25) Waterloo & Gare du Nord - Eurostar........*pair* 35
(26) Calais or Dover PAQUEBOTS ............................ 15
*Calais Rd., French St., Horn St., Railway Rd., Rising Bridge, Terminal Rd.,*
*Terminus Rd., The Link, Trafalgar Square, Undercliff. Prices from £10.*

**SLOGAN POSTMARKS**
(27) Le Shuttle, Folkestone to Calais........................... 15

**DOUBLE POSTMARKED COVERS**
The Channel Tunnel stamps were a joint Royal Mail/La Poste issue. Arrangements
were made for British collectors to obtain the French COQUELLES postmark at
the Philatelic Bureau by authority of La Poste, the French postal administration.
The Coquelles postmark was applied to the French stamps provided the covers had
at least one British Channel Tunnel stamp also affixed. The French Channel Tunnel
terminal is located at Coquelles.
(1) Covers with both sets (eight stamps) .................. 30
(2) Other combinations of English & French stamps... 15

*Pair of double-dated covers*

## 6th June 1994 – D-DAY
*25p Groundcrew reloading RAF Bostons; 25p Coastal bombardment/HMS Warspite;*
*25p Commandos landing on Gold Beach; 25p Infantry regrouping on Sword Beach;*
*25p Advancing inland from Ouistreham.*

**SPECIAL HANDSTAMPS** (1) Philatelic Bureau... 3 – *Royal Mail*
(2) First Day of Issue – Portsmouth.......................... 3 – *Royal Mail*
(3) First Day of Issue – London ................................ 3 – *Royal Mail*
(4) Operation 'Overlord' D-Day, BF 2398 PS ........ 12 15 *RAF FDC 21*
(5) Utah Beach, BF 2415 PS ..................................... 12 100 *Forces*
(6) Sword Beach, BF 2416 PS.................................... 12 110 *Forces*
(7) Gold Beach, BF 2417 PS..................................... 12 110 *Forces*
(8) Juno Beach, BF 2418 PS ..................................... 12 110 *Forces*
(9) Taking of Pegasus Bridge, BF 2419 PS.............. 12 15 *Forces(s)*
(10) Silencing of the Merville Battery, BF 2420 PS.. 12 15 *Forces(s)*
(11) 50th Anniversary of 'D' Day, BF 2422 PS ........ 12 100 *Forces*
(12) HMS Dryad, Portsmouth ................................... 12 20 *Royal Mint*
(13) D-Day, 1944-1994, Portsmouth.......................... 12 15 *Westminster*
(14) 50 Overlord, Southwick, Hampshire ................. 12 20 *Southwick P.O.*
(15) Operation Taxable, 617 Squadron...................... 12 200 *Cam S.C.*
(16) City of Portsmouth, D-Day, 50th Anniversary.. 12 60 *RM Portsmouth*
(17) D-Day Commemoration, Birmingham............... 12 10 *Royal Mail*
(18) D-Day + 50 (Eisenhower)................................... 12 15 *LFDC 124*
(19) D-Day, Southampton (square map) .................... 12 15 *VP 86*
(20) Spirit of Britain, London SW1 .......................... 12 15 *Bradbury*
(21) D-Day Museum, Portsmouth .............................. 12 60 *Arlington*
(22) Imperial War Museum, SE1 ............................... 12 12 *Benham*
(23) National Army Museum, Chelsea, SW3 ............ 12 25 *BenL44*
(24) Radio Times, D-Day Landings, Portsmouth ...... 12 10 *Benham*
(25) FEARLESS, Portsmouth ..................................... 12 20 *BLCS 95*
(26) D-Day Landings, Portsmouth ............................ 12 60 *BenC.I*
(27) D-Day, Tangmere............................................... 12 20 *Benham*
(28) Bletchley Park, Enigma Codebreakers............... 12 75 *Bletchley Trust*
(29) D-Day Preparations by Rail ............................... 12 20 *Dawn*
(30) Invasion of Europe, Portsmouth ........................ 12 50 *Cam S.C.*
(31) D-Day, News of the World, London E1............. 12 20 *CoverCraft*
(32) D-Day The Sun, London E1............................... 12 20 *CoverCraft*
(33) London Taxi Benevolent Assoc'n ...................... 12 20 *CoverCraft*
(34) D-Day, 1944-1994, Portsmouth (RAF Wings) .. 12 20 *CoverCraft*
(35) D-Day Commemoration, Southsea....................... 12 75 *CoverCraft*

**C.D.S POSTMARKS**
(36) Calais and Dover PAQUEBOTS.................*pair* 20
(37) Churchill, Bristol or Montgomery, Powys......... 20
(38) House of Commons or Lords .............................. 30
(39) Maritime Mail or Normandy (Guildford) ......... 20
(40) Portsmouth or Southampton ............................... 12
(41) Southwick – SHAEF Headquarters.................... 20
*Also: Battle, The Beach, Boston, Bulford Barracks, Dunkirk, Pathfinder*
*Village, RAF Scampton, Trenchard Lines, Victory Street. From £10.*

**SLOGAN POSTMARKS**
(42) Maritime Mail.................................................... 20
*In addition: Portsmouth 800; European Elections. Prices from £8.*

## 5th July 1994 – GOLF
*19p St. Andrews - The Old Course; 25p Muirfield - 18th Hole;*
*30p Carnoustie - Luckyslap; 35p Royal Troon - The Postage Stamp;*
*41p Turnberry - 9th Hole.*

**SPECIAL HANDSTAMPS** (1) Philatelic Bureau... 3 – *Royal Mail*
(2) First Day of Issue – Turnberry............................. 3 – *Royal Mail*
(3) First Day of Issue – London ................................ 3 – *Royal Mail*
(4) Royal and Ancient Golf Club, St. Andrews ....... 15 30 *LFDC 125*
(5) Golfer's Alphabet, St. Andrews .......................... 15 25 *VP 87*
(6) Gleneagles Hotel, Auchterarder.......................... 15 25 *Bradbury*

## Golf (contd.)

|  | | ordinary covers £ | official covers £ | |
|---|---|---|---|---|
| (7) | Tee Time, Philatelic Golf Society | 15 | 20 | *Bradbury* |
| (8) | H-C-E-G 250 Years, Muirfield | 15 | 30 | *HCEG(s)* |
| (9) | First Open, St. Georges, Sandwich | 15 | 12 | *BLCS 96* |
| (10) | The British Open, Greg Norman, Turnberry | 15 | 12 | *BLCS 96* |
| (11) | World's Oldest Golf Club, Muirfield | 15 | 10 | *Benham(s)* |
| (12) | St. Andrew's, Home of Golf | 15 | 25 | *Ben500(96)* |
| (13) | 250 Years of Golf, Carnoustie | 15 | 10 | *Benham(s)* |
| (14) | Mail on Sunday, British Open, Turnberry | 15 | 15 | *Benham* |
| (15) | 250 Years of Golf, Royal Troon | 15 | 10 | *Benham(s)* |
| (16) | Eighth Hole, Postage Stamp, Royal Troon | 15 | 50 | *CoverCraft* |
| (17) | No. 25 Squadron, BE 2429 PS | 8 | 15 | *RAF FDC 22* |

### C.D.S. POSTMARKS

| (18) | St. Andrews (19p); Gullane (25p); Carnoustie (30p); Troon (35p); or Turnberry (41p)......*each* | 45 | |
|---|---|---|---|
| (19) | Caddy | 200 | |
| (20) | The Fairway, The Green or The Links | 35 | |
| (21) | Gleneagles Hotel, Eagle or Par......*each* | 70 | |
| (22) | Leith Walk – 1744 home of H.C.E.G. | 25 | |

*Also: Ballybogy, Birkdale, Golf Road, Hoylake, Lytham St. Annes, Portrush, Prestwick, Sandwich, Wentworth. From £15.*

### SLOGAN POSTMARKS

| (23) | New Skoda Women's Scottish Open | 75 |
|---|---|---|

*TSB Athletics; BUPA; See the Clock/Make a Wish; Any Royal Mail slogans. Prices from £7.*

## 2nd August 1994 – SUMMERTIME

*19p Llanelwedd (Royal Welsh Show); 25p Wimbledon;*
*30p Cowes Week; 35p Lord's; 41p Braemar Highland Gathering*

| **SPECIAL HANDSTAMPS** (1) | Philatelic Bureau | 3 | – | *Royal Mail* |
|---|---|---|---|---|
| (2) | First Day of Issue – Wimbledon | 3 | – | *Royal Mail* |
| (3) | First Day of Issue – London | 4 | – | *Royal Mail* |
| (4) | Birthplace of Thomas Lord, Thirsk | 10 | 25 | *S.P.* |
| (5) | Memorial Cricket Match, NW8 | 10 | 25 | *S.P.* |
| (6) | Tribute to Lords, Derbyshire CCC | 10 | 25 | *S.P.* |
| (7) | Tribute to Lords, Durham CCC | 10 | 25 | *S.P.* |
| (8) | Tribute to Lords, Essex CCC | 10 | 25 | *S.P.* |
| (9) | Tribute to Lords, Glamorgan CCC | 10 | 25 | *S.P.* |
| (10) | Tribute to Lords, Gloucestershire CCC | 10 | 25 | *S.P.* |
| (11) | Tribute to Lords, Hampshire CCC | 10 | 25 | *S.P.* |
| (12) | Tribute to Lords, Kent CCC | 10 | 25 | *S.P.* |
| (13) | Tribute to Lords, Lancashire CCC | 10 | 25 | *S.P.* |
| (14) | Tribute to Lords, Leicestershire CCC | 10 | 25 | *S.P.* |
| (15) | Tribute to Lords, Middlesex CCC | 10 | 25 | *S.P.* |
| (16) | Tribute to Lords, Northamptonshire CCC | 10 | 25 | *S.P.* |
| (17) | Tribute to Lords, Nottinghamshire CCC | 10 | 25 | *S.P.* |
| (18) | Tribute to Lords, Somerset CCC | 10 | 25 | *S.P.* |
| (19) | Tribute to Lords, Surrey CCC | 10 | 25 | *S.P.* |
| (20) | Tribute to Lords, Sussex CCC | 10 | 25 | *S.P.* |
| (21) | Tribute to Lords, Warwickshire CCC | 10 | 25 | *S.P.* |
| (22) | Tribute to Lords, Worcestershire CCC | 10 | 25 | *S.P.* |
| (23) | Tribute to Lords, Yorkshire CCC | 10 | 25 | *S.P.* |
| (24) | Summertime at Lord's, NW8 | 10 | 15 | *VP 88* |
| (25) | Outside Edge, Nottingham | 10 | 10 | *Benham* |
| (26) | Yatching at Cowes | 10 | 15 | *Ben500(98)* |
| (27) | Braemar Gathering | 10 | 10 | *BLCS 98* |
| (28) | Royal Welsh Show, Llanelwedd | 10 | 10 | *BenL45* |
| (29) | Shetland Pony at Braemar | 10 | 10 | *BenL45* |
| (30) | YMCA, 150 Years, Dulverton | 10 | 20 | *Arlington* |
| (31) | National Association of Local Councils, WC1. | 10 | 10 | *LFDC 126* |
| (32) | Summertime Holidays by Train, Manchester | 10 | 15 | *Dawn* |
| (33) | Summertime Holidays by Rail, Leicester | 10 | 40 | *Dawn* |
| (34) | No.22 Squadron, BF 2431 PS | 10 | 12 | *RAF FDC 23* |
| (35) | GSG Technology Centre, Swindon | 10 | 225 | *CSG* |
| (36) | Postal Uniforms, National Postal Museum | 10 | – | *n.o.c.* |

### C.D.S. POSTMARKS

| (37) | Builth Wells (19p); Wimbledon (25p) Cowes (30p); St. John's Wood (35p); Braemar (41p) *each* | 15 | |
|---|---|---|---|

*Also: Bowling, Kennington, Over, Pavilion, Strawberry Hill, Summerhouse, Summerfield, Summerseat, Summertown. From £8.*

### SLOGAN POSTMARKS

| (38) | Tropical Places, Exotic Holiday | 12 |
|---|---|---|

*Also: Biggleswade Festival; Inverness; Perrier; McMillans; Wilde Weekend in Worthing; Collect British Stamps; Royal Mail slogans. From £7.*

## 27th September 1994 – MEDICAL DISCOVERIES

*25p Ultrasonic Imaging; 30p Scanning Electron Microscopy;*
*35p Magnetic Resonance Imaging; 41p Computed Tomography*

| **SPECIAL HANDSTAMPS** (1) | Philatelic Bureau | 3 | – | *Royal Mail* |
|---|---|---|---|---|
| (2) | First Day of Issue – Cambridge | 3 | – | *Royal Mail* |
| (3) | First Day of Issue – London | 8 | – | *Royal Mail* |
| (4) | Peak Practice, Whatstandwell | 8 | 10 | *BLCS 99* |
| (5) | Peak Practice, Wirksworth | 8 | 10 | *BLCS 99* |
| (6) | Peak Practice, Fritchley | 8 | 10 | *BLCS 99* |
| (7) | Peak Practice, Crich | 8 | 10 | *BLCS 99* |

## Medical Discoveries (contd.)

| | | ordinary covers £ | official covers £ | |
|---|---|---|---|---|
| (8) | The Lancet, London WC1 | 8 | 10 | BLCS 99 |
| (9) | St. Bartholomew's, London EC1 | 8 | 15 | Ben500(99) |
| (10) | St. George's Hospital, London SW17 | 8 | 10 | Sajal |
| (11) | Cystic Fibrosis, Bromley | 8 | 15 | Bradbury |
| (12) | BMA, Founded 1832, Worcester | 8 | 35 | Bradbury |
| (13) | BMA, Over 100,000 Members, WC1 | 8 | 35 | Bradbury |
| (14) | Florence Nightingale, SE1 | 8 | 10 | VP 89 |
| (15) | Royal College of Surgeons, WC2 | 8 | 10 | LFDC 127 |
| (16) | Glasgow Royal Maternity Hospital | 8 | 15 | GRMH |
| (17) | Blackburn Rovers UEFA Cup | 8 | 25 | Dawn |
| (18) | No.360 Squadron BF 2432 PS | 8 | 10 | RAF FDC 24 |

### C.D.S. POSTMARKS

| | | £ |
|---|---|---|
| (19) | Hospital Post Offices:- Benenden, Milford, Oswestry, Lancaster Moor or Edward VII | 15 |
| (20) | Glasgow Royal Infirmary | 25 |
| (21) | Harefield or Papworth – transplants | 10 |
| (22) | Harborne, Hammersmith or Paddington – Radiology work | 15 |
| (23) | Headington, Oxford – Electronic Microscope | 15 |

Also: Brentford, Cambridge, Glasgow, Healing, Lancing, Pill, New Invention, St. Clements, Oxford. £8.

### SLOGAN POSTMARKS

| | | £ |
|---|---|---|
| (24) | Zeneca (pharmaceuticals) | 15 |
| (25) | Health Education – Fresh Fruit & Veg | 15 |

In addition: Soft Rock Heart Radio; Royal Mail slogans. Prices from £7.

## 1st November 1994 – CHRISTMAS
*19p, 25p, 30p, 35p, 41p Children's Nativity Plays*

| | | | | |
|---|---|---|---|---|
| **SPECIAL HANDSTAMPS** (1) | Philatelic Bureau | 3 | – | Royal Mail |
| (2) | First Day of Issue – Bethlehem | 3 | – | Royal Mail |
| (3) | First Day of Issue – London | 3 | – | Royal Mail |
| (4) | Christmas Common | 10 | 15 | Ben500(100) |
| (5) | Hollytrees Museum, Colchester | 10 | 8 | BLCS 100 |
| (6) | The Nativity, Bethlehem | 10 | 8 | BLCS 100 |
| (7) | The Nativity, Nasareth | 10 | 8 | BLCS 100 |
| (8) | Wiseman's Bridge | 10 | 40 | Ben500(100a) |
| (9) | Christchurch Priory 1094-1994 | 10 | 25 | LFDC 128 |
| (10) | Bethlehem (angel and trumpet) | 10 | 15 | VP 90 |
| (11) | Santa Claus Distrib. Fund, Stoke Newington | 10 | 15 | G.K.Eldridge |
| (12) | National Postal Museum, Christmas 94 | 10 | 15 | Friends NPM |
| (13) | Happy Christmas, Royal Mail, EC1 | 10 | – | Royal Mail |
| (14) | Christmas Greetings, Lewes | 10 | 15 | FDP Co |
| (15) | Season's Greetings, Leeds United | 10 | 12 | Dawn |
| (16) | Aston Villa in Europe, Birmingham | 10 | 12 | Dawn |
| (17) | Salvation Army, Hackney, E8 | 10 | 12 | S.Army |
| (18) | No.78 Squadron, BF 2436 PS | 10 | 12 | RAF FDC 25 |
| (19) | Peterborough NVR, Wansford Station | 10 | 20 | Nene V. Rly |

### C.D.S. POSTMARKS

| | | £ |
|---|---|---|
| (20) | Nasareth or Holy Island | 20 |
| (21) | York – most famous Nativity play | 10 |

Also: Angel Hill, Brentwood Ave., Child's Hill, Christchurch, Jerusalem St Narberth, Playing Place, Shepherd's Bush, Shepherd's Well, St. Nicholas, Star, Star Cross. Prices from £6.

### SLOGAN POSTMARKS

| | | £ |
|---|---|---|
| (22) | Walt Disney's Snow White | 25 |

Also: Glasgow Concert Hall; Mercurycard Off Peak; Any Royal Mail slogans (postcode/dog etc). Prices from £5.

### £2.50 & £3.80 CHRISTMAS BOOKS OF STAMPS

| | | |
|---|---|---|
| With pair or block of four 19p & 25p stamps | ...pair | 7 |
| With complete panes of 19p & 25p stamps | .......pair | 15 |

## 17th January 1995 – CATS
*19p black cat; 25p Siamese & tabby; 30p ginger cat; 35p Abyssinian & tortoiseshell; 41p black & white cat*

| | | | | |
|---|---|---|---|---|
| **SPECIAL HANDSTAMPS** (1) | Philatelic Bureau | 3 | – | Royal Mail |
| (2) | First Day of Issue – Kitts Green | 3 | – | Royal Mail |
| (3) | First Day of Issue – London | 3 | – | Royal Mail |
| (4) | Your Cat Magazine, Peterborough | 15 | 20 | Benham |
| (5) | Cats, Woman & Home, SE1 | 15 | 20 | Benham |
| (6) | RSPCA, Horsham | 15 | 20 | BLCS 101 |
| (7) | Cats Protection League, Horsham | 15 | 20 | Benham |
| (8) | Cats Protection League, Kirkintilloch | 15 | 20 | Benham |
| (9) | Cats Protection League, Newtownards | 15 | 20 | Benham |
| (10) | Cats Protection League, Bridgend | 15 | 20 | Benham |
| (11) | Cats Protection League, Birmingham | 15 | 20 | BLCS 101 |
| (12) | Catstree, Bridgnorth | 15 | 50 | Ben500(101) |
| (13) | Catfield, Great Yarmouth | 15 | 20 | BLCS 101 |
| (14) | Catsham, Glastonbury | 15 | 20 | BLCS 101 |
| (15) | Catbrook, Chepstow | 15 | 20 | BLCS 101 |
| (16) | Catsash, Newport | 15 | 35 | BenSG25 |
| (17) | Philatelic Felines, Catsfield | 15 | 20 | VP 91 |
| (18) | Philatelic Felines, Catshill | 15 | 20 | LFDC 129 |
| (19) | Celebrating Cats, Catshill | 15 | 20 | Westminster |
| (20) | Wood Green Animal Shelters, Royston | 15 | 30 | Wood Green |

|  | ordinary covers £ | official covers £ |
|---|---|---|
| (21) Cool Cats Catalogue, Catsfield | 10 | 15 *FDP Co* |
| (22) Celebrating Cats, City of London | 10 | 25 *Bradbury* |
| (23) Postal Cats, National Postal Museum | 10 | – *n.o.c.* |
| (24) Tiger Squadron, Flying Pumas, BF 2439 PS | 10 | 15 *RAF FDC 26* |

**C.D.S. POSTMARKS**

| (25) Catfield, Catsfield, Catshill etc .................... *each* | 15 |  |
| (26) Earl's Court – Cat Show | 15 |  |
| (27) Horsham – RSPCA & CPL headquarters | 15 |  |

*Also: Catbrook, Catcot, Catforth, Catsworth, Lea Village, Mousehole, Whittington. From £12.*

**SLOGAN POSTMARKS** *Please control your dog; Collect British Stamps Prices from £10.*

## 14th March 1995 – SPRINGTIME

*19p Dandelions; 25p Sweet Chestnut Leaves; 30p Garlic Leaves; 35p Hazel Leaves; 41p Spring Grass*

| **SPECIAL HANDSTAMPS** (1) Philatelic Bureau... | 3 | – *Royal Mail* |
|---|---|---|
| (2) First Day of Issue – Springfield | 3 | – *Royal Mail* |
| (3) First Day of Issue – London | 3 | – *Royal Mail* |
| (4) Springtime, Wingfield | 10 | 12 *BLCS 102* |
| (5) Springtime, Swallownest | 10 | 12 *BLCS 102* |
| (6) Springtime, Birdbrook | 10 | 12 *BLCS 102* |
| (7) Springtime, Ducklington | 10 | 15 *Ben500(102)* |
| (8) Springtime, Featherstone | 10 | 12 *BLCS 102* |
| (9) Rupert, Bearwood | 10 | 12 *BLCS 102* |
| (10) Springtime Stamps, Springvale | 10 | 20 *LFDC 130* |
| (11) Springtime Stamps, Royal Botanic Gdns, Kew. | 10 | 15 *VP 92* |
| (12) Springtime, North Norfolk Railway | 10 | 12 *Dawn* |
| (13) Spring into the new Catalogue, Leaves Green.. | 10 | 12 *FDP Co* |
| (14) The 'Saints', BF 2458 PS | 10 | 12 *RAF FDC 27* |
| (15) Wansford Station, Peterborough | 10 | 20 *NVRly* |

**C.D.S. POSTMARKS**

| (16) Chestnut Grove or Hazel Grove | 15 |  |
| (17) Kew Gardens | 15 |  |
| (18) Springbank, Spring Grove or Springvale | 15 |  |
| (19) Spring Gardens or Springfield | 15 |  |

*Also: Grassmoor, Leaves Green, Long Shoot, Spring Corner, Spring Hill, Springside, Swallownest, Wrens Nest. Prices from £12.*

**SLOGAN POSTMARKS** *Tropical Places. Postcodes Spalding. Prices from £6.*

## 21st March 1995 - GREETINGS

*10 x 1st Class on the theme of Love & Kisses*

| **SPECIAL HANDSTAMPS** (1) Philatelic Bureau... | 3 | – *Royal Mail* |
|---|---|---|
| (2) First Day of Issue – Lover | 4 | – *Royal Mail* |
| (3) First Day of Issue – London | 4 | – *Royal Mail* |
| (4) Gretna Green | 12 | 25 *Bradbury* |
| (5) Loversall, Doncaster | 12 | 20 *BLCS 103* |
| (6) Darlington, Co. Durham | 12 | 20 *BLCS 103* |
| (7) Lovesgrove, Aberystwyth | 12 | 20 *BLCS 103* |
| (8) Loveston, Kilgetty | 12 | 20 *BLCS 103* |
| (9) Honeydon, Bedford | 12 | 20 *BLCS 103* |
| (10) Lover, Salisbury | 12 | 20 *BLCS 103* |
| (11) Lovington, Castle Cary | 12 | 20 *BLCS 103* |
| (12) Darlingscott, Shipston on Stour | 12 | 20 *BLCS 103* |
| (13) Kislingbury, Northampton | 12 | 20 *Ben500(103)* |
| (14) Hugglescote, Leicester | 12 | 20 *BenD234* |
| (15) Team Work, Royal Mail, Leeds | 12 | 25 *Royal Mail NE* |
| (16) Discovery Day, Dundee | 15 | – *n.o.c.* |

**C.D.S. POSTMARKS**

| (17) Big Top or Playing Place | 12 |  |
| (18) Greet, Gretna Green or Lover | 12 |  |

*Also: Darlington, Heartsease, Kishorn, Paradise, Portobello Rd. Prices from £8.*

*NB These stamps were re-issued on 13th February 1996 with Blue Fluor Phosphor*

## 11th April 1995 – NATIONAL TRUST

*19p 100 Years; 25p Protecting Land; 30p Conserving Art; 35p Saving Coast; 41p Repairing Buildings.*

| **SPECIAL HANDSTAMPS** (1) Philatelic Bureau... | 3 | – *Royal Mail* |
|---|---|---|
| (2) First Day of Issue – Alfriston | 3 | – *Royal Mail* |
| (3) First Day of Issue – London | 3 | – *Royal Mail* |
| (4) Queen Anne's Gate National Headquarters..... | 10 | – *Royal Mail* |
| (5) Attingham Park, Conserving Art | 10 | – *Royal Mail* |
| (6) St. David's, Saving Coastline | 10 | – *Royal Mail* |
| (7) Congleton, Repairing Buildings | 10 | – *Royal Mail* |
| (8) Crom, Enniskillen, Protecting Land | 10 | – *Royal Mail* |
| (9) Giant's Causeway, Bushmills (oval) | 10 | – *Royal Mail* |
| (10) Blickling Hall, Aylsham, Norfolk | 10 | – *Royal Mail* |
| (11) This England, Oakham, Rutland | 10 | 15 *VP 93* |
| (12) Country Houses Association, WC2 | 10 | 15 *LFDC 131* |
| (13) Steam Yacht Gondola, Coniston | 10 | 12 *BLCS 104* |
| (14) Brownsea Island, Poole | 10 | 12 *BLCS 104* |
| (15) Calke Abbey, Ticknall, Derby | 10 | 12 *Benham* |

*National Trust (contd.)*      **ordinary covers**    **official covers**

| | | £ | | £ | |
|---|---|---|---|---|---|
| (16) | Fountains, Abbey, Ripon | 10 | 15 | *Ben500(104)* |
| (17) | Powis Castle, Welshpool | 10 | 12 | *Benham* |
| (18) | Hidcote Manor, Chipping Camden | 10 | 12 | *Benham* |
| (19) | Giant's Causeway, Bushmills | 10 | 12 | *Benham* |
| (20) | The Old Post Office, Tintagel | 10 | 12 | *Benham* |
| (21) | The Clergy House, Alfriston | 10 | 12 | *Benham* |
| (22) | Chartwell, Westerham, Kent | 10 | 12 | *Benham* |
| (23) | The National Trust, Radio Times, W12 | 10 | 12 | *Benham* |
| (24) | George Stephenson's Birthplace, Wylam | 10 | 12 | *Dawn* |
| (25) | Supertrams, Sheffield | 10 | 12 | *Dawn* |
| (26) | The catalogue you can trust, Alfriston | 10 | 15 | *FDP Co* |
| (27) | Crathie Parish Church Centenary | 10 | 20 | *Pilgrim* |
| (28) | Llangollen Postal Museum | 10 | 50 | *Llangollen PM* |
| (29) | No.39 Squadron BF 2459 PS | 10 | 12 | *RAF FDC 28* |
| (30) | Port Ellen, Isle of Islay | 10 | – | *Royal Mail* |

**C.D.S. POSTMARKS**

| | | |
|---|---|---|
| (31) | Alfriston – first National Trust building | 15 |
| (32) | Atcham or Upton Megna – Attingham Park | 15 |
| (33) | Barmouth – first National Trust site | 15 |
| (34) | Haslemere – Robert Hunter (Founder) | 15 |
| (35) | Lower Shiplake – Canon Rawnsley (Founder) | 15 |
| (36) | St. David's (35p) or Scholar Green (41p) | 15 |
| (37) | Tintagel – National Trust Post Office | 15 |
| (38) | Wisbech – B/place Octavia Hill (Founder) | 15 |
| (39) | Land's End and John O'Groats | *pair* | 35 |

*In addition: Acorn Street, Bredon, Lacock, Montacute, Oak Tree, Oakhill, Petworth, Shipton-by-Beningbrough, Wylam.   Prices from £6.*

**SLOGAN POSTMARKS** *See the Clock etc.; Shetland Scottish Tourism.   Prices from £6.*

## 2nd May 1995 – VE DAY
*19p Liberation of Paris; 25p St. Paul's on VE night;*
*19p Red Cross ; 19p & 30p United Nations.*

| | **SPECIAL HANDSTAMPS** | | | |
|---|---|---|---|---|
| (1) | Philatelic Bureau | 3 | – | *Royal Mail* |
| (2) | First Day of Issue – Peace & Freedom, SW | 3 | – | *Royal Mail* |
| (3) | First Day of Issue – London | 3 | – | *Royal Mail* |
| (4) | First Day of Issue – VE DAY London EC4 | 3 | 3 | *DailyMirror(s)* |
| (5) | United Nations Association, Whitehall | 10 | 55 | *CoverCollection* |
| (6) | United Nations, Peacehaven | 10 | 12 | *BLCS 105* |
| (7) | United Nations, London SW1 | 10 | 10 | *BLCS 105* |
| (8) | Victory in Europe, London | 10 | 15 | *Ben500(105)* |
| (9) | Victory in Europe, Birmingham | 10 | 12 | *Benham* |
| (10) | Victory in Europe, Coventry | 10 | 12 | *Benham* |
| (11) | Victory in Europe, Edinburgh | 10 | 12 | *Benham* |
| (12) | Victory in Europe, Cardiff | 10 | 12 | *Benham* |
| (13) | Victory in Europe, Dover | 10 | 12 | *BLCS 105* |
| (14) | Daily Express, Hyde Park | 10 | 12 | *Benham* |
| (15) | The Mail on Sunday, Kensington | 10 | 12 | *Benham* |
| (16) | Victory in Europe, Radio Times, W12 | 10 | 12 | *Benham* |
| (17) | Victory in Europe, Whitehall (cigar) | 10 | 12 | *LFDC 132* |
| (18) | Peace & Freedom, EC4 | 10 | 15 | *VP 94* |
| (19) | British Medical Association | 10 | 15 | *Bradbury* |
| (20) | R J Mitchell Centenary Year, Southampton | 10 | 35 | *Bradbury(set 3)* |
| (21) | BBMF Commemoration, SW1 | 10 | 50 | *CoverCraft* |
| (22) | Enigma Codebreakers, Bletchley Park | 10 | 20 | *Arlington* |
| (23) | St. Dunstan's, London W1 | 10 | 55 | *Arlington* |
| (24) | Birmingham Evening Mail VE DAY | 10 | 20 | *Dawn* |
| (25) | Troops Return, Liverpool | 10 | 20 | *Dawn* |
| (26) | British Forces Postal Service 1000 | 10 | 75 | *Forces* |
| (27) | GB FDC Catalogue, Peacehaven | 10 | 15 | *FDP Co* |
| (28) | Llangollen Postal Museum | 10 | 40 | *Llangollen PM* |
| (29) | No 8 Squadron, BF 2460 PS | 10 | 12 | *RAF FDC 29* |
| (30) | Peterborough Rail 150 | 10 | 20 | *NVRly* |

**C.D.S. POSTMARKS**

| | | |
|---|---|---|
| (31) | Bladon, Churchill or Montgomery | 15 |
| (32) | House of Commons or Lords | 50 |
| (33) | London EC - St. Paul's Cathedral (25p) | 10 |
| (34) | Peacehaven, Cross in Hand or Hope | 15 |
| (35) | Tufton St SW1 - first meeting on UN | 15 |
| (36) | West Wellow - Florence Nightingale | 15 |

*Also: Biggin Hill, Cranwell, Falls Rd, The Maze, New York, Normandy, Wonersh, Victory St. From £10.*

## 6th June 1995 – SCIENCE FICTION
*25p The Time Machine; 30p The First Men in the Moon;*
*35p War of the Worlds; 41p The Shape of Things to Come.*

| | **SPECIAL HANDSTAMPS** | | | |
|---|---|---|---|---|
| (1) | Philatelic Bureau | 3 | – | *Royal Mail* |
| (2) | First Day of Issue – Wells | 3 | – | *Royal Mail* |
| (3) | First Day of Issue – London H G Wells SF | 3 | – | *Royal Mail* |
| (4) | Into the Future, Starboard Way, E14 | 12 | 10 | *BLCS 106* |
| (5) | Science Fiction, Star Road, W14 | 12 | 15 | *Ben500(107)* |
| (6) | War of the Worlds, Worlds End, Newbury | 12 | 15 | *BLCS 106* |
| (7) | Time and Space, Star | 12 | 10 | *Benham(s)* |
| (8) | Science Fiction, Radio Times, W12 | 12 | 15 | *Benham* |
| (9) | The First Men in the Moon, Bromley | 12 | 12 | *VP 95* |

111

**Science Fiction (contd.)**

| | ordinary covers £ | | official covers £ |
|---|---|---|---|
| (10) The War of the Worlds, Bromley | 12 | 25 | LFDC 133 |
| (11) H G Wells 1866-1946, Bromley | 12 | 25 | Cam.S.C. |
| (12) Blick, 70 Years Time Recording, Swindon | 12 | 25 | Blick |
| (13) Science Fiction Convention, Glasgow | 12 | 35 | CoverCollection |
| (14) Message from Mars, Bromley | 12 | 75 | CoverCraft |
| (15) Travel Back in Time, Wells | 12 | 15 | FDP Co |
| (16) No. IV (AC) Squadron BF 2469 PS | 12 | 15 | RAF FDC 30 |

**C.D.S. POSTMARKS**

| | | |
|---|---|---|
| (17) Bromley - birthplace of H. G. Wells | 15 | |
| (18) Sandgate, Sevenoaks, Woking or Wells | 15 | |

*Clockface, Eagle, Globe Rd, Greenwich, Horsell, New Invention, RAF Woodbridge, Starcoast World, The Rocket, Woking, Worlds End. From £12.*

## 8th August 1995 – SHAKESPEARE'S GLOBE THEATRE

*5 x 25p: The Swan Theatre 1595; The Rose Theatre 1587; The Globe Theatre 1599; The Hope Theatre 1613; The Globe Theatre 1614.*

**SPECIAL HANDSTAMPS**

| | | | |
|---|---|---|---|
| (1) Philatelic Bureau | 3 | – | Royal Mail |
| (2) First Day of Issue – Stratford upon Avon | 3 | – | Royal Mail |
| (3) First Day of Issue – Globe Theatre London | 3 | – | Royal Mail |
| (4) Henry V, The Barbican EC | 12 | 15 | BenSG26 |
| (5) Twelfth Night, The Barbican EC | 12 | 15 | BLCS 108 |
| (6) A Midsummer Night's Dream, Stratford | 12 | 15 | BLCS 108 |
| (7) Love's Labours Lost, Stratford | 12 | 15 | Ben500(108) |
| (8) Romeo and Juliet, Stratford | 12 | 15 | Benham |
| (9) Stratford Upon Avon (swan) | 12 | 15 | VP 96 |
| (10) Midsummer Night's Dream (portrait) Stratford | 12 | 15 | LFDC 134 |
| (11) Midsummer Night's Dream (ass) Stratford | 12 | – | Cam.S.C. |
| (12) Celebrating Shakespeare's New Globe | 12 | 20 | CoverCollection |
| (13) Stratford upon Avon (changeable date pmk) | 15 | – | Royal Mail |
| (14) Shakespeare's Globe, Bankside, SE1 | 12 | 20 | Bradbury |
| (15) Loughborough Grammar School | 12 | 20 | Bradbury |
| (16) Henry Purcell, City of Westminster | 12 | 25 | MusPhilCircle |
| (17) Blick Time Systems, Swindon | 12 | 25 | Blick |
| (18) The Hammers, Hamlet, Famous Locos E13 | 12 | 15 | Dawn |
| (19) The new replica Globe Theatre, South Bank | 12 | 15 | FDP Co |
| (20) Covercraft Tenth Anniversary Year | 12 | 15 | CoverCraft |
| (21) Guarding the Mail, National Postal Museum | 12 | – | Royal Mail |
| (22) Port Ellen, Isle of Islay | 12 | – | Royal Mail |
| (23) No.9 First Tornado Squadron BF 2470 PS | 12 | 15 | RAF FDC 31 |

**C.D.S. POSTMARKS**

| | | |
|---|---|---|
| (24) Blackfriars or Globe Road, London | 10 | |
| (25) London Bridge-nearest PO to the new Globe | 10 | |
| (26) Old Swan, Rose or Hope | 10 | |
| (27) Shakespeare St, Padiham Burnley | 10 | |
| (28) Stratford upon Avon | 10 | |

*Also: Llanfair, Macduff, Talke Pits, Theatre Square, The Circle. From £6.*

**SLOGAN POSTMARKS** *PO Charter, Stratford. Prices from £7.*

## 5th September 1995 – COMMUNICATIONS

*Rowland Hill: 19p Penny Postage; 25p Penny Black; Marconi: 41p Early wireless; 60p Marine safety & navigation.*

**SPECIAL HANDSTAMPS**

| | | | |
|---|---|---|---|
| (1) Philatelic Bureau | 3 | – | Royal Mail |
| (2) First Day of Issue – London EC (pillar box) | 3 | – | Royal Mail |
| (3) First Day of Issue – London (maltese cross) | 3 | – | Royal Mail |
| (4) Rowland Hill Fund - Philatelic Bureau | 10 | 125 | Royal Mail |
| (5) British Post Office Singapore '95 Edinburgh | 40 | – | Royal Mail |
| (6) Centenary First Wireless Message Chelmsford | 10 | 25 | LFDC 135 |
| (7) Bath (Maltese Cross) | 10 | 15 | VP 97 |
| (8) Radio Society of Great Britain, Herts | 10 | 45 | LFDC 135 |
| (9) Alexandra Palace, London N22 | 10 | 35 | Cam.S.C. |
| (10) Sir Rowland Hill, Kidderminster | 10 | 15 | BLCS 109 |
| (11) Sir Rowland Hill, Bath | 10 | 15 | Ben500(109) |
| (12) First Radio Message, Chelmsford (square) | 10 | 15 | Benham |
| (13) First Radio Message, Flatholm Island | 10 | 15 | BLCS 109 |
| (14) BT Portishead Radio, Highbridge | 10 | 60 | A. Hyde/BT |
| (15) ITN 40 Anniversary, WC2 | 10 | 30 | Arlington |
| (16) 60th Anniv TV Trans, Alexandra Palace | 10 | 15 | Dawn |
| (17) Navy & Army Equip Exhib BF 2484 PS | 10 | – | n.o.c. |
| (18) Blick Time Systems Ltd, Swindon | 10 | 25 | Blick |
| (19) SRH & GM making waves, Chelmsford | 10 | 15 | FDP Co |
| (20) Mail by Rail, Sheffield | 10 | 15 | Dawn |
| (21) First Roadside Pillar Box Carlisle | 10 | 100 | Carlisle PO |
| (22) Port Ellen, Isle of Islay | 10 | – | Royal Mail |
| (23) National Postal Museum (maltese cross) | 10 | – | n.o.c. |
| (24) No.32 Commun. Squadron BF 2471 PS | 10 | 12 | RAF FDC 32 |

**C.D.S. POSTMARKS**

| | | |
|---|---|---|
| (25) Bruce Grove - Rowland Hill/Bruce Castle | 15 | |
| (26) Great Baddow - Maroni Reseach laboratories | 15 | |
| (27) Kidderminster - Rowland Hill's birthplace | 15 | |
| (28) Mullion; Niton, IOW; or The Lizard | | |
|              - trans-Atlantic experiments | 15 | |

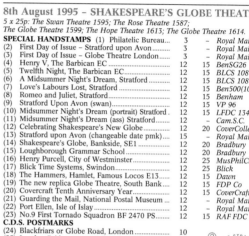

*Communications (contd.)* ordinary covers official covers
£ £

(29) Rathlin Island or Sandbanks - Marconi ........... 15
(30) Sanquhar - oldest Post Office ............................. 15
(31) Writtle - first radio broadcast............................ 15
*Also :Bath, Chelmsford, Hampstead Heath, Rowlands Castle,*
*Telephone Hse, any TPOs. From £10.*

**SLOGAN POSTMARKS**
(32) ACP Telecom, Birmingham.................................. 10
(33) Vodaphone Centre, Wolverhampton .................. 10
(34) Any postcode or radio station slogan........*each* 10
*In addition: Tropical Place-Teletex; Coins in cards; Please keep dogs inside. Prices from £7.*
**NB** *Five Colchester slogans exist - these were serviced 'by favour' and are therefore outside the scope*
*of this catalogue.*

Rugby League World Cup

## 3rd October 1995 - RUGBY LEAGUE
*19p Harold Wagstaff; 25p Gus Risman; 30p Jim Sullivan;*
*35p Billy Batten; 41p Brian Bevan.*

**SPECIAL HANDSTAMPS** (1)  Philatelic Bureau... 3 – *Royal Mail*
(2) First Day of Issue – Huddersfield ...................... 3 – *Royal Mail*
(3) First Day of Issue – London .............................. 3 – *Royal Mail*
(4) First Day of Issue – Headingley, Leeds ............. 3 200 *RM & NZ Post*
(5) Wigan Rugby League Football Club .................. 10 25 *LFDC 136*
(6) Halifax Rugby League Football Club ................. 10 15 *VP 98*
(7) Salford Rugby League Club................................ 10 15 *Dawn*
(8) Cent. of Rugby League, Bradford (rugby ball) .. 10 10 *Benham(s)*
(9) Cent. of Rugby League, Huddersfield (oval)...... 10 15 *BLCS 110*
(10) Centenary Rugby League, Leeds ........................ 10 15 *BLCS 110*
(11) Centenary Rugby League, Wigan ...................... 10 15 *BLCS 110*
(12) Cent. of Rugby League, Huddersfield (shield) .. 10 25 *Cam.S.C.*
(13) Association of  GB FDC Collectors, Kenton..... 10 150 *GBFDC GB1*
(14) Radio Times, Rugby League W12...................... 10 15 *Benham*
(15) Centenary Rugby League, Rugby....................... 10 15 *Ben500(110)*
(16) Blick Time Systems Ltd, Swindon ..................... 10 25 *Blick*
(17) Keep in Touch with your Collection, Rugby ..... 10 15 *FDP Co*
(18) In a League of its own, Huddersfield ................ 10 15 *FDP Co*
(19) Get a Kick out of Collecting, Playing Place....... 10 15 *FDP Co*
(20) Leeds Road, shared ground, Huddersfield ........ 10 15 *Dawn*
(21) Rugby League Centenary, Bradford (train)........ 10 15 *Dawn*
(22) Working with Epilepsy, Macclesfield ................. 10 200 *G.C. Comm*
(23) No 45 Squadron Flying Camels BF 2481 PS .... 10 15 *RAF FDC 33*

**C.D.S. POSTMARKS**
(24) Fartown, Huddersfield; Hessle Road, Hull; Irwell Rd,
Warrington; Salford City or Wigan - *connected*
*with players featured on the stamps* ........ *each* 15
(25) Rugby............................................................. 15
(26) Wembley or Wembley Pk - world cup venue.... 15
*Also: Bradford (or Wibsey Bankfoot, Bradford); Brighouse; Castleford; Halifax*
*(or Mount Pellon, Halifax); Hunslett; Duriding Lane, St. Helens; Englands Lane; Elland Rd, Leeds;*
*Mount Pleasant, Batley; Rothswell; The Ball; Wakefield; Watersheddings, Oldham; Workington. £10.*

**SLOGAN POSTMARKS**
(27) The Halifax Rugby League Centenary ............... 40

## 30th October 1995 – CHRISTMAS
*19p; 25p; 30p; 41p; 60p Robins*

**SPECIAL HANDSTAMPS** (1)  Philatelic Bureau... 3 – *Royal Mail*
(2) First Day of Issue – Bethlehem .......................... 3 – *Royal Mail*
(3) First Day of Issue – London .............................. 3 – *Royal Mail*
(4) Post Haste! for Christmas Nat Postal Museum. 10 20 *Friends of NPM*
(5) Christmas Greetings, York ................................. 10 15 *LFDC 137*
(6) Christmas, Canterbury...................................... 10 15 *VP 99*
(7) Happy Christmas, Royal Mail, EC1................... 10 – *Royal Mail*
(8) Happy Christmas, Radio Times, W12................ 10 15 *Benham*
(9) Happy Christmas, Fir Tree, Crook.................... 10 15 *BLCS 111*
(10) Yuletide Wishes, Snowdown, Dover.................. 10 15 *Ben500(111)*
(11) Merry Christmas, Hollybush, Ayr .................... 10 15 *BLCS 111*
(12) Christmas Greetings, Ivybridge, Devon ............ 10 15 *Ben500(111)*
(13) Seasons Greetings, Berry Hill, Coleford........... 10 12 *BLCS 111*
(14) Christmas Common, Oxford (cat) ..................... 10 15 *BLCS 111*
(15) Christmas Common, Oxfordshire ...................... 10 20 *Westminster*
(16) Merry Christms, Christmas Common................. 10 20 *R J Smith*
(17) Blick Time Systems Ltd, Swindon ..................... 10 25 *Blick*
(18) Christmas 1995, Waddington, Lincs .................. 10 30 *Cam.S.C.*
(19) Seasons Greetings, Middlesbrough.................... 10 25 *Dawn*
(20) Seasons Greetings, West Ham United ............... 10 25 *Dawn*
(21) Seasons Greetings, Nottingham Forest.............. 10 25 *Dawn*
(22) Bletchley Park, 50 Years this Christmas............ 10 20 *Bletchley PO*
(23) Christmas Greetings, St. Nicholas, Norfolk....... 10 15 *FDP Co*
(24) Loughborough Grammar School ........................ 10 20 *Bradbury*
(25) No 28 Squadron Hong Kong BF 2482 PS........ 10 15 *RAF FDC 34*

**C.D.S. POSTMARKS**
(26) Girton, Cambridge - HQ of 'Bird Life' .............. 10
(27) Holy Island or Nasareth ..............................*each* 15
(28) Robin's Lane, St. Helens.................................... 25
*Also: Canterbury, Fleet Street, Greet, Hollybush, Hollyhedge Road, Hopgrove,*
*Newbottle, Prettygate, Red Lodge, Robin Hood, Wing. Prices from £8.*

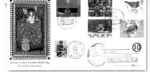

113

| | ordinary covers | official covers |
|---|---|---|
| **SLOGAN POSTMARKS** | £ | £ |
| (29) Happy Christmas Please Post Early .................. | 40 | |

*In addition: Thank you for Choosing Royal Mail. Prices from £8.*

**£2.40, £2.50 & £3.80 CHRISTMAS BOOKS OF STAMPS**
With pair or block of 19p, 25p & 60p stamps ......*set*    10
With complete panes of 19p & 25p stamps .......*pair*   15

---

## 25th January 1996 – ROBERT BURNS

*19p To A Mouse; 25p A Red, Red Rose; 41p Scots Wha Hae; 60p Auld Lang Syne*

| **SPECIAL HANDSTAMPS** | | |
|---|---|---|
| (1) Philatelic Bureau... | 3 | – *Royal Mail* |
| (2)   First Day of Issue – Dumfries ............................ | 3 | – *Royal Mail* |
| (3)   First Day of Issue – Glasgow, Scotland & NI... | 3 | – *Royal Mail* |
| (4)   First Day of Issue – London .............................. | 8 | – *Royal Mail* |
| (5)   Wee Sleekit Cowrin' etc, Kilmarnock................ | 10 | – *Royal Mail* |
| (6)   O, My Luve's Like a Red, Red Rose, Alloway .. | 10 | – *Royal Mail* |
| (7)   Scots Wha Hae, Dumfries .............................. | 10 | – *Royal Mail* |
| (8)   Should Auld Acquaintance etc, Ayr ................ | 10 | – *Royal Mail* |
| (9)   Spring Stampex (Red Red Rose), N1 .............. | 10 | – *Royal Mail* |
| (10) The Burns Federation, Dumfries (mausoleum). | 10 | 12 *LFDC 138* |
| (11) The Burns Federation, Alloway (portrait)......... | 10 | 12 *VP 100* |
| (12) To A Mouse, Mauchline, Ayrshire.................... | 10 | 15 *Bradbury* |
| (13) O My Luve's Like a Red, Red Rose, Dumfries . | 10 | 15 *Bradbury* |
| (14) Robert the Bruce, Bannockburn ...................... | 10 | 15 *Bradbury* |
| (15) Auld Lang Syne, Ellisland Farm, Dumfries ...... | 10 | 15 *Bradbury* |
| (16) Robert Burns, 1759-1796 Mauchline (lion)...... | 10 | 15 *Ben500(112)* |
| (17) Robert Burns Bicentenary, Alloway (mouse)... | 10 | 12 *BLCS 112* |
| (18) R.Burns, Writers' Museum, Edinburgh (rose)... | 10 | 12 *BLCS 112* |
| (19) Bicentenary of R. Burns, Dumfries (thistle)...... | 10 | 12 *BLCS 112* |
| (20) Robert Burns, Radio Times, W12 0TT............. | 10 | 12 *Benham* |
| (21) Rotary Club of Alloway, Ayr ............................ | 10 | 15 *Rotary* |
| (22) Robert Burns 1759-1796, Alloway (quill) ......... | 10 | 15 *Gem Covers* |
| (23) The Immortal Memory, Edinburgh.................... | 10 | 15 *Keith Prowse* |
| (24) Should auld acquaintance GB FDC Dumfries... | 10 | 15 *FDP Co* |
| (25) XV Squadron Tornado Weapons BF 2498 PS.. | 10 | 15 *RAF FDC 35* |

| **C.D.S. POSTMARKS** | | |
|---|---|---|
| (26) Alloway - birthplace of Robert Burns ................ | 10 | |
| (27) Bannockburn - Scots Wha Hae......................... | 10 | |
| (28) Burns Statue, Ayr............................................ | 20 | |
| (29) Dalswinton, Dunfermline, Kilmarnock or Tarbolton | | |
|   *connected with works featured on stamps* ....... | 10 | |
| (30) Dumfries - Burns died here in 1796.................. | 10 | |
| (31) Lincluden, Dumfries - Lincluden Abbey ........... | 10 | |
| (32) Mauchline - where Burns lived ......................... | 10 | |

*Also: Burnside, Burns Rd, Kirkoswald, Mousehole, Nicholson St Edinburgh, Poets Field, Rose, Sanquhar, Tam's Brig. Prices from £8.*

**SLOGAN POSTMARKS**
(33) Celebrate the Legend, Robert Burns ................    30
*Also: Luton Philatelic; Glasgow RCH; Strathclyde Univ.   Prices from £8.*

---

## 26th February 1996 – GREETINGS

*10 x 1st Class stamps featuring cartoons.*

| **SPECIAL HANDSTAMPS** | | |
|---|---|---|
| (1) Philatelic Bureau... | 3 | – *Royal Mail* |
| (2)   First Day of Issue – Titterhill ........................... | 3 | – *Royal Mail* |
| (3)   First Day of Issue – London ............................ | 8 | – *Royal Mail* |
| (4)   Titterhill, Haytons Bent (laughing pillar box) ... | 12 | 20 *Bradbury* |
| (5)   Greetings - Letterfearn, Kyle........................... | 12 | 15 *BLCS 113* |
| (6)   Greetings - Letterston, Haverfordwest............... | 12 | 15 *BLCS 113* |
| (7)   Greetings - Barking, Ipswich........................... | 12 | 15 *BLCS 113* |
| (8)   Greetings - Yapton, Arundel............................ | 12 | 15 *Ben500(113)* |
| (9)   Greetings - Purton, Swindon............................ | 12 | 15 *BenD245* |
| (10) Greetings - Braintree, Essex............................ | 12 | 15 *BLCS 113* |
| (11) Greetings - Purley, Reading............................. | 12 | 15 *BLCS 113* |
| (12) Greetings - Brington, Huntingdon..................... | 12 | 15 *BLCS 113* |
| (13) Greetings - Bonehill, Tamworth........................ | 12 | 15 *BLCS 113* |
| (14) Greetings - Nappa, Skipton.............................. | 12 | 15 *BLCS 113* |
| (15) The Cartoon Art Trust, London ......................... | 12 | – *n.o.c.* |
| (16) Greetings from Laughterton............................. | 12 | 15 *Gem Covers* |
| (17) Greetings from the 1996 Catalogue.................. | 12 | 20 *FDP Co* |
| (18) W H Smith Business Supplies, Andover ........... | 12 | 50 *WHS(Set3cards)* |
| (19) Royal Mail North East Team Work, Leeds........ | 12 | 25 *Royal Mail* |

| **C.D.S. POSTMARKS** | | |
|---|---|---|
| (20) Greet or Fleet Street.......................................*each* | 12 | |

*Also: Askham, Clockface, Crazies Hill, Fetcham, Idle, Laughterton, Lazy Hill,Letter, Little Snoring, Lover, Moneymore, Mumbles, New York, Penn, Point Clear, Witnesham, Yell.Prices from £8.*

**SLOGAN POSTMARKS**
(21) Walt Disney World.............................................    15
*In addition: Collect Stamps, Luton Philatelic. Prices from £7.*

There are thousands more pictures of
British first day covers at www.bfdc.co.uk

114

## 12th March 1996 – THE WILDFOWL & WETLANDS TRUST

*19p Muscovy Duckling; 25p Lapwing* **ordinary covers**   **official covers**
*30p White fronted Goose; 41p Swan*   £   £

**SPECIAL HANDSTAMPS** (1) Philatelic Bureau...

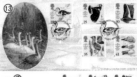

| | | |
|---|---|---|
| **SPECIAL HANDSTAMPS** (1) Philatelic Bureau... | 3 | – *Royal Mail* |
| (2) First Day of Issue – Slimbridge, Gloucester ..... | 3 | – *Royal Mail* |
| (3) First Day of Issue – London ........................ | 8 | – *Royal Mail* |
| (4) Wildfowl & Wetlands Trust, Slimbridge (oval) | 12 | 15 *Benham* |
| (5) Wildfowl & Wetlands Trust, The Mail ............. | 12 | 15 *Benham* |
| (6) Wildfowl & Wetlands Trust, Slimbridge ........... | 12 | 15 *BLCS 114* |
| (7) Wildfowl & Wetlands Trust, Washington ......... | 12 | 15 *BLCS 114* |
| (8) Wildfowl & Wetlands Trust, Arundel ............... | 12 | 15 *BenSG28* |
| (9) Wildfowl & Wetlands Trust, Caerlaverock....... | 12 | 15 *Ben500(114)* |
| (10) Wildfowl & Wetlands Trust, Welney............... | 12 | 15 *BLCS 114* |
| (11) Wildfowl & Wetlands Trust, Llanelli (heron) .. | 12 | 12 *Gem Covers* |
| (12) Wildfowl & Wetlands Trust, Llanelli (duck)..... | 12 | – *Royal Mail* |
| (13) Wildfowl & Wetland Birds, Sandy ................... | 12 | 15 *LFDC 139* |
| (14) Wildfowl & Wetland Birds, Malltraeth ........... | 12 | 15 *VP 101* |
| (15) Doncaster Rovers and Mallard, Doncaster....... | 12 | 15 *Dawn* |
| (16) GB First Day Collectors, Slimbridge ............... | 12 | 50 *GBFDC GB2* |
| (17) Birds of a Feather, Arundel ............................ | 12 | 15 *FDP Co* |
| (18) 202 Squadron, Search & Rescue BF 2499 PS .. | 12 | 10 *RAF FDC 36* |
| (19) Stratford (changeable date pmk depicts swan). | 12 | – *Royal Mail* |
| (20) Post Code Event, Team Work 96 Harrow........ | 12 | – *Royal Mail* |
| (21) 45th Anniversary of Fairey FDI BF 2502 PS..... | 12 | 150 *Forces* |

**C.D.S. POSTMARKS**

| | |
|---|---|
| (22) Arundel - Wildfowl & Wetlands centre ............ | 20 |
| (23) Slimbridge - Wildfowl & Wetlands Trust HQ .. | 15 |
| (24) Burscough (*Martin Mere*); Glencaple (*Caerlaverock*); Comber or Lisbane (*Castle Espie*); Llwynhendy or Llanelli; Welney; Washington .................. | 15 |
| (25) Malltraeth - home of Tunnicliffe...................... | 15 |
| (26) Sandy - RSPB headquarters ............................ | 15 |
| (27) Tring - British Trust for Ornitholgoy HQ ......... | 15 |

*In addition: Drake, Goose Green, The Pond, Waterside. Prices from £10.*

**SLOGAN POSTMARKS**

*Oilbank; Visit the Isle of Skye. Recycle Used Oil.  Prices from £10.*

---

## 16th April 1996 – 100 YEARS OF THE CINEMA

*19p Harrogate Odeon; 25p The Screen Kiss; 30p Cinema Ticket;*
*35p Pathe News; 41p 'Big Screen Showing', Manchester Odeon.*

| | | |
|---|---|---|
| **SPECIAL HANDSTAMPS** (1) Philatelic Bureau... | 3 | – *Royal Mail* |
| (2) First Day of Issue – London WC2................. | 3 | – *Royal Mail* |
| (3) First Day of Issue – London (Cinema 100)....... | 8 | – *Royal Mail* |
| (4) Leicester Square, WC2 (Superman) .................. | 10 | 15 *LFDC 140* |
| (5) Leicester Square, WC2 (Chaplin) ...................... | 10 | 15 *VP 102* |
| (6) Leicester Square, WC2 (Cinema 100 logo)....... | 10 | 25 *Cam.S.C.* |
| (7) The Harrogate Odeon................................... | 10 | 20 *Bradbury* |
| (8) The Projected Picture Trust, Bletchley.............. | 10 | 15 *Bletchley PO* |
| (9) Sense and Sensibility, Steventon ...................... | 10 | 20 *BenSG30* |
| (10) Centenary of the Cinema, Pinewood Studios.... | 10 | 15 *Ben500(115)* |
| (11) 100 Years of Cinema, Elstree ......................... | 10 | 15 *BLCS 115* |
| (12) 100 Years of Cinema, Shepperton .................. | 10 | 15 *BLCS 115* |
| (13) 100 Years of Going to Pictures, Ealing............ | 10 | 15 *BLCS 115* |
| (14) 100 British Cinema MOMI Museum, SE1........ | 10 | 15 *BenL46* |
| (15) Star Road, London W14................................ | 10 | 15 *Benham* |
| (16) Starboard Way, E14...................................... | 10 | 15 *Benham* |
| (17) Star Place, SE1............................................ | 10 | 15 *Benham* |
| (18) Star, Clydey ................................................ | 10 | 15 *Benham* |
| (19) Starcross, Exter ........................................... | 10 | 15 *Benham* |
| (20) Shepperton Studios....................................... | 10 | 15 *Gem Covers* |
| (21) Great Scott! 100 Years of Cinema, Windsor..... | 10 | 15 *Steven Scott* |
| (22) A Star Performer!, Star ................................. | 10 | 15 *FDP Co* |
| (23) RNLI Cinema Centenary, Star ........................ | 10 | 15 *StampSearchers* |
| (24) Bradford City on Film .................................. | 10 | 15 *Dawn* |
| (25) Warwickshire County Cricket, Edgbaston ....... | 10 | 65 *S.P.* |
| (26) No 617 Dam Busters Squadron ..................... | 10 | 10 *RAF FDC 37* |
| (27) SG (Stanley Gibbons) Strand WC2.................. | 10 | 10 *Benham* |
| (28) Post Haste! National Postal Musuem, EC......... | 10 | – *Royal Mail* |
| (29) 1746 Battle of Culloden 1996, Inverness .......... | 10 | 25 *Bradbury* |
| (30) 70th Birthday Celebrations, London SW1*...... | 10 | 25 *Bradbury* |
| (31) 70th Birthday Celebrations, Windsor*............. | 10 | 25 *Bradbury* |
| (32) 70th Birthday Celebrations, Balmoral* ........... | 10 | 25 *Bradbury* |
| (33) 70th Birthday Celebrations, Bruton St, SW1* .. | 10 | – *Benham* |
| (34) 70th Birthday, Queen St, W1*........................ | 10 | – *Benham* |
| (35) 70th Birthday, Windsor*............................... | 10 | – *Benham* |
| (36) 70th Birthday, Westminster Abbey, SW1*......... | 10 | – *Benham* |

\* *Sponsored primarily to coincide with the issue of the Royal Mail commemorative label to celebrate the Queen's 70th birthday.*

**C.D.S. POSTMARKS**

| | |
|---|---|
| (37) Bray, Denham Green, Ealing, Elstree, Iver Heath (Pinewood), Shepperton.................................. | 15 |
| (38) Barnet - first showing of a moving film ........... | 15 |
| (39) Harrogate; Oxford Street, Oldham or Manchester (featured on 19p, 30p and 41p values) ........... | 15 |

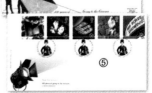

**Going to the Pictures (contd.)** ordinary covers official covers
£ £

(40) Hollywood or The Circle ........................................ 15
(41) Perry Bar, Birmingham - first Odeon ................. 15
(42) Regent St - 1st commercial screening of film.... 15
(43) Victoria St. SW1 - 1st Picture House................. 15

*Also: Attenborough, Borehamwood, Dorking, Hamilton, Leigh,*
*Long Shoot, Lover, South Bank Street,Waterloo Rd. Prices from £8.*

**SLOGAN POSTMARKS**
(44) Walt Disney World, Instant Win ......................... 15
*In addition: Blackpool Pleasure Beach; Trafford Park. Prices from £7.*

## 14th May 1996 – FOOTBALL LEGENDS
*19p 'Dixie' Dean; 25p Bobby Moore; 35p Duncan Edwards; 41p Billy Wright;*
*60p Danny Blanchflower.*

**SPECIAL HANDSTAMPS** (1) Philatelic Bureau... 3 – *Royal Mail*
(2) First Day of Issue – Wembley.............................. 3 – *Royal Mail*
(3) First Day of Issue – Philatelic Bureau................ 3 – *Royal Mail*
(4) First Day of Issue – Manchester ...................... 3 – *Royal Mail*
(5) First Day of Issue – London .............................. 12 – *Royal Mail*
(6) Bobby Moore, West Ham United ...................... 12 25 *Dawn*
(7) Billy Wright, Wolves & England........................ 12 20 *Dawn*
(8) Dixie Dean, Everton FC ..................................... 12 25 *Dawn*
(9) 60th Anniv 1st FA Semi-Final, Grimsby .......... 12 15 *Dawn*
(10) Manchester United FC Museum ...................... 12 25 *Dawn*
(11) Hull City 50 Years at Boothferry Park ............. 12 15 *Dawn*
(12) 25 Yrs Official Football Covers - 8 locations.... 12 35 *Dawn*
(13) A Celebration of Football, Wembley ................ 12 20 *Westminster*
(14) Autographed Editions, Wembley ...................... 12 20 *Westminster*
(15) Wembley, Middlesex (trophy) ........................... 12 15 *Gem Covers*
(16) Jackie Milburn, St. James' Park, Newcastle ...... 12 15 *FourPennyPost*
(17) Danny Blanchflower, Tottenham N17.............. 12 50 *G.Blanchflower*
(18) 1966 England Winners, Wembley (player) ....... 12 15 *LFDC 141*
(19) Football Legends, Bolton, Lancs...................... 12 15 *VP 103*
(20) Football Legends, Stoke on Trent (player) ....... 12 50 *Bradbury*
(21) Preston North End FC ....................................... 12 50 *Bradbury*
(22) Wolverhampton Wanderers (player)................ 12 30 *Bradbury*
(23) Football Heroes Wolverhampton (trophy & ball) 12 30 *Ben500(117)*
(24) Football Heroes, Wolverhampton (ball)............ 12 10 *Benham(s)*
(25) Football Heroes, The Mail on Sunday, Stoke ... 12 15 *Benham*
(26) Football Heroes, Stoke on Trent (ball) ............. 12 15 *BLCS 117*
(27) Football Heroes, Manchester (ball & flag) ........ 12 – *n.o.c.*
(28) Football Heroes, Manchester (ball & net).......... 12 10 *Benham(s)*
(29) Football Heroes, Everton Liverpool (ball) ......... 12 10 *Benham(s)*
(30) Football Heroes, Wembley (ball & flag)............. 12 20 *B'hamCoinCvr*
(31) Football Heroes, Tottenham (ball on banner) .. 12 10 *Benham(s)*
(32) England World Cup Winners, Sunday, E1 ........ 12 10 *Benham*
(33) Arsenal, FA Cup Winners, Highbury, N5 ........ 12 15 *BLCS 117*
(34) Evening Standard, Wembley .............................. 12 12 *RM/EveningStd*
(35) Brewers Fayre, Wembley .................................... 12 12 *RM/BrewFayre*
(36) Wembley (lettering in half circle plus ball)....... 12 10 *RM/MasterCard*
(37) Winning New Readers, Wembley ...................... 12 12 *FDP Co*
(38) RNLI Football Legends, Wembley ...................... 12 12 *StampSearchers*
(39) Matthew Sea Trials, Bristol............................... 12 55 *R Higgs*
(40) 80th Anniv No 54 Squadron BF 2581 PS.......... 12 12 *RAF FDC 38*

**C.D.S. POSTMARKS**
(41) County Rd, Liverpool - Everton (Dixie Dean).. 15
(42) Barking Rd, E13 - West Ham (Bobby Moore).. 15
(43) Trafford Pk - Man United (Duncan Edwards).. 15
(44) Staveley Rd. Wolverhampton - (Billy Wright).. 15
(45) Park Lne, Tottenham - (Danny Blanchflower). 20
(46) Benwell Grove (Newcastle), Elland Road (Leeds)
        Hillsborough (Sheffield), Priory Road (Liverpool)
        Radcliffe Rd (Nottingham), Villa Rd (Birmingham)
        all venues for Euro '96 ................. 15
(47) Wembley or Wembley Park............................... 15
*Also: Birkenhead, Bolton, Moore, Preston, Stoke on Trent.The Ball. Prices from £10.*
**SLOGAN POSTMARKS**
(48) Snickers - Proud to Sponsor Euro '96 ................ 15
*Also: Racial Equality, Europe Day, BBC Midlands Today, Trafford Park Centenary. Prices from £7*
*NB Royal Mail also issued a Prestige Book for the 1996 European Football*
*Championships on this date - these books also contained the new stamps in*
*various se-tenant and miniature sheet formats - please refer to definitive section*
*for prices.*

## 9th July 1996 – OLYMPIC GAMES
*5 x 26p: Olympic and Paralympic Teams 1996*

**SPECIAL HANDSTAMPS** (1) Philatelic Bureau... 3 – *Royal Mail*
(2) First Day of Issue – Much Wenlock................... 3 – *Royal Mail*
(3) First Day of Issue – London .............................. 8 – *Royal Mail*
(4) Meadowbank, Edinburgh.................................... 8 10 *Benham*
(5) Pond's Forge, Sheffield ..................................... 8 10 *Benham*
(6) Gateshead, Tyne & Wear ................................... 8 25 *Ben500(118)*
(7) Crystal Palace, London (running)...................... 8 15 *Ben500(118)*
(8) Crystal Palace, London (hurdles)...................... 8 10 *Benham*

### Olympic Games (contd.)

| | | ordinary covers £ | official covers £ | |
|---|---|---|---|---|
| (9) | Alexander Stadium, Perrybarr Birmingham...... | 8 | 8 | Benham |
| (10) | 100th Olympic Games, Wembley (torch) ......... | 8 | 17 | B'hamCoinCvr |
| (11) | Olympic Champion, Badminton ........................ | 8 | 10 | BLCS 118 |
| (12) | Henley on Thames .......................................... | 8 | 10 | BLCS 118 |
| (13) | The Mail on Sunday......................................... | 8 | 10 | Benham |
| (14) | Wembley (laurels)........................................... | 8 | 10 | VP 104 |
| (15) | Amateur Athletic Association, Birmingham ...... | 8 | 10 | LFDC 142 |
| (16) | Kodak, Hemel Hempstead ............................... | 8 | 10 | Gem Covers |
| (17) | Crystal Palace Gold Medal Winners, SE19 ...... | 8 | 10 | Westminster |
| (18) | Autographed Editions Crystal Palace, SE19...... | 8 | 18 | Westminster |
| (19) | Olympic Centenary 1896-1996 Crystal Palace.. | 8 | 15 | Keith Prowse |
| (20) | Olympic Centenary 1896-1996 Wembley .......... | 8 | 250 | Keith Prowse |
| (21) | Olympic Centenary 1896-1996 Hickstead ........ | 8 | 250 | Keith Prowse |
| (22) | Olympic Centenary 1896-1996 Henley ............. | 8 | 250 | Keith Prowse |
| (23) | Olympic Centenary 1896-1996 Bisley............... | 8 | 250 | Keith Prowse |
| (24) | Duke of Edinburgh's Award, Bewdley............... | 8 | 15 | Bredon Cvrs |
| (25) | Olympics and Paralympics, Crystal Essex ...... | 8 | 15 | Steven Scott 1 |
| (26) | To the Games by Train Barnsley........................ | 8 | 10 | Dawn |
| (27) | Running rings around competition, Runwell .... | 8 | 15 | FDP Co |
| (28) | Royal Tournament BF 1996 PS.......................... | 8 | 25 | Forces |
| (29) | RNLI Speedwell............................................... | 8 | 12 | StampSearchers |
| (30) | XI Squadron Swifter & Keener BF 2525 PS..... | 8 | 15 | RAF FDC 39 |

**C.D.S. POSTMARKS**

| (31) | Croydon – Headquarters of Paralympics ........... | 15 |
|---|---|---|
| (32) | London SE19 – Crystal Palace............................ | 15 |
| (33) | Much Wenlock – early olympic style games ...... | 15 |
| (34) | Wandsworth – British Olympic Assoc'n ............ | 15 |
| (35) | Wembley or Wembley Park – 1948 Olympics .. | 15 |

*Also: Anerley Rd., Badminton, Beetham, Boston, Birmingham, Chipping, Campden, Cosford Camp, Jump, Klondyke, Melbourne, New York, Paris Ave., Perry Bar, Sheriffhales, Silver End, Stoke Mandeville. Prices from £10.*

**SLOGAN POSTMARKS** *Trafford Park Centenary; New Postage Rates. Prices from £7.*

## 6th August 1996 – WOMEN OF ACHIEVEMENT
*20p Dorothy Hodgkin; 26p Margot Fonteyn; 31p Elisabeth Frink; 37p Daphne du Maurier; 43p Marea Hartman.*

**SPECIAL HANDSTAMPS**

| (1) | Philatelic Bureau... | 3 | – | Royal Mail |
|---|---|---|---|---|
| (2) | First Day of Issue – Fowey ............................. | 3 | – | Royal Mail |
| (3) | First Day of Issue – London ............................ | 8 | – | Royal Mail |
| (4) | Royal Academy of Dancing SW11.................... | 8 | 20 | LFDC 143 |
| (5) | Jane Eyre, Haworth Keighley............................ | 8 | 10 | VP 105 |
| (6) | Marea Hartman, AAA Birmingham ................... | 8 | 25 | LFDC 142 Spec |
| (7) | Margot Fonteyn (portrait), London EC1........... | 8 | 15 | Ben500(119) |
| (8) | Marea Hartman (portrait), Edgbaston B'ham ... | 8 | 15 | BenhamPilgrim |
| (9) | Daphne du Maurier (portrait), Par Cornwall .... | 8 | 12 | BLCS 119 |
| (10) | Dorothy Hodgkin (portrait), Oxford................. | 8 | 15 | BenhamPilgrim |
| (11) | Elisabeth Frink (portrait), Thurlow Suffolk....... | 8 | 15 | BenhamPilgrim |
| (12) | Ruth Rendell, Colchester ................................. | 8 | 10 | BLCS 119 |
| (13) | Votes for Women, Parliament Square SW1 ...... | 8 | 10 | BLCS 119 |
| (14) | Parliament Street, London SW1 ....................... | 8 | 15 | Steven Scott 2 |
| (15) | GBFDC Margot Fonteyn, Covent Garden ........ | 8 | 25 | GBFDC GB3 |
| (16) | Women's Royal Voluntary Service, SW19......... | 8 | 12 | Bredon Cvrs |
| (17) | St Thomas' Hospital, London SE1 ................... | 8 | 15 | Westminster |
| (18) | Autographed Editions, House of Lords SW1 .... | 8 | 50 | Westminster |
| (19) | Autographed Editions, BBC TV, London W12 | 8 | 20 | Westminster |
| (20) | Women's World Bowls, Leamington Spa ......... | 8 | 25 | Bradbury |
| (21) | Nurse Edith Cavell, Peterborough ................... | 8 | 12 | NVRly |
| (22) | Lisa Clayton's Voyage Around World, B'ham .. | 8 | 15 | JRiceStampCo |
| (23) | We Value Women of Achievement ................... | 8 | 12 | FDP Co |
| (24) | RNLI, Ladybank, Cupar.................................... | 8 | 15 | StampSearchers |
| (25) | 42 (Torpedo Bomber) Squadron BF 2528 PS ... | 8 | 15 | RAF FDC 40 |

**C.D.S. POSTMARKS**

| (26) | Fowey or Par - Daphne du Maurier ................... | 10 |
|---|---|---|
| (27) | Lady or Lady Margaret Rd ............................... | 10 |
| (28) | Reigate - birthplace of Margot Fonteyn............. | 10 |
| (29) | Shipston on Stour - Dorothy Hodgkin .............. | 10 |

*Also: Amwell St., Bodmin, Bristol, Cambridge, Canterbury, Coventry, Durham, Haworth, Manchester Airport, Oxford, Pill, Roman Rd., The Galleries, Tiptoe. Prices from £7*

**SLOGAN POSTMARKS** *Various Royal Mail slogans; Voters List. From £7.*

## 3rd September 1996 – CHILDREN'S TV
*20p Muffin the Mule: 26p Sooty; 31p Stingray; 37p The Clangers; 43p Dangermouse.*

**SPECIAL HANDSTAMPS**

| (1) | Philatelic Bureau ..... | 3 | – | Royal Mail |
|---|---|---|---|---|
| (2) | First Day of Issue – Alexandra Palace............... | 3 | – | Royal Mail |
| (3) | First Day of Issue – London ............................ | 8 | – | Royal Mail |
| (4) | Blue Peter, Shepherds Bush W12 ..................... | 10 | 100 | Royal Mail |
| (5) | Sooty, Blackpool............................................. | 10 | 15 | LFDC 144 |
| (6) | Treasure Island, Edinburgh .............................. | 10 | 15 | VP 106 |
| (7) | Just William, Bury Lancs ................................. | 10 | 15 | BLCS 120 |
| (8) | The Railway Children, Halstead, Kent............... | 10 | 15 | BLCS 120 |
| (9) | Bagpuss, The Mail, London W8.......................... | 10 | 35 | Benham |

| Children's Television (contd.) | ordinary covers £ | | official covers £ |
|---|---|---|---|
| (10) Children's TV (Mermaid) W1P 7LB................. | 10 | 25 | BenhamPilgrim |
| (11) Children's TV (Mule) Wood Lane W12............ | 10 | 25 | BenhamPilgrim |
| (12) Children's TV (Mouse) Cosgrove Hall............. | 10 | 25 | BenhamPilgrim |
| (13) Children's TV (Sooty) Guiseley, Leeds.............. | 10 | 25 | BenhamPilgrim |
| (14) Children's TV (Sooty) Child Okeford............... | 10 | 25 | BenhamPilgrim |
| (15) Children's TV (Clangers) Blean, Kent............... | 10 | 15 | Ben500(120) |
| (16) Children's TV (TV set) London WC2............... | 10 | 15 | Steven Scott 3 |
| (17) Big Stars/Small Screen, Autographed, Shipley. | 10 | 25 | Westminster |
| (18) Paddington Stn (Paddington Bear) W2............ | 10 | 15 | Westminster |
| (19) Booth Catalogue, Corsham Wilts...................... | 10 | 20 | FDP Co |
| (20) RNLI, Jubilee................................................. | 10 | 20 | StampSearchers |
| (21) Robin Hood, Nottingham (changeable date) ... | 12 | – | Royal Mail |
| (22) 29 Squadron (Energetic & Keen) BF 2540 PS . | 4 | 15 | RAF FDC 41 |

**C.D.S. POSTMARKS**

| | | |
|---|---|---|
| (23) Alexandra Pk Rd - 1st Children's TV broadcast....... | 12 | |
| (24) Blackpool - where Harry Corbett purchased Sooty.. | 12 | |
| (25) Grange Hill - famous children's TV series......... | 12 | |
| (26) Playing Place.................................................... | 12 | |
| (27) London W12 or Teddington - TV studios........... | 12 | |

*In addition: Baird Ave., Baker St., Blackwater, Blyton, Eccles, Edinburgh, Foxhole, Gotham, Mousehole, Mutley, Paddington, Pandy, Ramsbottom, Recreation Road, School Lane, Slough, Tobermory, Weedswood, Welbourne, Wellington, Wimbledon, Woodtop. Prices from £10.*

**SLOGAN POSTMARKS** *BBC; Kit Kat; Royal Mail; Severn Valley Rly; Wigan 750. From £8.*

## 1st October 1996 – CLASSIC CARS

*20p Austin Healey 100; 26p MG TD; 37p Triumph TR3; 43p Jaguar XK 120; 63p Morgan Plus 4.*

| SPECIAL HANDSTAMPS (1) Philatelic Bureau ..... | 3 | – | Royal Mail |
|---|---|---|---|
| (2) First Day of Issue – Beaulieu ...................... | 3 | – | Royal Mail |
| (3) First Day of Issue – London (vintage car) ........ | 3 | – | Royal Mail |
| (4) First Day of Issue – London (steering wheel)... | 8 | 8 | RM/Times |
| (5) Cent Emancipation Rally (map) – London ...... | 8 | – | Royal Mail |
| (6) Cent Emancipation Rally (map) – Brighton...... | 8 | – | Royal Mail |
| (7) British Motoring GB London ........................ | 8 | 12 | Royal Mint |
| (8) National Postal Museum .............................. | 10 | – | Royal Mail |
| (9) Heritage Motor Centre, Gaydon ................... | 10 | 25 | LFDC 145 |
| (10) London to Brighton Car Rally, Brighton .......... | 10 | 15 | VP 107 |
| (11) London to Brighton Car Rally, London ............ | 10 | 15 | VP 107 |
| (12) MG Owners' Club, Swavesey............................ | 10 | 20 | Bradbury |
| (13) National Motor Museum, Beaulieu................... | 10 | 15 | BLCS 121 |
| (14) Nigel Mansell, Silverstone............................... | 10 | 15 | BLCS 121 |
| (15) Genevieve, Hyde Park, London W2................... | 10 | 20 | B'hamCoinCvr |
| (16) Genevieve, Brighton....................................... | 10 | 20 | B'hamCoinCvr |
| (17) John Surtees, Goodwood, Sussex..................... | 10 | 15 | BenSG31 |
| (18) RAC, Pall Mall ............................................... | 10 | 15 | Benham |
| (19) A Tribute from Toyota, Redhill Surrey ............. | 10 | 15 | Benham |
| (20) A Tribute from Aston Martin, Newport Pagnell.. | 10 | 15 | Benham |
| (21) A Tribute from Landrover, Solihull.................. | 10 | 15 | Benham |
| (22) A Tribute from Lotus, Norwich........................ | 10 | 15 | Benham |
| (23) A Tribute from Vauxhall, Luton...................... | 10 | 15 | Benham |
| (24) A Tribute from Daimler, Coventry................... | 10 | 15 | Benham |
| (25) A Tribute from Rover Group, Birmingham ...... | 10 | 15 | Benham |
| (26) A Tribute from Morgan, Malvern..................... | 10 | 20 | Ben500(121) |
| (27) A Tribute from Jaguar, Coventry..................... | 10 | 15 | Benham |
| (28) A Tribute from Ford Motor Co, Dagenham ..... | 10 | 15 | Benham |
| (29) Practical Classics, Peterborough..................... | 10 | 15 | Benham |
| (30) Autographed - Motor Sport Legends, Aintree .. | 10 | 20 | Westminster |
| (31) Autographed - Classic Cars, Carr, Rotherham.. | 10 | 20 | Westminster |
| (32) Classic British Cars, Beaulieu ......................... | 10 | 20 | West Set of 5 |
| (33) 100th Anniv London-Brighton Rally Hyde Park.. | 10 | 15 | Westminster |
| (34) MG Car Club, Abingdon ................................ | 10 | 15 | FourPennyPost |
| (35) Aston Martin, Newport Pagnell ...................... | 10 | 80 | Bletchley PO |
| (36) 60th Anniv Morgan Four Wheeler, Malvern...... | 10 | 25 | GBFDC GB4 |
| (37) Great Scott - It's A Classic Hyde Park W2........ | 10 | 15 | Steven Scott 4 |
| (38) Silverstone, Northants.................................... | 10 | 20 | G Lovell |
| (39) British International Motor Show, NEC ............ | 10 | 20 | Arl'ton/T'graph |
| (40) National Exhibition Centre (changeable date) . | 10 | – | Royal Mail |
| (41) Driving Force, Booth Catalogue, Redcar........... | 10 | 15 | FDP Co |
| (42) RNLI Cargo, Carlisle ...................................... | 10 | 15 | StampSearchers |
| (43) Trafford Park Centenary, Manchester............. | 10 | 15 | Dawn |
| (44) Derby County Locomotive, Derby...................... | 10 | 15 | Dawn |
| (45) In Celebration of Lux, Malmesbury................. | 10 | 125 | D Pratten |
| (46) 80th Anniv. No. 9 Squadron BF 2541 PS 41.......... | 10 | 12 | RAF FDC 42 |
| (47) The Queen's Stamps, Mauritius, NPM .......... | 10 | – | Royal Mail |

**C.D.S. POSTMARKS**

| | | |
|---|---|---|
| (48) Abingdon - where MG TD was built.................. | 10 | |
| (49) Allesley - where Jaguar XK 120 was built.......... | 10 | |
| (50) Beaulieu - National Motor Museum ................ | 10 | |
| (51) Canley - home of Standard Triumph (TR3)...... | 10 | |
| (52) London & Brighton - car rally ....................pair | 20 | |
| (53) Longbridge - where Austin Healey 100 was built... | 10 | |

*Classic Cars (contd.)* | ordinary covers £ | official covers £

(54) Malvern Link - Morgan Plus Four was built..... 10
(55) NEC - Motor Show or Silverstone ..................... 20
(56) Royal Automobile Club, SW1 ......................... 50
*Also: Austin, Bentley, Cowley Centre, Dunlop, The Fender, Ford, Healey, Humber Rd, Leyland, Morganstown, Morris Green, Swavesey, Tickford St, Newport Pagnell, Trafford Park. Prices from £10.*

**SLOGAN POSTMARKS**
(57) Trafford Park ............................................. 15
*Also: Better Music Mix. PO Charter, Coventry. Prices from £7.*

## 28th October 1996 – CHRISTMAS
*2nd The Three Kings; 1st The Annunciation; 37p Journey to Nazareth; 43p The Nativity; 63p The Shepherds.*

**SPECIAL HANDSTAMPS** (1) Philatelic Bureau.... 3 – Royal Mail
(2) First Day of Issue – Bethlehem ......................... 3 – Royal Mail
(3) First Day of Issue – London ............................. 8 – Royal Mail
(4) Happy Christmas, Royal Mail, London EC1..... 8 – Royal Mail
(5) Westminster Abbey, SW1 ................................ 8 15 BLCS 122
(6) 900th Anniversary Norwich Cathedral............. 8 15 BLCS 122
(7) Season's Greetings, Jerusalem, Lincoln ............. 8 15 Ben500(122)
(8) Tidings of Great Joy, Nasareth ....................... 8 15 BLCS 122
(9) Unto us a King is born, Bethlehem ................ 8 15 Benham
(10) Jesus College Cambridge ............................ 8 25 LFDC 146
(11) The Christmas Story, Bethlehem.................... 8 15 VP 108
(12) Christmas Stamps, Bethlehem ..................... 8 20 CoverCraft
(13) Seasons Greetings, Angel Islington .............. 8 15 Steven Scott 5
(14) Autographed, Cathedral, Canterbury ............. 8 35 Westminster
(15) Christmas 1996 Bethlehem (star).................... 8 15 Westminster
(16) Booth Catalogue, St. Nicholas...................... 8 15 FDP Co.
(17) RNLI Christmas Common, Watlington.............. 8 15 StampSearchers
(18) No.18 Squadron Courage & Faith.................... 8 15 RAF FDC 43
(19) Heathrow Airport, 50th Anniversary ............. 8 30 Cam.S.C.
(20) Christmas 1996, Woodhall Spa, Lincs............. 8 30 Cam.S.C.
(21) The Queen's Stamps, Mauritius, NPM ............. 8 25 FriendsNPM

**C.D.S. POSTMARKS**
(22) Holy Island or Nasareth, Caernarfon........*each* 15
*Also: Angel Hill, Apple Cross, Cambridge, Capel St. Mary, Holytown, Lord Lane, Mary Pk, Noel Rd, Oaktree, Orangefield, Orange Tree, St. Nicholas, Shepherd's Bush, Shepherdswell, Threekingham. £7.*

**SLOGAN POSTMARKS** *Breast Cancer, Childline, Youth Service Week; Heart Check Week; Shopping by Post; The Beautiful South, Various Royal Mail slogans. Prices from £7.*

**£2.60 & £4 CHRISTMAS BOOKLETS**
With pair or block of 4 20p & 26p stamps........*pair* 10
With complete panes of 20p & 26p stamps .......*pair* 25

### SLOGAN POSTMARKS
With effect from November 1996 Royal Mail withdrew the re-posting facility for slogan postmarks. It is now therefore very difficult to obtain first day covers with all the stamps cancelled as described in the General Notes. Covers are known to exist, but not in sufficient quantity to warrant listing.

## 6th January 1997 – GREETINGS
*10 x 1st Class stamps featuring flowers.*

**SPECIAL HANDSTAMPS** (1) Philatelic Bureau.... 3 – Royal Mail
(2) First Day of Issue – Kew (Butterfly).................... 3 – Royal Mail
(3) First Day of Issue – London .............................. 10 – Royal Mail
(4) Greetings Stamps, Kew Gardens (rose)............. 12 15 Bradbury
(5) Greetings Flying Flowers, Staines .................... 12 15 BLCS 123
(6) Blooms of Bressingham, Norfolk ...................... 12 15 BLCS 123
(7) Blooms of Bressingham, Dorney Windsor........ 12 15 BenD290
(8) Blooms of Bressingham, Elton Peterborough.... 12 15 BLCS 123
(9) Wisley Gardens, Surrey................................... 12 20 BenhamPilgrim
(10) Greetings Gardening Direct, Chelmsford.......... 12 15 BLCS 123
(11) Royal Botanic Gardens, Edinburgh.................. 12 15 Ben500(123)
(12) Greetings Flower Girl, Romford ...................... 12 25 T Hurlstone
(13) Red, Red Rose - Robert Burns Alloway............ 12 – n.o.c.
(14) Autographed - Flowers, Kew Gardens.............. 12 27 Westminster: pair of covers
(15) Autographed - RHS Gardens, Wisley ............... 12 
(16) Floral Greetings, Kew Gardens (rose) ............. 12 20 Westminster: pair of covers
(17) Floral Greetings, Kew Gardens (daffodil) ......... 12 
(18) Floral Greetings, Kew Gardens (fuchsia) ......... 12 20 Westminster

**C.D.S. POSTMARKS**
(19) Botanic Gardens Belfast or Kew Gardens ....... 20
(20) Bloomfield or Flore or Flowery Field .............. 15
(21) Royal Hospital, Chelsea or Greet .................. 15
*Also: Garden Village, Moffat, Pleasure Gardens, Spalding  Prices from £10.*

## 21st January 1997 – THE GREAT TUDOR
*7 x 26p featuring portraits of Henry and his six wives.*

**SPECIAL HANDSTAMPS** (1) Philatelic Bureau.... 3 – Royal Mail
(2) First Day of Issue – Hampton Court.................. 3 – Royal Mail
(3) First Day of Issue – London .............................. 10 – Royal Mail
(4) Henry VIII & Six Wives, Peterboro' Cathedral .. 12 25 BenhamPilgrim

**Henry VIII (contd.)**

| | ordinary covers £ | sponsored covers £ |
|---|---|---|
| (5) Henry VIII & Six Wives, Sudeley Castle | 12 | 20 BenhamPilgrim |
| (6) Henry VIII & Six Wives, Windsor | 12 | 35 Ben500(124) |
| (7) Henry VIII & Six Wives, Tower of London | 12 | 20 BenSG32 |
| (8) Henry VIII & Six Wives, Hampton Ct Palace | 12 | 15 BLCS 124 |
| (9) Henry VIII & Six Wives, Hever Castle | 12 | 15 BLCS 124 |
| (10) Henry VIII & Six Wives, Dover Castle | 12 | 20 BenhamPilgrim |
| (11) Great Tudor (silhouette of Henry & wives) | 12 | 60 Westminster |
| (12) Hampton Court (silhouette Henry full length) | 12 | 15 Westminster |
| (13) 450th Anniv of Death (silhouette of Hampton Ct) | 12 | 7 Westminster(s) |
| (14) Hampton Ct (silhouette Henry head/shoulders) | 12 | 15 Westminster: |
| (15) 6 Wives of Henry Tudor (silhouette six wives) | 12 | 25 Set of 7 covers |
| (16) Birthplace of Henry VIII Greenwich | 12 | 15 LFDC 147 |
| (17) Henry VIII Hampton Wick | 12 | 15 VP 109 |
| (18) Autographed - Hampton Court Palace | 12 | 30 Westminster: |
| (19) Autographed - Tower of London EC3 | 12 | – pair of covers |
| (20) The Mary Rose Portsmouth | 12 | 6 Westminster(s) |
| (21) Henry VIII & Wives (Hampton Ct Palace) | 12 | 15 Cover Collection |
| (22) Henry VIII & Wives (Crown & Rose) The Mail | 12 | 15 Benham |
| (23) Henry VIII & Wives (Tudor Rose) Hampton Ct. | 12 | 20 Steven Scott 6 |
| (24) Henry VIII & Wives Kimbolton, Huntingdon | 12 | 25 Cam.S.C. |
| (25) Henry VIII School Coventry | 12 | 30 H.VIII School |
| (26) The Great Tudor, Tower Hill (rectangular) | 12 | 25 GBFDC GB5 |
| (27) Greetings Flower Girl, Romford | 12 | 20 T Hurlstone |
| (28) Tower Hill, London EC3 | 15 | – Royal Mail |
| (29) Portsmouth Philatelic Counter (Mary Rose) | 15 | – Royal Mail |
| (30) GWR Loco King Henry VIII Leamington Spa | 12 | 20 Dawn |
| (31) The Booth Catalogue, Henryd Gwynedd | 12 | 15 FDP Co |
| (32) RNLI Official Postmark, Six Bells | 12 | 15 StampSearchers |
| (33) No.7 Squadron, Farnborough | 12 | 12 RAF FDC 44 |

**C.D.S. POSTMARKS**

| | | |
|---|---|---|
| (34) Dunstable, Kimbolton, or Peterborough |||
|     - connections with Catherine of Aragon | 15 ||
| (35) Greenwich - birthplace of Henry VIII | 15 ||
| (36) Hampton, Hampton Wick or East Molesey | 15 ||
| (37) Seething Lane - near to Tower of London | 15 ||
| (38) Windsor - burial place of Henry VIII | 15 ||

*Also: Bolton Abbey, Broadway, Calais, Chelsea, Henry St., Howard Place, King's Est., King's Head, Maidenhead, Marlborough, Queen's Parade, Royal Parade, Seymour Hill, St. Georges, Tower Hill, Tudor Drive, Winchcombe. From £10.*

## 11th March 1997 - MISSIONS OF FAITH
*26p & 37p Saint Columba; 43p & 63p Saint Augustine.*

**SPECIAL HANDSTAMPS**

| | | |
|---|---|---|
| (1) Philatelic Bureau | 3 | – Royal Mail |
| (2) First Day of Issue – Isle of Iona | 4 | – Royal Mail |
| (3) First Day of Issue – London | 10 | – Royal Mail |
| (4) First Day of Issue – Durham | 10 | – Royal Mail |
| (5) First Day of Issue – St. Albans | 10 | – Royal Mail |
| (6) St. Columba 521-597, Iona | 10 | – n.s.c. |
| (7) Missions of Faith, Canterbury | 10 | 15 VP 110 |
| (8) Missions of Faith, Isle of Iona | 10 | 15 LFDC 148 |
| (9) Uckfield Philatelic Soc, Missions of Faith | 10 | 20 Uckfield PS |
| (10) Autographed Editions, Isle of Iona | 10 | 20 Westminster |
| (11) Missions of Faith, Canterbury Cathedral | 10 | 20 Westminster |
| (12) World's Oldest Wooden Church, Ongar | 10 | 20 T. Hurlstone |
| (13) St. Andrew's Church, Hornchurch, Essex | 10 | 20 T. Hurlstone |
| (14) St. Augustine's Church, Queensgate, SW7 | 10 | 15 Steven Scott 7 |
| (15) St. Columba, Iona Abbey, Isle of Iona | 10 | 15 BLCS 125 |
| (16) 597-1997 Canterbury | 10 | 15 BLCS 125 |
| (17) Lindisfarne, Holy Island | 10 | 15 Ben500(125) |
| (18) St.Augustine/English Heritage Canterbury | 10 | 15 BLCS 125 |
| (19) Downside, Bath | 10 | 35 St.Gregory's |
| (20) Any Royal Mail cathedral permanent h/s | 10 | – Royal Mail |
| (21) RNLI Missions of Faith, St. Columb, Cornwall | 10 | 15 StampSearchers |
| (22) St. Columba, Res Class 47, Newcastle | 10 | 20 Dawn |
| (23) No.14 Squadron, RAF's Crusades, Shoreham | 10 | 12 RAF FDC 45 |

**C.D.S. POSTMARKS**

| | | |
|---|---|---|
| (24) All Saints or Holy Island | 10 ||
| (25) Canterbury - St. Augustine first Archbishop | 10 ||
| (26) Dunkeld - Home of the St. Columba's relics | 10 ||
| (27) Isle of Iona - St. Columba's monastery | 10 ||
| (28) St. Augustine or St. Columb | 10 ||

*Also: Bede, Cliffs End, Coleraine, Edinburgh, Glasgow, Inverness, Jarrow, Londonderry, Morvern, Pagan Hill, The Priory, Rannoch, St. Cross, Saintfield, St. Peter's St (St. Albans), Urquhart,Whitby. From £7.*

## 21st April 1997 - GOLDEN WEDDING
*1st Class & 26p Golden Definitives*

**SPECIAL HANDSTAMPS**

| | | |
|---|---|---|
| (1) Philatelic Bureau | 3 | – Royal Mail |
| (2) First Day of Issue – Windsor | 3 | – Royal Mail |
| (3) First Day of Issue – London | 10 | – Royal Mail |
| (4) Westminster Abbey London SW1 | 10 | 15 Westminster |
| (5) Autographed Editions Westminster Abbey | 10 | 20 Westminster |
| (6) 50th Anniv Golden Wedding West. Abbey | 10 | 12 BLCS 128 |

*Golden Wedding (contd.)*                    **ordinary covers**    **sponsored covers**
£                    £

| (7) | Queen Street, London W1 | 10 | 15 | Ben500(128) |
| (8) | Golden Wedding Anniv Year Windsor | 10 | 15 | BenSG33 |
| (9) | 50th Anniv Golden Wedding Windsor | 10 | 15 | BLCS 128 |
| (10) | The Mail on Sunday | 10 | 15 | Benham |
| (11) | Golden Wedding Year Westminster Abbey | 10 | 10 | Bradbury |
| (12) | Golden Wedding Sandringham Norfolk | 10 | – | Royal Mail |
| (13) | Westminster Abbey London SW1 | 10 | 10 | Steven Scott 8 |
| (14) | Golden & Glorious National Postal Museum | 10 | – | NPM |
| (15) | Prototype Letterboxes Nat Postal Museum | 10 | – | NPM |
| (16) | Kendal & Windermere Railway, Kendal | 10 | 15 | Benham |
| (17) | Royal Mail London SW (permanent h/s) | 10 | – | Royal Mail |
| (18) | Royal Mail Windsor (permanent handstamp) | 10 | – | Royal Mail |

**C.D.S. POSTMARKS**

| (19) | Buckingham Palace, London SW1 | 150 | | |
| (20) | House of Commons or Lords | 15 | | |
| (21) | Queen Elizabeth Avenue | 15 | | |
| (22) | Windsor Castle, Windsor Berks | 125 | | |
| (23) | Windsor, Berks | 15 | | |

*In addition: Edinburgh. Prices from £6.*

## 13th May 1997 – TALES OF HORROR

*26p Dracula; 31p Frankenstein; 37p Dr Jekyll & Mr. Hyde;
43p The Hound of the Baskervilles.*

**SPECIAL HANDSTAMPS**

| (1) | Philatelic Bureau | 3 | – | Royal Mail |
| (2) | First Day of Issue – Whitby | 3 | – | Royal Mail |
| (3) | First Day of Issue – London | 10 | – | Royal Mail |
| (4) | Bram Stoker Society Whitby North Yorks | 10 | 15 | LFDC 149 |
| (5) | The Whitby Dracula Society | 10 | 15 | VP 111 |
| (6) | Carfax Estate, Purfleet Essex | 10 | 20 | Bradbury |
| (7) | Hound of the Baskervilles Princetown | 10 | 15 | Bradbury |
| (8) | Batman Close London W12 | 10 | 15 | GBFDC GB6 |
| (9) | Mary Shelley Frankenstein London SW17 | 10 | 15 | Ben500(126) |
| (10) | The Sherlock Holmes Museum London NW1 | 10 | 15 | BLCS 126 |
| (11) | Centenary of Dracula Bradford | 10 | 15 | BLCS 126 |
| (12) | Dr Jeykll & Mr Hyde Edinburgh | 10 | 20 | BenhamPilgrim |
| (13) | Tales of Terror Whitby | 10 | 15 | Westminster |
| (14) | Autographed Editions Mary Shelley | 10 | 25 | Westminster |
| (15) | Havering's Witch Queen Romford | 10 | 35 | T Hurlstone |
| (16) | Tales of Horror, Elstree | 10 | 60 | Cam.S.C. |
| (17) | Hound of the Baskervilles, Dartmoor | 10 | 60 | Cam.S.C. |
| (18) | Swains Lane Highgate N6 | 10 | 15 | CoverCollection |
| (19) | Birmingham Ghost Trails | 10 | 75 | GhostTrail |
| (20) | Sherlock Holmes Society of London | 10 | 15 | Steven Scott |
| (21) | Hound of the Baskervilles Baker Street | 10 | 12 | Steven Scott 9 |
| (22) | Visit of Endeavour Replica Whitby | 10 | 25 | B.Downham |
| (23) | RNLI Tales of Horror, Horrabridge, Devon | 10 | 12 | StampSearchers |
| (24) | Sunderland Champions FA Carling | 10 | 40 | Dawn |
| (25) | No.13 Squadron, We Assist by Watching | 10 | 12 | RAF FDC 46 |

**C.D.S. POSTMARKS**

| (26) | Hindhead - Conan Doyle wrote H of the B | 10 | | |
| (27) | Marlow - where Shelley wrote Frankenstein | 10 | | |
| (28) | Princetown - Hound of the Baskervilles | 10 | | |
| (29) | Purfleet or Whitby - Dracula settings | 10 | | |
| (30) | Westbourne - Stevenson wrote Dr J & Mr H | 10 | | |

*Also: Beast Banks, Bitteswell, Bournemouth,Cemetery, Cruden Bay,
Devil's Bdge, Edinburgh, Elstree, Golders Green, Hammerwich,
Headless Cross, Horrabridge, Houndsditch, Hyde, Shelley,
Stoneyhurst, Whitstable, Widecombe, Wolf's Castle. Prices from £7.*

## 10th June 1997 – ARCHITECTS OF THE AIR

*20p R J Mitchell (Spitfire); 26p R Chadwick (Lancaster); 37p R E Bishop (Mosquito);
43p G Carter (Meteor); 63p S Camm (Hunter).*

**SPECIAL HANDSTAMPS**

| (1) | Philatelic Bureau | 3 | – | Royal Mail |
| (2) | First Day of Issue – Duxford Cambridge | 3 | – | Royal Mail |
| (3) | First Day of Issue – London | 10 | – | Royal Mail |
| (4) | British Aerospace Farnborough | 10 | 15 | BAe/Royal Mail |
| (5) | Supermarine Spitfire R J Mitchell Duxford | 12 | 20 | BenhamPilgrim |
| (6) | Avro Lancaster Roy Chadwick Waddington | 12 | 15 | BLCS 129 |
| (7) | DeHaviland Mosquito R E Bishop Marham | 12 | 15 | BLCS 129 |
| (8) | Gloster Meteor W G Carter Manston | 12 | 20 | BenhamPilgrim |
| (9) | Hawker Hunter Sir Sidney Camm Leuchars | 12 | 15 | Ben500(129) |
| (10) | Supermarine Spitfire Southampton Int Airport | 12 | 15 | BenSG34 |
| (11) | Shuttleworth Collection Biggleswade | 12 | 15 | BLCS 129 |
| (12) | Supermarine Spitfire The Mail on Sunday | 12 | 15 | Benham |
| (13) | Royal Naval Air Station Culdrose | 12 | 15 | BenL47 |
| (14) | Architects of the Air Scampton Lincs | 12 | 20 | Westminster(set 5) |
| (15) | Architects of the Air Autographed Editions | 12 | 25 | Westminster |
| (16) | Home of the 617 Squadron Lossiemouth | 12 | 25 | LFDC 150 |
| (17) | The Dambusters 617 Squadron Scampton | 12 | 35 | LFDC 150 |
| (18) | Tribute to Aircraft Designers Farnborough | 12 | 15 | VP 112 |
| (19) | Bletchley Park | 12 | 50 | Bletchley PO |
| (20) | Lancaster Lancashire | 12 | 35 | RAF (P&P1) |
| (21) | Architects of the Air Biggin Hill | 12 | 15 | Steven Scott 10 |

121

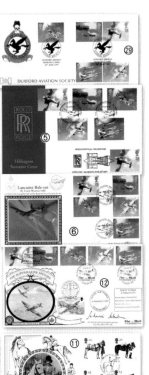

| *Architects of the Air (contd.)* | ordinary covers £ | sponsored covers £ | |
|---|---|---|---|
| (22) Battle of Britain Flight RAF Coningsby............ | 12 | 15 | *Steven Scott* |
| (23) Spitfire Way, Hounslow............................... | 12 | 15 | *GBFDC GB7* |
| (24) National Postal Museum City of London ......... | 12 | – | *n.s.c* |
| (25) Roy Chadwick Designer Scampton ................ | 12 | 35 | *Cam.S.C.* |
| (26) RJMitchell & Spitfire Duxford Cambridge........ | 12 | 35 | *Cam.S.C.* |
| (27) Architects of the Air Heathrow Airport............ | 12 | 35 | *Cam.S.C.* |
| (28) RAF Hornchurch Remembering the Few.......... | 12 | 25 | *T Hurlstone* |
| (29) Duxford Aviation Society Cambs................... | 12 | 25 | *T Hurlstone* |
| (30) Eurofighter 2000 GEC Marconi Stanmore ...... | 12 | 45 | *GEC-Marconi* |
| (31) City of Lancaster LMS loco6243 Lancaster ..... | 12 | 25 | *Dawn* |
| (32) Nene Valley Rly Return to Steam.................... | 12 | 20 | *NVRly* |
| (33) Heathrow Airport London, Houslow .............. | 12 | – | *n.s.c.* |
| (34) Royal Mail Gatwick ................................... | 12 | – | *n.s.c.* |
| (35) Booth Catalogue, Lancaster ....................... | 12 | 15 | *FDP Co* |
| (36) RNLI Lancaster ......................................... | 12 | 20 | *StampSearchers* |
| (37) No.19 Squadron Castle Bromwich ................ | 12 | 15 | *RAF FDC 47* |

**C.D.S. POSTMARKS**

| | | |
|---|---|---|
| (38) Cranwell - First flight of Meteor ................. | 12 | |
| (39) Duxford - RAF Spitfire base........................ | 12 | |
| (40) Eastleigh & Woolston - Spitfires built here...... | 12 | |
| (41) Edgware & Hatfield - Mosquitos built here ..... | 12 | |
| (42) Farnborough - British Aerospace & Air Show . | 12 | |
| (43) Hucclecote - Meteors built here................... | 12 | |
| (44) Kingston - Hawker Hunters built here ........... | 12 | |
| (45) Lancaster ............................................... | 12 | |
| (46) Leuchars - associated with Hawker Hunters ... | 12 | |
| (47) Lossiemouth & Scampton - Dambusters .......... | 12 | |
| (48) Manston - associated with Meteor ............... | 12 | |
| (49) Marham RAF Stn - associated with Mosquito.. | 12 | |
| (50) Newton Heath - Lancasters built here .............. | 12 | |

*In addition: Biggin Hill, Bletchley, Butt Lane, Churchill, Coningsby, Cranfield, Hawkinge, Herne Bay, North Berwick, Southampton, Victory St., Woodhall Spa. Prices from £10.*

## 8th July 1997 – ALL THE QUEEN'S HORSES

*20p Royal Mews (St Patrick); 26p Lifeguards (Thompson); 43p Blues & Royals (Janus); 63p Royal Mews (River Star).*

| **SPECIAL HANDSTAMPS** (1) Philatelic Bureau.... | 3 | – | *Royal Mail* |
|---|---|---|---|
| (2) First Day of Issue – Windsor ........................ | 3 | – | *Royal Mail* |
| (3) First Day of Issue – London ......................... | 10 | – | *Royal Mail* |
| (4) British Horse Society Stoneleigh ................... | 10 | 15 | *LFDC 151* |
| (5) British Horse Society Windsor Great Park........ | 10 | 15 | *VP 113* |
| (6) Household Cavalry London............................ | 10 | 20 | *Bradbury* |
| (7) Horse Guards Avenue SW1 (Banner at base) .. | 10 | 15 | *Ben500(130)* |
| (8) Horse Guards Avenue SW1 (circle)................ | 10 | 15 | *Westminster* |
| (9) Hyde Park Gardens W2................................ | 10 | 15 | *BLCS 130* |
| (10) Golden Wedding Horse Guards Ave .............. | 10 | 15 | *BenSG35* |
| (11) Pony Club Kenilworth ............................... | 10 | 15 | *BenL50* |
| (12) Badminton Gloucester (showjumper) ............ | 10 | 15 | *BLCS 130* |
| (13) Windsor Great Park (jockey on horseback)...... | 10 | 15 | *BLCS 130* |
| (14) The Guards Toy Soldier Centre..................... | 10 | 15 | *Steven Scott 11* |
| (15) King's Troop Royal Horse Artillery Whitehall.. | 10 | 15 | *FourPennyPost* |
| (16) The Coronation Coach Westminster Abbey...... | 10 | 15 | *T Hurlstone* |
| (17) Autographed Editions Badminton ................. | 10 | 20 | *Westminster* |
| (18) RNLI Horsehay Telford ............................. | 10 | 15 | *StampSearchers* |
| (19) No.203 Squadron Newquay Cornwall.............. | 10 | 15 | *RAF FDC 48* |
| (20) Vasco da Gama Sea Route to India, London .. | 10 | – | *n.s.c* |

**C.D.S. POSTMARKS**

| | | |
|---|---|---|
| (21) Broadway - Wellington Barracks ................... | 12 | |
| (22) Lancelot Pl. - Knightsbridge Barracks ............. | 12 | |
| (23) Victoria St. - Royal Mews .......................... | 12 | |
| (24) Windsor - where Queen's horses are trained .... | 12 | |

*Also: Badminton, Black Horse, Constantine, Duke Street, Guardhouse, Horsebridge, Horsehay, Horsefair, Horseman's Green, Kenilworth, King's Lynn, Queen's Dr., Queen's Parade, Stud Farm, Thompson, Whitehorse Hill. From £10*

## 12th August 1997 – POST OFFICES

*20p Haroldswick; 26p Painswick; 43p Beddgelert; 63p Ballyroney.*

| **SPECIAL HANDSTAMPS** (1) Philatelic Bureau.... | 3 | – | *Royal Mail* |
|---|---|---|---|
| (2) First Day of Issue – Wakefield ............................ | 3 | – | *Royal Mail* |
| (3) First Day of Issue – London ......................... | 10 | – | *Royal Mail* |
| (4) National Fed of SubPostmasters Wakefield ...... | 10 | 20 | *LFDC 152* |
| (5) National Fed of SubPostmasters Shoreham ...... | 10 | 15 | *VP 114* |
| (6) National Postal Museum Sub Post Offices ........ | 10 | – | *n.s.c* |
| (7) Britain's Post Office Heritage the NPM,........... | 10 | 15 | *Westminster* |
| (8) Autographed Editions Painswick Glos.............. | 10 | 25 | *Westminster* |
| (9) The Old Post Office Castle Combe.................... | 10 | 15 | *BLCS 131* |
| (10) Blisland Post Office Bodmin........................ | 10 | 15 | *BLCS 131* |
| (11) The Old Post Office Tintagel Cornwall ............ | 10 | 15 | *Ben500(131)* |
| (12) Sanquhar Post Office Dumfriesshire .............. | 10 | 12 | *BLCS 131* |
| (13) Earliest known posting of the 1d Black Bath ... | 10 | 15 | *Steven Scott 12* |
| (14) Hedge End Southampton ..................................... | 10 | 20 | *HedgeEnd PO* |
| (15) Haroldswick Post Office ............................. | 10 | – | *n.o.c.* |
| (16) Painswick Post Office ................................ | 10 | – | *n.o.c.* |

| Post Offices (contd.) | ordinary covers £ | sponsored covers £ | |
|---|---|---|---|
| (17) Beddgelert Gwynedd | 10 | 15 | GBFDC GB8 |
| (18) The Oldest Working Post Office Sanquhar | 10 | 15 | FourPennyPost |
| (19) Haroldswick Post Office - permanent h/s | 10 | – | n.s.c |
| (20) TPO Restoration Scheme Peterborough | 10 | 15 | NVRly |
| (21) Bicentenary of the Copper Penny Liverpool | 10 | 20 | B'hamCoinCvr |
| (22) Operation Pedestal Malta Gourock | 10 | 15 | RN CvrsGp 1-10 |
| (23) 750 Years Romford Market | 10 | 15 | T Hurlstone |
| (24) No.20 Squadron Netheravon Salisbury | 10 | 12 | RAF FDC 49 |
| (25) Post Office at Bletchley Park | 10 | 30 | Bletchley PO |
| (26) RNLI Sub Post Office Letters Ross-shire | 10 | 15 | StampSearchers |

**C.D.S. POSTMARKS**

| | | |
|---|---|---|
| (27) Ballyroney, Beddgelert, Haroldswick or Painswick Post Offices featured on the stamps | 12 | |
| (28) Sanquhar - Oldest working Post Office | 10 | |
| (29) Shoreham by Sea - Federation's HQ | 10 | |
| (30) Wakefield or Kirkgate - Fed founded here | 15 | |

*Also: Belstone, Carlisle (Mobile PO), Glenelg, Hargrave, Hilborough, Lanelli Hill, The Lizard, Maidford, RAC, Rowelton,Witcham, Spooner Row, Starcoast World, Thurcaston, Trafford Park, TPOs. From £7.*

## 9th September 1997 – ENID BLYTON'S FAMOUS FIVE

*20p Noddy; 26p Famous Five; 37p Secret Seven; 43p Faraway Tree; 63p Malory Towers.*

| SPECIAL HANDSTAMPS | | | |
|---|---|---|---|
| (1) Philatelic Bureau | 3 | – | Royal Mail |
| (2) First Day of Issue – Beaconsfield | 3 | – | Royal Mail |
| (3) First Day of Issue – London | 10 | – | Royal Mail |
| (4) First Day of Issue – Birmingham | 10 | – | Royal Mail |
| (5) Children's Stories for Sunny Days, Blyton | 12 | 20 | LFDC 153 |
| (6) World's Favourite Aunt, Blyton | 12 | 15 | VP 115 |
| (7) Centenary of Birth of Enid Blyton, Blyton | 12 | 15 | Westminster |
| (8) Autographed Editions Blyton | 12 | 20 | Westminster |
| (9) Enid Blyton Beaconsfield (teddy & doll) | 12 | 20 | Cam.S.C. |
| (10) Enid Blyton Corfe Castle | 12 | 15 | BLCS 132 |
| (11) Enid Blyton London W1 (Noddy) | 12 | 15 | BLCS 132 |
| (12) Enid Blyton Beaconsfield (open book) | 12 | 15 | BLCS 132 |
| (13) Enid Blyton Bickley, Bromley (Noddy) | 12 | 15 | Ben500(132) |
| (14) Enid Blyton Surbiton, Surrey | 12 | 15 | BenhamPilgrim |
| (15) Enid Blyton East Dulwich (pile of books) | 12 | 15 | BLCS 132 |
| (16) Enid Blyton The Mail on Sunday | 12 | 15 | Benham |
| (17) Variety Club London W1 | 12 | 15 | Benham |
| (18) Childhood Adventures, Childs Way NW11 | 12 | 15 | Steven Scott 13 |
| (19) Swan Libraries, Booksellers, Upminster | 12 | 20 | T Hurlstone |
| (20) Southampton, Hampshire | 12 | 15 | RAF (P&P2) |
| (21) RNLI Enid Blyton, Blyton Gainsborough | 12 | 15 | StampSearchers |
| (22) Operation Avalanche, Eastney, Southsea | 12 | 15 | RN CvrsGp 1-11 |
| (23) No.5 Squadron Famous Five Farnborough | 12 | 15 | RAF FDC 50 |

**C.D.S. POSTMARKS**

| | | |
|---|---|---|
| (24) Beaconsfield – home of Enid Blyton | 12 | |
| (25) Blyton, Gainsborough or Playing Place | 15 | |
| (26) East Dulwich – birthplace of Enid Blyton | 12 | |

*Also: Beckenham, Bourne End, Child's Hill, Corfe Castle, Fiveways. From £10*

## 27th October 1997 – CHRISTMAS

*2nd, 1st, 31p, 43p, 63p - Tom Smith's Christmas Crackers 1847-1997*

| SPECIAL HANDSTAMPS | | | |
|---|---|---|---|
| (1) Philatelic Bureau | 3 | – | Royal Mail |
| (2) First Day of Issue – Bethlehem | 3 | – | Royal Mail |
| (3) First Day of Issue – London | 10 | – | Royal Mail |
| (4) First Day of Issue – Birmingham | 10 | – | Royal Mail |
| (5) Happy Christmas Royal Mail London EC1 | 10 | – | Royal Mail |
| (6) Drury Lane WC2 (bells and holly) | 10 | 15 | BLCS 135 |
| (7) Norwich (crackers) | 10 | 15 | BLCS 135 |
| (8) Regent Street (boxed presents) | 10 | 15 | BLCS 135 |
| (9) Trafalgar Square (Christmas tree) | 10 | 15 | BLCS 135 |
| (10) Bethlehem (candle) | 10 | 15 | Ben500(135) |
| (11) Christmas Crackers Bethlehem | 10 | 15 | LFDC 155 |
| (12) Christmas Crackers 150 Years Nasareth | 10 | 15 | VP 117 |
| (13) Charles Dickens Rochester | 10 | 15 | Bradbury |
| (14) Christmas Crackers, Bangor | 10 | 30 | Blechley PO |
| (15) Happy Christmas, Rainham Royals | 10 | 20 | T Hurlstone |
| (16) Christmas Crackers, West Langdon, Dover | 10 | 15 | SouthernCvr.1 |
| (17) Great Scott, Crackers | 10 | 15 | Steven Scott 15 |
| (18) Christmas Cracker, Finsbury Square | 10 | 15 | Westminster |
| (19) Autographed Editions, Christmas Common | 10 | 25 | Westminster |
| (20) Snowdrop Close Hampton Middx | 10 | 15 | GBFDC GB10 |
| (21) Christmas Greetings HM Ships Abroad | 10 | 12 | RN CvrsGp 1-14 |
| (22) Santa Specials Nene Valley Railway | 10 | 15 | NVRly |
| (23) RNLI Christmas, St. Nicholas | 10 | 15 | StampSearchers |
| (24) Battle of Britain Flight, RAF Coningsby | 10 | 30 | Cam.S.C. |
| (25) No.72 Squadron, Upavon, Pewsey | 10 | 12 | RAF FDC 51 |
| (26) Queen's Stamps National Postal Museum | 10 | – | NPM |
| (27) Halifax, West Yorkshire | 10 | 15 | RAF (P&P4) |

123

| *Christmas (contd.)* | | ordinary covers | sponsored covers |
|---|---|---|---|
| **C.D.S. POSTMARKS** | | £ | £ |

(28) Heartease or Norwich - Tom Smith factory...... 12
(29) Bishop's Stortford, Colman Street EC2, Stockport
    all connected with Tom Smith's Crackers.. 10
(30) St Nicholas - Santa ................................................ 12
*Also: Holy Island, Nasareth. Prices from £7.*

**£2.60 & £4 CHRISTMAS BOOKLETS**
With pair or block of 4 20p & 26p stamps................ 5
With complete panes of 20p & 26p stamps.............. 10

## 13th November 1997 – QUEEN'S GOLDEN WEDDING
*20p & 43p Wedding day portrait; 26p & 63p Present day portrait*

**SPECIAL HANDSTAMPS**
| | | ordinary | sponsored | |
|---|---|---|---|---|
| (1) | Philatelic Bureau ...................... | 3 | – | *Royal Mail* |
| (2) | First Day of Issue – London SW Fifty Years..... | 3 | – | *Royal Mail* |
| (3) | First Day of Issue – London (bells & doves) .... | 10 | – | *Royal Mail* |
| (4) | First Day of Issue – Birmingham ..................... | 10 | – | *Royal Mail* |
| (5) | Queen & Duke of Ed 1947-1997 (W.Abbey)..... | 12 | 15 | *LFDC 154* |
| (6) | Golden Wedding West. Abbey (three bells) ...... | 12 | 15 | *VP 116* |
| (7) | Buckingham Palace Rd SW1 (showing Palace) .. | 12 | 20 | *BenhamPilgrim* |
| (8) | Westminster SW1 (showing Abbey)................... | 12 | 15 | *BLCS 134* |
| (9) | Crathie (showingBalmoral) .............................. | 12 | 15 | *BLCS 134* |
| (10) | Windsor (showing Castle) ................................. | 12 | 15 | *Ben500(134)* |
| (11) | 50th Wedd Anniv Congratulations, Romsey .... | 12 | 20 | *BenhamPilgrim* |
| (12) | Golden Wedd Anniv Congrat., Romsey ........... | 12 | 150 | *BenhamCoinCvr* |
| (13) | The Queen & the Duke of Ed, Windsor ........... | 12 | 20 | *BenhamCoinCvr* |
| (14) | Golden Wedding Year, Windsor........................ | 12 | 20 | *BenhamCoinCvr* |
| (15) | Royal Golden Wedd Year Congrat. Windsor..... | 12 | 15 | *BenSG36* |
| (16) | Royal Golden Wedding Anniv Ballater............. | 12 | 15 | *BLCS 134* |
| (17) | HM QEII HRH Prince Philip Westminster ....... | 12 | 15 | *BLCS 134* |
| (18) | Royal Golden Wedding Mail on Sunday ......... | 12 | 15 | *Benham* |
| (19) | Westminster Abbey (wreath) ............................ | 12 | 12 | *Steven Scott 15* |
| (20) | Westminster Abbey (text within bell)................ | 12 | 20 | *Cam.S.C.* |
| (21) | Royal Mews, Buckingham Palace Road (rose) . | 12 | 15 | *FourPennyPost* |
| (22) | 50th The Mall London SW1 ............................. | 12 | 15 | *Cover Collection* |
| (23) | Best Wishes/GBFDC Queen Elizabeth St........ | 12 | 15 | *GBFDC GB9* |
| (24) | Royal Naval Covers Group ............................... | 12 | 10 | *RN CvrsGp 1-12* |
| (25) | Autographed Editions, Westminster Abbey....... | 12 | 20 | *Westminster* |
| (26) | Britannia Royal Naval College ......................... | 12 | 15 | *Westminster* |
| (27) | Buckingham Palace Rd (hands) ........................ | 12 | 60 | *Bletchley PO* |
| (28) | Royal Mail Windsor - permanent handstamp... | 12 | – | *Royal Mail* |
| (29) | Royal Mail London SW - permanent h/s.......... | 12 | – | *Royal Mail* |
| (30) | Redhill Philatelic Society................................. | 12 | 15 | *Redhill PS* |
| (31) | Nat West Philatelic Society.............................. | 12 | 40 | *NatWest PS* |
| (32) | Uckfield Philatelic Society............................... | 12 | 15 | *Uckfield PS* |
| (33) | The Queen's Stamps National Postal Museum.. | 12 | 20 | *NPM* |
| (34) | Int Brotherhood Golden Fleece, Romford........ | 12 | 20 | *T Hurlstone* |
| (35) | Ardleigh House Comm. Assocn, Hornchurch.. | 12 | 20 | *T Hurlstone* |
| (36) | Havering Covers 150 Club ............................... | 12 | 15 | *T Hurlstone* |
| (37) | Sunderland Tyne & Wear................................. | 12 | 15 | *RAF (P&P3)* |
| (38) | Manchester City Royal Sovereign .................... | 12 | 15 | *Dawn* |
| (39) | RNLI Golden Wedding, Wedmore Somerset.... | 12 | 15 | *Stamp Searchers* |
| (40) | Happy Christmas Royal Mail London EC1 ...... | 12 | – | *Royal Mail* |
| (41) | No.11 Squadron, Farnborough Hants .............. | 12 | 15 | *RAF FDC 52* |
| (42) | 50th Anniv. Armstrong Whitworth, Baginton... | 12 | 20 | *RAF JSPCC* |

**C.D.S. POSTMARKS**
| (43) | Buckingham Palace............................................ | 150 | |
| (44) | Dartmouth - couple first met at RNCollege ...... | 10 | |
| (45) | House of Commons or House of Lords ............ | 20 | |
| (46) | Romsey - Honeymoon at Broadlands................ | 10 | |
| (47) | Queen Elizabeth Ave or Windsor .................... | 10 | |
| (48) | Windsor Castle................................................. | 250 | |

*Also: Broadway, Dolgellau,Duke St, Edinburgh, Gretna Grn,
Prince Consort Rd, Royal Pde. From £8.*

## 20th January 1998 – ENDANGERED SPECIES
*20p Dormouse; 26p Lady's slipper orchid; 31p Song thrush;
37p Shining ram's-horn snail; 43p Mole cricket; 63p Devil's bolete*

**SPECIAL HANDSTAMPS**
| (1) | Philatelic Bureau.... | 3 | – | *Royal Mail* |
| (2) | First Day of Issue – Selborne, Alton ................. | 3 | – | *Royal Mail* |
| (3) | First Day of Issue – London ............................ | 10 | – | *Royal Mail* |
| (4) | First Day of Issue – Birmingham ..................... | 10 | – | *Royal Mail* |
| (5) | Common dormouse, London Zoo ...................... | 12 | 15 | *BLCS 137* |
| (6) | Song Thrush, Sandy ......................................... | 12 | 15 | *BLCS 137* |
| (7) | Mole Cricket, London Zoo ............................... | 12 | 15 | *BLCS 137* |
| (8) | Devil's Bolete, Kew, Richmond ....................... | 12 | 15 | *BLCS 137* |
| (9) | Lady's Slipper Orchid, Kew, Richmond ........... | 12 | 15 | *Ben500(137)* |
| (10) | Shining Ram's-Horn Snail, Norwich................ | 12 | 20 | *BenhamPilgrim* |
| (11) | RSPB Saving the future, Sandy ....................... | 12 | 15 | *Benham* |
| (12) | Thames Salmon Trust Campaign ...................... | 12 | 15 | *BenL53* |
| (13) | Endangered Species, Selborne, Alton ............... | 12 | 20 | *LFDC 156* |
| (14) | Endangered Species, Sandy, Beds.................... | 12 | 15 | *VP 118* |
| (15) | Endangered Species, Grassington, Skipton ...... | 12 | 15 | *Bradbury* |
| (16) | Charles Lutwidge Do-do-Dodgson, Guildford.. | 12 | 15 | *Bradbury* |
| (17) | Birthplace of Lewis Carroll, Daresbury............ | 12 | 15 | *Bradbury* |
| (18) | Endangered Species, London Zoo (elephant)... | 12 | 15 | *Steven Scott* |

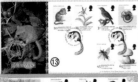

**Endangered Species (contd.)**

| | ordinary covers £ | sponsored covers £ | |
|---|---|---|---|
| (19) Endangered Species, Birdcage Walk, SW1 | 12 | 15 | *Steven Scott 16* |
| (20) Endangered Species, Mousehole | 12 | 20 | *Westminster* |
| (21) Autographed Editions Regents Park | 12 | 25 | *Westminster* |
| (22) Autographed Editions Attenborough | 12 | 25 | *Westminster* |
| (23) Ashford Stamp Shop | 12 | 20 | *SouthernCvr.2* |
| (24) Grassington Habitat of Lady's Slipper Orchid | 12 | 20 | *T Hurlstone* |
| (25) Ardleigh Green Habitat/Great Crested Newt | 12 | 20 | *T Hurlstone* |
| (26) Tusk Force Birmingham | 12 | – | *Royal Mail* |
| (27) Sinking of the Santorre Santarosa | 12 | 15 | *RN CvrsGp 2-1* |
| (28) No.43 Squadron, Fighting Cocks, Stirling | 12 | 15 | *RAF FDC 53* |
| (29) RNLI Mousehole | 12 | 15 | *Stamp Searchers* |

**C.D.S. POSTMARKS**

| | | | |
|---|---|---|---|
| (30) Botanic Gdns, Belfast, Kew Gardens or Mold | 15 | | |
| (31) Grassington - Lady's Slipper Orchid | 15 | | |
| (32) Lincoln or Selborne | 12 | | |

*Also: Attenborough, Mousehole, Otterburn, Snailbeach. Throstle Ln. From £10.*

## 3rd February 1998 – DIANA - PRINCESS OF WALES

*5 x 26p - Portraits of Diana*

| | | | |
|---|---|---|---|
| **SPECIAL HANDSTAMPS** (1) Philatelic Bureau | 3 | – | *Royal Mail* |
| (2) First Day of Issue – Kensington | 3 | – | *Royal Mail* |
| (3) Diana, Kens. Palace Gdns (roses & candle) | 10 | 30 | *BLCS 138* |
| (4) Diana, Kens. Palace Gdns (roses in bud) | 10 | 15 | *BenSG39* |
| (5) Diana, St. Paul's Cathedral (roses) | 10 | 50 | *BenhamPilgrim* |
| (6) Diana, Althorp (roses) | 10 | 15 | *Benham* |
| (7) Diana, Sandringham (roses) | 10 | 50 | *BenhamPilgrim* |
| (8) Diana, Cardiff (roses) | 10 | 30 | *BLCS 138* |
| (9) Diana, Kensington Palace Gdns | 10 | 15 | *Benham* |
| (10) Diana, St. Paul's Cathedral | 10 | 50 | *Ben(500)138* |
| (11) Diana, Althorp | 10 | 35 | *BenCoin* |
| (12) Diana, Sandringham | 10 | 30 | *BLCS 138* |
| (13) Diana, Cardiff | 10 | 30 | *BLCS 138* |
| (14) Diana, The Mail on Sunday | 10 | 15 | *Benham* |
| (15) Diana, KM Canterbury Kent | 10 | 15 | *Benham* |
| (16) Diana, St. Paul's Cathedral | 10 | 175 | *Benham* |
| (17) Diana, The People's Princess, Great Brington | 10 | 15 | *LFDC 160* |
| (18) Diana, Kensington (single rose in circle) | 10 | 15 | *VP 122* |
| (19) Queen of Hearts, Lewis Carroll Centenary | 10 | 25 | *Bradbury* |
| (20) Diana, Althorp (Althorp House) | 10 | 25 | *GtBringtonPO* |
| (21) Kensington, London W8 (Kensington Palace) | 10 | 20 | *Westminster* |
| (22) Autographed Editions, Kens. Palace Gdns | 10 | 35 | *Westminster* |
| (23) A Tribute to Diana, London E1 | 10 | 20 | *NewsOfWorld* |
| (24) A Tribute to Diana, Kensington | 10 | 15 | *CoverCraft* |
| (25) A Tribute to the People's Princess Kensington | 10 | 15 | *CoverCollection* |
| (26) Diana Commemoration London WC2 | 10 | 15 | *Steven Scott 17* |
| (27) England's Rose, Kensington | 10 | 40 | *CoverCraft* |
| (28) Diana Princess of Wales BFPS 3298 | 10 | 15 | *Forces* |
| (29) Althorp Northamptonshire | 10 | 15 | *T Hurlstone* |
| (30) Kensington Palace Gardens | 10 | 15 | *T Hurlstone* |
| (31) London SW1 Diana, Princess of Wales | 10 | 15 | *T Hurlstone* |
| (32) Kensington London W8, Princess of Wales | 10 | 15 | *T Hurlstone* |
| (33) The City of London, EC4 | 10 | 15 | *T Hurlstone* |
| (34) Limited Editions, Arundel | 10 | 15 | *T Hurlstone* |
| (35) England's Rose, Postcombe, Oxford | 10 | 15 | *FourPennyPost* |
| (36) Diana, Bletchley Park | 10 | 30 | *Bletchley PO* |
| (37) Capital of Wales, Cardiff | 10 | – | *Royal Mail* |
| (38) The Helping Hand, Diana Place, NW1 | 10 | 15 | *GBFDC GB* |
| (39) The Booth Catalogue | 10 | 12 | *FDP Co* |
| (40) Madame Tussaud's Baker Street | 10 | – | *n.s.c* |
| (41) London EC (St.Paul's) or London SW (Palace) | 10 | – | *n.s.c* |
| (42) North York Moors Railway, Pickering | 10 | 15 | *NYMoorsRly* |
| (43) Nene Valley Railway, Peterborough | 10 | 15 | *NVRly* |
| (44) HMShips Cornwall & Vanguard, Devonport | 10 | 15 | *RN CvrsGp 2-2* |
| (45) RNLI Althorp | 10 | 15 | *StampSearchers* |
| (46) Stirling | 10 | 30 | *RAF (P&P6)* |
| (47) NO.3 Squadron, Larkhill Salisbury | 10 | 20 | *RAF FDC 56* |

**C.D.S. POSTMARKS**

| | | | |
|---|---|---|---|
| (48) Buckingham Palace £60, or Windsor Castle | 175 | | |
| (49) Great Brington - Althorp | 60 | | |
| (50) Kensington High Street - Kensington Palace | 35 | | |
| (51) Sandringham | 275 | | |

*Also: Broadway, Earls Court, Elton, Forest Hall, Ludgate Circus,*
*The Jewel, Memorial Rd, Paris Ave., Princess Street, Sevenoaks,*
*Spencers Wood, Spencer Road, Wales   From £10.*

## 24th February 1998 - THE QUEEN'S BEASTS

*5x26p: Lion of England/Griffin of Edward III; Falcon of Plantagenet/Bull of Clarence;*
*Lion of Mortimer/Yale of Beaufort; Greyhound of Richmond/Dragon of Wales;*
*Unicorn of Scotland/Horse of Hanover*

| | | | |
|---|---|---|---|
| **SPECIAL HANDSTAMPS** (1) Philatelic Bureau | 3 | – | *Royal Mail* |
| (2) First Day of Issue – London SW1 (3 lions) | 3 | – | *Royal Mail* |
| (3) First Day of Issue – London (single lion) | 10 | – | *Royal Mail* |
| (4) First Day of Issue – Birmingham (Richard I) | 10 | – | *Royal Mail* |
| (5) Greyhound of Richmond | 10 | 15 | *BLCS 139* |

| Queen's Beasts (contd.) | ordinary covers £ | sponsored covers £ | |
|---|---|---|---|
| (6) The Yale of Beaufort, Lancaster | 10 | 20 | BenhamPilgrim |
| (7) The Silver Falcon, York | 10 | 20 | BenhamPilgrim |
| (8) The Scottish Unicorn, London SW1 | 10 | 15 | BLCS 139 |
| (9) The Lion of England, Oxford | 10 | 15 | BLCS 139 |
| (10) Richard I, Three Heraldic Leopards, Oxford .... | 10 | 15 | Ben(500)139 |
| (11) The Red Dragon of Wales, Caernarfon | 10 | 15 | BenhamCoinCvr |
| (12) The Griffin of Edward III, Windsor | 10 | 15 | BenSG40 |
| (13) Royal Armouries, Leeds | 10 | 15 | BLCS 139 |
| (14) The Heraldic Society, WC1 | 10 | 15 | LFDC 157 |
| (15) The Age of Chivalry, Windsor | 10 | 15 | VP 119 |
| (16) 650th Anniv Order of the Garter, Windsor | 10 | 30 | Bradbury |
| (17) Debrett's London SW6 | 10 | 25 | Bradbury |
| (18) The Queen's Beasts, Westminster Abbey | 10 | 15 | Westminster |
| (19) Autographed Editions, Westminster Abbey | 10 | 20 | Westminster |
| (20) City of Westminster, SW1 | 10 | 15 | RoyalMail/Mint |
| (21) The Heraldic City, London (changeable date).. | 10 | 20 | T Hurlstone |
| (22) Noak Hill Romford (changeable date) | 10 | 20 | T Hurlstone |
| (23) Herald's Place London SE11 | 10 | 15 | GBFDC GB11 |
| (24) Forgotten Beasts | 10 | 30 | PMPayne |
| (25) Order of the Garter, Buckingham Old Gaol ..... | 10 | 20 | Bletchley PO |
| (26) Queens Road Post Office, Bristol | 10 | – | n.s.c |
| (27) NatWest Philatelic Society | 10 | 30 | NWPhilSoc |
| (28) Queen's Beasts Historic Windsor | 10 | 20 | CoverCraft |
| (29) Henry V Lancaster | 10 | 15 | Steven Scott 18 |
| (30) Lincoln | 10 | 15 | RAF (P&P7) |
| (31) Dortmund-Ems Canal, Woodhall Spa | 10 | 20 | Cam S.C. |
| (32) The Flying Scotsman, Doncaster | 10 | 15 | Benham(s) |
| (33) Oldest Working Steam Loco, Liverpool | 10 | 15 | Dawn |
| (34) Mine Warfare Force in Gulf War | 10 | 15 | RN CvrsGp 2-3 |
| (35) RNLI Shieldfield | 10 | 15 | StampSearchers |
| (36) Lewis Carroll, Darlington | 10 | 25 | Bradbury |
| (37) No.23 Squadron, Gosport Hants | 10 | 15 | RAF FDC 54 |
| **C.D.S. POSTMARKS** | | | |
| (38) Arundel - home of the Earl Marshal | 10 | | |
| (39) Beaufort or Richmond | 10 | | |
| (40) Broadway, SW1 - Westminster Abbey | 10 | | |
| (41) Buckingham Palace or Windsor Castle | 125 | | |
| (42) House of Common or House of Lords | 25 | | |
| (43) Oxford - birthplace of Richard I | 10 | | |
| (44) Windsor or Windsor Great Park | 25 | | |

*Beast Bank, Clarence St. York, Falcon Lodge, Kew Gdns, Lion Green, Royal Pde, Shield Row. £7.*

## 24th March 1998 – LIGHTHOUSES

*20p St. John's Point; 26p the Smalls; 37p the Needles; 43p Bell Rock; 63p Eddystone*

| **SPECIAL HANDSTAMPS** | | | |
|---|---|---|---|
| (1) Philatelic Bureau | 3 | – | Royal Mail |
| (2) First Day of Issue – Plymouth | 3 | – | Royal Mail |
| (3) First Day of Issue – London | 10 | – | Royal Mail |
| (4) First Day of Issue – Birmingham | 10 | – | Royal Mail |
| (5) Flannan Lighthouse, Lewis | 12 | – | Royal Mail |
| (6) Grace Darling, Bamburgh | 12 | 15 | BLCS 141 |
| (7) The Original Eddystone, Plymouth | 12 | 15 | BLCS 141 |
| (8) The Smalls, St. Davids | 12 | 25 | BenhamPilgrim |
| (9) The Needles, Freshwater | 12 | 25 | BenhamPilgrim |
| (10) St. John's Point, Killough | 12 | 25 | BenhamPilgrim |
| (11) The Bell Rock, Arbroath | 12 | 15 | BLCS 141 |
| (12) 300th Anniv Eddystone Lighthouse | 12 | 15 | Ben(500)141 |
| (13) The Roman Pharos at Dover | 12 | 15 | BenL54 |
| (14) Belle Tout Lighthouse, Beachy Head | 12 | 25 | BenL55 |
| (15) 300 Years of the Eddystone Lighthouse | 12 | 15 | Westminster |
| (16) Autographed Editions, Eddystone | 12 | 20 | Westminster |
| (17) Corp. of Trinity House EC3 | 12 | 15 | LFDC 158 |
| (18) Corp. of Trinity House, Eddystone EC3 | 12 | 15 | VP 120 |
| (19) Seamark: Magazine about Lighthouses | 12 | 50 | Bradbury |
| (20) Skerries Court, Langley | 12 | 15 | GBFDC GB12 |
| (21) Belle Tout Eastbourne | 12 | 55 | HDMcIntyre |
| (22) A Guiding Light, Alum Bay | 12 | 15 | Steven Scott 19 |
| (23) Lighthouse, Reigate | 12 | 65 | Steven Scott |
| (24) Beacons Close E6 | 12 | 40 | PMPayne |
| (25) The Pharos Dover | 12 | 20 | PBarrett |
| (26) Beachy Head Eastbourne | 12 | 20 | UckPhilSoc |
| (27) Eddystone Lighthouse, Plymouth | 12 | 12 | JC Stamps |
| (28) Royal Mail Plymouth (changeable date) | 12 | – | Royal Mail |
| (29) RNLI Eddystone | 12 | 20 | StampSearchers |
| (30) Preserved Loco Eddystone | 12 | 20 | Dawn |
| (31) Lewis Carroll Beachy Head | 12 | 20 | Bradbury |
| (32) No201 Squadron, Gosport | 12 | 15 | RAF FDC 55 |
| (33) Hastings, East Sussex | 12 | 15 | RAF (P&P8) |
| (34) Royal Marines Act, Whitehall | 12 | 15 | RN CvrsGp 2-4 |
| (35) Leicester Synagogue | 12 | 35 | SKacher |
| **C.D.S. POSTMARKS** | | | |
| (36) Cawsand, Plymouth; Cliffburn, Arbroath; Dale; Killough; Totland Bay - nearest POs to lighthouses | 15 | | |
| (37) Lightouse or Seething Lane | 15 | | |

*Also: Fair Isles, Lightcliffe, Lightwater, Sandbanks, Seahouses. From £8.*

## 23rd April 1998 – COMEDIANS    ordinary cvrs    sponsored covers

*20p Tommy Cooper; 26p Eric Morecambe*
*37p Joyce Grenfell; 43p Les Dawson; 63p Peter Cook*

|  | ordinary cvrs £ | sponsored covers £ |
|---|---|---|
| **SPECIAL HANDSTAMPS** (1) Philatelic Bureau.... | 3 | – Royal Mail |
| (2) First Day of Issue – Morecambe ......................... | 3 | – Royal Mail |
| (3) First Day of Issue – London ............................... | 10 | – Royal Mail |
| (4) First Day of Issue – Birmingham ...................... | 10 | – Royal Mail |
| (5) Int. Stamp Exhibition, Stamp 98 Wembley ....... | 10 | – Royal Mail |
| (6) Stamp 98 Wembley ............................................ | 10 | 20 WalsallSecPrint |
| (7) Tommy Cooper, Caerphilly ................................ | 10 | 15 BenhamPilgrim |
| (8) Eric Morecambe, Morecambe............................. | 10 | 15 Ben500(142) |
| (9) Joyce Grenfell, London ...................................... | 10 | 15 BLCS 142 |
| (10) Les Dawson, Manchester.................................. | 10 | 20 BenhamPilgrim |
| (11) Peter Cook, Torquay ........................................ | 10 | 20 BenhamPilgrim |
| (12) Heroes of British Comedy The Mail, W8.......... | 10 | 15 Benham |
| (13) Comedy, London W1......................................... | 10 | 15 BLCS 142 |
| (14) Great British Comedy, Knightsbridge ............. | 10 | 35 Benham(Print) |
| (15) Great British Comedy, Cambridge.................... | 10 | 15 BenSG41 |
| (16) Great British Comedy, Slade............................ | 10 | 15 BLCS 142 |
| (17) Variety Club, London W1P............................... | 10 | 15 BenhamPilgrim |
| (18) Hell's Bells, Shepperton .................................. | 10 | 15 BLCS 142 |
| (19) Best of British Comedy, Morecambe................ | 10 | 15 LFDC 159 |
| (20) Oscar Wilde, Windermere ................................ | 10 | 15 VP 121 |
| (21) Tony Hancock, Birmingham............................. | 10 | 20 Bradbury |
| (22) British Comedy Greats, Blackpool .................. | 10 | 20 SculptureWks |
| (23) Britain's Comedy Legends ............................... | 10 | 15 Westminster |
| (24) Autographed Editions, London Palladium ........ | 10 | 25 Westminster |
| (25) Autographed Editions, Morecambe.................. | 10 | 25 Westminster |
| (26) Clowne, Chesterfield ....................................... | 10 | 10 GBFDC GB13 |
| (27) Comedians, Bletchley Park.............................. | 10 | 30 Bletchley PO |
| (28) Peter Cook, Satirist, London W1..................... | 10 | 15 T.Hurlstone |
| (29) Charlie Chaplin, Walworth, SE17 ................... | 10 | 15 T.Hurlstone |
| (30) Frankie Howerd, Eltham, SE........................... | 10 | 15 T.Hurlstone |
| (31) Laughter, the best Medicine............................ | 10 | 15 Steven Scott 20 |
| (32) Carry on Sergeant, Cambridge........................ | 10 | 25 Cam.S.C. |
| (33) Passport to Pimlico, Ealing W5....................... | 10 | 25 Cam.S.C. |
| (34) Caerffili, Caerffphilly...................................... | 10 | – Royal Mail |
| (35) Lewis Carroll, Rugby School............................ | 10 | 25 Bradbury |
| (36) No208 Squadron, Valley Holyhead.................. | 10 | 15 RAF FDC 57 |
| (37) RNLI Laughton................................................ | 10 | 15 StampSearchers |
| (38) HMS Hesperus, Bootle..................................... | 10 | 15 RN CvrsGp 2-6 |
| (39) Manchester...................................................... | 10 | 15 RAF (P&P9) |
| **C.D.S. POSTMARKS** | | |
| (40) Any Butlin's Holiday Camp ............................. | 25 | |
| (41) Caerphilly; Collyhurst; Fulham Rd; Morecambe | | |
|     or Torquay – birthplace or homes of comedians | | |
|     featured on stamps ............................................. | 15 | |
| (42) Giggleswick .................................................... | 15 | |

*Also: Coopers Rd., The Circle, Grenfell Rd., Knotty Ash, Pratts Bottom,*
*Reading, Shepherd's Bush.  £10.*

## 23rd June 1998 – NATIONAL HEALTH SERVICE
*20p Blood Donors; 26p Vaccinations; 43p Babies; 63p Outpatients.*

|  | ordinary cvrs £ | sponsored covers £ |
|---|---|---|
| **SPECIAL HANDSTAMPS** (1) Philatelic Bureau.... | 3 | – Royal Mail |
| (2) First Day of Issue – Tredegar ........................... | 3 | – Royal Mail |
| (3) First Day of Issue – London ............................. | 10 | – Royal Mail |
| (4) First Day of Issue – Birmingham ..................... | 10 | – Royal Mail |
| (5) National Blood Service, Watford....................... | 10 | 15 Benham |
| (6) The Royal Hospitals NHS Trust, Whitechapel . | 10 | 15 BLCS 143 |
| (7) Guy's & St.Thomas', London SE1...................... | 10 | 15 BLCS 143 |
| (8) Ebbw Vale, South Wales (portrait of Bevan).... | 10 | 15 BenL57 |
| (9) Trafford General Hospital, Manchester............. | 10 | 15 Ben500(143) |
| (10) NHS Edlington, Doncaster............................... | 10 | 15 LFDC 161 |
| (11) Florence Nightingale, East Wellow .................. | 10 | 15 VP 123 |
| (12) Heart of the Nations Healthcare, WC1............. | 10 | 20 Bradbury |
| (13) NHS Sydney Street, London SW3 .................... | 10 | 15 Steven Scott 21 |
| (14) 50th Anniv NHS, Tredegar .............................. | 10 | 15 Westminster |
| (15) Health Autographed, Tredegar ........................ | 10 | 20 Westminster |
| (16) William Beveridge, Westminster SW1 ............. | 10 | 20 T Hurlstone |
| (17) William Gladstone, Westminster SW1.............. | 10 | 20 T Hurlstone |
| (18) Gladstone Centenary, Hawarden Deeside......... | 10 | 20 T Hurlstone |
| (19) 50 years of getting better, Hale Gardens W3.... | 10 | 15 PMPayne |
| (20) The heart of the matter, Vale of Health NW3 .. | 10 | 10 GBFDC GB14 |
| (21) NatWest Philatelic Soc, St. Thomas' SE1 ......... | 10 | 15 NWPhilSoc |
| (22) Health in the Community, Uckfield.................. | 10 | 15 PBarrett |
| (23) National Health Service, Canterbury............... | 10 | 30 HDMcIntyre |
| (24) Ambrex Harrogate ASA .................................. | 10 | 25 WMAmbulance |
| (25) Scottish National Blood Transfusion ............... | 10 | 30 GlasgowBlood |
| (26) Carry On Nurse, Iver Bucks............................ | 10 | 25 Cam.S.C. |
| (27) MKCCG Milton Keynes.................................. | 10 | 25 Bletchley PO |
| (28) 100 Years Manufacturing, Enfield................... | 10 | 20 Arlington |
| (29) Royal Army Medical Corps ............................. | 10 | 20 Arlington |
| (30) The Most Famous Blood Donor, Birmingham . | 10 | 15 Bradbury |
| (31) Lewis Carroll Centenary, Oxford..................... | 10 | 25 Bradbury |
| (32) Leonard Cheshire, Westminster....................... | 10 | 15 WSORandle (s) |
| (33) Beverley .......................................................... | 10 | 15 RAF (P&P10) |

| Health Service (contd.) | ordinary covers £ | sponsored covers £ | |
|---|---|---|---|
| (34) HMS Scylla, Portsmouth | 6 | 10 | RN CvrsGp 2-7 |
| (35) Wimbledon Tennis, London SW19 | 6 | 20 | Arlington |
| (36) RNLI Healing | 6 | 10 | StampSearchers |
| (37) No55 Squadron, Castle Bromwich | 6 | 8 | RAF FDC 58 |
| (38) Nene Valley Railway | 6 | 8 | NVRly |

**C.D.S. POSTMARKS**

| | | |
|---|---|---|
| (39) Any hospital/infirmary postmark ..............*each* | 10 | |
| (40) Tredegar - birthplace of Aneurin Bevan ............ | 10 | |

*Also: Healing, Pill. from £8.*

## 21st July 1998 – MAGICAL WORLDS

*20p The Hobbit (J.R.R.Tolkien); 26p The Lion, the Witch & Wardrobe (C.S.Lewis); 37p The Phoenix and the Carpet (E.Nesbit); 43p The Borrowers (Mary Norton); 63p Through the Looking Glass (Lewis Carroll)*

**SPECIAL HANDSTAMPS**

| | | | |
|---|---|---|---|
| (1) Philatelic Bureau | 3 | – | Royal Mail |
| (2) First Day of Issue – Oxford | 3 | – | Royal Mail |
| (3) First Day of Issue – London | 10 | – | Royal Mail |
| (4) First Day of Issue – Birmingham | 10 | – | Royal Mail |
| (5) Aberdeen (cat: The Boggart) | 10 | 20 | RM Airletter |
| (6) Variety Club, London W1 | 10 | 15 | Benham |
| (7) Magical Worlds C.S.Lewis, Belfast | 10 | 15 | BLCS 144 |
| (8) Magical Worlds Lewis Carroll, Daresbury | 10 | 15 | BLCS 144 |
| (9) Magical Worlds E.Nesbit, Halstead, Kent | 10 | 15 | BLCS 144 |
| (10) Magical Worlds Mary Norton, Leighton Buzzard | 10 | 15 | BLCS 144 |
| (11) Magical Worlds J.R.R.Tolkien, Birmingham | 10 | 15 | Ben500(144) |
| (12) Centenary of the Birth of CS Lewis, Oxford | 10 | 15 | BenL58 |
| (13) Lewis Carroll, Oxford (Mad Hatter) | 10 | 25 | LFDC 162 |
| (14) 'Twas Brillig and the Slithy Toves, Oxford | 10 | 15 | VP 124 |
| (15) Birthplace of Lewis Carroll, Daresbury | 10 | 20 | Bradbury |
| (16) Alice Liddell, Lyndhurst Hants | 10 | 35 | Bradbury |
| (17) Lewis Carroll, Tom Quad, Oxford | 10 | 35 | Bradbury |
| (18) Sarehole Mill Inspired Tolkien, Birmingham | 10 | 25 | RMail B'ham |
| (19) Magical Worlds, Daresbury (open book) | 10 | 15 | Westminster |
| (20) Autographed Editions, Daresbury | 10 | 20 | Westminster |
| (21) Magical Authors, Guildford Surrey | 10 | 15 | Steven Scott |
| (22) St. Aldates, Oxford | 10 | 15 | Steven Scott 22 |
| (23) Yellow Brick Road Appeal, Newcastle | 10 | 20 | FourPennyPost |
| (24) Dillons Bookstore, Newcastle | 10 | 15 | FourPennyPost |
| (25) The Barley Field, Upminster Essex | 10 | 20 | T Hurlstone |
| (26) Dick Whittington, London | 10 | 20 | T Hurlstone |
| (27) Child's Way, London NW11 | 10 | 12 | GBFDC GB15 |
| (28) Paradise Place, London SE18 | 10 | 15 | PMPayne |
| (29) The Railway Children, Keighley | 10 | 35 | Cam S.C. |
| (30) HMS Quilliam, Belfast | 10 | 15 | RN CvrsGp 2-8 |
| (31) Belfast | 10 | 15 | RAF(P&P11) |
| (32) No27 Squadron, Hounslow | 10 | 10 | RAF FDC 59 |
| (33) Royal Tournament | 10 | 35 | Forces |
| (34) Blair Atholl Jamborette | 10 | 90 | Scouts |
| (35) Electrical Tramroad, Blackpool | 10 | 35 | Dawn |

**C.D.S. POSTMARKS**

| | | |
|---|---|---|
| (36) Guildford, Headington, Leighton Buzzard, Oxford - all associated with authors .................*each* | 12 | |
| (37) Llandudno or Lyndhurst - Alice Liddell .......*each* | 12 | |

*Also: Castle St., Belfast, Chessington, Child's Hill, Lewis Rd, Lewisham, Lilliput, Old Penshaw, Paradise, St. Mary's Bay, Underhill Circus. From £10*

## 25th August 1998 – CARNIVALS

*20p,26p,43p & 63p Scenes from the Notting Hill Carnival.*

**SPECIAL HANDSTAMPS**

| | | | |
|---|---|---|---|
| (1) Philatelic Bureau | 3 | – | Royal Mail |
| (2) First Day of Issue – London W11 (drum) | 3 | – | Royal Mail |
| (3) First Day of Issue – London (sax & bongo) | 10 | – | Royal Mail |
| (4) First Day of Issue – Birmingham | 10 | – | Royal Mail |
| (5) Notting Hill, W11 (face in sun) | 10 | 15 | RoyalMail/Mint |
| (6) London Celebrates Notting Hill (dancer) | 10 | 15 | Ben500(145) |
| (7) London Celebrations Notting Hill (dancer) | 10 | 15 | BLCS 145 |
| (8) London Celebrations Chinatown, W1 | 10 | 15 | BLCS 145 |
| (9) London Celebrations City Pageantry | 10 | 15 | BLCS 145 |
| (10) London Celebrations Pearly Kings & Queens | 10 | 15 | BLCS 145 |
| (11) Leicester Caribbean Carnival | 10 | 15 | LFDC 163 |
| (12) Notting Hill, London W11 (dancer) | 10 | 15 | VP 125 |
| (13) Carnival, Notting Hill (maracas) | 10 | 15 | Westminster |
| (14) Autographed Editions, Notting Hill | 10 | 20 | Westminster |
| (15) Largest Carnival in Europe, Notting Hill | 10 | 15 | Steven Scott 23 |
| (16) Europe's Largest Street Carnival | 10 | 15 | Cover Collection |
| (17) Carnival Notting Hill Gate | 10 | 20 | T Hurlstone |
| (18) Torchlight Carnival, Hornchurch | 10 | 20 | T Hurlstone |
| (19) The Spirit of Carnival, Notting Hill Gate | 10 | 10 | GBFDC GB16 |
| (20) Carnival, Notting Hill Gate (mask) | 10 | 15 | PMPayne |
| (21) Brazil Close, Beddington Croydon | 10 | 15 | PMPayne |
| (22) Come & Join the Dance, Daresbury | 10 | 25 | Bradbury |
| (23) No17 Squadron, Gosport | 10 | 15 | RAF FDC 60 |
| (24) RNLI postmark Merrymeet | 10 | 15 | Stamp Searchers |
| (25) Holiday on the Buses | 10 | 15 | Cam.SC |
| (26) HMS Wanderer, Devonport | 10 | 15 | RN CvrsGp 2-9 |

**Carnivals (contd.)**

| | | ordinary covers £ | sponsored covers £ |
|---|---|---|---|
| (27) | Lerwick ................................................ | 5 | 13 *RAF(P&P12)* |

**C.D.S. POSTMARKS**

| (28) | Notting Hill or Leicester - Caribbean Carnivals .... | 10 | |
| (29) | Ladbroke Grove or Portobello Rd - on route ........ | 10 | |

*Also: Bridgewater, Durham, Jamaica Street, Jamaica Road, Lerwick, Lewes, Lichfield, The Parade, Sloane Square, West India Dock. Prices from £7.*

## 29th September 1998 – SPEED

*20p Bluebird (Sir Malcolm Campbell); 26p Sunbeam (Sir Henry Seagrave);*
*30p Babs (John G Parry Thomas); 43p Railton Mobil Special (John R Cobb);*
*63p Bluebird (Donald Campbell)*

**SPECIAL HANDSTAMPS**

| (1) | Philatelic Bureau .... | 3 | – | *Royal Mail* |
|---|---|---|---|---|
| (2) | First Day of Issue – Pendine ............................... | 3 | – | *Royal Mail* |
| (3) | First Day of Issue – London ............................... | 10 | – | *Royal Mail* |
| (4) | First Day of Issue – Birmingham ....................... | 10 | – | *Royal Mail* |
| (5) | Sir Malcolm Campbell Castle Silverstone ......... | 12 | 15 | *BLCS 146* |
| (6) | Donald Cambell Horley ...................................... | 12 | 15 | *BLCS 146* |
| (7) | Sir Malcolm Campbell Castle Combe ............... | 12 | 15 | *BLCS 146* |
| (8) | Sir Malcolm Campbell Thruxton .......................... | 12 | 20 | *BenhamPilgrim* |
| (9) | Sir Malcolm Campbell Snetterton ...................... | 12 | 20 | *BenhamPilgrim* |
| (10) | Sir Malcolm Campbell Castle Donington ......... | 12 | 15 | *BLCS 146* |
| (11) | Sir Malcolm Campbell Pendine .......................... | 12 | 15 | *Ben500(146)* |
| (12) | Sir Malcolm Campbell Mail on Sunday ............. | 12 | 15 | *Benham* |
| (13) | National Motor Museum Beaulieu ...................... | 12 | 15 | *BenSG42* |
| (14) | Donald Campbell Bluebird Coniston ................. | 12 | 15 | *LFDC 164* |
| (15) | Land Speed Records Pendine .............................. | 12 | 15 | *VP 126* |
| (16) | Legends of Speed Pendine................................... | 12 | 15 | *Westminster* |
| (17) | Autographed Editions Silverstone ...................... | 12 | 15 | *Westminster* |
| (18) | Speedy Place London WC2.................................. | 12 | 15 | *Steven Scott 24* |
| (19) | Lakeland Motor Museum Holker Hall.............. | 12 | 15 | *Steven Scott* |
| (20) | Graham Hill Hendon ........................................... | 12 | 20 | *T Hurlstone* |
| (21) | Jim Clark Duns Berwickshire ............................. | 12 | 20 | *T Hurlstone* |
| (22) | Silverstone Golden Jubilee ................................. | 12 | 25 | *G Lovell* |
| (23) | Speed 98 Silverstone............................................ | 12 | 50 | *Bletchley PO* |
| (24) | Bluebird Don Wales Speed Record Attempt.... | 12 | 15 | *FourPennyPost* |
| (25) | Bentley Farnham.................................................. | 12 | 35 | *HDMcIntyre* |
| (26) | Genevieve Brighton.............................................. | 12 | 25 | *Cam S.C.* |
| (27) | Eric Morecambe................................................... | 12 | 25 | *Cam S.C.* |
| (28) | The Sound Barrier Heathrow Airport................. | 12 | 25 | *Cam S.C.* |
| (29) | Speed Heathrow Airport...................................... | 12 | 25 | *Cam S.C.* |
| (30) | Speedwell Street London...................................... | 12 | 15 | *PMPayne* |
| (31) | Hermes Way Wallington...................................... | 12 | 15 | *PMPayne* |
| (32) | Speed House Barbican......................................... | 12 | 12 | *GBFDC GB17* |
| (33) | Concorde Filton Bristol....................................... | 12 | - | *R Pratten* |
| (34) | Lewis Carroll Coniston ....................................... | 12 | 20 | *Bradbury* |
| (35) | Harrow.................................................................. | 12 | 15 | *RAF(P&P13)* |
| (36) | No12 Squadron, Salisbury................................... | 12 | 15 | *RAF FDC 61* |
| (37) | RNLI Postmark Speedwell................................... | 12 | 15 | *StampSearchers* |
| (38) | RAFLET Stamp Club............................................ | 12 | 15 | *RAFLET* |
| (39) | Liverpool FC Return to Europe .......................... | 12 | 15 | *Dawn* |
| (40) | The Fast Ball Instow Bideford............................ | 12 | 20 | *Instow PO* |
| (41) | A Tribute to the Brave Men....Scapa Flow........ | 12 | 15 | *RN CvrsGp 2-10* |

**C.D.S. POSTMARKS**

| (42) | Beaulieu - National Motor Museum ..................... | 15 | |
| (43) | Chislehurst - Birthplace of Malcolm Campbell...... | 15 | |
| (44) | Silverstone , Weybridge or RAC.......................... | 15 | |
| (45) | Pendine, Coniston or Windermere........................ | 15 | |

*The Drive, Elvington, Fort Augustus, Mansell Rd, The Rocket. From £10.*

## 2nd November 1998 – CHRISTMAS

*20p, 26p, 30p, 43p, 63p Angels*

**SPECIAL HANDSTAMPS**

| (1) | Philatelic Bureau .... | 3 | – | *Royal Mail* |
|---|---|---|---|---|
| (2) | First Day of Issue – Bethlehem ........................... | 3 | – | *Royal Mail* |
| (3) | First Day of Issue – London ............................... | 10 | – | *Royal Mail* |
| (4) | First Day of Issue – Birmingham ....................... | 10 | – | *Royal Mail* |
| (5) | Happy Christmas Royal Mail London EC1....... | 10 | – | *Royal Mail* |
| (6) | Hear the Christmas Angels Nasareth.................. | 10 | 15 | *BLCS 148* |
| (7) | Silent Night Holy Night Bethlehem ................... | 10 | 15 | *BLCS 148* |
| (8) | Sing Choirs of Angels Chrismas Common......... | 10 | 15 | *BLCS 148* |
| (9) | Born a King Wiseman's Bridge ........................... | 10 | 15 | *BLCS 148* |
| (10) | Gloria in Excelcis Angel Bank............................ | 10 | 15 | *Ben500(148)* |
| (11) | Bethlehem ............................................................ | 10 | 15 | *LFDC 165* |
| (12) | Nasareth ............................................................... | 10 | 15 | *VP 127* |
| (13) | Godshill Isle of Wight ........................................ | 10 | 15 | *Bradbury* |
| (14) | Christmas Greetings Lewis Carroll..................... | 10 | 15 | *Bradbury* |
| (15) | Autographed Editions Bethlehem ....................... | 10 | 20 | *Westminster* |
| (16) | Merry Christmas Bethlehem ............................... | 10 | 15 | *Westminster* |
| (17) | Canterbury Cathedral........................................... | 10 | 15 | *Steven Scott* |
| (18) | Angel Court London EC2..................................... | 10 | 15 | *Steven Scott 25* |
| (19) | The Angel Islington ............................................ | 10 | 15 | *T Hurlstone* |
| (20) | Chronic Pain South Ockendon ............................ | 10 | 15 | *T Hurlstone* |
| (21) | Bletchley Milton Keynes ..................................... | 10 | 25 | *Bletchley PO* |
| (22) | The Alhambra Theatre Bradford.......................... | 10 | 15 | *J Cook* |
| (23) | North Pole Road London W10 ............................ | 10 | 25 | *PMPayne* |
| (24) | St Nicholas Road London SE18........................... | 10 | 25 | *PMPayne* |

| Christmas (contd.) | ordinary covers £ | sponsored covers £ | |
|---|---|---|---|
| (25) Angel Lane London E15 | 10 | 12 | GBFDC GB18 |
| (26) The Salvation Army Kettering | 10 | 15 | DCopper |
| (27) Murder on the Orient Express | 10 | 25 | Cam S.C. |
| (28) Imperial War Museum Duxford | 10 | 25 | Cam S.C. |
| (29) Are You Being Served? Oxford Street | 10 | 25 | Cam S.C. |
| (30) Oxford | 10 | 15 | RAF(P&P14) |
| (31) No 31 Squadron, Farnborough | 10 | 10 | RAF FDC 62 |
| (32) RNLI Postmark Bethlehem | 10 | 15 | StampSearchers |
| (33) Christmas Angels Whitfield | 10 | 15 | PBarrett |
| (34) 25th Anniversary Tandy Walsall | 10 | 20 | Tandy |
| (35) The Midweek Club Farnborough | 10 | 25 | ROsborne |
| (36) Christmas Greetings HM Ships Plymouth | 10 | 15 | RN CvrsGp 2-11 |
| (37) Royal Mail New HQ Birmingham | 10 | 125 | Royal Mail |

**C.D.S. POSTMARKS**

| | | |
|---|---|---|
| (38) Angel Hill, Holy Island or Nasareth ............ *each* | 10 | |

*Also: Godshill, Chapel House, Jerusalem Street, Kew, Noel Road. Prices from £7*

# Millennium Stamps 1999-2001

To celebrate the new millennium Royal Mail devoted the whole of its special stamps programme for 1999 to British history and achievement over the past 1,000 years. Each stamp is numbered, the first issue being numbered 48, 47, 46 and 45 - the final set of the year being 4, 3, 2 and 1 - Royal Mail's countdown to the new millennium. The stamps for 2000 concentrates on Millennium funded projects such as the Eden Project. The Millennium Series ended in January 2001 with a set titled The Future.

## 1999 INVENTORS' TALE

### 12th January 1999 – INVENTORS' TALE

*20p Time, 26p Steam Power, 43p Photography, 63p Computers*

**SPECIAL HANDSTAMPS          SPONSOR**
**Price Guide Ordinary Covers £4-£9 / Sponsored Covers:**

| | | |
|---|---|---|
| (1) | FDI - Bureau | Royal Mail (n.s.c.) |
| (2) | FDI - Greenwich | Royal Mail (n.s.c.) |
| (3) | -do- non pictorial version | Royal Mail (n.s.c.) |
| (4) | Inventors' Tale Glasgow | Royal Mail (n.s.c.) |
| (5) | Steam Power Birmingham | Royal Mail (n.s.c.) |
| (6) | Photography Lacock ............£15 | Benham BLCS150 |
| (7) | Steam Power Newcastle ........£20 | Benham Pilgrim |
| (8) | Technology London SW7 ......£15 | Benham BLCS150 |
| (9) | Timekeeping Greenwich ........£15 | Benham BLCS150 |
| (10) | John Harrison Greenwich ......£25 | Benham Coin Mil.1 |
| (11) | John Harrison Foulby ............£25 | Benham 500(150) |
| (12) | Stonehenge ............................£20 | Benham Eng.Heritage |
| (13) | Steam Power Glasgow ..........£20 | Bradbury LFDC 166 |
| (14) | Steam Power Paddington ......£20 | Bradbury VP 128 |
| (15) | Robert Stephenson Newc'tle .£20 | Bradbury |
| (16) | Autographed Editions ............£25 | Westminster |
| (17) | Greenwich Millennium ..........£15 | Westminster |
| (18) | Lacock Chippenham ..............£30 | Steven Scott Plat.1 |
| (19) | Euston London ......................£20 | Steven Scott 26 |
| (20) | John Harrison Foulby ............£25 | FourpennyPost |
| (21) | Millennium Dome ..................£25 | T Hurlstone |
| (22) | Collosus ................................£35 | Bletchley PO |
| (23) | Trevithick Trust ....................£30 | J Henty |
| (24) | Bell Drive ..............................£30 | P M Payne |
| (25) | The Locomotive......................£30 | M Brazier (Pubs.1) |
| (26) | Engineers Way ......................£20 | GB19 |
| (27) | Homer Drive ..........................£35 | M J Kingsland |
| (28) | Power Road ............................£30 | P Sheridan |
| (29) | Timeball Tower......................£30 | H D MacIntyre |
| (30) | Shuttleworth Collection..........£20 | BritHerCollect |
| (31) | Charles Babbage ....................£20 | RN CvrsGpTDFC1-01 |
| (32) | Operation Pungent..................£20 | RN CvrsGpNFDC3-01 |
| (33) | East Grinstead Stamp Club....£25 | E GrinStampClub |
| (34) | Adhesive Postage Stamp........£25 | P Barrett |
| (35) | Sion Cop Whitehall ..............£20 | Benham/JS Medal 1 |
| (36) | The Wooden Horse ................£35 | Cam S.C. |
| (37) | Man in White Suit ..................£35 | Cam S.C. |
| (38) | Whisky Galore ......................£35 | Cam S.C. |
| (39) | Flying Scotsman ....................£35 | Cam S.C. |
| (40) | She Elstree Studios ................£35 | Cam S.C. |
| (41) | Satanic Rites Elstree ..............£35 | Cam S.C. |
| (42) | Total Eclipse Penzance ..........£35 | Bradbury |

**C.D.S. POSTMARKS Price Guide £10-£15**
(43) James Watt Dock, New Invention or The Rocket
(44) Clockface, Greenwich, Meridian Centre or Salisbury
(45) Any colliery pmk, Lacock, New Crofton or Smethwick
(46) Bletchley or Whitworth (Manchester)
(47) Science Museum

## 2nd February 1999 – TRAVELLERS' TALE
*20p Global travel, 26p Bicycle, 43p Linking the Nation,*
*63p Captain Cook - Exploration.*

### 1999 TRAVELLERS' TALE

| | | | |
|---|---|---|---|
| **SPECIAL HANDSTAMPS** | **SPONSOR** | | |

**Price Guide Ordinary Covers £4-£9 / Sponsored Covers:**

| | | | |
|---|---|---|---|
| (1) | FDI - Bureau | | *Royal Mail (n.s.c.)* |
| (2) | FDI - Coventry | | *Royal Mail (n.s.c.)* |
| (3) | -do- non pictorial version | | *Royal Mail (n.s.c.)* |
| (4) | Travellers' Tale Glasgow | | *Royal Mail (n.s.c.)* |
| (5) | Longbridge Birmingham | | *Royal Mail (n.s.c.)* |
| (6) | Air Travel Concorde | £20 | *Benham BLCS 151* |
| (7) | Linking the Nation Ports'th | £15 | *Benham BLCS 151* |
| (8) | Marton in Cleveland | £15 | *Benham BLCS 151* |
| (9) | Brunel, Paddington Station | £25 | *Benham 500(151)* |
| (10) | The Rocket Rainhill Prescot | £25 | *Benham Coin Mil.2* |
| (11) | Courthill Dumfries | £20 | *Benham Pilgrim* |
| (12) | English Heritage Tintagel | £20 | *Benham Eng.Heritage* |
| (13) | Global Travel Heathrow | £20 | *Bradbury LFDC 167* |
| (14) | Meriden Coventry | £20 | *Bradbury VP 129* |
| (15) | Sir Frank Whittle | £35 | *Bradbury* |
| (16) | Flying Scotsman | £35 | *Bradbury* |
| (17) | Global Travel The Comet | £30 | *Bradbury* |
| (18) | The Millennium Pall Mall | £15 | *Westminster* |
| (19) | Autographed Editions | £25 | *Westminster* |
| (20) | Sir Francis Drake Tavistock | £30 | *Steven Scott Plat.2* |
| (21) | Whittle Cranford Sleaford | £20 | *Steven Scott 27* |
| (22) | James Cook Marton | £25 | *FourpennyPost* |
| (23) | Luton Airport | £30 | *T Hurlstone* |
| (24) | James Cook Barking Essex | £30 | *T Hurlstone* |
| (25) | The Bike Man, Upminster | £30 | *T Hurlstone* |
| (26) | Mail Travels the World | £35 | *Bletchley PO* |
| (27) | The Travellers Rest | £25 | *M Brazier (Pubs.2)* |
| (28) | Ulysses Road | £40 | *P M Payne* |
| (29) | Great Malvern | £35 | *A Wright* |
| (30) | Captain Cook | £15 | *GB20* |
| (31) | Chichester Sussex | £30 | *M J Kingsland* |
| (32) | Transporter Bridge | £30 | *P Sheridan* |
| (33) | NYMR Millennium Stamps | £25 | *NYMRly* |
| (34) | St Andrew the Great | £30 | *B A Downham* |
| (35) | Supermarine S6 | £25 | *BritHerCollect* |
| (36) | Linking Nations Saltash | £25 | *RN CvrsGpTDFC1-02* |
| (37) | HMS Westcott | £25 | *RN CvrsGpNFDC3-02* |
| (38) | King George V loco | £25 | *Dawn* |
| (39) | Raflet Stamp Club | £25 | *RAFLET* |
| (40) | Anglo-Boer War Whitehall | £25 | *Benham/JS Medal 2* |
| (41) | Royal Mail Norwich | £30 | *Royal Mail* |
| (42) | Princess Diana Tribute | £25 | *Steven Scott* |
| (43) | The Belles of St.Trinians | £40 | *Cam S.C.* |
| (44) | Private's Progress | £40 | *Cam S.C.* |
| (45) | On The Buses | £40 | *Cam S.C.* |
| (46) | The Blue Lamp | £40 | *Cam S.C.* |
| (47) | Death of Howard Carter | £40 | *Cam S.C.* |
| (48) | Scott of the Antarctic | £40 | *Cam S.C.* |
| (49) | Dutch U-Boat Pens | £40 | *Cam S.C.* |
| (50) | Total Eclipse Torquay | £30 | *Bradbury* |

**C.D.S. POSTMARKS Price Guide £10-£15**

| | |
|---|---|
| (51) | Heathrow Airport, Luton, Filton or Glasgow Airport |
| (52) | Dumfries, Thornhill, Raleigh or Marton in Cleveland |
| (53) | Any TPO, station or junction postmark, Whitby |

## 2nd March 1999 – PATIENTS' TALE
*20p Vaccination, 26p Nursing, 43p Penicillin,*
*63p Test-tube baby.*

### 1999 PATIENTS' TALE

| | | | |
|---|---|---|---|
| **SPECIAL HANDSTAMPS** | **SPONSOR** | | |

**Price Guide Ordinary Covers £4-£9 / Sponsored Covers:**

| | | | |
|---|---|---|---|
| (1) | FDI - Bureau | | *Royal Mail (n.s.c.)* |
| (2) | FDI - Oldham | | *Royal Mail (n.s.c.)* |
| (3) | -do- non pictorial version | | *Royal Mail (n.s.c.)* |
| (4) | Patients' Tale Glasgow | | *Royal Mail (n.s.c.)* |
| (5) | QE Hospital Birmingham | | *Royal Mail (n.s.c.)* |
| (6) | Sir Alexander Fleming W2 | £25 | *Benham 500(153)* |
| (7) | Patients, Nursing W1 | £15 | *Benham BLCS 153* |
| (8) | In-vitro Fertilisation | £15 | *Benham BLCS 153* |
| (9) | Inoculations Berkeley | £25 | *Benham Pilgrim* |
| (10) | Penicillin Lochfield | £15 | *Benham BLCS 153* |
| (11) | Lambeth Palace Road | £20 | *Benham Coin Mil.3* |
| (12) | English Heritage Dover | £20 | *Benham Eng.Heritage* |
| (13) | Nursing Edinburgh | £20 | *Bradbury LFDC 168* |
| (14) | Patient Care WC1 | £20 | *Bradbury VP 130* |
| (15) | Aneurin Bevan Tredegar | £40 | *Bradbury* |
| (16) | Jenner Museum Berkeley | £50 | *Bradbury* |
| (17) | Festival of Medicine | £35 | *Bradbury (for BMA)* |
| (18) | The Millennium | £15 | *Westminster* |
| (19) | Autographed Editions | £25 | *Westminster* |
| (20) | 1st Test Tube Baby Oldham | £20 | *Steven Scott 28* |

## 1999 PATIENTS' TALE

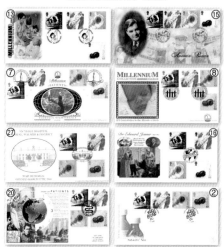

## 6th April 1999 – SETTLERS' TALE

*20p Migration to Scotland, 26p Pilgrim Fathers,*
*43p Colonisation of Australia, 63p Migration to UK.*

## 1999 SETTLERS' TALE

## 1999 WORKERS' TALE

## 4th May 1999 – WORKERS' TALE

*19p Weaver's Craft, 26p Mill Towns,*
*44p Shipbuilding, 64p City Finance.*

(7) Shipbuilding Belfast.................£15 *Benham*
(8) Mill Towns Blackburn...........£15 *Benham BLCS 155*
(9) City Finance, EC ......................£15 *Benham BLCS 155*
(10) Weaver's Craft..........................£20 *Benham Pilgrim*
(11) Barrow-in-Furness .................£25 *Ben500(155)*
(12) Shipbuilding & Tunnels.........£20 *Benham Coin Mil.5*
(13) Lindisfarne...............................£20 *Benham Eng.Heritage*
(14) Financial Trading, EC .............£20 *Bradbury LFDC 170*
(15) Lavenham, Suffolk...................£20 *Bradbury VP 132*
(16) Richard Arkwright ..................£40 *Bradbury*
(17) City of London.........................£15 *Westminster*
(18) Autographed Editions .............£25 *Westminster*
(19) Armoury Way, SW18 .............£20 *Steven Scott Plat.5*
(20) Great Western Dock ...............£30 *Steven Scott 30*
(21) Wallsend, Shipbuilding ..........£25 *FourpennyPost*
(22) Financial Capital .....................£25 *T Hurlstone*
(23) The Dry Dock Londonderry...£30 *M Brazier (Pubs.5)*
(24) Beehive Place ...........................£30 *PMPayne*
(25) Post Office Way, SW8..............£15 *GB23*
(26) Quarry Bank Mill Wilmslow .£55 *P Sheridan*
(27) The Dambusters........................£20 *BritHerCollect*
(28) Worker's Tales, London .........£20 *RN CvrsGpTDFC1-05*
(29) HMS Sheffield ..........................£20 *RN CvrsGpNFDC3-05*
(30) New Romney .............................£45 *H D MacIntyre*
(31) NatWest Philatelic Soc ...........£25 *NWPhilSoc*
(32) Operation Kindertransports...£40 *S Kacher*
(33) Salvation Army Sunbury........£20 *J A Deakins*
(34) National Postal Museum .......£25 *NPM (AGM 98 cvr)*
(35) Gallipoli 84th Anniversary....£20 *Benham/JS Medal 5*
(36) Andover....................................£20 *RAF(P&P17)*
(37) Total Eclipse Camborne .........£35 *Bradbury*
**C.D.S. POSTMARKS Price Guide £10-£15**
(38) Arkwright Town, Cranbrook, Saltaire, Lavenham,
(39) Cotton Tree, Lombard Street, Wool, Pounds, Jarrow
(40) Any Colliery pmk., Barrow, Belfast, Clydebank, Govan

## 1st June 1999 – ENTERTAINERS' TALE
*19p Freddie Mercury, 26p 1966 World Cup,*
*44p Doctor Who, 64p Charlie Chaplin.*
**SPECIAL HANDSTAMPS**      **SPONSOR**
Price Guide Ordinary Covers £4-£9 / Sponsored Covers:
(1) FDI - Bureau ..................................£ *Royal Mail (n.s.c.)*
(2) FDI - Wembley..............................£ *Royal Mail (n.s.c.)*
(3) -do- non pictorial version ............£ *Royal Mail (n.s.c.)*
(4) Hollywood, Birmingham ..............£ *Royal Mail (n.s.c.)*
(5) Entertainers' Tale Glasgow..........£ *Royal Mail (n.s.c.)*
(6) Birmingham Repertory .................£ *Royal Mail (n.s.c.)*
(7) Cinema Classics, Walworth ...£15 *BLCS 158*
(8) Football's Glory, Wembley......£15 *BLCS 158*
(9) Cult Television, London W1..£20 *Benham Pilgrim*
(10) Charity Concerts, Wembley ...£40 *Benham 500(158)*
(11) That's Entertainment, Ealing..£20 *Benham Coin Mil.6*
(12) Kenwood House.......................£20 *Benham Eng.Heritage*
(13) Cult Television, W12 .............£20 *Bradbury LFDC 171*
(14) Music Festival, Aldeburgh.....£20 *Bradbury VP 133*
(15) Lillie Langtry, Drury Lane .....£45 *Bradbury*
(16) 1966 World Cup, Wembley ....£20 *Bradbury (s)*
(17) Pop Culture, Wembley ...........£35 *Bradbury(LiveAid cvr)*
(18) The Millennium Wembley......£15 *Westminster*
(19) Autographed The Palladium ..£25 *Westminster*
(20) Autographed Wembley ...........£ *Westminster*
(21) Autographed Wood Lane.......£25 *Westminster*
(22) East Street London SE17 .......£30 *Steven Scott Plat.6*
(23) Olympic Way, Wembley ........£20 *Steven Scott 31*
(24) Baker Street, London NW1 ...£20 *Steven Scott*
(25) John Logie Baird, ....................£25 *FourpennyPost*
(26) Charlie Chaplin, .....................£30 *T Hurlstone*
(27) The King of Comedy, .............£30 *M Brazier (Pubs.6)*
(28) World Cup Rugby, .................£30 *P M Payne*
(29) Wimbledon .............................£35 *P M Payne*
(30) Football Lane Harrow............£20 *GB24*
(31) Auto Quest Stadium Widnes .£25 *P Sheridan*
(32) D-Day 1944-1999 Ramsgate ..£25 *BritHerCollect*
(33) Freddie Mercury......................£75 *Richard Gray*
(34) Entertaining at Wembley.......£20 *RN CvrsGpTDFC1-07*
(35) HMS Renown Devonport ......£20 *RN CvrsGpNFDC3-07*
(36) Augusta Rd Twickenham.......£30 *M J Kingsland*
(37) Home of Legends .....................£20 *P Barrett*
(38) American Express Brighton ...£20 *Woodford Sports Cvrs*
(39) Bobby Moore/West Ham .......£20 *Dawn*
(40) Toy & Model Shop, Margate ..£20 *Ashford Stamp Shop*
(41) Dr Who & Daleks,..................£45 *Cam S.C.*
(42) Leicester Square ......................£20 *A. Wright*
(43) The Somme, Whitehall ...........£20 *Benham/JS Medal 6*
(44) Aldershot.................................£20 *RAF(P&P18)*
(45) Total Eclipse, Helston .............£35 *Bradbury*

## 1999 WORKERS' TALE

## 1999 ENTERTAINERS' TALE

133

## 1999 ROYAL WEDDING

**C.D.S. POSTMARKS Price Guide £10-£15**
(46) Aldeburgh, Cults, Hollywood, West End
(47) Moore, Wembley, Wembley Park,
(48) Rock, Shepherd's Bush, World's End, Walworth

## 15th June 1999 – ROYAL WEDDING
*26p & 64p HRH Prince Edward & Miss Sophie Rhys-Jones.*

| SPECIAL HANDSTAMPS | SPONSOR |
|---|---|

**Price Guide Ordinary Covers £4-£9 / Sponsored Covers:**
(1) FDI - Bureau ................................. *Royal Mail (n.s.c.)*
(2) FDI - Windsor ............................... *Royal Mail (n.s.c.)*
(3) -do- non pictorial version ............ *Royal Mail (n.s.c.)*
(4) Sandringham, Norfolk .................. *Royal Mail (n.s.c.)*
(5) Buckingham Palace Rd .........£20 *Benham Coin Cover*
(6) Windsor (rose).........................£25 *Benham 500(161)*
(7) Royal Wedding, Windsor.......£15 *Benham BLCS 161*
(8) The Mail on Sunday ...............£15 *Benham*
(9) Windsor (Cypher) ...................£15 *Bradbury LFDC 178*
(10) Windsor (Chapel)...................£15 *Bradbury VP 140*
(11) Autographed Windsor ...........£25 *Westminster*
(12) Royal Wedding Windsor........£15 *Westminster*
(13) Castle Hill Windsor (Chapel).£15 *Steven Scott*
(14) Castle Hill Windsor (Heart) ..£15 *Steven Scott*
(15) St Georges Chapel (circle).........£20 *T Hurlstone*
(16) St Georges Chapel (oval)...........£20 *T Hurlstone*
(17) St Georges Chapel (rectangle)...£20 *T Hurlstone*
(18) Windsor (bells) .......................£20 *T Hurlstone*
(19) Prince Edward Road (roses) ..£20 *P M Payne*
(20) Prince Edward Road (cupid) .£15 *GB25*
(21) Windsor (rings) .......................£20 *BritHerCollect*
(22) Windsor (bells, horseshoes) ..£20 *RN CvrsGpTDFC1-08*
(23) Dracula Prince of Darkness....£35 *Cam S.C.*
(24) Victory in the Falklands ........£20 *RN CvrsGpNFDC3-08*
(25) Tavistock Cricket Club...........£20 *Stuart Mundy*
**C.D.S. POSTMARKS Price Guide £10-£15**
(26) Any Windsor pmk, Bagshot, Brenchley or Oxford
(27) Buckingham Palace or Windsor Castle £75 each

## 6th July 1999 – CITIZENS' TALE
*19p Votes for Women, 26p Right to Health,*
*44p Right to Learn, 64p Magna Carta.*

| SPECIAL HANDSTAMPS | SPONSOR |
|---|---|

**Price Guide Ordinary Covers £4-£9 / Sponsored Covers:**
(1) FDI - Bureau ................................. *Royal Mail (n.s.c.)*
(2) FDI - Powys Newtown ................. *Royal Mail (n.s.c.)*
(3) -do- non pictorial version ............ *Royal Mail (n.s.c.)*
(4) Education for All, Birmingham.... *Royal Mail (n.s.c.)*
(5) Citizens' Tale Glasgow ................ *Royal Mail (n.s.c.)*
(6) Votes for Women.....................£15 *Benham BLCS 162*
(7) Right to Health, Enfield...........£20 *Benham Pilgrim*
(8) Right to Learn, Lanark ...........£15 *Benham BLCS 162*
(9) First Rights, Runnymede.........£20 *Benham*
(10) Signing of the Magna Carta ...£25 *Benham 500(162)*
(11) People's Rights Parl. Sq .........£20 *Benham Coin Mil.7*
(12) Audley End ..............................£20 *Benham Eng.Heritage*
(13) Magna Carta 1215, Egham ....£20 *Bradbury LFDC 172*
(14) Parliament Square...................£20 *Bradbury VP 134*
(15) Emmeline Pankhurst ..............£35 *Bradbury*
(16) The Millennium Runnymede .£15 *Westminster*
(17) Autographed New Lanark......£25 *Westminster*
(18) Davidson Terrace, E7.............£20 *Steven Scott 32*
(19) Parliament Square, SW1........£30 *Steven Scott Plat.7*
(20) New Lanark..............................£25 *FourpennyPost*
(21) John Stuart Mill .......................£25 *T Hurlstone*
(22) Environmental Health.............£25 *T Hurlstone*
(23) Runnymede Hotel, Egham.....£20 *M Brazier (Pubs.7)*
(24) Milton Keynes Citizen............£20 *Bletchley PO*
(25) French Place, London E1.......£30 *P M Payne*
(26) Pankhurst Close, SE14...........£20 *GB26*
(27) Right to Vote, Widnes.............£20 *P Sheridan*
(28) Avro Lancaster Whitehall .....£20 *BritHerCollect*
(29) Citizens' Rights London ........£20 *RN CvrsGpTDFC1-09*
(30) HMS Shark Harwich ..............£20 *RN CvrsGpNFDC3-09*
(31) East Borough School...............£30 *EBorough Sch & PTA*
(32) South Cerney 999-1999 ..........£40 *South Cerney PO*
(33) 617 Sqn Woodhall Spa ..........£35 *Cam S.C.*
(34) Top Secret, Borehamwood......£35 *Cam S.C.*
(35) Carry on Teacher, Ealing........£35 *Cam S.C.*
(36) Compiegne, Whitehall............£20 *Benham/JS Medal 7*
(37) York ..........................................£20 *RAF(P&P19)*
(38) Total Eclipse, St. Just...............£35 *Bradbury*
**C.D.S. POSTMARKS Price Guide £10-£15**
(39) Egham, Salisbury, New Lanark or Newtown
(40) Manchester, Parliament Street, House of Commons
(41) Waterloo, Kielder

## 1999 CITIZENS' TALE

## 3rd August 1999 – SCIENTISTS' TALE
*19p Decoding DNA, 26p Darwin's Theory,*
*44p Faraday's Electricity, 64p Newton.*

**SPECIAL HANDSTAMPS**          **SPONSOR**
**Price Guide Ordinary Covers £4-£9 / Sponsored Covers:**
(1)  FDI - Bureau.................................. *Royal Mail (n.s.c.)*
(2)  FDI - Cambridge ........................... *Royal Mail (n.s.c.)*
(3)  -do- non pictorial version ............ *Royal Mail (n.s.c.)*
(4)  Scientists' Tale, Birmingham ........ *Royal Mail (n.s.c.)*
(5)  Scientists' Tale Glasgow .............. *Royal Mail (n.s.c.)*
(6)  Electricity, London SE1..........£15 *Benham*
(7)  Evoulution, Shrewsbury.........£20 *Benham Pilgrim*
(8)  Space Observation .................£15 *Benham BLCS 163*
(9)  Decoding DNA, Cambridge...£15 *Benham BLCS 163*
(10) The Royal Society ...................£20 *Benham 500(163)*
(11) Down House, Downe..............£20 *Benham Coin Mil.8*
(12) Battle Abbey ............................£20 *Benham Eng.Heritage*
(13) Theory of Evolution, SW7.......£20 *Bradbury LFDC 173*
(14) Sir Isaac Newton......................£20 *Bradbury VP 135*
(15) Charles Darwin, SW7.............£35 *Bradbury*
(16) The Hubble Telescope, SW7 .£45 *Bradbury*
(17) Festival of Medicine................£35 *Bradbury for BMA*
(18) Royal Institution, London .....£15 *Westminster*
(19) Autographed Newington ........£25 *Westminster*
(20) Jupiter Way, London N7 ......£30 *Steven Scott Plat.8*
(21) Moon Street, London N1.......£20 *Steven Scott 33*
(22) Michael Faraday, Southwark.£25 *FourpennyPost*
(23) Charles Darwin, SW7.............£25 *T Hurlstone*
(24) Sir Isaac Newton, Grantham.£25 *M Brazier (Pubs.8)*
(25) Turing Bombe, Bletchley .......£20 *Bletchley PO*
(26) Twining Ave, Middx ..............£25 *P M Payne*
(27) Pierre & Marie Curie .............£25 *P M Payne*
(28) Faraday Way, London SE18...£20 *GB27*
(29) Jodrell Bank Macclesfield......£25 *P Sheridan*
(30) Jodrell Bank Macclesfield......£20 *P Barrett*
(31) Birmingham (microscope).....£20 *RN CvrsGpTDFC1-10*
(32) HMS Dauntless .....................£20 *RN CvrsGpNFDC3-10*
(33) Lord of the Flies, Newquay....£35 *Cam S.C.*
(34) The Mindbenders, Chelsea....£35 *Cam S.C.*
(35) Dr Jekyll & Sister Hyde.........£35 *Cam S.C.*
(36) Miramshah, Whitehall............£20 *Benham/JS Medal 8*
(37) Total Eclipse, Falmouth .........£35 *Bradbury*
(38) Red Dwarf, London...............£25 *Steven Scott*
**C.D.S. POSTMARKS Price Guide £10-£15**
(39) Science Museum, Cambridge, Albermarle St., Teddington
(40) Faraday Avenue, Newton
(41) Colsterworth, Downe, Frankwell

## 11th August 1999 – TOTAL SOLAR ECLIPSE
*£2.56 Miniature Sheet comprising 4 x 64p Scientists' Tale.*
**SPECIAL HANDSTAMPS**          **SPONSOR**
**Price Guide Ordinary Covers £4-£9 / Sponsored Covers:**
(1)  FDI - Bureau.................................. *Royal Mail (n.s.c.)*
(2)  FDI - Falmouth ............................. *Royal Mail (n.s.c.)*
(3)  -do- non pictorial version ............ *Royal Mail (n.s.c.)*
(4)  Falmouth (oval) .......................£15 *Benham BLCS 164*
(5)  Falmouth (circle) .....................£15 *Benham BLCS 164*
(6)  Falmouth (circle) .....................£30 *Ben500(164)*
(7)  Falmouth (film strip) ...............£30 *Benham Coin C46*
(8)  Line of Totality, Falmouth .....£25 *Bradbury*
(9)  Line of Totality, Kingston.......£50 *Bradbury*
(10) Total Solar Eclipse ..................£15 *Westminster*
(11) Autographed, Isles of Scilly ...£25 *Westminster*
(12) Falmouth (sun)........................£20 *P Barrett*
(13) Land's End, Penzance.............£45 *S Wales Collectables*
(14) Eclipse Road ............................£20 *P M Payne*
(15) Walking on the Moon.............£20 *BritHerCollect*
(16) BAA Total Eclipse Truro ........ *Cam S.C. (n.s.c.)*
(17) Jodrell Bank Macclesfield......£25 *P Sheridan*
(18) Folland Midge, Hamble .........£25 *C Greaves*
**C.D.S. POSTMARKS Price Guide £15-£20**
(19) Falmouth, St. Ives, Greenwich, The Science Museum
(20) Shade, Blackshade

## 7th September 1999 – FARMERS' TALE
*19p Strip Farming, 26p Mechanical Farming,*
*44p Food from afar, 64p Satellite Agriculture.*
**SPECIAL HANDSTAMPS**          **SPONSOR**
**Price Guide Ordinary Covers £4-£9 / Sponsored Covers:**
(1)  FDI - Bureau.................................. *Royal Mail (n.s.c.)*
(2)  FDI - Laxton, Newark ................. *Royal Mail (n.s.c.)*
(3)  -do- non pictorial version ............ *Royal Mail (n.s.c.)*
(4)  Bull Ring Centre, Birmingham....... *Royal Mail (n.s.c.)*
(5)  Farmers' Tale Glasgow ................. *Royal Mail (n.s.c.)*
(6)  Strip Farming, Laxton ...........£15 *Benham BLCS 165*

### 1999 SCIENTISTS' TALE

### 1999 SOLAR ECLIPSE

## 1999 FARMERS' TALE

## 1999 SOLDIERS' TALE

(7) Mechanical Farming.................£15 *Benham BLCS 165*
(8) Food from afar.........................£20 *Benham*
(9) Satellite Agriculture.................£20 *Benham Pilgrim*
(10) Sir Walter Raleigh/Potato .....£20 *Benham 500(165)*
(11) The Changing Land, Laxton..£20 *Benham Coin Mil.9*
(12) English Heritage Kenilworth .£20 *Benham Eng.Heritage*
(13) Farmers, Stoneleigh ...............£20 *Bradbury LFDC 174*
(14) Farmers, Sheepscombe...........£20 *Bradbury VP 136*
(15) Robert Bakewell, Leicester.....£45 *Bradbury*
(16) NFU Shaftesbury Ave.............£15 *Westminster*
(17) Autographed Whitehall..........£25 *Westminster*
(18) Farm Lane London SW6.........£20 *Steven Scott 34*
(19) King William Street, EC4 ......£30 *Steven Scott Plat.9*
(20) Emmerdale, Esholt Shipley....£15 *Steven Scott*
(21) Jethro Tull, Reading...............£25 *FourpennyPost*
(22) Old Macdonalds Farm ...........£25 *T Hurlstone*
(23) The Farmers, Charlbury.........£25 *M Brazier (Pubs.9)*
(24) Farmers Road, London SE5 ..£25 *P M Payne*
(25) Farmer's Road London SE5...£20 *GB28*
(26) Congleton, Cheshire ..............£20 *P Sheridan*
(27) Farmer's Training...................£20 *RN CvrsGpTDFC1-11*
(28) HMS Swiftsure.......................£20 *RN CvrsGpNFDC3-11*
(29) Spitfire, Biggin Hill ...............£20 *BritHerCollect*
(30) Young Farmers.......................£25 *Ashford Stamp Shop*
(31) Eastry Sandwich.....................£30 *H D MacIntyre*
(32) Cowland Avenue, Enfield.......£25 *D Legg*
(33) Left, Right & Centre ..............£35 *Cam S.C.*
(34) The Elephant Man..................£35 *Cam S.C.*
(35) Arawazi, Whitehall .................£20 *Benham/JS Medal 9*
(36) Sikorski Museum....................£40 *Gen Sikorski Museum*
(37) Total Eclipse, Falmouth.........£35 *Bradbury*
**C.D.S. POSTMARKS Price Guide £10-£15**
(38) Farmers, Bull Farm, Cattle Market, Wheatfield
(39) Isle of Grain, Savacentre, Laxton

## 5th October 1999 – SOLDIERS' TALE

19p Bannockburn, 26p Civil War,
44p World Wars, 64p Peace keeping.

| SPECIAL HANDSTAMPS | SPONSOR |
|---|---|

**Price Guide Ordinary Covers £4-£9 / Sponsored Covers:**
(1) FDI - Bureau .................................. *Royal Mail (n.s.c.)*
(2) FDI - London SW......................... *Royal Mail (n.s.c.)*
(3) -do- non pictorial version ............ *Royal Mail (n.s.c.)*
(4) Soldiers', Tale, Birmingham.......... *Royal Mail (n.s.c.)*
(5) Soldiers, Tales, Glasgow............... *Royal Mail (n.s.c.)*
(6) Scottish Independence...........£20 *Benham Pilgrim*
(7) Civil War, Marston .................£15 *Benham BLCS 169*
(8) World Wars, Biggin Hill ........£20 *Benham*
(9) Peace Keeping, Whitehall.......£15 *Benham BLCS 169*
(10) Battle of Bannockburn...........£20 *Ben500(169)*
(11) Britain at War, Whitehall......£25 *Benham Coin Mil.10*
(12) Carisbrooke ...........................£20 *Benham Eng.Heritage*
(13) Soldiers, Sandhurst.................£20 *Bradbury LFDC 175*
(14) Soldiers, Whitehall.................£20 *Bradbury VP 137*
(15) Oliver Cromwell.....................£35 *Bradbury*
(16) Hastings Kent.........................£20 *Westminster*
(17) Autographed The Cenotaph...£25 *Westminster*
(18) Victory Way SE16...................£20 *Steven Scott 35*
(19) Battle Close SW19 ..................£30 *Steven Scott Plat.10*
(20) National Army Museum ........£15 *Steven Scott*
(21) Public Record Office, Kew.....£15 *Steven Scott*
(22) Lest We Forget, Whitehall .....£25 *FourpennyPost*
(23) Sir William Brereton, WC1....£25 *T Hurlstone*
(24) Oliver Cromwell.....................£35 *Cam S.C.*
(25) The Cenotaph.........................£35 *Cam S.C.*
(26) The Bold Dragoon ..................£25 *M Brazier (Pubs.10)*
(27) Oxf. & Bucks Bletchley ..........£25 *Bletchley PO*
(28) Russia Row, EC2 ....................£25 *P M Payne*
(29) Richard the Lionheart SW3....£25 *P M Payne*
(30) Cavalry Crescent, Hounslow ..£15 *GB30*
(31) To Our Glorious Dead............£20 *P Sheridan*
(32) Robert the Bruce.....................£20 *RN CvrsGpTDFC1-13*
(33) HMS Aurora & Catterick.......£20 *RN CvrsGpNFDC3-13*
(34) Handley Page Halifax..............£20 *BritHerCollect*
(35) Achilles Close SE1..................£30 *M J Kingsland*
(36) Start of World War II..............£20 *Benham/JS Medal 10*
(37) Total Eclipse, Falmouth.........£40 *Bradbury*
(38) Clarity of Vision .....................£45 *Helio*
(39) Ice Cold In Alex, Elstree .......£35 *Cam S.C.*
**C.D.S. POSTMARKS Price Guide £10-£15**
(40) Battle, The Barracks, Guardhouse, Wargrave
(41) Bannockburn, Aldershot, Naseby, Edgehill, Sandhurst
(42) Chelsea Royal Hospital, Sandhurst, Catterick Garrison

## 2nd November 1999 – CHRISTIANS' TALE

*19p Wesley, 26p King James Bible,*
*44p St. Andrews Pilgrimage, 64p First Christmas.*

**SPECIAL HANDSTAMPS          SPONSOR**
**Price Guide Ordinary Covers £4-£9 / Sponsored Covers:**

(1)   FDI - Bureau................................... *Royal Mail (n.s.c.)*
(2)   FDI - St. Andrews, Fife.................. *Royal Mail (n.s.c.)*
(3)   -do- non pictorial version ............. *Royal Mail (n.s.c.)*
(4)   Christians' Tale, Birmingham....... *Royal Mail (n.s.c.)*
(5)   Christians' Tales, Glasgow........... *Royal Mail (n.s.c.)*
(6)   Methodism, Epworth...............£15 *Benham BLCS 170*
(7)   Pilgrimage, St. Andrews..........£15 *Benham BLCS 170*
(8)   First Christmas, Bethlehem.....£20 *Benham Pilgrim*
(9)   The Bible, Hampton Court .....£20 *Benham*
(10) King James Bible, Edinburgh.£20 *Benham 500(170)*
(11) Trafalgar Square ......................£25 *Benham Coin Mil.11*
(12) Rievaulx Abbey.........................£20 *Benham Eng.Heritage*
(13) 1999 Christmas, Bethlehem ...£20 *Bradbury LFDC 176*
(14) 1999 Christmas, Nasareth .....£20 *Bradbury VP 138*
(15) John Wesley, Epworth...............£35 *Bradbury*
(16) Christians' Tale, Bethlehem ...£25 *Bradbury*
(17) Canterbury, Kent .....................£15 *Westminster*
(18) Autographed, Canterbury.......£25 *Westminster*
(19) Jerusalem Passage, EC1 .........£20 *Steven Scott 36*
(20) Reform Street, SW11...............£30 *Steven Scott Plat.11*
(21) St. Andrew's Cathedral ..........£25 *FourpennyPost*
(22) St. Andrew's Kaleidoscope.....£25 *T Hurlstone*
(23) St. Andrew's Fife ....................£25 *T Hurlstone*
(24) Merchant's Assoc'n..................£25 *T Hurlstone*
(25) The Pilgrim's Progress ...........£25 *M Brazier (Pubs.11)*
(26) Christians Code Bletchley ......£20 *Bletchley PO*
(27) Christian St, London E1........£25 *P M Payne*
(28) Christian St, London E1........£15 *GB31*
(29) Cathedrals Liverpool ..............£20 *P Sheridan*
(30) Christians' Tale, Bethlehem ...£20 *RN CvrsGpTDFC1-14*
(31) HMS Gloucester......................£20 *RN CvrsGpNFDC3-15*
(32) Vickers Wellington .................£20 *BritHerCollect*
(33) John Wesley, Oxford ..............£20 *P Barrett*
(34) Thomas Beckett.......................£30 *H D MacIntyre*
(35) Zionist Federation...................£50 *Zionist Federation*
(36) Happy Christmas, London........... *Royal Mail (n.s.c.)*
(37) Total Eclipse, Falmouth.........£35 *Bradbury*
(38) Laughter in Paradise, Elstree.£35 *Cam S.C.*
(39) Last Holiday, Elstree .............£35 *Cam S.C.*
(40) Guy Gibson, Woodhall Spa....£35 *Cam S.C.*
(41) Sinking of the Tirpitz .............£35 *Cam S.C.*
(42) Biggin Hill, Whitehall.............£20 *Benham/JS Medal 11*
(43) The Gunners Shot at Europe £20 *Dawn*
(44) Manchester Untd in Europe .£20 *Dawn*
**C.D.S. POSTMARKS Price Guide £10-£15**
(45) Holy Island, Nasareth, Angel Hill, St. Andrews
(46) Canterbury, Christchurch, Church, Epworth
(47) All Saints, All Hallows, Chapel Lane, Chapel Hill

---

## 7th December 1999 – ARTISTS' TALE

*19p World of Stage, 26p World of Music,*
*44p World of Literature, 64p New Worlds.*

**SPECIAL HANDSTAMPS          SPONSOR**
**Price Guide Ordinary Covers £4-£9 / Sponsored Covers:**

(1)   FDI - Bureau................................... *Royal Mail (n.s.c.)*
(2)   FDI - Stratford upon Avon .......... *Royal Mail (n.s.c.)*
(3)   -do- non pictorial version ............. *Royal Mail (n.s.c.)*
(4)   Artists' Tale, Birmingham............. *Royal Mail (n.s.c.)*
(5)   Artists' Tales, Glasgow................. *Royal Mail (n.s.c.)*
(6)   The Stage, Stratford ................£15 *Benham BLCS 171*
(7)   Music, Brook St, London W1 £20 *Benham*
(8)   Literature, Portsmouth............£15 *Benham BLCS 171*
(9)   New Worlds, Chelsea SW3.....£20 *Benham*
(10) Royal Academy of Music..........£20 *Benham Coin Mil.12*
(11) George Frideric Handel..........£20 *Benham 500(171)*
(12) Eng. Heritage Stonehenge.....£20 *Benham Eng.Heritage*
(13) William Shakespeare...............£20 *Bradbury LFDC 177*
(14) Glyndebourne, Lewes.............£20 *Bradbury VP 139*
(15) Charles Dickens, Rochester ...£35 *Bradbury*
(16) Autographed, Gadshill ...........£25 *Westminster*
(17) -do-, Royal Opera House.........£25 *Westminster*
(18) Stratford-upon-Avon ..............£15 *Westminster*
(19) Covent Garden, WC2...............£20 *Steven Scott 38*
(20) Handel Street, WC1................£30 *Steven Scott Plat.12*
(21) Gary Hume at Whitechapel....£25 *T Hurlstone*
(22) Leicester Sq, Theatre Land ...£25 *T Hurlstone*
(23) DanceStorm North East........£25 *FourpennyPost*
(24) The Charles Dickens..............£25 *M Brazier (Pubs.12)*
(25) Bletchley Park Post Office .....£20 *Bletchley PO*
(26) 400th Anniv Van Dyck..........£25 *P M Payne*

### 1999 CHRISTIANS' TALE

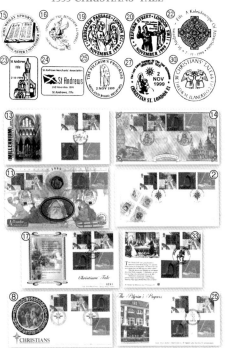

### 1999 ARTISTS' TALE

137

## 1999 ARTISTS' TALE

## 1999 MILLENNIUM TIMEKEEPER

### 14th Dec 1999 – MILLENNIUM TIMEKEEPER
*4 x 64p Globes/Time ~ Miniature Sheet*

| SPECIAL HANDSTAMPS | | SPONSOR |
|---|---|---|

**Price Guide Ordinary Covers £4-£9 / Sponsored Covers:**

*NB This Miniature Sheet was re-issued with a 'Stamp Show 2000' overprint on 1st March. Price with Stampex pmk £100*

### 6th JAN 2000 – NEW MILLENNIUM
*1st Class: Millennium Definitive*

| SPECIAL HANDSTAMPS | | SPONSOR |
|---|---|---|

**Price Guide Ordinary Covers £4-£9 / Sponsored Covers:**

*NB These stamps were also issued in stamp books - please see Definitive Section.*

## 2000 NEW MILLENNIUM

There are thousands more pictures of British first day covers at www.bfdc.co.uk where you can sort by stamp issue, theme, cover producer, stamp type etc. - and much more!

## 18th January 2000 – ABOVE & BEYOND

*19p Owl Centre Muncaster, 26p Space Science Centre Leicester,*
*44p Torrs Walkway/New Mills, 64p Seabird Centre, North Berwick.*

**SPECIAL HANDSTAMPS**    **SPONSOR**
**Price Guide Ordinary Covers £4-£9 / Sponsored Covers:**

(1)  FDI - Bureau .................................. *Royal Mail (n.s.c.)*
(2)  FDI - Muncaster, Ravenglass ....... *Royal Mail (n.s.c.)*
(3)  -do- non pictorial version ............ *Royal Mail (n.s.c.)*
(4)  Above & Beyond, Birmingham.... *Royal Mail (n.s.c.)*
(5)  Muncaster ................................. £15 *Benham BLCS 173*
(6)  Leicester ................................... £15 *Benham BLCS 173*
(7)  Matlock ...................................... £20 *Benham Pilgrim*
(8)  North Berwick .......................... £20 *Benham*
(9)  Matlock ...................................... £20 *Benham 500(173)*
(10) World of Birds, Sandy.............. £20 *Benham Coin Mill.1*
(11) Muncaster Castle...................... £20 *CoverCraft*
(12) Bolsover Castle ......................... £20 *Benham Eng.Heritage*
(13) Muncaster .................................. £20 *Bradbury LFDC 179*
(14) North Berwick .......................... £20 *Bradbury VP 134*
(15) The Future is Now .................. £20 *Bradbury*
(16) National Space Centre ........... £25 *Bradbury*
(17) Scottish Seabird Centre ...... £25 *Bradbury*
(18) The Millennium, Leicester .....£15 *Westminster*
(19) Autographed, RAF Cranwell..£25 *Westminster*
(20) Air Street, London W1 ..........£30 *Steven Scott Plat.12*
(21) Bird Street, London W1 ........£30 *Steven Scott 38*
(22) Hawk & Owl Trust.................£25 *FourpennyPost*
(23) The Oadby Owl ......................£25 *M Brazier (Pubs.13)*
(24) Flamingo Gardens, Northolt..£25 *P M Payne*
(25) Jupiter Way, London N7 .......£20 *GB33*
(26) Ullswater, Penrith...................£25 *P Sheridan*
(27) Walkway New Mills ...............£35 *Derbyshire Council*
(28) North Berwick ........................£20 *RN CvrsTDFC2-01*
(29) HMS Wilton ............................£20 *RN CvrsGpNFDC4-02*
(30) Death of Dickens, Rochester..£35 *Cam S.C.*
(31) Holly & Ivy, Shepperton........£35 *Cam S.C.*
(32) Zulu War, Whitehall...............£20 *Benham/JS Medal 13*
(33) Operation Millennium ...........£20 *Benham*
(34) Daleks Invasion Earth............£35 *Cam S.C.*

**C.D.S. POSTMARKS Price Guide £10-£15**
(35) Owlsmoor, Ravenglass, Leicester, Macclesfield, Starcross
(36) New Mills, Greenwich, North Berwick

*NB The 26p value was issued as a 1st Class NVI on 26th May ~*
*Please see page 142.*

## 1st February 2000 – FIRE & LIGHT

*19p Beacon Millennium, 26p Ffestiniog Railway,*
*44p Dynamic Earth, Edinburgh, 64p Croydon Skyline.*

**SPECIAL HANDSTAMPS**    **SPONSOR**
**Price Guide Ordinary Covers £4-£9 / Sponsored Covers:**

(1)  FDI - Bureau .................................. *Royal Mail (n.s.c.)*
(2)  FDI - Edinburgh............................ *Royal Mail (n.s.c.)*
(3)  -do- non pictorial version ............ *Royal Mail (n.s.c.)*
(4)  Birmingham................................... *Royal Mail (n.s.c.)*
(5)  Great Yarmouth ...................... £15 *Benham BLCS 174*
(6)  Ffestiniog.................................. £20 *Benham Pilgrim*
(7)  Edinburgh ................................ £15 *Benham BLCS 174*
(8)  Croydon .................................... £20 *Benham*
(9)  Edinburgh ................................ £20 *Benham 500(174)*
(10) Welsh Mountain Rail .............. £20 *Benham Coin Mill.2*
(11) Chiswick House........................ £20 *Benham Eng.Heritage*
(12) King's Cross, London ............. £20 *Bradbury LFDC 180*
(13) Victoria Station, London........ £20 *Bradbury VP 135*
(14) Porthmadog, Gwynedd ..........£20 *Bradbury*
(15) The Millennium, Met Office ..£15 *Westminster*
(16) Autographed, Met Office........£25 *Westminster*
(17) Phoenix Place, WC1 ...............£30 *Steven Scott Plat.13*
(18) Sunray Ave, London SE24.....£20 *Steven Scott 39*
(19) Our Dynamic Earth ................£20 *Steven Scott*
(20) Beacons, Great Yarmouth......£25 *FourpennyPost*
(21) Railwaymen's Arms ...............£20 *M Brazier (Pubs.14)*
(22) Jupiter Way, London N7 .......£20 *P M Payne*
(23) Railway Rise, London SE22 ..£15 *GB34*
(24) Bridge at Night, Widnes.........£25 *P Sheridan*
(25) Illuminations, Blackpool .......£25 *P Sheridan*
(26) Holyrood Park .........................£20 *RN CvrsGpTDFC2-02*
(27) HMS Welshman ......................£20 *RN CvrsGpNFDC4-03*
(28) Beacon Tower Bridge..............£20 *CoverCraft*
(29) Stealth Flight ...........................£20 *BritHerCollect*
(30) Limoges Aero-Engine..............£35 *Cam S.C.*
(31) Snowdon Mountain Railway .£20 *Dawn*
(32) Arakan Campaign, Whitehall £20 *Benham/JS Medal 14*

**C.D.S. POSTMARKS Price Guide £10-£15**
(33) Ffestiniog, Porthmadog, Croydon, Beacon, Thunder Lane
(34) Edinburgh, King's Cross, Caernarfon, Burnt Ash Lane

### 2000 ABOVE & BEYOND

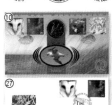

### 2000 FIRE & LIGHT

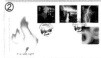

## 2000 WATER & COAST

### 7th March 2000 – WATER & COAST
*19p Durham Coast, 26p National Pondlife Liverpool,*
*44p Llanelli Coast, 64p Portsmouth Harbour.*

**SPECIAL HANDSTAMPS       SPONSOR**
Price Guide Ordinary Covers £4-£9 / Sponsored Covers:
(1)   FDI - Bureau .................................. *Royal Mail (n.s.c.)*
(2)   FDI - Llanelli ................................ *Royal Mail (n.s.c.)*
(3)   -do- non pictorial version ............ *Royal Mail (n.s.c.)*
(4)   Birmingham .................................. *Royal Mail (n.s.c.)*
(5)   Durham ...............................£15 *Benham BLCS 176*
(6)   Liverpool............................£20 *Benham Pilgrim*
(7)   Llanelli................................£15 *Benham BLCS 176*
(8)   Portsmouth .........................£20 *Benham*
(9)   Liverpool............................£20 *Benham 500(176)*
(10) Maritime Portsmouth ...........£20 *Benham Coin Mill.3*
(11) Eng. Heritage Stonehenge......£20 *Benham Eng.Heritage*
(12) Land's End, Penzance............£20 *Bradbury LFDC 181*
(13) Pondlife, Liverpool (frog) .......£20 *Bradbury VP 136*
(14) Pondlife, Liverpool (lily) .....£20 *Bradbury*
(15) Portsmouth Harbour 2000 .....£25 *Bradbury*
(16) The Millennium, Portsmouth ..£15 *Westminster*
(17) Autographed, Pembroke .......£25 *Westminster*
(18) Tideway Walk, SW8 ...............£30 *Steven Scott Plat.14*
(19) Pond Place, SW3 ..................£20 *Steven Scott 40*
(20) NEPA Durham .......................£20 *FourpennyPost*
(21) The Mary Rose, Portsmouth ..£20 *M Brazier (Pubs.15)*
(22) Ocean Street, London E1.......£25 *P M Payne*
(23) Puffin Close, Beckenham ......£20 *GB35*
(24) National Pondlife, Prescot ....£20 *P Sheridan*
(25) Turning the Tide, Durham .....£15 *CoverCraft*
(26) Water & Coast, Prescot.........£20 *RN CvrsGpTDFC2-03*
(27) HMS Wolverine .....................£20 *RN CvrsGpNFDC4-04*
(28) Bletchley Park Post Office .....£15 *Bletchley PO*
(29) Dover ....................................£30 *H D MacIntyre*
(30) Tidal Basin Road ...................£30 *M J Kingsland*
(31) Doodle Bugs, Whitehall.........£20 *BritHerCollect*
(32) I Was Monty's Double ...........£30 *Cam S.C.*
(33) Long, Short and the Tall .......£30 *Cam S.C.*
(34) Hendon.................................£20 *RAF(P&P19)*
(35) S.E.Asia Command ................£20 *Benham/JS Medal 15*
**C.D.S. POSTMARKS** Price Guide £10-£15
(36) Durham, Easington Colliery, Prescott, Llanelli, Portsmouth
(37) The Pond, Pathfinder Village, Waterbeach, Frogpool

## 2000 LIFE & EARTH

### 4th April 2000 – LIFE & EARTH
*2nd ECOS, Ballymena; 1st Web of Life, London Zoo,*
*44p Earth Centre, Doncaster; 64p Project SUZY Middlesbrough.*
**SPECIAL HANDSTAMPS       SPONSOR**
Price Guide Ordinary Covers £4-£9 / Sponsored Covers:
(1)   FDI - Bureau .................................. *Royal Mail (n.s.c.)*
(2)   FDI - Doncaster ............................ *Royal Mail (n.s.c.)*
(3)   -do- non pictorial version ............ *Royal Mail (n.s.c.)*
(4)   Birmingham .................................. *Royal Mail (n.s.c.)*
(5)   Ballymena .........................£20 *Benham Pilgrim*
(6)   London NW1.......................£15 *Benham BLCS 178*
(7)   Doncaster .........................£20 *Benham*
(8)   Middlesbrough ..................£15 *Benham BLCS 178*
(9)   Regents Park......................£20 *Benham Coin Mill.4*
(10) Biodiversity, London NW1......£20 *Benham 500(178)*
(11) Brodsworth Hall ....................£20 *Benham Eng.Heritage*
(12) Kew Gardens, Richmond ......£20 *Bradbury LFDC 182*
(13) Life & Earth, Ballymena........£20 *Bradbury VP 137*
(14) Kew Gardens (rose)...............£20 *Bradbury*
(15) ECOS, Ballymena...................£30 *Bradbury*
(16) 'SUZY' Middlesbrough ..........£25 *Bradbury*
(17) The Millennium, Kew...........£15 *Westminster*
(18) Autographed, Earth Centre ...£25 *Westminster*
(19) World's End Place, SW10 .....£20 *Steven Scott 41*
(20) Discovery Walk ....................£30 *Steven Scott Plat.16*
(21) The Reptile Trust, Newcastle .£20 *FourpennyPost*
(22) The Spider's Web, Aberdeen .£20 *M Brazier (Pubs.16)*
(23) Regent's Park, London NW1.£20 *P M Payne*
(24) Frog Lane, West Malling.......£15 *GB36*
(25) The Earth Centre, Doncaster .£15 *CoverCraft*
(26) Life & Earth, London ...........£20 *RN CvrsGpTDFC2-04*
(27) NATO ....................................£20 *RN CvrsGpNFDC4-05*
(28) Ness Botanic Gdns, Neston...£20 *P Sheridan*
(29) Nightingale, London SW12 ...£20 *J & M Arlington*
(30) E. London's Natural Habitat...£25 *T Hurlstone*
(31) Supermarine Walrus.............£20 *BritHerCollect*
(32) Met. Police Philatelic Soc......£20 *Bradbury*
(33) Blackburn..............................£20 *RAF(P&P20)*
(34) Operation Shingle ................£20 *Benham/JS Medal 16*
*A further seven handstamps were sponsored on this date to*
*coincide with the issue of the commemorative label featuring*

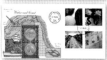

the Botanic Gardens of Wales ~ Please see definitive section.
**C.D.S. POSTMARKS Price Guide £10-£15**
(35) Acklam, Ballymena, Middlesbrough, Regents Park Road
(36) Doncaster, Primrose, Webheath

## 2nd May 2000 – ART & CRAFT
*2nd Ceramica, Stoke; 1st Tate Modern;*
*45p Cycle Network Artworks; 65p The Lowry, Salford.*

| SPECIAL HANDSTAMPS | SPONSOR |
| --- | --- |

**Price Guide Ordinary Covers £4-£9 / Sponsored Covers:**
(1)  FDI - Bureau .................................. *Royal Mail (n.s.c.)*
(2)  FDI - Salford ................................. *Royal Mail (n.s.c.)*
(3)  -do- non pictorial version ............ *Royal Mail (n.s.c.)*
(4)  Birmingham.................................... *Royal Mail (n.s.c.)*
(5)  Stoke on Trent ..........................£15 *Benham BLCS 180*
(6)  London SE1 .............................£20 *Benham Pilgrim*
(7)  Bristol ......................................£20 *Benham*
(8)  Salford .....................................£15 *Benham BLCS 180*
(9)  Fine Art Painting.....................£20 *Benham Coin Mill.5*
(10) Mother town of Potteries .......£20 *Benham 500(180)*
(11) Stokesay Castle........................£20 *Benham Eng.Heritage*
(12) Art & Craft, Burslem...............£20 *Bradbury LFDC 183*
(13) Art & Craft, St. Ives................£20 *Bradbury VP 138*
(14) Tower Bridge, London ............£25 *Bradbury*
(15) Ceramica, Burslem...................£25 *Bradbury*
(16) Tate Modern ...........................£15 *Westminster*
(17) Autographed, Tate Modern.....£25 *Westminster*
(18) Bankside, London SE1 ...........£30 *Steven Scott Plat.17*
(19) Tranquil Passage, SE3 ............£20 *Steven Scott 42*
(20) Coronation Street....................£15 *Steven Scott*
(21) L S Lowry in the N. East .......£20 *FourpennyPost*
(22) The Wobbly Wheel .................£20 *M Brazier (Pubs.17)*
(23) Turner, Temeraire St, SE16 ...£20 *P M Payne*
(24) Lowry Crescent, Mitcham ......£15 *GB37*
(25) The Lowry, Salford ................£15 *CoverCraft*
(26) Life & Earth, Salford.............£20 *RN CvrsGpTDFC2-05*
(27) HMS Conqueror......................£20 *RN CvrsGpNFDC4-06*
(28) The Lowry, Salford ...............£20 *P Sheridan*
(29) Art Centre of World ..............£25 *T Hurlstone*
(30) Gallery Road, SE21 ...............£25 *M J Kingsland*
(31) British Midland/Lufthansa.....£30 *Karl-Jurgen Schepers*
(32) B17 Football Loco .................£25 *Dawn*
(33) Bunbury Cricket Club ...........£25 *Woodford Sports*
(34) Arundel Castle Cricket Club..£25 *Woodford Sports*
(35) Ripon ......................................£20 *RAF(P&P21)*
(36) Operation Overlord ...............£20 *Benham/JS Medal 17*
(37) World WIZO Russell Sq........£40 *S Kacher*
**C.D.S. POSTMARKS Price Guide £10-£15**
(38) Salford, The Galleries, Raleigh, Dresden, Hanley, Barlaston
(39) Pottery Road, Stoke-on-Trent, Exchange Key (Salford).

## 22nd May 2000 – 'SMILERS' STAMPS
*Miniature Sheet issued for the 'Stamp Show 2000' containing a*
*reprinted version of the 1991 'Smiles' stamps and labels.*

| SPECIAL HANDSTAMPS | SPONSOR |
| --- | --- |

**Price Guide Ordinary Covers £4-£9 / Sponsored Covers:**
(1)  The Stamp Show 2000, SW5 ....... *Royal Mail (n.s.c.)*
(2)  Art & Entertainment.................... *Royal Mail (n.s.c.)*
(3)  Smilers, Stamp Show 2000 .....£20 *Benham (11 versions)*
*Other handstamps were sponsored on this date for the*
*'Artist's Palette' Souvenir Sheet. Please see Definitive Section.*

## 23rd May 2000 – THE QUEEN'S STAMPS
*Miniature Sheet issued for the 'Stamp Show 2000' containing a*
*reprinted version of the 1/3d 1953 Coronation stamp with a £1*
*denomination plus 4 Millennium Definitive Section.*

| SPECIAL HANDSTAMPS | SPONSOR |
| --- | --- |

**Price Guide Ordinary Covers £4-£9 / Sponsored Covers:**
(1)  FDI - Bureau .................................. *Royal Mail (n.s.c.)*
(2)  FDI - Westminster ......................... *Royal Mail (n.s.c.)*
(3)  -do- non pictorial version ............ *Royal Mail (n.s.c.)*
(4)  The Stamp Show 2000, SW5 ....... *Royal Mail (n.s.c.)*
(5)  Stamp Show - Royalty ................... *Royal Mail (n.s.c.)*
(6)  New £1 Coronation Stamp ....£25 *Bradbury*
(7)  Stamp Show, Earl's Court ......£20 *Benham BLCS 183*
(8)  Stamp Show, Westminster .....£20 *Benham BLCS 183*
(9)  Stamp Show, Westminster .....£20 *Benham*
(10) Coronation of Q. Elizabeth....£20 *Westminster*
(11) Lyceum Post Office.................£25 *P Sheridan*
(12) Stamp Show Earl's Court.......£25 *T Hurlstone*
(13) 160 Years Since First Stamp..£20 *P M Payne*
(14) The Penny Black, Bicester ....£25 *M Brazier (Pubs.19)*
(15) Royal Horticultural Society ...£35 *RHS*
**C.D.S. POSTMARKS Price Guide £10-£15**
(16) Balmoral, Buckingham Palace, Windsor Castle *(£150 each)*
(17) Windsor, Earls Court, Broadway

## 2000 ART & CRAFT

## 2000 THE QUEEN'S STAMPS

## 2000 SPECIAL RETAIL BOOK

## 2000 PEOPLE & PLACE

## 2000 STONE & SOIL

### 26th May 2000 – SPECIAL RETAIL BOOK

*Se-tenant pair of 1st Class stamps: Space Science Centre (Above & Beyond); Web of Life, London Zoo (Life & Earth). The Space Centre stamp was previously issued as a 26p, making this 1st Class value a new stamp.*

**SPECIAL HANDSTAMPS**     **SPONSOR**
Price Guide Ordinary Covers £4-£9 / Sponsored Covers:
| | | |
|---|---|---|
| (1) | FDI - Bureau | *Royal Mail (n.s.c.)* |
| (2) | FDI - Leicester | *Royal Mail (n.s.c.)* |
| (3) | -do- non pictorial version | *Royal Mail (n.s.c.)* |
| (4) | The Stamp Show 2000, SW5 | *Royal Mail (n.s.c.)* |
| (5) | Stamp Show - Technology | *Royal Mail (n.s.c.)* |
| (6) | Space Centre/London Zoo | £15 *Bradbury* |
| (7) | National SpaceCentre | £20 *Bradbury* |
| (8) | Space Leicester | £20 *Benham* |
| (9) | Above & Beyond, Space | £15 *Benham BLCS 184* |
| (10) | Life & Earth, NW1 | £15 *Benham BLCS 184* |
| (11) | Lyceum Post Office | £20 *P Sheridan* |
| (12) | Stamp Show Earl's Court | £25 *T Hurlstone* |
| (13) | deHaviland, Hatfield | £15 *Cam S.C.* |

### 6th June 2000 – PEOPLE & PLACE

*2nd Millennium Greens; 1st Gateshead Millennium Bridge; 45p Mile End Park, London; 65p On the Line (Greenwich)*

**SPECIAL HANDSTAMPS**     **SPONSOR**
Price Guide Ordinary Covers £4-£9 / Sponsored Covers:
| | | |
|---|---|---|
| (1) | FDI - Bureau | *Royal Mail (n.s.c.)* |
| (2) | FDI - Gateshead | *Royal Mail (n.s.c.)* |
| (3) | -do- non pictorial version | *Royal Mail (n.s.c.)* |
| (4) | People & Place, Birmingham | *Royal Mail (n.s.c.)* |
| (5) | Birmingham | £15 *Benham BLCS 185* |
| (6) | Gateshead | £15 *Benham BLCS 185* |
| (7) | London E14 | £20 *Benham Pilgrim* |
| (8) | Oxford | £20 *Benham* |
| (9) | Greenwich | £20 *Benham 500(185)* |
| (10) | Oxford | £20 *Benham Coin Mill.6* |
| (11) | Mt Grace Priory | £20 *Benham Eng.Heritage* |
| (12) | People & Place, London | £20 *Bradbury LFDC 184* |
| (13) | People & Place, Brighton | £20 *Bradbury VP 139* |
| (14) | Gateshead Millennium Bdge | £25 *Bradbury* |
| (15) | Sponsored Scooter Trek | £40 *Bradbury* |
| (16) | Trafalgar Square | £15 *Westminster* |
| (17) | Autographed, Hyde Park | £25 *Westminster* |
| (18) | Mile End Road, E1 | £15 *Steven Scott 43* |
| (19) | Meridian Road, SE7 | £30 *Steven Scott Plat.18* |
| (20) | We Shall Remember | £15 *Steven Scott* |
| (21) | Gateshead Millennium Bdge | £20 *FourpennyPost* |
| (22) | The Morris Man | £20 *M Brazier (Pubs.18)* |
| (23) | David Livingstone, E1 | £20 *P M Payne* |
| (24) | All Souls Place, W1 | £15 *GB38* |
| (25) | Baltic Centre, Gateshead | £15 *CoverCraft* |
| (26) | People & Place, Gateshead | £20 *RN CvrsGpTDFC2-06* |
| (27) | Operation Neptune | £20 *RN CvrsGpNFDC4-07* |
| (28) | Community Centre Widnes | £20 *P Sheridan* |
| (29) | Normandy Invasion | £20 *BritHerCollect* |
| (30) | Rowland Hill, Kidderminster | £25 *Assoc. of GBFDC 1* |
| (31) | Bletchley Park | £15 *Bletchley PO* |
| (32) | The Gilbert Collection | £20 *T Hurlstone* |
| (33) | Ramsgate | £35 *H D MacIntyre* |
| (34) | Old England XI, Hove | £30 *Woodford Sports* |
| (35) | Wistaston Jnr School | £25 *M Wilson* |
| (36) | Felixstowe | £20 *RAF(P&P22)* |
| (37) | V1 & V2 Assaults | £20 *Benham/JS Medal 18* |

**C.D.S. POSTMARKS Price Guide £10-£15**
(38) Gateshead, Greenwich, Mile End, Meridian Centre
(39) Playing Place, Daisy Hill, The Green or similar

### 4th July 2000 – STONE & SOIL

*2nd Strangford Stone, Killyleagh; 1st Trans-Pennine Trail; 45p Kingdom of Fife Cycleways; 65p Changing Places*

**SPECIAL HANDSTAMPS**     **SPONSOR**
Price Guide Ordinary Covers £4-£9 / Sponsored Covers:
| | | |
|---|---|---|
| (1) | FDI - Bureau | *Royal Mail (n.s.c.)* |
| (2) | FDI - Killyleagh | *Royal Mail (n.s.c.)* |
| (3) | -do- non pictorial version | *Royal Mail (n.s.c.)* |
| (4) | Birmingham | *Royal Mail (n.s.c.)* |
| (5) | Killyleagh | £15 *Benham BLCS 186* |
| (6) | Barnsley | £20 *Benham* |
| (7) | Glenrothes | £15 *Benham BLCS 186* |
| (8) | Birmingham | £20 *Benham Pilgrim* |
| (9) | Salisbury | £20 *Benham Coin Cover* |
| (10) | Barnsley | £20 *Benham 500(186)* |
| (11) | Pendennis Castle | £20 *Benham Eng.Heritage* |
| (12) | Stone & Soil, Barnsley | £20 *Bradbury LFDC 185* |
| (13) | Stone & Soil, Stonehenge | £20 *Bradbury VP 140* |

(14) Trans Pennine Trail ................£25 *Bradbury*
(15) Stonehenge ...............................£15 *Westminster*
(16) Autographed, Garden City.....£25 *Westminster*
(17) The Plantation, SE1................£20 *Steven Scott 44*
(18) English Grounds, SE1.............£30 *Steven Scott Plat.19*
(19) Long Distance Walkers..........£20 *FourpennyPost*
(20) The Rambler, Edale ................£20 *M Brazier (Pubs.20)*
(21) Rushmore Close, Bromley......£20 *P M Payne*
(22) Summer Olympics...................£20 *P M Payne*
(23) Stone .........................................£15 *GB39*
(24) Changing Places .....................£15 *CoverCraft*
(25) Stone & Soil, Glenrothes ......£20 *RN CvrsGpTDFC2-07*
(26) HMS Foylebank, Portland .....£20 *RN CvrsGpNFDC4-08*
(27) Ditton Brook, Widnes.............£25 *P Sheridan*
(28) Wimbledon Championships...£25 *Post Office Network*
(29) Wellington ...............................£20 *RAF(P&P23)*
(30) End of WWII, Whitehall ........£20 *Benham/JS Medal 19*
**C.D.S. POSTMARKS Price Guide £10-£15**
(31) Killyleagh, Strangford, Glenrothes, Kingdom Ctre, Southport
(32) Bluebell Hill, Stone, Stonesfield, Limestone Walk or similar

## 1st August 2000 – TREE & LEAF
*2nd Yews for the Millennium; Eden Project, St. Austell;*
*45p Millennium Seed Bank, Kew; 65p Forest for Scotland*
**SPECIAL HANDSTAMPS          SPONSOR**
**Price Guide Ordinary Covers £4-£9 / Sponsored Covers:**
(1)  FDI - Bureau...............................Royal Mail (n.s.c.)
(2)  FDI - St. Austell ..........................Royal Mail (n.s.c.)
(3)  -do- non pictorial version ............Royal Mail (n.s.c.)
(4)  Birmingham..................................Royal Mail (n.s.c.)
(5)  London SW7...........................£20 *Benham Pilgrim*
(6)  St. Austell..............................£15 *Benham BLCS 187*
(7)  Ardingley................................£20 *Benham*
(8)  Glasgow.................................£15 *Benham BLCS 187*
(9)  Sherwood...............................£20 *Benham Coin Cover*
(10) Glasgow.................................£20 *Benham*
(11) Walmer Castle.......................£20 *Benham Eng.Heritage*
(12) Kew (oak leaf)........................£20 *Bradbury LFDC 186*
(13) Kew (fern)..............................£20 *Bradbury VP 141*
(14) Wistow, Leics.........................£30 *Bradbury*
(15) Millennium Forest, Glasgow..£25 *Bradbury*
(16) Caverswall Garden.................£20 *Bradbury*
(17) The Millennium, New Forest.£15 *Westminster*
(18) Autographed, New Forest .....£25 *Westminster*
(19) Leafy Oak Road, SE12...........£30 *Steven Scott Plat.20*
(20) Sycamore Gdns, W6...............£20 *Steven Scott 45*
(21) Great North Forest ................£20 *FourpennyPost*
(22) Brave Old Oak, Towcester.....£20 *M Brazier (Pubs.21)*
(23) Rhodes Avenue, N22..............£20 *P M Payne*
(24) Isle of Pabay ..........................£15 *GB40*
(25) Yews for the Millennium........£15 *CoverCraft*
(26) Tree & Leaf, St. Austell .........£20 *RN CvrsGpTDFC2-08*
(27) HMS Euryalus, Plymouth.......£20 *RN CvrsGpNFDC4-09*
(28) Mersey Forest, Widnes...........£20 *P Sheridan*
(29) Molash, Canterbury ...............£25 *H D MacIntyre*
(30) Milton Keynes Philatelic Soc.£25 *M Brazier*
(31) Eden Project, St. Austell ........£35 *Mill.Com.Covers*
(32) Stranraer.................................£20 *RAF(P&P24)*
(33) HMS Amethyst, Whitehall .....£20 *Benham/JS Medal 20*
**C.D.S. POSTMARKS Price Guide £10-£15**
(34) Ardingly, Kew, Kew Gardens, Eden, St. Austell, Yew Tree
(35) Woodlands Park, The Forest, Pinewoods - or similar

## 4th August 2000 – QUEEN MOTHER
*Miniature Sheet celebrating the 100th Birthday of The Queen*
*Mother, containing 4 x 27p stamps depicting HM The Queen,*
*The Queen Mother, Prince Charles & Prince William*
**SPECIAL HANDSTAMPS          SPONSOR**
**Price Guide Ordinary Covers £4-£9 / Sponsored Covers:**
(1)  FDI - Bureau...............................Royal Mail (n.s.c.)
(2)  FDI - London SW1 .......................Royal Mail (n.s.c.)
(3)  -do- non pictorial version ............Royal Mail (n.s.c.)
(4)  Clarence House............................Royal Mail
(5)  The Queen Mother, SW1 ......£20 *Royal Mail/Royal Mint*
(6)  Life of the Century, Glamis ..£20 *Royal Mail*
(7)  Sandringham, Norfolk ................Royal Mail (n.s.c.)
(8)  St. James's ..............................£15 *Benham BLCS 188*
(9)  Westminster.............................£15 *Benham BLCS 188*
(10) Castle of Mey...........................£15 *Benham BLCS 188*
(11) Buckingham Pal Rd................£15 *Benham BLCS 188*
(12) Hundreth Birthday, Hitchin ..£20 *Benham*
(13) The Mail on Sunday................£20 *Benham*
(14) Grosvenor Gardens ................£20 *Benham*
(15) Glamis (lion) ...........................£25 *Benham Coin Cover*

## 2000 STONE & SOIL

## 2000 TREE & LEAF

## 2000 QUEEN MOTHER

## 2000 QUEEN MOTHER

| | | |
|---|---|---|
| (16) | Cinque Ports, Dover .................£20 | *Benham (Prestige Bk)* |
| (17) | Cinque Ports, Hythe ..................£20 | *Benham (Prestige Bk)* |
| (18) | Cinque Ports, Rye.....................£20 | *Benham (Prestige Bk)* |
| (19) | Cinque Ports, Walmer ..............£20 | *Benham (Prestige Bk)* |
| (20) | Cinque Ports, Hastings............£20 | *Benham* |
| (21) | Ancestral Home, Glamis .......£15 | *Bradbury LFDC 191* |
| (22) | Clarence House .......................£15 | *Bradbury VP 146* |
| (23) | St Paul's Walden ....................£15 | *Bradbury* |
| (24) | Clarence House .......................£15 | *Bradbury* |
| (25) | Windsor Berkshire ..................£15 | *Bradbury* |
| (26) | 100 Years, Clarence House....£15 | *Westminster* |
| (27) | 100th Birthday, Glamis..........£15 | *Westminster* |
| (28) | Majesty, Buck Palace Rd .......£15 | *Steven Scott* |
| (29) | Savoy Ct, Gilbert & Sullivan..£20 | *Steven Scott* |
| (30) | Queen of Hearts, Daventry ....£20 | *M Brazier (Pubs.22)* |
| (31) | Clarence House, SW1 ...........£20 | *T Hurlstone* |
| (32) | Windsor Castle .......................£20 | *T Hurlstone* |
| (33) | Elizabeth Way..........................£20 | *P M Payne* |
| (34) | Queen Elizabeth's Drive........£20 | *P M Payne* |
| (35) | Regal Way, Kenton .................£15 | *GB41* |
| (36) | Royal Naval Cvrs Plymouth....£20 | *RN CvrsGpTDFC2-09* |
| (37) | HMS Ark Royal, Rosyth........£20 | *RN CvrsGpNFDC4-10* |
| (38) | Halton Celebrates, Widnes ....£20 | *P Sheridan* |
| (39) | Prince William of Wales........£20 | *BritHeritCollections* |
| (40) | Moor House School Oxted....£20 | *BritHeritCollections* |
| (41) | Windsor...................................£20 | *BritHeritCollections* |
| (42) | Wedgwood, Barlaston ...........£20 | *Mill.Commem.Covers* |
| (43) | Raflet Stamp Club' ................£15 | *Raflet Stamp Club* |
| (44) | Colonel in Chief BF2611PS....£25 | *Group Capt Randle* |
| (45) | Colonel in Chief BF2612PS....£25 | *Group Capt Randle* |
| (46) | Colonel in Chief BF2613PS....£25 | *Group Capt Randle* |
| (47) | Colonel in Chief BF2614PS....£25 | *Group Capt Randle* |
| (48) | Colonel in Chief BF2615PS....£25 | *Group Capt Randle* |
| (49) | Colonel in Chief BF2616PS....£25 | *Group Capt Randle* |
| (50) | Colonel in Chief BF2617PS....£25 | *Group Capt Randle* |
| (51) | Colonel in Chief BF2618PS....£25 | *Group Capt Randle* |
| (52) | Internat'l Prisoners of War ...£15 | *Steven Scott* |
| (53) | Leonard Cheshire, Oxford .....£20 | *Cam S.C.* |
| (54) | Eden Project, St. Austell........£20 | *Mill.Commem.Covers* |

**C.D.S. POSTMARKS Price Guide £10-£15**
(55) Buckingham Palace, Windsor Castle *(each £200)*
(56) Glamis, Mey, Bowes, Windsor, Clarence Road Windsor
(57) Whitwell, Windsor Great Park, Hundred House,

## 2000 MIND & MATTER

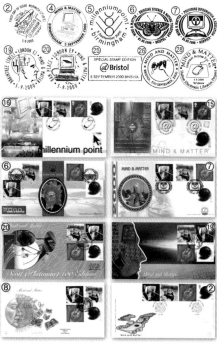

### 5th September 2000 – MIND & MATTER
*2nd Wildscreen at - Bristol; 1st Norfolk & Norwich Project;*
*45p Millennium Point, Birmingham; 65p SCRAN Edinburgh.*

| | **SPECIAL HANDSTAMPS** | **SPONSOR** |
|---|---|---|
| | Price Guide Ordinary Covers £4-£9 / Sponsored Covers: | |
| (1) | FDI - Bureau................................ | *Royal Mail (n.s.c.)* |
| (2) | FDI - Norwich .............................. | *Royal Mail (n.s.c.)* |
| (3) | -do- non pictorial version ............ | *Royal Mail (n.s.c.)* |
| (4) | Mind & Matter, Birmingham ...... | *Royal Mail (n.s.c.)* |
| (5) | millenniumpoint .......................£20 | *Royal Mail/MCC* |
| (6) | Bristol.......................................15 | *Benham BLCS 190* |
| (7) | Norwich.....................................15 | *Benham BLCS 190* |
| (8) | Birmingham ..............................20 | *Benham* |
| (9) | Edinburgh..................................20 | *Benham Pilgrim* |
| (10) | Bristol.......................................20 | *Benham Coin Cover* |
| (11) | Bristol.......................................20 | *Benham* |
| (12) | Eng. Heritage, Kirby Hall .........20 | *Benham Eng.Heritage* |
| (13) | Edinburgh..................................20 | *Bradbury LFDC 187* |
| (14) | Birmingham ..............................15 | *Bradbury VP 142* |
| (15) | www.britishfirstdaycovers.........35 | *Bradbury* |
| (16) | www.millenniumpoint.org.uk ..25 | *Bradbury* |
| (17) | Birmingham ..............................15 | *Westminster* |
| (18) | Autographed .............................25 | *Westminster* |
| (19) | Braintree Street, E2...................20 | *Steven Scott 46* |
| (20) | Ram Place, E9...........................30 | *Steven Scott Plat.21* |
| (21) | Norwich, Norfolk ......................20 | *Fourpenny Post* |
| (22) | The Boat Inn .............................20 | *M Brazier (Pubs.23)* |
| (23) | Botticelli, Venus Rd SE18 ........20 | *P M Payne* |
| (24) | Bristol Rd, London E7 .............15 | *GB41* |
| (25) | Special Stamp @ Bristol............15 | *CoverCraft* |
| (26) | Mind & Matter, Bristol .............20 | *RN CvrsGpTDFC2-09* |
| (27) | HMS Endymion, Portsmouth ..20 | *RN CvrsGpNFDC4-10* |
| (28) | Halton Electronic, Widnes .......20 | *P Sheridan* |
| (29) | Friends of NPM EC1 .................15 | *R. Pottle (postcards)* |
| (30) | Imjin River, Whitehall...............20 | *Benham/JS Medal 21* |
| (31) | Leonard Cheshire, Oxford.........30 | *Cam S.C.* |
| (32) | Pembroke BF 2609 PS .............20 | *RAF(P&P25)* |
| (33) | Eden Project, St Austell...........20 | *Eden Project* |

*A further seven handstamps were sponsored on this date to coincide with the issue of the fourth Retail Pane featuring a setenant pair of Trans-Pennine Trail & Eden Project stamps ~ Please see definitive section for details*
**C.D.S. POSTMARKS Price Guide £7-£10**
(33) Birmingham, Bristol, Edinburgh, Norwich

## 3rd October 2000 - BODY & BONE
*2nd Body/The Dome, Greenwich; 1st Hampden Pk, Glasgow; 45p Bath Spa; 65p Centre for Life, Newcastle.*

| SPECIAL HANDSTAMPS | | SPONSOR |
|---|---|---|
| **Price Guide Ordinary Covers £4-£9 / Sponsored Covers:** | | |
| (1) | FDI - Bureau | *Royal Mail (n.s.c.)* |
| (2) | FDI - Glasgow | *Royal Mail (n.s.c.)* |
| (3) | -do- non pictorial version | *Royal Mail (n.s.c.)* |
| (4) | Birmingham | *Royal Mail (n.s.c.)* |
| (5) | Greenwich | £15 *Benham BLCS 193* |
| (6) | Glasgow | £15 *Benham BLCS 193* |
| (7) | Bath | £20 *Benham* |
| (8) | Newcastle | £20 *Benham Pilgrim* |
| (9) | Bath | £20 *Benham Coin Cover* |
| (10) | Bath | £20 *Benham Coin Cover* |
| (11) | Cleeve Abbey | £20 *Benham Eng.Heritage* |
| (12) | Greenwich | £20 *Bradbury LFDC 188* |
| (13) | Greenwich | £15 *Bradbury VP 143* |
| (14) | Crystal Palace | £25 *Bradbury* |
| (15) | Bath's Spa Revival | £20 *Bradbury* |
| (16) | Hampden Stadium | £25 *Bradbury* |
| (17) | Sci & Nat History | £15 *Westminster* |
| (18) | Autographed, The Dome | £25 *Westminster* |
| (19) | Sportsbank St, SE6 | £20 *Steven Scott 47* |
| (20) | Hands Walk, E16 | £30 *Steven Scott Plat.22* |
| (21) | Life, Newcastle upon Tyne | £20 *FourpennyPost* |
| (22) | The Bath Tap, Bath | £20 *M Brazier (Pubs.24)* |
| (23) | Sir Francis Drake, E1 | £20 *P M Payne* |
| (24) | Bath | £15 *GB42* |
| (25) | Prime Meridian Greenwich | £15 *CoverCraft* |
| (26) | Hampden Park | £20 *RN CvrsGpTDFC2-10* |
| (27) | HMS Kenya | £20 *RN CvrsGpNFDC4-11* |
| (28) | Total Body Fitness, Widnes | £20 *P Sheridan* |
| (29) | Oldest Body & Bone | £15 *Assoc. of GBFDC 2* |
| (30) | Football at Wembley | £20 *Dawn* |
| (31) | Kidderminster Harriers | £20 *Dawn* |
| (32) | City are Back! Manchester | £20 *Dawn* |
| (33) | Burnley are Back in Div.One | £20 *Dawn* |
| (34) | Charlton are Back, SE7 | £20 *Dawn* |
| (35) | Any football permanent h/s | £20 *Dawn* |
| (36) | Kenya, 26th Anniversary | £20 *Benham/JS Medal 22* |
| (37) | Warwick | £20 *RAF(P&P26)* |
| (38) | Millennium Fair, Redhill | £20 *Redhill Philatelic Soc* |
| (39) | Polish Roman Catholic | £30 *J L Englert* |
| (40) | General Sikorski | £30 *J L Englert* |
| (41) | The Dome (changeable date) | *Royal Mail* |

**C.D.S. POSTMARKS Price Guide £10-£15**
(42) Millennium Dome, Mount Florida Glasgow, Hampden Park
(43) Glasgow, Bath, Newcastle, Orthopeadic Hospital

## 3rd October 2000 - CHRISTMAS Generic
**The first Generic Smilers Christmas stamps**
*A re-issue of the 1995 19p Robins Christmas stamp in sheets of 20 with labels & 1997 1st Class Crackers Christmas stamp in sheets of 10 with labels.*

| SPECIAL HANDSTAMPS | | SPONSOR |
|---|---|---|
| **Price Guide Ordinary Covers £4-£9 / Sponsored Covers:** | | |
| (1) | Bethlehem | £25 *Bradbury* |
| (2) | Hollybush | £15 *Benham BLCS 195* |
| (3) | Christmas Common | £15 *Benham BLCS 195* |

*These stamps were issued on the same day as the Body & Bone set. Therefore all of the Body & Bone handstamps (with the exception of the Bureau and Glasgow FDIs) were available for this issue. Conversely, the above three handstamps were also available for the Body & Bone issue.*

## 7th November 2000 - SPIRIT & FAITH
*2nd St. Edmundsbury Cathedral; 1st Church Floodlighting; 45p St. Patrick Ctre, Downpatrick; 65p Mystery Plays, York Minster*

| SPECIAL HANDSTAMPS | | SPONSOR |
|---|---|---|
| **Price Guide Ordinary Covers £4-£9 / Sponsored Covers:** | | |
| (1) | FDI - Bureau | *Royal Mail (n.s.c.)* |
| (2) | FDI - Downpatrick | *Royal Mail (n.s.c.)* |
| (3) | -do- non pictorial version | *Royal Mail (n.s.c.)* |
| (4) | Spirit & Faith, Birmingham | *Royal Mail (n.s.c.)* |
| (5) | Seasons Greetings Bethlehem | *Royal Mail (n.s.c.)* |
| (6) | Bury St Edmunds | £15 *Benham BLCS 194* |
| (7) | Walton-on-Thames | £20 *Benham Pilgrim* |
| (8) | Downpatrick | £15 *Benham BLCS 194* |
| (9) | York | £20 *Benham* |

### 2000 BODY & BONE

### 2000 CHRISTMAS Generic
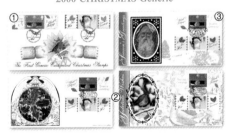

### 2000 SPIRIT & FAITH

## 2000 SPIRIT & FAITH

## 2000 SOUND & VISION

## 2001 THE FUTURE

(10) York Minster ............................£20 *Benham Coin Cover*
(11) Mystery Plays, York ................£20 *Benham*
(12) Belsay Hall................................£20 *Benham Eng.Heritage*
(13) Bethlehem ................................£20 *Bradbury LFDC 189*
(14) Nasareth ...................................£20 *Bradbury VP 144*
(15) The Saint Patrick Centre .......£30 *Bradbury*
(16) York Minster ............................£15 *Westminster*
(17) Autographed, York Minster ....£25 *Westminster*
(18) Christian St, E1......................£20 *Steven Scott 48*
(19) Cathedral Place, EC4 ............£30 *Steven Scott Plat.23*
(20) Church Floodlighting ..............£20 *FourpennyPost*
(21) The Minster Inn, York ...........£20 *M Brazier (Pubs.25)*
(22) 1st Xmas/3rd Millennium ....£20 *P M Payne*
(23) Faith Street, Bolton................£15 *GB43*
(24) St Edmundsbury Cathedral .....£15 *CoverCraft*
(25) Bletchley Park .........................£20 *Bletchley PO*
(26) Spirit & Faith, York ................£20 *RN CvrsGpTDFC2-11*
(27) HMS Fearless ...........................£20 *RN CvrsGpNFDC4-12*
(28) Church Floodlighting ..............£20 *P Sheridan*
(29) St Edmund, Greensted............£25 *T Hurlstone*
(30) St Martins Hill, Canterbury ...£30 *H D MacIntyre*
(31) HMS Petard..............................£35 *Cam S.C.*
(32) Sinking of the Tirpitz .............£35 *Cam S.C.*
(33) Concorde, Test & Delivery .....£35 *Cam S.C.*
(34) 60th Anniv Battle of Britain ...£35 *Cam S.C.*
(35) Suez, 44th Anniversary ..........£20 *Benham/JS Medal 23*
(36) London with SARO ...............£20 *RAF(P&P27)*
(37) Friends of NPMuseum ...........£25 *R G Pottle*
**C.D.S. POSTMARKS Price Guide £10-£15**
(38) Bury St. Edmunds, Nether Stowey, Downpatrick, York
(39) Holy Island, Angel Hill, St. Faith, Christchurch, Norwich

## 5th December 2000 – SOUND & VISION

*2nd Ringing in the Millennium; 1st Year of the Artist;
45p Canolfan Milenium,Cardiff; 65p Talent & Skills 2000.*

| SPECIAL HANDSTAMPS | SPONSOR |
|---|---|

**Price Guide Ordinary Covers £4-£9 / Sponsored Covers:**
(1) FDI - Bureau .................................. *Royal Mail (n.s.c.)*
(2) FDI - Cardiff ................................. *Royal Mail (n.s.c.)*
(3) -do- non pictorial version ............ *Royal Mail (n.s.c.)*
(4) Sound & Vision, Birmingham...... *Royal Mail (n.s.c.)*
(5) Seasons Greetings Bethlehem ..... *Royal Mail (n.s.c.)*
(6) Merry Christmas, Birmingham..... *Royal Mail (n.s.c.)*
(7) Happy Christmas, London EC1 .. *Royal Mail (n.s.c.)*
(8) Loughborough...........................£20 *Benham*
(9) Sheffield ..................................£20 *Benham Pilgrim*
(10) Cardiff ....................................£15 *Benham BLCS 196*
(11) London NW5 .........................£15 *Benham BLCS 196*
(12) London E1...............................£20 *Benham Coin Cover*
(13) Bridgwater ..............................£20 *Benham*
(14) Castle Acre.............................£20 *Benham Eng.Heritage*
(15) Shepherd's Bush .....................£20 *Bradbury LFDC 190*
(16) Shepherd's Bush .....................£15 *Bradbury VP 145*
(17) Taylor Bellfounders.................£25 *Bradbury*
(18) Royal Albert Hall ...................£15 *Westminster*
(19) Autographed, Abbey Road .....£25 *Westminster*
(20) Ringmore Rise, SE23..............£20 *Steven Scott 49*
(21) Theatre Street, SW11 .............£30 *Steven Scott Plat.24*
(22) Music/Arts Gateshead ...........£20 *FourpennyPost*
(23) The Five Bells, Bugbrooke .....£20 *M Brazier (Pubs.26)*
(24) Oxford Bell Ringers ...............£25 *M Brazier*
(25) Telephone Place, SW6 ...........£20 *P M Payne*
(26) Bell Street, NW1 ....................£15 *GB44*
(27) Year of the Artist, Sheffield ...£15 *CoverCraft*
(28) Four Lads who........................£15 *Assoc. of GBFDC 3*
(29) Sound & Vision, Cardiff........£20 *RN CvrsGpTDFC2-12*
(30) Bickleigh Plymouth................£20 *RN CvrsGpNFDC4-13*
(31) Chester Cathedral ..................£20 *P Sheridan*
(32) Whitechapel Bell Foundry .....£30 *T Hurlstone*
(33) SunsetSunrise School.............£35 *J L Englert*
(34) Concorde, Test & Delivery .....£35 *Cam S.C.*
(35) 60th Anniv Battle of Britain ...£35 *Cam S.C.*
(36) Borneo 38th Anniversary .......£20 *Benham/JS Medal 23*
**C.D.S. POSTMARKS Price Guide £10-£15**
(37) Eye, The Galleries, Six Bells
(38) Loughborough, Sheffield, Cardiff, London

## 16th January 2001 – THE FUTURE

*2nd Nuture Children (flower); 1st Listen to Children (tiger);
45p Teach Children (owl); 65p Children's Freedom (butterfly).*

| SPECIAL HANDSTAMPS | SPONSOR |
|---|---|

**Price Guide Ordinary Covers £4-£9 / Sponsored Covers:**
(1) FDI - Bureau .................................. *Royal Mail (n.s.c.)*
(2) FDI - Hope Valley ........................ *Royal Mail (n.s.c.)*
(3) -do- non pictorial version ............ *Royal Mail (n.s.c.)*
(4) The Future, Birmingham .............. *Royal Mail (n.s.c.)*

(5) Nuture Children ........................£15 *Benham BLCS 197*
(6) Listen to Children ..................£15 *Benham BLCS 197*
(7) Teach Children .........................£20 *Benham*
(8) Children's Freedom ...............£20 *Benham Pilgrim*
(9) A Child for the Future, N1.....£20 *Benham Coin Cover*
(10) The Earth's Children, N1 ......£20 *Benham*
(11) Savile Row, W1 ......................£20 *Benham Eng.Heritage*
(12) Greenwich ...............................£15 *Bradbury Sovereign 1*
(13) Greenwich ...............................£20 *Bradbury Britannia 1*
(14) Millennium, Hope Park .........£15 *Westminster*
(15) Autographed, Hope Close .....£25 *Westminster*
(16) Hope Park, Bromley Kent......£15 *Westminster*
(17) Child's Place, SW5..................£30 *Steven Scott Plat.25*
(18) Freedom Street, SW11 ...........£20 *Steven Scott 50*
(19) Hope Primary School..............£20 *FourpennyPost*
(20) Pattishall Primary School......£20 *M Brazier (Pubs.27)*
(21) Child's Place SW5 ..................£20 *P M Payne*
(22) Butterfly Lane, Elstree............£15 *GB45*
(23) CHF, Gateshead ......................£15 *CoverCraft*
(24) Hope for the Future, Hope ....£15 *RN CvrsGpTDFC2-13*
(25) HMS Porpoise, Gosport .........£15 *RN CvrsGpNFDC4-14*
(26) Rocket, Liverpool...................£40 *Buckingham Cvrs 1*
(27) The Future, Salisbury .............£20 *P Sheridan*
(28) Greenwich ...............................£25 *T Hurlstone*
(29) Iona Post Office 150 Anniv ...£20 *Royal Mail*
(30) South Georgia, Falkland Is....£20 *Benham/JS Medal 24*
(31) Duxford, Cambridge ...............£20 *BritHerCollections*
**C.D.S. POSTMARKS Price Guide £10-£15**
(32) Hope, Playing Place, Child's Hill, Child Okeford
(33) High Holborn (UNICEF)

## 2001 THE FUTURE

# Commemorative Issues 2001 to date

## 6th February 2001 – OCCASIONS
*5 x 1st Class: New Baby, Love, Cheers, Thanks & Welcome.*
**SPECIAL HANDSTAMPS**     **SPONSOR**
Price Guide Ordinary Covers £4-£9 / Sponsored Covers:
(1) FDI - Bureau................................ *Royal Mail (n.s.c.)*
(2) FDI - Merry Hill............................ *Royal Mail (n.s.c.)*
(3) -do- non pictorial version ............ *Royal Mail (n.s.c.)*
(4) Occasions, Birmingham.............. *Royal Mail (n.s.c.)*
(5) Childrey Wantage....................£15 *Benham BLCS 199*
(6) Greet Birmingham ...................£15 *Benham BLCS 199*
(7) Lover Salisbury ........................£20 *Benham*
(8) Thankerton Biggar....................£20 *Benham Pilgrim*
(9) Welcombe Bideford..................£20 *Benham*
(10) Greet Cheltenham...................£20 *Benham Coin Cover*
(11) Occasions..................................£20 *Benham 500(199)*
(12) Gretna Green ............................£20 *Bradbury Windsor 3*
(13) Autographed, Merryfield.........£25 *Westminster*
(14) Smiles Place, SE13..................£15 *Westminster*
(15) The Silver Jubilee ...................£15 *M Brazier (Pubs.28)*
(16) Silver Street, London ..............£15 *GB47*
(17) Lover Salisbury Wilts .............£25 *Buckingham Cvrs 2*
(18) N.I. Tourist Board....................£20 *P Sheridan*
(19) Hatton Garden .........................£20 *T Hurlstone*
(20) Friends of NPMuseum ...........£15 *NPM(postcard issue)*
(21) Boscombe Down .....................£20 *BritHerCollections*
**C.D.S. POSTMARKS Price Guide £10-£15**
(22) Lover, Silver Link

## 13th February 2001 – CATS & DOGS
*10 x 1st Class: Black & white photographic images.*
**SPECIAL HANDSTAMPS**     **SPONSOR**
Price Guide Ordinary Covers £4-£9 / Sponsored Covers:
(1) FDI - Bureau................................ *Royal Mail (n.s.c.)*
(2) FDI - Petts Wood........................... *Royal Mail (n.s.c.)*
(3) -do- non pictorial version ............ *Royal Mail (n.s.c.)*
(4) Cats & Dogs, Birmingham........... *Royal Mail (n.s.c.)*
(5) Catshill, Bromsgrove ..............£15 *Benham BLCS 200*
(6) Kittywell Braunton...................£20 *Benham Pilgrim*
(7) Catsfield, Battle.........................£20 *Benham*
(8) Catstree Bridgnorth .................£20 *Benham D372*
(9) Pant, Oswestry .........................£15 *Benham BLCS 200*
(10) Dog Little, Enniskillen...........£20 *Benham Pilgrim*
(11) Dog Big, Enniskillen...............£20 *Benham*
(12) Bonehill, Tamworth.................£20 *Benham*
(13) Barking, Ipswich.....................£20 *Benham Pilgrim*
(14) Pawlett, Bridgwater.................£20 *Benham Coin Cover*
(15) Cats Protection, Horsham.......£20 *Benham Pilgrim*
(16) Pett, Hastings ..........................£20 *Benham (500)200*
(17) Isle of Dogs..............................£15 *Bradbury Sovereign 2*
(18) Catshill......................................£15 *Bradbury Britannia 2*
(19) Battersea, London SW8..........£15 *Westminster*
(20) Autographed, Battersea...........£20 *Westminster*

## 2001 OCCASIONS

## 2001 CATS & DOGS

## 2001 THE WEATHER

(21) Battersea Sq, SW11 ...............£15 *Steven Scott 51*
(22) The Greyhound.......................£20 *M Brazier (Pubs.29)*
(23) Cat Hill, Barnet Herts............£15 *GB48*
(24) Our Dogs Manchester.............£15 *CoverCraft*
(25) Cats Ash, Newport..................£20 *Buckingham Cvrs 4*
(26) Black Dog, Crediton...............£20 *Buckingham Cvrs 4*
(27) PDSA Huyton, Liverpool.........£20 *P Sheridan*
(28) Your dog, Isle of Dogs............£25 *T Hurlstone*
(29) Your cat, Catford....................£25 *T Hurlstone*
(30) Celia Hammond Trust.............£25 *T Hurlstone*
(31) Lawton & Stokes ....................£25 *T Hurlstone*
(32) The Shackleton.......................£20 *BritHerCollections*
(33) Biggin Hill, Westerham..........£20 *BritHerCollections*
**C.D.S. POSTMARKS Price Guide £10-£15**
(34) Battersea, Dog & Gun, Isle of Dogs, Dog Kennel Lane
(35) Catsfield, Catshill, Barking, Terriers, Pett, Horsham
*Self-adhesive stamps issued in books of 10 1st Class stamps.*
*Some books contained an extra 2 x 1st definitives.*

## 13th March 2001 – THE WEATHER
*19p Rain; 27p Fair; 45p Stormy; 65p Very Dry/Set Fair.*
*Set of Stamps & Miniature Sheet issued on same date.*

| SPECIAL HANDSTAMPS | | SPONSOR |
|---|---|---|
| **Price Guide Ordinary Covers £4-£9 / Sponsored Covers:** | | |

(1) FDI - Bureau...................................... *Royal Mail (n.s.c.)*
(2) FDI - Fraserburgh ........................... *Royal Mail (n.s.c.)*
(3) -do- non pictorial version .............. *Royal Mail (n.s.c.)*
(4) The Weather, Birmingham............. *Royal Mail (n.s.c.)*
(5) Rainy Weather, Bracknell .....£20 *Benham Coin Cover*
(6) Fair Weather, Fair Isle ...........£20 *Benham Pilgrim*
(7) Stormy Weather, Oxford .......£20 *Benham 500(202)*
(8) Dry Weather, Reading.............£20 *Benham 500(202)*
(9) First Weather Map..................£20 *Benham Coin Cover*
(10) The Weather, Bracknell .........£20 *Benham 500(203)*
(11) First Weather Map..................£20 *Benham 500(203)*
(12) Wild Weather, Exton S'ton ....£15 *Benham BLCS 203*
(13) Wild Weather, Eastbourne.....£15 *Benham BLCS 203*
(14) RSPB Hope Farm....................£20 *Benham*
(15) Windygates ...........................£15 *Bradbury Sovereign 3*
(16) 150 Years Progress Reading...£20 *Bradbury Sovereign 3*
(17) Snowshill...............................£15 *Bradbury Britannia 3*
(18) Sunnyside..............................£15 *Bradbury Windsor 2*
(19) Autographed, Sunny Cresc....£15 *Westminster*
(20) Weatherley Close, E3 ............£15 *Steven Scott 52*
(21) Weather Cock ........................£20 *M Brazier (Pubs.30)*
(22) Sunbeam Rd, NW10...............£15 *GB48*
(23) Planting for Future, Uckfield..£15 *Buckingham Cvrs 5*
(24) Scottish Wildlife Trust.............£15 *CoverCraft*
(25) Windyridge Close, SW19.......£20 *P M Payne*
(26) 150 Years Weather Charts.....£15 *Dawn*
(27) British Weather London.........£10 *Assoc. of GBFDC 4*
(28) London's Maritime Borough .£20 *T Hurlstone*
(29) The Weather, Bracknell .........£15 *RN CvrsGp*
(30) Capt Walker Liverpool ..........£20 *RN CvrsGp*
(31) Manchester Weather Centre..£15 *P Sheridan*
(32) Exmouth Stamp Club.............£20 *Exmouth Stamp Club*
(33) Old England XI St Albans .....£20 *Woodford Sports*
(34) Grosvenor Square, W1..........£15 *BritHerCollections*
(35) Jade Crossing Fund.................£35 *Jade Crossing Fund*
(36) Gulf War, Kuwait Whitehall..£15 *Benham/JS Medal 25*
**C.D.S. POSTMARKS Price Guide £10-£15**
(37) Bracknell, Fair Isle, Sunnybrow, Windygates, Sunnyhill
(38) Puddletown, Windwhistle, Thunder Lane, Freezy Water
(39) Frazerburgh, Fog Lane, Gale Street, Rainhill - or similar

## 2001 THE WEATHER - Miniature Sheet

## 2001 SUBMARINES

## 10th April 2001 – SUBMARINES
*2nd Vanguard Class; 1st Swiftsure Class;*
*45p Unity Class; 65p Holland Class*

| SPECIAL HANDSTAMPS | | SPONSOR |
|---|---|---|
| **Price Guide Ordinary Covers £4-£9 / Sponsored Covers:** | | |

(1) FDI - Bureau.................................. *Royal Mail (n.s.c.)*
(2) FDI - Portsmouth.......................... *Royal Mail (n.s.c.)*
(3) -do- non pictorial version .......... *Royal Mail (n.s.c.)*
(4) Submarines, Birmingham............. *Royal Mail (n.s.c.)*
(5) Vanguard, Plymouth.............£15 *Benham BLCS 204*
(6) Swiftsure, Faslane..................£15 *Benham BLCS 204*
(7) Barrow-in-Furness (circle) ....£20 *Benham Coin Cover*
(8) Barrow-in-Furness (oval)......£25 *Benham 500(204)*
(9) Centenary, Portsmouth ..........£20 *Benham Coin Cover*
(10) Centenary, Barrow..................£20 *Benham*
(11) HMS Conquerors ...................£20 *Bradbury Sovereign 4*
(12) Nemo & the Nautilus.............£20 *Bradbury Britannia 4*
(13) Submarines, Portsmouth........£15 *Westminster*
(14) Submarines, Portsmouth........£15 *Westminster*
(15) Autographed, Portsmouth .....£25 *Westminster*

148

(16) Ocean Street, E1 ......................£15 *Steven Scott 53*
(17) The Nautilus, North Shields ..£20 *M Brazier (Pubs.31)*
(18) Target Close, Feltham..............£15 *GB50*
(19) RN Submarine Museum ........£25 *Buckingham Cvrs 6*
(20) Inst. of Marine Engineers.......£15 *CoverCraft*
(21) 20,000 Leagues Under Sea.....£20 *P M Payne*
(22) RN Submarine Service...........£15 *RN CvrsGp*
(23) HM Sub Spearfish...................£15 *RN CvrsGp*
(24) Dock Road Birkenhead .........£15 *P Sheridan*
(25) Enigma Code Breakers ..........£10 *Bletchley PO*
(26) Centenary Dover ....................£25 *H D McIntyre*
(27) Dive! Dive! Devonport.£25 *R G Howe*
(28) Cody War Kite BF2624PS......£85 *Group Capt Randle*
(29) Capture of Badajoz.................£20 *Benham/JS Medal 26*
(30) Mountbatten Plymouth ..........£20 *BritHerCollections*
(31) Gosport (changeable date).....£15 *RN CvrsGp*
(32) Faslane (changeable date)......£15 *RN CvrsGp*
(33) Vickerstown Barrow...............£30 *Cam S.C.*
(34) BF 2628 PS RN Sub Service ....... *British Forces (n.s.c.)*
(35) BF 2630 PS Bureau ...................... *British Forces (n.s.c.)*
**C.D.S. POSTMARKS Price Guide £10-£15**
(36) Clyde Submarine Base, Barrow in Furness, Clydebank,
(37) Drake Barracks, Gosport, Devonport, Holland on Sea

## 17th April 2001 – SUBMARINES Self Adhesive
*1st Swiftsure Class (x2) issued in self-adhesive stamp book with four 1st Class definitives*

**SPECIAL HANDSTAMPS**
**Price Guide Ordinary Covers £4-£9 / Sponsored Covers:**
(1) Barrow-in-Furness ..................£40 *Bradbury Sovereign 4*
(2) Barrow-in-Furness ..................£30 *Benham BLCS 205*
(3) Gosport....................................£35 *Benham*
(4) Chatham Kent.........................£30 *Benham BLCS 205*
(5) H M Submarine Affray ..........£30 *RN CvrsGp*
(6) Gosport (changeable date)........... *RN CvrsGp* (n.s.c.)
(7) Faslane (changeable date)........... *RN CvrsGp* (n.s.c.)
(8) Vickerstown Barrow...............£30 *Cam S.C.* *
* *Postmark same design as for the 10th April issue.*
**C.D.S. POSTMARKS Price Guide £10-£15**
(9) Barrow in Furness

## 15th May 2001 – BUSES
*5 x 1st Class featuring Classic Double-Decker Buses*
*Set of Stamps & Miniature Sheet issued on same date.*

**SPECIAL HANDSTAMPS**      **SPONSOR**
**Price Guide Ordinary Covers £4-£9 / Sponsored Covers:**
(1) FDI - Bureau............................ *Royal Mail (n.s.c.)*
(2) FDI - London WC2................... *Royal Mail (n.s.c.)*
(3) -do- non pictorial version ...... *Royal Mail (n.s.c.)*
(4) Double-Deckers, Birmingham...... *Royal Mail (n.s.c.)*
(5) Double-Deckers, Southall ......£15 *Benham BLCS 207*
(6) Double-Deckers, Guildford....£20 *Benham Pilgrim*
(7) Double-Deckers, Bristol .........£15 *Benham BLCS 208*
(8) Double-Deckers, W4................£15 *Benham BLCS 207*
(9) Double-Deckers, E4.................£15 *Benham BLCS 208*
(10) Double-Deckers, WC2.............£20 *Benham 500(208)*
(11) Stop Here, London SW1.......£20 *Benham 500(207)*
(12) Transportation .........................£20 *Benham Coin Cover*
(13) Leyland, Lancashire.................£20 *Bradbury Britannia 5*
(14) Leyland, Lancs.........................£20 *Bradbury Sovereign 5*
(15) Westminster, London .............£20 *Bradbury Windsor 5*
(16) Victoria, London ....................£15 *Westminster*
(17) Autographed, Victoria............£25 *Westminster*
(18) Oxford Street, W1 ..................£15 *Steven Scott 54*
(19) London's Transport Museum £15 *Steven Scott*
(20) Stagecoach, Perth....................£15 *M Brazier (Pubs.32)*
(21) Piccadilly Circus, W1 .............£15 *GB51*
(22) Buses, Bus Magazine ..............£40 *Buckingham Cvrs 7*
(23) Classic Bus, Edinburgh ..........£20 *CoverCraft*
(24) British Buses, London.............£15 *Assoc. of GBFDC 5*
(25) British Buses, Tuckingmill......£15 *RN CvrsGp*
(26) HMS/m Sickle .........................£15 *RN CvrsGp*
(27) British Bus Archives, Bury......£20 *P Sheridan*
(28) Electric Trams, Croydon.........£15 *Dawn*
(29) Electric Trams, Manchester ....£15 *Dawn*
(30) Manchester & Salford.............£15 *Dawn*
(31) Covent Garden .......................£25 *T Hurlstone*
(32) TransBus International ...........£10 *Bletchley PO*
(33) Code Breakers..........................£10 *Bletchley PO*
(34) Double Deckers, Victoria.......£30 *M J Kingsland*
(35) Buses of East Kent..................£20 *P J Barrett*
(36) Last Stand at Gandamak........£20 *Group Capt Randle*
(37) Red Arrows, Cranwell............£20 *BritHerCollections*
**C.D.S. POSTMARKS Price Guide £10-£15**
(38) Leyland, Paddington, Victoria St, Tuckingmill, Coach Rd
(39) Terminus Rd, Trafford Park, Herne Bay *etc*

## 2001 SUBMARINES

## 2001 BUSES

## 2001 FABULOUS HATS

### 5th June 2001 – OCCASIONS Generic Issue
*A re-issue of the February 2001 Occasions stamps issued in sheets of 20 1st Class stamps with labels attached: New Baby, Love, Cheers, Thanks & Welcome. These were also issued on 1st May with Customised Labels - Prices £10 - £15.*

**SPECIAL HANDSTAMPS       SPONSOR**
Price Guide Ordinary Covers £4-£9 / Sponsored Covers:
(1)  Letters Lochbroom .................£20  *Benham*
(2)  Lover Salisbury.......................£50  *Bradbury*
**C.D.S. POSTMARKS Price Guide £10-£15**
(3)  Silverstone, Silverdale, Silver Street

### 19th June 2001 – FABULOUS HATS
*Hats by the following designers: 1st Pip Hackett; 'E' Dai Rees; 45p Stephen Jones; 65p Philip Treacy.*

**SPECIAL HANDSTAMPS       SPONSOR**
Price Guide Ordinary Covers £4-£9 / Sponsored Covers:
(1)  FDI - Tallents House....................  *Royal Mail (n.s.c.)*
(2)  FDI - Ascot..................................  *Royal Mail (n.s.c.)*
(3)  -do- non pictorial version .........  *Royal Mail (n.s.c.)*
(4)  Fabulous Hats, Birmingham........  *Royal Mail (n.s.c.)*
(5)  Blackstock Road, N5...............£20  *Benham*
(6)  Belgravia, SW1 .......................£15  *Benham BLCS 209*
(7)  Gt. Western Road, W9...........£20  *Benham Pilgrim*
(8)  Great Queen Street, WC2 .....£15  *Benham BLCS 209*
(9)  Hat & Mitre Court, EC1 .......£20  *Benham 500(209)*
(10) Ascot ......................................£20  *Benham Coin Cover*
(11) Ascot Berks............................£15  *Bradbury Sovereign 6*
(12) Ascot Berkshire ......................£15  *Bradbury Britannia 6*
(13) Ascot Berkshire ......................£15  *Westminster*
(14) Autographed, Ascot ..................  *Westminster*
(15) Hat & Mitre Court, EC1 .......£15  *Steven Scott 55*
(16) The Boater, Luton Beds..........£20  *M Brazier (Pubs.33)*
(17) Hatters Lane............................£15  *GB52*
(18) Royal Ascot Ladies Day.........£25  *Buckingham Cvrs 9*
(19) British Hat Guild, Luton .......£25  *CoverCraft*
(20) Fabulous Hats, Stockport......£15  *RN CvrsGp*
(21) Falkland Islands ......................£15  *RN CvrsGp*
(22) Hat Works, Stockport............£20  *P Sheridan*
(23) Fabulous Hats Carnaby St .....£25  *T Hurlstone*
(24) Wimbledon, London SW1 .....£20  *P M Payne*
(25) Derby Street, London W1 .....£30  *M J Kingsland*
(26) Civil Defence Memorial.........£30  *C J Young*
(27) Bunbury Cricket Club ............£25  *Woodford Sports*
(28) Capture of Chuenpee .............£20  *Benham*
(29) Debden, Cambridgeshire .......£20  *BritHerCollections*
(30) Carrickfergus.........................£250  *Consignia*
**C.D.S. POSTMARKS Price Guide £10-£15**
(31) Ascot, Luton, Carnaby Street, Silk Street, Busby
(32) Hatt, Hatfield, Hatton, Top o' the Brow

### 3rd July 2001 – 'SMILERS' Generic Issue
*Reprinted version of the Miniature Sheet issued for the Stamp Show 2000 'Smilers' stamps plus revised label designs.*

**SPECIAL HANDSTAMPS       SPONSOR**
Price Guide Ordinary Covers £4-£9 / Sponsored Covers:
(1)  Smile with Mr Punch .............£30  *Bradbury*
(2)  Smilers Greetwell Lincoln......£20  *Benham*
(3)  Wimbledon Championships...£25  *Paul Inwood (pair)*

### 2001 PONDLIFE

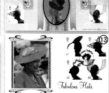

### 10th July 2001 – PONDLIFE
*1st Common Frong; 'E' Great Diving Beetle; 45p Stickleback; 65p Dragonfly.*

**SPECIAL HANDSTAMPS       SPONSOR**
Price Guide Ordinary Covers £4-£9 / Sponsored Covers:
(1)  FDI - Tallents House....................  *Royal Mail (n.s.c.)*
(2)  FDI - Oundle, Peterborough .......  *Royal Mail (n.s.c.)*
(3)  -do- non pictorial version ...........  *Royal Mail (n.s.c.)*
(4)  Pondlife, Birmingham...................  *Royal Mail (n.s.c.)*
(5)  Pondlife, Liverpool .................£15  *Benham BLCS 210*
(6)  Pondlife, Sutton Park .............£20  *Benham Pilgrim*
(7)  Pondlife, Barnes SW13 ..........£15  *Benham BLCS 210*
(8)  Pondlife, Alverley ...................£20  *Benham 500(210)*
(9)  Pondlife, Liverpool .................£20  *Benham Coin Cover*
(10) Pondersbridge, Huntingdon...£15  *Bradbury Sovereign 7*
(11) Fishers Pond, Eastleigh.........£25  *Bradbury Britannia 7*
(12) Freshwater Rd, London SW7 £15  *Westminster*
(13) Autographed, Pond Place .........  *Westminster*
(14) Pond Place, London SW3 .....£15  *Steven Scott 56*
(15) The Pike & Eel, Daventry .....£20  *M Brazier (Pubs.34)*
(16) Pond Street, London NW3.....£15  *GB53*
(17) Scotney Castle Garden...........£30  *Buckingham Cvrs 10*
(18) Scottish Wildlife Trust............£15  *CoverCraft*
(19) Pondlife, Poole Dorset ..........£15  *RN CvrsGp*
(20) Operation Husky.....................£15  *RN CvrsGp*
(21) Town Pond Runcorn ..............£20  *P Sheridan*

(22) Hampstead Heath, NW3 ........£20  *T Hurlstone*
(23) Vocal Pondlife ............................£25  *M J Kingsland*
(24) Frog Lane, Bristol ...................£25  *D Legg*
(25) Eden Project, St. Austell .......£30  *Mill.Commem.Covers*
(26) Rotary Club of London ...........£20  *Benham*
(27) Battle of Meeanee ..................£20  *Benham*
(28) Biggin Hill, Westerham .........£15  *BritHerCollections*
(29) Battle of Britain Mem Day .....£20  *Squadron Leader Hill*
**C.D.S. POSTMARKS Price Guide £10-£15**
(30) Watermeadow, Fishlake, The Pond, Fishponds, Frogmore
(31) Oundle, Fishers Pond, Waterside, Riverbank, Fishpool

## 4th September 2001 – PUNCH & JUDY
*6 x 1st: Policeman, Clown, Punch, Judy, Beadle & Crocodile.*
*Also issued on same day a Self Adhesive Stamp Book contain-*
*ing 6 x 1st: Mr Punch, Judy & 4 Definitives.*

**SPECIAL HANDSTAMPS          SPONSOR**
**Price Guide Ordinary Covers £4-£9 / Sponsored Covers:**
(1)  FDI - Tallents House ....................  *Royal Mail (n.s.c.)*
(2)  FDI - Blackpool ...........................  *Royal Mail (n.s.c.)*
(3)  -do- non pictorial version ............  *Royal Mail (n.s.c.)*
(4)  Punch & Judy, Birmingham .........  *Royal Mail (n.s.c.)*
(5)  Punch & Judy, Blackpool .........£15  *Benham BLCS 211*
(6)  Punch & Judy, Margate ...........£15  *Benham BLCS 212*
(7)  Punch & Judy, Brighton ........£20  *Benham Pilgrim*
(8)  Punch & Judy, Scarborough ...£20  *Benham 500*
(9)  Punch & Judy, Eastbourne .....£20  *Benham BLCS 211*
(10) Punch & Judy, Weston ...........£20  *Benham 500*
(11) Punch & Judy, Blackpool .......£20  *Benham Coin Cover*
(12) Birthplace of Mr Punch ..........£15  *Bradbury Sovereign 8*
(13) Covent Garden ........................£15  *Bradbury Britannia 8*
(14) Self Adhesives ..........................£30  *Bradbury Britannia 8*
(15) Blackpool, Lancashire .............£25  *Westminster*
(16) Autographed, Blackpool .........£25  *Westminster*
(17) Theatre Street, SW11 .............£15  *Steven Scott 57*
(18) Northampton ............................£20  *M Brazier (Pubs.35)*
(19) Croft New Ash Green ..............£15  *GB54*
(20) Punch & Judy Inn ....................£25  *Buckingham Cvrs 11*
(21) Puppeteers UK, Bicester ........£15  *CoverCraft*
(22) Punch & Judy Fellowship ......£15  *Bletchley PO*
(23) Harlequin Puppet Theatre ......£20  *P Sheridan*
(24) Punch & Judy, Covent Gdn ...£25  *T Hurlstone*
(25) Nat West Philatelic Society ...£25  *Nat West Phil Society*
(26) Punch & Judy, Margate ..........£25  *H D MacIntyre*
(27) East Grinstead Rotary Club ...£30  *E Grins'd Stamp Club*
(28) Debden, Saffron Walden ........£15  *BritHerCollections*
(29) Battle of Moodkee ..................£15  *Group Capt Randle*
**C.D.S. POSTMARKS Price Guide £10-£15**
(25) The Beach, South Shore, Seaside, The Pier, Loggerheads
(26) East Beach, Butlin's Camp, Funcoast World Skegness

## 2nd October 2001 – NOBEL PRIZES
*2nd Chemistry; 1st Economic Sciences; E Peace;*
*40p Medicine; 45p Literature; 65p Physics.*

**SPECIAL HANDSTAMPS          SPONSOR**
**Price Guide Ordinary Covers £4-£9 / Sponsored Covers:**
(1)  FDI - Tallents House ....................  *Royal Mail (n.s.c.)*
(2)  FDI - Cambridge ..........................  *Royal Mail (n.s.c.)*
(3)  -do- non pictorial version ............  *Royal Mail (n.s.c.)*
(4)  Nobel Prizes Birmingham ............  *Royal Mail (n.s.c.)*
(5)  FDI - Oxford ................................  *Royal Mail (n.s.c.)*
(6)  Brighton - Chemistry ...............£20  *Benham Pilgrim*
(7)  London WC2 - Econ Sciences ...£20  *Benham*
(8)  London EC1 - Peace .............£20  *Benham Coin Cover*
(9)  London NW1 -Medicine ........£20  *Benham (500)213*
(10) Literature - Oxford .................£15  *Benham BLCS 213*
(11) London SW7 - Physics ..........£15  *Benham BLCS 213*
(12) Alfred Nobel, Ardeer .............£20  *Bradbury Sovereign 9*
(13) Sir Winston Churchill ............£20  *Bradbury Britannia 9*
(14) Nobel Road, N18 ....................£15  *Westminster*
(15) Autographed, N18 ..................£25  *Westminster*
(16) Alfred Place, WC1 .................£20  *Steven Scott 58*
(17) The Swedish Flag, E1 ............£20  *M Brazier (Pubs.36)*
(18) Nobel House, SE5 ..................£15  *GB55*
(19) Cambridge ..............................£45  *Buckingham Cvrs 12*
(20) Rudyard Kipling, Burwash .....£35  *Buckingham Cvrs 12*
(21) Inst of Internat'l Affairs .........£15  *CoverCraft*
(22) Marconi Way, Southall ...........£20  *JFE Payne*
(23) The Washing Machine ............£20  *JFE Payne*
(24) Nobel Rd (changeable date) ..£20  *JFE Payne*
(25) Rudyard Kipling, Burwash .....£20  *P Sheridan*
(26) 5th Generation of Churchills ...£15  *Bletchley PO*
(27) Nobel Rd, N18 ........................£20  *Assoc. of GBFDC 6*
(28) Jean Henri Dunant ..................£20  *Britcross Ltd*
(29) Lech Walesa ............................£30  *J L Englert*
(30) Forever Heroes, Duxford .......£15  *BritHerCollections*

### 2001 PUNCH & JUDY

### 2001 NOBEL PRIZES

151

## 2001 FLAGS & ENSIGNS

(31) The Siege of Mooltan ...............£15 *Group Capt Randle*
(32) Northern Ireland, Armagh .....£20 *Royal Mail/RoyalMint*
**C.D.S. POSTMARKS Price Guide £10-£15**
(33) Churchill, Peacehaven, Science Museum,
(34) Cambridge, Oxford

## 22nd October 2001 – FLAGS & ENSIGNS
*(1) Miniature Sheet 4x1st: White Ensign; Union Flag;*
*        Jolly Roger; Chief of Defence Staff.*
*(2) Self Adhesive Stamp Book containing 6 x 1st Class Stamps:*
*        White Ensign, Jolly Roger & 4 Definitives.*
*(3) Prestige Stamp Book (see definitives section), which also*
*        contained the Flags & Ensigns miniature sheet.*

| SPECIAL HANDSTAMPS | SPONSOR |
|---|---|
| **Price Guide Ordinary Covers £4-£9 / Sponsored Covers:** | |

(1)  FDI - Tallents House.................... *Royal Mail (n.s.c.)*
(2)  FDI - Rosyth, Dunfermline .......... *Royal Mail (n.s.c.)*
(3)  -do- non pictorial version ............ *Royal Mail (n.s.c.)*
(4)  Flags & Ensigns Birmingham....... *Royal Mail (n.s.c.)*
(5)  Unseen & Unheard Birmingham.. *Royal Mail (n.s.c.)*
(6)  Faslane.....................................£20 *Benham (500)215*
(7)  Portsmouth ..............................£15 *Benham BLCS 215*
(8)  Whitehall..................................£15 *Benham BLCS 216*
(9)  Dartmouth ...............................£20 *Benham (500)214*
(10) Flags & ..., SW1.........................£15 *Benham BLCS 214*
(11) Flags & ..., Greenwich...............£15 *Benham BLCS 216*
(12) Flags & ..., Penzance ...............£20 *Benham D378*
(13) Flags & ..., Plymouth ................£20 *Benham*
(14) Flags & ..., Admiralty Arch.....£20 *Benham Coin Cover*
(15) Elgar, Lower Broadheath ......£20 *Bradbury (s)*
(16) Rule Britannia, Edinburgh .....£15 *Bradbury Windsor 11*
(17) Flags & Ensigns, Romsey ......£25 *Bradbury*
(18) Self Adhesive Stamps.............£25 *Bradbury*
(19) Unseen & Unheard, Barrow..£15 *Bradbury*
(20) Flags & Ensigns, Gosport......£15 *Westminster*
(21) Submarines, Gosport...............£15 *Westminster*
(22) Autographed, Gosport.............£25 *Westminster*
(23) Royal Standard Way................£15 *Steven Scott 59*
(24) The Union Jack, Rugby.............£20 *M Brazier (Pubs.37)*
(25) Victory Way London SE16.......£15 *GB56*
(26) RN Sub Museum, Gosport....£30 *Buckingham Cvrs 13*
(27) Admirals Flag Loft .................£20 *T Hurlstone*
(28) Historic Dockyard...................£20 *T Hurlstone*
(29) The Flag Insitute, York .........£20 *T Hurlstone*
(30) Battle of the Atlantic .............£20 *P Sheridan*
(31) Chatham 1901-2001................£30 *H D MacIntyre*
(32) The Boat Brewery .................£30 *A Sheriff*
(33) Peace in Kaffraria...................£15 *Group Capt Randle*
(34) Coningsby, Lincoln ................£15 *BritHerCollections*
(35) Corfu Channel Incident.........£15 *RN CvrsGp*
(36) Gosport (changeable date).....£20 *RN CvrsGp*
(37) Faslane (changeable date).....£20 *RN CvrsGp*
(38) HMS Petard.............................£25 *Cam S.C.*
(39) Royal Yacht Britannia ( -do- ) ..... *Royal Mail (n.s.c.)*
(40) Royal Mail Portsmouth ( -do- ) ... *Royal Mail (n.s.c.)*
(41) BF 2644 PS Forces Bureau........... *British Forces (n.s.c.)*
(42) Norfolk Philatelic Society ......£30 *Philatelic Society*
**C.D.S. POSTMARKS Price Guide £10-£15**
(43) St Andrews, St Georges Cross, Clyde Submarine Base
(43) Chatham, Union Street

## 2001 CHRISTMAS

## 6th November 2001 – CHRISTMAS
*2nd, 1st, E, 45p, & 65p Robins*

| SPECIAL HANDSTAMPS | SPONSOR |
|---|---|
| **Price Guide Ordinary Covers £4-£9 / Sponsored Covers:** | |

(1)  FDI - Tallents House.................... *Royal Mail (n.s.c.)*
(2)  FDI - Bethlehem ........................... *Royal Mail (n.s.c.)*
(3)  -do- non pictorial version ............ *Royal Mail (n.s.c.)*
(4)  Christmas, Birmingham ................ *Royal Mail (n.s.c.)*
(5)  Snowhill, Walcot, Bath ...............£15 *Benham BLCS 217*
(6)  Merry Hill, Wolverhampton ..£20 *Benham Pilgrim*
(7)  Christmas Common ....................£20 *Benham (500)217*
(8)  Frostrow, Sedbergh.................£20 *Benham Coin Cover*
(9)  Bird in Hand, Whiteshill .......£15 *Benham BLCS 217*
(10) Hadrian's Wall ..........................£20 *Benham Eng.Heritage*
(11) Nasareth ...................................£15 *Bradbury Sovereign 10*
(12) Bethlehem .................................£15 *Bradbury Britannia 10*
(13) Robins Lane, Norwich ...........£15 *Westminster*
(14) Autographed .............................£25 *Westminster*
(15) Holly Tree Close SW19 .........£15 *Steven Scott 60*
(16) The Robins, Bristol .................£20 *M Brazier (Pubs.38)*
(17) Robin Close, NW7 .................£15 *GB57*
(18) Robins, Midhurst....................£40 *Buckingham Cvrs 14*
(19) Pudding Lane, EC3..................£20 *CoverCraft*
(20) North Pole Road, W10 ..........£30 *M J Kingsland*
(21) Robins Lane, St. Helens ........£25 *P Sheridan*

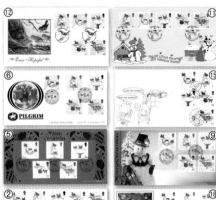

(22) Bletchley Park...........................£15  *Bletchley PO*
(23) Kings Cliffe, Peterborough .....£15  *BritHerCollections*
(24) Battle of Khoosh-Ab................£15  *Group Capt Randle*
(25) Target Tirpitz Lossiemouth....£25  *Cam S.C.*
**C.D.S. POSTMARKS Price Guide £10-£15**
(26) Robins Lane, Winter Gardens, Hollybush, Jerusalem St
(27) Holy Island, St. Nicholas-at-Wade, Nasareth

## 18th Dec 2001 – CARTOONS Generic Issue
*Reprinted version of the 1996 Cartoons Greetings stamps in
sheet format plus revised label designs.*

**SPECIAL HANDSTAMPS**　　　**SPONSOR**
**Price Guide Ordinary Covers £4-£9 / Sponsored Covers:**
(1)　Laughterton ............................£25  *Bradbury*
(2)　Lover, Salisbury.......................£20  *Benham BLCS 221*
(3)　Clock Face, St. Helens ...........£10  *Benham(s)*
(4)　World's End, Waterlooville.....£10  *Benham(s)*
(5)　Fetcham, Leatherhead　........£10  *Benham(s)*
(6)　Falstone, Hexham ..................£10  *Benham(s)*
(7)　Nutts Corner, Crumlin ..........£20  *Benham BLCS 221*
(8)　Braintree, Essex .....................£10  *Benham(s)*
(9)　Letters, Lochbroom ................£10  *Benham(s)*
(10) Ringmore, Kingsbridge ..........£10  *Benham(s)*
(11) Money More, Magherafelt......£10  *Benham(s)*

## 15th Jan 2002 – THE JUST SO STORIES
*10 x 1st Class:Whale, Camel, Rhinoceros, Leopard, Elephant,
Kangaroo, Armadillo, Crab, Cat and Butterfly.*

**SPECIAL HANDSTAMPS**　　　**SPONSOR**
**Price Guide Ordinary Covers £4-£9 / Sponsored Covers:**
(1)　FDI - Tallents House...............  *Royal Mail (n.s.c.)*
(2)　FDI - Burwash, Etchingham........  *Royal Mail (n.s.c.)*
(3)　-do- non pictorial version ........  *Royal Mail (n.s.c.)*
(4)　Rudyard Kipling Birmingham .....  *Royal Mail (n.s.c.)*
(5)　Cat...Wetwood, Stafford..........£15  *Benham BLCS 218*
(6)　Elephant...Ledbury..................£20  *Benham Coin Cover*
(7)　Rhinoceros..Church Stretton .£15  *Benham BLCS 218*
(8)　Butterfly...Palacefields ...........£20  *Benham Pilgrim*
(9)　Camel...Pity Me, Durham ......£10  *Benham (s)*
(10) Whale...Whale, Penrith ...........£20  *Benham Pilgrim*
(11) Kangaroo...Hopperton............£10  *Benham (s)*
(12) Armadillo...New Invention.......£15  *Benham 500(218)*
(13) Crab...Chacewater, Truro.......£20  *Benham Pilgrim*
(14) Leopard...Spott, Dunbar.........£20  *Benham Coin Cover*
(15) Rudyard, Leek, Staffs.............£20  *Bradbury Sovereign 11*
(16) Burwash (palette) .....................£40  *Westminster*
(17) Burwash (whale)......................£15  *Westminster*
(18) Autographed, Burwash ..........£25  *Westminster*
(19) The Rudyard Kipling ..............£20  *M Brazier (Rly.1)*
(20) Towcester Book Shop ............£20  *M Brazier (Pubs.39)*
(21) Cat Hill, Barnet ......................£15  *GB58*
(22) Bateman's, Home of Kipling..£30  *Buckingham Cvrs 15*
(23) Knowsley Safari Park .............£20  *P Sheridan*
(24) Kipling Society, Rottingdean .£15  *CoverCraft*
(25) Kipling Drive, SW19...............£30  *M J Kingsland*
(26) Zoological Gardens, Chester .£30  *A Sheriff*
(27) Kipling's Just So Stories.........£15  *Bletchley PO*
(28) Just So Stories, Humpage......£20  *Phil Stamp Covers 18*
(29) HMS Kipling, Glasgow ..........£15  *RN CvrsGp*
(30) Linton-on-Ouse .....................£15  *BritHerCollections*
(31) 2002 Anniversaries ................£20  *J F E Payne*
(32) Tales of Horror.......................£30  *Cam S.C.*
(33) London Aquarium...................£30  *T Hurlstone*
**C.D.S. POSTMARKS Price Guide £7-£10**
(34) Burwash, Rottingdean, Westward Ho!
(35) Crab Lane, Whale Hill, Camel's Head

## 6th Feb 2002 – QUEEN'S GOLDEN JUBILEE
*(1) 2nd, 1st, E, 45p & 65p Portraits of the Queen.*
*(2) **Gracious Accession** Prestige Stamp Book containing
reprinted versions of the 1¹/₂d and 2¹/₂d 1952 definitives
- see also Definitive Section.*

**SPECIAL HANDSTAMPS**　　　**SPONSOR**
**Price Guide Ordinary Covers £4-£9 / Sponsored Covers:**
(1)　FDI - Tallents House....................  *Royal Mail (n.s.c.)*
(2)　FDI - Windsor ..............................  *Royal Mail (n.s.c.)*
(3)　-do- non pictorial version ...........  *Royal Mail (n.s.c.)*
(4)　Golden Wedding, Birmingham ....  *Royal Mail (n.s.c.)*
(5)　Golden Jubilee, London (circle) ...  *Royal Mail (n.s.c.)*
(6)　Golden Jubilee, London (oval) .....  *Royal Mail (n.s.c.)*
(7)　Windsor, Berks .......................£15  *Benham BLCS 219*
(8)　Buckingham Palace Rd.........£15  *Benham BLCS 219*
(9)　Sandringham, Norfolk ...........£20  *Benham Pilgrim*
(10) Royal Mile, Edinburgh ...........£30  *Benham 500(219)*
(11) Balmoral, Ballater ..................£20  *Benham*
(12) Windsor (coat of arms) ..........£20  *Benham*
(13) King George VI.......................£20  *Benham*

# 2002

## 2002 THE JUST SO STORIES

## 2002 QUEEN'S GOLDEN JUBILEE

## 2002 QUEEN'S GOLDEN JUBILEE

## 2002 OCCASIONS

## 2002 BRITAIN'S COASTLINES

| | | |
|---|---|---|
| (14) | London (square).....................£20 | *Benham* |
| (15) | Edinburgh (square) ..................£20 | *Benham* |
| (16) | Buckingham Palace Rd ...........£20 | *Benham Coin Cover* |
| (17) | Westminster (Cathedral)........£15 | *Bradbury Sovereign 12* |
| (18) | A Gracious Accession, SW1 ..£20 | *Bradbury Windsor 15* |
| (19) | London SW1 (crown) ............£15 | *Westminster* |
| (20) | Windsor (palette) ...................£40 | *Westminster* |
| (21) | Autographed, Windsor............£20 | *Westminster* |
| (22) | Buckingham Palace Road.......£15 | *Steven Scott 61* |
| (23) | Canterbury...............................£15 | *Steven Scott* |
| (24) | Blandford Camp .....................£15 | *Steven Scott* |
| (25) | Princess Elizabeth ..................£20 | *M Brazier (Rly.2)* |
| (26) | Q. Elizabeth Elmley Castle ....£20 | *M Brazier (Pubs.40)* |
| (27) | Jubilee Way, London SW19...£15 | *GB59* |
| (28) | London SW1 (Palace).............£20 | *Buckingham Cvrs 16* |
| (29) | Sandringham ...........................£25 | *Buckingham Cvrs 16* |
| (30) | Windsor...................................£25 | *Buckingham Cvrs 16* |
| (31) | Windsor (Castle) ....................£15 | *CoverCraft* |
| (32) | Westminster (flowers) ............£25 | *P Sheridan* |
| (33) | Queen Street, Harwood..........£20 | *P M Payne* |
| (34) | Jubilee Place, London SW3 ...£20 | *P M Payne* |
| (35) | Windsor...................................£15 | *Assoc. of GBFDC 7* |
| (36) | Cranwell, Sleaford...................£15 | *BritHerCollections* |
| (37) | RN Covers, Plymouth..............£15 | *RN CvrsGp* |
| (38) | Q. Elizabeth II Square ...........£20 | *Phil Stamp Covers 19* |
| (39) | Jubilee Close, Castle Cary......£20 | *Phil Stamp Covers 20* |
| (40) | Mazel Tov ...............................£35 | *S Kacher* |
| (41) | Havengore Trust......................£25 | *T Hurlstone* |
| (42) | Tony Penberthy Benefit ..........£20 | *Woodford Sports* |
| (43) | Storming of Bomarsund.........£15 | *Group Capt Randle* |
| (44) | Windsor or SW1 (changeable date).. | *Royal Mail* |
| (45) | 2002 Anniversaries .................£15 | *P M Payne* |

**C.D.S. POSTMARKS Price Guide £7-£10**
(46) Jubilee Oak, Jubilee Fields, Jubilee Cresc, Queen's Parade
(47) Heathrow, Windsor, Windsor Great Park, Crathie
(48) Windsor Castle, Sandringham (each £100)

## 5th March 2002 – OCCASIONS
*5 x 1st: Moving House, Best Wishes, Hello, Love, New Baby*

| SPECIAL HANDSTAMPS | SPONSOR |
|---|---|

**Price Guide Ordinary Covers £4-£9 / Sponsored Covers:**

| | | |
|---|---|---|
| (1) | FDI - Tallents House.................... | *Royal Mail (n.s.c.)* |
| (2) | FDI - Merry Hill........................ | *Royal Mail (n.s.c.)* |
| (3) | -do- non pictorial version ............ | *Royal Mail (n.s.c.)* |
| (4) | Occasions Birmingham.............. | *Royal Mail (n.s.c.)* |
| (5) | Greetwell, Gainsborough ......£25 | *Benham 500(222)* |
| (6) | Birthorpe, Sleaford...............£15 | *Benham BLCS 222* |
| (7) | Bloomfield, Tipton .................£20 | *Benham Coin Cover* |
| (8) | Home Meadow, Worcester ...£20 | *Benham* |
| (9) | Love Lane, London N17 .......£15 | *Benham BLCS 222* |
| (10) | Gretna Green ..........................£15 | *Bradbury Windsor 12* |
| (11) | Merry Hill Rd (cake) .............£15 | *Westminster* |
| (12) | Merry Hill Rd (palette).........£40 | *Westminster* |
| (13) | Autographed, Merry Hill Rd £25 | *Westminster* |
| (14) | Best Wishes Great Occasion .£20 | *M Brazier* |
| (15) | Titanic Ship Yard, SW14.......£15 | *GB60* |
| (16) | Motherwell ..............................£15 | *Buckingham Cvrs* |
| (17) | Hugo Bicentenary, N19.........£20 | *P M Payne* |
| (18) | Flowergirl, Romford...............£20 | *T Hurlstone* |
| (19) | Heart in Hand Rd ...................£20 | *Phil Stamp Covers 21* |
| (20) | Duxford, Cambridge...............£20 | *BritHerCollections* |

**C.D.S. POSTMARKS Price Guide £7-£10**
(21) Lover, Greet, Weddington, Daisy Hill

## 19th March 2002 – BRITAIN'S COASTLINES
*10 x 27p Studland; Luskentyre; Dover; Padstow; Broadstairs; St.Abb's Head; Dunster; Newquay; Portrush; Conwy.*

| SPECIAL HANDSTAMPS | SPONSOR |
|---|---|

**Price Guide Ordinary Covers £4-£9 / Sponsored Covers:**

| | | |
|---|---|---|
| (1) | FDI - Tallents House.................... | *Royal Mail (n.s.c.)* |
| (2) | FDI - Poolewe........................... | *Royal Mail (n.s.c.)* |
| (3) | -do- non pictorial version ............ | *Royal Mail (n.s.c.)* |
| (4) | Coastlines, Birmingham.......... | *Royal Mail (n.s.c.)* |
| (5) | Dover, Kent ............................£15 | *Benham BLCS 223* |
| (6) | Padstow, Cornwall ..................£15 | *Benham BLCS 223* |
| (7) | Conwy......................................£20 | *Benham 500(223)* |
| (8) | Dunster, Minehead ..................£20 | *Benham Coin Cover* |
| (9) | Broadstairs, Kent....................£20 | *Benham Coin Cover* |
| (10) | Luskentyre, Harris ..................£20 | *Benham Pilgrim* |
| (11) | Newquay, Cornwall .................£10 | *Benham (s)* |
| (12) | Studland, Swanage..................£10 | *Benham (s)* |
| (13) | St. Abb's, Eyemouth ...............£20 | *Benham Pilgrim* |
| (14) | Portrush, Co. Antrim ..............£20 | *Benham Pilgrim* |
| (15) | Pembrokeshire Coast...............£15 | *Bradbury Sovereign 13* |
| (16) | Studland (sun and waves) ......£15 | *Westminster* |
| (17) | Studland (palette)....................£40 | *Westminster* |

(18) Autographed, Studland ..........£25 *Westminster*
(19) Port of London ........................£15 *Steven Scott 62*
(20) Bucket & Spade, Weston ......£20 *M Brazier (Pubs.41)*
(21) Shore Road, London E9........£15 *GB61*
(22) White Cliffs, Dover ................£30 *Buckingham Cvrs 17*
(23) St Michael's Mount................£20 *Buckingham Cvrs 17*
(24) Giant's Causeway...................£20 *P Sheridan*
(25) White Cliffs of Dover ............£30 *M J Kingsland*
(26) St Margaret's Bay ..................£30 *H D MacIntyre*
(27) Coastline Signals, Bletchley...£15 *Bletchley PO*
(28) Adnams, Southwold ..............£20 *Fourpenny Post*
(29) North Coates, Grimsby ..........£15 *BritHerCollections*
(30) Operation Paraquat ...............£15 *RN CvrsGp*
(31) Coast View, Bude...................£20 *Phil Stamp Covers 22*
(32) Baltasound, Unst (changeable date).. *Royal Mail*
(33) Giant's Causeway (changeable date). *Royal Mail*
(34) Battle of Balaklava.................£15 *Group Capt Randle*
(35) Relief of Lucknow..................£15 *Group Capt Randle*
(36) Ladies Curling Team .............£25 *T Hurlstone*
**C.D.S. POSTMARKS Price Guide £7-£10**
(37) Dunster, Portrush, Studland, Dover, Sandbanks, Padstow
(38) Broadstairs, Newquay, Harris, The Rock, The Harbour
(39) St Davids, Haverfordwest: Pemb. Coast Path 50th Anniversary

## 9th April 2002 – CIRCUS
*2nd Slack Wire Act; 1st Lion Tamer; E Trick Tri Cyclists;*
*40p Krazy Kar; 45p The Equestrienne.*
**SPECIAL HANDSTAMPS          SPONSOR**
**Price Guide Ordinary Covers £4-£9 / Sponsored Covers:**
(1)   FDI - Tallents House.....................*Royal Mail (n.s.c.)*
(2)   FDI - Clowne Chesterfield...........*Royal Mail (n.s.c.)*
(3)   -do- non pictorial version ...........*Royal Mail (n.s.c.)*
(4)   Circus, Big Top Birmingham.......*Royal Mail (n.s.c.)*
(5)   Westminster Bridge Rd, SE1 .£15 *Benham BLCS 224*
(6)   Blackfriar's Road, SE1 ...........£10 *Benham (s)*
(7)   London Bridge, SE1 ...............£20 *Benham Coin Cover*
(8)   Bank Hey Street, Blackpool...£20 *Benham (500)224*
(9)   Belle Vue, Manchester ...........£15 *Benham BLCS 224*
(10) Gerry Cottle's Circus..............£20 *Bradbury Sovereign 14*
(11) Circus Rd, NW8 (clown)........£15 *Westminster*
(12) Circus Rd, NW8  (palette)......£40 *Westminster*
(13) Autographed, Circus Rd  ........£25 *Westminster*
(14) Circus Place, London EC2....£15 *Steven Scott 63*
(15) Conjuror's Half Crown ..........£20 *M Brazier (Pubs.42)*
(16) Circus Road, NW8.................£15 *GB62*
(17) Great Circus Parade, SW1 .....£20 *Buckingham Cvrs 18*
(18) Circus Unlimited, Hemel........£20 *P Sheridan*
(19) Circus Friends Association.....£15 *CoverCraft*
(20) F14 Tomcat, Grosvenor Sq....£15 *BritHerCollections*
(21) HMS Hermes, Plymouth ........£15 *RN CvrsGp*
(22) Circus, Kings Langley..............£20 *Phil Stamp Covers 23*
(23) Circus of Horrors....................£25 *Cam S.C.*
(24) Concorde 33rd Anniversary........£25 *Cam S.C.*
(25) W Reid VC Memorial.............£25 *Cam S.C.*
(26) Capture of the Taku Forts......£25 *Group Capt Randle*
(27) Sir Walter Raleigh, Feltham...£20 *P M Payne*
(28) Old England XI, Hove ...........£15 *Woodford Sports*
**C.D.S. POSTMARKS Price Guide £7-£10**
(29) Big Top, Clowne, Chipperfield, Castle Circus or similar

## 23rd April 2002 – OCCASIONS Generic Issue
*Reprinted version of the  2002 Occasions stamps with labels.*
**SPECIAL HANDSTAMPS          SPONSOR**
**Price Guide Ordinary Covers £4-£9 / Sponsored Covers:**
(1)   Greetwell, Gainsborough ......£15 *Benham*
(2)   Gretna Green, Carlisle ..........£15 *Bradbury Windsor 12*
(3)   Alexander Dumas, SE5..........£15 *P M Payne*

## 25th April 2002 – THE QUEEN MOTHER
*1st The Queen Mother; E Queen Elizabeth; 45p Elizabeth,*
*Duchess of York; 65p Lady Elizabeth Bowes-Lyon*
**SPECIAL HANDSTAMPS          SPONSOR**
**Price Guide Ordinary Covers £4-£9 / Sponsored Covers:**
(1)   FDI - Tallents House.....................*Royal Mail (n.s.c.)*
(2)   FDI - London SW1 ......................*Royal Mail (n.s.c.)*
(3)   -do- non pictorial version ...........*Royal Mail (n.s.c.)*
(4)   Queen Mother, Sandringham.......*Royal Mail (n.s.c.)*
(5)   Castle of Mey ...........................£20 *Benham Pilgrim*
(6)   Glamis, Forfar ..........................£35 *Benham (500)228*
(7)   St James's, London SW1 .......£15 *Benham BLCS 228*
(8)   Buckingham Palace Rd...........£15 *Benham BLCS 228*
(9)   Windsor Berks ........................£20 *Benham Coin Cover*
(10) In Memoriam, Glamis.............£15 *Bradbury*
(11) In Memoriam, The Mall .........£15 *Bradbury*
(12) In Memoriam, Windsor ..........£15 *Bradbury Sovereign 21*
(13) In Memorian QM, Windsor...£15 *Westminster*
(14) Windsor  (palette) ..................£40 *Westminster*

2002

## 2002 CIRCUS

## 2002 THE QUEEN MOTHER

155

## 2002 AIRLINERS

(15) Autographed, Windsor............£25 *Westminster*
(16) A Lifetime Remembered........£15 *Steven Scott 64*
(17) Queen of Hearts, Daventry....£20 *M Brazier (Pubs.43)*
(18) Regal Way, Harrow ...............£15 *GB 64*
(19) Windsor................................£25 *Buckingham Cvrs 26*
(20) Memorial Tribute, Glamis......£15 *P Sheridan*
(21) Tribute to Queen Mother ......£15 *CoverCraft*
(22) Payne FDC Sympathy.............£20 *P M Payne*
(23) London SW1 ..........................£75 *H Athanassiades*
(24) Windsor (Lillies)....................£15 *Phil Stamp Covers*
(25) Windsor................................£20 *Cam S.C.*
(26) Life of Devotion and Joy........£20 *Bletchley PO*
(27) HMS Ark Royal......................£15 *RN CvrsGp*
(28) Yacht Britannia (changeable date)... *Royal Mail*
(29) Windsor (changeable date) ............ *Royal Mail*
(30) Buck Palace (changeable date) ...... *Royal Mail*
**C.D.S. POSTMARKS Price Guide £7-£10**
(31) Bowes, West Newton, Windsor, Mey, Glamis
(32) Windsor Great Park, Clarence Rd, Windsor, Walmer
(33) Windsor Castle, Buckingham Palace (£100 each)

## 2nd May 2002 – AIRLINERS
*(1) 2nd Airbus; 1st Concorde; E Trident; 45p VC10; 65p Comet.*
*(2) Miniature Sheet with above stamps;*
*(3) Self Adhesive Stamp Book containing 6 x 1st Class Stamps:*
*2 Concorde & 4 Definitives.*

| SPECIAL HANDSTAMPS | SPONSOR |
|---|---|

**Price Guide Ordinary Covers £4-£9 / Sponsored Covers:**
(1) FDI - Tallents House.................... *Royal Mail (n.s.c.)*
(2) FDI - Heathrow Airport............... *Royal Mail (n.s.c.)*
(3) -do- non pictorial version ............ *Royal Mail (n.s.c.)*
(4) Aircraft, Birmingham ................... *Royal Mail (n.s.c.)*
(5) Concorde, Filton Bristol .....£20 *Benham BLCS 227*
(6) Airbus, Broughton Chester.....£20 *Benham BLCS 226*
(7) Comet, Hatfield Herts.............£20 *Benham BLCS 225/6*
(8) Trident, St. James's London ..£20 *Benham*
(9) VC10, Brooklands...................£20 *Benham Pilgrim*
(10) Concorde, Heathrow..............£30 *Benham (500) 225*
(11) Commercial Jet Travel............£25 *Bradbury Windsor 13*
(12) Fifty Years Jet Travel .............£20 *Bradbury Sovereign 15*
(13) Self Adhesives, Hounslow......£35 *Bradbury Windsor 18*
(14) Airliners, Heathrow (plane)...£15 *Westminster*
(15) Airliners, Heathrow (palette).£40 *Westminster*
(16) Autographed, Heathrow .......£25 *Westminster*
(17) Evolution of Aircraft, W1......£20 *Steven Scott 65*
(18) The Spitfire, Stockton ...........£25 *M Brazier (Pubs.44)*
(19) Henri Coanda, Jetstar Way ....£20 *GB63*
(20) The Comet, Croydon ..............£40 *Buckingham Cvrs 19*
(21) Concorde, Heathrow..............£40 *Buckingham Cvrs 19*
(22) Liverpool Airport ...................£20 *P Sheridan*
(23) Airliners Commemoration......£25 *CoverCraft*
(24) Vulcan, Waddington..............£25 *BritHerCollections*
(25) Stansted, Essex......................£25 *T Hurlstone*
(26) Charles Lindberg...................£25 *P M Payne*
(27) Leonardo da Vinci .................£25 *P M Payne*
(28) Heathrow Airport...................£30 *Cam S.C.*
(29) Manston Airport....................£30 *H D MacIntyre*
(30) Gatwick Top Flight.................£25 *Assoc. of GBFDC 8*
(31) RAFLET Stamp Club...............£20 *P Barrett*
(32) Exter International Airport ....£20 *R Howe*
(33) Airliners, Concorde...............£20 *Phil Stamp Covers 25*
(34) Airliners, Comet Way.............£20 *Phil Stamp Covers 24*
(35) 26th Anniv Year Concorde ....£20 *Cam S.C.*
(36) Royal Mail, Gatwick...................... *Royal Mail (n.s.c.)*
(37) Bletchley Park Post Office .....£20 *Bletchley PO*
(38) Nimrod, BF2676PS.................£20 *Sqn Ldr Hill*
(39) VC10, BF2674PS....................£20 *Sqn Ldr Hill*
(40) Sinking of the Belgrano.........£20 *RN CvrsGp*
(41) Mildenhall.............................£40 *A Sherriff*
(42) Bunbury Cricket Club ............£25 *Woodford Sports*
(43) Attack on the Gate Pa ...........£20 *Group Capt Randle*
**C.D.S. POSTMARKS Price Guide £7-£10**
(44) Heathrow Terminal 2 or 4, Gatwick, Filton, Duxford,
(45) Manchester or Glasgow Airport, Hatfield, Biggin Hill

## 21st May 2002 – WORLD CUP FOOTBALL
*(1) Miniature Sheet 4 x 1st St. George Flag & Footballs plus*
*1 x 1st Crowned Lion of England.*
*(2) 1st Crowned Lion of England - in sheet format.*
*(3) Self Adhesive Stamp Book containing 6 x 1st Class Stamps:*
*2 St George Flag/Footballs & 4 Definitives.*
*(4) Generic Sheet of 20 x 1st (St George Flag) & 16 labels.*

| SPECIAL HANDSTAMPS | SPONSOR |
|---|---|

**Price Guide Ordinary Covers £4-£9 / Sponsored Covers:**
(1) FDI - Tallents House.................... *Royal Mail (n.s.c.)*
(2) FDI - Wembley.............................. *Royal Mail (n.s.c.)*
(3) -do- non pictorial version ............ *Royal Mail (n.s.c.)*

## 2002 AIRLINERS - Miniature Sheet

(4)   World Cup, Birmingham .............. *Royal Mail (n.s.c.)*
(5)   Football 2002, Highbury.........£15 *Benham BLCS 229*
(6)   Football 2002, Wembley.........£15 *Benham BLCS 230*
(7)   Football 2002, Liverpool ........£15 *Benham BLCS 230*
(8)   Football 2002, Manchester.....£15 *Benham BLCS 229*
(9)   Football 2002, Wembley.........£20 *Benham Coin Cover*
(10)  Football 2002, Wembley.........£20 *Benham Coin Cover*
(11)  Good Luck, Wembley .............£15 *Bradbury Sovereign 17*
(12)  Home of English Football ......£15 *Bradbury Windsor 16*
(13)  Self Adhesives, Wembley........£25 *Bradbury Sovereign 17*
(14)  Wembley (football) .................£15 *Westminster*
(15)  Wembley (palette).................£40 *Westminster*
(16)  Autographed, Wembley  ........£25 *Westminster*
(17)  Tom Finney, Preston......£15 *Steven Scott*
(18)  Good Luck to England ...........£15 *Steven Scott 66*
(19)  The Goal Post ..........................£20 *M Brazier (Pubs.45)*
(20)  Wembley Stadium ..................£15 *GB 65*
(21)  World Cup 2002, Wembley ...£40 *Buckingham Cvrs 20*
(22)  Becks - Good Luck..................£20 *P Sheridan*
(23)  Historic Wembley ..................£20 *CoverCraft*
(24)  World Cup 2002, Wembley ...£20 *T Hurlstone*
(25)  World Cup Qualifiers.............£20 *P M Payne*
(26)  World Cup, Korea - Japan......£25 *Cam S.C.*
(27)  Winners World Cup 1966 ......£25 *D Harper*
(28)  Englands Way .........................£15 *Phil Stamp Covers 26*
(29)  Korea Road, Preston...............£15 *Phil Stamp Covers 27*
(30)  Football Legends ....................£20 *M Jennings*
(31)  Best Wishes, Manchester.......£15 *Dawn*
(32)  M United (changeable date) ..£15 *Dawn*
(33)  Liverpool (changeable date)....£15 *Dawn*
(34)  Norwich (changeable date)....£15 *Dawn*
(35)  Typhoon, Duxford...................£15 *BritHerCollections*
(36)  First Solo Crossing Atlantic ...£15 *Group Capt Randle*
(37)  Reduction of Magdala ...........£15 *Group Capt Randle*
(38)  Royal Horticultural Society ...£25 *A W Mailing Services*
(39)  HMS Ardent.............................£15 *RN CvrsGp*
**C.D.S. POSTMARKS Price Guide £7-£10**
(40)  Wembley or Wembley Park, Trafford Park
(41)  The Ball, Ball Green, St George's Cross

## 5th June 2002 – GOLDEN JUBILEE
*1st Class Gold Self Adhesive Definitive.*
**SPECIAL HANDSTAMPS          SPONSOR**
**Price Guide Ordinary Covers £4-£9 / Sponsored Covers:**
(1)   Parliament Square...................£15 *Benham BLCS 231*
(2)   Canterbury..............................£15 *Benham BLCS 231*
(3)   Buckingham Palace Road.......£20 *Benham Coin Cover*
(4)   Westminster Abbey.................£25 *Benham (500)231*
(5)   Self Adhesives SW1 ...............£15 *Bradbury Windsor 19*
(6)   The Mall, London ...................£15 *Westminster*
(7)   Pall Mall, London SW1 .........£15 *Buckingham Cvrs*
(8)   Championships, Wimbledon ....£15 *New Malden PO*

## 16th July 2002 – COMMONWEALTH GAMES
*2nd Swimming; 1st Running; E Cycling; 47p Long-jumping;
68p Wheelchair athletics.*
**SPECIAL HANDSTAMPS          SPONSOR**
**Price Guide Ordinary Covers £4-£9 / Sponsored Covers:**
(1)   FDI - Tallents House...................... *Royal Mail (n.s.c.)*
(2)   FDI - Manchester........................... *Royal Mail (n.s.c.)*
(3)   -do- non pictorial version ............ *Royal Mail (n.s.c.)*
(4)   Manchester 2002........................... *Royal Mail (n.s.c.)*
(5)   Friendly Games, Birmingham ...... *Royal Mail (n.s.c.)*
(6)   Games 2002, Manchester......£15 *Benham BLCS 232*
(7)   Games 2002, Manchester......£20 *Benham Coin Cover*
(8)   Games 2002, Belfast...............£20 *Benham*
(9)   Games 2002, Edinburgh ........£20 *Benham*
(10)  Games 2002, London ............£15 *Benham BLCS 232*
(11)  Games 2002, Cardiff...............£20 *Benham*
(12)  Commonwealth Games .........£25 *Benham Gold(232)*
(13)  The 2002 Games .....................£15 *Bradbury Sovereign 16*
(14)  The Games, Manchester.........£15 *Westminster*
(15)  Manchester (palette)...............£40 *Westminster*
(16)  Autographed, Manchester  .....£20 *Westminster*
(17)  Friendly Games........................£15 *Steven Scott 67*
(18)  The Torch, Wembley ..............£20 *M Brazier (Pubs 46)*
(19)  Olympic Way, Wembley.........£15 *GB 66*
(20)  Henley (stop watch) ...............£15 *Buckingham Cvrs 21*
(21)  Henley (oars)...........................£15 *Buckingham Cvrs 21*
(22)  Manchester, The Games .........£15 *P Sheridan*
(23)  Wimbledon, London SW19 ....£15 *P M Payne*
(24)  The Friendly Games, Manch ..£20 *Cam S.C.*
(25)  Commonwealth Way...............£20 *M J Kingsland*
(26)  The Friendly Games ...............£15 *Phil Stamp Covers 28*
(27)  Royal Navy Athletics...............£15 *RN CvrsGp*
(28)  Spitfire, West Malling..............£15 *BritHerCollections*
(29)  The Fenian Raid ......................£15 *Group Capt Randle*
(30)  Anniversaries, Games Rd .......£20 *P M Payne*

## 2002 WORLD CUP FOOTBALL

## 2002 COMMONWEALTH GAMES

157

## 2002 PETER PAN

## 2002 BRIDGES OF LONDON

**C.D.S. POSTMARKS Price Guide £7-£10**
(31) M2002 Games Village (£50), Jump, Stoke Mandeville,
(32) any Manchester postmarks near to venues for the Games

## 20th August 2002 – PETER PAN

*2nd Tinkerbell; 1st Wendy, John & Michael; E Crocodile;
47p Peter Pan.*

| SPECIAL HANDSTAMPS | SPONSOR |
|---|---|
| **Price Guide Ordinary Covers £4-£9 / Sponsored Covers:** | |
| (1) FDI - Tallents House..................... | *Royal Mail (n.s.c.)* |
| (2) FDI - Hook................................... | *Royal Mail (n.s.c.)* |
| (3) -do- non pictorial version .......... | *Royal Mail (n.s.c.)* |
| (4) Peter Pan, Birmingham................ | *Royal Mail (n.s.c.)* |
| (5) Great Ormond Street .............£15 | *Benham BLCS 233* |
| (6) London ..................................£20 | *Benham Coin Cover* |
| (7) Kirriemuir ..............................£15 | *Benham BLCS 233* |
| (8) Edinburgh ..............................£25 | *Benham (500)233* |
| (9) Hook, Hampshire....................£20 | *Benham Pilgrim* |
| (10) Peter Pan, Kensington Gdns..£15 | *Bradbury Sovereign 22* |
| (11) Peter Pan, Hook ....................£15 | *Westminster* |
| (12) Hook (palette)........................£40 | *Westminster* |
| (13) Autographed, Hook ...............£25 | *Westminster* |
| (14) Peter Street, London W1.......£15 | *Steven Scott 68* |
| (15) The Peter Pan.........................£15 | *M Brazier (Pubs 47)* |
| (16) Barrie House, Addlestone .....£15 | *GB 67* |
| (17) Great Ormond Street .............£20 | *Buckingham Cvrs 27* |
| (18) Kensington Gardens...............£25 | *Buckingham Cvrs 27* |
| (19) Birthplace, Kirriemuir ..........£20 | *CoverCraft* |
| (20) Chicken Shed Theatre Co .....£15 | *P Sheridan* |
| (21) Hooks Close, SE15 ................£20 | *P M Payne* |
| (22) James Barrie, Kirriemuir........£25 | *Assoc. of GBFDC 9* |
| (23) Peter Pan, Bletchley Park......£15 | *Bletchley PO* |
| (24) Peter Pan, Kirriemuir...........£15 | *Phil Stamp Covers 29* |
| (25) Duke of York's Theatre .........£20 | *T Hurlstone* |
| (26) Lambert School, Hull.............£25 | *John Bryan* |
| (27) Concorde, Duxford ................£25 | *Cam S.C.* |
| (28) Phantom, Manston..................£15 | *BritHerCollections* |
| (29) The Capture of Coomassie.....£15 | *Group Capt Randle* |
| (30) U-43 Sinking off Brighton......£15 | *RN CvrsGp* |

**C.D.S. POSTMARKS Price Guide £7-£10**
(31) Kensington Church Street, Kirriemuir, Farnham
(32) Hook, Pan, Clockface

## 10th Sept 2002 – BRIDGES OF LONDON

*(1) 2nd Millennium Bridge; 1st Tower Bridge; E Westminster
Bridge; 47p Blackfriars Bridge; 68p London Bridge.*
*(2) Self Adhesive Stamp Book containing 6 x 1st Class Stamps:
2 Tower Bridge & 4 Definitives.*

| SPECIAL HANDSTAMPS | SPONSOR |
|---|---|
| **Price Guide Ordinary Covers £4-£9 / Sponsored Covers:** | |
| (1) FDI - Tallents House.................... | *Royal Mail (n.s.c.)* |
| (2) FDI - London SE1 ....................... | *Royal Mail (n.s.c.)* |
| (3) -do- non pictorial version .......... | *Royal Mail (n.s.c.)* |
| (4) Bridges of London, Birmingham . | *Royal Mail (n.s.c.)* |
| (5) Westminster Bridge.................£15 | *Benham BLCS 234* |
| (6) Tower Hill................................£20 | *Benham Coin Cover* |
| (7) Bankside..................................£15 | *Benham BLCS 234* |
| (8) London Bridge ........................£30 | *Benham (500)234* |
| (9) Blackfriars Road .....................£20 | *Benham Pilgrim* |
| (10) Tower Hill NVI Booklet........£20 | *Benham* |
| (11) Guildhall NVI Booklet ..........£20 | *Benham* |
| (12) Bridges of London (crest) .....£20 | *Bradbury Sovereign 18* |
| (13) Self Adhesives .......................£25 | *Bradbury Britannia 12* |
| (14) Riverview Road......................£15 | *Westminster* |
| (15) Riverview Road (palette) .......£40 | *Westminster* |
| (16) Autographed, Riverview Rd....£25 | *Westminster* |
| (17) London Bridges (Big Ben) ....£15 | *Steven Scott 69* |
| (18) The Giddy Bridge...................£15 | *M Brazier (Pubs 48)* |
| (19) The Square Arch ....................£20 | *GB 68* |
| (20) London Bridge........................£15 | *Buckingham Cvrs 22* |
| (21) Tower Bridge..........................£15 | *Buckingham Cvrs 22* |
| (22) Westminster Bridge................£25 | *P Sheridan* |
| (23) Structural Engineers ..............£20 | *CoverCraft* |
| (24) Tower Bridge .........................£20 | *T Hurlstone* |
| (25) Thomas Gainsborough ...........£20 | *P M Payne* |
| (26) London Bridges ......................£25 | *Cam S.C.* |
| (27) London SE1 ...........................£20 | *H D MacIntyre* |
| (28) London's Bridges....................£15 | *Assoc. of GBFDC 10* |
| (29) London Bridges ......................£20 | *N McInnes* |
| (30) Westminster Bridge................£15 | *Phil Stamp Covers 30* |
| (31) Tower Bridge..........................£15 | *Phil Stamp Covers 31* |
| (32) London Bridge Mustang.........£15 | *BritHerCollections* |
| (33) London's Fire Brigade............£20 | *Bletchley PO* |
| (34) Jade's Crossing, Detling .........£25 | *Jade Crossing Fund* |
| (35) Battle of Isandhlwana ...........£15 | *Group Capt Randle* |
| (36) HMS Warspite ........................£15 | *RN CvrsGp* |

C.D.S. POSTMARKS Price Guide £7-£10
(37) London Bridge, Blackfriars Rd, Westminster Bridge Rd
(38) Rising Bridge, Ironbridge, Thames View, New Bridge

## 24th September 2002 – ASTRONOMY
*(1) 4 x 1st: Planetary Nebula in Aquila & Norma;*
*Seyfert 2 Galaxy in Pegasus & Circinus.*
*(2) Across the Universe Prestige Stamp Book.*

| SPECIAL HANDSTAMPS | SPONSOR |
|---|---|

Price Guide Ordinary Covers £4-£9 / Sponsored Covers:
| | | |
|---|---|---|
| (1) | FDI - Tallents House.................... | *Royal Mail (n.s.c.)* |
| (2) | FDI - Star, Glenrothes................. | *Royal Mail (n.s.c.)* |
| (3) | -do- non pictorial version ........... | *Royal Mail (n.s.c.)* |
| (4) | Across the Universe, B'ham.......... | *Royal Mail (n.s.c.)* |
| (5) | Piccadilly...................................£20 | *Benham* |
| (6) | Greenwich ...............................£15 | *Benham BLCS 236* |
| (7) | Leicester ..................................£20 | *Benham Coin Cover* |
| (8) | Armagh ....................................£20 | *Benham* |
| (9) | Windsor....................................£15 | *Benham BLCS 236* |
| (10) | London W1...............................£20 | *Benham (500)236* |
| (11) | Macclesfield.............................£15 | *Benham* |
| (12) | Edinburgh ................................£15 | *Benham* |
| (13) | Macclesfield.............................£25 | *Bradbury Sovereign 19* |
| (14) | Space Shuttle, Cambridge ......£30 | *Bradbury Windsor 17* |
| (15) | Apollo Way, Birmingham.......£15 | *Westminster* |
| (16) | Apollo Way (palette) ..............£40 | *Westminster* |
| (17) | Autographed, Apollo Way........£25 | *Westminster* |
| (18) | Greenwich Observatory............£15 | *Steven Scott 70* |
| (19) | The North Star........................£15 | *M Brazier (Pubs 49)* |
| (20) | Starcross Street ........................£15 | *GB 69* |
| (21) | Jodrell Bank (oval)..................£15 | *Buckingham Cvrs 23* |
| (22) | Jodrell Bank (circle) ...............£15 | *Buckingham Cvrs 23* |
| (23) | The Blue Planet .......................£20 | *P Sheridan* |
| (24) | British Astronomical Ass'n ......£20 | *CoverCraft* |
| (25) | Sir William Ramsey ................£20 | *P M Payne* |
| (26) | Starfield Road .........................£20 | *M J Kingsland* |
| (27) | Greenwich Park, SE10.............£25 | *Cam S.C.* |
| (28) | Constellation St, Cardiff .........£15 | *Phil Stamp Covers 32* |
| (29) | HMS Echo ................................£15 | *RN Philatelic Society* |
| (30) | Attack on the Tirpitz ...............£15 | *RN CvrsGp* |
| (31) | The George Cross, SW1 ..........£15 | *Westminster* |
| (32) | Tempest, Manston....................£15 | *BritHerCollections* |
| (33) | Capture of Ali Musjid..............£15 | *Group Capt Randle* |

C.D.S. POSTMARKS Price Guide £7-£10
(34) Kennedy Centre, Greenwich, The Science Museum
(35) World's End, Meridian Centre, Star Cross, Seven Sisters

## 1st October 2002 – SMILERS GENERIC
*3 x 1st: Father Christmas; Teddy Bear; Dennis the Menace.*

| SPECIAL HANDSTAMPS | SPONSOR |
|---|---|

Price Guide Ordinary Covers £4-£9 / Sponsored Covers:
| | | |
|---|---|---|
| (1) | Smilers Issue, Bethlehem.......£20 | *Bradbury Windsor 22* |
| (2) | Bear Park, Durham..................£20 | *Benham (500)239* |
| (3) | Bearstead, Maidstone .............£15 | *Benham BLCS 239* |
| (4) | Bean, Dartford ........................£15 | *Benham BLCS 239* |

## 8th October 2002 – PILLAR TO POST
*2nd 1857 Decorative box; 1st 1874 Mainland box; E 1933*
*Airmail box; 47p 1939 Dual-aperture box; 68p 1980 New-style.*

| SPECIAL HANDSTAMPS | SPONSOR |
|---|---|

Price Guide Ordinary Covers £4-£9 / Sponsored Covers:
| | | |
|---|---|---|
| (1) | FDI - Tallents House................. | *Royal Mail (n.s.c.)* |
| (2) | FDI - Bishops Caundle .............. | *Royal Mail (n.s.c.)* |
| (3) | -do- non pictorial version ........... | *Royal Mail (n.s.c.)* |
| (4) | Pillar to Post, Birmingham.......... | *Royal Mail (n.s.c.)* |
| (5) | Pillar to Post, Solihull ............£20 | *Benham Pilgrim* |
| (6) | Pillar to Post, Windsor...........£15 | *Benham BLCS 238* |
| (7) | Pillar to Post, Edinburgh .......£20 | *Benham Coin Cover* |
| (8) | Pillar to Post, Salford .............£30 | *Benham (500)238* |
| (9) | Pillar to Post, London ............£15 | *Benham BLCS 238* |
| (10) | Letter Box Study Group ..........£20 | *Bradbury Sovereign 20* |
| (11) | Post Box Lane Abingdon.......£15 | *Westminster* |
| (12) | Post Box Lane (palette) .........£40 | *Westminster* |
| (13) | Autographed, Post Box Ln.......£25 | *Westminster* |
| (14) | Mount Pleasant.......................£15 | *Steven Scott 71* |
| (15) | The Pillar Box, EC1................£15 | *M Brazier (Pubs 50)* |
| (16) | Ye Olde Post Box Horsham ..£35 | *R Park* |
| (17) | Post Office Way, SW8.............£20 | *GB 70* |
| (18) | Bath Postal Museum................£30 | *Buckingham Cvrs 24* |
| (19) | Local Post, Runcorn................£20 | *P Sheridan* |
| (20) | First Pillar Box, EC1...............£20 | *CoverCraft* |
| (21) | Post Office Way, SW8.............£20 | *P M Payne* |
| (22) | Royal Hospital, Chelsea..........£20 | *FourpennyPost* |
| (23) | Folkestone...................................£30 | *H D MacIntyre* |
| (24) | Secret Postbox 111..................£25 | *Bletchley PO* |
| (25) | Botchergate, Carlisle...............£15 | *Phil Stamp Covers 33* |
| (26) | Exmouth Stamp Club..............£25 | *Exmouth Stamp Club* |

## 2002 ASTRONOMY

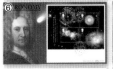

NORTHAMPTON

## 2002 PILLAR TO POST

## 2002 CHRISTMAS

## 2002 WILDINGS

(27) Box, Corsham............................£15 *Stick with Stamps*
(28) NatWest Philatelic Soc..............£25 *NW Phil Soc*
(29) Bath (changeable date)..........£15 *Buckingham Cvrs 24*
(30) "Dolphin", Portsmouth ...........£15 *RN CvrsGp*
(31) Lossiemouth, 617 Squadron ..£15 *BritHerCollections*
(32) Capture of Kabul ....................£15 *Group Capt Randle*
**C.D.S. POSTMARKS Price Guide £7-£10**
(33) Box, Send, Bishops Caundle, Sanquhar, Botchergate
(34) Mount Pleasant, Postbridge, Baltasound

---

## 5th November 2002 – CHRISTMAS
*2nd Spruce; 1st Holly; E Ivy; 47p Mistletoe; 68p Pine Cone*
**SPECIAL HANDSTAMPS          SPONSOR**
**Price Guide Ordinary Covers £4-£9 / Sponsored Covers:**
(1)  FDI - Tallents House....................  *Royal Mail (n.s.c.)*
(2)  FDI - Bethlehem ........................  *Royal Mail (n.s.c.)*
(3)  -do- non pictorial version ............  *Royal Mail (n.s.c.)*
(4)  Seasons Greetings, Bethlehem ....  *Royal Mail (n.s.c.)*
(5)  Christmas, Birmingham ...............  *Royal Mail (n.s.c.)*
(6)  Christmas, Bethlehem ............£15 *Benham BLCS 240*
(7)  Christmas, Nasareth ..............£20 *Benham Coin Cover*
(8)  Christmas, Shepherds Green .£15 *Benham BLCS 240*
(9)  Christmas, Star.........................£20 *Benham*
(10) Christmas, Wisemans Bridge .£20 *Benham (500)240*
(11) Christmas Kiss, Bethlehem.....£15 *Bradbury Sovereign 23*
(12) Holly Gardens, Margate ........£15 *Westminster*
(13) Holly Gardens (palette) .........£40 *Westminster*
(14) Autographed, Holly Gdns .....£25 *Westminster*
(15) Holly Way, Mitcham ..............£15 *Steven Scott 72*
(16) The Ivy Bush Inn, Llandybie .£15 *M Brazier (Pubs 51)*
(17) Robin Close, NW7 .................£15 *GB 71*
(18) Coventry Cathedral................£20 *Buckingham Cvrs 25*
(19) Trafalgar Square .....................£15 *P Sheridan*
(20) Peace & Goodwill, Bletchley £10 *Bletchley PO*
(21) Merry Christmas, Dartford.....£15 *Phil Stamp Covers*
(22) Mistletoe Green, Oxford........£15 *Phil Stamp Covers 34*
(23) Hollybush, Blackwood...........£15 *Stick with Stamps*
(24) Classic British Films, Ealing ..£25 *Cam S.C.*
(25) 617 Squadron, Lincoln .........£35 *Cam S.C.*
(26) Minewatchers, London ..........£15 *RN CvrsGp*
(27) Mildenhall, 15 Squadron.......£15 *BritHerCollections*
(28) Battle of Tel-el-Kebir ..............£15 *Group Capt Randle*
**C.D.S. POSTMARKS Price Guide £7-£10**
(29) Holy Island, Ivy Bush, Ivy Mount, Winter Gardens
(30) Hollybush, Holly Hall, Botanic Gardens, Woodberry Grove
(31) Holly Lane, Pinewoods, Berryhill, Holly Hedge

---

## 5th December 2002 – WILDINGS
*1p, 2p, 5p, 2nd, 1st, 30p, 37p, 47p, 50p Reprint of Wilding Definitives*
**SPECIAL HANDSTAMPS          SPONSOR**
**Price Guide Ordinary Covers £4-£9 / Sponsored Covers:**
(1)  FDI - Tallents House....................  *Royal Mail (n.s.c.)*
(2)  FDI - Windsor ..............................  *Royal Mail (n.s.c.)*
(3)  -do- non pictorial version ............  *Royal Mail (n.s.c.)*
(4)  Buckingham Palace Rd............£15 *Benham BLCS 241*
(5)  Portman Square ........................£20 *Benham*
(6)  Regent Street .............................£20 *Benham*
(7)  Old Bond Street........................£15 *Benham BLCS 241*
(8)  King Edward Street..................£20 *Benham Coin Cover*
(9)  Longford...................................£20 *Benham Pilgrim*
(10) High Wycombe .........................£20 *Benham Pilgrim*
(11) Basingstoke...............................£20 *Benham Pilgrim*
(12) The Octagon, Bath....................£20 *Benham*
(13) Wild about Wildings.................£25 *Bradbury Windsor 21*
(14) 1952 to 2002, George St.........£15 *Westminster*
(15) George Street, (palette)............£40 *Westminster*
(16) Autographed, George St .........£25 *Westminster*
(17) Westminster Abbey, SW1.......£15 *Westminster*
(18) Elizabethan Definitives............£20 *Buckingham Cvrs 28*
(19) George St, Portman Square ....£15 *P Sheridan*
(20) Bond Street, London W5 .......£15 *Phil Stamp Covers 35*
(21) Battles of El-Teb & Tamaai ....£15 *Group Capt Randle*
(22) Charlton Athletic......................£15 *Dawn*
**C.D.S. POSTMARKS Price Guide £7-£10**
(23) Portman Sq., Queen's Parade, Crown House, Throne

---

## 14th January 2003 – BIRDS of PREY
*5 x 1st Barn Owl; 5 x 1st Kestrel*

**SPECIAL HANDSTAMPS          SPONSOR**
Price Guide Ordinary Covers £4-£9 / Sponsored Covers:
(1)  FDI - Tallents House.................... *Royal Mail (n.s.c.)*
(2)  FDI - Hawkshead ........................ *Royal Mail (n.s.c.)*
(3)  -do- non pictorial version ............ *Royal Mail (n.s.c.)*
(4)  Birds of Prey, Birmingham........... *Royal Mail (n.s.c.)*
(5)  Birds of Prey, Newent ...........£20 *Benham Pilgrim*
(6)  Birds of Prey, Oakham...........£20 *Benham Pilgrim*
(7)  Birds of Prey, Ravenglass .......£20 *Benham (500)242*
(8)  Birds of Prey, Bangor ............£20 *Benham Coin Cover*
(9)  Birds of Prey, Carradale.........£20 *Benham*
(10) Birds of Prey, Edinburgh ........£20 *Benham*
(11) Birds of Prey, Thetford..........£15 *Benham BLCS 242*
(12) Birds of Prey, Sandy ..............£15 *Benham BLCS 242*
(13) Birds of Prey, Andover ...........£20 *Benham*
(14) Birds of Prey, Ringwood.........£20 *Benham Pilgrim*
(15) Birds of Prey, Sandy ..............£15 *Bradbury Sovereign 24*
(16) Barn Owl Close, Torquay......£15 *Westminster*
(17) Barn Owl Close (palette)........£40 *Westminster*
(18) Autographed, Barn Owl Cl ....£25 *Westminster*
(19) Bird in Bush Road .................£15 *Steven Scott 75*
(20) The Kestrel & the Falcon.......£20 *M Brazier (Rly.3)*
(21) The Barn Owl ........................£15 *M Brazier (Pubs 52)*
(22) Eagle Street, London WC1 ....£15 *GB 72*
(23) Barn Owl Ctre, Brockworth ..£30 *Buckingham Cvrs 29*
(24) Eagle Heights, Eynesford.......£30 *Buckingham Cvrs 29*
(25) The Hawk & Owl Trust.........£15 *CoverCraft*
(26) Hoo Farm................................£15 *P Sheridan*
(27) Barn Owl, Owlswick ..............£15 *Phil Stamp Covers 36*
(28) Wing, Leighton Buzzard.........£15 *Phil Stamp Covers 37*
(29) Eagle, Lincoln .......................£15 *Stick with Stamps*
(30) Many Hoots Owl Centre .......£20 *H D MacIntrye*
(31) Papagallos Restaurant ...........£15 *P M Payne*
(32) HMS/M Triumph, Gosport....£20 *RN CvrsGp*
(33) Expedition Against Mlanje.....£15 *Group Capt Randle*
(34) Expedition Benin Territory .....£15 *Group Capt Randle*
**C.D.S. POSTMARKS Price Guide £7-£10**
(35) Owlsmoor, Wing, Falconwood, Eagle, Sandy
(36) Hawkshead, Hawkswood, Hawkhurst, Falcon Lodge

## 21st January 2003 – FLOWERS Generic Issue
*Reprinted version of the 1997 Flowers Greetings stamps in sheet format plus revised label designs.*

**SPECIAL HANDSTAMPS          SPONSOR**
Price Guide Ordinary Covers £4-£9 / Sponsored Covers:
(1)  Botanical Fine Arts, Kew........£20 *Bradbury Windsor 23*
(2)  Smilers, Rettendon Common.£20 *Benham*
(3)  Smilers, Ardingly ..................£15 *Benham BLCS 243*
(4)  Smilers, St. Austell ................£20 *Benham Pilgrim*
(5)  Smilers, Torrington ...............£20 *Benham*
(6)  Smilers, Llanarthney...............£20 *Benham*
(7)  Smilers, Mevagissey ...............£20 *Benham Pilgrim*
(8)  Smilers, Woking .....................£20 *Benham*
(9)  Smilers, Kew............................£15 *Benham BLCS 243*
(10) Smilers, Chelsea.....................£20 *Benham (500)243*
(11) Smilers, Harrogate .................£20 *Benham Pilgrim*

## 4th February 2003 – OCCASIONS
*(1) 6 x 1st: Gold Star; I Love You; Angel; Yes; Oops!; I did it!*
*(2) 6 x 1st Stamps as above with generic labels.*

**SPECIAL HANDSTAMPS          SPONSOR**
Price Guide Ordinary Covers £4-£9 / Sponsored Covers:
(1)  FDI - Tallents House.................... *Royal Mail (n.s.c.)*
(2)  FDI - Merry Hill........................... *Royal Mail (n.s.c.)*
(3)  -do- non pictorial version ............ *Royal Mail (n.s.c.)*
(4)  Occasions, Birmingham................ *Royal Mail (n.s.c.)*
(5)  Flowerdown, Winchester.......£15 *Benham BLCS 244*
(6)  Angel Bank, Ludlow................£20 *Benham (500)244*
(7)  May Street, London.................£20 *Benham Pilgrim*
(8)  Jump, Barnsley.........................£20 *Benham Coin Cover*
(9)  Star, Glenrothes.......................£20 *Benham*
(10) Loversall, Doncaster ..............£15 *Benham BLCS 244*
(11) Gretna Green, Carlisle ...........£15 *Bradbury Sovereign 25*
(12) Angel Street, Worcester .........£15 *Westminster*
(13) Angel Street (palette)..............£40 *Westminster*
(14) Autographed, Angel Street .....£25 *Westminster*
(15) The True Lovers Knot .............£15 *M Brazier (Pubs 53)*
(16) Donkey Lane, Enfield .............£15 *GB 73*
(17) Just Married, Sandwich Kent.£15 *Buckingham Cvrs 30*
(18) Tickenham, Clevedon..............£15 *Phil Stamp Covers 38*
(19) Lover, Salisbury.......................£20 *Stick with Stamps*
(20) Nostradamus............................£15 *P M Payne*
**C.D.S. POSTMARKS Price Guide £7-£10**
(21) Angel Hill, Playing Place, Lover, Gretna Green, Send, Mark

## 2003 BIRDS of PREY

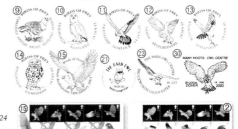

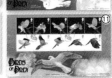

## 2003 OCCASIONS

161

## 2003 DNA: The SECRET of LIFE

## 2003 FUN FRUIT & VEG

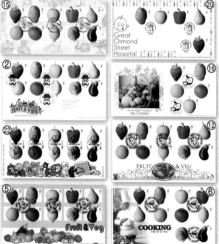

### 25th Feb 2003 – DNA: The SECRET of LIFE

*(1) 2nd End of the Beginning; 1st Comparative Genetics;*
*E Cracking the Code; 47p Genetic Eng; 68p Medical Futures.*
*(2) Microcosmos Prestige Stamp Book.*

**SPECIAL HANDSTAMPS                SPONSOR**
**Price Guide Ordinary Covers £4-£9 / Sponsored Covers:**
| | | |
|---|---|---|
| (1) | FDI - Tallents House..................... | *Royal Mail (n.s.c.)* |
| (2) | FDI - Cambridge ........................... | *Royal Mail (n.s.c.)* |
| (3) | -do- non pictorial version ............ | *Royal Mail (n.s.c.)* |
| (4) | Secret of Life, Birmingham........... | *Royal Mail (n.s.c.)* |
| (5) | Cambridge (fingerprint) .........£20 | *Royal Mail/Royal Mint* |
| (6) | London W1 .............................£15 | *Benham BLCS 245* |
| (7) | London W12 ............................£20 | *Benham (500)245* |
| (8) | Harley Street, London W1.....£20 | *Benham* |
| (9) | Belfast .......................................£20 | *Benham* |
| (10) | Edinburgh ...............................£20 | *Benham Coin Cover* |
| (11) | Cambridge ...............................£15 | *Benham BLCS 245* |
| (12) | Harwell, Didcot.......................£20 | *Benham Pilgrim* |
| (13) | Discovery of DNA...................£15 | *Bradbury Sovereign 26* |
| (14) | Secret of Life, Cambridge .....£15 | *Westminster* |
| (15) | Cambridge (palette) ...............£40 | *Westminster* |
| (16) | Autographed, Cambridge.......£25 | *Westminster* |
| (17) | Discovery Walk, London E1 .£15 | *Steven Scott 76* |
| (18) | The Eagle, Cambridge .............£15 | *M Brazier (Pubs 54)* |
| (19) | Discovery Walk,SE1 ................£15 | *GB 74* |
| (20) | Cambridge ...............................£30 | *Buckingham Cvrs 31* |
| (21) | Genetic Interest Group ...........£15 | *P Sheridan* |
| (22) | Chemistry, Whitchurch...........£15 | *Phil Stamp Covers 39* |
| (23) | Crick, Northampton ................£20 | *Stick with Stamps* |
| (24) | Code, Bletchley Park ...............£15 | *Bletchley PO* |
| (25) | Secret of Life, Cambridge ......£10 | *Assoc. of GBFDC 11* |
| (26) | Cavendish Laboratory ............£25 | *Cam S.C.* |
| (27) | William Harvery, E11 ............£15 | *P M Payne* |
| (28) | HMS Ark Royal.......................£15 | *RN CvrsGp* |
| (29) | The Relief of Chitral ...............£15 | *Group Capt Randle* |

**C.D.S. POSTMARKS Price Guide £7-£10**
(30) Crick, Cambridge, Watson Way, Weston Favell

### 4th March 2003 – 'HELLO' Self Adhesive

*1st Occasions Hello (x2) issued in self-adhesive stamp book*
*with four 1st Class definitives*

**SPECIAL HANDSTAMPS                SPONSOR**
**Price Guide Ordinary Covers £4-£9 / Sponsored Covers:**
| | | |
|---|---|---|
| (1) | Hounslow, Middlesex..............£15 | *Bradbury Windsor 26* |
| (2) | Greetwell, Lincoln ..................£15 | *Benham BLCS 247* |
| (3) | Waverton, Chester ..................£15 | *Benham BLCS 247* |
| (4) | Flyford Flavell, Worcester .....£20 | *Benham* |
| (5) | HMS Vanguard........................£15 | *RN CvrsGp* |

### 25th March 2003 – FUN FRUIT & VEG

*10 x 1st Strawberry, Potato, Apple, Pepper, Pear, Orange,*
*Tomato, Lemon, Sprout, Aubergine.*

**SPECIAL HANDSTAMPS                SPONSOR**
**Price Guide Ordinary Covers £4-£9 / Sponsored Covers:**
| | | |
|---|---|---|
| (1) | FDI - Tallents House..................... | *Royal Mail (n.s.c.)* |
| (2) | FDI - Pear Tree, Derby ................. | *Royal Mail (n.s.c.)* |
| (3) | -do- non pictorial version ............ | *Royal Mail (n.s.c.)* |
| (4) | Fun Fruit & Veg, Birmingham..... | *Royal Mail (n.s.c.)* |
| (5) | Pear Tree, Derby.....................£15 | *Benham BLCS 248* |
| (6) | Pepper Arden, Northalleton ..£15 | *Benham BLCS 248* |
| (7) | Brusselton, Shildon.................£20 | *Benham* |
| (8) | Garden Village, Hull...............£20 | *Benham* |
| (9) | Chipping, Preston....................£20 | *Benham Coin Cover* |
| (10) | Appleby, Scunthorpe ..............£20 | *Benham Pilgrim* |
| (11) | Ripe, Lewes .............................£20 | *Benham* |
| (12) | Bittering, Dereham.................£20 | *Benham (500)248* |
| (13) | Grove, Canterbury ..................£20 | *Benham* |
| (14) | Strawberry Valley....................£20 | *Benham* |
| (15) | Covent Garden ........................£15 | *Bradbury Sovereign 27* |
| (16) | Appletree, Daventry................£15 | *Westminster* |
| (17) | Appletree (palette)..................£40 | *Westminster* |
| (18) | Autographed, Appletree.........£25 | *Westminster* |
| (19) | Sainsburys ...............................£15 | *M Brazier (Pubs 55)* |
| (20) | Great Ormond Street .............£25 | *Buck' Cvrs 32 (pair)* |
| (21) | Eat for Health, Covent Gdn ..£15 | *P Sheridan* |
| (22) | Appledore, Ashford................£15 | *Phil Stamp Covers 40* |
| (23) | Covent Garden ........................£25 | *Cam S.C.* |
| (24) | Sainsbury Drury Lane .............£20 | *A Bard* |
| (25) | Sticker St. Austell....................£20 | *A Bard* |
| (26) | Child's Place, London .............£20 | *H Athanassiades* |
| (27) | Greens Turriff..........................£15 | *Stick with Stamps* |
| (28) | Operation Iceberg ...................£15 | *RN CvrsGp* |
| (29) | Brecknock Museum.................£30 | *Brecknock Mus (pair)* |

**C.D.S. POSTMARKS Price Guide £7-£10**
(30) Strawberry Hill, Orange Tree, Pear Tree, Apple Cross, Ripe
(31) The Allotments, The Orchards, Orchard Way, Jersey Farm

## 29th April 2003 - EXTREME ENDEAVOURS
*(1) 2nd Amy Johnson; 1st Everest Team; E Freya Stark;*
*42p Ernest Shackleton; 47p Francis Chichester;*
*68p Robert Falcon Scott.*
*(2) Self Adhesive Stamp Book containing 6 x 1st Class Stamps:*
*2 Everest & 4 Definitives.*

### 2003 EXTREME ENDEAVOURS

| SPECIAL HANDSTAMPS | SPONSOR |
|---|---|
| **Price Guide Ordinary Covers £4-£9 / Sponsored Covers:** | |

(1) FDI - Tallents House..................... *Royal Mail (n.s.c.)*
(2) FDI - Plymouth ............................. *Royal Mail (n.s.c.)*
(3) -do- non pictorial version ............ *Royal Mail (n.s.c.)*
(4) Ext. Endeavours, Birmingham ..... *Royal Mail (n.s.c.)*
(5) Amy Johnson, Hull .................£15 *Benham BLCS 250*
(6) Edmund Hillary, SW1............£20 *Benham*
(7) Francis Chichester, WC1 .......£20 *Benham (500)250*
(8) Francis Chichester .................£20 *Benham Coin Cover*
(9) Robert Falcon Scott................£20 *Benham*
(10) Ernest Shackleton ..................£15 *Benham BLCS 250*
(11) Ascent of Everest, SW1.........£20 *Benham BLCS 251*
(12) Ascent of Everest, SW1.........£15 *Benham BLCS 251*
(13) Amy Johnson, Derby .............£20 *Benham BLCS 250*
(14) Conquest of Everest, SW1......£20 *Bradbury Sovereign 28*
(15) Amy Johnson Memorabilia ....£15 *Anniv & Events 9*
(16) Self Adhesives, London .........£20 *Bradbury Windsor 29*
(17) Everest Place ..........................£15 *Westminster*
(18) Everest Place (palette)............£40 *Westminster*
(19) Autographed, Everest Place ...£25 *Westminster*
(20) The Three Compasses ............£20 *M Brazier (Pubs 56)*
(21) Shackleton House, SE1 .........£20 *GB 75*
(22) Conquest of Mount Everest ...£20 *Buckingham Cvrs 33*
(23) Price's Candles, Bedford........£20 *P Sheridan*
(24) Mountain Ash .........................£15 *Phil Stamp Covers 42*
(25) Endeavour Way, SW19..........£25 *Assoc. of GBFDC 12*
(26) Polemarch St, Seaham ...........£15 *Stick with Stamps*
(27) RRS Discovery, Dundee ........£15 *Stick with Stamps*
(28) Dulwich College, SE21 ..........£20 *CoverCraft*
(29) High Peak, Derby....................£25 *Cam S.C.*
(30) Self Adhesive Booklet ............£15 *A Bard*
(31) Summit, Littleborough ...........£15 *A Bard*
(32) Greenwich, London SE1 ........£20 *H D MacIntyre*
(33) Endeavour Way, Barking .......£15 *Steven Scott*
(34) Endeavour High School .........£20 *J Bryan*
(35) Endeavour Way, SW19..........£15 *P M Payne*
(36) HMS Scott, Devonport...........£15 *RN CvrsGp*
(37) Capture of Coomassie ............£15 *Group Capt Randle*
**C.D.S. POSTMARKS Price Guide £7-£10**
(38) Summit, Chichester, The Heights, North Pole Rd, The Camp
(39) any Hull pmk, Croydon, Buckingham Palace (£75)

## 20th May 2003 - WILDINGS
*4p, 8p, 10p, 20p, 28p, 34p, E, 42p, 68 Reprint of Wilding*
*Definitives*

| SPECIAL HANDSTAMPS | SPONSOR |
|---|---|
| **Price Guide Ordinary Covers £4-£9 / Sponsored Covers:** | |

(1) FDI - Tallents House..................... *Royal Mail (n.s.c.)*
(2) FDI - Windsor .............................. *Royal Mail (n.s.c.)*
(3) -do- non pictorial version ............ *Royal Mail (n.s.c.)*
(4) Wildings, Old Bond Street......£25 *Benham (500)252*
(5) Wildings, Regent Street...........£20 *Benham Pilgrim*
(6) Wildings, Portman Square......£20 *Benham Coin Cover*
(7) Wildings, King Edward St ......£20 *Benham Pilgrim*
(8) Wildings, London SW1..........£20 *Benham BLCS 252*
(9) Wildings, Longford .................£20 *Benham Coin Cover*
(10) Wildings, High Wycombe......£15 *Benham BLCS 252*
(11) Wildings, Basingstoke ...........£15 *Benham BLCS 252*
(12) Wildings, The Octagon, Bath £20 *Benham BLCS 252*
(13) Wilding Revivals, Windsor.....£25 *Bradbury Windsor 24*
(14) Autographed, George Street ...£25 *Westminster*
(15) George Street (palette)...........£40 *Westminster*
(16) Wilding Defins, George St .....£15 *Westminster*
(17) Elizabethan Definitives..........£15 *Buckingham Cvrs*
(18) Wilding Defins Portman Sq ...£15 *P Sheridan*
(19) Old Bond Street, W5..............£15 *Phil Stamp Covers 43*
(20) Chelsea, SW3 ..........................£25 *Royal Hort. Society*
**C.D.S. POSTMARKS Price Guide £7-£10**
(21) Portman Sq., Throne, Windsor, Innsworth

### 2003 WILDINGS

## 2003 CORONATION

## 2nd June 2003 – CORONATION
*10 x 1st Scenes from the 1953 Coronation. Also issued on the same day the* **A Perfect Coronation** *Prestige Stamp Book.*

| SPECIAL HANDSTAMPS | SPONSOR |
|---|---|
| **Price Guide Ordinary Covers £4-£9 / Sponsored Covers:** | |

(1)  FDI - Tallents House.................... *Royal Mail (n.s.c.)*
(2)  FDI - London SW1 ...................... *Royal Mail (n.s.c.)*
(3)  -do- non pictorial version ............ *Royal Mail (n.s.c.)*
(4)  Long Live the Queen, EC1......... *Royal Mail (n.s.c.)*
(5)  Coronation Anniversary, SW1..... *Royal Mail (n.s.c.)*
(6)  Coronation, Birmingham ............. *Royal Mail (n.s.c.)*
(7)  Westminster - horses ..............£15 *Benham BLCS 253*
(8)  Westminster - coach ...............£30 *Benham (500)253*
(9)  Westminster - crown & lion ..£20 *Benham*
(10)  Westminster - rose & thistle..£20 *Benham*
(11)  Westminster - 50th Anniv .....£20 *Benham Pilgrim*
(12)  Westminster - Abbey ..............£20 *Benham*
(13)  London SW1 - crown ............£20 *Benham Coin Cover*
(14)  Buck Palace Rd - lion ...........£15 *Benham BLCS 253*
(15)  God Save the Queen ..............£20 *Benham*
(16)  Buck Palace Rd - emblems ....£20 *Benham Pilgrim*
(17)  50th Anniv of Coronation.....£15 *Bradbury Sovereign 29*
(18)  Westminster Abbey.................£15 *Westminster*
(19)  Abbey (palette).......................£40 *Westminster*
(20)  Autographed, Abbey .............£25 *Westminster*
(21)  Coronation Road, E13 ...........£15 *Steven Scott*
(22)  The Crown & Sceptre ...........£15 *M Brazier (Pubs 57)*
(23)  Coronation, Euston.................£15 *M Brazier (Rly.4)*
(24)  Coronation Road, E13 ...........£15 *GB 76*
(25)  Westminster Abbey, SW1......£15 *Buckingham Cvrs 34*
(26)  Buckingham Palace, SW1 ......£15 *Buckingham Cvrs 34*
(27)  Express Newspapers, SW1....£15 *Buckingham Cvrs*
(28)  Heraldry Society, SW1...........£20 *CoverCraft*
(29)  Queen Elizabeth St, SE1 .......£15 *P Sheridan*
(30)  £1 The Coronation, SW1.......£15 *Phil Stamp Covers 45*
(31)  Windsor...................................£15 *Phil Stamp Covers 44*
(32)  Coronation Court....................£10 *Assoc. of GBFDC 13*
(33)  Coronation Chair, SW1 .........£10 *Stick with Stamps*
(34)  Coronation Crown, SW1.......£10 *Stick with Stamps*
(35)  Westminster Abbey, SW1......£15 *Cam S.C.*
(36)  Happy Birthday, Wawne ........£20 *J Bryan*
(37)  Three Crowns...........................£15 *P M Payne*
(38)  Coronation Tram, Blackpool £20 *Dawn*
(39)  HMS Invincible, London .....£15 *RN CvrsGp*
(40)  Morris Light Commercial......£20 *DTL Enterprises*
(41)  Battle of Omdurman...............£15 *Group Capt Randle*
(42)  Battle of Battle of Atbara ......£15 *Group Capt Randle*
(43)  Royal Hospital Haslar............£20 *R F John*
**C.D.S. POSTMARKS Price Guide £7-£10**
(44)  Scone, Coronation
(45)  Throne, Coronation Parade, Queen's Parade or similar
(46)  Buckingham Palace, Windsor Castle (£75 each)

## 2003 PRINCE WILLIAM

## 17th June 2003 – PRINCE WILLIAM
*28p, E, 47p, 68p Photographic portraits of the Prince*
| SPECIAL HANDSTAMPS | SPONSOR |
|---|---|
| **Price Guide Ordinary Covers £4-£9 / Sponsored Covers:** | |

(1)  FDI - Tallents House.................... *Royal Mail (n.s.c.)*
(2)  FDI - Cardiff ................................ *Royal Mail (n.s.c.)*
(3)  -do- non pictorial version ............ *Royal Mail (n.s.c.)*
(4)  21st Birthday, Birmingham ...... *Royal Mail (n.s.c.)*
(5)  Prince William, St. Andrews..£15 *Benham BLCS 255*
(6)  Prince William, Windsor .......£15 *Benham BLCS 255*
(7)  Prince William, W2................£20 *Benham (500)255*
(8)  Prince William, SW1 .............£20 *Benham Coin Cover*
(9)  Windsor...................................£15 *Bradbury Sovereign 31*
(10)  Highgrove House, Tetbury .....£15 *Westminster*
(11)  St Andrews, Fife ....................£15 *Westminster*
(12)  St Andrews (palette)...............£40 *Westminster*
(13)  Autographed, St Andrews ....£25 *Westminster*
(14)  Prince of Wales Road.............£15 *Steven Scott*
(15)  Windsor Castle .......................£15 *M Brazier (Pubs 58)*
(16)  William Road, NW1 ...............£15 *GB 77*
(17)  Caernarfon ..............................£30 *Buckingham Cvrs 35*
(18)  Caernarfon ..............................£15 *P Sheridan*
(19)  Fort William ...........................£15 *Phil Stamp Covers 46*
(20)  Prince of Wales, Windsor......£15 *Stick with Stamps*
(21)  Prince of Wales Road.............£15 *P M Payne*
(22)  Sailing Ship Prince William...£15 *RN CvrsGp*
(23)  National Ecumenical ..............£20 *Methodist Philat. Soc*
(24)  John Wesley, Epworth............£20 *Methodist Philat. Soc*
(25)  The Attack on Fort Lubwas...£15 *Group Capt Randle*
**C.D.S. POSTMARKS Price Guide £7-£10**
(26)  Eton, St. Andrews, Cardiff, Windsor, Great Brington
(27)  Caernarfon, Tetbury, Paddington (Born St. Mary's Hosp),
(28)  Princes Avenue, William Street, or similar

## 15th July 2003 - SCOTLAND

*(1) 2nd Loch Assynt, Sutherland; 1st Ben More, Isle of Mull; E Rothiemurchus, Cairngorms; 42p Dalveen Pass, Lowther Hills; 47p Glenfinnan Viaduct, Lochaber; 68p Papa Little, Shetlands
(2) Self Adhesive Stamp Book containing 6 x 1st Class Stamps: 2 Ben More & 4 Definitives.*

**SPECIAL HANDSTAMPS**  **SPONSOR**
**Price Guide Ordinary Covers £4-£9/Sponsored Covers:**

| | | |
|---|---|---|
| (1) | FDI - Tallents House..................... | *Royal Mail (n.s.c.)* |
| (2) | FDI - London Baltasound............. | *Royal Mail (n.s.c.)* |
| (3) | -do- non pictorial version ............ | *Royal Mail (n.s.c.)* |
| (4) | Scotland, Birmingham ................. | *Royal Mail (n.s.c.)* |
| (5) | Papa Little, Baltasound...........£15 | *Benham BLCS 256* |
| (6) | Aviemore....................................£20 | *Benham Coin Cover* |
| (7) | Glenfinnan..................................£15 | *Benham BLCS 256* |
| (8) | Crianlarich..................................£20 | *Benham* |
| (9) | Ullapool......................................£20 | *Benham (500)256* |
| (10) | Wanlockhead, Biggar ...............£20 | *Benham Pilgrim* |
| (11) | Ben More, Isle of Mull............£15 | *Benham BLCS 257* |
| (12) | Crianlarich..................................£20 | *Benham* |
| (13) | Ben More, Isle of Mull............£20 | *Benham (500)257* |
| (14) | Beautiful Britain, Edinburgh...£15 | *Bradbury Sovereign 30* |
| (15) | Self Adhesives, Alloway...........£15 | *Bradbury Windsor 32* |
| (16) | Fort William..............................£15 | *Westminster* |
| (17) | Fort William (palette)..............£40 | *Westminster* |
| (18) | Autographed, Fort William ......£25 | *Westminster* |
| (19) | Aberdeen Place, NW8..............£15 | *Steven Scott* |
| (20) | Scotland Place, EC1 ................£15 | *GB 78* |
| (21) | Loch Ness, Inverness ...............£20 | *Buckingham Cvrs 36* |
| (22) | Glenfinnan Viaduct .................£15 | *P Sheridan* |
| (23) | Drumnadrochit, Inverness .....£15 | *Phil Stamp Covers 47* |
| (24) | Thistle St., Edinburgh.............£15 | *Stick with Stamps* |
| (25) | Beauties of Scotland...............£20 | *Cam S.C.* |
| (26) | Dalmally....................................£20 | *H D MacIntyre* |
| (27) | Naval Base, Faslane.................£15 | *RN CvrsGp* |
| (28) | Scott's View, Melrose .............£15 | *A Bard* |
| (29) | Letters, Lochbroom Garve.....£15 | *A Bard* |
| (30) | Steyn's War Cabinet ...............£15 | *Group Capt Randle* |

**C.D.S. POSTMARKS Price Guide £7-£10**
(31) The Scotlands, Glenfinnan, Aviemore, Lochside
(32) Leadhills, Lochinver, Highland Dykes, Aith, Thistle Hill

## 29 July 2003 - CROSSWORDS Generic Issue

*Reprinted version of the 1996 Cartoons Greetings stamps in sheet format plus labels featuring Crosswords in miniature.*
**SPECIAL HANDSTAMPS**  **SPONSOR**
**Price Guide Ordinary Covers £4-£9/Sponsored Covers:**
(1)  Crosswords on Stamps ................. *Bradbury Windsor 35*

## 12th August 2003 - PUB SIGNS

*1st The Station; 'E' Black Swan; 42p The Cross Keys; 47p The Mayflower; 68p The Barley Sheaf*
**SPECIAL HANDSTAMPS**  **SPONSOR**
**Price Guide Ordinary Covers £4-£9 / Sponsored Covers:**

| | | |
|---|---|---|
| (1) | FDI - Tallents House..................... | *Royal Mail (n.s.c.)* |
| (2) | FDI - Cross Keys, Hereford .......... | *Royal Mail (n.s.c.)* |
| (3) | -do- non pictorial version ............ | *Royal Mail (n.s.c.)* |
| (4) | Pub Signs, Birmingham ............... | *Royal Mail (n.s.c.)* |
| (5) | Rotherham..................................£15 | *Benham BLCS 258* |
| (6) | Leicester....................................£30 | *Benham (500)258* |
| (7) | Southsea.....................................£20 | *Benham Coin Cover* |
| (8) | Lincoln .....................................£15 | *Benham BLCS 258* |
| (9) | Bodmin......................................£20 | *Benham Pilgrim* |
| (10) | The Inn Sign Society ...............£20 | *Bradbury Sovereign 32* |
| (11) | Cross Keys, Hereford ...............£15 | *Westminster* |
| (12) | Cross Keys, (palette) ...............£40 | *Westminster* |
| (13) | Autographed, Q.Victoria St ...£25 | *Westminster* |
| (14) | Autographed, Cross Keys ........ | *Westminster* |
| (15) | Lords Cricket Ground...........£15 | *Steven Scott* |
| (16) | Original Pub Cover Series......£15 | *M Brazier (Pubs 60)* |
| (17) | Taverners Way, E4..................£15 | *GB 79* |
| (18) | Shepherd Neame......................£25 | *Buckingham Cvrs 37* |
| (19) | Beer & Pub Assoc, SW8........£20 | *CoverCraft* |
| (20) | The Crown, Widnes.................£15 | *P Sheridan* |
| (21) | Beer, Seaton .............................£15 | *Phil Stamp Covers 48* |
| (22) | Drinker's End Gloucester......£15 | *Stick with Stamps* |
| (23) | Captain Ridley's Billets ..........£15 | *Bletchley PO* |
| (24) | The Big Match, Manchester...£15 | *Dawn* |
| (25) | The Scapehouse Inn ...............£40 | *R C Productions* |
| (26) | Life of 'HMS Black Swan' ....£15 | *RN CvrsGp* |
| (27) | Real Ale Tasting Soc, WC1....£20 | *P M Payne* |
| (28) | Pubs & Stars of Jazz...............£15 | *P M Payne* |
| (29) | Relief of Peking.......................£15 | *Group Capt Randle* |

**C.D.S. POSTMARKS Price Guide £7-£10**
(30) Beer, Barley Mow, Brewery Road, Cross Keys
(31) Old Swan, Royal Oak, Black Bull

### 2003 SCOTLAND

### 2003 PUB SIGNS

## 2003 TRANSPORTS of DELIGHT

## 18th Sept 2003 – TRANSPORTS of DELIGHT

*(1) 1st Meccano Constructor Biplane; E Wells-Brimtoy*
*Clockwork Omnibus; 42p Hornby Clockwork Locomotive;*
*47p Dinky Ford Zephyr; 68p Mettoy Space Ship Eagle*
*(2) Miniature Sheet.*
*(3) Self Adhesive Stamp Book containing 6 x 1st Class Stamps:*
*2 Meccano Biplane & 4 Definitives.*

| SPECIAL HANDSTAMPS | SPONSOR |
|---|---|
| **Price Guide Ordinary Covers £4-£9 / Sponsored Covers:** | |
| (1) FDI - Tallents House..................... | *Royal Mail (n.s.c.)* |
| (2) FDI - Toye, Downpatrick............ | *Royal Mail (n.s.c.)* |
| (3) -do- non pictorial version ............ | *Royal Mail (n.s.c.)* |
| (4) Transports of Delight, Stampex ... | *Royal Mail (n.s.c.)* |
| (5) Stampex 50th Anniversary.....£20 | *Royal Mail/Stampex* |
| (6) Birmingham............................... | *Royal Mail (n.s.c.)* |
| (7) Epping.................................£15 | *Benham BLCS 260* |
| (8) Margate................................£15 | *Benham BLCS 260* |
| (9) Northampton...........................£15 | *Benham BLCS 261* |
| (10) Liverpool.............................£20 | *Benham Coin Cover* |
| (11) TLiverpool ...........................£15 | *Benham BLCS 259* |
| (12) York ....................................£20 | *Benham (500)259* |
| (13) Duxford...............................£20 | *Benham Coin Cover* |
| (14) Beaulieu...............................£20 | *Benham (500)260* |
| (15) Corgi Leicester.....................£15 | *Benham BLCS 259* |
| (16) Hornby Lancaster ..................£15 | *Bradbury Sovereign 33* |
| (17) Hornby Lancaster ..................£15 | *Bradbury Windsor 30* |
| (18) Self Adhesives, Hornby..........£15 | *Bradbury Windsor 31* |
| (19) Hornby Close, London ...........£15 | *Westminster* |
| (20) Hornby Close (palette)...........£40 | *Westminster* |
| (21) Autographed, Hornby Cl.......£25 | *Westminster* |
| (22) www.scificollector.co.uk ........£15 | *Steven Scott* |
| (23) Orient Way, London E5........£15 | *GB 80* |
| (24) Hornby, Margate ..................£50 | *Buckingham Cvrs 38* |
| (25) Hornby, Stampex ..................£50 | *Buckingham Cvrs 38* |
| (26) Pollock's Toy Museum...........£20 | *P Sheridan* |
| (27) Toy & Hobby Association.....£20 | *CoverCraft* |
| (28) Bletchley Park Post Office ....£15 | *Bletchley PO* |
| (29) Hornby, Lancaster ................£15 | *Phil Stamp Covers 50* |
| (30) Eagle, Lincoln .....................£15 | *Phil Stamp Covers 49* |
| (31) Dinky Trams & Buses...........£20 | *Dawn* |
| (32) Memory Lane, Leicester........£20 | *Stick with Stamps* |
| (33) Transport Revisited...............£20 | *P M Payne* |
| (34) Barry Potter Toy Collectors ..£20 | *M Brazier (Pubs.61)* |
| (35) Duke Ellington......................£20 | *P M Payne* |
| (36) Ford Centenary, Dagenham...£20 | *D T L Enterprises* |
| (37) Recapture of Kumassi............£15 | *Group Capt Randle* |
| (38) Off Tripoli, Faslane..............£15 | *RN CvrsGp* |
| **C.D.S. POSTMARKS Price Guide £7-£10** | |
| (39) The Rocket, Playing Place, Hornby, Eagle, Model Village | |

## 30 Sept 2003 – ROBINS Generic Issue

*Reprinted version of the 2001 1st Class Christmas Robins*
*stamps in sheet format plus labels.*

| SPECIAL HANDSTAMPS | SPONSOR |
|---|---|
| **Price Guide Ordinary Covers £4-£9 / Sponsored Covers:** | |
| (1) Christmas Common.................£20 | *Benham* |
| (2) Christmas, Bethlehem ............£10 | *Bradbury Windsor 37* |
| (3) RAF Coltishall.......................£10 | *British Forces* |

## 7th October 2003 - BRITISH MUSEUM

*2nd Coffin of Denytenamun; 1st Alexander the Great;*
*'E' Sutton Hoo Helmet; 42p Sculpture of Parvati;*
*47p Mask of Xiuhtecuhtli; 68p Hoa Hakananai'a*

| SPECIAL HANDSTAMPS | SPONSOR |
|---|---|
| **Price Guide Ordinary Covers £4-£9 / Sponsored Covers:** | |
| (1) FDI - Tallents House................... | *Royal Mail (n.s.c.)* |
| (2) FDI - London WC1 ..................... | *Royal Mail (n.s.c.)* |
| (3) -do- non pictorial version ............ | *Royal Mail (n.s.c.)* |
| (4) London WC1 ............................... | *Royal Mail* |
| (5) Birmingham............................... | *Royal Mail (n.s.c.)* |
| (6) Great Russell St (Egyptian)....£20 | *Benham Coin Cover* |
| (7) British Museum .....................£20 | *Benham (500)262* |
| (8) British Museum (coin) ...........£20 | *Benham* |
| (9) Great Russell St (snake) ........£20 | *Benham Pilgrim* |
| (10) British Museum (circle).........£10 | *Benham BLCS 262* |
| (11) British Museum (oval) ..........£10 | *Benham BLCS 262* |
| (12) 250 Years British Museums ...£10 | *Bradbury Sovereign 34* |
| (13) British Museums (helmet)......£10 | *Westminster* |
| (14) British Museums (palette) ......£40 | *Westminster* |
| (15) Autographed, Museums..........£20 | *Westminster* |
| (16) 250 Years of Excellence.........£10 | *Steven Scott* |
| (17) Museum Tavern, WC1 ...........£15 | *M Brazier (Pubs.62)* |
| (18) Headstone Road, Harrow.......£10 | *GB 81* |
| (19) Egyptian Art ........................£15 | *P Sheridan* |
| (20) The British Museum ..............£10 | *Phil Stamp Covers 51* |
| (21) Museum Street.......................£20 | *Assoc. of GBFDC 14* |
| (22) Sutton Hoo, Woodbridge ......£10 | *Stick with Stamps* |

## 2003 BRITISH MUSEUM

(23) Sloane Square, SW1 ...............£10 *A Bard*
(24) Woodnesborough ....................£20 *H D McIntyre*
(25) Canford School, Wimborne ...£20 *T Hurlstone*
(26) Morris Traveller, Cowley ........£20 *D T L Enterprises*
(27) HMS Unruly..............................£10 *RN CvrsGp*
(28) Concorde Farewell Flight .......£20 *Buckingham Cvrs*
**C.D.S. POSTMARKS Price Guide £7-£10**
(29) Russell Square, Elgin, Sutton, The Galleries, Sloane Sq.

## 4th November 2003 - CHRISTMAS
*2nd Ice Spiral; 1st Icicle Star; 'E' Wall of Frozen Snow;*
*53p Ice Ball; 68p Ice Hole; £1.12 Snow Pyramids*
*Also issued on same date 2nd & 1st Generic Sheets*
**SPECIAL HANDSTAMPS          SPONSOR**
**Price Guide Ordinary Covers £4-£9 / Sponsored Covers:**
(1)  FDI - Tallents House.....................*Royal Mail (n.s.c.)*
(2)  FDI - Bethlehem ............................*Royal Mail (n.s.c.)*
(3)  -do- non pictorial version ............*Royal Mail (n.s.c.)*
(4)  Seasons Greetings, Bethlehem......*Royal Mail (n.s.c.)*
(5)  Christmas, Snow Hill, B'ham.......*Royal Mail (n.s.c.)*
(6)  Chilwell, Nottingham..............£20 *Benham Coin Cover*
(7)  Frostrow, Sedbergh .................£15 *Benham*
(8)  Crystal Peaks, Sheffield..........£15 *Benham*
(9)  Winterburn, Skipton ...............£30 *Benham (500)267*
(10) Snowhill, Enniskillen .............£10 *Benham BLCS 267*
(11) Cold Blow, Narberth ...............£10 *Benham BLCS 267*
(12) Bethlehem.................................£15 *Bradbury Sovereign 35*
(13) Snowball Hill, Maidenhead ...£10 *Westminster*
(14) Snowball Hill (palette)...........£40 *Westminster*
(15) Autographed, Snowball Hill ..£20 *Westminster*
(16) St Nicholas Rd, SE18.............£10 *Steven Scott*
(17) Wise Man, Dorchester ..........£15 *M Brazier (Pubs.63)*
(18) Snowy Fielder Waye...............£20 *GB 82*
(19) Freezywater, Enfield ..............£20 *P Sheridan*
(20) Merry Christmas, Dartford.....£10 *Phil Stamp Covers*
(21) Cold Christmas, Ware ............£10 *Phil Stamp Covers 52*
(22) Freezywater, Enfield ..............£10 *ABC-FDC*
(23) Bletchley Park ........................£10 *Bletchley PO*
(24) Hector Berlioz ........................£10 *P M Payne*
(25) Loch Striven, Dunoon ...........£10 *RN CvrsGp*
**C.D.S. POSTMARKS Price Guide £7-£10**
(26) Freezywater, Winter Gdns, North Pole Rd, Frosterley

## 19 Dec 2003 - RUGBY WORLD CHAMPIONS
*1st Flags; 1st Team Circle; 68p World Cup; 68p Rear of Team*
**SPECIAL HANDSTAMPS          SPONSOR**
**Price Guide Ordinary Covers £4-£9 / Sponsored Covers:**
(1)  FDI - Tallents House.....................*Royal Mail (n.s.c.)*
(2)  FDI - Twickenham ........................*Royal Mail (n.s.c.)*
(3)  -do- non pictorial version ............*Royal Mail (n.s.c.)*
(4)  Congratulations, Birmingham ......*Royal Mail (n.s.c.)*
(5)  England Rugby, WC2 ..............£20 *Benham*
(6)  England Rugby, SW1 ...............£15 *Benham BLCS 270*
(7)  England Rugby, Twick'ham ...£20 *Benham*
(8)  England Rugby, Rugby............£20 *Benham*
(9)  World Champions.....................£20 *Benham*
(10) World Champions, Leics .......£15 *Bradbury Sovereign 44*
(11) Birthplace of Rugby ................£15 *Anniv & Events 21*
(12) Leicester Tigers.......................£20 *Bradbury*
(13) Rugby.......................................£15 *Westminster*
(14) Rugby (palette).......................£40 *Westminster*
(15) Autographed, Rugby ..............£25 *Westminster*
(16) Twickenham ............................£15 *Steven Scott*
(17) William Webb Ellis, Rugby ...£15 *M Brazier (Pubs.65)*
(18) Northampton Saints................£15 *M Brazier (Sports.1)*
(19) GB Covers, Kenton.................£25 *GB 84*
(20) England Rugby World Cup .....£35 *Buckingham Cvrs 41*
(21) Rugby School ..........................£15 *CoverCraft*
(22) World Champions, Rugby ......£15 *Phil Stamp Cvrs 52a*
**C.D.S. POSTMARKS Price Guide £7-£10**
(23) Twickenham, Rugby

## 13th Jan 2004 – CLASSIC LOCOMOTIVES
*(1) 20p Talyllyn Railway; 28p Bo'ness & Kinneil Railway;*
*E Great Central Railway; 42p Severn Valley Railway;*
*47p Bluebell Railway; 68p Keighley & Worth Valley Rly*
*(2) Miniature Sheet.*
**SPECIAL HANDSTAMPS          SPONSOR**
**Price Guide Ordinary Covers £4-£9 / Sponsored Covers:**
(1)  FDI - Tallents House.....................*Royal Mail (n.s.c.)*
(2)  FDI - York...................................*Royal Mail (n.s.c.)*
(3)  -do- non pictorial version ............*Royal Mail (n.s.c.)*
(4)  2004 Penydarren Merthyr Tydfil .*Royal Mail (n.s.c.)*
(5)  New Street Birmingham.............*Royal Mail (n.s.c.)*
(6)  Tywyn, Gwynedd....................£20 *Benham BLCS 269*
(7)  Bo'ness, West Lothian............£25 *Benham Pilgrim*
(8)  Loughborough...........................£20 *Benham BLCS 269*

### 2003 CHRISTMAS

### 2003 RUGBY WORLD CHAMPIONS

### 2004 CLASSIC LOCOMOTIVES

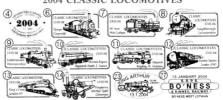

167

## 2004 CLASSIC LOCOMOTIVES

(9) Kidderminster ..........................£15 *Benham(s)*
(10) Horsted Keynesx .....................£20 *Benham BLCS 268*
(11) Haworth, Keighley .................£15 *Benham(s)*
(12) Euston Station, NW1 ............£20 *Benham BLCS 268*
(13) King's Cross, N1 ......................£25 *Benham Coin Cover*
(14) Penydarren, Merthyr Tydfil....£30 *Benham (500)268*
(15) King's Cross, London .............£20 *Bradbury Sovereign 36*
(16) King's Cross, London .............£20 *Westminster*
(17) Penydarren, Merthyr Tydfil....£20 *Westminster*
(18) Penydarren, Merthyr Tydfil....£20 *Westminster*
(19) Penydarren (palette) ...............£40 *Westminster*
(20) Autographed, Penydarren......£30 *Westminster*
(21) Charing Cross.........................£15 *Steven Scott*
(22) The North Western.................£20 *M Brazier (Pubs.64)*
(23) King Arthur Close, SE15 .......£20 *GB 83*
(24) Railway Magazine, SE1 .........£30 *Buckingham Cvrs 201*
(25) Great Central Railway............£30 *Buckingham Cvrs 201*
(26) National Railway Museum....£25 *Buckingham Cvrs 201*
(27) Bo'ness & Kinneil Railway ....£20 *CoverCraft*
(28) Keighley & Worth Valley ......£20 *P Sheridan*
(29) Classic Locos, Bridgnorth .....£15 *Phil Stamp Covers 53*
(30) Classic Locos, York ...............£15 *Phil Stamp Covers 54*
(31) Railtrail Tours, Leek, Staffs....£20 *Dawn*
(32) Canterbury.............................£20 *H D MacIntyre*
(33) Flying Scotsman, Euston .......£25 *Assoc. of GBFDC 15*
(34) London Victoria .....................£25 *Cam S.C.*
(35) Bletchley Park Post Office .....£15 *Bletchley PO*
(36) Rheilffordd Talyllyn Rly.........£25 *Talyllyn Rly Company*
(37) Wrenn Railways Collectors....£30 *B Fentiman*
(38) NATO Atlantic Squadron ......£15 *RN CvrsGp*
(39) Royal Navy Football Assoc'n.£15 *R F John*
(40) Chattanooga Choo Choo........£15 *P M Payne*
**C.D.S. POSTMARKS Price Guide £7-£10**
(41) Keighley, Bewdley, Loughborough, Bo'ness
(42) Uckfield, Ffestiniog, Tywyn, Railway Road

### 30th January 2004 – 'HELLO' Generic Issue
*1st Occasions Hello stamp + labels to mark the Hong Kong Stamp Expo and Year of the Monkey*
**SPECIAL HANDSTAMPS        SPONSOR**
**Price Guide Ordinary Covers £4-£9 / Sponsored Covers:**
(1) Year of the Monkey...............£10 *Bradbury Windsor 42*

### 3rd February 2004 – OCCASIONS
*(1) 5 x 1st Entertaining Envelopes; (2) Generic Sheet*
**SPECIAL HANDSTAMPS        SPONSOR**
**Price Guide Ordinary Covers £4-£9 / Sponsored Covers:**
(1) FDI - Tallents House...................... *Royal Mail (n.s.c.)*
(2) FDI - Merry Hill......................... *Royal Mail (n.s.c.)*
(3) -do- non pictorial version ............ *Royal Mail (n.s.c.)*
(4) Valentine Road, Birmingham....... *Royal Mail (n.s.c.)*
(5) Happisburgh, Norwich..........£15 *Benham Pilgrim*
(6) Penn, High Wycombe ............£10 *Benham BLCS 271*
(7) Lovington, Castle Cary............£10 *Benham BLCS 271*
(8) Newsome, Huddersfield.........£15 *Benham (500)271*
(9) Babel, Landovery ....................£15 *Benham Coin Cover*
(10) Gretna Green ..........................£10 *Bradbury Sovereign 37*
(11) Letter Box Lane, Sevenoaks ..£10 *Westminster*
(12) -do- Autographed Editions.....£15 *Westminster*
(13) -do- (palette design)................£40 *Westminster*
(14) Postling, Hythe ......................£15 *Buckingham.Cvrs 202*
(15) Laughterton, Lincoln..............£10 *Phil Stamp Covers 55*
**C.D.S. POSTMARKS Price Guide £7-£10**
(16) Greet, Manchester Airport, Send, Duckworth Lane

### 26th February 2004 – LORD of the RINGS
*10 x 1st Map of Middle Earth; Lothlorien Forest; Fellowship of the Ring; Rivendell; Bag End; Orthanc; Doors of Durin; Barad-dur; Minas Tirith; Fanghorn Forest.*
**SPECIAL HANDSTAMPS        SPONSOR**
**Price Guide Ordinary Covers £4-£9 / Sponsored Covers:**
(1) FDI - Tallents House...................... *Royal Mail (n.s.c.)*
(2) FDI - Oxford............................. *Royal Mail (n.s.c.)*
(3) -do- non pictorial version ............ *Royal Mail (n.s.c.)*
(4) Stampex - Lord of the Rings ....... *Royal Mail (n.s.c.)*
(5) Ryde, Isle of Wight .................£20 *Benham BLCS 272*
(6) Arrow, Alcester.......................£20 *Benham*
(7) Elphin, Lairg............................£25 *Benham Coin Cover*
(8) Forest Green, Dorking ...........£20 *Benham*
(9) Spellbrook...............................£20 *Benham Pilgrim*
(10) Battlefield, Shrewsbury ..........£20 *Benham BLCS 272*
(11) Treeton, Rotherham ...............£20 *Benham*
(12) Crow Bank, Wallsend ............£20 *Benham Pilgrim*
(13) Mountain, Holyhead ..............£30 *Benham (500)272*
(14) Shirehampton, Bristol ............£20 *Benham Pilgrim*
(15) Tolkien Society, Sarehole.......£20 *Anniv & Events 14*

## 2004 OCCASIONS

## 2004 LORD of the RINGS

(16) Enchanted World....................£20 *Bradbury Sovereign 38*
(17) Sarehole Mill...........................£15 *Westminster*
(18) -do- (palette design)................£40 *Westminster*
(19) -do- Autographed Editions.....£25 *Westminster*
(20) Middle Way, London SW1 ....£15 *Steven Scott*
(21) Eagle and Child, Oxford.........£20 *M Brazier (Pubs.66)*
(22) Ring Road, London W12.........£15 *GB 85*
(23) King Arthur, Machynlleth ......£20 *P Sheridan*
(24) Ringwould, Deal.....................£15 *Buckingham Cvrs 203*
(25) Rings End, Wisbech................£15 *Buckingham Cvrs 203*
(26) Sarehole Mill..........................£15 *Phil Stamp Covers 56*
(27) Oxford...................................£15 *Phil Stamp Covers 57*
(28) Spring Stampex, MCC............£10 *MachinCollectorsClub*
(29) Spring Stampex, N1 ..............£15 *Royal Mail*
(30) Lords of the Strings ...............£15 *P M Payne*
(31) George Cross 56th Anniv.......£15 *RN CvrsGp*
**C.D.S. POSTMARKS Price Guide £7-£10**
(32) The Shires, Wolvercote, Ringmer, Underhill Circus
(33) Oxford, High Holborn, Hurst Green, Edgbaston

## 16th March 2004 – NORTHERN IRELAND
*(1) 2nd Ely Island, Lough Erne; 1st Giant's Causeway;*
*E Slemish, Antrim Mountains; 42p Banns Road, Mourne*
*Mountains; 47p Glenelly Valley, Sperring; 68p Islandmore,*
*Strangford Lough.*
*(2) Self Adhesive Stamp Book containing 6 x 1st Class*
*Stamps: 2 Giant's Causeway & 4 Definitives.*
**SPECIAL HANDSTAMPS          SPONSOR**
**Price Guide Ordinary Covers £4-£9 / Sponsored Covers:**
(1)   FDI - Tallents House.....................*Royal Mail (n.s.c.)*
(2)   FDI - Garrison, Enniskillen.........*Royal Mail (n.s.c.)*
(3)   -do- non pictorial version ....*Royal Mail (n.s.c.)*
(4)   Northern Ireland, Birmingham....*Royal Mail (n.s.c.)*
(5)   Ballymena, County Antrim ....£10 *Benham BLCS 273*
(6)   Bushmills, County Antrim......£10 *Benham Coin Cover*
(7)   Newcastle, County Down......£20 *Benham (500)273*
(8)   Enniskillen...............................£10 *Benham BLCS 273*
(9)   Downpatrick.............................£15 *Benham*
(10) Omagh, County Tyrone .........£15 *Benham Pilgrim*
(11) Belfast.....................................£15 *Bradbury Sovereign 39*
(12) Self Adhesives .......................£10 *Bradbury Windsor 40*
(13) A British Journey, Bushmills..£10 *Westminster*
(14) -do- (palette design)................£40 *Westminster*
(15) -do- Autographed Editions.....£20 *Westminster*
(16) Ireland Place, N22 ..................£10 *Steven Scott*
(17) Saint Molaise Tower...............£10 *GB 86*
(18) Glens of Antrim, Glenariff.....£10 *P Sheridan*
(19) White Park Bay, Bushmills...£30 *Buckingham Cvrs 204*
(20) Northern Ireland, Belfast .......£15 *Phil Stamp Covers 58*
(21) Hunt Class, Belfast.................£10 *RN CvrsGp*
(22) Giants Causeway - permanent ...... *Royal Mail (n.s.c.)*
(23) Battle of Maldon ....................£15 *Heritage of Britain 1*
*NB The **Letters by Night** Prestige Stamp Book was also issued*
*on 16th March. Therefore Northern Ireland covers may also*
*exist with postmarks listed below.*
**C.D.S. POSTMARKS Price Guide £7-£10**
(24) Bushmills, Antrim, Warrenpoint, Strangford
(25) Strabane, Draperstown, Monea, Ballykeel

## 16th March 2004 – LETTERS BY NIGHT
*Prestige Stamp Book with four stamp panes including Classic*
*Locomotives stamps (Jan 2004) and Pub Signs - The Station*
*(Aug 2003).* **Values for set of 4 covers.**
**SPECIAL HANDSTAMPS          SPONSOR**
**Price Guide Ordinary Covers £20 / Sponsored Covers:**
(1)   FDI - Tallents House.....................*Royal Mail (n.s.c.)*
(2)   FDI - London NW10 ...................*Royal Mail (n.s.c.)*
(3)   -do- non pictorial version ............*Royal Mail (n.s.c.)*
(4)   New Street, Birmingham.............*Royal Mail (n.s.c.)*
(5)   Letters by Night, Crewe.........£40 *Benham*
(6)   Letters by Night, Newcastle...£40 *Benham*
(7)   Letters by Night, Calisle ........£40 *Benham*
(8)   Letters by Night, Edinburgh ..£40 *Benham*
(9)   Letters by Night, Euston.........£40 *Benham*
(10) The Night Mail, York..............£40 *Buckingham Cvrs*
(11) Final Journey of TPO Bristol .£40 *P Sheridan*
(12) Royal Scot Class, Glasgow.....£40 *M Brazier*
(13) Letters by Night, Bristol .........£40 *Phil Stamp Covers 59*
*NB **Northern Ireland** stamps were also issued on 16th March.*
*Therefore Letters by Night covers may also exist with*
*postmarks listed above.*
**C.D.S. POSTMARKS Price Guide £10 (each cover)**
(14) The Station, Railway Road, Penzance, Kidderminster

### 2004 NORTHERN IRELAND

### 2004 LETTERS BY NIGHT

169

## 2004 ENTENTE CORDIALE

Entente Cordiale

## 2004 OCEAN LINERS

### 6th April 2004 – ENTENTE CORDIALE
*28p Lace 1; 57p Coccinelle.*

| SPECIAL HANDSTAMPS | SPONSOR |
|---|---|

**Price Guide Ordinary Covers £4-£9 / Sponsored Covers:**
(1) FDI - Tallents House.................... *Royal Mail (n.s.c.)*
(2) FDI - London SW1 ..................... *Royal Mail (n.s.c.)*
(3) -do- non pictorial version .......... *Royal Mail (n.s.c.)*
(4) Entente Cordiale 1904-2004........ *Royal Mail/Royal Mint*
(5) Premier Jour, Paris...................... *See note below*
(6) Twinned Lyon - Birmingham ....... *Royal Mail (n.s.c.)*
(7) King Charles St, SW1.............£10 *Benham BLCS 277*
(8) Parliament Sqe, SW1.............£20 *Benham (500)277*
(9) Knightsbridge, SW1 ...............£10 *Benham BLCS 277*
(10) London-Paris Rail Link .........£10 *Bradbury Sovereign 42*
(11) London SW1 ...........................£10 *Westminster*
(12) -do- (palette design)................£40 *Westminster*
(13) -do- Autographed Editions.....£20 *Westminster*
(14) Allied Way, London W3........£10 *Steven Scott*
(15) Concorde, Filton, Bristol .......£15 *M Brazier (Pubs)*
(16) Bleriot Road, Hounslow ........£10 *GB 87*
(17) L'Entente Cordiale, SW1.......£15 *Buckingham Cvrs 205*
(18) Entente Cordiale, SW1 ..........£15 *Phil Stamp Covers 60*
(19) Grecian Cresc, SE19..............£10 *P M Payne*
(20) Hunt Class, Belfast..................£10 *RN CvrsGp*
(21) Battle of Stamford Bridge.......£15 *Heritage of Britain 2*
**C.D.S. POSTMARKS Price Guide £7-£10**
(22) Paris Avenue, Dunkirk, Calais Road, Britannia
**DOUBLE POSTMARKED COVERS**
The Entente Cordiale stamps were a joint Royal Mail/LaPoste
issue. Arrangements were made for British collectors to
obtain the Paris postmark (see item 5 above) at Tallents
House by authority of LaPoste, the French postal administration. The Paris postmark was applied to the French stamps
provided the covers had the Royal Mail's Entente Cordiale
stamps also affixed

### 13th April 2004 – OCEAN LINERS
*(1) 1st RMS Queen Mary 2 (2004); E SS Canberra;*
*42p RMS Queen Mary (1936); 47p RMS Mauretania;*
*57p SS City of New York; 68p PS Great Western.*
*(2) Miniature Sheet*
*(3) Self Adhesive Stamp Book containing 6 x 1st Class*
*Stamps: 2 Queen Mary 2 & 4 Definitives.*

| SPECIAL HANDSTAMPS | SPONSOR |
|---|---|

**Price Guide Ordinary Covers £4-£9 / Sponsored Covers:**
(1) FDI - Tallents House.................... *Royal Mail (n.s.c.)*
(2) FDI - Southampton ..................... *Royal Mail (n.s.c.)*
(3) -do- non pictorial version .......... *Royal Mail (n.s.c.)*
(4) Spanning the Oceans.................. *Royal Mail/Mint*
(5) Canberra Way, Birmingham ....... *Royal Mail (n.s.c.)*
(6) RMS Queen Mary 2, S'ton....£20 *Benham BLCS 279*
(7) SS Canberra, Belfast...............£20 *Benham BLCS 278*
(8) RMS Queen Mary ...................£20 *Benham BLCS 278*
(9) RMS Mauretania, Wallsend....£25 *Benham Coin Cover*
(10) SS City of New York.............£25 *Benham (500)278*
(11) PS Great Western, Bristol .....£20 *Benham Pilgrim*
(12) Ocean Liners, Liverpool........£20 *Bradbury Sovereign 40*
(13) Ocean Liners, Glasgow .........£15 *Bradbury Windsor 36*
(14) Self Adhesives, Ocean Liners £15 *Bradbury Windsor 41*
(15) Ocean Liners, Southampton..£15 *Westminster*
(16) -do- (palette design)................£25 *Westminster*
(17) -do- Autographed Editions.....£25 *Westminster*
(18) Tilbury Road, E10 ..................£15 *Steven Scott*
(19) Southampton............................£15 *Buckingham Cvrs 206*
(20) QM2, Southampton.................£25 *Buckingham Cvrs 206*
(21) Crown & Anchor.....................£15 *M Brazier (Pubs.67)*
(22) Merchant Navy Class .............£15 *M Brazier (Rly.9A)*
(23) Great Western Rd, W9............£15 *GB 88*
(24) Cunard, Southampton.............£15 *P Sheridan*
(25) Belfast .......................................£15 *Phil Stamp Covers 61*
(26) Southampton............................£15 *Phil Stamp Covers 62*
(27) Southampton............................£15 *Assoc. of GBFDC 16*
(28) Bristol .......................................£20 *H D Macintyre*
(29) Queen Mary 2 Southampton .£15 *RN CvrsGp*
(30) Cruise Control, Bletchley ......£15 *Bletchley PO*
(31) Flight Approach.......................£10 *P M Payne*
(32) Battle of Hastings....................£15 *Heritage of Britain 3*
**C.D.S. POSTMARKS Price Guide £7-£10**
(33) Southampton, Bristol, Belfast, Glasgow, Sea Lane
(34) Sea Street, Quarterdeck, Seaview, The Harbour

## 25 May 2004 – ROYAL HORTICULTURAL SOC.
*(1) 2nd Dianthus; 1st Dahlia; E Clematis;*
*42p Miltonia; 47p Lilium; 68p Delphinium*
*(2) Miniature Sheet  (3) Prestige Stamp Book Stamps*
*(4) Generic Sheet of 20 x 1st Class + labels.*

**SPECIAL HANDSTAMPS          SPONSOR**
**Price Guide Ordinary Covers £4-£9 / Sponsored Covers:**
| | | |
|---|---|---|
| (1) | FDI - Tallents House..................... | *Royal Mail (n.s.c.)* |
| (2) | FDI - Wisley, Woking .................. | *Royal Mail (n.s.c.)* |
| (3) | -do- non pictorial version ............ | *Royal Mail (n.s.c.)* |
| (4) | RHS 1804-2004 ............................ | *Royal Mail/Mint* |
| (5) | Chelsea Flower Show FDI............ | *Royal Mail* |
| (6) | Chelsea Flower Show RHS ......... | *Royal Mail* |
| (7) | Canberra Way, Birmingham........ | *Royal Mail (n.s.c.)* |
| (8) | Chelsea, London...................... | £20 | *Benham (500)281* |
| (9) | Knutsford, Cheshire................. | £20 | *Benham Coin Cover* |
| (10) | Great Torrington, Devon....... | £15 | *Benham* |
| (11) | Wisley, Woking....................... | £10 | *Benham BLCS 281* |
| (12) | Rettendon, Chelmsford .......... | £10 | *Benham BLCS 281* |
| (13) | Harrogate, N. Yorkshire ........ | £15 | *Benham* |
| (14) | Kew Gardens, Richmond ...... | £15 | *Bradbury Sovereign 41* |
| (15) | Chelsea, London.................... | £15 | *Bradbury Windsor 43* |
| (16) | Flower Girl, Chelsea............... | £15 | *Bradbury Windsor 44* |
| (17) | Royal Horticultural Society ... | £15 | *Westminster* |
| (18) | -do- (palette design)............... | £40 | *Westminster* |
| (19) | -do- Autographed Editions... | £25 | *Westminster* |
| (20) | Chelsea Embankment ............ | £15 | *Steven Scott* |
| (21) | RHS Chelsea ........................... | £15 | *Buckingham Cvrs 207* |
| (22) | RHS Wisley ............................. | £15 | *Buckingham Cvrs 207* |
| (23) | The Tulip................................ | £15 | *M Brazier (Pubs.69)* |
| (24) | Wisley Road, SW11................ | £10 | *GB 89* |
| (25) | Flowers & Plants Ass'n ......... | £10 | *P Sheridan* |
| (26) | Chelsea .................................... | £15 | *Phil Stamp Covers 63* |
| (27) | The Glory of the Garden....... | £15 | *Phil Stamp Covers 65* |
| (28) | Wisley, Woking....................... | £15 | *Phil Stamp Covers 64* |
| (29) | Battle of the Standard ........... | £15 | *Heritage of Britain 4* |
| (30) | Mount Everest Expedition .... | £20 | *ABC-FDC* |
| (31) | Poland - United Europe......... | £25 | *J L Englert* |
| (32) | HMS Coventry........................ | £15 | *RN CvrsGp* |

**C.D.S. POSTMARKS Price Guide £7-£10**
(33)  Chelsea Royal Hospital, Botanical Gardens, Primrose
(34)  New Covent Gdn, Ripley, Garden Village, Rose Lane

## 15th June 2004 – WALES
*(1) 2nd Barmouth Bridge; 1st Hyddgen, Plynlimon;*
*40p Brecon Beacons; 43p Pen-pych, Rhondda Valley;*
*47p Rhewl, Dee Valley; 68p Marloes Sands.*
*(2) Self Adhesive Stamp Book containing 6 x 1st Class*
*Stamps: 2 Hyddgen, Plynlimon & 4 Definitives.*

**SPECIAL HANDSTAMPS          SPONSOR**
**Price Guide Ordinary Covers £4-£9 / Sponsored Covers:**
| | | |
|---|---|---|
| (1) | FDI - Tallents House..................... | *Royal Mail (n.s.c.)* |
| (2) | FDI - Llanfair................................ | *Royal Mail (n.s.c.)* |
| (3) | -do- non pictorial version ............ | *Royal Mail (n.s.c.)* |
| (4) | Prince of Wales Lane, B'ham....... | *Royal Mail (n.s.c.)* |
| (5) | Machynlleth, Powys................ | £10 | *Benham BLCS 285* |
| (6) | Llangollen, Clwyd .................. | £20 | *Benham (500)284* |
| (7) | Snowdonia, Barmouth .......... | £20 | *Benham Coin Cover* |
| (8) | Marloes, Pembrokeshire ........ | £15 | *Benham* |
| (9) | Brecon, Powys ........................ | £10 | *Benham BLCS 284* |
| (10) | Blaenrhonnda, Glamorgan... | £20 | *Benham* |
| (11) | Machynlleth, Powys.............. | £10 | *Benham BLCS 284* |
| (12) | Tenby, Dyfed ......................... | £10 | *Bradbury Sovereign 43* |
| (13) | Merthyr Tydfil....................... | £10 | *Bradbury Windsor 45* |
| (14) | Brecon, Powys ....................... | £10 | *Westminster* |
| (15) | -do- (palette design)............... | £40 | *Westminster* |
| (16) | -do- Autographed Editions.... | £20 | *Westminster* |
| (17) | Prince of Wales Road, NW5... | £10 | *Steven Scott* |
| (18) | The National Trust.................. | £30 | *Buckingham Cvrs 208* |
| (19) | The Welsh Harp ..................... | £10 | *M Brazier (Pubs.70)* |
| (20) | Owens Way, London SE23.... | £10 | *GB 90* |
| (21) | Portmeirion............................. | £10 | *P Sheridan* |
| (22) | Cymru - Wales, Cardiff .......... | £10 | *Phil Stamp Covers 66* |
| (23) | Battle of Lewes ...................... | £15 | *Heritage of Britain 5* |
| (24) | HMS Cardiff............................ | £10 | *RN CvrsGp* |

**C.D.S. POSTMARKS Price Guide £7-£10**
(25)  Barmouth, Brecon, Marloes, Wales, Blaenrrhondda
(26)  Llangollen, Rhewl, Machynlleth

### 2004 ROYAL HORTICULTURAL SOCIETY

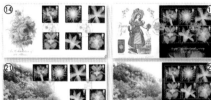

### 2004 WALES

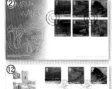

At www.bfdc.co.uk/postmarks you can download FREE files showing illustrations of virtually every special handstamp for all the commemorative stamp issues listed in this catalogue.

## 2004 RULE BRITANNIA

## 27 July 04 – RULE BRITANNIA Generic Issue
*1st Union Jack stamp + labels featuring all things British*

**SPECIAL HANDSTAMPS**          **SPONSOR**
Price Guide Ordinary Covers £4-£9 / Sponsored Covers:
(1) Rule Britannia, W1 .................£20 *Benham BLCS 287*
(2) Rule Britannia, SW1 ..............£20 *Benham (500)287*
(3) Union Jack Generic Issue......£25 *Bradbury Britannia 17*
(4) Smilers, Union Jack, Flagg .....£15 *Phil Stamp Covers*
(5) 55th Anniversary The Comet £20 *Group Capt Randle*

## 10th August 2004 – ROYAL SOCIETY of ARTS
*1st Sir Rowland Hill; 40p William Shipley;*
*43p RSA Examinations; 47p Appartus for sweeping chimnies;*
*57p Eric Gill's typeface; 68p Zero Waste.*

## 2004 ROYAL SOCIETY of ARTS

**SPECIAL HANDSTAMPS**          **SPONSOR**
Price Guide Ordinary Covers £4-£9 / Sponsored Covers:
(1) FDI - Tallents House.................... *Royal Mail (n.s.c.)*
(2) FDI - London WC2.................... *Royal Mail (n.s.c.)*
(3) -do- non pictorial version ............ *Royal Mail (n.s.c.)*
(4) Rowland Hill, Birmingham.......... *Royal Mail (n.s.c.)*
(5) John Adam Street, WC2 ........£10 *Benham BLCS 286*
(6) Henrietta Street, WC2............£15 *Benham (500)286*
(7) Millbank, SW1 ........................£10 *Benham*
(8) Kensington Gore, SW1 ..........£15 *Benham Coin Cover*
(9) Regent Street, Cambridge ......£10 *Benham*
(10) Kidderminster ...........................£10 *Benham BLCS 286*
(11) The 1851 Great Exhibition ....£10 *Bradbury Sovereign 45*
(12) RSA John Adam Street ..........£10 *Westminster*
(13) -do- (palette design)................£40 *Westminster*
(14) -do- Autographed Editions....£20 *Westminster*
(15) RSA John Adam Street ..........£10 *Steven Scott*
(16) Anniversary, London WC2 ....£30 *Buckingham Cvrs 209*
(17) The Printers Devil, Fleet St....£15 *M Brazier (Pubs.71)*
(18) Milton Keynes Philatelic Soc.£10 *M Brazier*
(19) Smart Street............................£10 *GB 91*
(20) Assoc. Chimney Sweeps ........£15 *P Sheridan*
(21) 250 Anniversary, WC2...........£10 *Phil Stamp Covers 67*
(22) RSA Stoke on Trent ...............£15 *T Hurlstone*
(23) Battle of Evesham ...................£15 *Heritage of Britain 6*
(24) New Orleans Walk ..................£10 *P M Payne*
(25) Alexandra Athanassiades.......£10 *P M Payne*
(26) Op. Pedestal Gourock............£10 *RN CvrsGp*
**C.D.S. POSTMARKS** Price Guide £7-£10
(27) Kidderminster, Shipley, Trafalgar Square

## 2004 WOODLAND ANIMALS

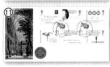

## 16th Sept 2004 – WOODLAND ANIMALS
*10 x 1st: Pine marten, Roe deer, Badger, Yellow-necked mouse,*
*Wild cat, Red squirrel, Stoat, Natterer's bat, Mole, Fox*

**SPECIAL HANDSTAMPS**          **SPONSOR**
Price Guide Ordinary Covers £4-£9 / Sponsored Covers:
(1) FDI - Tallents House.................... *Royal Mail (n.s.c.)*
(2) FDI - Woodland, Bhp Auckland. *Royal Mail (n.s.c.)*
(3) -do- non pictorial version ............ *Royal Mail (n.s.c.)*
(4) Stampex Woodland Animals....... *Royal Mail (n.s.c.)*
(5) Autumn Stampex ........................... *Royal Mail (n.s.c.)*
(6) Fox Green, Birmingham............... *Royal Mail (n.s.c.)*
(7) Great Molewood, Hertford .....£15 *Benham*
(8) Badger, Burnhill Green............£15 *Benham*
(9) Mousehole, Penzance..............£20 *Benham (500)288*
(10) Bats Corner, Farnham.............£15 *Benham*
(11) Catshill, Bromsgrove ..............£20 *Benham Coin Cover*
(12) Foxholes, Driffield...................£15 *Benham BLCS 288*
(13) Nutgrove, Blandford Forum ..£15 *Benham BLCS 288*
(14) Stotfield, Lossiemouth............£15 *Benham*
(15) Deerhurst, Gloucester ............£20 *Benham Coin Cover*
(16) Marten, Marlborough..............£15 *Benham*
(17) Badger's Mount, Sevenoaks ..£15 *Bradbury Sovereign 46*
(18) Woodland Walk .......................£15 *Westminster*
(19) -do- (palette design)................£40 *Westminster*
(20) -do- Autographed Editions....£25 *Westminster*
(21) Highwood Gardens, Ilford .....£15 *Steven Scott*
(22) Brownsea Island, Poole .........£12 *Buckingham Cvrs 210*
(23) Dinefwr Deer Park..................£12 *Buckingham Cvrs 210*
(24) The Squirrel, Cannock ...........£15 *M Brazier (Pubs.72)*
(25) British Deer Society................£15 *P Sheridan*
(26) Woodlands, Harrow Middx ...£15 *GB 92*
(27) Stoat's Nest Village.................£15 *Phil Stamp Covers 69*
(28) Badger, Wolverhampton........£15 *Phil Stamp Covers 68*
(29) Naturewatch HQ.....................£20 *Naturewatch*
(30) Wildlife across the Park..........£15 *Bletchley PO*
(31) Scouting, Harwick ..................£30 *I Tack*
(32) Woodland Animals, Extinct...£15 *P M Payne*
(33) Battle of Stirling Bridge .........£15 *Heritage of Britain 7*
**C.D.S. POSTMARKS Price Guide** £7-£10
(34) Mole Hill Green, Mousehole, Foxhole, Woodland
(35) Beddgelert, Kinloch Rannoch, New Deer, Deerpark

172

## 5th Oct 2004 – SCOTTISH PARLIAMENT
*Miniature Sheet containing 1 x 2nd, 2 x 1st, 2 x 40p, Scottish Country Pictorial stamps*

**SPECIAL HANDSTAMPS      SPONSOR**
**Price Guide Ordinary Covers £4-£9 / Sponsored Covers:**

| | | |
|---|---|---|
| (1) | Tallents House | *Royal Mail (n.s.c.)* |
| (2) | Edinburgh EH99 | *Royal Mail (n.s.c.)* |
| (3) | -do- non pictorial version | *Royal Mail (n.s.c.)* |
| (4) | Scotland Street, Birmingham | *Royal Mail (n.s.c.)* |
| (5) | Holyrood (lion) | £10 *Benham BLCS 289* |
| (6) | Holyrood (thistle) | £15 *Benham (500)289* |
| (7) | Holyrood | £10 *Benham BLCS 289* |
| (8) | Scottish Parliament | £10 *Bradbury Sovereign 49* |
| (9) | New Scottish Parliament | £13 *Buckingham Cvrs 213* |
| (10) | The Scottish Parliament | £10 *Phil Stamp Covers 70* |
| (11) | City of Edinburgh | £10 *M Brazier* |
| (12) | HMS's Catterick & Aurora | £10 *RN CvrsGp* |

**C.D.S. POSTMARKS Price Guide £50**
(13) The Scottish Parliament

## 12th Oct 2004 – CRIMEAN WAR
*2nd   Private McNamara,(Charge at Battle of Balaclava)*
*1st    Piper Muir, (Amphibious raid on Kerch & Yenikale)*
*40p   Sgt Major Edwards, (Gallant action at Inkerman)*
*57p   Sgt Powell, (Battles of Alma and Inkerman)*
*68p   Sgt Major Poole,(Front Line at Battle of Inkerman)*
*£1.12 Sgt Glasgow,(Gun Battery, Sebastopol)*

**SPECIAL HANDSTAMPS      SPONSOR**
**Price Guide Ordinary Covers £4-£9 / Sponsored Covers:**

| | | |
|---|---|---|
| (1) | FDI - Tallents House | *Royal Mail (n.s.c.)* |
| (2) | FDI - London SW3 | *Royal Mail (n.s.c.)* |
| (3) | -do- non pictorial version | *Royal Mail (n.s.c.)* |
| (4) | Balaclava Road, Birmingham | *Royal Mail (n.s.c.)* |
| (5) | Crimean War Research Soc | £15 *Bradbury Sovereign 47* |
| (6) | Royal Leicestershire Reg | £20 *Bradbury* |
| (7) | Alma Road, London E4 | £15 *Westminster* |
| (8) | -do- (palette design) | £40 *Westminster* |
| (9) | -do- Autographed Editions | £20 *Westminster* |
| (10) | Victoria Cross Road | £15 *Westminster* |
| (11) | Inkerman Road, NW5 | £10 *Steven Scott* |
| (12) | National Army Museum | £20 *Buckingham Cvrs 211* |
| (13) | Hyde Park, London W1 | £20 *Buckingham Cvrs 211* |
| (14) | The Victoria Cross | £15 *M Brazier (Pubs.73)* |
| (15) | Bomb, Lucas Avenue | £10 *GB 93* |
| (16) | CWRS, London SW1 | £15 *P Sheridan* |
| (17) | Alma Cut, St. Albans | £15 *Phil Stamp Covers 71* |
| (18) | Inkerman Road, NW5 | £10 *Assoc. of GBFDC 17* |
| (19) | HMS's Catterick & Aurora | £10 *RN CvrsGp* |
| (20) | Crimean War Victoria Cross | £10 *RN CvrsGp* |
| (21) | CWRS, Sowerby Bridge | £10 *P M Payne* |
| (22) | Battle of Falkirk | £15 *Heritage of Britain 8* |
| (23) | The Buffs, Canterbury | £30 *H D Macintyre* |
| (24) | The Fall of Sevastopol | £15 *Benham* |
| (25) | The Treaty of Paris | £15 *Benham* |
| (26) | Expedition to Kerch | £15 *Benham* |
| (27) | The Battle of Inkerman | £15 *Benham* |
| (28) | The Battle of Balaklava | £15 *Benham* |
| (29) | The Battle of Alma | £15 *Benham* |
| (30) | K2 1954-2004 Cho Oyu | £10 *ABC-FDC* |

**C.D.S. POSTMARKS Price Guide £7-£10**
(31) Battle, Raglan, Chelsea Royal Hospital, West Wellow
(32) Aldershot, Gun Hill, Alma Vale

## 2nd November 2004 – CHRISTMAS
*(1) 2nd, 1st, 40p, 57p, 68p, £1.12 'Father Christmas'*
*(2) Miniature Sheet*
*(3) Generic Sheet containing 2nd and 1st Class stamps.*

**SPECIAL HANDSTAMPS      SPONSOR**
**Price Guide Ordinary Covers £4-£9 / Sponsored Covers:**

| | | |
|---|---|---|
| (1) | FDI - Tallents House | *Royal Mail (n.s.c.)* |
| (2) | FDI - Bethlehem | *Royal Mail (n.s.c.)* |
| (3) | -do- non pictorial version | *Royal Mail (n.s.c.)* |
| (4) | Father Christmas, Tallents Hse | *Royal Mail (n.s.c.)* |
| (5) | Snow Hill, Birmingham | *Royal Mail (n.s.c.)* |
| (6) | Seasons Greetings, Bethlehem | *Royal Mail (n.s.c.)* |
| (7) | Toys Hill, Edenbridge | £10 *Benham BLCS 291* |
| (8) | Christmas Street, SE1 | £15 *Benham 500(292)* |
| (9) | Yule Tide Close, NW10 | £15 *Benham BLCS 292* |
| (10) | Rudolf Road, London E13 | £10 *Benham BLCS 291* |
| (11) | Winerley, Sandbach | £15 *Benham 500(291)* |
| (12) | St Nicholas, Goodwick | £15 *Benham Coin Cover* |
| (13) | St Nicholas, Cardiff | £10 *Bradbury Sovereign 48* |
| (14) | Yuletide Close (palette) | £40 *Westminster* |
| (15) | -do- Autographed Editions | £10 *Westminster* |
| (16) | Angel Street, EC1 | £10 *Steven Scott* |
| (17) | Bloomsbury, WC1 | £13 *Buckingham Cvrs 212* |
| (18) | Christmas Common | £13 *Buckingham Cvrs 212* |

### 2004 SCOTTISH PARLIAMENT

### 2004 CRIMEAN WAR

### 2004 CHRISTMAS

## 2005 FARM ANIMALS

### 11th January 2005 – FARM ANIMALS
*(1) 10 x 1st British Saddleback Pig; Khaki Campbell Duck;*
*Suffolk Punch; Shorthorns; Border Collie; Chicks; Suffolk*
*Sheep; Bagot Goat; Norfolk Black Turkeys; Emden Geese.*
*(2) Generic Sheet of 20 x 1st Class stamps (2 of each design).*

**SPECIAL HANDSTAMPS    SPONSOR**
**Price Guide Ordinary Covers £4-£9 / Sponsored Covers:**
(1) FDI - Tallents House..................... *Royal Mail (n.s.c.)*
(2) FDI - Paddock, Huddersfield...... *Royal Mail (n.s.c.)*
(3) -do- non pictorial version ............ *Royal Mail (n.s.c.)*
(4) Farmers Walk, Birmingham ........ *Royal Mail (n.s.c.)*
(5) Trumpington, Cambridge.......£15 *Benham BLCS 293*
(6) Bentley Heath, Solihull..........£15 *Benham*
(7) Market Hill, Woodbridge ......£20 *Benham Coin Cover*
(8) Stoneleigh Park, Kenilworth..£15 *Benham*
(9) Llangwm, Corwen....................£20 *Benham 500(293)*
(10) Frampton, Boston ..................£15 *Benham BLCS 293*
(11) Llanelwedd, Builth Wells ......£15 *Benham*
(12) Bovey Tracey.........................£15 *Benham*
(13) Great Eversden, Cambridge ..£15 *Benham*
(14) Gelly, Clynderwen..................£15 *Benham*
(15) Farmers, Llanwrda.................£15 *Bradbury Sovereign 50*
(16) Farm Lane (palette design) ....£15 *Westminster*
(17) -do- Autographed Editions.....£40 *Westminster*
(18) Horseshoe Lane......................£15 *GB 95*
(19) Kentish Town City Farm .......£15 *P Sheridan*
(20) Sowerby Bridge, N. Yorks.....£15 *Buckingham Cvrs 214*
(21) Thirsk, N. Yorks......................£20 *Buckingham Cvrs 214*
(22) Farm Animals on Pub Signs ..£15 *M Brazier (Pubs.75)*
(23) Farm Animals, Hereford ........£10 *Phil Stamp Covers 74*
(24) Farm Animals, Woolley .........£10 *Phil Stamp Covers 75*
(25) HMS/m Tallyho .....................£10 *RN CvrsGp*
(26) Battle of Boroughbridge.........£15 *Heritage of Britain 10*
**C.D.S. POSTMARKS Price Guide £7-£10**
(27) Goose Green, Bull Farm, Sheepwash, Fieldgate etc

## 2005 FARM ANIMALS - Generic Sheet

## 2005 SOUTH WEST ENGLAND

### 8th February 2005 – SOUTH WEST ENGLAND
*2nd Old Harry Rocks, Studland; 1st Wheal Coates, St. Agnes;*
*40p Start Point, Start Bay; 43p Horton Down, Wilts;*
*57p Chiselcombe, Exmoor; 68p St. James's Stone, Lundy.*

**SPECIAL HANDSTAMPS    SPONSOR**
**Price Guide Ordinary Covers £4-£9 / Sponsored Covers:**
(1) FDI - Tallents House..................... *Royal Mail (n.s.c.)*
(2) FDI - The Lizard, Helston.. ........ *Royal Mail (n.s.c.)*
(3) -do- non pictorial version ............ *Royal Mail (n.s.c.)*
(4) Cornwall Rd, Birmingham ........ *Royal Mail (n.s.c.)*
(5) Studland, Swanage, Dorset ....£10 *Benham*
(6) St. Agnes, Cornwall ...............£10 *Benham BLCS 294*
(7) Hallsands, Kingsbridge...........£15 *Benham 500(294)*
(8) Avebury, Marlborough ...........£10 *Benham BLCS 294*
(9) Lynmouth, Devon ...................£10 *Benham*
(10) Bideford to Lundy Island ......£15 *Benham Coin Cover*
(11) Penzance, Cornwall ...............£10 *Bradbury Sovereign 51*
(12) The Lizard (palette design) ....£40 *Westminster*
(13) -do- Autographed Editions.....£15 *Westminster*
(14) Stourhead, Warminster..........£30 *Buckingham Cvrs 215*
(15) Cornwall Road, SE1...............£10 *Steven Scott*
(16) Lynmouth Road, N2...............£10 *GB 96*
(17) SW England, Penzance..........£15 *Phil Stamp Covers 76*
(18) The White Horse, Uffington ..£10 *P Sheridan*
(19) Air, Rail, Sea, Bristol .............£15 *Cam S.C.*
(20) South West Naval Base .........£10 *RN CvrsGp*
(21) Battle of Neville's Cross.........£15 *Heritage of Britain 11*
**C.D.S. POSTMARKS Price Guide £7-£10**
(22) St. Agnes, Studland, Torcross, Bideford, Penzance etc

## 2005 JANE EYRE

### 24th February 2005 – JANE EYRE
*(1) 2nd Mr Rochester; 1st Jane; 40p Jane at George Inn;*
*57p Adele and Jane; 68p & £1.12 Jane at Lowton School.*
*(2) Miniature Sheet & (3) Prestige Stamp Book.*

**SPECIAL HANDSTAMPS    SPONSOR**
**Price Guide Ordinary Covers £4-£9 / Sponsored Covers:**
(1) FDI - Tallents House..................... *Royal Mail (n.s.c.)*

(2) FDI - Haworth Parsonage............ *Royal Mail (n.s.c.)*
(3) -do- non pictorial version ............ *Royal Mail (n.s.c.)*
(4) Hay-on-Wye................................... *Royal Mail/Royal Mint*
(5) Spring Stampex ............................ *Royal Mail (n.s.c.)*
(6) Stampex, Jane Eyre........................ *Royal Mail (n.s.c.)*
(7) Eyre Rd., Birmingham.................... *Royal Mail (n.s.c.)*
(8) Norton Conyers, Ripon...........£10 *Benham BLCS 296*
(9) The Parsonage, Haworth .......£15 *Benham Coin Cover*
(10) Cowan Bridge School ..............£10 *Benham BLCS 296*
(11) Thornton, Bradford................£10 *Benham BLCS 295*
(12) Tunstall, Carnforth..................£10 *Benham BLCS 295*
(13) Wycoller, Colne, Lancs...........£15 *Benham 500(295)*
(14) Jane Eyre - Charlotte Bronte .£15 *Bradbury Sovereign 53*
(15) Bronte Grove (palette)............£40 *Westminster*
(16) -do- Autographed Editions.....£20 *Westminster*
(17) BS, Haworth, Keighley...........£15 *Buckingham Cvrs 216*
(18) Bronte Parsonage Museum ....£15 *Buckingham Cvrs 216*
(19) Wuthering Heights Inn ..........£10 *M Brazier (Pubs.76)*
(20) Society of Authors, SW10 ......£10 *P Sheridan*
(21) Chestnut Lane, N20.................£10 *GB 97*
(22) Eyre Street Hill, EC1...............£10 *Steven Scott*
(23) Safety Matches, Rochester .....£15 *Phil Stamp Covers 77*
(24) Aspirin, Gateshead..................£10 *Phil Stamp Covers 78*
(25) Charlotte Bronte, York ..........£10 *Cotswold*
(26) Literature & Fables, SE5 .......£10 *P M Payne*
(27) Loss of HMS Dainty................£10 *RN CvrsGp*
(28) Battle of Otterburn .................£15 *Heritage of Britain 12*
**C.D.S. POSTMARKS Price Guide £7-£10**
(29) Thornton, Rochester, Haworth, Rawdon, Gateshead

## 15th March 2005 – MAGIC
*(1) 1st Heads or Tails; 40p Rabbit and Top Hat; 47p Scarves;
68p Ace of Hearts; £1.12 Fezzes.*
*(2) Generic Sheet of 20 x 1st Class stamps (and labels).*
**SPECIAL HANDSTAMPS          SPONSOR**
**Price Guide Ordinary Covers £4-£9 / Sponsored Covers:**
(1) FDI - Tallents House.................... *Royal Mail (n.s.c.)*
(2) FDI - London NW1.................... *Royal Mail (n.s.c.)*
(3) -do- non pictorial version ............ *Royal Mail (n.s.c.)*
(4) Daniels Road, Birmingham.......... *Royal Mail (n.s.c.)*
(5) Stephenson Way, NW1..........£10 *Benham BLCS 299*
(6) Southport ..............................£10 *Benham BLCS 299*
(7) Selly Oak, Birmingham .........£15 *Benham 500(299)*
(8) St. Austell, Cornwall...............£15 *Benham Coin Cover*
(9) Glasgow .................................£15 *Benham Coin Cover*
(10) A Century of Magic ................£15 *Bradbury Sovereign 54*
(11) The Magic Circle Centenary ...£25 *Bradbury*
(12) Stephenson Way (palette) ......£40 *Westminster*
(13) -do- Autographed Editions.....£15 *Westminster*
(14) Prestolee, Bolton ....................£13 *Buckingham Cvrs 217*
(15) Conjurors 1/2 Crown, Poole...£14 *M Brazier (Pubs.77)*
(16) Hand Court, WC1 ...................£10 *GB 98*
(17) Stephenson Way, NW1..........£10 *Steven Scott*
(18) Wandsworth ..........................£15 *Phil Stamp Covers 79*
(19) Bletchley Park Post Office .....£10 *Bletchley PO*
(20) Magic through the Ages...........£10 *P M Payne*
(21) Merlin Close, Croydon...........£15 *Assoc. of GBFDC 18*
(22) Operation Marstrike................£10 *RN CvrsGp*
(23) Battle of Shrewsbury ..............£10 *Heritage of Britain 13*
**C.D.S. POSTMARKS Price Guide £7-£10**
(24) Bunny, Hatt, King's Cross

## 22nd March 2005 – CASTLES
*50p Carrickfergus & Windsor; £1 Caernarfon & Edinburgh*
**SPECIAL HANDSTAMPS          SPONSOR**
**Price Guide Ordinary Covers £4-£9 / Sponsored Covers:**
(1) FDI - Tallents House.................... *Royal Mail (n.s.c.)*
(2) FDI - Windsor.......................... *Royal Mail (n.s.c.)*
(3) -do- non pictorial version ............ *Royal Mail (n.s.c.)*
(4) Castle Road, Birmingham .......... *Royal Mail (n.s.c.)*
(5) Carrickfergus ...........................£15 *Benham BLCS 300*
(6) Edinburgh ...............................£15 *Benham BLCS 300*
(7) Windsor...................................£20 *Benham Coin Cover*
(8) Caernarfon ..............................£15 *Benham(500)300*
(9) 50th Anniversary of Castles...£15 *Bradbury Sovereign 52*
(10) Windsor (palette design).........£40 *Westminster*
(11) -do- Autographed Editions......£25 *Westminster*
(12) QEII High Values ...................£30 *Buckingham Cvrs 218*
(13) British Castles Windsor .........£15 *M Brazier (Pubs.78)*
(14) Windsor Way, London W14...£15 *GB DWX*
(15) The Windsor Castle ................£15 *Steven Scott*
(16) The 1955 Castle Definitives ...£15 *P Sheridan*
(17) The Castle Definitives ............£15 *Phil Stamp Covers 80*
(18) Second Battle of Sirte .............£10 *RN CvrsGp*
(19) Battle of St. Albans .................£15 *Heritage of Britain 14*
**C.D.S. POSTMARKS Price Guide £7-£10**
(20) Windsor, Caernarfon, Edinburgh, Carrickfergus

## 2005 JANE EYRE

## 2005 MAGIC

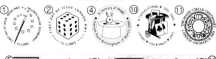

## 2005 CASTLES

## 2005 ROYAL WEDDING

## 8th April 2005 – ROYAL WEDDING

*2 x 30p; 2 x 68p Prince Charles & Mrs Camilla Parker Bowles in Miniature Sheet format.*

**SPECIAL HANDSTAMPS    SPONSOR**
Price Guide Ordinary Covers £4-£9 / Sponsored Covers:
(1) FDI - Tallents House.................... *Royal Mail (n.s.c.)*
(2) FDI - Windsor... ......................... *Royal Mail (n.s.c.)*
(3) -do- non pictorial version ......... *Royal Mail (n.s.c.)*
(4) Prince of Wales, Birmingham ...... *Royal Mail (n.s.c.)*
(5) Royal Wedding, Windsor........£15 *Benham BLCS 301*
(6) Charles & Camilla .................£15 *Benham BLCS 301*
(7) Tudor Rose, Windsor...............£20 *Benham(500)301*
(8) Royal Wedding Celebrations .£15 *Bradbury Sovereign 62*
(9) Windsor (palette design)........£40 *Westminster*
(10) -do- Autographed Editions.....£20 *Westminster*
(11) Majesty Magazine, Windsor...£35 *Buckingham Cvrs 227*
(12) The Guildhall, Windsor ........£15 *M Brazier*
(13) Royal Wedding .....................£15 *Phil Stamp Covers 84*
(14) Rotary, Romford....................£10 *T Hurlstone*
(15) Rotary, Brentford ..................£10 *T Hurlstone*
(16) Battle of Towton....................£15 *Heritage of Britain 9*
(17) No.32 (The Royal) Squadron £10 *S Hill*
(18) HMS Glowworm.....................£10 *RN CvrsGp*
**C.D.S. POSTMARKS Price Guide £7-£10**
(19) Windsor, Windsor Great Park, Wales, Caernarfon
*The Royal Wedding was postponed from 8th April to 9th April as a mark of respect for Pope John Paul II's funeral. Royal Mail therefore agreed that all sponsors of postmarks could obtain a free postmark for 9th April provided it was of an identical design (except of course for the date). Double dated covers also exist - these will fetch a premium over the prices listed above.*

## 2005 WORLD HERITAGE SITES

## 21st April 2005 – WORLD HERITAGE SITES

*2nd, Hadrian's Wall; 2nd Uluru-Kata Tjuta; 1st Stonehenge; 1st Wet Tropics Queensland; 47p Blenheim Palace; 47p Greater Blue Mountains; 68p Heart of Neolithic, Orkney; 68p Purnululu National Park*
*Also issued on same day: Pacific Explorer Generic Sheet with 20 x Hello Stamps and labels.*

**SPECIAL HANDSTAMPS    SPONSOR**
Price Guide Ordinary Covers £4-£9 / Sponsored Covers:
(1) FDI - Tallents House.................... *Royal Mail (n.s.c.)*
(2) FDI - Blenheim Palace... ............. *Royal Mail (n.s.c.)*
(3) -do- non pictorial version ......... *Royal Mail (n.s.c.)*
(4) Stonehenge, Amesbury ............... *Royal Mail (n.s.c.)*
(5) Stonehenge Croft, Birmingham .. *Royal Mail (n.s.c.)*
(6) Hounslow, West London .......£15 *Benham Coin Cover*
(7) Invergowrie, Dundee..............£10 *Benham*
(8) The Strand, London WC2.......£10 *Benham BLCS 302*
(9) Great Russell Street, WC1 .....£10 *Benham*
(10) Prehistoric Britain, Salisbury .£10 *Benham*
(11) Roman Britain, Carlisle..........£10 *Benham*
(12) Year of the Sea, Greenwich ...£10 *Benham BLCS 302*
(13) Year of the Sea, South'ton .....£10 *Benham BLCS 302*
(14) Stonehenge..............................£10 *Bradbury Sovereign 55*
(15) Blenheim (palette design)......£10 *Westminster*
(16) -do- Autographed Editions.....£40 *Westminster*
(17) Blenheim Palace.....................£20 *Buckingham Cvrs 219*
(18) Captain Cook ........................£25 *Buckingham Cvrs 219*
(19) Bark Endeavour......................£20 *Buckingham Cvrs 219*
(20) The Hadrian, Wall .................£10 *M Brazier (Pubs.79)*
(21) Stonehenge, Salisbury ...........£10 *P Sheridan*
(22) Barrier Approach, SE7...........£10 *GB 99*
(23) Dean's Yard, London SW1 ....£15 *Steven Scott*
(24) World Heritage Sites, Perth ...£15 *Phil Stamp Covers 81*
(25) Battle of Blore Heath .............£15 *Heritage of Britain 15*
(26) Bombardment of Tripoli.........£10 *RN CvrsGp*
**C.D.S. POSTMARKS Price Guide £7-£10**
(27) Heddon on the Wall, Stromness, Woodstock, Amesbury
*This was a joint issue with Australia Post. Pairs of covers exist with both sets of stamps. Priced approx double the above.*

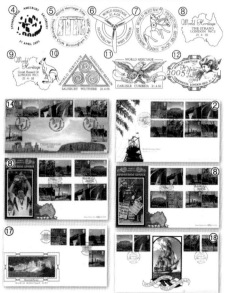

## 2005 TROOPING THE COLOUR

## 7th June 2005 – TROOPING THE COLOUR

*2nd Ensign of Scots Guard; 1st H M the Queen; 42p Trumpeter, Household Cavalry; 60p Welsh Guards Sgt; 68p H M the Queen as Colonel of the Coldstream Guards; £1.12 H M the Queen with the Duke of Edinburgh. Stamps and Miniature Sheet.*

**SPECIAL HANDSTAMPS    SPONSOR**
Price Guide Ordinary Covers £4-£9 / Sponsored Covers:
(1) FDI - Tallents House.................... *Royal Mail (n.s.c.)*
(2) FDI - London SW1... .................. *Royal Mail (n.s.c.)*
(3) -do- non pictorial version ......... *Royal Mail (n.s.c.)*
(4) Queen's Road, Birmingham......... *Royal Mail (n.s.c.)*
(5) Horse Guards Avenue, SW1..£10 *Benham BLCS 304*

(6)   Whitehall, SW1 ........................£10   *Benham BLCS 303*
(7)   St. James's St., SW1 .................£10   *Benham BLCS 303*
(8)   Buckingham Palace Rd ...........£15   *Benham(500)303*
(9)   Tower Hill, EC3 ........................£15   *Benham(500)304*
(10) Birdcage Walk, SW1 ................£10   *Benham BLCS 304*
(11) Horse Guards Ave ...................£15   *Bradbury Sovereign 56*
(12) 1805-2005, London ..........................   *Bradbury (n.s.c.)*
(13) London SW1 (palette) ...........£40   *Westminster*
(14) -do- Autographed Editions.....£20   *Westminster*
(15) Buckingham Palace Road........£15   *Steven Scott*
(16) The Mall, SW1 ........................£13   *Buckingham Cvrs 220*
(17) Horse Guards Parade, SW1...£13   *Buckingham Cvrs 220*
(18) The Royal & The Parade.......£10   *M Brazier (Pubs.80)*
(19) Coldstream (Gdns) Guards....£10   *GB 100*
(20) Trooping the Colour...............£10   *P Sheridan*
(21) The Parade, SW1....................£10   *Assoc. of GBFDC 19*
(22) Trooping the Colour...............£15   *Phil Stamp Covers 82*
(23) Trooping the Colour...............£15   *Phil Stamp Covers 83*
(24) Rotary Club of London..........£20   *Bradbury*
(25) Battle of Northampton...........£15   *Heritage of Britain 16*
(26) Trooping the BP Colour ........£10   *Bletchley PO*
(27) 61st Anniversary D-Day +1...£10   *RN CvrsGp*
(28) Kangchenjunga, Watford.......£15   *ABC-FDC*
(29) Makalu 1955, Mt Pleasant ....£15   *ABC-FDC*
(30) Annapurna South Face.........£15   *ABC-FDC*
(31) BFPO 1000 .............................£25   *British Forces PO*
**C.D.S. POSTMARKS Price Guide £7-£10**
(32) Coldstream, Windsor, Trafalgar Square
(33) Queensway, Queens Parade, Queen's Drive, March

## 21st June 05 – WHITE ENSIGN Generic Issue
*1st White Ensign stamp + labels featuring signal flags*
**SPECIAL HANDSTAMPS**      **SPONSOR**
**Price Guide Ordinary Cvrs £3-£5 / Sponsored Covers:**
(1)   Horatio Nelson .......................£15   *Bradbury Windsor 55*
(2)   The White Ensign, Flagg........£15   *Phil Stamp Covers*
(3)   Wimbledon .......................................   *Royal Mail (n.s.c.)*

## 5th July 2005 – END OF THE WAR
*Miniature Sheet comprising of:*
*1st Floodlit St. Paul's; 5 x 1st Gold Definitives*
**SPECIAL HANDSTAMPS**      **SPONSOR**
**Price Guide Ordinary Covers £3-£5 / Sponsored Covers:**
(1)   FDI - Tallents House....................£   *Royal Mail (n.s.c.)*
(2)   FDI - Peacehaven ..........................£   *Royal Mail (n.s.c.)*
(3)   -do- non pictorial version ............£   *Royal Mail (n.s.c.)*
(4)   St Pauls London EC4....................£   *Royal Mail (n.s.c.)*
(5)   Winston Drive, Birmingham .......   *Royal Mail*
(6)   Whitehall, London SW1........£10   *Benham BLCS 305*
(7)   St Pauls, London SW1 ...........£10   *Benham BLCS 305*
(8)   Peacehaven, East Sussex....£15   *Benham(500)305*
(9)   Peace, London SW1 ...............£15   *Bradbury Sovereign 57*
(10) St. Paul's (palette design) ....£40   *Westminster*
(11) -do- Autographed Editions....£15   *Westminster*
(12) Victory Road, SW19 ..............£10   *Steven Scott*
(13) Peace on Earth, EC4 ............£15   *Buckingham Cvrs 221*
(14) The Soldiers Return...............£10   *M Brazier (Pubs.81)*
(15) Wall End Road, E6.................£10   *GB 101*
(16) End of War, London .............£10   *P Sheridan*
(17) Victory Walk ..........................£10   *Phil Stamp Covers 84*
(18) End of War BF 2865 PS........£10   *Forces BFPS*
(19) 60th Anniv End of War .........£10   *Bletchley PO*
(20) End of War BF 2867 PS........£10   *RN CvrsGp*
(21) Battle of Barnet ......................£15   *Heritage of Britain 18*
**C.D.S. POSTMARKS Price Guide £7-£10**
(22) Montgomery, Peacehaven, Wargrave, Bletchley,
(23) Churchill, Woodstock, King George Road

## 19th July 2005 – BRITISH MOTORCYCLES
*1st Norton F1; 40p BSA Rocket; 42p Vincent Black Shadow;*
*47p Triumph Twin Speed; 60p Brough Superior;*
*68p Royal Enfield*
**SPECIAL HANDSTAMPS**      **SPONSOR**
**Price Guide Ordinary Cvrs £3-£5 / Sponsored Covers:**
(1)   FDI - Tallents House....................£   *Royal Mail (n.s.c.)*
(2)   FDI - Solihull ................................£   *Royal Mail (n.s.c.)*
(3)   -do- non pictorial version ............£   *Royal Mail (n.s.c.)*
(4)   Sheen Road, Birmingham ...........   *Royal Mail*
(5)   Wolverhampton ........................£   *Benham*
(6)   Birmingham ...............................£20   *Benham Coin Cover*
(7)   Stevenage ..................................£15   *Benham*
(8)   Coventry ....................................£20   *Benham(500) 306*
(9)   Nottingham ...............................£15   *Benham BLCS 306*
(10) Redditch ....................................£15   *Benham BLCS 306*
(11) Automobile Association.........£15   *Bradbury Sovereign 58*

## 2005 TROOPING THE COLOUR

## 2005 END OF THE WAR

## 2005 BRITISH MOTORCYCLES

## 2005 BRITISH MOTORCYCLES

(12) Brands Hatch (palette)...........£40 *Westminster*
(13) -do- Autographed Editions.....£25 *Westminster*
(14) Motorcycles, Norwich...........£15 *Steven Scott*
(15) Beaulieu.....................................£12 *Buckingham Cvrs 222*
(16) Classic Bike, Silverstone......£12 *Buckingham Cvrs 222*
(17) Stirling Moss, Aintree.............£15 *Buckingham Cvrs 222*
(18) The Norton & the Sun Inn.....£15 *M Brazier (Pubs.82)*
(19) Harley Davidson, Towcester...£15 *M Brazier*
(20) Biko Close, Uxbridge..............£10 *GB 102*
(21) Sammy Miller Motorcycles....£25 *P Sheridan*
(22) TMC Southfield Rd, W4........£25 *H D MacIntyre*
(23) Silverstone, Towcester............£20 *G Lovell*
(24) Motorcycles, Birmingham .....£20 *Phil Stamp Covers 86*
(25) Ace Corner, NW10.................£15 *Farrukh Jamil Covers*
(26) Ace Corner, NW10.................£15 *Farrukh Jamil Covers*
(27) Brough Superior, Tonbridge...£35 *W H Pugh*
(28) AJS, Andover...........................£35 *W H Pugh*
(29) BSA, Southampton ..................£35 *W H Pugh*
(30) Verralls, Haywards Heath .....£35 *W H Pugh*
(31) Royal Enfield, Moreton..........£35 *W H Pugh*
(32) Post Office Urgent Despatch .£10 *Bletchley PO*
**C.D.S. POSTMARKS Price Guide £7-£10**
(33) Brereton, Small Heath, Allesley, Sherwood, The Rocket
(34) Redditch, Brough, Silverstone, Norton, Enfield, Dunlop

## 2005 LONDON 2012

### 5th August 2005 – LONDON 2012
*Miniature Sheet comprising of: 1st Athlete; 1st Javelin;*
*1st Basketball; 1st Swimming; 2 x 1st Triumphant Athlete*
**SPECIAL HANDSTAMPS          SPONSOR**
**Price Guide Ordinary Covers £3-£5 / Sponsored Covers:**
(1)   FDI - Tallents House....................  *Royal Mail (n.s.c.)*
(2)   FDI - London E15.......................  *Royal Mail (n.s.c.)*
(3)   -do- non pictorial version ...........  *Royal Mail (n.s.c.)*
(4)   London Road, Birmingham .........  *Royal Mail*
(5)   2012 (Finishing Line)............£10  *Benham BLCS 310*
(6)   2012 (Javelin) ...........................£15  *Benham(500) 310*
(7)   2012 (Swimming) .....................£10  *Benham*
(8)   2012 (Runner)............................£15  *Benham BLCS 310*
(9)   2012 (Basketball) .....................£10  *Benham*
(10)  Hat Trick for London...............£15  *Bradbury Sovereign 64*
(11)  Host City, E15 (palette)..........£40  *Westminster*
(12)  -do- Autographed Editions.....£15  *Westminster*
(13)  London Wins Stratford..........£10  *Steven Scott*
(14)  2012 (torch)...............................£13  *Buckingham Cvrs 228*
(15)  Raffles, Romford.......................£10  *M Brazier (Pubs.84)*
(16)  Olympic Way, Wembley.......£10  *GB 104*
(17)  It's London Host City 2012 ...£15  *P Sheridan*
(18)  London Host City .....................£15  *Phil Stamp Covers*
(19)  Soc of Olympic Collectors ....£10  *Soc of Olympic Coll.*
(20)  Congratultions, York ..............£10  *Cotswold*
(21)  Havering Sports Council .......£15  *T Hurlstone*
(22)  HMS Belfast ..............................£10  *RN CvrsGp*
**C.D.S. POSTMARKS Price Guide £7-£10**
(23)  Stratford, City (London)

### 23rd August 2005 – CHANGING TASTES
*2nd Rice; 1st Tea; 42p Sushi; 47p Pasta; 60p Chips;*
*68p Apples*
**SPECIAL HANDSTAMPS          SPONSOR**
**Price Guide Ordinary Covers £3-£5 / Sponsored Covers:**
(1)   FDI - Tallents House....................  *Royal Mail (n.s.c.)*
(2)   FDI - Cookstown .........................  *Royal Mail (n.s.c.)*
(3)   -do- non pictorial version ...........  *Royal Mail (n.s.c.)*
(4)   Oliver Street, Birmingham ..........  *Royal Mail*
(5)   Ashdown Forest, E. Sussex ....£10  *Benham BLCS 309*
(6)   Guiseley, Leeds........................£15  *Benham(500) 309*
(7)   Hillingdon, Uxbridge ..............£10  *Benham*
(8)   St. Austell, Cornwall................£10  *Benham BLCS 309*
(9)   Victoria, London SW1.............£15  *Benham Coin Cover*
(10)  Chagford, Devon ......................£10  *Benham*
(11)  Covent Garden ........................£10  *Bradbury Sovereign 59*
(12)  Curry Rise (palette)................£40  *Westminster*
(13)  -do- Autographed Editions.....£15  *Westminster*
(14)  Curry Rise, NW7.....................£10  *Steven Scott*
(15)  Great British Food, W1 .........£30  *Buckingham Cvrs 223*
(16)  The Bramley Apple...................£15  *M Brazier (Pubs.83)*
(17)  Cooksway, Hatfield ................£10  *GB 103*
(18)  Vegetarian Society ..................£15  *P Sheridan*
(19)  Cookham, Maidenhead............£15  *Phil Stamp Covers 87*
(20)  Nando's, South Bank SE1.......£15  *ABC FDC*
(21)  Food you can trust, Iceland....£15  *W H Pugh*
(22)  Changing Rations ....................£10  *Bletchley PO*
(23)  Battle of Bosworth ..................£15  *Heritage of Britain 20*
(24)  HMS Hero ................................£10  *RN CvrsGp*
**C.D.S. POSTMARKS Price Guide £7-£10**
(25)  Bramley, Strawberry Hill, Curry Rivel, Isle of Grain
(26)  Wheatley, Rowelton, New Covent Garden, Sugar Island

## 2005 CHANGING TASTES

## 15th September 2005 – CLASSIC ITV

*(1) 2nd Inspector Morse; 1st Emmerdale; 42p Rising Damp;*
*47p Avengers; 60p South Bank Show;*
*68p Who wants to be a Millionaire*
*(2) Generic Sheet of 20 x 1st Class stamps.*

**SPECIAL HANDSTAMPS**       **SPONSOR**
**Price Guide Ordinary Covers £3-£5 / Sponsored Covers:**
(1)  FDI - Tallents House................. *Royal Mail (n.s.c.)*
(2)  FDI - London SE19.................... *Royal Mail (n.s.c.)*
(3)  -do- non pictorial version ........... *Royal Mail (n.s.c.)*
(4)  Stampex, London N1 ................ *Royal Mail*
(5)  Stampex ITV, London N1 .......... *Royal Mail*
(6)  Broad Street, Birmingham ......... *Royal Mail*
(7)  Oxford............................£10 *Benham BLCS 311*
(8)  The Woolpack, Harewood .....£15 *Benham Coin Cover*
(9)  Burley Road, Leeds...............£10 *Benham*
(10) Elstree, Borehamwood ..........£15 *Benham(500) 311*
(11) Upper Ground, SE1...............£10 *Benham BLCS 311*
(12) Grays Inn Road, WC.............£10 *Benham*
(13) Commercial TV, Manchester.£10 *Bradbury Sovereign 60*
(14) South Bank (palette) .............£40 *Westminster*
(15) -do- Autographed .................£15 *Westminster*
(16) Gray's Inn Road, WC2..........£10 *Steven Scott*
(17) TV Times, SE1 .....................£20 *Buckingham Cvrs 224*
(18) 50 Years of Classic ITV .........£20 *Buckingham Cvrs 224*
(19) The Sweeney, Charlton..........£15 *M Brazier (Pubs.85)*
(20) Cooper Road, London ...........£10 *GB 105*
(21) Police Station Lane, Herts .....£10 *GB 105*
(22) National Museum, Bradford..£15 *P Sheridan*
(23) Classic ITV, Watchet..............£15 *Phil Stamp Covers 85*
(24) Scott's View, Melrose.............£10 *ABC-FDC*
(25) Riot of Steam 150 Years........£10 *Dawn*
(26) HMS Valient .........................£10 *RN CvrsGp*
(27) Battle of East Stoke ...............£15 *Heritage of Britain 21*
**C.D.S. POSTMARKS Price Guide £7-£10**
(28) Harewood, South Bank, Esholt, Oxford, Woodsley
(29) Teddington, Blackfriars Road, Elstree

## 4th October 2005 – SMILERS

*6 x 1st featuring small versions of the previously issued*
*'Smilers' stamps: Hello, Love, Union Jack, Teddy Bear,*
*Flowers and Robin. (Self Adhesives issued in Stamp Book)*

**SPECIAL HANDSTAMPS**       **SPONSOR**
**Price Guide Ordinary Covers £3-£5 / Sponsored Covers:**
(1)  FDI - Tallents House.................. *Royal Mail (n.s.c.)*
(2)  FDI - Windsor ........................ *Royal Mail (n.s.c.)*
(3)  -do- non pictorial version ........... *Royal Mail (n.s.c.)*
(4)  Garden Village, Hull .............£10 *Benham*
(5)  Greet, Cheltenham................£10 *Benham BLCS 312*
(6)  Lovington, Castle Cary..........£10 *Benham BLCS 312*
(7)  Flagg, Buxton ......................£10 *Benham D461*
(8)  Bearwood, Leominster..........£15 *Benham Coin Cover*
(9)  Birdwood, Gloucester ..........£15 *Benham(500) 312*
(10) Teddy Bears Picnic ..............£15 *Bradbury Windsor 57*
(11) Bearwood, Birmingham........£15 *Buckingham Cvrs 229*
(12) Stamp Bk, Greetham............£15 *Phil Stamp Covers 9*
(13) 1st Pictorial Defins, York ......£10 *Cotswold*

## 6th October 2005 – CRICKET (The Ashes)

*2 x 1st; 2 x 68p Scenes from the 2005 Ashes*
**SPECIAL HANDSTAMPS**       **SPONSOR**
**Price Guide Ordinary Covers £3-£5 / Sponsored Covers:**
(1)  FDI - Tallents House.................. *Royal Mail (n.s.c.)*
(2)  FDI - London SE11.................... *Royal Mail (n.s.c.)*
(3)  -do- non pictorial version ........... *Royal Mail (n.s.c.)*
(4)  Edgbaston, Birmingham .............. *Royal Mail*
(5)  Birmingham..........................£10 *Benham BLCS 316*
(6)  Manchester...........................£15 *Benham(500) 316*
(7)  Nottingham...........................£15 *Benham Coin Cover*
(8)  London SE11 .........................£15 *Benham BLCS 316*
(9)  Hambledon............................£15 *Bradbury Sovereign 70*
(10) London SE11 (palette)............£40 *Westminster*
(11) -do- Autographed ...................£15 *Westminster*
(12) Ashes Come Home, Oval ........£15 *Buckingham Cvrs*
(13) Test Match, W Bridgford.......£10 *M Brazier (Pubs.87)*
(14) Cricketers Arms Rd, Enfield ..£10 *GB 107*
(15) Victory, The Oval....................£10 *Cotswold*
(16) Bletchley Park........................£10 *Bletchley PO*
(17) Winning the Ashes..................£10 *Phil Stamp Covers*
(18) Mine Counter Measures .........£10 *RN CvrsGp*
**C.D.S. POSTMARKS Price Guide £7-£10**
(19) St. John's Wood, Edgbaston, Old Trafford, Trent Bridge
(20) Kennington

**2005 CLASSIC ITV**

**2005 SMILERS**

**2005 CRICKET (The Ashes)**

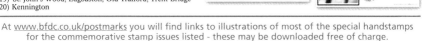

## 2005 TRAFALGAR

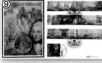

## 2005 CHRISTMAS

### 18th October 2005 – TRAFALGAR
*(1) 2 x 1st, 2 x 42p, 2 x 68p Battle of Trafalgar*
*(2) Miniature Sheet*
*(3) Prestige Stamp Book*

**SPECIAL HANDSTAMPS      SPONSOR**
**Price Guide Ordinary Covers £3-£5 / Sponsored Covers:**
| | | | |
|---|---|---|---|
| (1) | FDI - Tallents House | | *Royal Mail (n.s.c.)* |
| (2) | FDI - Portsmouth | | *Royal Mail (n.s.c.)* |
| (3) | -do- non pictorial version | | *Royal Mail (n.s.c.)* |
| (4) | Burnham Thorpe | | *Royal Mail* |
| (5) | Nelson Road, Birmingham | | *Royal Mail* |
| (6) | Trafalgar Square, WC2 | £15 | *Benham BLCS 313* |
| (7) | Burnham Thorpe | £15 | *Benham BLCS 313* |
| (8) | Merton, London SW19 | £15 | *Benham BLCS 314* |
| (9) | St. Paul's Churchyard, EC4 | £25 | *Benham Coin Cover* |
| (10) | Portsmouth | £30 | *Benham(500) 314* |
| (11) | Whitehall, London SW1 | £15 | *Benham BLCS 314* |
| (12) | Trafalgar Square, London | £15 | *Bradbury Sovereign 61* |
| (13) | H M Naval Base | £15 | *Westminster* |
| (14) | -do- Palette Design | £40 | *Westminster* |
| (15) | -do- Autographed | £25 | *Westminster* |
| (16) | Trafalgar Square, London | £15 | *Steven Scott* |
| (17) | The Victory, Portsmouth | £13 | *Buckingham Cvrs 225* |
| (18) | HMS Victory, Chatham | £13 | *Buckingham Cvrs 225* |
| (19) | The Trafalgar, Hythe | £15 | *M Brazier (Pubs.86)* |
| (20) | Victory Way, London | £15 | *GB 106* |
| (21) | Royal Naval Museum | £15 | *P Sheridan* |
| (22) | Portsmouth | £15 | *Phil Stamp Covers 89* |
| (23) | Nelson | £15 | *Phil Stamp Covers 90* |
| (24) | Victory Place, E14 | £20 | *Assoc. of GBFDC 20* |
| (25) | Southsea, Hants | £20 | *H D Macintyre* |
| (26) | Trafalgar BF 2878 PS | £15 | *Forces* |
| (27) | Eng Expects BF 2885 PS | £15 | *Forces* |
| (28) | Trafalgar 1805 Matapan | £15 | *Bletchley PO* |
| (29) | Battle of Flodden | £20 | *Heritage of Britain 22* |

**C.D.S. POSTMARKS Price Guide £7-£10**
(30) Trafalgar Sq, Nelson, Trafalgar Rd, Portsmouth, Merton
(31) Burnham Market, The Quarterdeck, Deal, HMS Nelson

### 1st November 2005 – CHRISTMAS
*(1) Madonna & Child through the eyes of different cultures:*
*2nd Haiti; 1st & 42p Europe; 60p North American Indian;*
*68p India; £1.12 Australian Aborigine.*
*(2) Miniature Sheet*
*(3) Generic Sheet with 2nd and 1st Class Robin stamps.*

**SPECIAL HANDSTAMPS      SPONSOR**
**Price Guide Ordinary Covers £3-£5 / Sponsored Covers:**
| | | | |
|---|---|---|---|
| (1) | FDI - Tallents House | | *Royal Mail (n.s.c.)* |
| (2) | FDI - Bethlehem | | *Royal Mail (n.s.c.)* |
| (3) | -do- non pictorial version | | *Royal Mail (n.s.c.)* |
| (4) | Mary Street, Birmingham | | *Royal Mail (n.s.c.)* |
| (5) | Wiseman's Bridge, Narberth | £10 | *Benham BLCS 319* |
| (6) | Christchurch, Newport | £15 | *Benham(500) 318* |
| (7) | Bethlehem, Llandeilo | £15 | *Benham BLCS 318* |
| (8) | Maryhill, Isle of Lewis | £10 | *Benham BLCS 318* |
| (9) | Stableford, Newcastle | £15 | *Benham Coin Cover* |
| (10) | Shepherdswell, Dover | £15 | *Benham(500) 319* |
| (11) | Madonna and Child | £15 | *Bradbury Sovereign 63* |
| (12) | Noel Street, W1 Palette | £40 | *Westminster* |
| (13) | -do- Autographed | £25 | *Westminster* |
| (14) | North Pole Road, W10 | £10 | *Steven Scott* |
| (15) | 1300 Years, Wells | £10 | *Buckingham Cvrs 226* |
| (16) | Christmas, Canterbury | £12 | *Buckingham Cvrs 226* |
| (17) | Season's Greetings | | *Royal Mail (n.s.c.)* |
| (18) | St Katherine's Way, E1 | £10 | *GB 108* |
| (19) | Holytown | £10 | *P Sheridan* |
| (20) | Christmas Robins, Ware | £10 | *Phil Stamp Covers 10* |
| (21) | Bethlehem (angel) | £15 | *Phil Stamp Covers 92* |
| (22) | Bethlehem (crown) | £15 | *Phil Stamp Covers 91* |
| (23) | Madonna and Child, York | £10 | *Cotswold* |
| (24) | York Minster | £10 | *Cotswold* |
| (25) | Allendale, Hexham | £15 | *T Beaumont* |
| (26) | Philatelic Music Circle | £15 | *G Datson* |
| (27) | Bletchley Park Post Office | £10 | *Bletchley PO* |
| (28) | Wolver'ton Art Gallery | £10 | *Royal Mail (n.s.c.)* |
| (29) | H M Ships at Christmas | £10 | *RN CvrsGp* |
| (30) | Battle of Solway Moss | £15 | *Heritage of Britain 23* |

**C.D.S. POSTMARKS Price Guide £7-£10**
(31) Holy Island, Canterbury, Bethlehem, Jerusalem Street

---

All of the colour illustrations in this catalogue have been taken from my website www.bfdc.co.uk
Many of the items will still be available - there are over 29,000 British FDCs online.
Obviously I cannot illustrate all of them in this catalogue - so if you are looking for a cover and
cannot find it within these pages, please try www.bfdc.co.uk

## 10th January 2006 – ANIMAL TALES

*(1) 2nd Jeremy Fisher; 2nd Kipper; 1st Enormous Crocodile;*
*1st Paddington Bear; 42p Boots; 42p White Rabbit;*
*68p The Very Hungry Caterpillar; 68p Maisy.*
*(2) Generic Sheet with 20 x Paddington Bear stamps.*

**SPECIAL HANDSTAMPS          SPONSOR**
**Price Guide Ordinary Covers £3-£5 / Sponsored Covers:**
(1)   FDI - Tallents House...................... *Royal Mail (n.s.c.)*
(2)   FDI - Mousehole........................... *Royal Mail (n.s.c.)*
(3)   -do- non pictorial version ........... *Royal Mail (n.s.c.)*
(4)   Dogpool Lane, Birmingham ........ *Royal Mail (n.s.c.)*
(5)   Inkpen, Hungerford.................£10 *Benham BLCS 319*
(6)   Paddington, Warrington ........£10 *Benham*
(7)   Near Sawrey, Ambleside........£15 *Benham Coin Cover*
(8)   Llandaff, Cardiff ....................£15 *Benham (500) 319*
(9)   Stratford-upon-Avon ..............£15 *Benham (500) 319*
(10) Daresbury, Warrington ...........£10 *Benham BLCS 319*
(11) Catshill, Bromsgrove ..............£10 *Benham BLCS 319*
(12) Mousehole, Penzance...............£10 *Benham BLCS 319*
(13) Animal Tales, London............£15 *Bradbury Sovereign 65*
(14) Paddington St, W1 (Palette) ...£40 *Westminster*
(15) -do- Autographed ...................£20 *Westminster*
(16) Paddington, London W2 .......£10 *Steven Scott*
(17) A Bear Called Paddington.....£15 *Buckingham Cvrs 231*
(18) Paddington, London W2 .......£15 *Buckingham Cvrs 231*
(19) The White Rabbit, Maidstone£15 *M Brazier (Pubs.89)*
(20) Animal Tales, Waverton ........£20 *P Sheridan*
(21) Snapper...............................£15 *Phil Stamp Covers 93*
(22) Windsor Gardens ...................£15 *Phil Stamp Covers 91*
(23) 1st Stamp Issue 2006, York ...£10 *Cotswold*
(24) Bletchley Park Post Office .....£10 *Bletchley PO*
(25) Battle of Pinkie......................£15 *Heritage of Britain 24*
(26) HMS Gallant............................£10 *RN CvrsGp*
**C.D.S. POSTMARKS Price Guide £7-£10**
(27) Bunny, Catfield, Mousehole, Frogmore
(28) Paddington, Hawkshead

## 7th February 2006 – ENGLAND

*12 x 1st: Cardigan Mill Valley; Beachy Head; St. Paul's*
*Cathedral; Brancaster; Derwent Edge; Robin Hood's Bay;*
*Buttermere; Chipping Campden; St. Boniface Down;*
*Chamberlain Square Birmingham*

**SPECIAL HANDSTAMPS          SPONSOR**
**Price Guide Ordinary Covers £3-£5 / Sponsored Covers:**
(1)   FDI - Tallents House...................... *Royal Mail (n.s.c.)*
(2)   FDI - Tea Green, Luton .............. *Royal Mail (n.s.c.)*
(3)   -do- non pictorial version ......... *Royal Mail (n.s.c.)*
(4)   Chamberlain Sq, Birmingham...... *Royal Mail (n.s.c.)*
(5)   St Paul's Churchyard..............£10 *Benham BLCS 320*
(6)   Brancaster Staithe...................£15 *Benham (500) 320*
(7)   Bamford, Hope Valley...........£10 *Benham*
(8)   Birmingham............................£10 *Benham*
(9)   Robin Hood's Bay, Whitby ....£10 *Benham*
(10) Church Stretton, Shropshire...£10 *Benham*
(11) Buttermere, Cockermouth......£10 *Benham BLCS 320*
(12) Chipping Campden, Glos .......£10 *Benham*
(13) Eastbourne, East Sussex ........£10 *Benham*
(14) Cowes, Isle of Wight..............£10 *Benham Coin Cover*
(15) England & St George ............£15 *Bradbury Sovereign 66*
(16) St Paul's Courtyard ...............£10 *Westminster*
(17) -do- Autographed ...................£20 *Westminster*
(18) London - New York ...............£15 *Westminster*
(19) Ramblers, Eastbourne ............£20 *Buckingham Cvrs 232*
(20) Ramblers, Buttermere............£15 *Buckingham Cvrs 232*
(21) Birmingham - Beachy Head ..£10 *M Brazier (Rly.14)*
(22) Buttermere Lake.....................£10 *P Sheridan*
(23) Journeys End (ointment) .......£15 *Phil Stamp Covers 95*
(24) Journeys End (boots)..............£15 *Phil Stamp Covers 94*
(25) HMS Orwell............................£10 *RN CvrsGp*
(26) Defeat of Spanish Armada.....£15 *Heritage of Britain*
**C.D.S. POSTMARKS Price Guide £7-£10**
(27) Church Stretton, Chipping Campden, Brancaster,
(28) Robin Hoods Bay, Bamford, Birmingham, East Dean

## 23rd February 2006 – BRUNEL

*(1) 1st Royal Albert Bridge, Saltash; 40p Box Tunnel;*
*42p Paddington Station; 47p PSS Great Eastern;*
*60p Clifton Suspension Bridge; 68p Maidenhead Bridge*
*(2) Miniature Sheet*
*(3) Prestige Stamp Book*
**SPECIAL HANDSTAMPS          SPONSOR**
**Price Guide Ordinary Covers £3-£5 / Sponsored Covers:**
(1)   FDI - Tallents House...................... *Royal Mail (n.s.c.)*
(2)   FDI - Bristol................................. *Royal Mail (n.s.c.)*
(3)   -do- non pictorial version ............ *Royal Mail (n.s.c.)*
(4)   Brunel Close, Birmingham........... *Royal Mail (n.s.c.)*

**2006 ANIMAL TALES**

**2006 ENGLAND**

**2006 BRUNEL**

## 2006 BRUNEL

(5)  Brunel - Stampex....................£15 *Royal Mail*
(6)  Spring Stampex......................£15 *Royal Mail*
(7)  Engineer - Paddington ...........£20 *Royal Mail*
(8)  Clifton Suspension Bridge.....£15 *Benham BLCS 321*
(9)  Maidenhead Bridge................£20 *Benham(500) 322*
(10) Box Tunnel, Corsham ...........£15 *Benham BLCS 321*
(11) Royal Albert Bridge, Saltash..£15 *Benham BLCS 322*
(12) Paddington Station ................£20 *Benham Coin Cover*
(13) Great Eastern, Millwall..........£15 *Benham BLCS 322*
(14) Saltash, Cornwall ..................£15 *Bradbury Sovereign 67*
(15) Brunel Road, W3 (Palette).....£40 *Westminster*
(16) -do- Autographed ...................£20 *Westminster*
(17) Great Western Railway ...........£15 *Westminster*
(18) Paddington..............................£35 *Buckingham Cvrs 233*
(19) Saltash ...................................£25 *Buckingham Cvrs 233*
(20) The Enterprise - Bristol .........£15 *M Brazier (Pubs.90)*
(21) Brunel University ...................£15 *P Sheridan*
(22) Brunel Road, London W3.....£10 *Steven Scott*
(23) Portsea, Portsmouth ..............£15 *Phil Stamp Covers 97*
(24) Millwall, London E14 ...........£15 *Phil Stamp Covers 96*
(25) Saltash Cornwall ...................£10 *Cotswold*
(26) Brunel Road, London W3.....£10 *GB 109*
(27) Britain Street, Portsea ...........£10 *ABC FDC*
(28) Battle of Newburn Ford.........£15 *Heritage of Britain 25*
(29) 2006 Anniversaries ................£10 *P M Payne*
(30) HMS Bicester..........................£10 *RN CvrsGp*
**C.D.S. POSTMARKS Price Guide £7-£10**
(31) Saltash, Box, Paddington, Clifton Village, Maidenhead
(32) .................

## 1st March 2006 – WELSH ASSEMBLY
*Miniature Sheet containing 1 x 2nd, 2 x 1st, 2 x 68p, Welsh Country Pictorial stamps*

| SPECIAL HANDSTAMPS | SPONSOR |
|---|---|

Price Guide Ordinary Covers £3-£5 / Sponsored Covers:
(1)  Tallents House...............................*Royal Mail (n.s.c.)*
(2)  Cardiff...........................................*Royal Mail (n.s.c.)*
(3)  -do- non pictorial version ............*Royal Mail (n.s.c.)*
(4)  Daffodil Way, Birmingham...........*Royal Mail (n.s.c.)*
(5)  Llanberis, Caernarfon.............£10 *Benham BLCS 325*
(6)  Caernarfon...............................£15 *Benham Coin Cover*
(7)  Builth Wells.............................£15 *Benham (500)325*
(8)  Cardiff.....................................£10 *Benham BLCS 325*
(9)  Cardiff Bay, Cardiff (Palette) .£40 *Westminster*
(10) -do- Autographed ...................£15 *Westminster*
(11) Cardiff.....................................£10 *Buckingham Cvrs 234*
(12) Cardiff/Caerdydd....................£10 *Phil Stamp Covers 98*
(13) Cymru, Cardiff ........................£10 *Cotswold*
(14) Battle of Powick Bridge.........£10 *Heritage of Britain*
(15) RFA Fort George......................£10 *RN CvrsGp*
**C.D.S. POSTMARKS Price Guide £7-£10**
(16) National Assembly for Wales (English or Welsh version)
(17) Cardiff, St. Davids

## 7th Mar 2006 – Fruit & Veg Generic Issue
*20 x 1st Strawberry, Potato, Apple, Pepper, Pear, Orange, Tomato, Lemon, Sprout, Aubergine + labels*

| SPECIAL HANDSTAMPS | SPONSOR |
|---|---|

Price Guide Ordinary Covers £3-£5 / Sponsored Covers:
(1)  Saffron Walden, Essex ...........£10 *Benham 500(326)*
(2)  Winchester, Hampshire .........£10 *Benham BLCS 326*
(3)  Wells, Somerset ......................£10 *Benham BLCS 326*
(4)  Covent Garden .......................£10 *Buckingham Cvrs 32*
(5)  Potato Town .............................£10 *Phil Stamp Covers 12*

## 21st March 2006 – ICE AGE MAMMALS
*1st Sabre-Tooth Cat; 42p Giant Deer; 47p Woolly Rhino; 68p Woolly Mammoth; £1.12 Cave Bear*

| SPECIAL HANDSTAMPS | SPONSOR |
|---|---|

Price Guide Ordinary Covers £3-£5 / Sponsored Covers:
(1)  FDI - Tallents House....................*Royal Mail (n.s.c.)*
(2)  FDI - Tea Green, Luton ...............*Royal Mail (n.s.c.)*
(3)  -do- non pictorial version ............*Royal Mail (n.s.c.)*
(4)  Coldbath Road, Birmingham.......*Royal Mail (n.s.c.)*
(5)  Ilford ......................................£15 *Benham Coin Cover*
(6)  Lowestoft ...............................£10 *Benham BLCS 327*
(7)  Lancaster.................................£15 *Benham 500(327)*
(8)  Burton-on-Trent .....................£10 *Benham BLCS 327*
(9)  Torquay ..................................£10 *Benham*
(10) London ...................................£15 *Bradbury Sovereign 69*
(11) Cromwell Road (Palette) ........£40 *Westminster*
(12) -do- Autographed ...................£15 *Westminster*
(13) Bearsted, Maidstone ..............£12 *Buckingham Cvrs 235*
(14) Iceland & The Great Stone ...£10 *M Brazier (Pubs.91)*
(15) Save the Rhino........................£10 *P Sheridan*
(16) Piltdown .................................£15 *Phil Stamp Covers 99*

## 2006 WELSH ASSEMBLY

## 2006 ICE AGE MAMMALS

(17) Cromwell Road, SW7..................... *GB 110*
(18) Bletchley Park Post Office ........... *Bletchley PO*
(19) Battle of Edgehill ........................... *Heritage of Britain*
(20) HMS Bulldog.................................. *RN CvrsGp*
**C.D.S. POSTMARKS Price Guide £7-£10**
(21) Freezywater, Frosterley, Coldstream, or similar
(22) Ilford, Deerpark, Bearsden, New Deer, Bear Flat etc

## 18th April 2006 – QUEEN'S 80th BIRTHDAY
*2 x 2nd; 2 x 1st; 2 x 44p; 2 x 72p Portraits of the Queen*

**SPECIAL HANDSTAMPS**     **SPONSOR**
Price Guide Ordinary Covers £3-£5 / Sponsored Covers:
(1) FDI - Tallents House.................... *Royal Mail (n.s.c.)*
(2) FDI - Windsor ............................... *Royal Mail (n.s.c.)*
(3) -do- non pictorial version ............ *Royal Mail (n.s.c.)*
(4) Queens Drive, Birmingham .......... *Royal Mail (n.s.c.)*
(5) Sandringham, Norfolk ...........£15 *Benham 500(328)*
(6) London SW1............................£10 *Benham BLCS 328*
(7) Windsor Berkshire ..................£10 *Benham BLCS 328*
(8) Crathie, Ballater.....................£15 *Benham Coin Cover*
(9) Edinburgh ...............................£10 *Benham*
(10) Buckingham Palace Rd..........£15 *Bradbury Sovereign 71*
(11) Bruton Street (Palette) ...........£40 *Westminster*
(12) -do- Autographed ...................£15 *Westminster*
(13) Buckingham Palace ...............£10 *Westminster*
(14) Windsor, Berkshire ................£15 *Buckingham Cvrs 236*
(15) The Crown and Sceptre.........£10 *M Brazier (Pubs.92)*
(16) Buckingham Palace Road........£10 *P Sheridan*
(17) Windsor.................................£15 *Phil Stamp Cvrs 100*
(18) London 80 .............................£10 *Cotswold*
(19) Grenadier Street, E16............£10 *GB 111*
(20) Bletchley Park Post Office .....£10 *Bletchley PO*
(21) Jewish Community..................£10 *ABC-FDC*
(22) Stanley Gibbons 150 .............£15 *Stanley Gibbons*
(23) Battle of Braddock Down ......£10 *Heritage of Britain 26*
(24) HMS Sandown .......................£10 *RN CvrsGp*
**C.D.S. POSTMARKS Price Guide £7-£10**
(25) Throne, Britannia, Windsor, Queen's Rd or similar
(26) Windsor Castle, Buckingham Palace (£50)

## 25th May 2006 – Washington Stamp Expo
*Generic Sheet: 1st Hello + labels depicting US Post Box*
**Price Guide Ordinary Cvrs £10 - £15 / No Sponsored Covers**

## 6th June 2006 – WORLD CUP WINNERS
*(1) 1st England; 42p Italy; 44p Argentina; 50p Germany;*
*64p France; 72p Brazil*
*(2) Generic Sheet with 20 x England World Cup Winners.*

**SPECIAL HANDSTAMPS**     **SPONSOR**
Price Guide Ordinary Covers £3-£5 / Sponsored Covers:
(1) FDI - Tallents House.................... *Royal Mail (n.s.c.)*
(2) FDI - Balls Park, Hertford .......... *Royal Mail (n.s.c.)*
(3) -do- non pictorial version ............ *Royal Mail (n.s.c.)*
(4) Bobby Moore, OBE .................£15 *Royal Mail*
(5) Hurst Street, Birmingham ............ *Royal Mail (n.s.c.)*
(6) Wembley (Ball).......................£10 *Benham BLCS 329*
(7) Wembley (Boots)....................£15 *Benham Coin Cover*
(8) A Glorious Past, Wembley.....£10 *Benham BLCS 329*
(9) England 4 - W Germany 2.....£15 *Bradbury Sovereign 73*
(10) Wembley (silhouette) ............£10 *Westminster*
(11) Champion Rd, SE26...............£10 *Westminster*
(12) -do- Autographed ...................£15 *Westminster*
(13) Wembley .................................£10 *Buckingham Cvrs 238*
(14) World Cup Willie....................£10 *Buckingham Cvrs 238*
(15) Football Lane, Harrow............£10 *GB 112*
(16) The Ball, Widnes ...................£10 *P Sheridan*
(17) Referees' Association .............£10 *P Sheridan*
(18) World Cup Winners ...............£15 *Phil Stamp Cvrs 101*
(19) Football Tavern, Derby ..........£10 *M Brazier (Pubs.93)*
(20) World Cup Winners ...............£10 *Assoc. of GBFDC 21*
(21) footballcovers.co.uk ...............£10 *Dawn*
(22) Bletchley Park .......................£10 *Bletchley PO*
(23) Numerical Symmetry..............£10 *Royal Mail (n.s.c.)*
(24) Battle of Hopton Heath .........£10 *Heritage of Britain 27*
**C.D.S. POSTMARKS Price Guide £7-£10**
(25) Wembley, The Ball, New England, Gerrards Cross
(26) Moore, Ramsey, Charlton or similar

## 20th June 2006 – MODERN ARCHITECTURE
*1st 30 St. Mary Axe, London; 42p Maggies Centre, Dundee;*
*44p Selfridges, Birmingham; 50p Downland Gridshell,*
*Chichester; 64p An Turas, Isle of Tiree; 72p The Deep, Hull*
**SPECIAL HANDSTAMPS**     **SPONSOR**
Price Guide Ordinary Covers £3-£5 / Sponsored Covers:
(1) FDI - Tallents House.................... *Royal Mail (n.s.c.)*
(2) FDI - Balls Park, Hertford .......... *Royal Mail (n.s.c.)*
(3) -do- non pictorial version ............ *Royal Mail (n.s.c.)*

## 2006 QUEEN'S 80th BIRTHDAY

## 2006 WORLD CUP WINNERS

## 2006 MODERN ARCHITECTURE

## 2006 MODERN ARCHITECTURE

## 2006 NATIONAL PORTRAIT GALLERY

## 2006 YEAR of the THREE KINGS

(4)  The Bull Ring, Birmingham ......... *Royal Mail (n.s.c.)*
(5)  Birmingham.................................... *Benham BLCS 330*
(6)  Oban, Argyll.................................. *Benham 500(330)*
(7)  Portland Place, London W1........ *Benham Coin Cover*
(8)  Chichester, West Sussex .........£10 *Benham BLCS 330*
(9)  St Mary Axe (palette) .............£40 *Westminster*
(10)  -do- Autographed ...................£15 *Westminster*
(11)  Architectural Review .............£20 *Buckingham Cvrs 239*
(12)  The Gherkin .............................£10 *GB 113*
(13)  Glasgow Science Centre........£20 *P Sheridan*
(14)  St. Mary Axe............................£15 *Phil Stamp Cvrs 102*
(15)  Maggie's, Dundee .(postcard) £15 *Maggie's Cancer Care*
(16)  1st Ascent of Manaslu............£10 *ABC FDC*
(17)  1st Ascent of LHOTSE ..........£10 *ABC FDC*
(18)  Indian Ocean Deployment.....£10 *RN CvrsGp*
**C.D.S. POSTMARKS Price Guide £7-£10**
(19)  Downlands, Scarinish (Isle of Tiree), Lowgate (Hull),
(20)  Singleton (Chichester), City of London, New Buildings

### 4th July 2006 – SMILERS Generic Issue
*6 x 1st small 'Smilers' stamps with labels: Hello, Love, Union Jack, Teddy Bear, Flowers and Robin. (Self Adhesives)*
**SPECIAL HANDSTAMPS                SPONSOR**
**Price Guide Ordinary Covers £3-£5 / Sponsored Covers:**
(1)  Buckingham Palace Rd..........£10 *Benham BLCS 331*
(2)  Giggleswick .............................£10 *Phil Stamp Covers 14*

### 18 July 06  NATIONAL PORTRAIT GALLERY
*10 x 1st: Sir Winston Churchill; Joshua Reynolds; T S Elliot; Mrs Pankhurst; Virginia Woolf; Sir Walter Scott; Mary Seacole; William Shakespeare; Dame Cicely Saunders; Charles Darwin*
**SPECIAL HANDSTAMPS                SPONSOR**
**Price Guide Ordinary Covers £3-£5 / Sponsored Covers:**
(1)  FDI - Tallents House.................... *Royal Mail (n.s.c.)*
(2)  FDI - London WC2 ..................... *Royal Mail (n.s.c.)*
(3)  -do- non pictorial version ............ *Royal Mail (n.s.c.)*
(4)  London WC2 ............................£15 *Royal Mail*
(5)  Rowlands Rd, Birmingham....... *Royal Mail (n.s.c.)*
(6)  Plympton, Plymouth ...............£10 *Benham BLCS 332*
(7)  Trafalgar Square.......................£15 *Benham Coin Cover*
(8)  Southwark, SE1 .......................£10 *Benham BLCS 332*
(9)  Walmer, Deal ...........................£10 *Benham (500)332*
(10)  Great Britons on Canvas.......£10 *Westminster*
(11)  St Martin's Place (palette) .....£10 *Westminster*
(12)  -do- Autographed ...................£15 *Westminster*
(13)  International Churchill Soc ....£25 *Buckingham Cvrs 240*
(14)  National Portrait Gallery.......£12 *Buckingham Cvrs 240*
(15)  Royal Soc Portrait Painters....£10 *P Sheridan*
(16)  St Martin's Place ....................£15 *Phil Stamp Cvrs 103*
(17)  Portraits of Pub Signs.............£10 *M Brazier (Pubs.95)*
(18)  From Paint to Pixel.................£10 *Bletchley PO*
(19)  HMS Enterprise - Caen .........£10 *RN CvrsGp*
(20)  Battle of Chalgrove .................£10 *Heritage of Britain*
**C.D.S. POSTMARKS Price Guide £7-£10**
(21)  Trafalgar Square, Plympton, East Coker, Sydenham
(22)  Shrewsbury, Melrose, Manchester, Churchill.

### 31st Aug 2006 – YEAR of the THREE KINGS
*Miniature Sheet: £3 Definitive plus reproductions of 1d definitives for each of the Three Kings.*
**SPECIAL HANDSTAMPS                SPONSOR**
**Price Guide Ordinary Covers £3-£5 / Sponsored Covers:**
(1)  FDI - Tallents House.................... *Royal Mail (n.s.c.)*
(2)  FDI - Threekingham, Sleaford .... *Royal Mail (n.s.c.)*
(3)  -do- non pictorial version ............ *Royal Mail (n.s.c.)*
(4)  King's Heath, Birmingham........... *Royal Mail (n.s.c.)*
(5)  Dean's Yard, SW1...................£10 *Benham BLCS 334*
(6)  Buckingham Gate, SW1 .........£15 *Benham (500) 334*
(7)  Three King's Yard, W1............£10 *Westminster*
(8)  Three King's Yard (palette)....£40 *Westminster*
(9)  -do- Autographed ...................£15 *Westminster*
(10)  Windsor ....................................£15 *Buckingham Cvrs 241*
(11)  Kingsdown ...............................£20 *Buckingham Cvrs 241*
(12)  Windsor.....................................£20 *P Sheridan*
(13)  Three Kings Yard, EC4 ..........£10 *Assoc. of GBFDC 22*
(14)  The Three Kings ......................£10 *M Brazier (Pubs.96)*
(15)  London SW1 (Vacancy)........£15 *Phil Stamp Cvrs 104*
(16)  Baldwins...................................£10 *ABC-FDC*
(17)  70 Years Hertz Chumash ......£10 *I Balcombe*
(18)  First Convoy "Dervish".........£10 *RN CvrsGp*
(19)  Battle of Adwalton Moor ......£10 *Heritage of Britain*
**C.D.S. POSTMARKS Price Guide £12-£15**
(20)  Windsor, Windsor Great Park, Throne
(21)  House of Commons, House of Lords

## 21st Sept 2006 – VICTORIA CROSS
*(1) 1st Brave Gurkha; 1st Boy VC; 64p Midshipman;*
*64p Army Doctor; 72p Feared Lost; 72p Colditz Hero*
*(2) Miniature Sheet; (3) Prestige Stamp Book*
**SPECIAL HANDSTAMPS**
**Price Guide Ordinary Covers £3-£5 / Sponsored Covers:**
(1) FDI - Tallents House.................... *Royal Mail (n.s.c.)*
(2) FDI - Potters Bar ......................... *Royal Mail (n.s.c.)*
(3) -do- non pictorial version ............ *Royal Mail (n.s.c.)*
(4) Stampex, London N1 .................... *Royal Mail (n.s.c.)*
(5) Stampex, Victoria Cross .............. *Royal Mail (n.s.c.)*
(6) Hyde Park.................................... *Royal Mail (n.s.c.)*
(7) Victoria Road, Birmingham......... *Royal Mail (n.s.c.)*
(8) Whitehall, SW1.....................£10 *Benham BLCS 335*
(9) Chelsea, SW3 ......................£15 *Benham (500)335*
(10) Lambeth Road, SE1...............£10 *Benham Coin Cover*
(11) For Valour, Duxford..............£10 *Benham Pilgrim*
(12) Portsmouth ............................£10 *Benham BLCS 337*
(13) Hyde Park...............................£10 *Benham BLCS 335*
(14) Hyde Park...............................£10 *Westminster*
(15) Hyde Park (palette) ................£40 *Westminster*
(16) -do- Autographed............................ *Westminster*
(17) Hyde Park (canon) ................£12 *Buckingham Cvrs 242*
(18) Hyde Park (VC).....................£12 *Buckingham Cvrs 242*
(19) Warrior, London E12.............£20 *GB 115*
(20) Victoria Square .....................£12 *Assoc. of GBFDC 23*
(21) Victoria Cross Society...........£12 *P Sheridan*
(22) Malet Lambert School ...........£12 *Malet Lambert School*
(23) Mereworth, Maidstone...........£15 *Phil Stamp Crs 105/6*
(24) Thornton Heath, Surrey ........£10 *M Brazier (Pubs.97)*
(25) For Valour BF 2934 PS .........£10 *Forces BFPO777*
(26) Captain Fenton John Aylmer.£10 *ABC FDC*
(27) BF 2916 PS.............................£10 *RNPS*
(28) Bletchley Park........................£10 *Bletchley PO*
(29) Zeebrugge Raid......................£10 *H D MacIntyre*
(30) RAFLET Stamp Club.............£10 *RAFLET*
(31) St. Sepulchre .........................£10 *T Wyard*
(32) Albert Ball.............................£50 *Trent College, Notts*
(33) VC to Cornwell & Lucas.......£10 *RN CvrsGp*
(34) Battle of Lansdowne Hill ......£10 *Heritage of Britain*
**C.D.S. POSTMARKS Price Guide £7-£10**
(35) Battle, Battle Hill, Wargrave, Woolwich and similar
(35) Buckingham Palace (£75)

## 3rd Oct 2006 – SOUNDS of BRITAIN
*1st Bollywood and Bhangra; 42p Africa and the Caribbean;*
*50p Celtic; 72p Jazz and Blues; £1.19 Latin American*
**SPECIAL HANDSTAMPS        SPONSOR**
**Price Guide Ordinary Covers £3-£5 / Sponsored Covers:**
(1) FDI - Tallents House.................... *Royal Mail (n.s.c.)*
(2) FDI - Rock, Kidderminster .......... *Royal Mail (n.s.c.)*
(3) -do- non pictorial version ............ *Royal Mail (n.s.c.)*
(4) Osbourne Rd, Birmingham.......... *Royal Mail (n.s.c.)*
(5) Harpswell, Gainsborough.......£10 *Benham BLCS 338*
(6) Fiddlers Hamlet, Epping........£10 *Benham BLCS 338*
(7) Rock, Kidderminster...............£15 *Benham (500)338*
(8) Rock Street (palette)................£40 *Westminster*
(9) -do- Autographed ....................£15 *Westminster*
(10) The Stables, Milton Keynes ...£12 *Buckingham Cvrs 243*
(11) The Louis Armstrong..............£10 *M Brazier (Pubs.98)*
(12) India Way, London W12.........£12 *GB 116*
(13) Dublin Street, Liverpool........£12 *P Sheridan*
(14) the brindley, Runcorn ............£12 *P Sheridan*
(15) Sound, Nantwich ...................£15 *Phil Stamp Crs 107*
(16) CDT Design, London WC1....£12 *CDT Design Ltd*
(17) Children in Need, Pudsey.......£20 *Gerald Lovell*
(18) HMS Roebuck Commissions.£10 *RN CvrsGp*
(19) Battle of Roundhay Down .....£10 *Heritage of Britain*
**C.D.S. POSTMARKS Price Guide £7-£10**
(20) Rock, Elton, Wembley, Glastonbury, Knebworth

## 17th Oct 2006 – SPECIAL MOMENTS
*(1) 1st New Baby; 1st Best Wishes; 1st Thank You; 1st*
*Balloons; 1st Fireworks; 1st Champagne*
*(2) Generic Sheet - of 20 stamps plus matching labels*
**SPECIAL HANDSTAMPS        SPONSOR**
**Price Guide Ordinary Covers £3-£5 / Sponsored Covers:**
(1) FDI - Tallents House.................... *Royal Mail (n.s.c.)*
(2) FDI - Grinshill, Shrewsbury ........ *Royal Mail (n.s.c.)*
(3) -do- non pictorial version ............ *Royal Mail (n.s.c.)*
(4) Love Lane, Birmingham.............. *Royal Mail (n.s.c.)*
(5) Kittywell, Braunton..................£10 *Benham (500)340*
(6) Bangor .....................................£10 *Benham BLCS 340*
(7) Glass, Huntly...........................£10 *Benham BLCS 340*
(8) Soar, Brecon............................£10 *Benham Coin Cover*
(9) Joydenswood, Dartford ...........£12 *Buckingham Cvrs 247*
(10) Giggleswick ...........................£15 *Phil Stamp Crs 15*

### 2006 VICTORIA CROSS
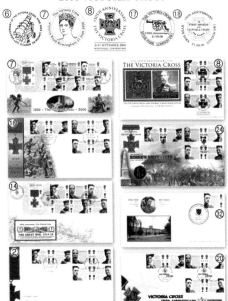

### 2006 SOUNDS of BRITAIN

### 2006 SPECIAL MOMENTS

185

## 2006 CHRISTMAS

## 2006 LEST WE FORGET

## 2006 CELEBRATING SCOTLAND

Most of your questions will be answered in the
General Notes at the beginning of this catalogue.

## 7th Nov 2006 – CHRISTMAS

*(1) 2nd Snowman; 2nd (Large) Snowman; 1st Santa;*
*1st (Large) Santa; 72p Reindeer; £1.19 Christmas Tree*
*(2) Miniature Sheet;*
*(3) Generic Sheet with 2nd (small) & 1st (small) values*

| SPECIAL HANDSTAMPS | | SPONSOR |
|---|---|---|

**Price Guide Ordinary Covers £3-£5  /  Sponsored Covers:**

| | | |
|---|---|---|
| (1) | FDI - Tallents House................... | *Royal Mail (n.s.c.)* |
| (2) | FDI - Bethlehem ........................... | *Royal Mail (n.s.c.)* |
| (3) | -do- non pictorial version ............ | *Royal Mail (n.s.c.)* |
| (4) | St. Nicholas Gdns, Birmingham.. | *Royal Mail (n.s.c.)* |
| (5) | Rudolph Road, E13 ...............£10 | *Benham BLCS 341* |
| (6) | Snowhill, Enniskillen .............£15 | *Benham (500) 342* |
| (7) | St. Nicholas, Goodwick........£10 | *Benham BLCS 342* |
| (8) | Yuletide Close, NW10............£15 | *Benham (500) 341* |
| (9) | St. Nicholas St SE8 (palette).£40 | *Westminster* |
| (10) | -do- Autographed ....................£15 | *Westminster* |
| (11) | Bath Postal Museum...............£12 | *Buckingham Cvrs 244* |
| (12) | 40 Years, Bethlehem...............£12 | *Buckingham Cvrs 244* |
| (13) | Christmas Puppy, NW10 .......£10 | *GB 117* |
| (14) | Donna's, Blackpool ................£10 | *P Sheridan* |
| (15) | Happy Christmas, York .........£10 | *Cotswold* |
| (16) | Star, Glenrothes.....................£15 | *Phil Stamp Cvrs 109* |
| (17) | Cold Christmas, Ware ............£15 | *Phil Stamp Cvrs 108* |
| (18) | Generic Smilers ......................£15 | *Phil Stamp Cvrs 16* |
| (19) | YZWFN COKZR ....................£10 | *Bletchley PO* |
| (20) | Christmas Greetings, EC1............ | *Royal Mail (n.s.c.)* |
| (21) | Seasons Greetings, Bethlehem..... | *Royal Mail (n.s.c.)* |
| (22) | MCC - Lord's Ground.............£10 | *Bletchley PO* |
| (23) | HM Ships Abroad...................£10 | *RN CvsGp* |
| (24) | Battle of Newbury...................£10 | *Heritage of Britain* |

**C.D.S. POSTMARKS Price Guide £7-£10**
(25) Noel Rd, Holy Island, Jerusalem St, North Pole Road

## 9th Nov 2006 – LEST WE FORGET

*(1) 1st Poppy; 4 x 72p Country Pictorials*
*(2) Generic Sheet of 20 Poppy stamps and labels*

| SPECIAL HANDSTAMPS | | SPONSOR |
|---|---|---|

**Price Guide Ordinary Covers £3-£5  /  Sponsored Covers:**

| | | |
|---|---|---|
| (1) | FDI - Tallents House................... | *Royal Mail (n.s.c.)* |
| (2) | FDI - London SW1 ....................... | *Royal Mail (n.s.c.)* |
| (3) | -do- non pictorial version ............ | *Royal Mail (n.s.c.)* |
| (4) | Poppy Lane, Birmingham ............ | *Royal Mail (n.s.c.)* |
| (5) | Chelsea, London SW3 ...........£10 | *Benham BLCS 343* |
| (6) | Whitehall, London SW1........£15 | *Benham (500) 343* |
| (7) | Whitehall, London SW1A.......£10 | *Westminster* |
| (8) | Whitehall (palette) ..................£40 | *Westminster* |
| (9) | Whitehall Autographed..........£15 | *Westminster* |
| (10) | London SW1 ...........................£12 | *Buckingham Cvrs 245* |
| (11) | London SW1, Cenotaph........£12 | *Buckingham Cvrs 245* |
| (12) | The Falklands Conflict............£10 | *Buckingham Cvrs* |
| (13) | Wargrave Road, Harrow.........£10 | *GB 118* |
| (14) | The Earl Haig, Birmingham...£10 | *M Brazier (Pubs 99)* |
| (15) | Western Front Association.....£10 | *P Sheridan* |
| (16) | The Cenotaph, SW1 ...............£15 | *Phil Stamp Cvrs 110* |
| (17) | The Cenotaph, SW1 ...............£15 | *Phil Stamp Cvrs 17* |
| (18) | Lest We Forget BF 2950 PS...£10 | *BFPO Inglis Barracks* |
| (19) | Malet Lambert School ............£10 | *Malet Lambert School* |
| (20) | Battle of Winceby...................£10 | *Heritage of Britain* |

**C.D.S. POSTMARKS Price Guide £7-£10**
(21) Wargrave, Battle, Dunkirk

## 14th Nov 2006 – Belgica Stamp Expo
*Generic Sheet: 1st Hello + labels depicting thematics*
**Price Guide Ordinary Cvrs £10 - £15 / No Sponsored Covers**

## 30th Nov 2006 – CELEBRATING SCOTLAND
*2 x 1st Scottish Pictorials; 72p St. Andrew; Edinburgh Castle*

| SPECIAL HANDSTAMPS | | SPONSOR |
|---|---|---|

**Price Guide Ordinary Covers £3-£5  /  Sponsored Covers:**

| | | |
|---|---|---|
| (1) | FDI - Tallents House................... | *Royal Mail (n.s.c.)* |
| (2) | FDI - St. Andrews........................ | *Royal Mail (n.s.c.)* |
| (3) | -do- non pictorial version ............ | *Royal Mail (n.s.c.)* |
| (4) | St. Andrews, Birmingham ............ | *Royal Mail (n.s.c.)* |
| (5) | St. Andrews ............................£10 | *Benham BLCS 345* |
| (6) | Edinburgh ..............................£15 | *Benham (500) 345* |
| (7) | St. Andrews (palette)..............£40 | *Westminster* |
| (8) | -do- Autographed ...................£15 | *Westminster* |
| (9) | Edinburgh (castle)..................£12 | *Buckingham Cvrs 246* |
| (10) | St. Andrews (thistle)...............£12 | *Buckingham Cvrs 246* |
| (11) | St. Andrews (fish)...................£15 | *Phil Stamp Cvrs 111* |
| (12) | Age of Steam, Paddington .....£15 | *Westminster* |
| (13) | HMS Vanguard.......................£10 | *RN CvsGp* |
| (14) | The Storming of Bristol .........£10 | *Heritage of Britain* |

**C.D.S. POSTMARKS Price Guide £7-£10**
(15) Edinburgh, St. Andrews, The Scotlands
(16) The Scottish Parliament

## 9th Jan 2007 – THE BEATLES

*(1) 2 x 1st; 2 x 64p; 2 x 72p Beatles Album Sleeves*
*(2) Miniature Sheet 4 x 1st Beatles Memorabilia*

**SPECIAL HANDSTAMPS          SPONSOR**
Price Guide Ordinary Covers £3-£5  / Sponsored Covers:
| | | | |
|---|---|---|---|
| (1) | FDI - Tallents House.................... | Royal Mail (n.s.c.) |
| (2) | FDI - Liverpool ........................... | Royal Mail (n.s.c.) |
| (3) | -do- non pictorial version ............ | Royal Mail (n.s.c.) |
| (4) | Abbey Road, Birmingham ............. | Royal Mail (n.s.c.) |
| (5) | Liverpool ...............................£10 | Benham BLCS 347 |
| (6) | Mathew St...............................£10 | Benham BLCS 346 |
| (7) | Abbey Rd...............................£15 | Benham 500(346) |
| (8) | Carnaby St ............................£15 | Benham 500(347) |
| (9) | Spirit of the 60s Abbey Rd .....£10 | Westminster |
| (10) | -do- (palette)........................£40 | Westminster |
| (11) | -do- Autographed ..................£15 | Westminster |
| (12) | Cavern Club...........................£12 | Buckingham Cvrs 301 |
| (13) | Penny Lane, Liverpool...........£12 | Buckingham Cvrs 301 |
| (14) | Peppers, etc Liverpool............£10 | M Brazier |
| (15) | Abbey Road, NW8 ..................£10 | GB 119 |
| (16) | Abbey Rd, Westminster...........£15 | Phil Stamp Cvrs 112 |
| (17) | Penny Lane, L18 ....................£15 | Phil Stamp Cvrs 113 |
| (18) | Liverpool Music City..............£10 | P Sheridan |
| (19) | Strawberry Fields...................£10 | Royal Mail (n.s.c.) |
| (20) | Liverpool (silhouettes) ...........£10 | Cotswold |
| (21) | Legends..60s, Penny Lane .....£10 | New Stamp Centre |
| (22) | Legends..60s, Abbey Road ....£10 | New Stamp Centre |
| (23) | The Mersey Beat, Liverpool .£10 | Royal Mail (n.s.c.) |
| (24) | Bletchley Park PO..................£10 | Bletchley PO |
| (25) | Creative Quarter, Folkestone.£10 | Chaucer Covers |
| (26) | Final World Concert Tour....£10 | ABC-FDC* |
| (27) | First Recording Contract.......£10 | ABC-FDC* |
| (28) | World's Most Famous Group..£10 | ABC-FDC* |
| (29) | Rooftop Concert......................£10 | ABC-FDC* |
| (30) | Members of British Empire....£10 | ABC-FDC* |
| (31) | Album Cover Photo Shoot.....£10 | ABC-FDC* |
| (32) | Famous Zebra Crossing..........£10 | ABC-FDC* |

\* *Postmarks are all the same style*

| | | | |
|---|---|---|---|
| (33) | Battle of Nantwich..................£10 | Heritage of Britain |
| (34) | Battle of Cheriton...................£10 | Heritage of Britain |
| (35) | Royal Navy Anniversaries......£10 | RN CvsGp |

**C.D.S. POSTMARKS Price Guide £7-£10**
(36) Liverpool, Abbey Road, Rock, Elstead

## 16th Jan 2007 – Love Advert Book

*1 x 1st Love stamp (with elliptical perfs)*

**SPECIAL HANDSTAMPS          SPONSOR**
Price Guide Ordinary Covers £3-£5  / Sponsored Covers:
| | | | |
|---|---|---|---|
| (1) | Lover, Salisbury.............................. | Benham BLCS 348 |
| (2) | Rose, Truro..................................... | Benham 500(348) |

## 1st Feb 2007 – SEA LIFE

*10 x 1st Jellyfish, Starfish, Anemone, Bass, Ray, Octopus,*
*Mussels, Seal, Crab, Sun Star*

**SPECIAL HANDSTAMPS          SPONSOR**
Price Guide Ordinary Covers £3-£5  / Sponsored Covers:
| | | | |
|---|---|---|---|
| (1) | FDI - Tallents House.................... | Royal Mail (n.s.c.) |
| (2) | FDI - Seal Sands ........................ | Royal Mail (n.s.c.) |
| (3) | -do- non pictorial version ............ | Royal Mail (n.s.c.) |
| (4) | Seal Close, Birmingham ............... | Royal Mail (n.s.c.) |
| (5) | Sea Life, Brighton ..................£10 | Benham |
| (6) | Sea Life, Weymouth ................£10 | Benham BLCS 349 |
| (7) | Sea Life, Scarborough .............£10 | Benham BLCS 349 |
| (8) | Sea Life, Blackpool..................£15 | Benham 500(349) |
| (9) | Marine St, SE16 (palette).......£40 | Westminster |
| (10) | -do- Autographed ...................£15 | Westminster |
| (11) | Sea Life, Fishguard .................£15 | Buckingham Cvrs 302 |
| (12) | Pub Signs, Brighton ................£10 | M Brazier |
| (13) | Seal, Sevenoaks .......................£15 | Phil Stamp Cvrs 114 |
| (14) | The Deep, Hull ........................£10 | Cotswold |
| (15) | Bletchley Park PO....................£10 | Bletchley PO |
| (16) | Battle of Cropredy Bridge ......£10 | Heritage of Britain |
| (17) | Tranquility Aquatic Centre.....£15 | T Hurlstone |
| (18) | London Aquarium.....................£15 | T Hurlstone |
| (19) | Loss of HMS Welshman........£10 | RN CvsGp |

**C.D.S. POSTMARKS Price Guide £7-£10**
(20) Seaside, Musselburgh, Crabs Cross, Crabs Lane

## 13th Feb 2007 – THE SKY AT NIGHT

*1st Saturn Nebula C55; 1st Eskimo Nebula C39;*
*50p Cat's Eye Nebula C6; 50p Helix Nebula C63;*
*72p Flaming Star Nebula C31; 72p The Spindle C53*

**SPECIAL HANDSTAMPS          SPONSOR**
Price Guide Ordinary Covers £3-£5  / Sponsored Covers:
| | | | |
|---|---|---|---|
| (1) | FDI - Tallents House.................... | Royal Mail (n.s.c.) |
| (2) | FDI - Star, Glenrothes................ | Royal Mail (n.s.c.) |
| (3) | -do- non pictorial version ............ | Royal Mail (n.s.c.) |

### 2007 THE BEATLES

### 2007 SEA LIFE

### 2007 THE SKY AT NIGHT

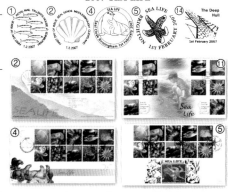

## 2007 THE SKY AT NIGHT

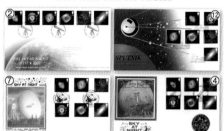

| | | |
|---|---|---|
| (4) | Moore Crescent, Birmingham...... | *Royal Mail (n.s.c.)* |
| (5) | Sky at Night, Greenwich.............. | *Royal Mail (n.s.c.)* |
| (6) | Sky at Night, Pinner.................... | *Benham BLCS 350* |
| (7) | Sky at Night, Macclesfield ........... | *Benham 500(350)* |
| (8) | Sky at Night, Star Glenrothes...... | *Benham BLCS 350* |
| (9) | BAA ................................................ | *Bradbury Sovereign 83* |
| (10) | Star Street (palette)................£40 | *Westminster* |
| (11) | -do- Autographed ....................£15 | *Westminster* |
| (12) | Sputnik, Jodrell Bank.............£13 | *Buckingham Cvrs 303* |
| (13) | North Star, Northampton .....£10 | *M Brazier* |
| (14) | WYAS, Pontefract..................£10 | *Cotswold* |
| (15) | Horsehead Nebula, SW14.....£10 | *GB 120* |
| (16) | Pex Hill Observatory.............£10 | *P Sheridan* |
| (17) | GBFDC Warrington ...............£10 | *Assoc. of GBFDC* |
| (18) | Planet Park ............................£15 | *Phil Stamp Cvrs 115* |
| (19) | Flaming Star Nebula, W9.......£10 | *W H Pugh* |
| (20) | Seven Sisters, Selsey..............£15 | *W H Pugh* |
| (21) | Battle of Marston Moor.........£10 | *Heritage of Britain* |
| (22) | HMS Tasman ...........................£10 | *RN CvsGp* |
| (23) | Carpetbagger Aviation Mus ...£10 | *Bletchley PO* |

**C.D.S. POSTMARKS Price Guide £7-£10**
(24)  Moore, Greenwich, Selsey, Chelford

## 2007 WORLD of INVENTION

### 1st March 2007 – WORLD of INVENTION
*1st Telford - Bridges; 1st Stephenson - Railways;*
*64p Bell - Telephone; 64p Baird - Television;*
*72p Berners-Lee - World-Wide Web; 72p Space Tourism*
*(2) Miniature Sheet;   (3) Prestige Stamp Book*
**SPECIAL HANDSTAMPS**          **SPONSOR**
**Price Guide Ordinary Covers £3-£5  / Sponsored Covers:**

| | | |
|---|---|---|
| (1) | FDI - Tallents House.................... | *Royal Mail (n.s.c.)* |
| (2) | FDI - Menai Bridge .................... | *Royal Mail (n.s.c.)* |
| (3) | -do- non pictorial version ......... | *Royal Mail (n.s.c.)* |
| (4) | Spring Stampex ............................ | *Royal Mail (n.s.c.)* |
| (5) | -do- World of Invention ............ | *Royal Mail (n.s.c.)* |
| (6) | Telford Way, Birmingham............ | *Royal Mail (n.s.c.)* |
| (7) | Tim Berners-Lee SW14............£10 | *Benham* |
| (8) | Rowland Hill, Kidderminster.£10 | *Benham* |
| (9) | George Stephenson, Wylam ..£10 | *Benham BLCS351* |
| (10) | Thomas Telford, Langholm....£10 | *Benham BLCS351* |
| (11) | Logie Baird, Helensburgh.....£10 | *Benham Coin Cover* |
| (12) | Alex Grah Bell, Edinburgh....£10 | *Benham (500)351* |
| (13) | Discovery Walk (palette).......£40 | *Westminster* |
| (14) | -do- Autographed ...................£15 | *Westminster* |
| (15) | Concorde, Heathrow..............£10 | *Buckingham Cvrs 304* |
| (16) | Jet Engine, Cranwell ..............£10 | *Buckingham Cvrs 304* |
| (17) | Stephenson's Rocket...............£20 | *P Sheridan* |
| (18) | New Invention.........................£15 | *Phil Stamp Cvrs 117* |
| (19) | Cogges, Witney.......................£15 | *Phil Stamp Cvrs 116* |
| (20) | Bletchley Park Post Office .....£10 | *Bletchley PO* |
| (21) | Goodenough College...............£10 | *Bletchley PO* |
| (22) | Int Polar Year, Cambridge .....£25 | *R Hurst* |
| (23) | Post Office Way.......................£10 | *P M Payne* |
| (24) | HMS Exeter...............................£10 | *RN CvsGp* |
| (25) | Battle of Aberdeen .................£10 | *Heritage of Britain* |

**C.D.S. POSTMARKS Price Guide £7-£10**
(26)  New Invention, Science Museum
(27)  Ironbridge, Helensburgh, James Watt Dock

### 1st March 2007 – Glorious Wales
*Generic Sheet of 20 x 1st Welsh Dragon + labels.*
**SPECIAL HANDSTAMPS**          **SPONSOR**
**Price Guide Ordinary Covers £3-£5  / Sponsored Covers:**

| | | |
|---|---|---|
| (1) | Telford Way, Birmingham............ | *Royal Mail (n.s.c.)* |
| (2) | Llanberis, Caernarfon.............£15 | *Benham BLCS 354* |
| (3) | Caerphilly ................................£15 | *Benham BLCS 354* |
| (4) | Giggleswick ..............................£15 | *Phil Stamp Cvrs* |

### 22nd March 2007 – ABOLITION of SLAVERY
*1st William Wilberforce; 1st Olaudah Equiano;*
*50p Granville Sharpe; 50p Thomas Clarkson;*
*72p Hannah More; 72p Ignacious Sancho*
**SPECIAL HANDSTAMPS**          **SPONSOR**
**Price Guide Ordinary Covers £3-£5  / Sponsored Covers:**

| | | |
|---|---|---|
| (1) | FDI - Tallents House.................... | *Royal Mail (n.s.c.)* |
| (2) | FDI - Hull .................................... | *Royal Mail (n.s.c.)* |
| (3) | -do- non pictorial version ............ | *Royal Mail (n.s.c.)* |
| (4) | Slave Trade, Liverpool.................. | *Royal Mail (n.s.c.)* |
| (5) | Freeman Street, Birmingham....... | *Royal Mail (n.s.c.)* |
| (6) | Parliament Square, SW1.........£10 | *Benham BLCS 355* |
| (7) | Dean's Yard, SW1....................£10 | *Benham (500)355* |
| (8) | Hull ..........................................£10 | *Benham BLCS 355* |
| (9) | High Street, Hull.....................£10 | *Westminster* |
| (10) | -do- (palette)...........................£40 | *Westminster* |
| (11) | -do- Autographed ...................£15 | *Westminster* |
| (12) | Settlement of Jamestown.......£10 | *Buckingham Cvrs 305* |
| (13) | Wilberforce Arms, Hull..........£10 | *M Brazier* |
| (14) | Garrison Close .........................£10 | *GB 121* |

## 2007 ABOLITION of SLAVERY

188

(15) Hull ............................................£10 *Cotswold*
(16) Freeland, Witney .....................£15 *Phil Stamp Cvrs 118*
(17) Memorial 2007, Hyde Park....£10 *Bletchley PO*
(18) Thomas Clarkson, Wisbech ...£20 *Fenland Stamp Club*
(19) HMS Birmingham...................£10 *RN CvsGp*
(20) Second Battle of Newbury .....£10 *Heritage of Britain*
**C.D.S. POSTMARKS Price Guide £7-£10**
(21)House of Commons/Lords, Jamaica Road, Wisbech

## 23rd April 2007 – CELEBRATING ENGLAND
*(1) Miniature Sheet: 2 x 1st English Pictorials;*
*78p St. George; Parliament*
*(2) Generic Sheet of 20 x 1st Lion & Shield + labels.*
**SPECIAL HANDSTAMPS           SPONSOR**
**Price Guide Ordinary Covers £3-£5 / Sponsored Covers:**
(1)  FDI - Tallents House.....................*Royal Mail (n.s.c.)*
(2)  FDI - St Georges, Telford.............*Royal Mail (n.s.c.)*
(3)  -do- non pictorial version ............*Royal Mail (n.s.c.)*
(4)  St. Georges Street, Birmingham .. *Royal Mail (n.s.c.)*
(5)  Trafalgar Square, WC2...........£10 *Benham*
(6)  Horse Guards Parade, SW1....£10 *Benham (500)356*
(7)  Westminster, SW1..................£10 *Benham Coin Cover*
(8)  Stratford-upon-Avon .............£10 *Benham BLCS 356*
(9)  St. Georges Way, SE15 .........£10 *Westminster*
(10) -do- W1 (palette)...................£40 *Westminster*
(11) -do- W1 Autographed ...........£15 *Westminster*
(12) Mother of Parliament.............£10 *Buckingham Cvrs 306*
(13) Stratford upon Avon...............£10 *Buckingham Cvrs 306*
(14) Floral Trail, Harrogate ...........£10 *Cotswold*
(15) Soc of St George Folkestone .£15 *P Sheridan*
(16) St Georges Chapel ................£15 *Phil Stamp Cvrs 119*
(17) George Lane, E18 ..................£30 *Bank of Scotland PS*
(18) Newcastle upon Tyne............£15 *Royal Mail*
(19) Battle of Auldearn..................£10 *Heritage of Britain*
(20) Task Force South Atlantic .....£10 *RN CvsGp*
**C.D.S. POSTMARKS Price Guide £7-£10**
(21) St George (and similar), New England Way
(22) House of Commons/Lords, Parliament Street

## 15th May 2007 – BESIDE THE SEASIDE
*1st Ice Cream; 46p Sand Castle; 48p Merry-go-round;*
*54p Beach Huts; 69p Deck Chairs; 78p Donkey Rides.*
**SPECIAL HANDSTAMPS           SPONSOR**
**Price Guide Ordinary Covers £3-£5 / Sponsored Covers:**
(1)  FDI - Tallents House.....................*Royal Mail (n.s.c.)*
(2)  FDI - Blackpool ............................*Royal Mail (n.s.c.)*
(3)  -do- non pictorial version ............*Royal Mail (n.s.c.)*
(4)  Sandy Way, Birmingham...............*Royal Mail (n.s.c.)*
(5)  Brighton, East Sussex.............£10 *Benham BLCS 358*
(6)  Blackpool, Lancashire............£10 *Benham BLCS 358*
(7)  Weymouth, Dorset..................£10 *Benham (500)357*
(8)  Beachy Rd, E3 (palette) .........£40 *Westminster*
(9)  -do- W1 Autographed ............£15 *Westminster*
(10) Blackpool...............................£10 *Buckingham Cvrs 307*
(11) Scarborough ..........................£10 *Cotswold*
(12) Shell Road, SE13 ..................£10 *GB 122*
(13) Water Park, Blackpool...........£15 *P Sheridan*
(14) Margate..................................£15 *Phil Stamp Cvrs 120*
(15) Battle of Naseby ....................£15 *Heritage of Britain*
(16) Falkland War .........................£10 *RN CvsGp*
**C.D.S. POSTMARKS Price Guide £7-£10**
(17)  Seaside, The Beach, Great Yarmouth (or other resorts)

## 17th May 2007 – WEMBLEY STADIUM
*(1) Miniature Sheet: 1st Lion; 2 x 2nd; 2 x 78p Eng. Pictorials*
*(2) Generic Sheet: 20 x 1st Lion and labels.*
**SPECIAL HANDSTAMPS           SPONSOR**
**Price Guide Ordinary Covers £3-£5 / Sponsored Covers:**
(1)  FDI - Tallents House.....................*Royal Mail (n.s.c.)*
(2)  FDI - Wembley ............................*Royal Mail (n.s.c.)*
(3)  -do- non pictorial version ............*Royal Mail (n.s.c.)*
(4)  Wembley Grove, Birmingham.......*Royal Mail (n.s.c.)*
(5)  Legendary Venue, Wembley ..£10 *Benham (500)359*
(6)  New Era, Wembley .................£10 *Benham BLCS 359*
(7)  A Glorious Past, Wembley .....£15 *Benham Coin Cover*
(8)  Wembley Middlesex................£10 *Westminster*
(9)  -do- (palette).............................£40 *Westminster*
(10) -do- W1 Autographed ...........£15 *Westminster*
(11) New Wembley Stadium ..........£10 *Buckingham Cvrs 308*
(12) Wembley Stadium ..................£15 *Phil Stamp Cvrs 121*
(13) Smilers, Giggleswick..............£15 *Phil Stamp Cvrs 19*
(14) Battle of Alford ......................£15 *Heritage of Britain*
(15) MCC England v W Indies .....£10 *Bletchley PO*
(16) San Carlos Water ..................£10 *RN CvsGp*
(17) 1st Flight British Bulldog........£10 *Group Capt Randle*
**C.D.S. POSTMARKS Price Guide £7-£10**
(18) Wembley, Moore, The Ball, Ramsey, New England Road

# 2007

## 2007 CELEBRATING ENGLAND

## 2007 BESIDE THE SEASIDE

## 2007 WEMBLEY STADIUM

## 2007 MACHIN ANNIVERSARY

## 5th June 2007 – MACHIN ANNIVERSARY

*(1) Miniature Sheet: 1st Arnold Machin; 1st First Machin Stamp; £1 Violet; £1 Ruby*
*(2) Prestige Stamp Book. (3) Retail Book of 6 x 1st Class*
*(4) Generic Sheet: 20 x 1st Arnold Machin and labels.*

| SPECIAL HANDSTAMPS | SPONSOR |
|---|---|

**Price Guide Ordinary Covers £3-£5 / Sponsored Covers:**

| | | |
|---|---|---|
| (1) | FDI - Tallents House.................... | *Royal Mail (n.s.c.)* |
| (2) | FDI - Windsor ............................... | *Royal Mail (n.s.c.)* |
| (3) | -do- non pictorial version ............ | *Royal Mail (n.s.c.)* |
| (4) | FDI - Stoke-on-Trent .................... | *Royal Mail (n.s.c.)* |
| (5) | -do- non pictorial version ............ | *Royal Mail (n.s.c.)* |
| (6) | St Martin's-le-Grand .................... | *Royal Mail (n.s.c.)* |
| (7) | Oakhill, Stoke-on-Trent ............... | *Royal Mail (n.s.c.)* |
| (8) | Machin Road, Birmingham.......... | *Royal Mail (n.s.c.)* |
| (9) | A Timeless Classic ........................ | *British Postal Museum* |
| (10) | Windsor, Berkshire ................£15 | *Benham (500)361* |
| (11) | Old Street, London EC1........£15 | *Benham Coin Cover* |
| (12) | Piccadilly, London W1............£10 | *Benham BLCS 361* |
| (13) | Old Brompton Road, SW7....£10 | *Benham D508* |
| (14) | Kensington Gore, SW7 ...........£10 | *Benham* |
| (15) | Stoke-on-Trent.......................£10 | *Benham BLCS 361* |
| (16) | Arnold Road, London E3.......£10 | *Westminster* |
| (17) | -do- (palette).........................£40 | *Westminster* |
| (18) | -do- W1 Autographed .............£15 | *Westminster* |
| (19) | 40th Anniversary, SW1...........£10 | *Buckingham Cvrs 309* |
| (20) | British Icon, Windsor.............£10 | *Buckingham Cvrs 309* |
| (21) | Society of Sculptors ................£10 | *P Sheridan* |
| (22) | Stoke-on-Trent.......................£15 | *Phil Stamp Cvrs 122* |
| (23) | MCC Windsor.........................£10 | *S J Downes* |
| (24) | Battle of Langport...................£15 | *Heritage of Britain* |
| (25) | Devonport Naval Base............£10 | *RN CvsGp* |

**C.D.S. POSTMARKS Price Guide £7-£10**
(26) Eccleshall, Windsor, Barlaston, Stoke on Trent

## 2007 GRAND PRIX

## 3rd July 2007 – GRAND PRIX

*1st Graham Hill; 1st Stirling Moss; 54p Jackie Steward;*
*54p Jim Clark; 78p James Hunt; 78p Nigel Mansell.*

| SPECIAL HANDSTAMPS | SPONSOR |
|---|---|

**Price Guide Ordinary Covers £3-£5 / Sponsored Covers:**

| | | |
|---|---|---|
| (1) | FDI - Tallents House.................... | *Royal Mail (n.s.c.)* |
| (2) | FDI - Silverstone.......................... | *Royal Mail (n.s.c.)* |
| (3) | -do- non pictorial version ............ | *Royal Mail (n.s.c.)* |
| (4) | Brooklands, Weybridge ................ | *Royal Mail (n.s.c.)* |
| (5) | Mansell Close, Birmingham.......... | *Royal Mail (n.s.c.)* |
| (6) | Castle Donington ...................£15 | *Benham (500)365* |
| (7) | Silverstone, Towcester............£15 | *Benham Coin Cover* |
| (8) | Brooklands Rd, Weybridge ....£10 | *Benham BLCS 365* |
| (9) | Silverstone (palette)................£40 | *Westminster* |
| (10) | -do- W1 Autographed .............£15 | *Westminster* |
| (11) | Nigel Mansell, Silverstone......£10 | *Buckingham Cvrs 310* |
| (12) | Silverstone ..............................£15 | *G Lovell* |
| (13) | Grand Prix Cars Association .£20 | *P Sheridan* |
| (14) | Silverstone Close ....................£20 | *GB 123* |
| (15) | Grand Prix, Silverstone..........£15 | *Phil Stamp Cvrs 123* |
| (16) | Rolling Stone, Brands Hatch .£15 | *W H Pugh* |
| (17) | GP 100, Donington Park........£15 | *W H Pugh* |
| (18) | Father & Son, Silverstone.......£15 | *W H Pugh* |
| (19) | Let Yourself Innovate.............£10 | *Bletchley PO* |
| (20) | Silverstone ..............................£10 | *Chaucer Covers* |
| (21) | Subaru......................................£25 | *M Porter* |
| (22) | Battle of Kilsyth......................£15 | *Heritage of Britain* |
| (23) | HMS Triumph..........................£10 | *RN CvsGp* |

**C.D.S. POSTMARKS Price Guide £7-£10**
(24) Silverstone, Fawkham (Brands Hatch), RAC

## 2007 HARRY POTTER

## 17th July 2007 – HARRY POTTER

*(1) 1st Philosoher's Stone; 1st Chamber of Secrets;*
*1st Prisoner of Azkaban; 1st Goblet of Fire; 1st Order of the*
*Phoenix; 1st Half Blood Prince; 1st Deathly Hallows*
*(2) Miniature Sheet: 1st Gryffindor; 1st Hufflepuff;*
*1st Hogwarts; 1st Ravenclaw; 1st Slytherin*
*(3) Generic Sheet: 20 x 1st Stamps from Miniature Sheet*

| SPECIAL HANDSTAMPS | SPONSOR |
|---|---|

**Price Guide Ordinary Covers £3-£5 / Sponsored Covers:**

| | | |
|---|---|---|
| (1) | FDI - Tallents House.................... | *Royal Mail (n.s.c.)* |
| (2) | FDI - Broom ................................. | *Royal Mail (n.s.c.)* |
| (3) | -do- non pictorial version ............ | *Royal Mail (n.s.c.)* |
| (4) | Phoenix Rise, Birmingham.......... | *Royal Mail (n.s.c.)* |
| (5) | Gryffindor, Bracknell .............£10 | *Benham BLCS 365* |
| (6) | Hufflepuff, London W1 ...........£10 | *Benham BLCS 367* |
| (7) | Ravenclaw, London N1............£10 | *Benham BLCS 365* |
| (8) | Slytherin, Chipping Sodbury...£10 | *Benham BLCS 367* |
| (9) | Hogwarts, Alnwick ..................£15 | *Benham (500)366* |
| (10) | Hogwarts Express, N1..............£10 | *Benham BLCS 368* |
| (11) | Kings Cross 9 3/4....................£10 | *Buckingham Cvrs 317* |

(12) Alnwick (owl) ...........................£10 *Buckingham Cvrs 317*
(13) Goathland, North Yorks........£10 *Cotswold*
(14) The Potter Magic, Radcliffe ...£10 *P Sheridan*
(15) Magic of Books, Radcliffe ......£10 *P Sheridan*
(16) Harri Potta, Potters Bar.................. *n.o.c.\**
(17) Sch of Wizardry Potters Bar...£15 *Phil Stamp Cvrs 125*
(18) Harri Potta, Broome Bungay........ *n.o.c.\**
(19) Sch of Flying, Broome............£15 *Phil Stamp Cvrs 126*
(20) Quidditch Lane, Cambourne.£15 *ABC FDC-FDC*
(21) Hogwarts, Spellbrook..............£15 *ABC FDC-FDC*
(22) Mimbus, Dosthill.....................£15 *ABC FDC-FDC*
(23) Mugglewick, Durham ...........£15 *ABC FDC-FDC*
(24) Wizards, Bloomsbury ............£50 *Phil Stamp Cvrs*
(25) Operation Mascot ...................£10 *RN CvsGp*
(26) Battle of Philphaugh...............£15 *Heritage of Britain*
(27) Battle of Rowton Heath.........£15 *Heritage of Britain*
*\* Postmarks withdrawn - covers may exist - but not officials*
**C.D.S. POSTMARKS Price Guide £7-£10**
(28) Broom, Dursley, Potters Bar, Kings Cross, Owlsmoor

## 26th July 2007 – SCOUTS
*1st Looking to the Moon; 46p Rock Climbing;*
*48p Planting a Tree; 54p Archery Practice;*
*69p Piloting an Aircraft; 78p Celebrating 100 Years*
**SPECIAL HANDSTAMPS          SPONSOR**
**Price Guide Ordinary Covers £3-£5  / Sponsored Covers:**
(1)   FDI - Tallents House.....................*Royal Mail (n.s.c.)*
(2)   FDI - Brownsea Island .................*Royal Mail (n.s.c.)*
(3)   -do- non pictorial version .............*Royal Mail (n.s.c.)*
(4)   Gilwell Park..............................£15 *Royal Mail/Mint*
(5)   Scout Close, Birmingham............*Royal Mail (n.s.c.)*
(6)   21st World Jamboree..............£15 *Benham (500)369*
(7)   Robert Baden-Powell...............£10 *Benham BLCS 369*
(8)   Brownsea Island (tents)...........£10 *Benham BLCS 369*
(9)   Brownsea Island (camp fire) .£10 *Westminster*
(10) Brownsea Island (palette) ......£40 *Westminster*
(11) -do- W1 Autographed ............£15 *Westminster*
(12) Brownsea Island (tent)............£10 *Buckingham Cvrs 311*
(13) Brownsea Island (tent)............£10 *Cotswold*
(14) Brownsea Island (compass) ...£10 *Assoc. of GBFDC*
(15) Scouting, Shrewsbury..............£10 *Henry Pugh*
(16) Bletchley Park Post Office .....£10 *Bletchley PO*
(17) Gilwell Park............................£15 *Phil Stamp Cvrs 124*
(18) Concorde, Heathrow...................*Westminster*
(19) Loss of HMS Vestal.................£10 *RN CvsGp*
(20) Battle of Stow on the Wold ...£15 *Heritage of Britain*
(21) Battle of Philphaugh................£15 *Heritage of Britain*
**C.D.S. POSTMARKS Price Guide £7-£10**
(22) Sandbanks, Chingford, Godalming, Writtle

## 4th September 2007 – BIRDS
*1st White-Tailed Eagle; 1st Bearded Tit; 1st Red Kite;*
*1st Cirl Bunting; 1st Marsh Harrier; 1st Avocet; 1st Bittern;*
*1st Dartford Warbler; 1st Corncrake; 1st Peregrine*
**SPECIAL HANDSTAMPS          SPONSOR**
**Price Guide Ordinary Covers £3-£5  / Sponsored Covers:**
(1)   FDI - Tallents House.....................*Royal Mail (n.s.c.)*
(2)   FDI - Dartford ...............................*Royal Mail (n.s.c.)*
(3)   -do- non pictorial version ............*Royal Mail (n.s.c.)*
(4)   Osprey Road, Birmingham...........*Royal Mail (n.s.c.)*
(5)   Eastbridge, Saxmundham.......£10 *Benham BLCS 370*
(6)   Symonds Yat Rock, Coleford £15 *Benham Coin Cover*
(7)   Exmouth, Devon .....................£15 *Benham (500)370*
(8)   Balranald, Uist ........................£10 *Benham BLCS 370*
(9)   Bird Street, W1 (palette) ........£40 *Westminster*
(10) -do- Autographed ...................£15 *Westminster*
(11) Keswick, Cumbria ...................£10 *Buckingham Cvrs 312*
(12) The Red Kite, London EC2....£15 *GB 124*
(13) Bittern Close, WA7 .................£40 *Assoc. of GBFDC*
(14) Bletchley Park Post Office .....£10 *Bletchley PO*
(15) The Dartford Warbler .............£15 *Phil Stamp Cvrs 127*
(16) HMS Roberts - Taomina .......£10 *RN CvsGp*
(17) Battle of Rowton Heath..........£15 *Heritage of Britain*
(18) Siege of Colchester ................£15 *Heritage of Britain*
**C.D.S. POSTMARKS Price Guide £7-£10**
(19) Eagle, Wing, Sandy, Hawkshead

# 2007

## 2007 SCOUTS

## 2007 BIRDS

191

## 2007 ARMY UNIFORMS

### 20th September 2007 – ARMY UNIFORMS
(1) 1st NCO Royal Military Police 1999;
   1st Tank Commander 5th Royal Tank Regiment 1944;
   1st Observer Royal Field Artillery 1917;
   78p Rifleman 95th Rifles 1813;
   78p Grenadier Royal Regiment of Foot of Ireland 1704;
   78p Trooper Earl of Oxford's Horse 1661
(2) Prestige Stamp Book

**SPECIAL HANDSTAMPS**      **SPONSOR**
Price Guide Ordinary Covers £3-£5 / Sponsored Covers:
| | | | |
|---|---|---|---|
| (1) | FDI - Tallents House..................... | | Royal Mail (n.s.c.) |
| (2) | FDI - Boot ................................... | | Royal Mail (n.s.c.) |
| (3) | -do- non pictorial version ............ | | Royal Mail (n.s.c.) |
| (4) | Falkland Way, Birmingham......... | | Royal Mail (n.s.c.) |
| (5) | Army Uniforms, Stampex............. | | Royal Mail (n.s.c.) |
| (6) | Autumn, Stampex ........................ | | Royal Mail (n.s.c.) |
| (7) | London SW1............................... | £10 | Benham BLCS 372 |
| (8) | Belfast ...................................... | £10 | Benham BLCS 373 |
| (9) | Edinburgh ................................. | £10 | Benham BLCS 372 |
| (10) | Cardiff...................................... | £15 | Benham Coin Cover |
| (11) | Whitehall, SW1.......................... | £10 | Benham (500) 372 |
| (12) | Armoury Road (swords) ........ | £10 | Westminster |
| (13) | Armoury Road (palette).......... | £40 | Westminster |
| (14) | -do- Autographed................... | £15 | Westminster |
| (15) | The Chosen Men, Ilford ........ | £10 | Buckingham Cvrs 313 |
| (16) | Eden Camp, Malton ................ | £10 | Cotswold |
| (17) | Guards Road, Windsor ........... | £15 | GB 125 |
| (18) | Tank Museum, Bovington ..... | £10 | P Sheridan |
| (19) | 40th Anniv Launch of QE2.... | £10 | Buckingham Cvrs |
| (20) | Salisbury................................... | £15 | Phil Stamp Cvrs 128 |
| (21) | General Anders, SW7............. | £15 | Polish Philatelic Soc |
| (22) | The Cheshire Regiment.......... | £15 | British Forces |
| (23) | Frome Stamp Club................... | £10 | Frome Stamp Club |
| (24) | HMS Leda Sunk...................... | £10 | RN CvsGp |
| (25) | Battle of Dunbar...................... | £15 | Heritage of Britain |

**C.D.S. POSTMARKS** Price Guide £7-£10
(26) Bovington Camp, Battle, Garrison

### 16th October 2007 – DIAMOND WEDDING
(1) Six stamps depicting photos of the Queen & Prince Philip:
   1st 2006; 1st 1997; 54p 1980; 54p 1969; 78p 1961; 78p 1947
(2) Miniature Sheet: Royal Family 2 x 1st; 69p and 78p

**SPECIAL HANDSTAMPS**      **SPONSOR**
Price Guide Ordinary Covers £3-£5 / Sponsored Covers:
| | | | |
|---|---|---|---|
| (1) | FDI - Tallents House E&P .......... | | Royal Mail (n.s.c.) |
| (2) | FDI - Windsor 1947-2007............ | | Royal Mail (n.s.c.) |
| (3) | -do- non pictorial version .......... | | Royal Mail (n.s.c.) |
| (4) | 1947-2007, London SW1............. | | Royal Mail (n.s.c.) |
| (5) | Prince Philip Close, Birmingham | | Royal Mail (n.s.c.) |
| (6) | Windsor, Berks ....................... | £10 | Benham BLCS 374 |
| (7) | Buckingham Palace Rd SW1. | £10 | Benham BLCS 375 |
| (8) | Westminster, SW1.................. | £10 | Benham BLCS 374 |
| (9) | Balmoral, Ballater .................. | £15 | Benham Coin Cover |
| (10) | Westminster, London SW1.... | £10 | Westminster |
| (11) | Westminster SW1 (palette) .... | £40 | Westminster |
| (12) | -do- Autographed.................. | £15 | Westminster |
| (13) | Windsor .................................. | £10 | Buckingham BCC 105 |
| (14) | London SW1 ........................... | £10 | Buckingham Cvrs 314 |
| (15) | Windsor, Berks ....................... | £10 | Buckingham BCC 105 |
| (16) | Diamond Estate, SW17........... | £15 | GB 126 |
| (17) | Cotswold & Stuart, York........ | £10 | Cotswold |
| (18) | 60 Windsor (ring)................... | £15 | Phil Stamp Cvrs 129 |
| (19) | E & P Bletchley Park ............. | £15 | Bletchley PO |
| (20) | Battle of Worcester................. | £15 | Heritage of Britain |
| (21) | HMS Furious........................... | £10 | RN CvsGp |

**C.D.S. POSTMARKS** Price Guide £7-£10
(22) The Diamond, Throne, Windsor, Edinburgh, Queensway

## 2007 DIAMOND WEDDING

### 6th November 2007 – CHRISTMAS
(1) 2nd Peace; 2nd (Large) Peace; 1st Goodwill;
   1st (Large) Goodwill; 78p Joy; £1.24 Glory
(2) Miniature Sheet
(3) Generic Sheet with 2nd, 1st and 78p stamps + labels
(4) 2nd, 1st Madonna and Child

**SPECIAL HANDSTAMPS**      **SPONSOR**
Price Guide Ordinary Covers £3-£5 / Sponsored Covers:
| | | | |
|---|---|---|---|
| (1) | FDI - Tallents House..................... | | Royal Mail (n.s.c.) |
| (2) | FDI - Bethlehem .......................... | | Royal Mail (n.s.c.) |
| (3) | -do- non pictorial version............ | | Royal Mail (n.s.c.) |
| (4) | Wesley Road, Birmingham........... | | Royal Mail (n.s.c.) |
| (5) | Holywell Common.................. | £10 | Benham BLCS 379 |
| (6) | Wing, Buckinghamshire.......... | £10 | Benham BLCS 377 |
| (7) | Peacehaven, East Sussex........ | £10 | Benham BLCS 376 |
| (8) | Bethlehem ............................... | £10 | Benham BLCS 379 |
| (9) | Christmas Common.................. | £10 | Benham BLCS 377 |
| (10) | Nasareth ................................... | £15 | Benham Coin Cover |

## 2007 CHRISTMAS

(11) Angel Walk, W6 (palette).......£40 *Westminster*
(12) -do- Autographed...................£15 *Westminster*
(13) Bethlehem.................................£10 *Buckingham Cvrs 315*
(14) Edward Elgar, Worcester.......£10 *Buckingham Cvrs 315*
(15) Dickens World, Chatham.......£10 *Buckingham Cvrs 315*
(16) Happy Xmas, York .................£10 *Cotswold*
(17) Happy Christmas, Harrow .....£15 *GB 127/8*
(18) Church, Lancashire.................£15 *Assoc. of GBFDC*
(19) Angels, Midhurst W Sussex ...£15 *P Sheridan*
(20) Bethlehem .............................£15 *Phil Stamp Cvrs 130*
(21) Bletchley Park Angels ............£10 *Bletchley PO*
(22) Dutch Raid on the Medway...£15 *Heritage of Britain*
(23) The Assault on Suez ..............£10 *RN CvsGp*
**C.D.S. POSTMARKS Price Guide £7-£10**
(24) Noel Road, Holy Island, Bethlehem

## 8th November 2007 – LEST WE FORGET
*(1) 1st Poppy; 4 x 78p Country Pictorials*
*(2) Generic Sheet of 20 Poppy stamps and labels*
**SPECIAL HANDSTAMPS          SPONSOR**
**Price Guide Ordinary Covers £3-£5  / Sponsored Covers:**
(1) FDI - Tallents House...................... *Royal Mail (n.s.c.)*
(2) FDI - London SW1 ....................... *Royal Mail (n.s.c.)*
(3) -do- non pictorial version ............ *Royal Mail (n.s.c.)*
(4) Monument Road, Birmingham .... *Royal Mail (n.s.c.)*
(5) Grosvenor Street, W1.............£10 *Benham D522*
(6) The Strand, WC2....................£10 *Benham BLCS 381*
(7) Chelsea, SW3 .........................£10 *Benham BLCS 380*
(8) Whitehall, SW1......................£15 *Benham (500) 380*
(9) Whitehall, SW1 (palette) .......£40 *Westminster*
(10) -do- Autographed...................£15 *Westminster*
(11) Passchendaele, SW1 ..............£10 *Buckingham Cvrs 316*
(12) For Ever England, SW1.........£10 *Buckingham Cvrs 316*
(13) Western Front Association......£15 *P Sheridan*
(14) The Cenotaph.........................£15 *Phil Stamp Cvrs 131*
(15) MCC Lord's Ground .............£10 *Bletchley PO*
(16) Battle of Sedgemoor ..............£15 *Heritage of Britain*
(17) Operation Torch......................£10 *RN CvsGp*
**C.D.S. POSTMARKS Price Guide £7-£10**
(18) Wargrave, Battle, Battlehill

## 30 November 2007 – Glorious Scotland
*Generic Sheet of 20 x 1st Scottish Lion + labels.*
**SPECIAL HANDSTAMPS          SPONSOR**
**Price Guide Ordinary Covers £3-£5  / Sponsored Covers:**
(1) Fort William ...............................£15 *Benham BLCS 382*
(2) Kyle of Lochalsh.....................£15 *Benham (500) 382*
(3) Edinburgh ..............................£15 *Benham BLCS 382*

## 8th January 2008 – JAMES BOND
*(1) 1st Casino Royale; 1st Dr. No;*
*    54p Goldfinger; 54p Diamonds are Forever;*
*    78p From Russia with Love; 78p For Your Eyes Only*
*(2) Miniature Sheet with above stamps*
**SPECIAL HANDSTAMPS          SPONSOR**
**Price Guide Ordinary Covers £3-£5  / Sponsored Covers:**
(1) FDI - Tallents House...................... *Royal Mail (n.s.c.)*
(2) FDI - London SE1....................... *Royal Mail (n.s.c.)*
(3) -do- non pictorial version ............ *Royal Mail (n.s.c.)*
(4) Bond Street, Birmingham........... *Royal Mail (n.s.c.)*
(5) Fleet Street, EC4 (passport)....£15 *Benham (500) 384*
(6) Pall Mall, SW1 (cocktail) ......£15 *Benham (500) 385*
(7) Green Street, Mayfair (IF).....£10 *Benham BLCS 383*
(8) Whitehall, SW1 (gun)............£10 *Benham Coin Cover*
(9) Vauxhall Cross, SE1 (007) ....£10 *Benham BLCS 384*
(10) Ebury Street, SW1 (car)........£15 *Benham (500) 383*
(11) Bond Street, E15 (gun) ..........£10 *Westminster*
(12) -do- Autographed...................£15 *Westminster*
(13) Bond Street, W1 (cocktail) ....£10 *Buckingham Cvrs 318*
(14) Mayfair, W1 (dice) ................£10 *Buckingham Cvrs 318*
(15) Dover (diver)..........................£10 *Buckingham Cvrs 318*
(16) Bond Street, (book) ...............£10 *Steven Scott*
(17) Target Close, Feltham............£15 *GB 129*
(18) Leo Casino, Liverpool............£10 *P Sheridan*
(19) 007 Ebury Street......................£25 *Fleming Publications*
(20) James Bond, London W1 .......£10 *Cotswold*
(21) 007 Ian Fleming, Bletchley ....£10 *Bletchley PO*
(22) Top Secret? Dartford ..............£15 *Phil Stamp Cvrs 134*
(23) 006$^{1}/_{2}$ Kew Richmond ...........£15 *Phil Stamp Cvrs GA1*
(24) Sevenhampton .........................£15 *Phil Stamp Cvrs AQ3*
(25) Tyne Bridge, Newcastle ..........£15 *Buckingham Cvrs*
(26) HM Submarine Sturgeon .......£10 *RN CvsGp*
**C.D.S. POSTMARKS**
None serviced in quantities of 20 or more

**2007 LEST WE FORGET**

**2008 JAMES BOND**

## 2008 WORKING DOGS

## 2008 KINGS

## 2008 NORTHERN IRELAND

## 15th January 2008 – NEW STYLE SMILERS

*(1) 10 x Round style Smilers labels with Hello, Love and Union Flag stamps*
*(2) Stamp book with 2 x Love stamps and St. Valentines labels*

**SPECIAL HANDSTAMPS           SPONSOR**
**Price Guide Ordinary Covers £3-£5 / Sponsored Covers:**
(1) Lover, Salisbury (rose) ..............£10 *Benham BLCS 386*
(2) Cherwell River, Oxford ..........£10 *Benham BLCS 387*
(3) Love Lane, Birmingham ........£15 *Benham (500) 386*
(4) Gretna Green ............................£10 *Benham BLCS 386*

## 5th February 2008 – WORKING DOGS

*1st Assistance Dog; 46p Mountain Rescue; 48p Police Dog; 54p Customs Dog; 69p Sheepdog; 78p Guide Dog*

**SPECIAL HANDSTAMPS           SPONSOR**
**Price Guide Ordinary Covers £3-£5 / Sponsored Covers:**
(1) FDI - Tallents House.....................*Royal Mail (n.s.c.)*
(2) FDI - Round Green ......................*Royal Mail (n.s.c.)*
(3) -do- non pictorial version ...........*Royal Mail (n.s.c.)*
(4) St Bernards Road, Birmingham... *Royal Mail (n.s.c.)*
(5) Police Dog, Spennymoor.......£10 *Benham BLCS 388*
(6) Sheep Dog, Kendal .................£15 *Benham (500) 388*
(7) Mountain Rescue, Denbigh.....£15 *Benham Coin Cover*
(8) Dog Kennel...Autographed.....£15 *Westminster*
(9) New Scotland Yard ................£10 *Buckingham Cvrs 319*
(10) Sheep Dog Society, Bedford ..£15 *P Sheridan*
(11) Guide Dogs, Reading..............£15 *P Sheridan*
(12) Dogs for Disabled, Banbury...£15 *P Sheridan*
(13) Dog Lane, NW10 ....................£15 *GB 130*
(14) Thrive, London N2.................£10 *ABC FDC*
(15) First Working Dogs, Hull ......£10 *Cotswold*
(16) Working Dogs, Barking .........£15 *Phil Stamp Cvrs GA2*
(17) -do- Newfoundland.................£15 *Phil Stamp Cvrs 136*
(18) Royal Mail Rathbone Place ......... *Royal Mail (n.s.c.)*
(19) Royal Mail Mount Pleasant .......... *Royal Mail (n.s.c.)*
(20) HMS Antelope Sinks U-41 ....£10 *RN CvsGp*

**C.D.S. POSTMARKS Price Guide £7-£10**
(21) Dog & Gun, Dog Kennel Lane, Isle of Dogs, Barking

## 28th February 2008 – KINGS

*(1) 1st Henry IV; 1st Henry V; 54p Henry VI; 54p Edward IV; 69p Edward V; 69p Richard III*
*(2) Miniature Sheet: 1st Owain Glyn Dwr; 1st Battle of Agincourt; 54p Battle of Tewkesbury; 78p William Caxton*

**SPECIAL HANDSTAMPS           SPONSOR**
**Price Guide Ordinary Covers £3-£5 / Sponsored Covers:**
(1) FDI - Tallents House.....................*Royal Mail (n.s.c.)*
(2) FDI - Tewkesbury ........................*Royal Mail (n.s.c.)*
(3) -do- non pictorial version ...........*Royal Mail (n.s.c.)*
(4) Rose Road, Birmingham............... *Royal Mail (n.s.c.)*
(5) FDI - Westminster, SW1 ........£15 *Royal Mail Cachet Cvr*
(6) FDI - Spring Stampex, N1 .......... *Royal Mail (n.s.c.)*
(7) Spring Stampex, N1 ...................... *Royal Mail (n.s.c.)*
(8) Westminster, SW1...................£10 *Benham BLCS 390*
(9) Tower Hill, EC3.......................£15 *Benham (500) 389*
(10) Lancaster...............................£15 *Benham (500) 390*
(11) York ........................................£10 *Benham BLCS 389*
(12) Autographed, Monarch Rd ....£15 *Westminster*
(13) Battle of Agincourt.................£10 *Buckingham Cvrs 320*
(14) Richard III, York....................£10 *Buckingham Cvrs 320*
(15) Richard III Society.................£15 *P Sheridan*
(16) Houses of Lancaster & York.£15 *Assoc. of GBFDC*
(17) Kings & Queens, York...........£10 *Cotswold*
(18) St. Albans...............................£15 *Phil Stamp Cvrs 137*
(19) Tewkesbury............................£15 *Phil Stamp Cvrs AQ4*
(20) Houses of Lancaster & York.£15 *J Bevan Pubs 105*
(21) Operation Granby ...................£10 *RN CvsGp*

**C.D.S. POSTMARKS Price Guide £7-£10**
(22) York, Lancaster, Battle

## 28th February 2008 – Smilers Book

*(1) 6 X 1st: Hello, Flower, Union Flag, Balloons, Fireworks, Champagne - with elliptical perfs*

**SPECIAL HANDSTAMPS           SPONSOR**
**Price Guide Ordinary Covers £3-£5 / Sponsored Covers:**
(1) Britannia, Bacup ........................... *Benham*
(2) Pontypool (Concorde) ................. *Benham*

## 11th March 2008 – NORTHERN IRELAND

*(1) Miniature Sheet: 2 x 1st Carrickfergus; Giant's Causeway; 78p St.Patrick; Queen's Bridge, Belfast*
*(2) Generic Sheet of 20 x 1st Lion & Shield + labels.*

**SPECIAL HANDSTAMPS           SPONSOR**
**Price Guide Ordinary Covers £3-£5 / Sponsored Covers:**
(1) FDI - Tallents House.....................*Royal Mail (n.s.c.)*
(2) FDI - Downpatrick.......................*Royal Mail (n.s.c.)*
(3) -do- non pictorial version ...........*Royal Mail (n.s.c.)*

| (4) | St Patrick's Close, Birmingham ... | *Royal Mail (n.s.c.)* |
|---|---|---|
| (5) | Queen's Bridge, Belfast | £10 *Benham BLCS 392* |
| (6) | Queen's Island, Belfast | £15 *Benham (500) 393* |
| (7) | Carrickfergus | £15 *Benham (500) 392* |
| (8) | Downpatrick | £10 *Benham BLCS 392* |
| (9) | Autographed, Belfast Rd | £15 *Westminster* |
| (10) | Downpatrick - celtic pattern | £10 *Buckingham Cvrs 322* |
| (11) | Bushmills - shamrock | £10 *Buckingham Cvrs 322* |
| (12) | Phil goes to Cushendun | £15 *Phil Stamp Cvrs* |
| (13) | The Harp, Bridgnorth | £15 *J Bevan Pubs 106* |
| (14) | HMS Naiao | £10 *RN CvsGp* |

**C.D.S. POSTMARKS Price Guide £7-£10**
(15) Carrickfergus, Bushmills, Belfast

## 2008 – S.O.S. RESCUE AT SEA

## 13th March 2008 – S.O.S. RESCUE AT SEA
*1st Barra; 46p Appledore; 48p Portland; 54p St Ives;
69p Lee-on-Solent; 78p Tenby.*
**SPECIAL HANDSTAMPS          SPONSOR**
**Price Guide Ordinary Covers £3-£5 / Sponsored Covers:**

| (1) | FDI - Tallents House | *Royal Mail (n.s.c.)* |
|---|---|---|
| (2) | FDI - Poole, Dorset | *Royal Mail (n.s.c.)* |
| (3) | -do- non pictorial version | *Royal Mail (n.s.c.)* |
| (4) | Portland Road, Birmingham | *Royal Mail (n.s.c.)* |
| (5) | Southampton - lifebuoy | £10 *Benham BLCS 394* |
| (6) | Poole - lifeboat | £10 *Benham BLCS 394* |
| (7) | Devonport Royal Dockyard | £15 *Benham (500) 394* |
| (8) | Autographed, Mayday Rd | £15 *Westminster* |
| (9) | RNLI - Tenby | £10 *Buckingham Cvrs 321* |
| (10) | RNLI - St.Ives | £10 *Buckingham Cvrs 321* |
| (11) | RNLI - Appledore | £10 *Buckingham Cvrs 321* |
| (12) | Maritime & Coastguard | £10 *Buckingham Cvrs 321* |
| (13) | RNLI - Isle of Barra | £10 *Buckingham Cvrs 321* |
| (14) | Mayday Gardens, SW3 | £15 *GB 131* |
| (15) | Port William Inshore Rescue | £15 *P Sheridan* |
| (16) | Whitby | £10 *Cotswold* |
| (17) | Sea Rescue, Seaham | £15 *Phil Stamp Cvrs 139* |
| (18) | Rescue at Sea, Wincham | £15 *Phil Stamp Cvrs GA3* |
| (19) | Mayday, Dover | £10 *Steven Scott* |
| (20) | Lifeboat Inn, Blackpool | £15 *J Bevan Pubs 107* |
| (21) | Assault on Letpan | £10 *RN CvsGp* |

**C.D.S. POSTMARKS Price Guide £7-£10**
(22) Portland, Lighthouse, Cromer

## 1st April 2008 – Territorial Army
*Commemorative Stamp Sheet of 10 1st Class Union Flag
stamps and TA Stamp Labels*
**SPECIAL HANDSTAMPS          SPONSOR**
**Price Guide Ordinary Covers £3-£5 / Sponsored Covers:**

| (1) | Wilton, Salisbury | £15 *Royal Mail* |
|---|---|---|
| (2) | Whitehall | £15 *Benham* |

## 2008 TERRITORIAL ARMY

## 15th April 2008 – INSECTS
*1st Adonis Blue; 1st Southern Damselfly; 1st Red Barbed Ant;
1st Barberry Carpet Moth; 1st Stag Beetle; 1st Hazel Pot Beetle;
1st Field Cricket; 1st Silver-spotted Skipper; 1st Purbeck Mason
Wasp; 1st Nobel Chater*
**SPECIAL HANDSTAMPS          SPONSOR**
**Price Guide Ordinary Covers £3-£5 / Sponsored Covers:**

| (1) | FDI - Tallents House | *Royal Mail (n.s.c.)* |
|---|---|---|
| (2) | FDI - Crawley, West Sussex | *Royal Mail (n.s.c.)* |
| (3) | -do- non pictorial version | *Royal Mail (n.s.c.)* |
| (4) | Crawley Walk, Birmingham | *Royal Mail (n.s.c.)* |
| (5) | Endangered Insects, NW1 | £15 *Benham (500) 395* |
| (6) | -do, London SW7 | £10 *Benham BLCS 395* |
| (7) | -do, Peterborough | £10 *Benham BLCS 395* |
| (8) | -do, Sheffield | £15 *BenhamCoin Cover* |
| (9) | Autographed, Butterfly Lane | £15 *Westminster* |
| (10) | Canvey Island | £10 *Buckingham Cvrs 323* |
| (11) | Butterfly Lane, Elstree | £15 *GB 132* |
| (12) | Bugbrooke (Butterfly) | £15 *Phil Stamp Cvrs 140* |
| (13) | Bugbrooke (Bees) | £15 *Phil Stamp Cvrs GA4* |
| (14) | The Red Admiral, Leicester | £15 *J Bevan Pubs 108* |
| (15) | George Cross, Malta | £10 *RN CvsGp* |

**C.D.S. POSTMARKS Price Guide £7-£10**
(16) St. Bees, Bugbrooke, Selborne, Bugthorpe

## 2008 INSECTS

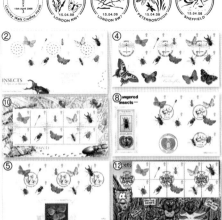

## 13th May 2008 – Ice Cream Self Adhesive
*1st Seaside:Ice Cream (x 2) issued in self-adhesive stamp book
with four 1st Class definitives*
**SPECIAL HANDSTAMPS          SPONSOR**
**Price Guide Ordinary Covers £3-£5 / Sponsored Covers:**

| (1) | Summer Holidays Brighton | £15 *Benham* |
|---|---|---|
| (2) | Summer Holidays Blackpool | £15 *Benham* |

## 2008 CATHEDRALS

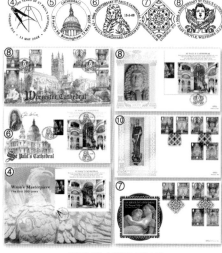

### 13th May 2008 – CATHEDRALS
*(1) 1st Lichfield Cathedral; 48p Belfast Cathedral;*
*50p Gloucester Cathedral; 56p St Davids Cathedral;*
*72p Westminster Cathedral; 81p St Magnus Cathedral*
*(2) Miniature Sheet: 2 x 1st, 2x 81p St Paul's Cathedral*

| SPECIAL HANDSTAMPS | SPONSOR |
|---|---|
| Price Guide Ordinary Covers £3-£5 / Sponsored Covers: | |
| (1) FDI - Tallents House | *Royal Mail (n.s.c.)* |
| (2) FDI - London EC4 | *Royal Mail (n.s.c.)* |
| (3) -do- non pictorial version | *Royal Mail (n.s.c.)* |
| (4) 300 Years St Paul's £15 | *Royal Mail/Royal Mint* |
| (5) St Paul's Rd, Birmingham | *Royal Mail (n.s.c.)* |
| (6) St Paul's (Wren portrait) £12 | *Benham BLCS 397* |
| (7) Lichfield £12 | *Benham BLCS 396* |
| (8) East Knoyle £17 | *Benham (500) 397* |
| (9) St.Davids £12 | *Benham BLCS 396* |
| (10) Kirkwall, Orkney £17 | *Benham (500) 396* |
| (11) St Pauls £10 | *Buckingham Cvrs 324* |
| (12) Gloucester Cathedral £10 | *Buckingham Cvrs 324* |
| (13) Cathedral View, Guildford £15 | *GB 133* |
| (14) St Paul's, Churchyard £15 | *P Sheridan* |
| (15) Gloucester £10 | *Cotswold* |
| (16) Salisbury £15 | *Phil Stamp Cvrs GA5* |
| (17) York £15 | *Phil Stamp Cvrs 141* |
| (18) Autographed, Holy Cross £15 | *Westminster* |
| (19) Hope Street, Liverpool £15 | *Assoc. of GBFDC* |
| (20) Cathedrals London £15 | *J Bevan Pubs 109* |
| (21) HM Sub Undaunted £10 | *RN CvsGp* |
| **C.D.S. POSTMARKS** Price Guide £7-£10 | |
| (22) St Paul's Rd, Christchurch, Bishops Castle, Gloucester | |

## 2008 CLASSIC FILMS

### 10th June 2008 – CLASSIC FILMS
*(1) 1st Carry on Sergeant; 48p Dracula; 50p Carry on Cleo;*
*56p The Curse of Frankenstein; 72p Carry on Screaming;*
*81p The Mummy*
*(2) Stamp Book: 6 x 1st Definitives*

| SPECIAL HANDSTAMPS | SPONSOR |
|---|---|
| Price Guide Ordinary Covers £3-£5 / Sponsored Covers: | |
| (1) FDI - Tallents House | *Royal Mail (n.s.c.)* |
| (2) FDI - Bray, Maidenhead | *Royal Mail (n.s.c.)* |
| (3) -do- non pictorial version | *Royal Mail (n.s.c.)* |
| (4) James Rd, Birmingham | *Royal Mail (n.s.c.)* |
| (5) Guildford (Sgt Major) £12 | *Benham* |
| (6) Iver Heath (clapper board) £12 | *Benham BLCS 399* |
| (7) Swain's Lane (vampire) £12 | *Benham BLCS 399* |
| (8) Bray (mummy) £17 | *Benham (500) 399* |
| (9) Shepperton (film reel) £10 | *Buckingham Cvrs 325* |
| (10) Elstree (clapper board £10 | *Buckingham Cvrs 325* |
| (11) Wardour Street, London W1 £15 | *GB 134* |
| (12) Autographed, Water Oakley £15 | *Westminster* |
| (13) Woolton Picture House £15 | *P Sheridan* |
| (14) The Flicks, Cheltenham £15 | *J Bevan Pubs 110* |
| (15) Sidmouth £15 | *Phil Stamp Cvrs GA6* |
| (16) Falklands War £10 | *RN CvsGp* |
| **C.D.S. POSTMARKS** Price Guide £7-£10 | |
| (17) Shepperton, Hammerwich, Iver Heath, Bray | |

## 2008 AIR DISPLAYS

### 17th July 2008 – AIR DISPLAYS
*(1) 1st Red Arrows; 48p RAF Falcons; 50p Red Arrows;*
*56p Vulcan; 72p Parachutist; 81p Hendon Air Race*
*(2) Generic Sheet of 20 x 1st Red Arrows*

| SPECIAL HANDSTAMPS | SPONSOR |
|---|---|
| Price Guide Ordinary Covers £3-£5 / Sponsored Covers: | |
| (1) FDI - Tallents House | *Royal Mail (n.s.c.)* |
| (2) FDI - Farnborough | *Royal Mail (n.s.c.)* |
| (3) -do- non pictorial version | *Royal Mail (n.s.c.)* |
| (4) Trenchard House £20 | *Royal Mail/Royal Mint* |
| (5) Concord Rd, Birmingham | *Royal Mail (n.s.c.)* |
| (6) Farnborough £12 | *Benham BLCS 401* |
| (7) Duxford £12 | *Benham* |
| (8) Biggin Hill £17 | *Benham (500) 401* |
| (9) Avro Vulcan £10 | *Buckingham Cvrs 326* |
| (10) Air Displays, Farnborough £10 | *Buckingham Cvrs* |
| (11) Airfield Way £15 | *GB 135* |
| (12) Autographed, Scampton £15 | *Westminster* |
| (13) Southport Airshow £15 | *P Sheridan* |
| (14) Farnborough £15 | *Cotswold* |
| (15) Red Arrows, Lutterworth £15 | *J Bevan Pubs 111* |
| (16) Air Displays, Farnborough £15 | *Phil Stamp Cvrs GA7* |
| (17) New Brighton, Wallasey £25 | *Assoc. of GBFDC* |
| (18) RAFLET Stamp Club £15 | *RAFLET* |
| (19) RAF 90th Bletchley Park £15 | *Bletchley PO* |
| (20) Attack on "Tirpitz" £15 | *RN CvsGp* |
| (21) Postwatch Midlands | *Royal Mail (n.s.c.)* |
| **C.D.S. POSTMARKS** Price Guide £7-£10 | |
| (22) Biggin Hill, Duxford, Farnborough, Cosford | |

## 24th July 2008 – 1908 Olympics
*Commemorative Stamp Sheet of 10 1st Class Union Flag stamps and Olympic Stamp Labels*
**SPECIAL HANDSTAMPS        SPONSOR**
**Price Guide Ordinary Covers £3-£5  / Sponsored Covers:**
(1)  White City W12 (wreath) .......£15  *Royal Mail (n.s.c.)*
(2)  Windsor....................................£15  *Benham*
(3)  White City W12 (runner) .......£15  *Benham*

## 5th August 2008  – Beijing Expo
*Generic Sheet: 1st Hello + labels depicting Chinese lanterns*
**Price Guide Ordinary Cvrs £10 - £15 / No Sponsored Covers**

## 22nd August 2008 – OLYMPIC HANDOVER
*Miniature Sheet: 1st National Stadium, Beijing; 1st London Eye; 1st Tower of London; 1st Corner Tower, Forbidden City*
**SPECIAL HANDSTAMPS        SPONSOR**
**Price Guide Ordinary Covers £3-£5  / Sponsored Covers:**
(1)   FDI - Tallents House...................  *Royal Mail (n.s.c.)*
(2)   FDI - London E15 .........................  *Royal Mail (n.s.c.)*
(3)   -do- non pictorial version ............  *Royal Mail (n.s.c.)*
(4)   Radcliffe Drive, Birmingham........  *Royal Mail (n.s.c.)*
(5)   White City..............................£15  *Benham Coin Cover*
(6)   Stratford E15...........................£17  *Benham (500) 403*
(7)   Wembley ..................................£12  *Benham BLCS 403*
(8)   Autographed, Trafalgar Sq .....£15  *Westminster*
(9)   London W12 ...........................£10  *Buckingham Cvrs 327*
(10)  Onwards to London, E15.......£10  *Buckingham Cvrs 327*
(11)  Olympic Games Handover ....£15  *Cotswold*
(12)  Games Road, Barnet...............£15  *Benham*
(13)  Games, Wembley....................£15  *J Bevan Pubs 112*
(14)  Beijing, London SW1............£15  *Benham*
(15)  The Games, Andover..............£15  *Phil Stamp Cvrs GA8*
(16)  Manchester PTA.....................£15  *T Barnett*
(17)  HMS Hood ..............................£15  *RN CvsGp*
**C.D.S. POSTMARKS Price Guide £7-£10**
(18)  Fence, Badminton

## 18th September 2008 – RAF UNIFORMS
*(1) 1st Drum Major RAF Central Band 2007; 1st Helicopter Rescue Winchman 1984; 1st Hawker Hunter Pilot 1951; 81p Lancaster Air Gunner 1944; 81p Plotter WAAF 1940; 81p Pilot 1918*
*(2) Prestige Stamp Book*
**SPECIAL HANDSTAMPS        SPONSOR**
**Price Guide Ordinary Covers £3-£5  / Sponsored Covers:**
(1)   FDI - Tallents House...................  *Royal Mail (n.s.c.)*
(2)   FDI - London NW9 .....................  *Royal Mail (n.s.c.)*
(3)   -do- non pictorial version ............  *Royal Mail (n.s.c.)*
(4)   Autumn Stampex, RAF.................  *Royal Mail (n.s.c.)*
(5)   Autumn Stampex ..........................  *Royal Mail (n.s.c.)*
(6)   Gibson Road, Birmingham ..........  *Royal Mail (n.s.c.)*
(7)   Cranwell, Sleaford...................£15  *Benham BLCS 404*
(8)   Brize Norton, Oxfordshire .....£10  *Benham*
(9)   Northolt, Ruislip....................£12  *Benham Coin Cover*
(10)  Biggin Hill, Kent....................£17  *Benham (500) 404*
(11)  Peter Twiss...............................£10  *Buckingham Cvrs 328*
(12)  Air Street, London W1 ..........£15  *GB 137*
(13)  Autographed, Lincoln ...........£15  *Westminster*
(14)  Helicopter Museum .................£15  *P Sheridan*
(15)  Yorkshire Air Museum...........£15  *Cotswold*
(16)  RAF 1918-2008.......................£15  *Bletchley PO*
(17)  Woodvale, Formby................£45  *Assoc. of GBFDC*
(18)  Biggin Hill...............................£15  *Phil Stamp Cvrs GA9*
(19)  The Pilot, Coventry.................£15  *J Bevan Pubs 113*
(20)  Tripoli, 67th Anniversary......£15  *RN CvsGp*
(21)  RAFLET Stamp Club..............£25  *RAFLET*
**C.D.S. POSTMARKS Price Guide £7-£10**
(22)  Biggin Hill, Cranwell (or any other RAF station pmk)

## 29th Sept 2008 – COUNTRY DEFINITIVES
*(1) Miniature Sheet: 9 x 1st Regionals*
*(2) Prestige Stamp Book   (3) Glorious UK Generic Sheet*
**SPECIAL HANDSTAMPS        SPONSOR**
**Price Guide Ordinary Covers £3-£5  / Sponsored Covers:**
(1)   FDI - Tallents House...................  *Royal Mail (n.s.c.)*
(2)   FDI - Gloucester ...........................  *Royal Mail (n.s.c.)*
(3)   -do- non pictorial version ............  *Royal Mail (n.s.c.)*
(4)   25 Years of £1 Coin London .£20  *Royal Mail/Royal Mint*
(5)   Union Street, Birmingham ..........  *Royal Mail*
(6)   Britannia .....................................£12  *Benham BLCS 407*
(7)   London (lion)...........................£12  *Benham D539*
(8)   London SW (union flag).........£17  *Benham (500) 407*
(9)   Belfast .......................................£12  *Benham BLCS 406*
(10)  Edinburgh ...............................£17  *Benham (500) 406*
(11)  Cardiff ......................................£12  *Benham BLCS 406*
(12)  Ireland, Scotland, Wales etc ..£10  *Buckingham Cvrs 329*

### 2008 OLYMPIC HANDOVER

### 2008 RAF UNIFORMS

### 2008 COUNTRY DEFINITIVES

## 2008 WOMEN of DISTINCTION

## 2008 SMILERS for KIDS

## 2008 CHRISTMAS

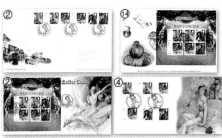

## 2008 LEST WE FORGET

See 30,000 more GB FDCs at: www.bfdc.co.uk

---

(13) Autographed, Lincoln ............£15 *Westminster*
(14) London (union flag) ...............£15 *J Bevan Pubs 114*
(15) Windsor ..................................£15 *Phil Stamp Cvrs 142*
*250th Anniversary of Birth of Nelson:*
(16) British Forces 3024.................£15 *RN Philatelic Officer*
(17) British Forces 3067.................£15 *RN CvsGp*
(18) Burnham Thorpe (outline).....£15 *Benham*
(19) Burnham Thorpe (portrait)....£15 *Benham*
(20) Burnham Thorpe (birthplace)£15 *Buckingham Cvrs*
(21) Battle of Newbury...................£15 *Heritage of Britain*
**C.D.S. POSTMARKS Price Guide £7-£10**
(22) Cardiff, Belfast, Edinburgh, Glasgow

## 14th Oct 2008 – WOMEN of DISTINCTION
*1st Millicent Garrett Fawcett; 48p Elizabeth Garrett Anderson; 50p Marie Stopes; 56p Eleanor Rathbone; 72p Claudia Jones; 81p Barbara Castle*
**SPECIAL HANDSTAMPS        SPONSOR**
**Price Guide Ordinary Covers £3-£5 / Sponsored Covers:**
(1)  FDI - Tallents House...................  *Royal Mail (n.s.c.)*
(2)  FDI - Gloucester ..........................  *Royal Mail (n.s.c.)*
(3)  -do- non pictorial version ............  *Royal Mail (n.s.c.)*
(4)  Suffrage Street, Smethwick..........  *Royal Mail (n.s.c.)*
(5)  Downing St, SW1A.................£15  *Benham BLCS 409*
(6)  Parliament Square.................£17  *Benham (500) 409*
(7)  Equality for Women .............£10  *Buckingham Cvrs 330*
(8)  Autographed, Ladywell.........£15  *Westminster*
(9)  Women's Rights......................£15  *J Bevan Pubs 143*
(10) Boadicea St, London N1.......£15  *GB 138*
(11) Pills, Bristol.........................£15  *Assoc. of GBFDC*
(12) WW2 Veteran, Bletchley.......£15  *Bletchley PO*
(13) Ladywell (angel) ..................£15  *Phil Stamp Cvrs GA10*
(14) Ladywell (handbag) .............£15  *Phil Stamp Cvrs 143*
(15) Trident Missile Sub .............£15  *RN CvsGp*
**C.D.S. POSTMARKS Price Guide £7-£10**
(16) The University, Liverpool, Newnham, Cambridge,
(17) House of Lords, House of Commons

## 18th October 2008 – Smilers for Kids
*Four stamp sheets: Almond Blossom (Flower Fairies); Peter Rabbit (Beatrix Potter); Noddy; Mr Happy (Mr Men)*
**SPECIAL HANDSTAMPS        SPONSOR**
**Price Guide Ordinary Covers £3-£5 / Sponsored Covers:**
(1)  Fairyfield Ave, Birmingham.........  *Royal Mail (n.s.c.)*
(2)  Croydon (Fairy) ......................£12  *Benham*
(3)  London W8 (Rabbit) ..............£12  *Benham*

## 4th November 2008 – CHRISTMAS
*2nd Ugly Sisters; 2nd (Large) Ugly Sisters; 1st Genie; 1st (Large) Genie; 50p Captain Hook; 81p Wicked Queen*
**SPECIAL HANDSTAMPS        SPONSOR**
**Price Guide Ordinary Covers £3-£5 / Sponsored Covers:**
(1)  FDI - Tallents House...................  *Royal Mail (n.s.c.)*
(2)  FDI - Bethlehem ..........................  *Royal Mail (n.s.c.)*
(3)  -do- non pictorial version ............  *Royal Mail (n.s.c.)*
(4)  Whittington Rd, Birmingham.......  *Royal Mail (n.s.c.)*
(5)  Waterloo Rd, London SE1.....£15  *Benham BLCS 410*
(6)  Drury Lane, London WC2.....£15  *Benham BLCS 410*
(7)  Covent Garden, WC2............£17  *Benham (500) 410*
(8)  Christmas Common.................£15  *Benham BLCS 411*
(9)  Aldwych, London WC2 .........£17  *Benham (500) 411*
(10) Autographed, Drury Lane ......£15  *Westminster*
(11) Southampton ........................£10  *Buckingham Cvrs 331*
(12) Canterbury..............................£10  *Buckingham Cvrs 331*
(13) Happy Christmas, Leeds.........£15  *Cotswold*
(14) Christmas Wishes, Harrow ....£15  *GB 139*
(15) Aladdin's Lamp, Darlaston ....£15  *J Bevan Pubs 144*
(16) 60 Years Panto, Pontefract ....£15  *P Sheridan*
(17) Grand Theatre, Blackpool......£15  *P Sheridan*
(18) Drury Lane (panto horse) ......£15  *Phil Stamp Cvrs 144*
(19) Drury Lane (angel) ................£15  *Phil Stamp Cvrs GA11*
(20) HM Ships Abroad ..................£15  *RN CvsGp*

## 6th November 2008 – LEST WE FORGET
*(1) 1st Poppy; 4 x 81p Country Pictorials*
*(2) Generic Sheet of 20 Poppy stamps and labels*
*(3) 2006, 2007, 2008 Poppy stamps in setenant format*
**SPECIAL HANDSTAMPS        SPONSOR**
**Price Guide Ordinary Covers £3-£5 / Sponsored Covers:**
(1)  FDI - Tallents House...................  *Royal Mail (n.s.c.)*
(2)  FDI - London SW1 ......................  *Royal Mail (n.s.c.)*
(3)  -do- non pictorial version ............  *Royal Mail (n.s.c.)*
(4)  Remembering Glorious Dead......  *Royal Mail (n.s.c.)*
(5)  Monument Road, Birmingham ....  *Royal Mail (n.s.c.)*
(6)  Buckingham Palace Road.......£15  *Benham Coin Cover*
(7)  Parliament Square...................£15  *Benham BLCS 414*
(8)  The Mall, SW1A....................£15  *Benham BLCS 413*

(9)  Whitehall, SW1A......................£20 *Benham (500) 413*
(10) Autographed, Whitehall..........£15 *Westminster*
(11) London SW1 (Cenotaph)......£10 *Buckingham Cvrs 332*
(12) London SW1 (poppy) ............£10 *Buckingham Cvrs 332*
(13) The Poppy, Shirley..................£15 *J Bevan Pubs 145*
(14) Western Front Association.....£15 *P Sheridan*
(15) The Cenotaph, London SW1.£15 *Phil Stamp Cvrs 145*
(16) Operation Muskateer .............£15 *RN CvsGp*
**C.D.S. POSTMARKS Price Guide £7-£10**
(17) Battle, Battle Hill, Battlefield Road, Commons, Lords

## 14th Nov 2008 – Prince of Wales
*Commemorative Stamp Sheet of 10 1st Class Union Flag*
*stamps and Prince of Wales Labels*
**SPECIAL HANDSTAMPS**     **SPONSOR**
Price Guide Ordinary Covers £3-£5 / Sponsored Covers:
(1)  Prince Charles Close .............£15 *Royal Mail*
(2)  Tetbury 60th (oval) .................£15 *Benham*
(3)  Tetbury 60th (circle)...............£15 *Benham*

## 13th January 2009 – DESIGN CLASSICS
*(1) 1st Supermarine Spitfire; 1st Mini Skirt; 1st Mk1 Mini;*
    *1st Anglepoise Lamp; 1st Concorde; 1st K2 Telephone Kiosk;*
    *1st Polypropylene Chair; 1st Penguin Books;*
    *1st London Underground Map; 1st Routemaster Bus*
*(2) Generic Sheet of 20 Mini stamps and labels*
**SPECIAL HANDSTAMPS**     **SPONSOR**
Price Guide Ordinary Covers £3-£5 / Sponsored Covers:
(1)  FDI - Tallents House.................... *Royal Mail (n.s.c.)*
(2)  FDI - Longbridge .......................... *Royal Mail (n.s.c.)*
(3)  -do- non pictorial version ............ *Royal Mail (n.s.c.)*
(4)  Austin Rise, Longbridge ............... *Royal Mail (n.s.c.)*
(5)  50th Anniv Mini Longbridge......£20 *Royal Mail/Royal Mint*
(6)  Longbridge (Mini Motor)......£15 *Benham BLCS Sp14*
(7)  London (Union Flag) ..............£15 *Benham Coin Cover*
(8)  Trafalgar Sq (Routemaster) ...£15 *Benham BLCS 416*
(9)  Duxford (Spitfire)....................£20 *Benham (500) 416*
(10) Filton (Concorde)....................£15 *Benham BLCS 416*
(11) Scampton (Red Arrows) .........£12 *Benham*
(12) Heritage Motor Museum ........£10 *Buckingham Cvrs 333*
(13) Filton (changeable date) ........£10 *Buckingham Cvrs*
(14) Autographed, Bow Street........£15 *Westminster*
(15) Concorde 002 Filton...............£15 *Cam S.C.*
(16) Longbridge (Mini side on) .....£15 *Cotswold*
(17) Spitfire Way, London N1 .......£15 *GB 140*
(18) Cowley, Oxford.......................£15 *Assoc. of GBFDC*
(19) Telephone Kiosk, Bletchley ...£15 *Bletchley PO*
(20) Rainham (Concorde).............£15 *J Bevan Pubs 146*
(21) Strand (model on chair).......£15 *Phil Stamp Cvrs GA12*
(22) Strand (Phil Stamp) ................£15 *Phil Stamp Cvrs 146*
**C.D.S. POSTMARKS Price Guide £7-£10**
(23) Longbridge

## 22nd January 2009 – ROBERT BURNS
*Miniature Sheet: 1st A Man's a Man for a' that;*
*1st Burns Portrait; 2nd, 1st, 50p, 81p Scottish pictorials*
**SPECIAL HANDSTAMPS**     **SPONSOR**
Price Guide Ordinary Covers £3-£5 / Sponsored Covers:
(1)  FDI - Tallents House.................... *Royal Mail (n.s.c.)*
(2)  FDI - Alloway, Ayr ....................... *Royal Mail (n.s.c.)*
(3)  -do- non pictorial version ............ *Royal Mail (n.s.c.)*
(4)  Burns Close, Redditch ................ *Royal Mail (n.s.c.)*
(5)  Alloway, For auld lang syne...£20 *Royal Mail/Royal Mint*
(6)  Edinburgh (thistle) .................£15 *Benham*
(7)  Alloway (portrait)....................£15 *Benham BLCS 418*
(8)  Dumfries (Burns with quill)...£10 *Buckingham Cvrs 334*
(9)  Alloway (quill) .......................£10 *Buckingham Cvrs 334*
(10) Autographed, Alloway............£15 *Westminster*
(11) Alloway (portrait)....................£15 *J Bevan Pubs 147*
(12) Burns World Federation .........£15 *P Sheridan*
(13) Should auld Acquaintance .....£35 *Royal Bank of Scot*
(14) Robert Burns, Dumbarton.....£25 *J Moir Nelson*
(15) Alloway (mouse)......................£15 *Phil Stamp Cvrs 147*
(16) Battle of Killiecrankie ............£15 *Heritage of Britain*
**C.D.S. POSTMARKS Price Guide £7-£10**
(17) Burns Statue, Alloway, Ayr, Kilmarnock, Mauchline etc

## 12th February 2009 – CHARLES DARWIN
*(1) 1st Charles Darwin; 48p Marine Iguana; 50p Finches;*
    *56p Atoll; 72p Bee Orchid; Orang-utan.*
*(2) Mini Sheet: 1st Flightless Cormorant; 1st Giant Tortoise*
    *and Cactus Finch; 81p Marine Iguana; 81p Mockingbird*
*(3) Prestige Stamp Book*
**SPECIAL HANDSTAMPS**     **SPONSOR**
Price Guide Ordinary Covers £3-£5 / Sponsored Covers:
(1)  FDI - Tallents House.................... *Royal Mail (n.s.c.)*
(2)  FDI - Shrewsbury......................... *Royal Mail (n.s.c.)*
(3)  -do- non pictorial version ............ *Royal Mail (n.s.c.)*

## 2009 DESIGN CLASSICS

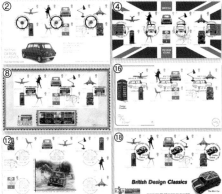

## 2009 ROBERT BURNS

## 2009 CHARLES DARWIN

## 2009 CELEBRATING WALES

## 2009 CONCORDE

## 2009 INDUSTRIAL REVOLUTION

(4)  Downe, Orpington, Kent........£20  *Royal Mail/Royal Mint*
(5)  Darwin House, Birmingham...........  *Royal Mail (n.s.c.)*
(6)  Plymouth (HMS Beagle)........£15  *Benham Coin Cover*
(7)  Regent's Park (iguana) ...........£20  *Benham (500) 420*
(8)  Carlton House (portrait)........£15  *Benham BLCS 420*
(9)  Piccadilly (apes)................£15  *Benham Coin Cover*
(10) Downe (Darwin's finch) .......£20  *Benham (500) 419*
(11) Shrewsbury (portrait) .............£15  *Benham BLCS 419*
(12) Beagle Project, Lawrenny......£10  *Buckingham Cvrs 335*
(13) Cambridge.................................£10  *Buckingham Cvrs 335*
(14) Autographed, Shrewsbury .....£15  *Westminster*
(15) Charles Darwin, Shrewsbury .£15  *J Bevan Pubs 148*
(16) Friends of the Earth................£15  *P Sheridan*
(17) Darwin Road, London W5 ....£15  *GB 141*
(18) Darwin, Bletchley Park..........£15  *Bletchley PO*
(19) Apethorpe ................................£15  *Phil Stamp Cvrs GA13*
(20) Shrewsbury ..............................£15  *Phil Stamp Cvrs 148*
**C.D.S. POSTMARKS Price Guide £7-£10**
(21) Cambridge, The Lizard, Frankwell, Falmouth, Shrewsbury

### 26th Feb 2009 – CELEBRATING WALES
*(1) Miniature Sheet: 2 x 1st Welsh Flag; Welsh Dragon;*
*2 x 78p St.David; Welsh Assembly*

| SPECIAL HANDSTAMPS | SPONSOR |
| --- | --- |

**Price Guide Ordinary Covers £3-£5 / Sponsored Covers:**
(1)  FDI - Tallents House....................  *Royal Mail (n.s.c.)*
(2)  FDI - St Davids .............................  *Royal Mail (n.s.c.)*
(3)  -do- non pictorial version .............  *Royal Mail (n.s.c.)*
(4)  Spring Stampex ..........................  *Royal Mail (n.s.c.)*
(5)  Spring Stampex - Wales ...............  *Royal Mail (n.s.c.)*
(6)  St. Davids Drive, Birmingham .....  *Royal Mail (n.s.c.)*
(7)  Cardiff (dragon)......................£15  *Benham BLCS 422*
(8)  St David's (celtic design) ........£18  *Benham (500) 422*
(9)  Great Little Trains of Wales ..£10  *Buckingham Cvrs 336*
(10) St. David's (dragon) ................£10  *Buckingham Cvrs 336*
(11) Autographed, Cardiff...............£15  *Westminster*
(12) Cardiff (Dragon)....................£15  *Phil Stamp Cvrs GA14*
(13) Cardiff (Welsh Dragon) .........£15  *J Bevan Pubs 149*
(14) Great Little Trains, Tywyn .....£10  *Buckingham Cvrs*
(15) Battle of Dunkeld....................£15  *Heritage of Britain*
**C.D.S. POSTMARKS Price Guide £7-£10**
(16) Cambridge, The Lizard, National Assembly of Wales

### 2nd March 2009 – Concorde
*Generic Sheet of 20 x 1st Concorde + Concorde labels.*

| SPECIAL HANDSTAMPS | SPONSOR |
| --- | --- |

**Price Guide Ordinary Covers £3-£5 / Sponsored Covers:**
(1)  Filton (silhoutte Concorde)....£20  *Royal Mail/Royal Mint*
(2)  Filton (square)..........................£50  *Benham (Set of 4)*
(3)  Heathrow Airport....................£35  *Benham (Pair)*
(4)  Filton (changeable date) ........£15  *Benham*
(5)  Concorde 002 (-do-)................£15  *Cam S.C.*

### 10th Mar 2009 – INDUSTRIAL REVOLUTION
*1st Matthew Boulton; 1st James Watt; 50p Richard Arkwright;*
*50p Josiah Wedgwood; 56p George Stephenson;*
*56p Henry Maudslay; 72p James Brindley; 72p John McAdam*

| SPECIAL HANDSTAMPS | SPONSOR |
| --- | --- |

**Price Guide Ordinary Covers £3-£5 / Sponsored Covers:**
(1)  FDI - Tallents House ....................  *Royal Mail (n.s.c.)*
(2)  FDI - Steam Mills, Cinderford .....  *Royal Mail (n.s.c.)*
(3)  -do- non pictorial version .............  *Royal Mail (n.s.c.)*
(4)  Brindley Wharf, Birmingham .......  *Royal Mail (n.s.c.)*
(5)  Stephenson Drive, Birmingham...  *Royal Mail (n.s.c.)*
(6)  Burslem (vase) ..........................£15  *Benham BLCS 423*
(7)  Birmingham (mills)..................£20  *Benham (500) 423*
(8)  Darlington (Locomotion).......£15  *Benham BLCS 423*
(9)  George Stephenson, Shildon .£10  *Buckingham Cvrs 337*
(10) Autographed, New Canal St.....£15  *Westminster*
(11) Industry Terrace, SW9 ...........£15  *GB142*
(12) Saltaire......................................£15  *Cotswold*
(13) Dudley (teapot)........................£15  *Phil Stamp Cvrs 149*
(14) London (mills) .........................£15  *J Bevan Pubs 150*
(15) Bletchley Park Post Office .....£15  *Bletchley PO*
(16) Battle of Preston.....................£15  *Heritage of Britain*
**C.D.S. POSTMARKS Price Guide £7-£10**
(17) James Watt Dock
    ***British Designs Stamp Book (also issued 10th March):***
(18) Piccadilly (Telephone kiosk)...£15  *Phil Stamp Cvrs 424*
(19) Charing Cross (Routemaster) .£18  *Benham (500) 424*

With effect from The Tudors issue, I am no
longer listing CDS postmarks

See postmark images at: www.bfdc.co.uk/postmarks

Most of your questions will be answered in
the Introduction commencing on Page 1.

## 13 March 2009 – Castles of Northern Ireland
*Generic Sheet of 20 x 1st Northern Ireland + Castle labels.*
**SPECIAL HANDSTAMPS          SPONSOR**
Price Guide Covers £3-£5  / Sponsored Covers:
(1)  Belfast ..........................................£15  Benham

## 21st April 2009 – THE TUDORS
*(1) 1st Henry VII; 1st Henry VIII; 62p Edward VI;*
*    62p Lady  Jane Grey; 81p Mary I; 81p Elizabeth I*
*(2) Miniature Sheet: 1st Mary Rose; 1st Field of Cloth of Gold;*
*    90p Royal Exchange; 90p Sir Francis Drake*
**SPECIAL HANDSTAMPS          SPONSOR**
Price Guide Ordinary Covers £3-£5  / Sponsored Covers:
(1)   FDI - Tallents House....................  Royal Mail (n.s.c.)
(2)   FDI - London SE10......................  Royal Mail (n.s.c.)
(3)   -do- non pictorial version ...........  Royal Mail (n.s.c.)
(4)   Greenwich (Tower).................£25  Royal Mail/Mint
(5)   Hampton Court (timeline) .....£10  Royal Mail cachet cover
(6)   Hampton Court (Tudor rose) £45  Royal Mail Medal cover
(7)   Tudor Road, Birmingham ............  Royal Mail (n.s.c.)
(8)   Portsmouth (Mary Rose) .......£15  Benham BLCS 427
(9)   Hatfield (Queen Elizabeth)....£15  Benham (500) 426
(10) London SE (Henry VIII)........£15  Benham
(11) Cornhill (Grasshopper)..........£15  Benham (500) 427
(12) Tower Hill (Tudor Rose) .......£15  Benham BLCS 426
(13) Last Tudor Queen, Hatfield...£12  Buckingham Cvrs 338
(14) Mary Rose, Portsmouth .........£12  Buckingham Cvrs 338
(15) Povr.Defender Portsmouth....£15  Buckingham Cvrs 109
(16) Autographed, Bosworth Cl.....£15  Westminster
(17) Hampton Ct (Tudor Rose) .....£15  Cotswold
(18) Tudor Way, London ...............£15  GB 143
(19) House of Tudor, London.......£15  J Bevan Pubs 151
(20) Mary Rose, Portsmouth .........£15  P Sheridan
(21) Chopwell, Newcastle ..............£15  Phil Stamp Cvrs 150
(22) Sir Francis Drake, Tavistock .£15  Phil Stamp Cvrs GA15
(23) Bletchley Park PO...................£15  Bletchley Park PO
(24) St Paul's School......................£15  ABC-FDC
        *British Designs Stamp Book 2 (also issued 21st April):*
(26) Austin Rise Longbridge .................  Royal Mail (n.s.c.)
(27) Longbridge, Birmingham........£15  Benham BLCS 428
(28) Fawkham, Longfield................£15  Benham 500 (428)

## 30th April  2009 – Smilers for Kids (2)
*Four stamp sheets: Wild Cherry (Flower Fairies); Jeremy Fisher*
*(Beatrix Potter); Big Ears (Noddy); Miss Sunshine (Mr Men)*
**SPECIAL HANDSTAMPS          SPONSOR**
Price Guide Ordinary Covers £3-£5  / Sponsored Covers:
(1)   Croydon (Fairy) ......................£12  Benham
(2)   London W8 (Frog)...................£12  Benham

## 19th May 2009 – PLANTS & KEW GARDENS
*(1) 10 x 1st: Round-headed Leek; Floating Water-plantain;*
*    Lady's Slipper Orchid; Dwarf Milkwort; Marsh Saxifrage;*
*    Downy Woundwort; Upright Spurge; Sea Knotgrass;*
*    Deptford Pink.*
*(2) Kew Gardens Miniature Sheet: 1st Palm House; 1st*
*    Millennium Seed Bank; 81p Pagoda; 81p Sackler Crossing*
**SPECIAL HANDSTAMPS          SPONSOR**
Price Guide Ordinary Covers £3-£5  / Sponsored Covers:
(1)   FDI - Tallents House....................  Royal Mail (n.s.c.)
(2)   FDI - Kew, Richmond...................  Royal Mail (n.s.c.)
(3)   -do- non pictorial version ...........  Royal Mail (n.s.c.)
(4)   Kew Gardens 250....................£20  Royal Mail/Mint
(5)   Botany Walk, Birmingham .........£15  Benham
(6)   Action for Species, Liverpool £15  Benham BLCS 429
(7)   Kew (Palm House)..................£15  Benham 500 (430)
(8)   Kew (Pagoda)...........................£15  Benham BLCS 430
(9)   Action for Species, Bodelva...£15  Benham (500) 429
(10) Kew, Botanic Gardens .........£12  Buckingham Cvrs 339
(11) Kent Wildlife Trust ................£12  Buckingham Cvrs 339
(12) Autographed, Richmond.........£15  Westminster
(13) Kew Green, Richmond .........£15  GB 144
(14) Plants, London.........................£15  J Bevan Pubs 152
(15) Sefton Park Liverpool ............£15  P Sheridan
(16) Kew Gardens............................£15  Phil Stamp Cvrs 152
(17) Wortwell, Harleston ...............£15  Phil Stamp Cvrs 151
(18) Bletchley Park PO...................£15  Bletchley Park PO

## 21st May  2009 – Flower Arrangers
*Stamp Book: 1st Iris; 1st Tulipa; 4 x 1st Definitives*
**SPECIAL HANDSTAMPS          SPONSOR**
Price Guide Ordinary Covers £3-£5  / Sponsored Covers:
(1)   Kew Gardens, Birmingham....£12  Royal Mail (n.s.c.)
(2)   Halstead (Tulip)......................£12  Benham (500) 431
(3)   London EC2 (Iris)...................£12  Benham BLCS 431

**2009 THE TUDORS**

**2009 PLANTS & KEW GARDENS**

## 2009 MYTHICAL CREATURES

## 2009 POST BOXES

## 2009 FIRE & RESCUE

See postmark images at: www.bfdc.co.uk/postmarks

202

## 16th June 2009 – MYTHICAL CREATURES
*1st Unicorns; 1st Dragons; 62p Giants; 62p Pixies;*
*90p Mermaids; 90p Fairies*

**SPECIAL HANDSTAMPS** **SPONSOR**
Price Guide Ordinary Covers £3-£5 / Sponsored Covers:
(1)   FDI - Tallents House................... *Royal Mail (n.s.c.)*
(2)   FDI - Dragonby, Scunthorpe........... *Royal Mail (n.s.c.)*
(3)   -do- non pictorial version ........... *Royal Mail (n.s.c.)*
(4)   Unicorn Hill, Redditch ................. *Royal Mail (n.s.c.)*
(5)   Sea, Illminster ..........................£15 *Benham BLCS 432*
(6)   Fairy Cross, Bideford...............£15 *Benham 500 (432)*
(7)   Ivor the Engine.........................£12 *Buckingham Cvrs 340*
(8)   Autographed, Dragon's Green .£15 *Westminster*
(9)   Unicorn Walk, Greenhithe ....£15 *GB 145*
(10) Mythical Creatures, London..£15 *J Bevan Pubs 153*
(11) Wookey Hole Caves ...............£15 *P Sheridan*
(12) Cottingley, Bingley ..................£15 *Assoc. of GBFDC*
(13) Elveden...................................£15 *Phil Stamp Cvrs AQ5*
(14) Dragonby (Dragon)................£15 *Phil Stamp Cvrs 153*
(15) Dragonby (Unicorn) ..............£15 *Phil Stamp GA16*
(16) Bletchley Park Post Office ....£15 *Bletchley Park PO*
(17) Battle of Prestonpans .............£15 *Heritage of Britain*

## 21st July 2009 – Moon Landing
*Commemorative Stamp Sheet of 10 1st Class Union Flag*
*stamps and 40th Anniversary of Moon Landing labels*
**SPECIAL HANDSTAMPS** **SPONSOR**
Price Guide Ordinary Covers £3-£5 / Sponsored Covers:
(1)   Buckingham Palace Road.......£15 *Benham (500) SpG65*
(2)   Exploration Drive Leicester...£15 *Benham BLCS Sp20*

## 3rd August 2009 – Thaipex Stamp Expo
*Generic Sheet: 1st Hello + labels depicting tuk-tuk*
**Price Guide Ordinary Cvrs £10 - £15 / No Sponsored Covers**

## 18th August 2009 – POST BOXES
*(1) Mini Sheet: 1st George V Wall Box; 56p Edward VII*
*Ludlow Box; 81p Victorian Lamp Box; 90p Elizabeth II*
*Wall Box.*
*(2) Prestige Stamp Book*
**SPECIAL HANDSTAMPS** **SPONSOR**
Price Guide Ordinary Covers £3-£5 / Sponsored Covers:
(1)   FDI - Tallents House................... *Royal Mail (n.s.c.)*
(2)   FDI - Wakefield ............................ *Royal Mail (n.s.c.)*
(3)   -do- non pictorial version ............ *Royal Mail (n.s.c.)*
(4)   FDI - Tallents Hse (mailcoach) .. *Royal Mail (n.s.c.)*
(5)   FDI - London EC1......................... *Royal Mail (n.s.c.)*
(6)   -do- non pictorial version ............ *Royal Mail (n.s.c.)*
(7)   Hill Street, Birmingham .............. *Royal Mail (n.s.c.)*
(8)   London WC1 (Victoria)..........£15 *Benham*
(9)   Windsor (Letter Box) .............£15 *Benham BLCS 433*
(10) Southampton (George VI) .....£15 *Benham BLCS 433*
(11) Wakefield (1809 Letter Box) .£15 *Benham 500 (433)*
(12) London EC1A (Postman).......£15 *Benham*
(13) Bath Postal Museum...............£12 *Buckingham Cvrs 342*
(14) Autographed, London ECIV...£15 *Westminster*
(15) Letter Box Lane, Sevenoaks ..£15 *GB 146*
(16) Wakefield (Pillar Box)............£15 *J Bevan Pubs 154*
(17) Wakefield Post Boxes.............£12 *Cotswold*
(18) Sheridan Philatelic Covers.....£15 *P Sheridan*
(19) Box, Corsham.........................£15 *Phil Stamp Cvrs 154*
(20) Birmingham Philatelic Soc.....£30 *Birmingham Phil Soc*
(21) Burnley v Manchester Utd ......£15 *N.Eng SHCentre*
(22) Second Battle of Falkirk........£15 *Heritage of Britain*
      *Concorde Stamp Book (also issued 18th August):*
(23) Concorde Tower .....................£15 *Royal Mail (n.s.c.)*
(24) Heathrow ...............................£18 *Benham*

## 1st September 2009 – FIRE & RESCUE
*1st Firefighting; 54p Chemical Fire; 56p Emergency Service;*
*62p Flood Rescue; 81p Search and Rescue; 90p Fire Safety*
**SPECIAL HANDSTAMPS** **SPONSOR**
Price Guide Ordinary Covers £3-£5 / Sponsored Covers:
(1)   FDI - Tallents House................... *Royal Mail (n.s.c.)*
(2)   FDI - Hose, Melton Mowbray ..... *Royal Mail (n.s.c.)*
(3)   -do- non pictorial version ............ *Royal Mail (n.s.c.)*
(4)   Moreton-in-Marsh ....................... *Royal Mail/Royal Mint*
(5)   Fire Station Road, Birmingham .. *Royal Mail (n.s.c.)*
(6)   Chester, Cheshire ....................£15 *Benham 500 (436)*
(7)   Union Street, London SE1.....£15 *Benham BLCS 436*
(8)   Auxiliary Fire Service.............£12 *Buckingham Cvrs 343*
(9)   AFS Auxiliary Fire Service.....£12 *Buckingham Cvrs 343*
(10) Autographed, Herts ................£15 *Westminster*
(11) Fire Bell Lane, Surbiton ........£15 *GB 147*
(12) Wolverhampton .......................£15 *J Bevan Pubs 155*
(13) Engine Lane, Liverpool .........£15 *Assoc. of GBFDC*
(14) Sleaford, Lincs .......................£15 *P Sheridan*

(15) Hose ...........................................£15  *Phil Stamp Cvrs 155*
(16) Germany Invades Poland .......£15  *Polish Institute*
(17) Battle of Culloden ...................£15  *Heritage of Britain*

## 17th Sept 2009 – ROYAL NAVY UNIFORMS
*(1) 1st Flight Deck Officer 2009; 1st Captain 1941;*
*1st Second Officer WRNS 1918; 90p Able Seaman 1880;*
*90p Royal Marines 1805; 90p Admiral 1795*
*(2) Prestige Stamp Book*

| SPECIAL HANDSTAMPS | SPONSOR |
| --- | --- |

**Price Guide Ordinary Covers £3-£5 / Sponsored Covers:**
(1)  FDI - Tallents House.......................  *Royal Mail (n.s.c.)*
(2)  FDI - Portsmouth..........................  *Royal Mail (n.s.c.)*
(3)  -do- non pictorial version ...........  *Royal Mail (n.s.c.)*
(4)  Admiral's Way, Rowley Regis.......  *Royal Mail (n.s.c.)*
(5)  Autumn Stampex ..........................  *Royal Mail (n.s.c.)*
(6)  -do- Royal Navy Uniforms...........  *Royal Mail (n.s.c.)*
(7)  Greenwich (ship's wheel).......£15  *Benham 500 (437)*
(8)  Portsmouth (anchor) ..............£15  *Benham BLCS 437*
(9)  Faslane (Navy Emblem) ........£15  *Benham Coin Cover*
(10) Devonport (White Ensign).....£15  *Benham Coin Cover*
(11) HMS Warrior...........................£12  *Buckingham Cvrs 344*
(12) Autographed, Whitehall..........£15  *Westminster*
(13) Nelson Place, London............£15  *GB 148*
(14) Portsmouth (Nelson)..............£15  *J Bevan Pubs 156*
(15) Western Approaches, L'pool £15  *Assoc. of GBFDC*
(16) Historical Maritime Society...£25  *P Sheridan*
(17) Admiralty Library....................£15  *Cotswold*
(18) HMS Phil, Portsmouth............£15  *Phil Stamp Cvrs 156*
(19) Russia Invades Poland ...........£15  *Polish Institute*
(20) Battle of Britain .......................£15  *Heritage of Britain*
     *Mini Skirt Stamp Book (also issued 17th September):*
(21) Knightsbridge Rd, Solihull .....£15  *Royal Mail (n.s.c.)*
(22) Chelsea, London SW3 ............£18  *Benham*
(23) Blackheath, London SE3 .......£18  *Benham*

## 18th September 2009 – Big Ben
*Commemorative Stamp Sheet of 10 1st Class Union Flag*
*stamps and 150th Anniversary of Big Ben labels*

| SPECIAL HANDSTAMPS | SPONSOR |
| --- | --- |

**Price Guide Ordinary Covers £3-£5 / Sponsored Covers:**
(1)  Big Ben (Bell)...........................£15  *Royal Mail/Royal Mint*
(2)  Parliament Square...................£15  *Benham BLCSsp22*
(3)  Parliament Sq (clock face) ....£15  *Benham SPG 68*
(4)  Autumn Stampex.....................£15  *Royal Mail (n.s.c.)*

## 7th Oct 2009 – Cambridge University
*Commemorative Stamp Sheet of 10 1st Fireworks stamps and*
*800th Anniversary of Cambridge University labels*

| SPECIAL HANDSTAMPS | SPONSOR |
| --- | --- |

**Price Guide Ordinary Covers £3-£5 / Sponsored Covers:**
(1)  Cambridge (Shield).................£15  *Benham BLCSsp23*

## 8th Oct 2009 – EMINENT BRITONS
*(1) 1st Fred Perry; 1st Henry Purcell; 1st Sir Matt Busby;*
*1st William Gladstone; 1st Mary Wollstonecraft;*
*1st Sir Arthur Conan Doyle; 1st Donald Campbell;*
*1st Judy Fryd; 1st Samuel Johnson; 1st Sir Martin Ryle*

| SPECIAL HANDSTAMPS | SPONSOR |
| --- | --- |

**Price Guide Ordinary Covers £3-£5 / Sponsored Covers:**
(1)  FDI - Tallents House.....................  *Royal Mail (n.s.c.)*
(2)  FDI - Britannia Bacup ...................  *Royal Mail (n.s.c.)*
(3)  -do- non pictorial version ............  *Royal Mail (n.s.c.)*
(4)  Gladstone Road, Birmingham......  *Royal Mail (n.s.c.)*
(5)  Edinburgh (Holmes)...............£15  *Benham BLCS 440*
(6)  London (music) .......................£15  *Benham BLCS 440*
(7)  Manchester (football).............£15  *Benham 500 (440)*
(8)  Coniston (Bluebird) ................£15  *Benham 500 (440)*
(9)  Sherlock Holmes, Baker St....£12  *Buckingham Cvrs 345*
(10) Matt Busby, Manchester........£12  *Buckingham Cvrs 345*
(11) Autographed, Whitehall.........£15  *Westminster*
(12) Shakespeare Way, Feltham....£15  *GB 149*
(13) Westminster (Conductor)....£15  *J Bevan Pubs 157*
(14) Gladstone St, Liverpool........£15  *Assoc. of GBFDC*
(15) Bosom Buddies, Widnes.......£15  *P Sheridan*
(16) Coniston ................................£15  *Phil Stamp Cvrs 157*
(17) Sir Matt Busby, Manchester ..£15  *NE Special H Centre*

## 21st October 2009  – Italia Stamp Expo
*Generic Sheet: 1st Hello + labels depicting Italian landmarks*
**Price Guide Ordinary Cvrs £10 - £15 / No Sponsored Covers**

At www.bfdc.co.uk you will find over 30,000
British FDCs available.  This visual resource
allows you to search by cover producer, cover
series, stamp type, postmark - and much more.

## 2009 ROYAL NAVY UNIFORMS

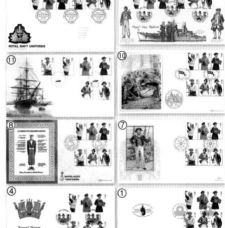

## 2009 EMINENT BRITONS

203

## 2009 OLYMPICS

## 2009 CHRISTMAS

## 2010 CLASSIC ALBUM COVERS

See postmark images at: www.bfdc.co.uk/postmarks

## 22nd October 2009 – OLYMPICS

*(1) 1st Canoe Slalom; 1st Paralympic Games: Archery;*
*1st Athletics: Track; 1st Aquatics; 1st Paralympic Games:*
*Boccia; 1st Judo; 1st Paralympic Games: Equestrian;*
*1st Badminton; 1st Weightlifting; 1st Basketball*
*(2) Commemorative Sheet with all 10 stamps*

**SPECIAL HANDSTAMPS**     **SPONSOR**
Price Guide Ordinary Covers £3-£5 / Sponsored Covers:

| | | |
|---|---|---|
| (1) | FDI - Tallents House.................... | *Royal Mail (n.s.c.)* |
| (2) | FDI - Badminton........................... | *Royal Mail (n.s.c.)* |
| (3) | -do- non pictorial version ............ | *Royal Mail (n.s.c.)* |
| (4) | Countdown to London .................. | *Royal Mail/Royal Mint* |
| (5) | Archers Close, Birmingham......... | *Royal Mail (n.s.c.)* |
| (6) | Sporting Disciplines (flag).....£15 | *Benham BLCS 441* |
| (7) | -do- London (fireworks)..........£15 | *BenhamBLCSsp24* |
| (8) | -do- London (runner).............£15 | *Benham BLCS 441* |
| (9) | -do- Greenwich (equestrian)..£15 | *Benham 500 (441)* |
| (10) | -do- Broxbourne (canoe).......£12 | *Benham 500 (441)* |
| (11) | Yngling Team, Weymouth.....£15 | *Buckingham Cvrs 341* |
| (12) | Ben Ainslie, Falmouth............£12 | *Buckingham Cvrs 341* |
| (13) | Autographed, Stratford E15....£15 | *Westminster* |
| (14) | Stratford E15............................£15 | *Westminster* |
| (15) | London (shuttlecock).............£15 | *Cotswold* |
| (16) | English Field Archery.............£15 | *P Sheridan* |
| (17) | Wembley .................................£15 | *J Bevan Pubs 158* |
| (18) | Kuzushi Judo, Slough.............£15 | *Kuzushi Judo Club* |

## 3rd November 2009 – CHRISTMAS

*(1) 2nd Madonna; 2nd (Large) Madonna; 1st Madonna and*
*Child; 1st (Large) Madonna and Child; 56p Joseph;*
*90p Wise Man; £1.35 Shepherd*
*(2) Miniature Sheet; (3) Generic Sheet; (4) Stamp Books*

**SPECIAL HANDSTAMPS**     **SPONSOR**
Price Guide Ordinary Covers £3-£5 / Sponsored Covers:

| | | |
|---|---|---|
| (1) | FDI - Tallents House.................... | *Royal Mail (n.s.c.)* |
| (2) | FDI - Bethlehem .......................... | *Royal Mail (n.s.c.)* |
| (3) | -do- non pictorial version ............ | *Royal Mail (n.s.c.)* |
| (4) | Seasons Greetings, Bethlehem ... | *Royal Mail (n.s.c.)* |
| (5) | Noel Avenue, Birmingham ......... | *Royal Mail (n.s.c.)* |
| (6) | Rye, East Sussex ......................£15 | *Benham 500 (442)* |
| (7) | Upavon, Pewsey........................£15 | *Benham BLCS 442* |
| (8) | Ormesby, Great Yarmouth.......£15 | *Benham Coin Cover* |
| (9) | Staveley, Keswick....................£15 | *Benham BLCS 443* |
| (10) | Minehead, Somerset ...............£12 | *Benham 500 (443)* |
| (11) | Glossop, Derbyshire ...............£12 | *Buckingham Cvrs 346* |
| (12) | Stained Glass Museum, Ely ...£12 | *Buckingham Cvrs 346* |
| (13) | Autographed, Mistletoe Grn...£15 | *Westminster* |
| (14) | Christmas Lane, Farnham .....£15 | *GB 150* |
| (15) | York Glaziers Trust ................£15 | *Cotswold* |
| (16) | Westminster Cathedral...........£15 | *P Sheridan* |
| (17) | London (angels) .....................£15 | *J Bevan Pubs 159* |
| (18) | Staining, Blackpool.................£15 | *Phil Stamp Cvrs 158* |
| (19) | Marshal Jozef Pilsudski..........£15 | *Polish Institute* |

## 4th November 2009 – Monaco Stamp Expo

*Generic Sheet: 1st Hello + labels depicting Italian landmarks*
Price Guide Ordinary Cvrs £10 - £15 / No Sponsored Covers

## 30th November 2009 – Castles of Scotland

*Generic Sheet of 20 x 1st Scottish flag + Castle labels.*

**SPECIAL HANDSTAMPS**     **SPONSOR**
Price Guide Ordinary Covers £3-£5 / Sponsored Covers:

| | | |
|---|---|---|
| (1) | Edinburgh (Castle)..................£15 | *Benham BLCS sp26* |
| (2) | Flying Scotsman .....................£15 | *Buckingham Cvrs* |

## 7th Jan 2010 – CLASSIC ALBUM COVERS

*(1) 1st The Division Bell; 1st A Rush of Blood to the Head;*
*1st Parklife; 1st Power Corruption and Lies; 1st Let It Bleed;*
*1st London Calling; 1st Tubular Bells; 1st IV;*
*1st Screamadelica; 1st Ziggy Stardust*
*(2) Souvenir Sheet   (3) Prestige Stamp Book*

**SPECIAL HANDSTAMPS**     **SPONSOR**
Price Guide Ordinary Covers £3-£5 / Sponsored Covers:

| | | |
|---|---|---|
| (1) | FDI - Tallents House.................... | *Royal Mail (n.s.c.)* |
| (2) | FDI - Oldfield ............................. | *Royal Mail (n.s.c.)* |
| (3) | -do- non pictorial version ............ | *Royal Mail (n.s.c.)* |
| (4) | Plant Street, Cradley Heath....... | *Royal Mail (n.s.c.)* |
| (5) | Glastonbury, Somerset...........£15 | *Benham BLCS 445* |
| (6) | Isle of Wight ..........................£15 | *Benham BLCS 446* |
| (7) | Park Lane, London..................£15 | *Benham 500 (446)* |
| (8) | Reading, Berkshire .................£15 | *Benham BLCS 445* |
| (9) | Engineers Way, Wembley......£12 | *Benham 500 (445)* |
| (10) | The 02 Greenwich ..................£15 | *Buckingham Cvrs 401* |
| (11) | Pirate Radio, Frinton on Sea .£12 | *Buckingham Cvrs 401* |
| (12) | Autographed, Bowie Street ....£15 | *Westminster* |
| (13) | Regal Way, Harrow .................£15 | *GB 151* |
| (14) | Classic Album Art, London ...£15 | *Cotswold* |

(15) Music Industries Association..£15 *P Sheridan*
(16) London (Gramophone) .........£15 *J Bevan Pubs 160*
(17) Sound, Nantwich ....................£15 *Phil Stamp Cvrs 159*
(18) Bells Lane, Liverpool .............£15 *Assoc. of GBFDC*
(19) Rolling Stones, London .........£15 *P Barrett*
(20) Pink Floyd The Division Bell..£15 *New Stamp Centre*
(21) Classic Albums, Brixton.........£15 *Peter Barrett*
(22) Royal Bank of Scotland .........£15 *RBS Philatelic Society*
    *Olympics Stamp Book No.1 (also issued 7th January):*
(23) Birmingham (Judo)..................£18 *Royal Mail (n.s.c.)*
(24) Stratford E15 (Archery)..........£18 *Benham BLCS 448*
(25) London W2 (Union flag)........£18 *Benham BLCS 448*

## 26th January 2010 – SMILERS
*(1) 1st Aeroplane; 1st Car; 1st Royal Seal; 1st Birthday Cake;*
*1st Train; 1st Ocean Liner; 1st Poppy; 1st Present;*
*'Europe' Bird carrying letter; 'World' Plane with Hello banner*
*(2) Generic Sheet containing mixture of above stamps*

**SPECIAL HANDSTAMPS**    **SPONSOR**
Price Guide Ordinary Covers £3-£5 / Sponsored Covers:
(1) FDI - Tallents House.....................*Royal Mail (n.s.c.)*
(2) FDI - Happy Valley, Malvern.......*Royal Mail (n.s.c.)*
(3) -do- non pictorial version ............*Royal Mail (n.s.c.)*
(4) Crown Street Birmingham ...........*Royal Mail (n.s.c.)*
(5) London WC (Flag)...................£15 *Benham BLCS 449*
(6) London SW1 (Crown) ...........£15 *Benham (500) 449*
(7) London W2 (Car)...................£15 *Benham*
(8) Croydon (Aeroplane) .............£15 *Benham BLCS 449*
(9) Liverpool...................................£12 *Buckingham Cvrs 402*
(10) Derby (Steam engine).............£15 *J Bevan Pubs 161*
(11) Revolution & Restoration .....£15 *Westminster*
(12) Up Helly AA, Lerwick ...........£15 *Up Helly AA*
(13) St Magnus Cathedral....................*Royal Mail (n.s.c.)*

## 2nd February 2010 – GIRLGUIDING
*1st Rainbows; 56p Brownies; 81p Guides; 90p Senior Section*

**SPECIAL HANDSTAMPS**    **SPONSOR**
Price Guide Ordinary Covers £3-£5 / Sponsored Covers:
(1) FDI - Tallents House.....................*Royal Mail (n.s.c.)*
(2) FDI - Guide, Blackburn ...............*Royal Mail (n.s.c.)*
(3) -do- non pictorial version ............*Royal Mail (n.s.c.)*
(4) HQ Girlguiding 100 Years.....£15 *Royal Mail/Royal Mint*
(5) Venture Way, Birmingham .........*Royal Mail (n.s.c.)*
(6) London W2 (Baden-Powell)..£15 *Benham BLCS 450*
(7) Chesterfield (Guide) ..............£15 *Benham (500) 450*
(8) Crystal Palace (100).................£12 *Buckingham Cvrs 403*
(9) Autographed, Rainbow Ave ..£15 *Westminster*
(10) Crystal Palace (Cake) .............£15 *Cotswold*
(11) Birmingham (Rainbow) ...........£15 *J Bevan Pubs 162*
(12) Crystal Palace (Guide) ...........£15 *Phil Stamp GA17*

## 25 February 2010 – THE ROYAL SOCIETY
*(1) 1st Robert Boyle; 1st Isaac Newton; 1st Benjamin Franklin;*
*1st Edward Jenner; 1st Charles Babbage;*
*1st Alfred Russell Wallace; 1st Joseph Lister; 1st Ernest*
*Rutherford; 1st Dorothy Hodgkin; 1st Nicholas Shackleton*
*(2) Prestige Stamp Book*

**SPECIAL HANDSTAMPS**    **SPONSOR**
Price Guide Ordinary Covers £3-£5 / Sponsored Covers:
(1) FDI - Tallents House.....................*Royal Mail (n.s.c.)*
(2) FDI - London SW1 .......................*Royal Mail (n.s.c.)*
(3) -do- non pictorial version ............*Royal Mail (n.s.c.)*
(4) London (If I have seen. . .) ....£15 *Royal Mail/Royal Mint*
(5) Newton Road, Birmingham.........*Royal Mail (n.s.c.)*
(6) Stampex (Royal Society crest) ....*Royal Mail (n.s.c.)*
(7) Stampex (Magnifying glass) .........*Royal Mail (n.s.c.)*
(8) Carlton House Terrace...........£15 *Benham*
(9) Cambridge (Telescope) ..........£15 *Benham*
(10) London EC2 (Key)..................£15 *Benham (500) 451*
(11) London SW1 (Cow) ...............£15 *Benham BLCS 451*
(12) London SW1 (Planets)............£15 *Benham BLCS 452*
(13) London SW1.............................£12 *Buckingham Cvrs 404*
(14) Autographed, Royal Parade ...£15 *Westminster*
(15) Catalyst Science Discovery ....£15 *P Sheridan*
(16) Evolution Wallace Road........£15 *GB 152*
(17) Cambridge (Newton)..............£15 *J Bevan Pubs 163*
(18) Chemistry, Whitchurch...........£15 *Phil Stamp Cvrs 160*
    *Olympics Stamp Book No.2 (also issued 25th February):*
(19) Birmingham (Basketball)........£18 *Royal Mail (n.s.c.)*
(20) Stratford E15 (Runner)...........£18 *Benham (500) 453*
(21) Stratford E15 (Basketball)......£18 *Benham BLCS 453*

## 1st March 2010 – Castles of Wales
*Generic Sheet of 20 x 1st Wales + Castle labels.*

**SPECIAL HANDSTAMPS**    **SPONSOR**
Price Guide Ordinary Covers £3-£5 / Sponsored Covers:
(1) Caernarfon ................................£15 *Benham*

### 2010 SMILERS

### 2010 GIRLGUIDING

### 2010 THE ROYAL SOCIETY

## 2010 BATTERSEA DOGS & CATS HOME

## 2010 THE STEWARTS

## 2010 MAMMALS

## 2010 KING GEORGE V ACCESSION

### 11th Mar 2010 – BATTERSEA DOGS & CATS
*10 x 1st Dogs and Cats*
**SPECIAL HANDSTAMPS          SPONSOR**
**Price Guide Ordinary Covers £3-£5 / Sponsored Covers:**
(1)  FDI - Tallents House ..................... *Royal Mail (n.s.c.)*
(2)  FDI - London SW8 ....................... *Royal Mail (n.s.c.)*
(3)  -do- non pictorial version ............. *Royal Mail (n.s.c.)*
(4)  Battersea - 150 Years ............. £10 *Royal Mail/Royal Mint*
(5)  Dogkennel Lane, Halesowen ....... *Royal Mail (n.s.c.)*
(6)  London SW8 (dog) ................. £15 *Benham (500) 454*
(7)  Ash, Sevenoaks (cat) ............. £15 *Benham BLCS 454*
(8)  Black Dog, Crediton ............... £15 *Buckingham Cvrs 405*
(9)  Catstree, Bridgnorth ............. £15 *Buckingham Cvrs 405*
(10) Autographed, Battersea SW8 .£15 *Westminster*
(11) Missing Pets Register ............ £15 *P Sheridan*
(12) Norton, Suffolk ...................... £15 *J Bevan Pubs 163*
(13) Halewood, Liverpool ............. £15 *Assoc. of GBFDC*
(14) Battersea ............................. £15 *Phil Stamp Cvrs 161*
(15) Thrive .................................. £15 *ABC FDC*
(16) Iron Mike Tyson, Wigan ........ £15 *Dawn Covers*

### 23th March 2010 – THE STEWARTS
*(1) 1st James I; 1st James II; 1st James III; 62p James IV;*
*62p James V; 81p Mary; 81p James VI*
*(2) Miniature Sheet: 1st St Andrews University; 1st College of*
*Surgeons; 81p Court of Session; 81p John Knox*
**SPECIAL HANDSTAMPS          SPONSOR**
**Price Guide Ordinary Covers £3-£5 / Sponsored Covers:**
(1)  FDI - Tallents House ..................... *Royal Mail (n.s.c.)*
(2)  FDI - Linlithgow ........................... *Royal Mail (n.s.c.)*
(3)  -do- non pictorial version ............. *Royal Mail (n.s.c.)*
(4)  Stirling Castle (timeline) ........ £10 *Royal Mail cachet cover*
(5)  Linlithgow (thistle) ................. £45 *Royal Mail Medal cover*
(6)  James Road, Birmingham ............. *Royal Mail (n.s.c.)*
(7)  Edinburgh (thistle) ................. £15 *Benham (500) 456*
(8)  Perth (unicorn) ...................... £15 *Benham (500) 455*
(9)  Scone (Scottish lion) ............. £15 *Benham BLCS 455*
(10) St Andrews (flag) .................. £15 *Benham BLCS 456*
(11) Mary Queen Scots Jedburgh . £15 *Buckingham Cvrs 406*
(12) Scottish Reformation ............ £15 *Buckingham Cvrs 406*
(13) Autographed, Stewart St ........ £15 *Westminster*
(14) Stirling (thistle) ..................... £15 *Cotswold*
(15) Stewart Street, London N14 . £15 *GB 153*
(16) Stewarton .............................. £15 *Phil Stamp Cvrs 162*
(17) Edinburgh .............................. £15 *J Bevan Pubs 164*

### 6th April 2010 – Pink Floyd
*Souvenir Sheet with 10 x 1st Pink Floyd Division Bell*
**SPECIAL HANDSTAMPS          SPONSOR**
**Price Guide Ordinary Covers £15 / Sponsored Covers:**
(1)  Britannia Row, Islington ........ £25 *Benham*
(2)  Ely, Cambridgeshire ............... £25 *Benham*

### 13th April 2010 – MAMMALS
*1st Humpback Whale; 1st Wildcat; 1st Brown Long-eared Bat;*
*1st Polecat; 1st Sperm Whale; 1st Water Vole; 1st Greater*
*Horseshoe Bat; 1st Otter; 1st Dormouse; 1st Hedgehog*
**SPECIAL HANDSTAMPS          SPONSOR**
**Price Guide Ordinary Covers £3-£5 / Sponsored Covers:**
(1)  FDI - Tallents House ..................... *Royal Mail (n.s.c.)*
(2)  FDI - Batts Corner, Farnham ...... *Royal Mail (n.s.c.)*
(3)  -do- non pictorial version ............. *Royal Mail (n.s.c.)*
(4)  Otter Croft, Birmingham ............. *Royal Mail (n.s.c.)*
(5)  Sidlesham, Chichester ............ £15 *Benham (500) 460*
(6)  N Petherwin, Launceston ...... £15 *Benham BLCS 460*
(7)  Scottish Wildcat ..................... £15 *Buckingham Cvrs 407*
(8)  British Hedgehog Society ...... £15 *Buckingham Cvrs 407*
(9)  Autographed, Otter Walk ...... £15 *Westminster*
(10) Whales Yard .......................... £15 *GB 154*
(11) The Mammal Society .............. £15 *P Sheridan*
(12) Farnham ................................ £15 *J Bevan Pubs 165*
(13) Otterspool, Liverpool ............ £15 *Assoc. of GBFDC*
(14) Mousehole ............................. £15 *Phil Stamp Cvrs 163*

### 6th May 2010 – KING GEORGE V
*1st Queen Elizabeth & King George V;*
*£1 King George V Downey and Mackennal Heads*
**SPECIAL HANDSTAMPS          SPONSOR**
**Price Guide Ordinary Covers £3-£5 / Sponsored Covers:**
(1)  FDI - Tallents House ..................... *Royal Mail (n.s.c.)*
(2)  FDI - Sandringham ..................... *Royal Mail (n.s.c.)*
(3)  -do- non pictorial version ............. *Royal Mail (n.s.c.)*
(4)  Royal Philatelic Collection ... £35 *Royal Mail Ingot Cvr*
(5)  George St, Birmingham ............... *Royal Mail (n.s.c.)*
(6)  George V (Portrait - circle) .... £15 *Benham BLCS 461*
(7)  George V (Portrait - oval) ...... £15 *D593*
(8)  Philatelist King (Crown) ........ £15 *Benham (500) 461*

(9) Festival of Stamps (Dolphins)..£15 *Benham BLCS 462*
(10) Festival of Stamps ..................£15 *Benham Coin Cover*
(11) GvR (shield) Windsor ............£15 *Buckingham Cvrs 408*
(12) Autographed, London SW1...£15 *Westminster*
(13) GvR, London SW1 .................£15 *Westminster*
(14) King George V College ...........£15 *P Sheridan*
(15) King George V Birmingham ..£15 *J Bevan Pubs 166*
(16) National Police Dog Trials.....£15 *Lincs Police Dog Stn*

## 8th May 2010 – FESTIVAL OF STAMPS
*(1) Miniature Sheet: 2 x 1st Wembley; 2 x £1 Seahorses*
*(2) 6th May Accession Miniature Sheet with overprint*
*(3) London 2010 Exhibition Souvenir Sheet (mixed definitives)*
*(4) Prestige Stamp Book  (5) Smilers Generic Sheet*
*(5) London 2010 Exhibition Generic Sheet*
**SPECIAL HANDSTAMPS        SPONSOR**
**Price Guide Ordinary Covers £3-£5  / Sponsored Covers:**
(1) FDI - Tallents House.....................*Royal Mail (n.s.c.)*
(2) FDI - London N1...........................*Royal Mail (n.s.c.)*
(3) -do- non pictorial version .............*Royal Mail (n.s.c.)*
(4) The King's Stamps, London N1....*Royal Mail (n.s.c.)*
(5) London 2010 Festival of Stamps. *Royal Mail (n.s.c.)*
(6) George St, Birmingham................*Royal Mail (n.s.c.)*
(7) Festival of Stamps (Dolphins)..£15 *Benham*
(8) Festival of Stamps, SW1A .....£15 *Benham*
(9) Islington, London N1.............£15 *Benham (500) 463*
(10) London (Tower Bridge).........£15 *Benham*
(11) London (Magnifying Glass) ...£15 *Benham BLCS 463*
(12) Islington (Maltese Cross)........£15 *Buckingham Cvrs 409*
(13) Autographed, London SW1 ...£15 *Westminster*
(14) GvR, London SW1 .................£15 *Westminster*
(15) London (Britannia)................£15 *Cotswold*
(16) British Empire, Wembley .....£15 *P Sheridan*
(17) Wembley ...............................£15 *Phil Stamp Cvrs 164*
(18) National Police Dog Trials.....£15 *Lincs Police Dog Stn*
(19) Chesterfield FC ......................£15 *North England SHC*

## 13th May 2010 – BRITAIN ALONE
*(1) 1st Churchill; 1st Land Girls; 60p Home Guard;*
*60p Evacuees; 67p Air Raid Wardens; 67p Women in*
*Factories; 97p Royal Broadcast; 97p Fire Service*
*(2) Miniature Sheet - Dunkirk  (3) Prestige Stamp Book*
**SPECIAL HANDSTAMPS        SPONSOR**
**Price Guide Ordinary Covers £3-£5  / Sponsored Covers:**
(1) FDI - Tallents House.....................*Royal Mail (n.s.c.)*
(2) FDI - Dover, Kent..........................*Royal Mail (n.s.c.)*
(3) -do- non pictorial version .............*Royal Mail (n.s.c.)*
(4) Britain Alone, London N1............*Royal Mail (n.s.c.)*
(5) Dunkirk 70th Anniv, Dover .........*Royal Mail (n.s.c.)*
(6) Churchill Rd, Birmingham...........*Royal Mail (n.s.c.)*
(7) Dover (Coat of Arms) ..............£15 *Benham BLCS468*
(8) London (Evacuee)....................£15 *Benham*
(9) London (Fireman)...................£15 *Benham*
(10) London SE1 (Soldier) .............£15 *Benham BLCS 467*
(11) Westerham (Churchill) ..........£15 *Benham (500) 467*
(12) Dunkirk Little Ships, Dover ..£15 *Buckingham Cvrs 410*
(13) Churchill Centre, Oxford.......£15 *Buckingham Cvrs 410*
(14) Land Girls, Womenswold ......£15 *Buckingham Cvrs*
(15) Autographed, Churchill Walk.£15 *Westminster*
(16) Warden Rd, London NW5.....£15 *GB 154*
(17) Surviving the Blitz, Stockport.£15 *P Sheridan*
(18) Britain Alone, London ...........£15 *J Bevan Pubs 167*
(19) Churchill, Winscombe.............£15 *Phil Stamp Cvrs 165*

## 18th May 2010 – Halley's Comet
*Commemorative Stamp Sheet of 10 Union Flag stamps and*
*Halley's Comet labels*
**SPECIAL HANDSTAMPS        SPONSOR**
**Price Guide Ordinary Covers £3-£5  / Sponsored Covers:**
(1) Shoreditch (Halley portrait) ..£15 *Benham*

## 15th June 2010 – THE STUARTS
*(1) 1st James I; 1st CharlesI; 60p Charles II; 60p James II;*
*67p William III; 67p Mary II; 88p Anne*
*(2) Miniature Sheet: 1st William Harvey; 60p Civil War;*
*88p John Milton; 97p Castle Howard*
**SPECIAL HANDSTAMPS        SPONSOR**
**Price Guide Ordinary Covers £3-£5  / Sponsored Covers:**
(1) FDI - Tallents House.....................*Royal Mail (n.s.c.)*
(2) FDI - Royal Oak, Filey ................*Royal Mail (n.s.c.)*
(3) -do- non pictorial version .............*Royal Mail (n.s.c.)*
(4) Kensington Palace (timeline).£15 *Royal Mail cachet cover*
(5) Stuarts Road, Birmingham.........*Royal Mail (n.s.c.)*
(6) London SW1 (Crown) .............£15 *Benham BLCS 470*
(7) Stuarts, London .......................£15 *Benham (500) 471*
(8) Naseby (Roundhead)...............£15 *Benham BLCS 471*
(9) Whitehall (Charles I)...............£15 *Benham (500)470*

# 2010

## 2010 FESTIVAL OF STAMPS

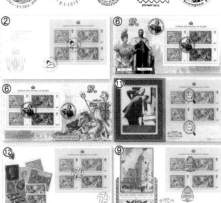

## 2010 BRITAIN ALONE

## 2010 THE STUARTS

## 2010 THE STUARTS (contd)

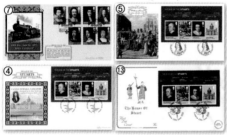

(10) Dunbar, East Lothian..............£15 *Buckingham Cvrs 411*
(11) Restoration, London WC1 .....£15 *Buckingham Cvrs 411*
(12) Autographed, Churchill Walk .£15 *Westminster*
(13) London (Rose and Thistle) ......£15 *Cotswold*
(14) Stuart Street, London N14.....£15 *GB 155*
(15) Wigtown, Newton Stewart.....£15 *Phil Stamp Cvrs 167*
(16) Worcester (Charles I).............£15 *J Bevan Pubs 168*
(17) Middleton Railway..................£15 *Buckingham Covers*
   *Mammals Stamp Book (also issued 15th June):*
(18) Hedgetree Croft, Birmingham...... *Royal Mail (n.s.c.)*
(19) Earsham (Otter) ........................... *Benham BLCS 472*
(20) Haddenham, (Hedgehog)............. *Benham (500) 472*

### 8th July 2010 – Grand Prix
*Commemorative Stamp Sheet of 10 1st Class Union Flag*
*stamps and British World Champion Grand Prix Drivers labels.*
**SPECIAL HANDSTAMPS          SPONSOR**
**Price Guide Ordinary Covers £3-£5 / Sponsored Covers:**
(1) Brands Hatch Rd, Fawkham .£15 *Benham*
(2) Silverstone, Towcester............£15 *Benham*

### 27th July 2010 – OLYMPICS
*(1) 1st Rowing; 1st Shooting; 1st Modern Pentathlon;*
   *1st Taekwondo; 1st Cycling; 1st Table Tennis; 1st Hockey;*
   *1st Football; 1st Goalball; 1st Boxing*
*(2) Retail Stamp Book: 1st Football; 1st Cycling (self adhesives)*
**SPECIAL HANDSTAMPS          SPONSOR**
**Price Guide Ordinary Covers £3-£5 / Sponsored Covers:**

## 2010 OLYMPICS

(1) FDI - Tallents House...................... *Royal Mail (n.s.c.)*
(2) FDI - Rowington, Warwick ......... *Royal Mail (n.s.c.)*
(3) -do- non pictorial version ............ *Royal Mail (n.s.c.)*
(4) Countdown to London 2012 .£15 *Royal Mail/Royal Mint*
(5) Raleigh Close, Birmingham ......... *Royal Mail (n.s.c.)*
(6) London (Olympic flame).......£15 *Benham*
(7) London (Medallists) ...............£15 *Benham*
(8) Greenwich Park, London......£15 *Benham*
(9) Wembley (Stadium) ................£15 *Benham*
(10) Rebecca Adlington Mansfield.£15 *Buckingham Cvrs 412*
(11) Nicole Cooke, Wick ...............£15 *Buckingham Cvrs 412*
(12) Autographed, Stratford ..........£15 *Westminster*
(13) London 2012 (Bike) ...............£15 *Cotswold*
(14) Mountain Bike Association....£15 *P Sheridan*
(15) Games, Wembley.....................£15 *J Bevan Pubs 169*
   *Olympics Stamp Book No.3 (also issued 27th July):*
(16) Tennis Court, Birmingham...£15 *Royal Mail (n.s.c.)*
(17) Dorney, Windsor....................£15 *Benham*

### 10th August 2010 – London Eye
*Commemorative Stamp Sheet of 10 1st Class Union Flag*
*stamps and London Eye labels*
**SPECIAL HANDSTAMPS          SPONSOR**
**Price Guide Ordinary Covers £3-£5 / Sponsored Covers:**
(1) 10th Anniversary, London .....£15 *Benham*

### 19 Aug 2010 – GREAT BRITISH RAILWAYS
*1st LMS Coronation Class; 1st BR Class 9F;*
*67p GWR King Class; 67p LNER Class A1;*
*97p SR King Arthur Class; 97p LMS NCC Class WT*
**SPECIAL HANDSTAMPS          SPONSOR**
**Price Guide Ordinary Covers £3-£5 / Sponsored Covers:**
(1) FDI - Tallents House...................... *Royal Mail (n.s.c.)*
(2) FDI - Swindon.............................. *Royal Mail (n.s.c.)*
(3) -do- non pictorial version ............ *Royal Mail (n.s.c.)*
(4) Railway Road, Birmingham ......... *Royal Mail (n.s.c.)*
(5) King Class Loco, Swindon .....£15 *Benham*
(6) BR Class 9F Loco, York ........£15 *Benham*
(7) Kings Cross, N1.......................£15 *Buckingham Cvrs 413*
(8) Waterloo, SE1 .........................£15 *Buckingham Cvrs 413*
(9) Euston, NW1 ...........................£15 *Buckingham Cvrs 413*
(10) Paddington W2 .......................£15 *Buckingham Cvrs 413*
(11) Swindon...................................£15 *Buckingham Cvrs 413*
(12) Autographed, Swindon ..........£15 *Westminster*
(13) King Arthur Close, SE15 .......£15 *GB 156*
(14) Balcombe, West Sussex..........£15 *Cotswold*
(15) Crewe Heritage Centre ..........£15 *P Sheridan*
(16) Great British Rlys, Evesham..£15 *J Bevan Pubs 170*
(17) Vulcan Foundry.......................£15 *Assoc. of GBFDC*
(18) York ........................................£15 *Phil Stamp Cvrs 168*
(19) Flower Festival, Wisbech.....£15 *Trevor Dyke*

## 2010 GREAT BRITISH RAILWAYS

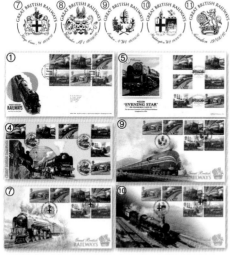

## 15th Sept 2010 – SPITFIRE Self Adhesive
*1st Spitfire Design Icon (x 2) issued in self-adhesive stamp*
*book with four 1st Class definitives. Also issued on same date:*
*Generic Sheet with 20 x 1st gummed Spitfire stamps and labels*

**SPECIAL HANDSTAMPS          SPONSOR**
**Price Guide Ordinary Covers £3-£5 / Sponsored Covers:**
| | | |
|---|---|---|
| (1) | Spitfire Road, Birmingham .......... | *Royal Mail (n.s.c.)* |
| (2) | Autumn Stampex ........................... | *Royal Mail (n.s.c.)* |
| (3) | Biggin Hill, Westerham..........£15 | *Benham* |
| (4) | Croydon, Surrey .....................£15 | *Benham* |
| (5) | Stanmore, Middlesex ..............£15 | *Benham* |
| (6) | Ruislip, Middlesex..................£15 | *Benham* |

## 16 Sept 2010 – MEDICAL BREAKTHROUGHS
*1st Beta-blockers; 58p Penicillin; 60p Hip-replacement;*
*67p Artificial lens implant; 88p Malaria parasite;*
*97p Computed tomograhy scanner*

**SPECIAL HANDSTAMPS          SPONSOR**
**Price Guide Ordinary Covers £3-£5 / Sponsored Covers:**
| | | |
|---|---|---|
| (1) | FDI - Tallents House.................... | *Royal Mail (n.s.c.)* |
| (2) | FDI - Paddington ......................... | *Royal Mail (n.s.c.)* |
| (3) | -do- non pictorial version ............ | *Royal Mail (n.s.c.)* |
| (4) | Fleming Road, Birmingham......... | *Royal Mail (n.s.c.)* |
| (5) | Autumn Stampex .......................... | *Royal Mail (n.s.c.)* |
| (6) | Autumn Stampex Medical ........... | *Royal Mail (n.s.c.)* |
| (7) | Edinburgh ...................................£15 | *Benham* |
| (8) | Tavistock Square, WC1...........£15 | *Benham* |
| (9) | London, SW7 ...........................£15 | *Buckingham Cvrs 414* |
| (10) | Autographed, A Fleming Rd..£15 | *Westminster* |
| (11) | Joint Action, London WCA2.£15 | *P Sheridan* |
| (12) | Oxford.......................................£15 | *J Bevan Pubs 171* |
| (13) | Last BR Steam Loco, Swindon.... | *Royal Mail (n.s.c.)* |
| (14) | British Steam Locos, Swindon..... | *Royal Mail (n.s.c.)* |

## 17th Sept 2010 – GARDEN BIRDS
*1st Blue Tit; 1st Goldfinch; 1st House Sparrow;*
*1st Robin; 1st Starling; 1st Wood Pigeon*

**SPECIAL HANDSTAMPS          SPONSOR**
**Price Guide Ordinary Covers £3-£5  / Sponsored Covers:**
| | | |
|---|---|---|
| (1) | FDI - Tallents House.................... | *Royal Mail (n.s.c.)* |
| (2) | FDI - Bristol................................ | *Royal Mail (n.s.c.)* |
| (3) | -do- non pictorial version ............ | *Royal Mail (n.s.c.)* |
| (4) | Birdbrook Road, Birmingham...... | *Royal Mail (n.s.c.)* |
| (5) | Autumn Stampex .......................... | *Royal Mail (n.s.c.)* |
| (6) | Autumn Stampex Birds................. | *Royal Mail (n.s.c.)* |
| (7) | Sandy, Bedfordshire................£15 | *Benham* |
| (8) | Thetford, Norfolk ....................£15 | *Benham* |
| (9) | Holmfirth, Huddersfield .........£15 | *Buckingham Cvrs 416* |
| (10) | Garden Village, Sheffield.......£15 | *Buckingham Cvrs 416* |
| (11) | Kelder Water .............................£15 | *P Sheridan* |

## 12th Oct 2010 – WINNIE-the-POOH
*1st with Christopher Robin; 58p with Piglet; 60p with Rabbit;*
*67p with Eeyore; 88p with Friends; 97p with Tigger*
*Miniature Sheet: 1st, 60p, 88p, 97p*

**SPECIAL HANDSTAMPS          SPONSOR**
**Price Guide Ordinary Covers £3-£5  / Sponsored Covers:**
| | | |
|---|---|---|
| (1) | FDI - Tallents House.................... | *Royal Mail (n.s.c.)* |
| (2) | FDI - Hartfield............................. | *Royal Mail (n.s.c.)* |
| (3) | -do- non pictorial version ............ | *Royal Mail (n.s.c.)* |
| (4) | Bearwood, Birmingham............... | *Royal Mail (n.s.c.)* |
| (5) | St John's Wood (balloon).......£15 | *Benham* |
| (6) | Chelsea (boy with book)..........£15 | *Benham* |
| (7) | Hampstead (bee on flower) ...£15 | *Benham* |
| (8) | Hartfield (hearts).....................£15 | *Benham* |
| (9) | Ashdown Forest, Hartfield .....£15 | *Buckingham Cvrs 415* |
| (10) | Story Time, Buckingham.........£15 | *Buckingham Cvrs 415* |
| (11) | Autographed, Stories Rd........£15 | *Westminster* |
| (12) | Milne Gardens, SE9 ...............£15 | *GB 157* |
| (13) | Treehouse Appeal, Ipswich ....£15 | *P Sheridan* |
| (14) | Pooh Corner, Hartfield ..........£15 | *Steven Scott* |
| (15) | Wilton, York...........................£15 | *J Bevan Pubs 172* |
| (16) | Hartfield (balloon) ..................£15 | *Phil Stamp Cvrs 169* |
| (17) | Cycling, Manchester..................... | *Royal Mail (n.s.c.)* |
| (18) | Athletics Track, Oxford ................ | *Royal Mail (n.s.c.)* |
| | **Olympics Stamp Book No. 4 (also issued 12th October):** | |
| (19) | London Road, Birmingham......... | *Royal Mail (n.s.c.)* |
| (20) | Wembley ......................................... | *Benham* |

### 2010 SPITFIRE

### 2010 MEDICAL BREAKTHROUGHS

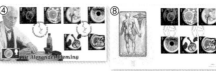

### 2010 GARDEN BIRDS

### 2010 WINNIE-the-POOH

Teddy goes fishing

---

Keep up to date with all the latest Royal Mail stamp issues at:
# www.bfdc.co.uk

# N. C. Porter
## ....*fine first day covers*

*N. C. Porter . Farnham House . 2 Beedingwood Drive . Forest Road . Colgate*
*Horsham . West Sussex RH12 4TE (Telephone 01293 851174)*
*norman@normanporter.me.uk*

We have been producing British first day covers since 1978 and specialise in circular date stamp (cds) postmarked covers. All our covers are offered through our **FREE NEWSLETTER** which is published periodically to cover all British commemorative stamp issues. We offer a prompt service at very competitive prices. If you would like to receive our Newsletter please contact us (details above) giving your name and address. We also offer a Wants List service but specialise mainly in slogan and cds postmarks.

**Here is just a brief selection of some of the covers from our stock:**

*(£)*

| | | |
|---|---|---:|
| 2009 | *Plants (Miniature Sheet) .................................Ardingly cds* | 9.50 |
| 2009 | *Plants (Miniature Sheet) .............................Kew Gardens cds* | 10.00 |
| 2009 | *Plants (10 stamps) ...................................Fleur-de-Lis cds* | 9.50 |
| 2009 | *The Age of Tudors (Mini Sheet) .........................Greenwich cds* | 9.50 |
| 2009 | *The Age of Tudors (6 stamps) ..........................Tudor Parade cds* | 9.50 |
| 2009 | *Celebrating Wales (Mini Sheet) .......National Assembly cds (in Welsh) RARE* | 20.00 |
| 2009 | *Celebrating Wales (Mini Sheet) ......National Assembly cds (in English) RARE* | 20.00 |
| 2009 | *Darwin (Miniature Sheet) ...............................Frankwell cds* | 10.00 |
| 2009 | *Darwin (6 stamps) ......................................Frankwell cds* | 10.00 |
| 2009 | *Darwin (Miniature Sheet) ...............................Cambridge cds* | 9.50 |
| 2009 | *Darwin (6 stamps) ......................................Cambridge cds* | 9.50 |
| 2009 | *Darwin (Miniature Sheet) ............Milford Haven cds (replica Beagle )* | 10.00 |
| 2009 | *Darwin (6 stamps) ..................Milford Haven cds (replica Beagle )* | 10.00 |
| 2009 | *Burns 250th Anniversary ..................Burns Statue, Ayr cds SUPERB* | 15.00 |
| 1981 | *Jaguar Drivers Club (Official) .........Signed by Lofty England & Bill Lyons* | 12.00 |
| 1981 | *Butterflies .........................National Butterfly Museum SLOGAN* | 15.00 |
| 1982 | *Youth ...................................Scouts help others SLOGAN* | 12.00 |
| 1982 | *Theatre ........................Eden Court Highlands Theatre SLOGAN* | 15.00 |
| 1982 | *Cars ....................................Hella of Banbury SLOGAN* | 25.00 |
| 1984 | *Christmas .......................Halfpenny Green Xmas 1984 SLOGAN* | 20.00 |
| 1985 | *British Composers ..............Hereford Cathedral Restoration SLOGAN* | 20.00 |
| 1988 | *Welsh Bible ..................................Jesus is Alive SLOGAN* | 25.00 |
| 1989 | *Games and Toys .....................Save the Children Week SLOGAN* | 20.00 |
| 1989 | *Microscopes ...........................Army Blood Supply SLOGAN* | 10.00 |
| 1989 | *The Lord Mayor s Show .....................Autumn Stampex SLOGAN* | 10.00 |
| 1990 | *Gallantry...........................RAF Finningley Air Show SLOGAN* | 8.00 |
| 1994 | *Channel Tunnel ...................................Le Shuttle SLOGAN* | 7.00 |
| 1994 | *D-Day .......................European Parliament Elections SLOGAN* | 8.00 |
| 1994 | *Medical Discoveries ..................Zeneca 75th Anniversary SLOGAN* | 8.00 |

*CONTACT US NOW AND RECEIVE OUR FREE NEWSLETTER AND*
*START COLLECTING THE FINEST CDS COVERS AVAILABLE*

# Definitive Issues

Please also read the Introduction Notes at the beginning of this catalogue.

## 1. PRICES & CONDITION

**1839-1936** Prices vary considerably, according to condition, for all early definitives on first day covers. The prices quoted are for good covers with clear postmarks. Unless otherwise stated prices are for plain covers. Superb examples may realise a better price whilst covers in poor condition will fetch less.

**1936-1970** Prices are given for both plain and illustrated covers, with any postmark. Where relevant postmarks are known to exist these have been listed. The prices quoted are for good covers with clear postmarks.

**1970 to date** First day covers for this period are usually available unaddressed (or with small printed labels etc.) and the prices reflect this. Prices are also given for the more sought after Windsor postmarks and for covers with any other type of postmark. Where relevant special handstamps were sponsored for specific issues, these have also been listed as have any official/sponsored covers (see Introduction Notes at the beginning of this catalogue).

## 2. FORMAT & SCOPE

This Section has been sub-divided as follows:

*New Stamps*
*To Pay & Frama Labels*
*New Services*
*Commemorative Labels*
*Retail Book Panes*
*Prestige Stamp Book Panes*
*Channel Islands Occupation issues*
*Stamp Book Panes*
*Varieties (changes to phosphor, perfs, gum, paper etc.)*
*Self Adhesives*
*Regionals*
*Country Pictorial Definitives*
*Stamp Coils*

Where the first day of issue is known, all new definitive stamps have been listed. With effect from the new Machin definitives issued in 1967 the Post Office provided first day of issue facilities for most new values and colour changes. Varieties in perforations, phosphors, papers etc are also listed where known. However these are not recognised as new stamps by Royal Mail and are therefore only available with permanent pictorial handstamps or CDS postmarks.

*A selection of GPO/Royal Mail first day covers for definitive stamp issues 1967 - 2004*

211

*Values (1839-1936) are for plain covers except where stated.*

### Queen Victoria (1837-1901)

| | £ |
|---|---|
| 5 Dec 1839 Uniform 4d Post | 350 |
| 10 Jan 1840 First DayUniversal Penny Post | 750 |
| 6 May 1840 The Mulready 1d Stationery | 2,500 |
| 6 May 1840 1d Black (imperf.) | 20,000 |
| 8 May 1840 2d Blue (imperf.) | 25,000 |
| 22 Feb 1855 2d Blue (perforated, Plate 4) | 2,500 |
| 7 Mar 1865 6d Deep Lilac | 1,800 |
| 1 Oct 1870 ¹/₂d Rose Red (small format) | |
| on Asylum cover | 1,200 |
| printed on postcard | 600 |
| 12 Apr 1872 6d Deep Chestnut | 1,500 |
| 1 Sep 1873 1s Green | 2,500 |
| 1 Jan 1880 1d Venetian Red | 1,750 |
| 24 May 1881 1s Orange Brown (Imp Crown) | 5,500 |

Jubilee Issues

| | £ |
|---|---|
| 24 May 1887 ¹/₂d Orange | 2,500 |
| 5d Dull Purple & Blue | 1,250 |
| 15 Sep 1892 4¹/₂d Green & Carmine | 3,000 |
| 17 Apr 1900 ¹/₂d Blue-green | 950 |

Uniform Penny Postage Jubilee - official envelopes

| | £ |
|---|---|
| 16 May 1890 Guildhall handstamp (No. 1) | 50 |
| 2 Jul 1890 South Kensington (No. 6) | 30 |
| -do- (Nos. 4 or 5) | 70 |
| -do- (Nos. 2 or 3) | 50 |
| All five h/s on one cover | 150 |

### King Edward VII (1901-1910)

| | £ |
|---|---|
| 1 Jan 1902 ¹/₂d Blue-green | 75 |
| 1d Red | 75 |
| 2¹/₂d Blue | 250 |
| 6d Purple | 350 |
| The above 4 values on one cover | 1,200 |
| -do- with Parliament Street C.D.S. | 1,250 |
| 1 Nov 1909 4d Brown-orange (on postcard) | 600 |
| 12 Jul 1911 4d Orange | 1,200 |

### King George V (1910-1936)

Downey Head (Imperial Crown Watermark)

| | £ |
|---|---|
| 22 Jun 1911 ¹/₂d Green | 75 |
| -do- Junior Philatelic Soc. cover | 325 |
| ¹/₂d Green – printed on postcard | 75 |
| 1d Red | 60 |
| ¹/₂d & 1d on one cover | 200 |
| -do- Westminster Abbey C.D.S. | 2,500 |
| -do- Windsor C.D.S. | 2,500 |
| 1 Jan 1912 Redrawn ¹/₂d and 1d | 1,200 |

Profile Head (Royal Cypher Watermark)

| | £ |
|---|---|
| 17 Jan 1913 ¹/₂d Green | 1,500 |
| 8 Oct 1912 1d Red | 1,200 |
| 15 Oct 1912 1¹/₂d Red-brown | 700 |
| -do- Int. Stamp Exhib. h/s | 800 |

| | £ |
|---|---|
| 20 Aug 1912 2d Orange | 600 |
| 18 Oct 1912 2¹/₂d Blue | 500 |
| -do- Int. Stamp Exhib. h/s | 950 |
| 9 Oct 1912 3d Violet | 1,600 |
| 15 Jan 1913 4d Grey-green | 1,600 |
| 30 Jun 1913 5d Brown & 9d Agate | 3,250 |
| 1 Aug 1913 6d Purple **or** 7d Olive | 2,750 |
| 8d Black-yellow | 2,900 |
| 10d Turquoise | 3,000 |
| 1s Bistre | 3,000 |
| 8 Mar 1934 ¹/₂d,1d,1¹/₂d ......Harrison Printing | 750 |

Profile Head (Block Cypher Watermark)

| | £ |
|---|---|
| 10 Oct 1924 2¹/₂d Blue & 3d Violet | 2,750 |
| 23 Oct 1924 4d Grey-green | 3,250 |
| 17 Oct 1924 5d Brown | 4,250 |
| 11 Nov 1924 9d Olive-green | 5,000 |
| 28 Nov 1924 10d Blue | 6,000 |

High values – 'Sea Horses'

| | £ |
|---|---|
| 30 Jun 1913 2s 6d Brown | 2,400 |
| 16 Oct 1934 2s 6d Brown re-engraved issue | 3,500 |

Photogravure (Block Cypher Watermark)

| | £ |
|---|---|
| 19 Nov 1934 ¹/₂d Green ............(illust. cvr £40) | 15 |
| 14 Feb 1935 ¹/₂d Green (small format) | 1,600 |
| 24 Sep 1934 1d Scarlet ............(illust. cvr £40) | 15 |
| 30 Apr 1935 1d Red (sideways wmk) | 2,250 |
| 20 Aug 1934 1¹/₂d Red-brown ....(illust. cvr £50) | 15 |
| 7 Feb 1935 1¹/₂d Red-brown (small format) | 1,600 |
| 21 Jan 1935 2d Orange ............(illust. cvr £90) | 40 |
| 30 Apr 1935 2d Orange (sideways wmk) | 2,750 |
| 18 Mar 1935 2¹/₂d Blue | 30 |
| 3d Violet | 40 |
| 2¹/₂d & 3d - one cover | 95 |
| 2 Dec 1935 4d Grey-green | 80 |
| 9d Olive-green | 100 |
| 4d & 9d - one cover | 250 |
| 22 Feb 1936 5d Yellow-brown | 750 |
| *covers exist with 17th Feb pmk* | |
| 24 Feb 1936 10d Turquoise-blue | 800 |
| 26 Feb 1936 1s Bistre-brown | 600 |
| Set of 9 or 11 covers | 1,800 |
| All 11 values on one cover | 3,500 |

*Values from KEVIII are for plain or illustrated covers where known. ('n.k.' = not known)*

| | plain covers £ | illus. covers £ |
|---|---|---|

### King Edward VIII (1936)

| | plain covers £ | illus. covers £ |
|---|---|---|
| 1 Sep 1936 ¹/₂d, 1¹/₂d & 2¹/₂d | 15 | 125 |
| -do- King Edward, Banff C.D.S. | 125 | n.k. |
| -do- Windsor C.D.S. | 160 | 500 |
| -do- Kingstanding C.D.S. | n.k. | 200 |
| -do- Buckingham Gate C.D.S. | 100 | n.k. |
| 14 Sep 1936 1d | 20 | 150 |
| -do- King Edward, Banff C.D.S. | 120 | n.k. |
| -do- Windsor C.D.S. | 120 | n.k. |
| All 4 values on one cover | 100 | n.k. |

### King George VI (1936-1952)

Low values – original issue

| | plain covers £ | illus. covers £ |
|---|---|---|
| 10 May 1937 ¹/₂d, 1d & 2¹/₂d .....................(1) | 10 | 35 |
| -do- Windsor pmk | n.k. | 100 |
| -do- Kingstanding, B'ham pmk | 40 | 100 |
| 30 Jul 1937 1¹/₂d Red-brown | 10 | 50 |
| 31 Jan 1938 2d Orange | 15 | 35 |
| 3d Violet | 15 | 35 |
| 2d & 3d - on one cover | 30 | 80 |
| 21 Nov 1938 4d Grey-green | 20 | n.k. |
| 5d Brown | 20 | n.k. |
| 4d & 5d - on one cover | 50 | n.k. |
| -do- Windsor pmk | 200 | n.k. |
| 30 Jan 1939 6d Purple | 40 | n.k. |

| | plain covers £. | illus cvrs £. |
|---|---|---|

## King George VI (1936-1952) contd.

| | | |
|---|---|---|
| 27 Feb 1939 7d Emerald-green.......................... | 25 | n.k. |
| 8d Carmine............................... | 25 | n.k. |
| 7d & 8d - on one cover................ | 55 | 200 |
| -do- Windsor pmk ...................... | 220 | n.k. |
| 1 May 1939 9d Olive-green.......................... | 80 | n.k. |
| 10d Turquoise-blue...................... | 90 | n.k. |
| 1s Bistre-brown ............................. | 90 | n.k. |
| 9d, 10d, & 1s - on one cover ...... | 275 | n.k. |
| 29 Dec 1947 11d Plum.................................... | 35 | 100 |
| Set of 15 values ........................ | 1,750 | n.k. |

### High values – 'Arms' Design

| | | |
|---|---|---|
| 4 Sep 1939 2s 6d Brown.............................. | 1250 | n.k. |
| 9 Mar 1942 2s 6d Yellow-green ...................... | 950 | n.k. |
| 21 Aug 1939 5s Red..................................... | 500 | n.k. |
| 30 Oct 1939 10s Dark blue ....................(2) | 1,750 | n.k. |
| 30 Nov 1942 10s Ultramarine............................ | 2,750 | n.k. |
| 1 Oct 1948 £1 Brown.................................. | 250 | n.k. |

### Low values – change to pale colours

| | | |
|---|---|---|
| 1 Sep 1941 ¹/₂ d Pale green..................................... | 25 | n.k. |
| 11 Aug 1941 1d Pale scarlet............................ | 20 | 100 |
| 28 Sep 1942 1¹/₂ d Pale red-brown ...................... | 45 | n.k. |
| 6 Oct 1941 2d Pale orange ........................... | 50 | n.k. |
| 21 Jul 1941 2¹/₂ d Pale ultramarine ..................... | 35 | 125 |
| 3 Nov 1941 3d Pale violet ........................... | 85 | n.k. |
| Set of six covers................................... | 225 | n.k. |
| | | |
| 2 Oct 1950 4d Light ultramarine .......................... | 20 | 75 |
| | | |
| 3 May 1951 **Low values – colour changes:** | | |
| ¹/₂ d, 1d, 1¹/₂ d, 2d, 2¹/₂ d...............(3) | 10 | 40 |
| ditto Battersea C.D.S. pmk ............... | 20 | 80 |
| **'Festival' High values:** | | |
| 2s 6d, 5s, 10s, £1* ............................. | 250 | 675 |
| ditto Battersea pmk*........... | n.k. | 900 |
| * (on one cover or set of four covers) | | |

## Queen Elizabeth II £.s.d. issues (1952-1970)

### Low values

| | | |
|---|---|---|
| 5 Dec 1952 **1¹/₂ d, 2¹/₂ d** ......................................(4) | 5 | 20 |
| -do- with Windsor postmark ............ | 25 | 60 |
| -do- with Buckingham Palace pmk.. | 125 | 175 |
| 6 Jul 1953 **5d, 8d, 1s** ........................ | 10 | 40 |
| 31 Aug 1953 **¹/₂ d, 1d, 2d** ........................ | 10 | 40 |
| 2 Nov 1953 **4d, 1s 3d, 1s 6d** ........................ | 25 | 125 |
| 18 Jan 1954 **3d, 6d, 7d** ........................ | 25 | 75 |
| 8 Feb 1954 **9d, 10d, 11d** ........................ | 40 | 150 |
| Set on matching covers.................... | 150 | 600 |
| 9 Feb 1959 **4¹/₂ d new value** ........................ | 15 | 200 |

### 'Castles' High values

| | | |
|---|---|---|
| 1 Sep 1955 **10s, £1** – on one or two covers ........ | 200 | 450 |
| **10s, £1** – Edinburgh C.D.S. ............... | – | 625 |
| **10s** only – Edinburgh C.D.S. ............. | 200 | – |
| **£1** only – Windsor Castle C.D.S...... | 250 | – |
| 23 Sep 1955 **2s 6d, 5s** – on one or two covers ...... | 75 | 400 |
| **2s 6d** only – Carrickfergus C.D.S. ...... | 75 | 450 |
| **5s** only – Caernarfon C.D.S............. | 150 | – |
| **Set of 4** on matching covers............. | 275 | 1750 |

| | Windsor postmark £ | other pmk £ |
|---|---|---|

## All values are now for illustrated covers

### New Style (Machin Head) Definitives

| | | |
|---|---|---|
| 5 Jun 1967 **4d, 1s, 1s 9d** ........................(5) | 10 | 2 |
| 8 Aug 1967 **3d, 9d, 1s 6d** ........................(6) | 10 | 2 |
| 5 Feb 1968 **¹/₂ d, 1d, 2d, 6d** ........................(7) | 10 | 2 |
| 1 Jul 1968 **5d, 7d, 8d, 10d** ........................(8) | 10 | 2 |
| 6 Jan 1969 **4d Red & 8d Turquoise**..............(9) | 10 | 2 |
| 5 Mar 1969 **2s 6d, 5s, 10s, £1** ..........................(10) | 8 | 15 |
| -do- Stampex special handstamp...... | – | 25 |
| -do- Stampex official cover.............. | – | 35 |

*Remember, for each stamp issue there can be several different designs of first day cover.*

213

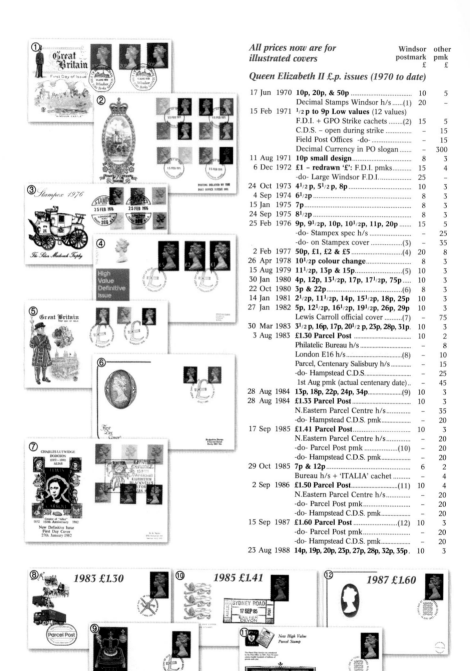

| | | All prices now are for illustrated covers | Windsor postmark £ | other pmk £ |
|---|---|---|---|---|

**Queen Elizabeth II £.p. issues (1970 to date)**

| Date | | Description | Windsor postmark £ | other pmk £ |
|---|---|---|---|---|
| 17 Jun | 1970 | **10p, 20p, & 50p** | 10 | 5 |
| | | Decimal Stamps Windsor h/s ......(1) | 20 | – |
| 15 Feb | 1971 | **1/2 p to 9p Low values** (12 values) | | |
| | | F.D.I. + GPO Strike cachets ........(2) | 15 | 5 |
| | | C.D.S. – open during strike ............. | – | 15 |
| | | Field Post Offices  -do- ...................... | – | 15 |
| | | Decimal Currency in PO slogan ...... | – | 300 |
| 11 Aug | 1971 | **10p small design**............................. | 8 | 3 |
| 6 Dec | 1972 | **£1 – redrawn '£'**: F.D.I. pmks......... | 15 | 4 |
| | | -do- Large Windsor F.D.I................. | 25 | – |
| 24 Oct | 1973 | **41/2 p, 51/2 p, 8p** .............................. | 10 | 3 |
| 4 Sep | 1974 | **61/2p** ................................................ | 8 | 3 |
| 15 Jan | 1975 | **7p**.................................................... | 8 | 3 |
| 24 Sep | 1975 | **81/2p** ................................................ | 8 | 3 |
| 25 Feb | 1976 | **9p, 91/2p, 10p, 101/2p, 11p, 20p** ...... | 15 | 5 |
| | | -do- Stampex spec h/s ...................... | – | 25 |
| | | -do- on Stampex cover ................(3) | – | 35 |
| 2 Feb | 1977 | **50p, £1, £2 & £5** ...........................(4) | 20 | 8 |
| 26 Apr | 1978 | **101/2p colour change**......................... | 8 | 3 |
| 15 Aug | 1979 | **111/2p, 13p & 15p** ........................(5) | 10 | 3 |
| 30 Jan | 1980 | **4p, 12p, 131/2p, 17p, 171/2p, 75p** ..... | 10 | 3 |
| 22 Oct | 1980 | **3p & 22p**......................................(6) | 8 | 3 |
| 14 Jan | 1981 | **21/2p, 111/2p, 14p, 151/2p, 18p, 25p** | 10 | 3 |
| 27 Jan | 1982 | **5p, 121/2p, 161/2p, 191/2p, 26p, 29p** | 10 | 3 |
| | | Lewis Carroll official cover .........(7) | – | 75 |
| 30 Mar | 1983 | **31/2 p, 16p, 17p, 201/2 p, 23p, 28p, 31p.** | 10 | 3 |
| 3 Aug | 1983 | **£1.30 Parcel Post** ......................... | 10 | 2 |
| | | Philatelic Bureau h/s ........................ | – | 8 |
| | | London E16 h/s ..............................(8) | – | 10 |
| | | Parcel, Centenary Salisbury h/s ........... | – | 15 |
| | | -do- Hampstead C.D.S. ...................... | – | 25 |
| | | 1st Aug pmk (actual centenary date).. | – | 45 |
| 28 Aug | 1984 | **13p, 18p, 22p, 24p, 34p**.................(9) | 10 | 3 |
| 28 Aug | 1984 | **£1.33 Parcel Post** ......................... | 10 | 3 |
| | | N.Eastern Parcel Centre h/s............. | – | 35 |
| | | -do- Hampstead C.D.S. pmk.................. | – | 20 |
| 17 Sep | 1985 | **£1.41 Parcel Post** ......................... | 10 | 3 |
| | | N.Eastern Parcel Centre h/s............. | – | 20 |
| | | -do- Parcel Post pmk ..................(10) | – | 20 |
| | | -do- Hampstead C.D.S. pmk.................. | – | 20 |
| 29 Oct | 1985 | **7p & 12p**......................................... | 6 | 2 |
| | | Bureau h/s + 'ITALIA' cachet ......... | – | 4 |
| 2 Sep | 1986 | **£1.50 Parcel Post**......................(11) | 10 | 4 |
| | | N.Eastern Parcel Centre h/s............. | – | 20 |
| | | -do- Parcel Post pmk...................... | – | 20 |
| | | -do- Hampstead C.D.S. pmk.................. | – | 20 |
| 15 Sep | 1987 | **£1.60 Parcel Post** ....................(12) | 10 | 3 |
| | | -do- Parcel Post pmk...................... | – | 20 |
| | | -do- Hampstead C.D.S. pmk.................. | – | 20 |
| 23 Aug | 1988 | **14p, 19p, 20p, 23p, 27p, 28p, 32p, 35p.** | 10 | 3 |

| | Ordinary covers £ | Sponsored covers £ | |
|---|---|---|---|
| 18 Oct 1988 **£1, £1.50, £2, £5 'Castles' High Values** | | | |
| FDI, Bureau special h/s | 20 | – | *Royal Mail* |
| FDI, Windsor special h/s | 25 | – | *Royal Mail* |
| Carrickfergus h/s | 30 | 60 | *Benham* |
| Caernarfon h/s | 30 | 60 | *Benham* |
| Edinburgh h/s (13) | 30 | 60 | *Benham* |
| Windsor h/s | 30 | 60 | *Benham* |
| Set of 4 with appropriate h/s | 25 | | |
| Windsor Castle C.D.S. | 220 | | |
| Carrickfergus C.D.S. | 250 | | |
| Windsor C.D.S. | 150 | | |
| Caernarfon or Edinburgh C.D.S. | 150 | | |
| Set of 4 with appropriate CDS | 200 | | |
| 22 Aug 1989 **Non-Value Indicators:** 1st, 2nd (14) | 15 | *(Windsor pmk)* | |
| 26 Sep 1989 15p, 20p, 24p, 29p, 30p, 34p, 37p | 10 | *(Windsor pmk)* | |
| 10 Jan 1990 **Penny Black Anniversary** | | | |
| *See commemorative issues (10 Jan 1990) &* | | | |
| *booklet panes (30 Jan & 3 May 1990).* | | | |
| 7 Aug 1990 **Non-Value Indicators:** 1st, 2nd | 10 | *(Windsor pmk)* | |
| 4 Sep 1990 10p, 17p, 22p, 26p, 27p, 31p, 33p (15) | 10 | *(Windsor pmk)* | |
| 10 Sep 1991 6p, 18p, 24p, 28p, 34p, 35p, 39p (16) | 10 | *(Windsor pmk)* | |
| -do- 'New Postage Rates' slogan | 20 | | |
| 24 Mar 1992 **Security Printing 'Castles':** | | | |
| **£1, £1.50, £2 & £5** | | | |
| FDI, Bureau h/s | 20 | – | *Royal Mail* |
| FDI, Windsor h/s | 20 | – | *Royal Mail* |
| Carrickfergus h/s | 25 | 35 | *Benham* |
| Caernarfon h/s | 25 | 35 | *Benham* |
| Edinburgh h/s | 25 | 35 | *Benham* |
| Windsor h/s (17) | 25 | 35 | *Benham* |
| 'Security Printing' Windsor | 35 | 75 | *Bradbury* |
| Windsor CDS | 35 | | |
| Windsor Castle CDS | 150 | | |
| Other relevant CDS | 35 | | |
| Set of 4 with relevant CDS | 35 | | |
| 2 Mar 1993 **£10 Britannia:** | | | |
| FDI, Bureau h/s | 18 | – | *Royal Mail* |
| FDI, Windsor | 20 | – | *Royal Mail* |
| FDI, London | 25 | – | *Royal Mail* |
| Windsor h/s (Britannia) | 25 | 45 | *Bradbury* |
| £10 Britannia, Porth h/s (18) | 25 | 45 | *Benham* |
| £10 Dover h/s | 25 | 45 | *Benham* |
| Britannia Way h/s | 25 | 45 | *Benham* |
| Spring Stampex h/s | 40 | | |
| National Postal Museum h/s | 50 | | |
| Britannia, Pounds or Brailes CDS | 45 | | |
| Maritime Mail or Paquebot CDS | 35 | | |
| Windsor CDS | 40 | | |
| Windsor Castle CDS | 150 | | |
| 26 Oct 1993 19p, 25p, 29p, 36p, 38p, 41p (19) | 4 | *(Windsor pmk)* | |
| -do- 'New Postage Rates' slogan | 10 | | |
| 9 Aug 1994 **60p Airmail (new value in bkt)** | 4 | *(Windsor pmk)* | |
| 22 Aug 1995 **£1 (small format) & £3 Carrickfergus Castle** | | | |
| FDI, Bureau h/s | 5 | – | *Royal Mail* |
| FDI, Bureau (lions) h/s | 5 | – | *Royal Mail* |
| FDI, Windsor h/s (20) | 5 | – | *Royal Mail* |
| FDI, London h/s | 5 | – | *Royal Mail* |
| FDI, Carrickfergus h/s | 5 | – | *Royal Mail* |
| Carrickfergus (harp) h/s | 5 | 10 | *Benham* |
| Carrickfergus (heraldic) h/s | 5 | 10 | *Benham* |
| Carrickfergus CDS | 15 | – | |
| 25 Jun 1996 20p, 26p, 31p, 37p, 39p, 43p, 63p (21) | 5 | *(Windsor pmk)* | |
| New Postage Rates slogan | 12 | – | |
| 21 Apr 1997 **Golden Definitives 1st & 26p** *See commemorative issues.* | | | |
| *See also booklet pane section.* | | | |
| 10 Mar 1998 **'Wilding' reprints 20p, 26p, 37p** | 5 | *(Windsor pmk)* | |
| Windsor (National Emblems) (22) | 5 | 40 | *Bradbury* |
| *See Prestige Booklets (Definitive Portrait) section.* | | | |
| 19 Jan 1999 **European NVI 'E'** | 3 | *(Windsor pmk)* | |
| Waterloo Station h/s | 3 | 8 | *Benham* |
| Ashford (Eiffel Tower) h/s (23) | 3 | 8 | *Benham* |

215

16 Feb 1999 **Large Style Machin 1st NVIs x 3**.... 5 *(Windsor pmk)*
Windsor (Gateway) h/s.................(1) 5 20 *Bradbury*
*See Prestige Booklets (Profile on Print) section.*

9 Mar 1999 **£1.50, £2, £3, £5 Small Format**........ 15 *(Windsor pmk)*
King Edward Street h/s ....................... 15 28 *Benham*
London SW1 (lions) h/s ..............(2) 15 23 *Benham*
London W1 (lions) h/s........................ 15 25 *Benham*
Edinburgh (Scottish lion) h/s ............. 15 28 *Benham*
Balmoral (Scottish lion) h/s ............ 15 23 *Benham*
Cardiff (Welsh Dragon) h/s............... 15 28 *Benham*
Conwy (Welsh Dragon) h/s............... 15 23 *Benham*
Belfast (Hand) h/s ............................. 15 28 *Benham*
William Shakespeare h/s................... 15 28 )*Benham*
Dylan Thomas h/s .............................. 15 ) *Set of*
Robert Burns h/s................................ 15 ) *Four*
Jonathan Swift h/s............................. 15 ) *Covers*

20 Apr 1999 **7p, 38p, 44p, 64p** ............................. 4 *(Windsor pmk)*
London SW (Beefeater) h/s .........(3) 4 20 *Bradbury*

6 Jan 2000 **Millennium Definitive 1st Class**
*See commemorative issues & booklet pane section.*

25 Apr 2000 **8p, 33p, 40p, 41p, 45p, 65p** ............. 4 *(Windsor pmk)*
London (Buckingham Pal) h/s ....(4) 4 15 *Bradbury*

22 May 2000 **Stamp Show Exhibition Souvenir Miniature Sheet**
Philatelic Bureau h/s........................... 6
Earl's Court h/s ................................... 6
-do- Art & Entertainment h/s .......... 20
Stamp Capital of the World h/s ..(5) 7 25 *Bradbury*
Westminster Abbey h/s...................... 7 12 *Westminster*
Earl's Court Security Print h/s.......... 7 12 *CoverCraft*
Stamp Show 2000 h/s........................ 7 12 *T Hurlstone*
Dr Who/Stamp Show 2000 h/s........ 7 12 *Steven Scott*
Lyceum Post Office h/s ..................... 7 12 *P Sheridan*
Artist's Palette, Picadilly h/s.............. 7 12 *Benham*
Artist's Palette, Earl's Court h/s........ 7 12 *Benham*
Artist's Palette, Strand h/s ................ 7 12 *Benham*
Artist's Palette, Kidderminster h/s .. 7 12 *Benham*
Earl's Court cds pmk h/s.................... 10

6 Feb 2002 **'Wilding' reprints 2nd & 1st Class**
A Gracious Accession h/s.............(6) 7 25 *Bradbury*
Various special handstamps .............. 5
*See commemorative issues of same date for full*
*details of postmarks & Prestige Stamp Book section.*

5 Jun 2002 **Gold Definitive 1st Class Self Adhesive** (7)
Various special handstamps......from 5
*See commemorative issues for postmark details.*

4 Jul 2002 **37p, 42p, 47p, 68p**
Tallents House (Arms) h/s................. 4 - *Royal Mail*
Windsor (Coat of Arms) h/s.............. 4 - *Royal Mail*
Windsor (Castle) h/s ......................... 4 12 *Bradbury*

4 Jul 2002 **E, 42p, 68p Self Adhesives**
Hampton Wick h/s........................(8) 4 12 *Bradbury*

5 Dec 2002 **'Wilding' reprints Miniature Sheet No.1**
Various special handstamps......from 8
*See commemorative issues for postmark details.*

27 Mar 2003 **52p, £1.12 Universal Rates NVIs Self Adhesive**
Tallents House (Arms) h/s................. 5 - *Royal Mail*
Windsor (Coat of Arms) h/s.............. 5 - *Royal Mail*
Universal Rates Birmingham h/s...... 4 - *Royal Mail*
Europe & Worldwide h/s ............(9) 4 12 *Bradbury*
New NVI definitives London h/s..... 4 12 *MachinColl*
RMS Titanic, Belfast h/s.................... 4 12 *Benham*
SS Great Britain, Southampton h/s .. 4 12 *Benham*
SS Great Britain, Bristol ................... 4 12 *Benham*
English Channel, Dover...................... 4 12 *Benham*
Aviation, Southampton....................... 4 12 *Benham*
Universal Airmail, Send..................... 4 12 *Phil Stamp*

6 May 2003 **34p New Postage Rate**
Tallents House (Arms) h/s................. 2 - *Royal Mail*
Windsor (Arms) h/s...................(10) 2 - *Royal Mail*
Stoke on Trent (Crown) h/s .............. 3 10 *Phil Stamp*

20 May 2003 **'Wilding' reprints Miniature Sheet No.2**
Various special handstamps......from 8
*See commemorative issues for postmark details.*

| | Ordinary covers £ | Sponsored covers £ |
|---|---|---|

**1 Jul   2003  £1.50, £2, £3, £5 Iriodin Ink**

| | | |
|---|---|---|
| Tallents House (Arms) h/s................. | 15 | – Royal Mail |
| Windsor (Arms) h/s............................ | 16 | – Royal Mail |
| Great Britons Portsmouth h/s........... | 17 | 20 Benham |
| Great Britons Althorp h/s................. | 17 | 20 Benham |
| Great Britons Blenheim h/s ............. | 17 | 20 Benham |
| Great Britons Downe h/s.................. | 17 | 20 Benham |
| High Values Hastings h/s.................. | 17 | 20 Benham |
| London Transport h/s......................... | 17 | 20 Benham |
| High Values Stoke h/s ...............(11) | 17 | 20 Phil Stamp |

**1 Apr  2004  7p, 35p, 39p, 40p, 43p**

| | | |
|---|---|---|
| Tallents House (Arms) h/s................. | 3 | – Royal Mail |
| Windsor (Arms) h/s....................(12) | 4 | – Royal Mail |
| Stoke-on-Trent.................................... | 5 | 10 Phil Stamp |

**1 Apr  2004  43p Universal Postcard Rate**

| | | |
|---|---|---|
| Tallents House (Arms) h/s................. | 3 | – Royal Mail |
| Windsor (Arms) h/s............................ | 4 | – Royal Mail |
| Birmingham h/s.................................. | 5 | – Royal Mail |
| London h/s........................................... | 5 | 12 Bradbury |
| Croydon h/s ........................................ | 5 | 12 Benham |
| Southampton h/s ............................... | 5 | 12 Benham |
| Falmouth h/s....................................... | 5 | 12 Benham |
| Woking h/s.......................................... | 5 | 12 Phil Stamp |

**5 Apr  2005  9p, 35p, 46p**

| | | |
|---|---|---|
| Tallents House (Arms) h/s................. | 3 | – Royal Mail |
| Windsor (Arms) h/s....................(13) | 4 | – Royal Mail |
| Stoke-on-Trent.................................... | 5 | 10 Phil Stamp |

**28 Mar 2006  37p, 44p, 49p, 72p**

| | | |
|---|---|---|
| Tallents House (Arms) h/s .........(14) | 3 | – Royal Mail |
| Windsor (Arms) h/ ............................ | 4 | – Royal Mail |
| Stoke-on-Trent.................................... | 5 | 10 Phil Stamp |
| Machin Road Birmingham................. | 5 | – Royal Mail |

**1 Aug  2006  Pricing in Proportion: 2nd Small, 2nd Large, 1st Small, 1st Large; Make-up Values 12p, 14p**

| | | |
|---|---|---|
| Tallents House (Arms) h/s................. | 3 | – Royal Mail |
| Windsor (Arms) h/s............................ | 4 | – Royal Mail |
| Birmingham...............................(15) | 10 | – Royal Mail |
| The Strand .......................................... | 10 | 15 Benham |
| London EC........................................... | 10 | 15 Benham |
| Mailcoach Bristol............................... | 10 | 15 Benham |
| Stoke-on-Trent.................................... | 10 | 15 Phil Stamp |
| Bird Stamp Society, Swansea............ | 10 | – n.o.c. |

**15 Aug 2006  PiP: 2nd Small, 1st Small ~ Self Adhesives**

| | | |
|---|---|---|
| Windsor or other running h/s........... | 6 | |

**12 Sep  2006  PiP: 2nd Large, 1st Large ~ Self Adhesives**

| | | |
|---|---|---|
| Windsor or other running h/s........... | 6 | |

**27 Mar 2007  16p, 48p, 50p, 54p, 78p**

| | | |
|---|---|---|
| Tallents House (Arms) h/s................. | 4 | – Royal Mail |
| Windsor (Arms) h/s....................(16) | 5 | – Royal Mail |
| Q Elizabeth Rd, Birmingham.....(17) | 10 | – Royal Mail |

**5 Jun   2007  £1 Ruby - 40th Anniversary of Machins**

| | | |
|---|---|---|
| Various special handstamps......from | 5 | |
| *See commemorative issues for postmark details.* | | |

**1 Apr  2008  15p, 56p, 81p**

| | | |
|---|---|---|
| Tallents House (Arms) h/s................. | 4 | – Royal Mail |
| Windsor (Arms) h/s............................ | 5 | – Royal Mail |
| Q Elizabeth Rd, Birmingham.....(18) | 10 | – Royal Mail |
| London Cry God for Harry................ | 10 | – Royal Mail |

**17 Feb 2009  Security Features: 2nd, 2nd Large, 1st 1st Large, 50p £1, £1.50, £2, £3, £5**

*Prices for all values on one cover or pair of covers:*

| | | |
|---|---|---|
| Tallents House (Arms) h/s................. | 15 | – Royal Mail |
| Windsor (Arms) h/s............................ | 15 | – Royal Mail |
| Q Elizabeth Rd, Birmingham ........... | 25 | – Royal Mail |
| Security Features, Windsor ........(19) | 25 | 35 Benham |
| Security Features, London SW1 ....... | 25 | – Benham |
| Security Features, London SE1 ........ | 25 | – Benham |

**31 Mar 2009  17p, 22p, 62p, 90p**

| | | |
|---|---|---|
| Tallents House (Arms) h/s................. | 4 | – Royal Mail |
| Windsor (Arms) h/s............................ | 5 | – Royal Mail |
| Q Elizabeth Rd, Birmingham ........... | 10 | – Royal Mail |
| London Cry God for Harry ............... | 10 | – Royal Mail |
| New Machin Definitives, Windsor... | 10 | 15 Benham |

| | | | Ordinary covers £ | Sponsored covers £ |
|---|---|---|---|---|
| 17 Nov 2009 | **Recorded Signed For: 1st, 1st Large** | | | |
| | Tallents House (Arms) h/s | | 4 | – Royal Mail |
| | Windsor (Arms) h/s | | 5 | – Royal Mail |
| | Q Elizabeth Rd, Birmingham.....(20) | | 10 | – Royal Mail |
| | Farringdon Rd, London EC1A | | 10 | 15 Benham |
| 30 Mar 2010 | **60p, 67p, 88p, 97p, £1.46, E, W** | | | |
| | Tallents House (Arms) h/s | | 4 | – Royal Mail |
| | Windsor (Arms) h/s | | 5 | – Royal Mail |
| | Q Elizabeth Rd, Birmingham.....(21) | | 10 | – Royal Mail |
| | London Cry God for Harry | | 10 | – Royal Mail |
| | George V: The Philatelist King | | 10 | 15 Benham |
| 26 Oct 2010 | **Special Delivery: up to 100g & 500g** | | | |
| | Tallents House (Arms) h/s | | 15 | – Royal Mail |
| | Windsor (Arms) h/s | | 17 | – Royal Mail |
| | Q Elizabeth Rd, Birmingham | | 20 | – Royal Mail |
| | ..........*More details to follow in next edition* | | | |

## Wilding Revival Stamps

① The 'Castles' high value definitives showing Carrickfergus, Caernarvon, Edinburgh and Windsor Castles have been popular with collectors ever since they were first issued by the Post Office in 1955. They also feature the portrait of the Queen by Dorothy Wilding.

To mark their 50th anniversary these stamps were re-issued by Royal Mail in 2005 with decimal denominations. Both sets of stamps feature on this fabulous cover.

**Price £45    Stock Code 16065**

Royal Mail has also re-issued the £sd low value 'Wilding' definitives with decimal values.

(2) 1998 The Definitive Portrait - From prestige stamp book ............£45   2262
(3) 2002 A Gracious Accession - From prestige stamp book .............£25   5062
(4) 2002 Wildings Reprints - Miniature Sheet No. 1   .................£25   25522
(5) 2003 Wildings Reprints - Miniature Sheet No. 2   .................£25   8329

Order online at www.bfdc.co.uk using the stock codes above, or send cheque to:

A G BRADBURY   3 LINK ROAD   STONEYGATE   LEICESTER   LE2 3RA

218

**POSTAGE DUES** *(plain envelopes)* £

| | | £ |
|---|---|---|
| 20 Apr 14 | ½d Green (postcard) | 750 |
| | 1d Red (cover or postcard) | 500 |
| | 2d Black | 700 |
| | 5d Brown | 1,500 |
| 23 Dec 20 | 4d Dull grey-green | 1,000 |
| 1 Oct 24 | 1½d Chestnut | 500 |
| 7 Jun 56 | 1d Violet-blue | 900 |
| 1 Oct 68 | 8d Red | 750 |

**TO PAY LABELS** *(Illustrated envelopes)*

| | | £ |
|---|---|---|
| 17 Jun 70 | **To Pay Labels: 10p, 20p, 50p, £1** | 500 |
| | **To Pay Labels: ½p, 1p, 2p, 3p, 4p, 5p** | |
| 15 Feb 71 | Authentic C.D.S. postmarks | 750 |
| 11 Mar 71 | Official issue date C.D.S. pmks | 125 |
| 2 Apr 73 | **£5 To Pay Label** | 450 |
| 21 Aug 74 | **7p To Pay Label** .....................(1) | 50 |
| 18 Jun 75 | **11p To Pay Label** ...................(2) | 40 |
| 9 Jun 82 | **1p-£5 To Pay Labels:** | |
| | Stratford permanent h/s | 400 |
| | Any CDS on one or two covers | 30 |
| 15 Feb 94 | **To Pay Labels: 1p-£5** (9 values) | |
| | First Day of Issue – London EC3 | 25 |
| | To Pay Labels, Windsor special h/s | 25 |
| | -do- Bradbury official cover ............(4) | 50 |
| | Tower of London special h/s | 25 |
| | -do- Benham official pair of covers ...(6) | 35 |
| | Authentic Surcharge/C.O.D. pmk .....(5) | 125 |

**FRAMA LABELS** *(Illustrated envelopes)*

| | | £ |
|---|---|---|
| 1 May 84 | **Frama Labels: ½p-16p** | |
| | (32 values) on six covers: | |
| | Philatelic Bureau spec h/s | 20 |
| | Cambridge special h/s | 25 |
| | London EC special h/s | 25 |
| | Southampton special h/s | 25 |
| | Windsor special h/s | 20 |
| | Set: 6 covers with related CDS | 100 |
| | Set on one cover with CDS ............(3) | 75 |
| 28 Aug 84 | **Frama Labels: 16½p & 17p** | |
| | Philatelic Counter handstamps | 2 |

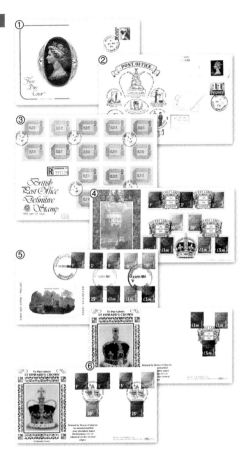

| | | £ |
|---|---|---|
| 1 Aug 1883 | **6d Parcel Service** | 750 |
| 9 Sep 1911 | **Coronation UK First Aerial Post** | |
| | ½d Green (Postcard) | 55 |
| | ½d -do- Privilege card in violet | 250 |
| | 1d Red (Envelope) | 80 |
| | 1d -do- Privilege envelope in violet | 350 |
| 25 Jan 1912 | **Wilkinson Meter Mail** | 300 |
| 1 Feb 1961 | **Recorded Delivery** ...............(10) | 60 |
| 16 Sep 1968 | **Two Tier Post** pair of covers | 10 |
| | -do- Windsor postmark | 30 |
| 24 Nov 1975 | **SpeedPost** Brighton or Bexhill pmks.....(11) | 35 |
| 24 Jan 1977 | **SpeedPost** Extension of service | 150 |
| 12 Oct 1998 | **Special Delivery** | 15 |
| 14 Feb 2002 | **Automated Postage Labels** Set of seven. | 90 |
| 15 Jan 2004 | **SmartStamp Service** Set of eight | 95 |
| 31 Mar 2009 | **Post and Go Labels** Set of five .........(12) | 10 |

## Commemorative Labels

|  |  | Ordinary covers £ | Sponsored covers £ |
|---|---|---|---|
| 27 Jul 94 | **£1 Bank of England** | | |
| | Bank of Eng (1694–1994) | 10 | 25 Royal Mail |
| | Bank of Eng (Britannia) ....(1) | 10 | 25 Bradbury |
| | 300 Years Bank of Eng | 10 | 20 Benham |
| | Stock Exch or Britannia CDS .. | 35 | – |
| 16 May 95 | **£1 Spitfire** | | |
| | Stoke on Trent | 5 | 15 Royal Mail |
| | Southampton (signature) ....(2) | 5 | 20 Bradbury |
| | Southampton Spitfire | 5 | 10 Benham |
| | Stoke Mitchell Designer | 5 | 10 Benham |
| | Mitchell BF 2465 PS | 5 | – |
| | VE Day BBMF, SW1 | 5 | 20 CoverCraft |
| | Biggin Hill or Eastleigh CDS .. | 10 | – |
| | Butt Lane, Stoke CDS | 10 | – |
| 16 Apr 96 | **£1 Queen's Birthday** | | |
| | Westminster Abbey | 5 | 10 Benham |
| | Bruton Street, SW1 | 5 | 10 Benham |
| | Queen Street, W1 | 5 | 10 Benham |
| | Windsor spec h/s | 5 | 10 Benham |
| | London SW1 ..........................(3) | 5 | 20 Bradbury |
| | Balmoral | 5 | 20 Bradbury |
| | Windsor (Castle) | 5 | 20 Bradbury |
| | Windsor CDS | 8 | – |
| 12 Feb 97 | **£1.04 Hong Kong** | | |
| | Farewell Chinatown | 6 | 15 Benham |
| | Parliament Square | 6 | 10 Benham |
| | London SW1 | 6 | 10 Benham |
| | Chinatown W1 (junk)..........(4) | 6 | 15 Bradbury |
| | BFPO Hong Kong CDS | 25 | – |
| | Any relevant CDS | 10 | – |
| 21 Oct 97 | **£1.04 Commonwealth** | | |
| | Edinburgh (circ. text) | 5 | 10 Benham |
| | Edinburgh (rect. text) | 5 | 10 Benham |
| | Edinburgh (building) | 5 | 10 Benham |
| | Edinburgh (thistle) | 5 | 12 Bradbury |
| | Any Edinburgh CDS | 8 | – |
| 14 Nov 98 | **£1.04 Prince of Wales** | | |
| | 50th Birthday Tetbury | 5 | 15 Royal Mail |
| | Tetbury, Glos | 5 | 10 Benham |
| | Balmoral | 5 | 10 Benham |
| | Windsor | 5 | 10 Benham |
| | Caernarfon | 5 | 10 Benham |
| | Balmoral ..........................(5) | 5 | 12 Bradbury |
| | The Mall, SW1 | 5 | 12 Westminster |
| | St. Pauls | 5 | 12 Westminster |
| | RN Covers | 5 | 20 RN CvrsGp |
| | Any relevant CDS pmk | 8 | – |
| 12 May 99 | **£1.04 Berlin Airlift** | | |
| | Brize Norton Carterton | 5 | 15 Royal Mail |
| | Watford | 5 | 10 Benham |
| | Oakington, Cambridge | 5 | 10 Benham |
| | Lyneham RAF Station | 5 | 10 Benham |
| | Brize Norton, Oxford | 5 | 10 Benham |
| | RAF Lyneham ......................(6) | 5 | 12 Bradbury |
| | Oakington, Cambs | 5 | 10 RN CvrsGp |
| | HMS Glasgow | 5 | 10 RN CvrsGp |
| | RAF Abingdon | 5 | 10 Cam.SC |
| | RAF Museum, NW9 | 5 | 10 Westminster |
| | Settle Rd, E13 | 5 | 12 PM Payne |
| | Any relevant CDS pmk | 8 | – |
| 1 Oct 99 | **£1.04 Rugby World Cup** | | |
| | Caerdydd, Cardiff | 5 | 15 Royal Mail |
| | Rugby 1999, Twickenham | 5 | 10 Benham |
| | Rugby 1999, Cardiff | 5 | 10 Benham |
| | Rugby 1999, Edinburgh | 5 | 10 Benham, |
| | Rugby 1999, Belfast | 5 | 10 Benham |
| | Birthplace of Rugby ...........(7) | 5 | 12 Bradbury |
| | Rugby, the Cup | 5 | 12 PM Payne |
| | Cardiff, Wales | 5 | 10 Westminster |
| | Widnes Vikings RLFC | 5 | 10 P Sheridan |

|  |  | Ordinary covers £ | Sponsored covers £ |
|---|---|---|---|
|  | Rugby Street | 5 | 20 GBFDC |
|  | Royal Naval Rugby | 5 | 10 RN CvrsGp |
| 21 Mar 00 | **£1.04 Postman Pat** |  |  |
|  | Keswick | 5 | 10 Benham |
|  | London SW13 | 5 | 10 Benham |
|  | Leeds | 5 | 10 Benham |
|  | Colne | 5 | 10 Benham |
|  | Children's Favourite............(8) | 5 | 20 Bradbury |
|  | Pattishall Post Office | 5 | 12 M Brazier |
| 4 Apr 00 | **£1.04 Botanical** |  |  |
|  | Llanarthne | 5 | 10 Benham |
|  | Llanarthne (bee) | 5 | 10 Benham |
|  | Kew, Richmond | 5 | 10 Benham |
|  | Westonbirt, Tetbury | 5 | 10 Benham |
|  | Llanarthne | 5 | 10 Benham |
|  | Kew, Richmond ..................(9) | 5 | 12 Bradbury |
|  | Llanarthney | 5 | 12 Royal Mail |
| 29 Jan 01 | **£1.62 Queen Victoria -** |  |  |
|  | **prices for complete label and six stamps** |  |  |
|  | Victoria Centenary.............(10) | 6 | 25 Bradbury |
|  | The Strand | 6 | 10 Westminster |
|  | Kensington | 6 | 10 Westminster |
|  | Autographed Editions | 6 | – Westminster |
|  | 1st Ever Self Adhesive | 6 | – Internetstamps |
|  | East Cowes (circle) | 6 | – Benham |
|  | Windsor | 6 | – Benham |
|  | East Cowes | 6 | – Benham |
|  | East Cowes (oval) | 6 | – Benham |
|  | London SW1 | 6 | – Benham |
|  | Self Adhesive Stamp Bks | 6 | – n.o.c. |
|  | Battle of Assaye | 6 | – Benham |

## Retail Book Panes

*The four special Retail Books issued in 1999-2000 contain two panes of stamps, viz: one pane of eight 1st Class definitives and one pane of two special stamps.*
*Values are for covers with the special stamp pane only.*

### 12th May 1999 Special Retail Book No.1
*26p Pilgrim Fathers & 26p Mill Towns*
**Price Guide Ordinary Covers £2-£3/Official Covers:**
(1)  Millennium Bklt Edinburgh ............£15 Benham
(2)  Millennium Bklt Bolton ...................£15 Benham
(3)  Millennium Bklt Greenwich ............£15 Benham
(4)  Millennium Bklt Plymouth..... (11) £15 Benham
(5)  Windsor Berks....................................£15 Bradbury

### 21st Sept 1999 Special Retail Book No.2
*2 x 26p Farmers' Tale*
**Price Guide Ordinary Covers £2-£3/Official Covers:**
(1)  Millennium Bklt Detling..................£15 Benham
(2)  Millennium Bklt Belfast...................£15 Benham
(3)  Millennium Bklt Cardiff...................£15 Benham
(4)  Millennium Bklt Stoneleigh ... (12) £15 Benham
(5)  Windsor Berks....................................£15 Bradbury

### 26th May 2000 Special Retail Book No.3
*1 x 1st Space Centre & 1x 1st Web of life* (13) *(As the Space Centre stamp was a new issue, i.e. a 1st Class NVI, please see Commemorative Section for details of this issue)*

### 5th Sept 2000 Special Retail Book No.4
*1 x 1st Trans Pennine Trail & 1 x 1st Eden Project*
**Price Guide Ordinary Covers £2-£3/Official Covers:**
(1)  St. Austell (Arms) .............................£15 Benham
(2)  St. Austell (Swirls)............................£15 Benham
(3)  St. Austell (Deocorative Border).....£15 Benham
(4)  Millennium Bklt, Liverpool.............£15 Benham
(5)  Pennine Trail, Barnsley........... (14) £20 Bradbury
(6)  Garden of Eden, St. Austell .............£20 Bradbury
(7)  Eden Project, St. Austell ...................£20 Mill Comm Cvrs

See thousands more British first day covers at www.bfdc.co.uk

✗ **Incomplete Panes**

✓ **Complete Panes**

✓ **Complete Panes**

✓ **Complete Panes**

✓ *Prices are for the set of four covers with the complete pane of stamps plus descriptive/pictorial panel affixed to the covers, e.g. 2nd Wedgwood set illustrated alongside.* ✗ *Covers with the stamps only, e.g. 1st Wedgwood set, are worth considerably less. Sponsored covers exist for most issues - these are worth at least a 50% premium, often more.*

| | | £ |
|---|---|---|
| **1 Dec 1969 £1 Stamps for Cooks** | | |
| (1) Milk Marketing special h/s | | 95 |
| **24 May 1972 £1 Wedgwood** (1) | | |
| (2) Bureau special h/s | | 75 |
| (3) Barlaston special h/s | | 110 |
| **16 Apr 1980 £3 Wedgwood** (2) | | |
| (4) Bureau special h/s | | 30 |
| (5) Barlaston special h/s | | 40 |
| Burslem CDS | | 150 |
| **19 May 1982 £4 Stanley Gibbons** | | |
| (6) Bureau special h/s | | 25 |
| (7) London WC FDI h/s | | 35 |
| (8) Plymouth special h/s | | 45 |
| London WC special h/s | | 45 |
| **14 Sep 1983 £4 Royal Mint** | | |
| (9) Bureau special h/s | | 35 |
| (10) Llantrisant special h/s | | 50 |
| **4 Sep 1984 £4 Christian Heritage** (3) | | |
| (11) Bureau special h/s | | 25 |
| (12) Canterbury special h/s | | 30 |
| (13) St. Mary le Strand h/s | | 50 |
| (14) St. James Piccadilly h/s | | 50 |
| Christian Heritage slogan | | 75 |
| Holy Island CDS or similar | | 55 |
| **8 Jan 1985 £5 The Times** | | |
| (15) Bureau special h/s | | 25 |
| (16) London WC special h/s | | 30 |
| Times 1785-1985 slogan pmk | | 80 |
| Fleet Street CDS | | 80 |
| **18 Mar 1986 £5 British Rail** | | |
| (17) Crewe special h/s | | 35 |
| (18) Bureau special h/s | | 25 |
| T.P.O. pmks | | 60 |
| Railway slogans or CDS | | 50 |
| **3 Mar 1987 £5 P & O** | | |
| (19) Bureau special h/s | | 35 |
| (20) Falmouth special h/s | | 45 |
| (21) Spring Stampex special h/s | | 75 |
| Maritime Mail CDS | | 85 |
| Appropriate CDS | | 55 |
| Clydebank slogan | | 95 |
| **9 Feb 1988 £5 Financial Times** | | |
| (22) Bureau special h/s | | 30 |
| (23) London EC4 special h/s | | 40 |
| Fleet Street C.D.S. | | 80 |
| **21 Mar 1989 £5 Scots Connection** (4) | | |
| (24) Bureau special h/s | | 15 |
| (25) Inverness special h/s | | 30 |
| Appropriate CDS pmks | | 45 |
| Visit Isle of Skye slogan | | 45 |
| **20 Mar 1990 £5 London Life** | | |
| (26) Bureau special h/s | | 15 |
| (27) Tower Hill special h/s | | 25 |
| (28) Stamp World special h/s | | 35 |
| (29) Victorian Heritage h/s | | 35 |
| Set of four different handstamps | | 35 |
| Relevant CDS or slogans | | 50 |
| **19 Mar 1991 £6 Agatha Christie** | | |
| (30) Bureau special h/s | | 20 |
| (31) Marple special h/s | | 45 |
| (32) Orient Express h/s | | 45 |
| (33) Sunningdale special h/s | | 45 |
| Set of four different handstamps | | 45 |
| Torquay CDS | | 60 |
| Bite out of Crime slogan | | 35 |

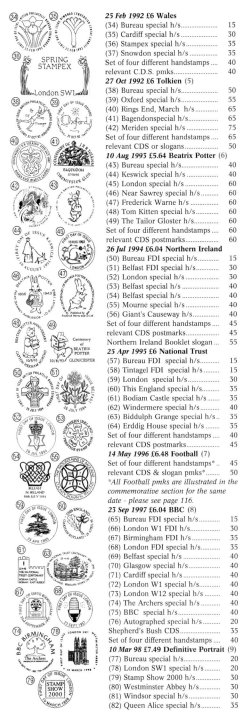

### 25 Feb 1992 £6 Wales
| | |
|---|---|
| (34) Bureau special h/s.................... | 15 |
| (35) Cardiff special h/s.................... | 30 |
| (36) Stampex special h/s................ | 35 |
| (37) Snowdon special h/s................ | 35 |
| Set of four different handstamps .... | 40 |
| relevant C.D.S. pmks........................ | 40 |

### 27 Oct 1992 £6 Tolkien (5)
| | |
|---|---|
| (38) Bureau special h/s.................... | 50 |
| (39) Oxford special h/s.................... | 55 |
| (40) Rings End, March  h/s............ | 65 |
| (41) Bagendon special h/s............... | 65 |
| (42) Meriden special h/s ................ | 75 |
| Set of four different handstamps .... | 65 |
| relevant CDS or slogans.................. | 50 |

### 10 Aug 1993 £5.64 Beatrix Potter (6)
| | |
|---|---|
| (43) Bureau special h/s.................... | 40 |
| (44) Keswick special h/s................. | 40 |
| (45) London special h/s .................. | 60 |
| (46) Near Sawrey special h/s.......... | 60 |
| (47) Frederick Warne h/s ............... | 60 |
| (48) Tom Kitten special h/s............. | 60 |
| (49) The Tailor Gloster h/s............. | 60 |
| Set of four different handstamps .... | 60 |
| relevant CDS postmarks.................. | 60 |

### 26 Jul 1994 £6.04 Northern Ireland
| | |
|---|---|
| (50) Bureau FDI special h/s............ | 15 |
| (51) Belfast FDI special h/s............ | 30 |
| (52) London special h/s.................. | 30 |
| (53) Belfast special h/s .................. | 40 |
| (54) Belfast special h/s .................. | 40 |
| (55) Mourne special h/s.................. | 40 |
| (56) Giant's Causeway h/s.............. | 40 |
| Set of four different handstamps .... | 45 |
| relevant CDS postmarks.................. | 45 |
| Northern Ireland Booklet slogan .. | 55 |

### 25 Apr 1995 £6 National Trust
| | |
|---|---|
| (57) Bureau FDI  special h/s.......... | 15 |
| (58) Tintagel FDI  special h/s........ | 15 |
| (59) London  special h/s................. | 30 |
| (60) This England special h/s.......... | 35 |
| (61) Bodiam Castle special h/s........ | 35 |
| (62) Windermere special h/s........... | 40 |
| (63) Biddulph Grange special h/s... | 35 |
| (64) Erddig House special h/s ....... | 35 |
| Set of four different handstamps .... | 40 |
| relevant CDS postmarks.................. | 45 |

### 14 May 1996 £6.48 Football (7)
| | |
|---|---|
| Set of four different handstamps* .. | 45 |
| relevant CDS & slogan pmks*....... | 50 |

*All Football pmks are illustrated in the commemorative section for the same date - please see page 116.

### 23 Sep 1997 £6.04 BBC (8)
| | |
|---|---|
| (65) Bureau FDI special h/s........... | 15 |
| (66) London W1 FDI h/s................. | 30 |
| (67) Birmingham FDI h/s............... | 35 |
| (68) London FDI special h/s.......... | 35 |
| (69) Belfast special h/s .................. | 40 |
| (70) Glasgow special h/s................. | 40 |
| (71) Cardiff special h/s .................. | 40 |
| (72) London W1 special h/s............ | 40 |
| (73) London W12 special h/s .......... | 40 |
| (74) The Archers special h/s .......... | 40 |
| (75) BBC special h/s...................... | 40 |
| (76) Autographed special h/s.......... | 20 |
| Shepherd's Bush CDS...................... | 35 |
| Set of four different handstamps .... | 40 |

### 10 Mar 98 £7.49 Definitive Portrait (9)
| | |
|---|---|
| (77) Bureau special h/s.................... | 20 |
| (78) London SW1 special h/s......... | 20 |
| (79) Stamp Show 2000 h/s.............. | 30 |
| (80) Westminster Abbey h/s............ | 30 |
| (81) Windsor special h/s................. | 30 |
| (82) Queen Alice special h/s.......... | 35 |

223

**Definitive Portrait (Contd)** (10)    **£**
(83) Bond Street special h/s ........ 30
(84) Earl's Court special h/s ....... 30
(85) Portman Square h/s ............. 30
(86) King Edward Street h/s ........ 30
(87) Longford special h/s ............ 30
Set of four different handstamps ... 35

**13 Oct 1998 £6.16 Speed** (11)
(88) FDI - Bureau h/s ................. 15
(89) FDI - Chislehurst h/s ........... 20
(90) FDI - London h/s ................ 30
(91) Pendine special h/s ............. 30
(92) Pendine (flags) h/s ............. 30
(93) Beaulieu special h/s ............ 30
(94) Duxford special h/s ............ 30
(95) Coniston special h/s ........... 30
(96) Chislehurst special h/s ........ 30
Set of four different handstamps ... 30

**16 Feb 1999 £7.49 Profile on Print** (12)
*NB Five panes/covers in this set*
(97) FDI - Bureau h/s ................. 20
(98) FDI - London SW1 h/s ........ 20
(99) Windsor h/s ..................... 35
(1) Self Adhesive, Windsor h/s ... 35
(2) Machin Portrait h/s ............ 35
(3) Piccadilly W1 h/s ............... 35
(4) Millbank, SW1 h/s ............. 35
(5) High Wycombe h/s ............. 35
(6) Stoke on Trent h/s ............. 35
(7) Walsall h/s ...................... 35
(8) Parkhouse Street SE5 h/s ..... 35
Set of five different handstamps .... 35

**21 Sept 99 £6.99 World Changers** (13)
*NB Five panes/covers in this set*
(9) FDI - Bureau h/s ................. 20
(10) FDI - Downe h/s ............... 20
(11) Exhibition Road, SW7 h/s .... 30
(12) Birmingham New Age h/s .... 30
(13) Charles Darwin h/s ............ 30
(14) Michael Faraday h/s ........... 30
(15) Alan Turing h/s ................ 30
(16) Edward Jenner h/s ............. 30
(17) Moon Street, N1 h/s .......... 30
Set of five different handstamps .... 30

**15 Feb 2000 £7.70 Special by Design**
(18) FDI - Bureau h/s ................ 15
(19) FDI - London SW5 h/s ........ 15
(20) Buckingham Palace Rd h/s ... 25
(21) Nat Postal Musuem h/s ....... 25
(22) Belfast special h/s .............. 25
(23) Edinburgh special h/s ......... 25
(24) Cardiff special h/s ............. 25
(25) Earl's Court special h/s ....... 25
(26) London EC4 special h/s ...... 25
(27) Westminster Abbey h/s ....... 25
(28) Earl's Court h/s ................ 25
Set of four different handstamps ... 25

**4 Aug 2000 £7.03 Queen Mother**
Set of four different handstamps* . 25
*All Queen Mother pmks are illustrated
in the commemorative section for the
same date - please see page 143.*

**18 Sept 2000 £7 A Treasury of Trees**
(29) FDI - Bureau h/s ................ 15
(30) FDI - Llangernyw h/s .......... 15
(31) Kew Gardens h/s ............... 30
(32) Sherwood Forest h/s ........... 25
(33) London SW7 h/s ............... 25
(34) Cardiff h/s ...................... 25
(35) Glasgow h/s ..................... 25
(36) Ardingly h/s .................... 25
(37) London SW7 h/s ............... 25
(38) Birmingham h/s ................ 25

At *www.bfdc.co.uk*
you will find superb albums
to house your British first
day covers and Smilers stamp
sheets.

## Channel Islands Occupation Issues

| | plain covers £ | illus cvrs £ |
|---|---|---|
| **Guernsey Bisects** | | |
| 27 Dec 1940 2d Orange George V (Profile) | 125 | – |
| 2d Orange George V (Gravure) | 90 | – |
| 2d Orange George VI | 35 | – |
| 2d Orange Centenary | 25 | – |
| **Guernsey 'ARMS' issues** | | |
| 7 Apr 1941 ¹/₂d green | 10 | 50 |
| 11 Mar 1942 -do- on Bluish French Banknote paper | 300 | – |
| 18 Feb 1941 1d scarlet | 10 | 50 |
| 9 Apr 1942 -do- on Bluish French Banknote paper | 100 | – |
| 12 Apr 1944 2¹/₂d blue (63) | 20 | 75 |
| All 3 values on one cover with correct dates | 100 | – |
| **Jersey 'VIEWS' issues** | | |
| 1 Jun 1943 ¹/₂d green | 10 | 40 |
| 1 Jun 1943 1d scarlet | 10 | 40 |
| 1 Jun 1943 ¹/₂d & 1d on one cover | 20 | 60 |
| 8 Jun 1943 1¹/₂d brown (62) | 15 | 50 |
| 8 Jun 1943 2d orange-yellow | 15 | 50 |
| 8 Jun 1943 1¹/₂d & 2d on one cover | 25 | 80 |
| 29 Jun 1943 2¹/₂d blue | 15 | 75 |
| 29 Jun 1943 3d violet | 15 | 75 |
| 29 Jun 1943 2¹/₂d & 3d on one cover | 25 | 125 |
| All 6 values on one cover with correct dates for each pair | 45 | – |
| **Jersey 'ARMS' issues** | | |
| 29 Jan 1942 ¹/₂d green (61) | 10 | 50 |
| 1 Apr 1941 1d red | 10 | 50 |
| Both stamps on one cover with correct dates | 80 | – |

225

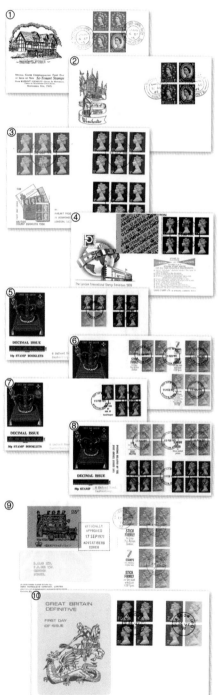

## Stamp Book Panes

*Book panes are included if some or all of the stamps are new or different (e.g. se-tenant formats, perfs, phosphors, gums, papers etc) to those previously issued. Prices are for the complete panes on cover - as per illustrations.*

|  | plain covers £ | illus. cvrs £ |
|---|---|---|
| 3 May51 **1s Book:** (4 x ¹/₂d; 4 x 1d; 4 x 1¹/₂d)..... | - | 200 |
| 15 July 63 **2s Holiday Book:** 4 x 2¹/₂d .................. | 40 | 100 |
| Se-tenant 3 x ¹/₂d + 2¹/₂d........................ | 30 | 90 |
| 6 Sep 63 **2s Book reprint:** 2 panes as above (1).. | 50 | 90 |
| 1 Jul 64 **2s Holiday Book:** Se-tenant 2 x 2¹/₂d + 2 x ¹/₂d | | |
| Se-tenant pane tourist pmks .........*each* n.k. | | 10 |
| Holiday resort slogan pmks ..................... | 10 | 25 |
| 21 Jun 65 **6s Book:** 6 x 4d ......................................... | 100 | 175 |
| 16 Aug 65 **2s Book:** 2 panes: | | |
| (2 x 1d + 2 x 3d) + (4 x 4d) .............. | 50 | 150 |
| Se-tenant pane only (2) ...................... | 15 | 70 |
| 6 Dec 65 **2s Christmas Book:** 4 x 3d .................... | 100 | 275 |
| 21 Sep 67 **6s Machin Book:** 6 x 4d...................... | 5 | 100 |
| 25 Mar 68 **10s Livingstone Book:** 3 panes Stampex pmk: | | |
| (6 x 4d; 6 x 3d; 6 x 1d) ...................... | 10 | 100 |
| 6 Apr 68 **2s Machin Book:** 2 panes: | | |
| (2 x 1d + 2 x 3d)+(4 x 4d) ...................... | 20 | 70 |
| 10 Jul 68 **4s 6d Cutty Sark Book:** 2 panes: | | |
| (6 x 4d)+(6 x 1d) .................................. | 20 | 110 |
| 16 Sep 68 **2s Book:** 2 panes: | | |
| (4 x 4d)+(2 x 4d + 2 L) ...................... | 5 | 20 |
| -do- Windsor postmark............................ | 8 | 30 |
| **4s 6d Golden Hind Book:** 3 panes: | | |
| 2 @ (6 x 4d)+(6 x 1d)........................ | 10 | 70 |
| **10s Scott Book:** 3 panes: | | |
| (6 x 4d)+(6 x 5d)+(4 x 1d + 2 x 4d) (3) | 15 | 100 |
| 16 Oct 68 **6s Woodpecker Book:** 6 x 4d ............... | 15 | 110 |
| 27 Nov68 **5s Ightham Mote Book:** 6 x 5d ............. | 15 | 110 |
| 8 Jan 69 **4s 6d QE2 Bklt:** two panes* ................... | 15 | 80 |
| **10s Mary Kingsley Book:** three panes* | 20 | 80 |
| *10s known with 6 January date* | | |
| 28 Feb 69 **6s Barn Owl Book:** 6 x 4d ...................... | 10 | 80 |
| 3 Mar 69 **2s Book:** two panes* ............................. | 5 | 80 |
| **As 16 Sep 1968 but 4d colour change to red.* | | |
| 3 Mar 70 **5s Philympia Book:** | | |
| 6 x 5d Stampex pmk (4) .......................... | 5 | 60 |

*L = Label; CB = Centre Band Phos SB = Side Band Phos*

|  | Windsor Postmark £ | Other Pmks £ |
|---|---|---|
| 15 Feb 71 **New Decimal Books:** | | |
| 10p Pillar Boxes (2 x 2p + 2 x ¹/₂p) (5) | | |
| +(2 x 1p + 2 x 1¹/₂p) Vertical format | | |
| 25p Omnibus (5 x 2¹/₂p + L)+(4 x 2¹/₂p + 2 L) | | |
| +(5 x ¹/₂p + L) (6) | | |
| 30p Curlew (5 x 3p + L) (7) | | |
| 50p Bindweed (6 x 3p)+(4 x 3p + 2 x 2¹/₂p SB) | | |
| +(5 x 2¹/₂p CB + L)+(5 x ¹/₂p + L) (8) | | |
| Set of 10 panes ................................. | 100 | 50 |
| Set of 3 se-tenant panes.......................... | 40 | 15 |
| 14 Jul 71 **10p Book:** (2 x 2p + 2 x ¹/₂p) (10) | | |
| +(2 x 1p + 2 x 1¹/₂p) Horizontal..... | 450 | 400 |
| 23 Jul 71 **30p Bk:** (5 x 3p + L imperf in margin*).... | 350 | 200 |
| 17 Sep 71 **25p Book:** (5 x 2¹/₂p + L)+(4 x 2¹/₂p + 2 L) | | |
| +(5 x ¹/₂p + L) (9) | | |
| Labels imperf in margin* – 3 panes....... | n.k. | 150 |
| **50p Book:** (5 x 2¹/₂p CB + L)+(5 x ¹/₂p + L) | | |
| Labels imperf in margin* – 2 panes....... | 180 | 125 |
| **Changes introduced as an aid to the blind.* | | |
| 24 Dec 71 **25p & 50p Christmas Books:** | | |
| **25p** (5 x ¹/₂p + L)+(5 x 2¹/₂p + L)+(4 x 2¹/₂p + 2 L) | | |
| **50p** (5 x 2¹/₂p + L) – *different to 25p booklet* | | |
| Four panes with Southampton pmk ...... | n.k. | 95 |
| 14 Nov71 **50p Book:** Two panes (11) ..................... | 140 | 80 |
| (5 x 3¹/₂p + L)+(5 x 3p CB + L) | | |
| 30 Jan 74 **30p Book:** 5 x 3 CB p + L ..................... | n.k. | 50 |

| | Windsor Postmark £ | Other Pmks £ |
|---|---|---|
| 9 Oct 74 **45p Book:** 5 x 4$^1$/2p + L (12) | 150 | 70 |
| 23 Oct 74 **35p Book:** 5 x 3$^1$/2p phos + L | 100 | 60 |
| 10 Mar76 **10p Book:** 2 x $^1$/2p; 3 x 1p; 1 x 6p | 3 | 1 |
| -do- Telecom h/s (official cover) (13) | – | 15 |
| 14 Jul 76 **65p, 85p** (10 x 6$^1$/2p)+(10 x 8$^1$/2p) (14) | 100 | 45 |
| 26 Jan 77 **50p Books:** 2 @ | | |
| (2 x $^1$/2p; 2 x 1p; 2 x 6$^1$/2p; 4 x 8$^1$/2p) | | |
| Pair of mirror image panes | 12 | 4 |
| 13 Jun 77 **50p Books:** 2 @ (2 x 1p; 3 x 7p; 3 x 9p) | | |
| Pair of mirror image panes | 8 | 4 |
| **70p & 90p Books:** (10 x 7p)+(10 x 9p) | 20 | 9 |
| **30p & 60p Sachet Books** | 150 | – |
| **10p Book:** Reprint:narrow selvedge | – | 60 |
| 8 Feb 78 **10p Bk:** (2 x $^1$/2p; 2 x 1p; 1 x 7p + L) | 2 | 1 |
| 15 Nov78 **£1.60 Xmas Book:** (10 x 9p; 10 x 7p) | 5 | 2 |
| 5 Feb 79 **70p Book:** (10 x 7p) Kedleston Hall; | | |
| **90p Book:** (10 x 9p) Tramway Museum, Crich. | | |
| Derby CDS **or** Postcode pmk (pair) (15) | – | 150 |
| Kedleston CDS & Crich CDS (pair) | – | 125 |
| *Issued in conjunction with the opening of* | | |
| *Derby Mechanised Letter Office.* | | |
| 28 Aug 79 **50p Books:** (2 x 2p; 2 x 8p; 3 x 10p + L) | | |
| Pair of mirror image panes | 5 | 2 |
| 3 Oct 79 **80p & £1 Books:** (10 x 8p)+(10 x 10p) | 6 | 3 |
| 17 Oct 79 **10p 'London 1980'**(2 x 1p; 1 x 8p + L) | 2 | 1 |
| -do- 'London 1980' slogan pmk | – | 3 |
| 14 Nov79 **£1.80 Xmas Book:** (10 x 10p; 10 x 8p). | 3 | 2 |
| BPE Wembley special h/s | – | 6 |
| 4 Feb 80 **50p Books:** (3 x 2p; 2 x 10p; 2 x 12p + L) | | |
| Pair of mirror image panes | 8 | 3 |
| 4 Feb 80 **£1 & £1.20:** (10 x 10p)+(10 x 12p) | 10 | 4 |
| 25 Jun 80 **50p Chambon:** (as 4th February) | | |
| Pair of mirror image panes | 80 | 70 |
| 27 Aug80 **10p Chambon: 'London 1980'** | 2 | 1 |
| 12 Nov80 **£2.20 Xmas Bk:** (10 x 12p; 10 x 10p) | 4 | 3 |
| 26 Jan 81 **50p Books:** (1 x $^1$/2p;1 x 1p; 3 x 11$^1$/2p; 1 x 14p) | | |
| Pair of mirror image panes | 5 | 2 |
| 26 Jan 81 **£1.15 & £1.40:** (10x11$^1$/2p)+(10x14p) | 6 | 3 |
| 6 May81 **£1.30 National Stamp Day Book:** | 3 | 1 |
| Birmingham or British Library h/s | – | 3 |
| Cameo Stamp Centre special h/s | – | 3 |
| London EC special h/s | – | 3 |
| Pair of mirror image panes | 7 | 2 |
| 26 Aug81 **50p Books:** (3 x 2$^1$/2p; 2 x 4p; 3 x 11$^1$/2p) | | |
| Pair of mirror image panes (16) | 7 | 2 |
| 11 Nov81 **£2.55 Xmas:** (10 x 11$^1$/2p; 10 x 14p) | 7 | 3 |
| 1 Feb 82 **50p Books:** (1 x $^1$/2p; 4 x 3p; 3 x 12$^1$/2p) | | |
| Pair of mirror image panes | 4 | 1 |
| 1 Feb 82 **£1.25 & £1.55 Books:** | | |
| (10 x 12$^1$/2p)+(10 x 15$^1$/2p) | 6 | 3 |
| **£1.43 Book:** (4 x 12$^1$/2p + 6 x 15$^1$/2p) | | |
| Pair of mirror image panes (17) | 8 | 2 |
| 10 Nov82 **£2.55 Xmas Book:** | | |
| (10 x 12$^1$/2p; 10 x 15$^1$/2p) | 6 | 3 |
| Star, Glenrothes CDS | – | 15 |
| *Sold at 30p discount. Star printed on reverse.* | | |
| 5 Apr 83 **50p Glos 'Old Spot' Book:** | 2 | 1 |
| (2 x 1p; 3 x 3$^1$/2p; 3 x 12$^1$/2p) | | |
| Cotswold Farm Park special h/s | – | 5 |
| -do- Benham official cvr | – | 10 |
| **£1.60 Book:** (10 x 16p) | 5 | 3 |
| **£1.46 Books:** (4 x 12$^1$/2p; 6 x 16p) | | |
| Pair of mirror image panes | 10 | 4 |
| 10 Aug83 **£1.45 Discount Book:** (10 x 16p) | 7 | 3 |
| *Sold at 15p discount + printed 'D' on reverse.* | | |
| 9 Nov83 **£2.20 Christmas Book:** (20 x 12$^1$/2p) | 5 | 2 |
| -do- Aladdin WC2 special handstamp | – | 15 |
| *30p discount with star printed on reverse.* | | |
| 3 Sep 84 **£1.54 Books:** (4 x 13p; 6 x 17p) | | |
| Pair of mirror image panes | 5 | 3 |
| **50p Books:** (3 x 1p; 2 x 4p; 3 x 13p) | 3 | 1 |
| **£1.30 & £1.70:** (10 x 13p)+(10 x 17p) | 15 | 6 |

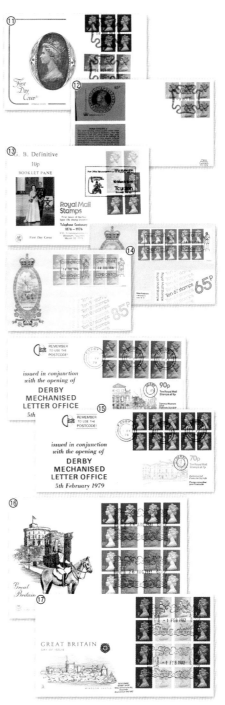

| | Windsor Postmark £ | Other Pmks £ |
|---|---|---|

5 Mar85 **£1.55 Discount Book:** (10 x 17p) ......... 7 — 3
*Sold at 15p discount + printed 'D' on reverse.*

4 Nov85 **50p Discount Book:** (3 x 17p + L)........ 3 — 1
*Sold at a 1p discount with star printed on reverse.*

14 Jan 86 **£1.20 Book:** (10 x 12p)........................... 6 — 2
**£1.50 Books:** (4 x 12p; 6 x 17p) (1)
Pair of mirror image panes...................... 10 — 4

29 Jul 86 **50p Book: (2** x 1p; 4 x 12p) ..................... 2 — 1
**£1 Book:** (6 x 17p) *2p discount* .................. 7 — 3

12 Aug 86 **50p Book:** (3 x 17p + label) *1p disc..* 2 — 1
*Different to 4 Nov 1985 issue - no Star underprint*

20 Oct 86 **50p 'Roman Britain' Book:**
(1p + 13p; 2 x 18p) ..................................... 2 — 1
St. Albans h/s or Porchester CDS (2) .. – — 4
**50p 'Pond Life' Book:**
(1p + 2 x 5p; 3 x 13p) ............................. 2 — 1
Pond CDS .... – — 4
**£1** (1 x 13p; 5 x 18p) *3p discount* ......... 3 — 2
**£1.30 & £1.80:** (10 x 13p)+(10 x 18p)... 12 — 5

2 Dec 86 **£1.20 Xmas Book:** (10 x 13p)............. 5 — 3
*10p discount with Star printed on reverse*
Glastonbury special handstamps ............ – — 6

27 Jan 87 **2 x 50p, £1, £1.30 Books:** – set of 4 ...... 35 — 25
*As 20 Oct 1986 but with new phosphor ink.*

14 Apr 87 **£1.80 Book:** (10 x 18p) ACP .................. 5 — 2

4 Aug 87 **52p** (4 x 13p); **72p** (4 x 18p); **£1.04** (4 x 26p);
**£1.30** (10 x 13p); **£1.80** (10 x 18p)......... 30 — 20
*Printed with a selvedge around all four sides.*
*giving the appearance of small 'sheetlets'. Issued*
*on trial at Bristol, Nottingham, Preston & York.*
Set of five with any of these pmks ......... – — 30

29 Sep 87 **50p Mount Stewart Book:** (3)
(1 x 1p, 2 x 5p, 3 x 13p) ........................... 2 — 1
Belfast pmk. (Mount Stewart) ................ – — 3
**£1 Sherlock Holmes Book:** (4)
(1 x 13p; 5 x 18p) *3p discount* ................ 3 — 2
Baker St. C.D.S. ........................................... – — 25
*Produced with straight edges*
*(i.e. outer long edges had no perforations).*

23 Aug 88 **56p** (4 x 14p); **76p** (4 x 19p); **£1.08** (4 x 27p);
**£1.40** (10 x 14p); **£1.90** (10 x 19p)......... 25 — 15
*Issued on trial at Bristol, Nottingham,*
*Preston & York.*
Set of five with any of these pmks (5)... – — 30

5 Sep 88 **50p** (1 x 14p; 2 x 19p + L) *2p disc.* (7). 2 — 1
**£1** (2 x 14p; 4 x 19p) *4p discount* ......... 3 — 2
**£1.40 & £1.90** (10 x 14p)+(10 x 19p) (6) 10 — 7

11 Oct 88 **56p, 76p, £1.08, £1.40, £1.90** Set ........... 30 — 10
*As 23 Aug issue, but selvedge replaced by*
*straight edges at top and bottom of stamp panes.*
**Bklts: £1.40, £1.90** Pair............................ 15 — 8
*Questa – the first 14p and 19p litho printings.*

24 Jan 89 **Bklts: 56p, 76p** ........................................ 4 — 2
*As 23 Aug 1988 but with three straight edges.*

25 Apr 89 **£1** (2 x 14p; 4 x 19p) *4p discount* ......... 4 — 2
-do- Walsall Security Printers spec h/s . – — 6
-do- Walsall C.D.S. pmk ............................ – — 30
*Walsall Security Printers with straight edges*

26 Jun 89 **£1.90** (10 x 19p) Jumelle Press.............. 5 — 2
10 Jul 89 **£1.40** (10 x 14p) Jumelle Press.............. 4 — 2
22 Aug 89 **Non-Value Indicator Books:** Set of 4... 20 — 15
**56p** (4 x 2nd) & **76p** (4 x 1st) Walsall
**£1.40** (10 x 2nd) **£1.90** (10 x 1st) Harrison
19 Sep 89 **Non-Value Indicator Books:**
**£1.40**(10 x 2nd),**£1.90**(10 x 1st)Questa . 10 — 7
2 Oct 89 **50p Book:** (2 x 15p; 1 x 20p + label) .... 2 — 1
**£1 Book:** (5 x 20p + label) ...................... 3 — 2
**£1.16 Airmail Book:** (4 x 29p) .................. 3 — 2
28 Nov89 **60p Book:** (4 x 2nd) – Harrison*.......... 15 — –
5 Dec 89 **80p Book:** (4 x 1st) – Harrison*............ 25 — –
*\*Three straight edges (top, right and bottom).*

228

| | Windsor Postmark £ | Other Pmks £ |
|---|---|---|

30 Jan 90 **Penny Black Anniv. Books:** Set of 4 .... | 20 | 8
   60p (4 x 15p); **80p** (4 x 20p); (8)
£1.50 (10 x 15p); £2 (10 x 20p) (9)
**Penny Black Anniv. Books:** Set of 3 .... | 16 | 7
   50p (2 x 15p; 1 x 20p + L) – Harrison Printers (10)
£1 (5 x 20p + L) – Harrison Printers (11)
£1 (5 x 20p + L) – Walsall Printers

17 Apr 90 **Penny Black Anniv. Books:** Set of 3 .... | 20 | 12
   80p (4 x 20p) Harrison 3 straight edges
£1.50 (10 x 15p) Questa full perfs
£2 (10 x 20p) Questa full perfs
**Standard definitives:**
£1.16 (4 x 29p) 3 straight edges ............. | 4 | 2

12 Jun 90 **Penny Black Anniv. Books:** Pair ........ | 10 | 4
   £1.50 (10 x 15p) Walsall – 3 straight edges
£2 (10 x 20p) Walsall – 3 straight edges

7 Aug 90 **Non-Value Indicator Books:** Set of 8 .... | 40 | 25
   60p (4 x 2nd); 80p (4 x 1st); Walsall Printers
£1.50 (10 x 2nd); £2 (10 x 1st) Walsall Printers
£1.50 (10 x 2nd); £2 (10 x 1st) Harrison Printers
£1.50 (10 x 2nd); £2 (10 x 1st) Questa Printers

4 Sep 90 **50p Book:** (3 x 17p) *1p discount* (12)... | 2 | 1
   £1 Book: (2 x 17p; 3 x 22p) (13)......... | 3 | 1

17 Sep 90 **£1.24 Book:** (4 x 31p) Walsall ................ | 3 | 2

6 Aug 91 **Non-Value Indicator Book:** Set of 7 .... | 25 | 12
   68p (4 x 2nd); 88p (4 x 1st) Walsall
£1.70 (10 x 2nd); £2.20 (10 x 1st) Walsall
£1.70 (10 x 2nd); £2.20 (10 x 1st) Questa
£2.20 (10 x 1st) Harrison

10 Sep 91 **50p & £1 Book:**
   (2 x 24p; 2 x 1p);(4 x 24p; 2 x 2p) ........ | 4 | 3
   -do- 'New Postage Rates' slogan ............. | – | 6

16 Sep 91 **£1.32,£1.56**(4 x 33p);(4 x 39p) Walsall. | 7 | 3
   -do- with 'New Postage Rates' slogan.... | – | 10

28 Jul 92 **78p Kelloggs Book:** 2 x 39p ..................... | 10 | 3

8 Sep 92 **£1.32 Book:** (4 x 33p) Dextrin Gum ....... | 4 | 2

22 Sep 92 **£1.80 NVI Book:** (10 x 2nd Class)......... | 6 | 3
   *Harrison: straight edges at the top & bottom.*

9 Feb 93 **£2.40 NVI Book:** (10 x 1st Class) .......... | 6 | 3
   *Walsall: straight edges at the top & bottom.*
£1 Book: (4 x 24p; 2 x 2p) ...................... | 4 | 2
   *Walsall ACP with straight edges at left & right.*

16 Mar 93 **£1.80 NVI Book:** (10 x 2nd Class)......... | 6 | 3
   *Walsall ACP straight edges at the top & bottom.*

6 Apr 93 **Non-Value Indicator Books:** Set of 5... | 18 | 10
   96p (4 x 1st); £2.40 (10 x 1st) Harrison
72p (4 x 2nd); £2.40 (10 x 1st)* Walsall
£1.80 (10 x 2nd) Questa
   *Perfs all round with elliptical perfs.*
   **Walsall £2.40 – two phos. bands.*

17 Aug 93 **96p NVI Book:** (4 x 1st) Walsall ........... | 4 | 2

7 Sep 93 **72p NVI Book:** (4 x 2nd) Harrison ....... | 4 | 2

1 Nov 93 **50p** (2 x 25p) Harrisons; £1 (4 x 25p) Walsall;
   £2 (8 x 25p) Harrisons Set of 3 ................... | 10 | 5
£2.50 NVI Book: (10 x 1st Class) .............. | 6 | 3
   *Questa with elliptical perfs*
**Overseas Rates Books:** Walsall
£1.40 (4 x 35p); £1.64 (4 x 41p) (14) .... | 8 | 4

25 Jan 94 **50p** (2 x 25p) Harrisons;
   £1 (4 x 25p) Walsall ......................... | 10 | 3

22 Feb 94 **£1.90, £2.50 NVI:** (10 x 2nd);(10 x 1st) | 8 | 5
   *Walsall Printers with elliptical perfs*

26 Apr 94 **£1 Book:** (4 x 25p) Harrison ................. | 5 | 3
   Any Airport postmark........................... | – | 6

9 Aug 94 **60p Airmail Rate Book:**........................... | 6 | 3
   Any relevant CDS postmark .................. | – | 6

4 Apr 95 **£2.50 NVI Book:** (10 x 1st) Harrison.... | 7 | 3

16 May 95 **£1 R J Mitchell Book:** (4 x 25p 2 PB) .. | 3 | 2
   Any Spitfire/VE Day special h/s.............. | – | 3
   Any relevant CDS postmark .................. | – | 6

6 Jun 95 **50p, £2** (2 x 25p); (8 x 25p 2 PB) ......... | 6 | 4

5 Oct 95 **£1.40** (4 x 35p) - Walsall (BF)................. | 6 | –

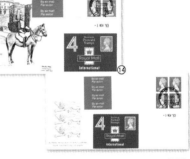

| | | Windsor Postmark £ | Other Pmks £ |
|---|---|---|---|
| 12 Dec 95 | **76p** (4 x 2nd) - Walsall (BF)................... | 5 | – |
| | **£1.90** (10 x 2nd) - Harrison (BF).......... | 6 | – |
| 16 Jan 96 | **£1, £2**(4 x 25p);(8 x 25p) Questa (BF).. | 8 | – |
| 19 Feb 96 | **£2.50 Walt Disney Book:** | | |
| | 10 x 1st *(First Scratch Card Bklt)* .......... | 5 | – |
| 20 Feb 96 | **£2 Book:** (8 x 25p) - Harrison (BF)....... | 5 | – |
| 19 Mar 96 | **£1.64 Book:** (4 x 41p) Walsall (BF)....... | – | 5 |
| | **£2.40 Book:** (4 x 60p) Walsall (BF)....... | 5 | 5 |
| 8 Jul 96 | **£1** (3 x 26p; 20p; 2 x 1p) & **£2** (7 x 26p; 20p) | | |
| | **£1.48** (4 x 37p) & **£2.52** (4 x 63p) ........ | 10 | 8 |
| | -do- New Bklets Windsor spec h/s (20) | 15 | – |
| 21 Apr 97 | **Gold Definitives Books:** | | |
| | **£2.60** (10 x 1st Class) – Harrison | | |
| | **£2.60** (10 x 1st Class) – Walsall......pair | 10 | 5 |
| | -do- golden wedding pmks*........... (21) | 15 | 15 |
| | *See commemorative section for full details of pmks* | | |
| 29 Apr 97 | **£2 Book:** (10 x 2nd) Harrison.................... | 5 | 2 |
| 26 Aug 97 | **£1.04** (4 x 1st); 80p (4 x 2nd); | | |
| | **£1.48** (4 x 37p); **£2.52** (4 x 63p) .......set | 15 | 10 |
| 18 Nov 97 | **£2.60** (10 x 1st) Harrison-lay flat gum .. | 6 | 3 |
| | **£2.60** (10 x 1st) Harrison .................... | 5 | 2 |
| | **£2.60** (10 x 1st) Walsall ......................... | 5 | 2 |
| 5 May 98 | **£1.20 Book:** (4 x 30p) Walsall.............. | 5 | 2 |
| 1 Dec 98 | **Change to gravure printing process:** | | |
| | **£2** (10 x 2nd) & **£2.60** (10 x 1st).......... | 10 | 4 |
| | **£1** (3 x 26p; 1 x 20p; 2 x 1p + 2 L) ... | 5 | 2 |
| | **£2** (7 x 26p; 1 x 20p) ......................... | 6 | 2 |
| 19 Jan 99 | **European NVI 'E'** (4 x E) ..................... | 6 | 2 |
| 26 Apr 99 | **£1** (3 x 26p; 1 x 19p; 1 x 1p, 1 x 2p + L). | 3 | 2 |
| | **£1.52** (4 x 38p)................................. | 4 | 2 |
| | **£2** (7 x 26p; 1 x 19p) ........................ | 6 | 3 |
| | **£2.56** (4 x 64p)................................ | 6 | 3 |
| 6 Jan 00 | **£2.60** (10 x 1st Millennium) Walsall ...... | 6 | 4 |
| | **£2.60** (10 x 1st Millennium) Questa ...... | 6 | 4 |
| 27 Apr 00 | **£1** (3 x 1st; 1 x 2nd) ......................... | 3 | 2 |
| | **£2** (6 x 1st; 2 x 2nd) ......................... | 4 | 2 |
| | **£1.60** (4 x 40p) ................................. | 5 | 3 |
| | **£2.60** (4 x 65p)................................. | 6 | 3 |
| 29 Jan 01 | **Set of 7 Self Adhesive Stamp Bks** (22) | 30 | 25 |
| | **£3.24** (12 x 1st) Walsall; **£3.24** (12 x 1st) Questa; | | |
| | **£2.28** (12 x 2nd) Questa; | | |
| | **£2.70** (10 x 1st) Questa; **£1.90** (10 x 2nd) Questa; | | |
| | **£1.14** (6 x 1st) Walsall; **£1.90** (6 x 2nd) Walsall | | |
| 17 Apr 01 | **£1** (Text change on label) ...................... | 3 | 2 |

**N.B.** *With effect from July 2002, stamp books contained self-adhesive stamps with the matrix (or selvedge) stripped away from the backing paper. It is therefore impossible to affix a complete pane of stamps to covers other than by using glue. I have therefore decided not to list these.*

## Stamp Varieties on FDC

*This section includes changes of watermark, paper, perforations, phosphor, gum etc. where the dates of issue are known. Similar changes to stamps from stamp book panes are included in the Prestige Stamp Book Panes and Stamp Book Panes Sections.*

| | | plain covers £ | illus. covers £ |
|---|---|---|---|
| 17 Jul 1956 | **3d** St. Edward Crown wmk ............. | 275 | – |
| 19 Nov 1957 | **¹/2d, 1d, 1¹/2d, 2d, 2¹/2d, 3d** ........... | 40 | 80 |
| | *Graphite lines printed under the gum as an experiment in automatic letter sorting at Southampton.* | | |
| 4 Dec 1958 | **2d** Multiple Crowns wmk ................. | 150 | – |
| 23 Dec 1958 | **6d** Multiple Crowns wmk ................. | 150 | – |
| 24 Mar 1959 | **9d** Multiple Crowns wmk ................. | 200 | – |
| 18 Nov 1959 | **¹/2d,1d,1¹/2d,2d,2¹/2d,3d,4d,4¹/2d** ... | 40 | 100 |
| | *Phos-Graphite: Similar to above with the addition of phosphor bands on the front - Southampton pmk.* (31) | | |

|  | plain covers £ | illus. covers £ |
|---|---|---|
| 27 Jun 1960 **6d** Phosphor | – | 400 |
| 6 Jul 1960 **¹/2d, 1d, 1¹/2d, 2d, 2¹/2d,** | | |
| **3d, 4d, 6d, 1s3d** Phosphor | – | 135 |
| *Phosphor Sorting Machine - Southampton pmk.* | | |
| 17 May 1965 **4d** Deep Ultramarine | 30 | 75 |
| **3d** Deep Lilac Phosphor (32) | 30 | 75 |
| *Covers are known with earlier dates:* | | |
| *28th April (4d) and 29th April (3d).* | | |
| 30 Dec 1966 **10d** Phosphor | 150 | – |
| 15 Feb 1967 **7d** Phosphor | 400 | – |
| 9 Jun 1967 **5d** Phosphor | 175 | – |
| 28 Jun 1967 **8d, 1s** Phosphor | 300 | – |
| **'CASTLES' HIGH VALUES:** | | |
| **Unwatermarked Paper** | | |
| 6 Dec 1967 **£1** London Underground cvr (33) | – | 900 |
| **£1** Plain cover with CDS pmk | 200 | – |
| 16 Apr 1968 **5s and 10s** (34) | 575 | – |
| 4 Jun 1968 **2s 6d** Chalky Paper | 150 | 350 |
| 3 Jul 1968 **2s 6d** (35) | n.k. | 600 |
| 28 Aug 1968 **1s 6d** PVA Gum | – | 175 |
| 16 Sep 1968 **4d** Phosphor | 10 | 25 |
| 29 Nov 1968 **9d** PVA Gum | – | 175 |
| 10 Dec 1969 **1s 6d** Phosphor | 1 | 10 |

|  | Windsor Postmark £ | Other Pmks £ |
|---|---|---|
| 17 Jun 1970 **10p, 20p, 50p & £1** | | |
| (Recess printed in sheets of 100) | 800 | 600 |
| 16 Nov 1970 **1s 9d** PVA Gum | – | 175 |
| 23 Aug 1972 **3p** Gum Arabic | – | 60 |
| 13 Sep 1972 **2¹/2p** Gum Arabic (36) | – | 60 |
| 22 Sep 1972 **¹/2p** Gum Arabic | – | 40 |
| 31 Oct 1972 **4p** Gum Arabic | – | 70 |
| 1 Feb 1973 **50p** All Over Phosphor (37) | – | 80 |
| 6 Jun 1973 **6p** Gum Arabic | – | 130 |
| 8 Aug 1973 **2¹/2p** PVA/Dextrin Gum | – | 25 |
| 22 Aug 1973 **3¹/2p** PVA/Dextrin Gum | – | 60 |
| 10 Sep 1973 **3p** Phosphor: Centre Band | 15 | 5 |
| 10 Sep 1973 **3p** Gum Arabic | | |
| **+ 1p, 2p, 3p** PVA/Dextrin Gum | 80 | 30 |
| 27 Sep 1973 **£1** Bradbury Contractors Paper | – | 750 |
| 9 Oct 1973 **¹/2p** PVA/Dextrin Gum | – | 60 |
| 30 Oct 1973 **6p** PVA/Dextrin Gum | – | 125 |
| 12 Nov 1973 **4p, 10p** PVA/Dextrin Gum | – | 125 |
| 30 Nov 1973 **20p** Bradbury Contractors Paper | – | 450 |
| 20 Feb 1974 **50p** Bradbury Contractors Paper | – | 450 |
| 22 Mar 1974 **9p** PVA/Dextrin Gum | – | 150 |
| 5 Jun 1974 **1¹/2p, 5p** PVA/Dextrin Gum | – | 40 |
| 24 Jun 1974 **3¹/2p** Phosphor: Centre Band | 30 | 6 |
| 13 Nov 1974 **4¹/2p** Experimental Phosphor, | 25 | 3 |
| Cambridge, Aberdeen | | |
| or Norwich pmks *each* | – | 30 |
| *(Stamps on sale at these Post Offices)* | | |
| 15 Jan 1975 **7p** Phosphor: Two Bands | 2 | 1 |
| -do- with phosphor omitted | 20 | 8 |
| 17 Mar 1975 **5¹/2p** Phosphor: Centre Band | 4 | 1 |
| 21 May 1975 **2¹/2p** Phosphor: Two Bands | 10 | 4 |
| 24 Sep 1975 **6¹/2p** Cent. Band, **8¹/2p** Two Bands . | 2 | 1 |
| 24 Mar 1976 **8¹/2p** Experimental Phosphor | 2 | 1 |
| 26 Jan 1977 **9p** All Over Phosphor | – | 125 |
| 31 Oct 1977 **6p, 7p, 9p, 10p** Halley Press | 250 | 175 |
| 20 Aug 1979 **8p** Phosphor: Centre Band | 2 | 1 |
| 20 Aug 1979 **10p** Phos Coated Paper + 2 Bands).. | 2 | 1 |
| 10 Oct 1979 **1p, 2p, 5p, 20p** New Phos Paper.... | 2 | 1 |
| 12 Dec 1979 **1p, 2p** PCP + **8p** Enschedé | 2 | 1 |
| 4 Feb 1980 **10p** Phosphor: Centre Band | 2 | 1 |
| 4 Feb 1980 **10p** Phosphor Coated Paper | 75 | 25 |
| 21 May 1980 **2p, 5p** Questa, **20p** Waddington, | | |
| **50p** non-phos | 2 | 1 |
| 27 Aug 1980 **11p** Phosphor Coated Paper | 3 | 2 |
| 22 Oct 1980 **3p + 22p** PCP1 & PCP2 | 10 | 5 |
| 10 Dec 1980 **¹/2 p** Phosphor Coated Paper | 2 | 1 |

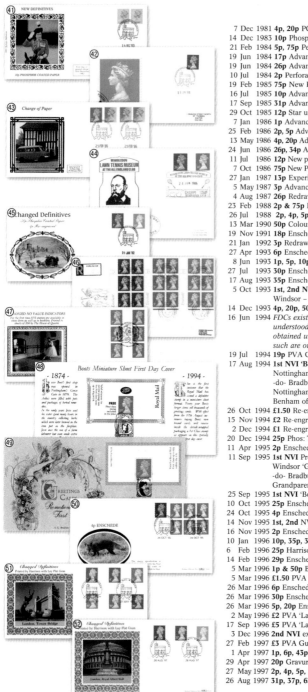

| | | Postmark: | Windsor £ | Other £ |
|---|---|---|---|---|
| 7 Dec | 1981 | **4p, 20p** PCP Waddington printing.... | 15 | 5 |
| 14 Dec | 1983 | **10p** Phosphor Coated Paper.......(41) | 2 | 1 |
| 21 Feb | 1984 | **5p, 75p** Perforation change ............... | 2 | 1 |
| 19 Jun | 1984 | **17p** Advanced Coated Paper............ | 2 | 1 |
| 19 Jun | 1984 | **26p** Advanced Coated Paper ......(42) | 75 | – |
| 10 Jul | 1984 | **2p** Perforation change........................ | 2 | 1 |
| 19 Feb | 1985 | **75p** New Paper.................................... | 150 | – |
| 16 Jul | 1985 | **10p** Advanced Coated Paper............. | 2 | 1 |
| 17 Sep | 1985 | **31p** Advanced Coated Paper............. | 2 | 1 |
| 29 Oct | 1985 | **12p** Star underprint ........................... | 2 | 1 |
| 7 Jan | 1986 | **1p** Advanced Coated Paper ............... | 2 | 1 |
| 25 Feb | 1986 | **2p, 5p** Advanced Coated Paper...(43) | 2 | 1 |
| 13 May | 1986 | **4p, 20p** Adv. Coated Paper - Questa .. | 2 | 1 |
| 24 Jun | 1986 | **26p, 34p** Adv. Coated Paper ........(44) | 2 | 1 |
| 11 Jul | 1986 | **12p** New phosphor ink....................... | 40 | 25 |
| 7 Oct | 1986 | **75p** New Paper, 28p ACP................... | 5 | 2 |
| 27 Jan | 1987 | **13p** Experimental phosphor .............. | 4 | |
| 5 May | 1987 | **3p** Advanced Coated Paper ............... | 2 | 1 |
| 4 Aug | 1987 | **26p** Redrawn value........................... | 20 | 6 |
| 23 Feb | 1988 | **2p & 75p** Redrawn values.................. | 2 | 1 |
| 26 Jul | 1988 | **2p, 4p, 5p, 75p** Harrison printing.... | 2 | 1 |
| 13 Mar | 1990 | **50p** Colour variation ....................... | 5 | 1 |
| 19 Nov | 1991 | **18p** Enschedé printing....................... | 2 | 1 |
| 21 Jan | 1992 | **3p** Redrawn value, 50p ACP.......(45) | 2 | 1 |
| 27 Apr | 1993 | **6p** Enschedé printing ........................ | 2 | 1 |
| 8 Jun | 1993 | **1p, 5p, 10p** Enschedé printings..(46) | 2 | 1 |
| 27 Jul | 1993 | **30p** Enschedé printing ...................... | 2 | 1 |
| 17 Aug | 1993 | **35p** Enschedé printing ...................... | 2 | 1 |
| 5 Oct | 1993 | **1st, 2nd NVIs** in Sheet Format......... | 2 | 1 |
| | | Windsor – Tudor Rose h/s .........(47) | 3 | – |
| 14 Dec | 1993 | **4p, 20p, 50p** Enschedé printings...... | 3 | 2 |
| 16 Jun | 1994 | *FDCs exist with 2nd Class NVI stamps. It is understood that these experimental stamps were obtained under dubious circumstances and as such are outside the scope of this catalogue.* | | |
| 19 Jul | 1994 | **19p** PVA Gum/Harrison ..................... | 3 | 2 |
| 17 Aug | 1994 | **1st NVI 'Boots'** Promotional Label .. | 2 | 1 |
| | | Nottingham 'B' spec h/s...................... | – | 3 |
| | | -do- Bradbury official cover ......(48) | – | 15 |
| | | Nottingham 'NVI' spec h/s................. | – | 3 |
| | | Benham official cover ......................... | – | 8 |
| 26 Oct | 1994 | **£1.50** Re-engraved ............................... | 150 | – |
| 15 Nov | 1994 | **£2** Re-engraved.................................. | 150 | – |
| 2 Dec | 1994 | **£1** Re-engraved.................................. | 150 | – |
| 20 Dec | 1994 | **25p** Phos: Two Bands Harrison........ | 2 | 1 |
| 11 Apr | 1995 | **2p** Enschedé printing ........................ | 2 | 1 |
| 11 Sep | 1995 | **1st NVI** Promotional Label .............. | 2 | 1 |
| | | Windsor 'G' spec h/s........................... | 3 | – |
| | | -do- Bradbury official cover .......(49) | 10 | – |
| | | Grandparents Day slogan.................... | – | 5 |
| 25 Sep | 1995 | **1st NVI** 'Boots' Blue Fluor ............... | 5 | 5 |
| 10 Oct | 1995 | **25p** Enschede/changed gum ............. | – | 5 |
| 24 Oct | 1995 | **4p** Enschede Blue Fluor..............(50) | 5 | – |
| 14 Nov | 1995 | **1st, 2nd NVIs** Blue Fluor.................. | 6 | – |
| 16 Nov | 1995 | **2p** Enschede printing Blue Fluor...... | 5 | – |
| 10 Jan | 1996 | **10p, 35p, 38p** Enschede Blue Fluor . | 6 | – |
| 6 Feb | 1996 | **25p** Harrison printing Blue Fluor...... | 5 | – |
| 14 Feb | 1996 | **29p** Enschede printing Blue Fluor .... | 5 | – |
| 5 Mar | 1996 | **1p & 50p** Blue Fluor .......................... | 5 | – |
| 5 Mar | 1996 | **£1.50** PVA 'Lay-Flat' Gum.................. | – | 5 |
| 26 Mar | 1996 | **6p** Enschede printing Blue Fluor....... | 5 | – |
| 26 Mar | 1996 | **30p** Enschede printing Blue Fluor .... | 5 | – |
| 26 Mar | 1996 | **5p, 20p** Enschede Blue Fluor............ | 5 | – |
| 2 May | 1996 | **£2** PVA 'Lay-Flat' Gum...................... | 25 | – |
| 17 Sep | 1996 | **£5** PVA 'Lay-Flat' Gum ...................... | 15 | – |
| 3 Dec | 1996 | **2nd NVI** extended phos ..................... | 2 | 1 |
| 27 Feb | 1997 | **£3** PVA Gum...................................... | 100 | – |
| 1 Apr | 1997 | **1p, 6p, 43p, 50p £1** Gravure............. | 5 | 3 |
| 29 Apr | 1997 | **20p** Gravure ...................................... | 4 | 2 |
| 27 May | 1997 | **2p, 4p, 5p, 10p, 30p, 39p** Grav..(51) | 4 | 2 |
| 26 Aug | 1997 | **31p, 37p, 63p** Gravure ................(52) | 4 | 2 |

| Postmark: | Windsor £ | Other £ |
|---|---|---|
| 29 Jul 1997 **£1.50, £2, £3 & £5 Castles** Enschedé | | |
| Windsor permanent special h/s......... | 15 | – |
| Windsor h/s *(Benham official £20)*.. | 15 | – |
| Edinburgh *(Benham official £20)* ..... | – | 15 |
| Caernarfon *(Benham official £20)* .... | – | 15 |
| Carrickfergus *(Benham official £20)* | – | 15 |
| Appropriate CDS pmks ...................... | 25 | 25 |
| 18 Nov 1997 **1st NVIs** Sheet Format/Walsall .(53) | 2 | 1 |
| **26p** Harrison 'Lay-Flat' Gum............. | 2 | 1 |
| 20 Apr 1999 **19p** De La Rue ................................ | 2 | 1 |
| **20p** 2 Phos De La Rue....................... | 2 | 1 |
| 5 Oct 1999 **'E' NVI** Ex Sheet/DeLaRue...........(54) | 2 | 1 |
| 11 Apr 2000 **£1.50, £2, £3 & £5** DeLaRue | | |
| Windsor permanent special h/s......... | 15 | – |
| Cardiff *(Benham official £20)* ........... | – | 15 |
| Edinburgh *(Benham official £20)* ..... | – | 15 |
| Belfast *(Benham official £20)* ........... | – | 15 |
| London EC1 *(Benham official £20)* . | – | 15 |
| High Wycombe *(Benham off. £20)* ... | – | 15 |
| Appropriate CDS pmks ...................... | 20 | 20 |
| 9 May 2002 **1st & 2nd** Enschede...................(55) | 5 | 1 |
| 4 Jul 2002 **Gold 1st Class** Enschede.................. | 5 | 1 |
| 18 Mar 2003 **1st & 2nd** Walsall ............................... | 5 | 1 |
| 1 Jul 2003 **Gold 1st Class** DeLaRue............(56) | 5 | 1 |
| 10 May 2005 **35p** DeLaRue ........................................ | 5 | 1 |

## Self Adhesives - Experimental Issues

| | ordinary covers | sponsored covers |
|---|---|---|
| | £ | £ |
| 10 Feb 1974 **Self Adhesive Labels:** | | |
| ¹/₂p, 1p, 1¹/₂p, | | |
| (3p + 5p), (¹/₂p + 5p) ........(1) 350 | | |
| | | |
| 19 Jun 1974 **Self Adhesive Labels:** | | |
| 3p, 3¹/₂p..............................(2) 50 | | |
| | | |
| 19 Oct 1993 **Self Adhesive Stamps: 1st Class NVI** | | |
| FDI – Philatelic Bureau......... 5 | - | *Royal Mail* |
| FDI – Newcastle................(4) 5 | - | *Royal Mail* |
| FDI – 1st London ................... 5 | - | *Royal Mail* |
| Windsor (Britannia) .............. 10 | 15 | *Bradbury* |
| Windsor (Arms) ............. (3) 10 | 15 | *Bradbury* |
| Newcastle (Cathedral).......... 10 | 15 | *Benham* |
| Walsall Security h/s .............. 10 | 20 | *Walsall* |
| Lickey End Bromsgrove......... 10 | - | *Royal Mail* |
| New Postage Rates slogan ..... 10 | | |
| Complete pane on cover ....... 20 | - | |
| 18 Mar 1997 **Self Adhesive Stamps: 1st & 2nd NVIs Horizontal** | | |
| FDI – Philatelic Bureau......... 3 | - | *Royal Mail* |
| FDI – Glasgow...................(5) 3 | - | *Royal Mail* |
| FDI – London .......................... 3 | - | *Royal Mail* |
| Windsor (Arms) ..................... 5 | 10 | *Bradbury* |
| Windsor (Castle) ..................... 5 | 8 | *Benham* |
| 6 Apr 1998 **1st & 2nd Class NVIs Vertical (rolls of 200) - Enschede** | | |
| Windsor (Arms) ..................... 5 | 10 | *Bradbury* |
| Windsor special h/s................ 5 | 8 | *Benham* |
| Glasgow special h/s .............. 5 | 8 | *Benham* |
| Clydebank special h/s............. 5 | 8 | *RN Cvrs Gp* |
| 22 Jun 1998 **1st & 2nd Class NVIs Vertical (sheets of 100) - Walsall** | | |
| Windsor (Arms) ..................... 5 | 10 | *Bradbury* |
| -do- with 'dagger' perfs........... 75 | - | |
| 16 Feb 1999 **1st Class NVI Large White ex** *Profile on Print* **PSBklt** | | |
| Windsor (Arms) ..................... 5 | 10 | *Bradbury* |
| 4 Sep 2000 **1st & 2nd Class NVIs New style business sheets of 100** | | |
| Windsor (Castle) h/s................ 5 | | |

**N.B. For later self-adhesive definitive issues
please refer to:
New Stamp Issues Section (new values etc), or
Stamp Varieties Section (different printers etc).**

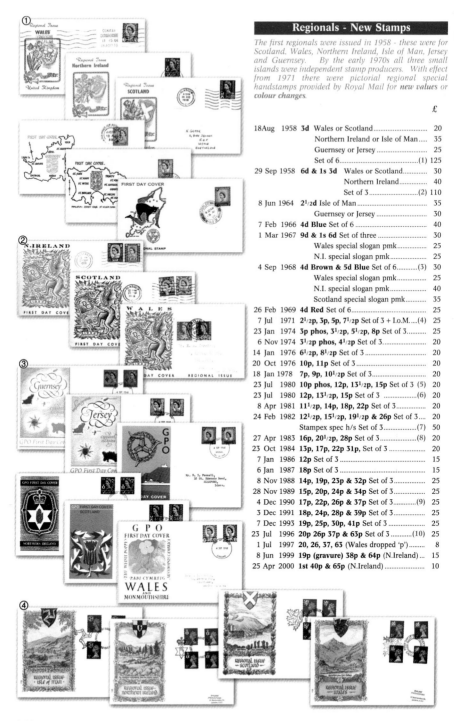

## Regionals - New Stamps

*The first regionals were issued in 1958 - these were for Scotland, Wales, Northern Ireland, Isle of Man, Jersey and Guernsey. By the early 1970s all three small islands were independent stamp producers. With effect from 1971 there were pictorial regional special handstamps provided by Royal Mail for **new values** or **colour changes**.*

£

| | | |
|---|---|---:|
| 18Aug 1958 | **3d** Wales or Scotland | 20 |
| | Northern Ireland or Isle of Man | 35 |
| | Guernsey or Jersey | 25 |
| | Set of 6 ...........................(1) | 125 |
| 29 Sep 1958 | **6d & 1s 3d** Wales or Scotland | 30 |
| | Northern Ireland | 40 |
| | Set of 3 ...........................(2) | 110 |
| 8 Jun 1964 | **2¹/₂d** Isle of Man | 35 |
| | Guernsey or Jersey | 30 |
| 7 Feb 1966 | **4d Blue** Set of 6 | 40 |
| 1 Mar 1967 | **9d & 1s 6d** Set of three | 30 |
| | Wales special slogan pmk | 25 |
| | N.I. special slogan pmk | 25 |
| 4 Sep 1968 | **4d Brown & 5d Blue** Set of 6 ..........(3) | 30 |
| | Wales special slogan pmk | 25 |
| | N.I. special slogan pmk | 40 |
| | Scotland special slogan pmk | 35 |
| 26 Feb 1969 | **4d Red** Set of 6 | 25 |
| 7 Jul 1971 | **2¹/₂p, 3p, 5p, 7¹/₂p** Set of 3 + I.o.M. ....(4) | 25 |
| 23 Jan 1974 | **3p phos, 3¹/₂p, 5¹/₂p, 8p** Set of 3 | 25 |
| 6 Nov 1974 | **3¹/₂p phos, 4¹/₂p** Set of 3 | 20 |
| 14 Jan 1976 | **6¹/₂p, 8¹/₂p** Set of 3 | 20 |
| 20 Oct 1976 | **10p, 11p** Set of 3 | 20 |
| 18 Jan 1978 | **7p, 9p, 10¹/₂p** Set of 3 | 20 |
| 23 Jul 1980 | **10p phos, 12p, 13¹/₂p, 15p** Set of 3 (5) | 20 |
| 23 Jul 1980 | **12p, 13¹/₂p, 15p** Set of 3 ...........(6) | 20 |
| 8 Apr 1981 | **11¹/₂p, 14p, 18p, 22p** Set of 3 | 20 |
| 24 Feb 1982 | **12¹/₂p, 15¹/₂p, 19¹/₂p & 26p** Set of 3 .... | 20 |
| | Stampex spec h/s Set of 3 ...........(7) | 50 |
| 27 Apr 1983 | **16p, 20¹/₂p, 28p** Set of 3 ...........(8) | 20 |
| 23 Oct 1984 | **13p, 17p, 22p 31p**, Set of 3 | 20 |
| 7 Jan 1986 | **12p** Set of 3 | 15 |
| 6 Jan 1987 | **18p** Set of 3 | 15 |
| 8 Nov 1988 | **14p, 19p, 23p & 32p** Set of 3 | 25 |
| 28 Nov 1989 | **15p, 20p, 24p & 34p** Set of 3 | 25 |
| 4 Dec 1990 | **17p, 22p, 26p & 37p** Set of 3 ...........(9) | 25 |
| 3 Dec 1991 | **18p, 24p, 28p & 39p** Set of 3 | 25 |
| 7 Dec 1993 | **19p, 25p, 30p, 41p** Set of 3 | 25 |
| 23 Jul 1996 | **20p 26p 37p & 63p** Set of 3 ...........(10) | 25 |
| 1 Jul 1997 | **20, 26, 37, 63** (Wales dropped 'p') | 8 |
| 8 Jun 1999 | **19p (gravure)** 38p & 64p (N.Ireland) ... | 15 |
| 25 Apr 2000 | **1st 40p & 65p** (N.Ireland) | 10 |

*Values are for illustrated covers with regional pmks.*
*Philatelic Bureau handstamps are worth half catalogue*
*value.*

*Set of 6 = Wales, Scotland, Northern Ireland,*
*Guernsey, Jersey & Isle of Man*
*Set of 3 = Wales, Scotland & Northern Ireland*

£

| Date | Description | £ |
|---|---|---|
| 29 Jan 1963 | **3d, 6d, 1s 3d** Scotland (phos) | 100 |
| 15 Jul 1963 | **3d** Isle of Man chalky paper | 400 |
| 7 Feb 1966 | **4d Blue** Scotland - phosphor | 8 |
| 9 Jun 1967 | **3d** Lilac Jersey - phosphor | 250 |
| 5 Sep 1967 | **4d Blue** Jersey - phosphor | 250 |
| 28 Sep 1970 | **9d** Scotland unwatermarked paper | 20 |
| 22 Sep 1972 | **2$^{1}/_{2}$p** Scottish Gum Arabic | 60 |
| 22 Sep 1972 | **2$^{1}/_{2}$p** Welsh Gum Arabic | 60 |
| 14 Dec 1972 | **3p** Scottish Gum Arabic | 60 |
| 6 Jun 1973 | **3p** Welsh Gum Arabic | 60 |
| 21 May 1975 | **5$^{1}/_{2}$p phos** Set of 3 | 10 |
| 2 Nov 1983 | **16p** Scotland ACP | 1 |
| 10 Jan 1984 | **12$^{1}/_{2}$p, 16p** Wales Perf change | 2 |
| 28 Feb 1984 | **12$^{1}/_{2}$p, 16p** N.I. Perf change | 4 |
| 25 Jun 1985 | **17p** Scotland PCP/PVA | 2 |
| 4 Dec 1985 | **31p** Scotland Re-drawn lion | 250 |
| 25 Feb 1986 | **17p** Wales ACP | 2 |
| 25 Feb 1986 | **17p** N.I. ACP | 2 |
| 29 Apr 1986 | **12p, 17p, 31p** Scot: perf & paper change | 2 |
| 9 Sep 1986 | **17p** N.I. Redrawn Crown | 175 |
| 4 Nov 1986 | **13p** Scotland 'Questa' printing | 1 |
| 28 Nov 1986 | **13p** N.I. Redrawn Crown | 75 |
| 27 Jan 1987 | **Advanced Coated Paper, Questa:** | |
| | Scotland: 22p, 26p, 28p | |
| | Wales 26p, 28p, 31p & N.I. 26p, 28p | 6 |
| 14 Apr 1987 | **13p** Coated Papers Ltd. Set of 3 | 5 |
| | **31p** N.I. ACP | 2 |
| 14 Apr 1987 | **13p** Wales Dextrim gum | 12 |
| 29 Mar 1988 | **18p Scotland & Wales** | |
| | Henry & Leigh Slater paper - pair | 2 |
| 25 Apr 1989 | **19p** Scotland Coated Papers Ltd | 2 |
| 20 Jun 1989 | **19p** Wales Coated Papers Ltd | 2 |
| 14 May 1991 | **22p, 26p, 37p** Scot: Coated Papers | 3 |
| | **22p** Wales Coated Papers Ltd | 2 |
| 18 Feb 1993 | **28p** Scottish Perf Error 13$^{1}/_{2}$ x 14 | 45 |
| 3 Oct 1995 | **19p** Scottish Blue Fluor | 5 |
| 19 Oct 1995 | **19p** Welsh Blue Fluor | 5 |
| 1 Feb 1996 | **19p** N.Ireland Blue Fluor | 5 |
| 5 Mar 1996 | **25p** N.Ireland Blue Fluor | 5 |
| 30 Apr 1996 | **41p** Welsh Blue Fluor | 5 |
| 1 Jul 1997 | **20p, 26p, 37p, 63p** Walsall: Scot & NI | 4 |

| | | Ordinary covers £ | Sponsored £ |
|---|---|---|---|
| 23 Apr 01 | **2nd, 1st, E, 65p** | | |
| | Philatelic Bureau................... | 3 | – *Royal Mail* |
| | Cry God for Harry................ | 3 | – *Royal Mail* |
| | St George & Dragon........... | 3 | 40 *RM Ingot cvr* |
| | Shakespeare Country........... | 3 | – *Royal Mail* |
| | First Pictorials Windsor ..(4) | 3 | 12 *Bradbury* |
| | St George's Day .....(3) | 3 | 12 *Bradbury* |
| | London (Three Lions)....(3) | 3 | 10 *Westminster* |
| | London (Shield)................... | 3 | 10 *Westminster* |
| | London (Acorn)................... | 3 | 10 *Westminster* |
| | London (Tudor Rose).......... | 3 | 10 *Westminster* |
| | London (flag)...................... | 3 | 10 *Westminster* |
| | Cardiff (flag)....................... | 3 | 10 *Westminster* |
| | Edinburgh (flag).................. | 3 | 10 *Westminster* |
| | Belfast (flag)........................ | 3 | 10 *Westminster* |
| | St George's Day .................. | 3 | 10 *P Sheridan* |
| | Westminster......................(1) | 3 | 10 *Benham* |
| | Windsor ............................... | 3 | 10 *Benham* |
| | Bishopswood ....................... | 3 | 10 *Benham* |
| | Lancaster ............................. | 3 | 10 *Benham* |
| | Bond Street W1 .................. | 3 | 10 *Benham* |
| | William Shakespeare ......(2) | 3 | 10 *Benham* |
| | Windsor Berks..................... | 3 | 10 *Benham* |
| | Buckingham Palace Rd ......... | 3 | 10 *Benham* |
| | Battle of Waterloo ............... | 3 | 10 *Benham* |
| | Blockading Zeebrugge .......... | 3 | 10 *RNCoversGp* |
| 4 Jul 02 | **68p** | | |
| | Tallents House.................... | 3 | – *Royal Mail* |
| | Cry God for Harry ............... | 3 | – *Royal Mail* |
| 14 Oct 03 | **2nd, 1st, E, 68p White Borders** | | |
| | Tallents House .................(8) | 3 | – *Royal Mail* |
| | Cry God for Harry ............... | 5 | – *Royal Mail* |
| | London (3 Lions) ................ | 3 | 10 *PhilStamps* |
| | Bakewell (Crowned Lion) ... | 3 | 10 *Benham* |
| | Castlerigg (Stones) ..........(5) | 3 | 10 *Benham* |
| | London (Concorde).........(6) | 3 | 10 *Benham* |
| | Newport (Acorns) ............(7) | 3 | 10 *Benham* |
| | London (Map)...................... | 3 | 10 *Westminster* |
| 11 May 04 | **40p** | | |
| | Tallents House.................... | 2 | – *Royal Mail* |
| | Cry God for Harry .............. | 3 | – *Royal Mail* |
| | London (Oak Leaves)........... | 3 | 8 *PhilStamps* |
| 5 Apr 05 | **42p** | | |
| | Tallents House.................... | 2 | – *Royal Mail* |
| | Cry God for Harry .............. | 3 | – *Royal Mail* |
| | Macduff............................... | 3 | 8 *PhilStamps* |
| 10 May 05 | **42p De La Rue**................. | 4 | |
| 28 Mar 06 | **44p, 72p** | | |
| | Tallents House.................... | 2 | – *Royal Mail* |
| | Cry God for Harry .............. | 3 | – *Royal Mail* |
| | Windsor............................... | 3 | 8 *PhilStamps* |
| 27 Mar 07 | **48p, 78p** | | |
| | Tallents House.................... | 2 | – *Royal Mail* |
| | Cry God for Harry .............. | 3 | – *Royal Mail* |
| 01 Apr 08 | **50p, 81p** | | |
| | Tallents House.................... | 2 | – *Royal Mail* |
| | Cry God for Harry .............. | 3 | – *Royal Mail* |
| 31 Mar 09 | **56p, 90p** | | |
| | Tallents House.................... | 2 | – *Royal Mail* |
| | Cry God for Harry .............. | 3 | – *Royal Mail* |
| 30 Mar 10 | **60p, 97p** | | |
| | Tallents House.................... | 2 | – *Royal Mail* |
| | Cry God for Harry ..........(9) | 3 | – *Royal Mail* |

| | Ordinary covers | | Sponsored |
|---|---|---|---|
| | | £ | £ |
| 8 Jun 99 | **2nd, 1st, E, 64p** | | |
| | Philatelic Bureau .................. | 3 | – Royal Mail |
| | People of the Country .....(4) | 3 | – Royal Mail |
| | First Scottish Defins ............. | 3 | 20 Bradbury |
| | Lochawe (Lion) ...............(3) | 3 | 10 Benham |
| | Glencoe (Thistle) ............(2) | 3 | 10 Benham |
| | Glasgow (Flag) ....................... | 3 | 10 Benham |
| | Ballater (Tartan) .................. | 3 | 10 Benham |
| | Edinburgh (Celtic pattern) ...(1) | 3 | 10 Benham |
| | Braemar (Celtic border) ............ | 3 | 10 Benham |
| | Edinburgh (Thistle) ............... | 3 | 10 Westminster |
| | Walsall ................................. | 3 | – |
| | Cricket World Cup ................ | 3 | 10 SPublicity |
| | Scottish Parliament cds ........ | 25 | – |
| 25 Apr 00 | **65p** | | |
| | Philatelic Bureau .................. | 3 | – Royal Mail |
| | People of the Country ......... | 3 | – Royal Mail |
| | New 65p Edinburgh ............. | 3 | 10 Bradbury |
| 5 Jun 02 | **2nd, 1st** De La Rue ........... | 3 | |
| 4 Jul 02 | **68p** | | |
| | Talelnts House ...................... | 3 | – Royal Mail |
| | People of the Country ......... | 3 | – Royal Mail |
| 14 Oct 03 | **2nd, 1st, E, 68p White Borders** | | |
| | Tallents House ...................... | 3 | – Royal Mail |
| | People of the Country .....(7) | 5 | – Royal Mail |
| | Edinburgh (Sporran) ............ | 3 | 10 PhilStamps |
| | Glencoe (Stag) ...................... | 3 | 10 Benham |
| | Edinburgh (Lion) ............(6) | 3 | 10 Benham |
| | Isle of Skye (Thistle) ............ | 3 | 10 Benham |
| | Isle of Lewis (Stones) .....(5) | 3 | 10 Benham |
| | Edinburgh (Map) ................. | 3 | 10 Westminster |
| 11 May 04 | **40p** | | |
| | Tallents House ...................... | 2 | – Royal Mail |
| | People of the Country .....(8) | 3 | – Royal Mail |
| | Edinburgh (Thistle) ............... | 3 | 8 PhilStamps |
| 5 Apr 05 | **42p** | | |
| | Tallents House ...................... | 2 | – Royal Mail |
| | People of the Country ......... | 3 | – Royal Mail |
| | Macduff ............................... | 3 | 8 PhilStamps |
| 10 May 05 | **42p** De La Rue ...................... | 4 | |
| 28 Mar 06 | **44p, 72p** | | |
| | Tallents House ...................... | 2 | – Royal Mail |
| | People of the Country ......... | 3 | – Royal Mail |
| | Windsor ............................... | 3 | 8 PhilStamps |
| 27 Mar 07 | **48p, 78p** | | |
| | Tallents House ...................... | 2 | – Royal Mail |
| | People of the Country ......... | 3 | – Royal Mail |
| 01 Apr 08 | **50p, 81p** | | |
| | Tallents House ...................... | 2 | – Royal Mail |
| | People of the Country ......... | 3 | – Royal Mail |
| 31 Mar 09 | **56p, 90p** | | |
| | Tallents House ...................... | 2 | – Royal Mail |
| | People of the Country ......... | 3 | – Royal Mail |
| 30 Mar 10 | **60p, 97p** | | |
| | Tallents House ...................... | 2 | – Royal Mail |
| | People of the Country .....(9) | 3 | – Royal Mail |

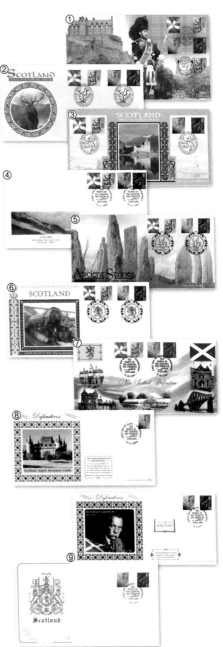

At _www.bfdc.co.uk_ you will find around
35,000 different British first day covers -
many still available for sale.  These are all
illustrated on the website.  You can search
or browse by cover producer and series,
stamp types, themes, issue dates etc
**PREPARE TO BE AMAZED!!**

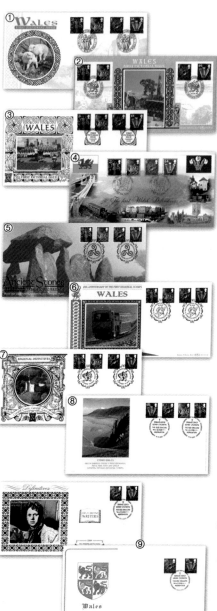

| | | Ordinary covers | | Sponsored |
|---|---|---|---|---|
| | | | £ | £ |
| 8 Jun 99 | **2nd, 1st, E, 64p** | | | |
| | Philatelic Bureau.................. | | 3 | – *Royal Mail* |
| | The Red Dragon................... | | 3 | – *Royal Mail* |
| | First Welsh Definitives....(4) | | 3 | 20 *Bradbury* |
| | Pormeirion (Dragon) .......(2) | | 3 | 10 *Benham* |
| | Builth Wells (Daffodils) ..(1) | | 3 | 10 *Benham* |
| | Caerphilly (Leeks) ............... | | 3 | 10 *Benham* |
| | Caernarvon (P of Wales) ........ | | 3 | 10 *Benham* |
| | Cardiff (Celtic border).....(3) | | 3 | 10 *Benham* |
| | Cardiff (Dragon) .................. | | 3 | 10 *Westminster* |
| | Walsall...................................... | | 3 | – |
| | Cricket World Cup.............. | | 3 | 10 *SPublicity* |
| 25 Apr 00 | **65p** | | | |
| | Philatelic Bureau.................. | | 2 | – *Royal Mail* |
| | The Red Dragon................... | | 3 | – *Royal Mail* |
| | New 65p Cardiff .................. | | 3 | 10 *Bradbury* |
| 4 Jul 02 | **68p** | | | |
| | Tallents House...................... | | 2 | – *Royal Mail* |
| | The Red Dragon................... | | 3 | – *Royal Mail* |
| 4 Mar 03 | **1st De La Rue**..................... | | 3 | |
| 28 May 03 | **2nd De La Rue**..................... | | 3 | |
| 14 Oct 03 | **2nd, 1st, E, 68p White Borders** | | | |
| | Tallents House...................... | | 3 | – *Royal Mail* |
| | The Red Dragon.............(8) | | 5 | – *Royal Mail* |
| | Cardiff (Dragon) .................. | | 3 | 10 *PhilStamps* |
| | Llanrwst (Leek) .................... | | 3 | 10 *Benham* |
| | Cardigan ........................(5) | | 3 | 10 *Benham* |
| | Llanberis (Daffodil)..........(6) | | 3 | 10 *Benham* |
| | Cardiff (Dragon) ............(7) | | 3 | 10 *Benham* |
| | Cardiff (Map) ...................... | | 3 | 10 *Westminster* |
| 11 May 04 | **40p** | | | |
| | Tallents House...................... | | 2 | – *Royal Mail* |
| | The Red Dragon................... | | 3 | – *Royal Mail* |
| | Cardiff (Dragon) .................. | | 3 | 10 *PhilStamps* |
| 5 Apr 05 | **42p** | | | |
| | Tallents House...................... | | 2 | – *Royal Mail* |
| | The Red Dragon................... | | 3 | – *Royal Mail* |
| | Macduff................................ | | 3 | 8 *PhilStamps* |
| 10 May 05 | **42p De La Rue**.................... | | 4 | |
| 28 Mar 06 | **44p, 72p** | | | |
| | Tallents House...................... | | 2 | – *Royal Mail* |
| | The Red Dragon................... | | 3 | – *Royal Mail* |
| | Windsor................................ | | 3 | 8 *PhilStamps* |
| 27 Mar 07 | **48p, 78p** | | | |
| | Tallents House...................... | | 2 | – *Royal Mail* |
| | The Red Dragon................... | | 3 | – *Royal Mail* |
| 01 Apr 08 | **50p, 81p** | | | |
| | Tallents House...................... | | 2 | – *Royal Mail* |
| | The Red Dragon................... | | 3 | – *Royal Mail* |
| 31 Mar 09 | **56p, 90p** | | | |
| | Tallents House...................... | | 2 | – *Royal Mail* |
| | The Red Dragon................... | | 3 | – *Royal Mail* |
| 30 Mar 10 | **60p, 97p** | | | |
| | Tallents House...................... | | 2 | – *Royal Mail* |
| | The Red Dragon .............(9) | | 3 | – *Royal Mail* |

At *www.bfdc.co.uk* you will find superb
albums to house your British first day
covers and Smilers stamp sheets.

| | | Ordinary covers | | Sponsored |
|---|---|---|---|---|
| | | | £ | £ |
| 6 Mar 01 | **2nd, 1st, E, 65p** | | | |
| | Philatelic Bureau | 3 | | – Royal Mail |
| | At Dusk Horizons | 3 | | – Royal Mail |
| | NI Pictorial Stamps ........(1) | 3 | | 12 Bradbury |
| | Bushmills (rectangle) ......(4) | 3 | | 10 Benham |
| | Bushmills (oval) | 3 | | 10 Benham |
| | Belleek Enniskillen .........(2) | 3 | | 10 Benham |
| | Bushmills (circle) | 3 | | 10 Benham |
| | Lisburn | 3 | | 10 Benham |
| | Belfast | 3 | | 10 Benham |
| | Newcastle .........................(3) | 3 | | 10 Benham |
| | Battle of Trafalgar | 3 | | 10 Benham |
| 4 Jul 02 | **68p** | | | |
| | Tallents House | 2 | | – Royal Mail |
| | At Dusk Horizons | 3 | | – Royal Mail |
| 15 Oct 02 | **'E' De La Rue** | 3 | | |
| 14 Oct 03 | **2nd, 1st, E, 68p White Borders** | | | |
| | Tallents House | 2 | | – Royal Mail |
| | At Dusk Horizons ...........(7) | 5 | | – Royal Mail |
| | Belfast (Leprechaun) | 3 | | 10 PhilStamps |
| | Belfast (Harp) ..............(6) | 3 | | 10 Benham |
| | Cookstown (Flax) .........(5) | 3 | | 10 Benham |
| | Portrush (Cross) | 3 | | 10 Benham |
| | Londonderry (Hand) | 3 | | 10 Benham |
| | Belfast (Map) | 3 | | 10 Westminster |
| 11 May 04 | **40p** | | | |
| | Tallents House | 2 | | – Royal Mail |
| | At Dusk Horizons | 3 | | – Royal Mail |
| | Belfast (Flower) | 3 | | 8 PhilStamps |
| 5 Apr 05 | **42p** | | | |
| | Tallents House | 2 | | – Royal Mail |
| | At Dusk Horizons | 3 | | – Royal Mail |
| | Macduff | 3 | | 8 PhilStamps |
| 26 Jul 05 | **42p De La Rue** | 4 | | |
| 28 Mar 06 | **44p, 72p** | | | |
| | Tallents House | 2 | | – Royal Mail |
| | At Dusk Horizons | 3 | | – Royal Mail |
| | Windsor | 3 | | 8 PhilStamps |
| 27 Mar 07 | **48p, 78p** | | | |
| | Tallents House | 2 | | – Royal Mail |
| | At Dusk Horizons | 3 | | – Royal Mail |
| 01 Apr 08 | **50p, 81p** | | | |
| | Tallents House | 2 | | – Royal Mail |
| | At Dusk Horizons | 3 | | – Royal Mail |
| 31 Mar 09 | **56p, 90p** | | | |
| | Tallents House | 2 | | – Royal Mail |
| | At Dusk Horizons | 3 | | – Royal Mail |
| 30 Mar 10 | **60p, 97p** | | | |
| | Tallents House | 2 | | – Royal Mail |
| | At Dusk Horizons ...........(8) | 3 | | – Royal Mail |

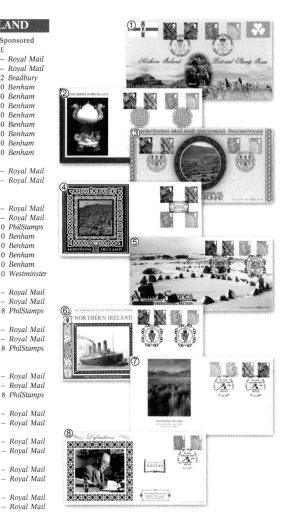

| | | | |
|---|---|---|---|
| 16 Sep 1968 | .1st 5d . . .2nd 4d | 5 Apr 1983 | . .1st 16p . .2nd 12$\frac{1}{2}$p | 26 Apr 1999 | . .1st 26p . .2nd 19p |
| 15 Feb 1971 | .1st 3p . . .2nd 2$\frac{1}{2}$p | 3 Sep 1984 | . .1st 17p . .2nd 13p | 27 Apr 2000 | . .1st 27p . .2nd 19p |
| 10 Sep 1973 | .1st 3$\frac{1}{2}$p .2nd 3p | 4 Nov 1985 | . . .1st 17p . .2nd 12p | 8 May 2003 | . .1st 28p . .2nd 20p |
| 24 Jun 1974 | .1st 4$\frac{1}{2}$p .2nd 3$\frac{1}{2}$p | 20 Oct 1986 | . . .1st 18p . .2nd 13p | 1 Apr 2004 | . .1st 28p . .2nd 21p |
| 29 Sep 1975 | .1st 8$\frac{1}{2}$p .2nd 6$\frac{1}{2}$p | 5 Sep 1988 | . . .1st 19p . .2nd 14p | 7 Apr 2005 | . .1st 30p . .2nd 21p |
| 13 Jun 1977 | .1st 9p . . .2nd 7p | 2 Oct 1989 | . .1st 20p . .2nd 15p | 3 Apr 2006 | . .1st 32p . .2nd 23p |
| 20 Aug 1979 | .1st 10p . .2nd 8p | 17 Sep 1990 | . .1st 22p . .2nd 17p | 2 Apr 2007 | . .1st 34p . .2nd 24p |
| 4 Feb 1980 | . .1st 12p . .2nd 10p | 16 Sep 1991 | . .1st 24p . .2nd 18p | 7 Apr 2008 | . .1st 36p . .2nd 27p |
| 26 Jan 1981 | . .1st 14p . .2nd 11$\frac{1}{2}$p | 1 Nov 1993 | . .1st 25p . .2nd 19p | 6 Apr 2009 | . .1st 39p . .2nd 30p |
| 1 Feb 1982 | . .1st 15$\frac{1}{2}$p 2nd 12$\frac{1}{2}$p | 8 Jul 1996 | . . . .1st 26p . .2nd 20p | 6 Apr 2010 | . .1st 41p . .2nd 32p |

239

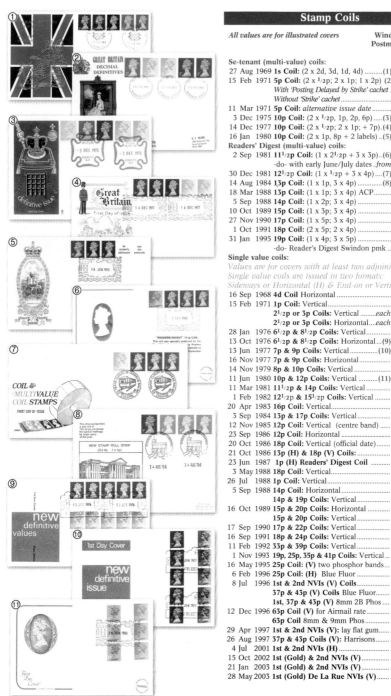

## Stamp Coils

| *All values are for illustrated covers* | Windsor Postmark £ | Other Pmks £ |
|---|---|---|
| **Se-tenant (multi-value) coils:** | | |
| 27 Aug 1969 **1s Coil:** (2 x 2d, 3d, 1d, 4d) .........(1) | 10 | 3 |
| 15 Feb 1971 **5p Coil:** (2 x 1/2p; 2 x 1p; 1 x 2p) (2) | | |
|     *With 'Posting Delayed by Strike' cachet* . | 10 | 3 |
|     *Without 'Strike' cachet* ............................... | n.k. | 10 |
| 11 Mar 1971 **5p Coil:** *alternative issue date* .......... | n.k. | 12 |
| 3 Dec 1975 **10p Coil:** (2 x 1/2p, 1p, 2p, 6p) .....(3) | 10 | 3 |
| 14 Dec 1977 **10p Coil:** (2 x 1/2p; 2 x 1p; + 7p).(4) | 10 | 3 |
| 16 Jan 1980 **10p Coil:** (1p, 8p + 2 labels) ..(5) | 10 | 3 |
| **Readers' Digest (multi-value) coils:** | | |
| 2 Sep 1981 **11 1/2p Coil:** (1 x 2 1/2p + 3 x 3p)..(6) | 10 | 2 |
|     -do- with early June/July dates .*from* | n.k. | 20 |
| 30 Dec 1981 **12 1/2p Coil:** (1 x 1/2p + 3 x 4p)....(7) | 10 | 2 |
| 14 Aug 1984 **13p Coil:** (1 x 1p, 3 x 4p) .............(8) | 10 | 2 |
| 18 Mar 1988 **13p Coil:** (1 x 1p; 3 x 4p) ACP......... | 25 | 10 |
| 5 Sep 1988 **14p Coil:** (1 x 2p; 3 x 4p) ................. | 10 | 2 |
| 10 Oct 1989 **15p Coil:** (1 x 3p; 3 x 4p) ................. | 10 | 2 |
| 27 Nov 1990 **17p Coil:** (1 x 5p; 3 x 4p) ................. | 10 | 2 |
| 1 Oct 1991 **18p Coil:** (2 x 5p; 2 x 4p) ................. | 10 | 2 |
| 31 Jan 1995 **19p Coil:** (1 x 4p; 3 x 5p) ................. | 10 | 2 |
|     -do- Reader's Digest Swindon pmk .. | – | 10 |
| **Single value coils:** | | |
| *Values are for covers with at least two adjoining stamps.* | | |
| *Single value coils are issued in two formats:* | | |
| *Sideways or Horizontal (H) & End-on or Vertical (V)* | | |
| 16 Sep 1968 **4d Coil** Horizontal .............................. | 300 | – |
| 15 Feb 1971 **1p Coil:** Vertical................................... | – | 600 |
|     **2 1/2p or 3p Coils:** Vertical .......*each* | 600 | 500 |
|     **2 1/2p or 3p Coils:** Horizontal....*each* | 600 | 500 |
| 28 Jan 1974 **6 1/2p & 8 1/2p Coils:** Vertical............... | n.k. | 150 |
| 13 Oct 1976 **6 1/2p & 8 1/2p Coils:** Horizontal...(9) | 250 | 80 |
| 13 Jun 1977 **7p & 9p Coils:** Vertical...............(10) | 125 | 45 |
| 16 Nov 1977 **7p & 9p Coils:** Horizontal................. | 250 | 45 |
| 14 Nov 1979 **8p & 10p Coils:** Vertical ................. | 125 | 45 |
| 11 Jun 1980 **10p & 12p Coils:** Vertical ..........(11) | 50 | 40 |
| 11 Mar 1981 **11 1/2p & 14p Coils:** Vertical .......... | 50 | 35 |
| 1 Feb 1982 **12 1/2p & 15 1/2p Coils:** Vertical .......... | 50 | 25 |
| 20 Apr 1983 **16p Coil:** Vertical............................. | 20 | 3 |
| 3 Sep 1984 **13p & 17p Coils:** Vertical ................... | 40 | 3 |
| 12 Nov 1985 **12p Coil:** Vertical (centre band) ...... | 8 | 2 |
| 23 Sep 1986 **12p Coil:** Horizontal ......................... | 5 | 2 |
| 20 Oct 1986 **18p Coil:** Vertical (official date)......... | 15 | – |
| 21 Oct 1986 **13p (H) & 18p (V) Coils:** ................... | 30 | 7 |
| 23 Jun 1987 **1p (H) Readers' Digest Coil** .......... | 5 | 2 |
| 3 May 1988 **18p Coil:** Vertical................................ | 5 | 2 |
| 26 Jul 1988 **1p Coil:** Vertical............................... | 5 | 2 |
| 5 Sep 1988 **14p Coil:** Horizontal .......................... | 8 | 3 |
|     **14p & 19p Coils:** Vertical................... | 8 | 3 |
| 16 Oct 1989 **15p & 20p Coils:** Horizontal ............. | 6 | 2 |
|     **15p & 20p Coils:** Vertical ................. | 6 | 2 |
| 17 Sep 1990 **17p & 22p Coils:** Vertical ................. | 5 | 4 |
| 16 Sep 1991 **18p & 24p Coils:** Vertical ................. | 5 | 4 |
| 11 Feb 1992 **33p & 39p Coils:** Vertical ................. | 5 | 3 |
| 1 Nov 1993 **19p, 25p, 35p & 41p Coils:** Vertical .. | 8 | 4 |
| 16 May 1995 **25p Coil: (V)** two phosphor bands... | 5 | 2 |
| 6 Feb 1996 **25p Coil: (H)** Blue Fluor .................. | 10 | – |
| 8 Jul 1996 **1st & 2nd NVIs (V) Coils**.................. | 5 | 3 |
|     **37p & 43p (V) Coils** Blue Fluor........... | 6 | 4 |
|     **1st, 37p & 43p (V)** 8mm 2B Phos .... | 30 | – |
| 12 Dec 1996 **63p Coil (V)** for Airmail rate ............. | 5 | 2 |
|     **63p Coil** 8mm & 9mm Phos ................ | 12 | – |
| 29 Apr 1997 **1st & 2nd NVIs (V):** lay flat gum...... | 6 | 3 |
| 26 Aug 1997 **37p & 43p Coils (V):** Harrisons...... | 8 | 4 |
| 4 Jul 2001 **1st & 2nd NVIs (H)** ....................... | 4 | 3 |
| 15 Oct 2002 **1st (Gold) & 2nd NVIs (V)**............... | 4 | 3 |
| 21 Jan 2003 **1st (Gold) & 2nd NVIs (V)**............... | 4 | 3 |
| 28 May 2003 **1st (Gold) De La Rue NVIs (V)**....... | 4 | 3 |

# Benham
## First Day Cover Clubs

**Joining a Benham Club brings nothing but benefits -**
- *covers reserved for you at special low club prices,*
- *30 day money-back guarantee*
- *the right to cancel at any time.*

Call 0844 994 9400 or visit www.benham.co.uk — *To enrol in any of these clubs, please tick the appropriate box. Club price per cover is as listed below.*

**SOLD OUT**

### Gold 500 Series
This is our most prestigious series. Each cover bears the full set of stamps in the issue featured, together with an appropriate image framed by a **22ct gold-blocked border**. The series is issued in a strictly **limited edition of 500 hand-numbered** covers, considerably enhancing their collectability.

☐ ✓ I will pay £16, saving £1.50 per cover. **GOLD01M**

### BLCS 5000 Series
Benham Luxury Cover Series. Established in 1985, this is one of our longest-running clubs. The individually designed covers reflect the excitement and colour of each Royal Mail issue with an appropriate image and a specially sponsored pictorial handstamp. Bearing the full set of stamps, these fine covers are understandably popular amongst collectors.

BLCS467A £12.95 ☐ ✓ I will pay £10.65, saving £2.30 per cover. **B001M**

### BLCS 5000 Signed Series
A limited number of the BLCS 5000 cover is available signed by a personality closely associated with the theme of the stamp issue. Recent signatories have included actress Susan Hampshire (Britain Alone), Radio presenter John Humphries (Castles of Wales) and Angela Rippon (Festival of Stamps sheet).

BLCSSP32S2 £18.50 ☐ ✓ I will pay £16.60, saving £1.30 per cover. **SIG01M**

**SOLD OUT**

### Main Coin Cover Series
This is one of our most popular clubs, the special feature of which is that each cover encapsulates a coin reflecting the issue theme or even dating from the era the stamps are commemorating. Some of our greatest successes have been covers with historic coins from as long ago as the Roman era. The cover illustrated contains a 1910 George V halfpenny.

☐ ✓ I will pay £15.70, saving £1.80 per cover. **COIN1M**

### Jennifer Toombs Hand Painted Series
This club will appeal to both the philatelist and the collector. Jennifer Toombs is a highly-respected artist and stamp designer. Each cover in this series, bearing the full stamp issue, is individually painted and signed by her, making it a unique work of art and therefore highly collectable.

HP0846 £50 ☐ ✓ I will pay £43.50, saving £6.50 per cover. **COL140**

---

## order form
Send completed coupon to: **FREEPOST RLXY-YGSH-EXGT, The Benham Group, Folkestone, CT19 4RG**

☐ I enclose my cheque/PO. made payable to BENHAM for the first cover (+ £1.75 p&p) £
☐ OR debit my card for the first cover (and subsequent instalments at the time of despatch)

| Code | Description | Qty | £ |
|------|-------------|-----|---|
|  |  |  |  |
|  |  |  |  |
| UK postage per order (*overseas postage will be charged at cost) £ |  |  | 2.50 |
| I enclose my cheque/PO. made payable to BENHAM for £ |  |  |  |

*Instalments will be despatched as covers are issued. All orders are subject to availability. If you are not satisfied you may return the item(s) within 30 days in good condition for a refund.*

Signature _____
Date _____
Name _____
Address _____
_____
Postcode _____
Tel No. _____
Email: _____

**OR** debit my Card Number:
☐☐☐☐ ☐☐☐☐ ☐☐☐☐ ☐☐☐☐ (Maestro only)

| Valid From | Expires | Issue No. (Maestro only) | Security No. |

*(A clear photocopy of this form is acceptable if you don't wish to cut up your magazine)*

**MEDIA CODE:** BCA1009A

# STAMP ORGANISER
## Bringing Stamp Collecting to the 21st Century

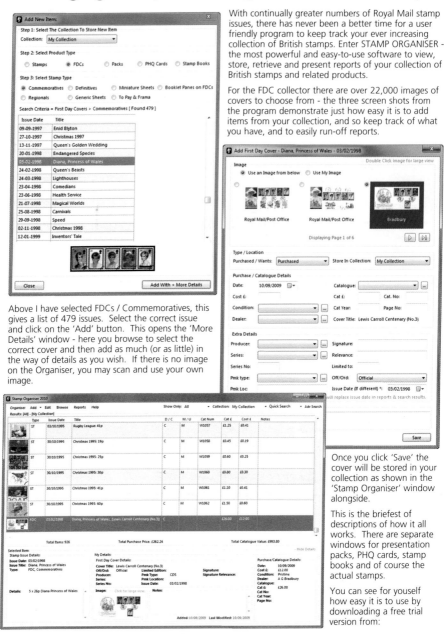

With continually greater numbers of Royal Mail stamp issues, there has never been a better time for a user friendly program to keep track your ever increasing collection of British stamps. Enter STAMP ORGANISER - the most powerful and easy-to-use software to view, store, retrieve and present reports of your collection of British stamps and related products.

For the FDC collector there are over 22,000 images of covers to choose from - the three screen shots from the program demonstrate just how easy it is to add items from your collection, and so keep track of what you have, and to easily run-off reports.

Above I have selected FDCs / Commemoratives, this gives a list of 479 issues. Select the correct issue and click on the 'Add' button. This opens the 'More Details' window - here you browse to select the correct cover and then add as much (or as little) in the way of details as you wish. If there is no image on the Organiser, you may scan and use your own image.

Once you click 'Save' the cover will be stored in your collection as shown in the 'Stamp Organiser' window alongside.

This is the briefest of descriptions of how it all works. There are separate windows for presentation packs, PHQ cards, stamp books and of course the actual stamps.

You can see for youself how easy it is to use by downloading a free trial version from:

## www.bfdc.co.uk/so - for a free trial version

244

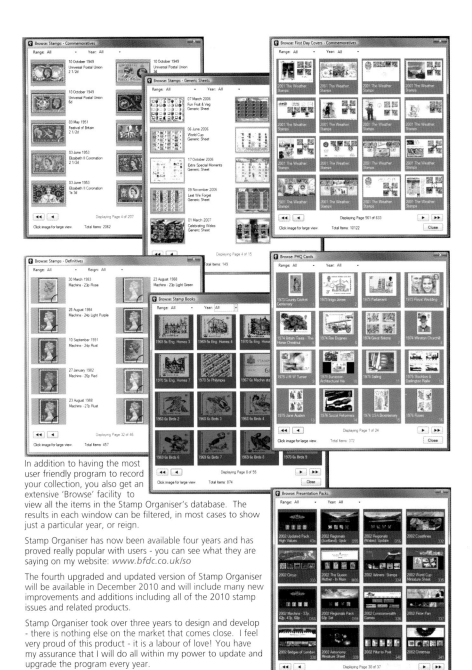

In addition to having the most user friendly program to record your collection, you also get an extensive 'Browse' facility to view all the items in the Stamp Organiser's database. The results in each window can be filtered, in most cases to show just a particular year, or reign.

Stamp Organiser has now been available four years and has proved really popular with users - you can see what they are saying on my website: *www.bfdc.co.uk/so*

The fourth upgraded and updated version of Stamp Organiser will be available in December 2010 and will include many new improvements and additions including all of the 2010 stamp issues and related products.

Stamp Organiser took over three years to design and develop - there is nothing else on the market that comes close. I feel very proud of this product - it is a labour of love! You have my assurance that I will do all within my power to update and upgrade the program every year.

**Stamp Organiser is available from BFDC Ltd., Royal Mail and all good stamp shops.**

System Requirements:    Windows: XP (Service Pack 2 and above), Vista, 7
                        128Mb RAM
                        500Mb of disk space
                        Screen resolution (minimum requirement) 1024 x 768
Mac Version - release date soon - we are working on this.

*Adrian Bradbury.*

245

# Index for Commemorative Issues

Add a touch of class to your collection

www.bfdc.co.uk   Stock Code 34553

www.bfdc.co.uk

## Discover a whole new world of British First Day Covers and Smilers Stamp Sheets